Words Their Way®

Words Their Way®

Word Study for Phonics, Vocabulary, and Spelling Instruction

SIXTH EDITION

Donald R. Bear
Iowa State University

Marcia Invernizzi
University of Virginia

Shane Templeton
University of Nevada, Reno

Francine Johnston
University of North Carolina at Greensboro

PEARSON

Boston · Columbus · Indianapolis · New York · San Francisco · Upper Saddle River
Amsterdam · Cape Town · Dubai · London · Madrid · Milan · Munich · Paris · Montreal · Toronto
Delhi · Mexico City · Sao Paulo · Sydney · Hong Kong · Seoul · Singapore · Taipei · Tokyo

Vice President & Publisher: Jeffery W. Johnston
Executive Editor: Meredith D. Fossel
Senior Development Editor: Max Effenson Chuck
Editorial Assistant: Maria Feliberty
Program Manager: Karen Mason
Project Manager: Cynthia DeRocco/Christina Taylor
Executive Marketing Manager: Krista Clark
Editorial Production Service: MPS North America LLC
Manufacturing Buyer: Deidra Skahill
Electronic Composition: Jouve
Interior Design: MPS North America LLC
Art Director: Diane Lorenzo
Illustrator: Francine Johnston

Credits and acknowledgments borrowed from other sources and reproduced, with permission, in this textbook appear on appropriate page within text.

Library of Congress Cataloging-in-Publication Data
Bear, Donald R.
  Words their way: word study for phonics, vocabulary, and spelling instruction/Donald R. Bear, Iowa State University, Marcia Invernizzi, University of Virginia, Shane Templeton, University of Nevada, Reno, Francine Johnston, University of North Carolina at Greensboro. —Sixth Edition.
    pages cm
  Rev. ed. of: Words their way / Donald R. Bear ... [et al.]
  Includes bibliographical references and index.
  ISBN 978-0-13-399633-3—ISBN 0-13-399633-6   1. Word recognition.   2. Reading--Phonetic method.
3. English language—Orthography and spelling.   I. Invernizzi, Marcia.   II. Templeton, Shane.
III. Johnston, Francine R.   IV. Bear, Donald R. Words their way.   V. Title.
  LB1050.44.B43 2015
  372.46'2—dc23

                                                                              2015008892

5   18

PEARSON

ISBN-10: 0-13-399633-6
ISBN-13: 978-0-13-399633-3

This book is dedicated to
the memory of our teacher,
Edmund H. Henderson.

Donald R. Bear
Marcia Invernizzi
Shane Templeton
Francine Johnston

Letter from the Authors

Dear Educator,

It is an honor for the authors of ***Words Their Way®: Word Study for Phonics, Vocabulary, and Spelling Instruction*** to present the sixth edition of this seminal text on word study. Accompanying this edition is an online resource, PDToolkit for *Words Their Way®*, featuring classroom video, printable sorts and games, online interactive sorts, assessment tools, and applications all in one place. These tools will help you to effectively implement word study instruction in your classroom.

For the sixth edition, the authors highlight a few key ideas presented in *Words Their Way*.

Donald

Words Their Way presents a developmental approach that makes word study more efficient and responsive. This approach to word study integrates phonics, spelling, and vocabulary because of the reciprocal nature of literacy: what students learn in spelling transfers to reading, and what they learn in reading transfers to spelling and vocabulary. These are not, therefore, three separate and unrelated areas of instruction. Integrating phonics, vocabulary, and spelling instruction with a developmental approach contributes, we hope, to deep and rewarding learning and teaching.

Marcia

Words Their Way has gotten teachers to think about phonics, spelling, and vocabulary instruction from a completely different point of view. Teachers welcome our student-centered, minds-on, active approach that considers word study not only as an integral part of literacy development, but also as an integral vehicle for fostering critical thinking. Effective word study lessons pose questions and involve students in solving problems through careful analysis, reflection, and discussion. The questions teachers pose during words study—such as, "Why do some words end in a silent *e*?"—encourage an investigative mindset, and give purpose for engaging in word study activities such as word sorts. The language we use when we talk with students about words has a powerful influence on their self-efficacy as learners. This is in sharp contrast to most phonics and spelling programs that merely ask students to memorize relationships, rules, and words.

Shane

Words Their Way helps teachers provide their students with the breadth and depth of exploration necessary to construct knowledge about words over time—from individual letters to sound, from groups of letters to sound, and from groups of letters to meaning. Awareness and appreciation of how children construct this knowledge empowers and emboldens many teachers to advocate for developmental instruction in word study specifically and in literacy more generally. This understanding is now being applied to instruction in vocabulary—in particular, general academic vocabulary and domain-specific vocabulary.

Francine

Students learn best when they are working with content that is in their "Zone of Proximal Development" or window of opportunity. *Words Their Way* offers an assessment-driven developmental guide for word study that helps teachers to differentiate instruction to meet children's needs and provides the resources to do so.

Bring your colleagues and come join us in the most active edition of *Words Their Way*® yet. We wish you happy sorting with your students!

Sincerely,

Donald R. Bear   **Marcia Invernizzi**   **Shane Templeton**   **Francine Johnston**

About the Authors

Donald R. Bear is director of the Duffelmeyer Reading Clinic in the School of Education, Iowa State University, where he and his students teach and assess students who are experiencing difficulties learning to read and write. A former elementary teacher, Donald currently researches literacy development with a special interest in students who speak different languages. He partners with schools and districts to think about how to assess and conduct literacy instruction.

Marcia Invernizzi is executive director of the McGuffey Reading Center in the Curry School of Education at the University of Virginia. She and her multilingual doctoral students enjoy exploring developmental universals in non-English orthographies. A former English and reading teacher, Marcia extends her experience working with children who experience difficulties learning to read and write to numerous intervention programs, such as Virginia's Early Intervention Reading Initiative and Book Buddies.

Shane Templeton is Foundation Professor Emeritus of Literacy Studies in the College of Education at the University of Nevada, Reno. A former classroom teacher at the primary and secondary levels, his research focuses on the development of orthographic and vocabulary knowledge. He has written several books on the teaching and learning of reading and language arts and is a member of the Usage Panel of the *American Heritage Dictionary*.

Francine Johnston is retired from the School of Education at the University of North Carolina at Greensboro, where she coordinated the reading master's program and directed a reading clinic for struggling readers. Francine is a former first grade teacher and reading specialist, and she continues to work with schools as a consultant.

Brief Contents

Contents

CHAPTER 1 Developmental Word Knowledge   2

CHAPTER 2 Getting Started   22

CHAPTER 3 Organizing for Word Study   48

CHAPTER 4 Word Study for Learners in the Emergent Stage   90

CHAPTER 5 Word Study for Beginners in the Letter Name-Alphabetic Stage 146

CHAPTER 8 Word Study for Advanced Readers and Writers   276

Activities

Preface

I see and I forget. I hear and I remember. I do and I understand.

—Confucius

Word study involves "doing" things with words—examining, manipulating, comparing, and categorizing—and offers students the opportunity to make their own discoveries about how words work. When teachers use this practical, hands-on way to study words with students, they create tasks that focus students' attention on critical features of words: sound, pattern, and meaning.

Words Their Way is a developmental approach to phonics, vocabulary, and spelling instruction. Guided by an informed interpretation of spelling errors and other literacy behaviors, *Words Their Way* offers a systematic, teacher-directed, child-centered plan for the study of words from kindergarten to high school. Step by step, the chapters explain exactly how to provide effective word study instruction. The keys to this research-based approach are knowing your students' literacy progress, organizing for instruction, and implementing word study.

NEW to This Edition

- **NEW:** To enhance thoughtful discussions, a chart in Chapter 3 offers sample questions to guide problem solving, reflection, application, and transfer.

- **NEW:** Ideas for teaching proofreading and dictionary skills have been developed for each level.

- **NEW:** Common Core State Standards are listed for each activity.

- **NEW:** Word study websites and resources are expanded for this edition.

- **NEW:** Academic vocabulary is introduced with accompanying vocabulary activities.

- **NEW:** Coverage of oral vocabulary is enhanced with additional activities at all stages.

- **NEW:** More assessments for the emergent stage have been added.

- **NEW:** A newly designed marginal icon connects the reader to specific videos, sorts, or assessments on PDToolkit.

- **NEW:** Activities have been added, and many have been revised.

- **NEW:** Photos have been pulled from videos and appear in the book, further enhancing the interconnectedness between the text and the media.

- **NEW:** References throughout the book pertaining to student demographics and the latest research pertaining to word study have been updated.

PDToolkit for *Words Their Way*®

A website with media tools accompanies *Words Their Way*, sixth edition. Together with the text, the website provides the tools you need to carry out word study instruction that will motivate and engage your students and help them succeed in literacy learning.

The PDToolkit for *Words Their Way*® is available free for twelve months with the password that comes with this book. After twelve months, your subscription must be renewed. Be sure to explore and download the resources available at the website. The following resources are currently available:

- **NEW**: In addition to all new footage presented with the fifth edition of *Words Their Way*®, the classroom footage added to the sixth edition shows you teachers using word study at all of stages of development, including English learners and PreK–K and secondary students.

- An assessment tool provides downloadable inventories and feature guides, as well as interactive classroom composites that help you monitor your students' development throughout the year.

- Prepared word sorts and games for each stage will help you get started with word study in your classroom.

- A Create Your Own feature allows you to modify and create sorts and games and online computers.

- Word sorts that can be used with interactive whiteboards are available for each stage.

   We will continue to add new other resources.

Knowing Your Students

Chapter 1 provides you with foundational information on word study and the research in orthography and literacy development that led to this word study approach. Then, Chapter 2 presents assessment and evaluation tools, walking you step by step through the process of determining your students' instructional level and focusing your word study instruction appropriately. After you administer one of the spelling inventories, you will be able to compile a feature guide for each of your students that will help you identify their stage and the word study features they are ready to master. The classroom composite will identify which students have similar instructional needs, allowing you to plan wisely and effectively for word study grouping.

The website includes progress monitoring charts and spell checks, enabling you to determine the effectiveness of instruction on a regular basis and to modify it as needed. On the PD Toolkit for *Words Their Way®* you will find assessment resources to download, including:

- Primary Spelling Inventory, feature guide, error guide, and classroom composite
- Elementary Spelling Inventory, feature guide, error guide, and classroom composite
- Upper-Level Spelling Inventory, feature guide, and classroom composite
- Spelling-by-Stage Organizational Chart
- Qualitative Spelling Checklist
- Emergent Class Record and other emergent assessments
- Word Feature Inventory
- McGuffey Qualitative Spelling Inventory
- Kindergarten Spelling Inventory and Analysis
- Progress monitoring charts
- Spell checks

Organizing for Instruction

Chapter 3 outlines the most effective ways to organize word study for classroom instruction. We suggest activities for small groups, partners, and individuals that can be incorporated into weekly routines that will help you manage leveled groups for instruction at all grade levels. We also describe a continuum of support that will help you plan and implement lessons to maximize classroom time. Tips are provided to help guide discussions about words.

Implementing Word Study

Once you have assessed your students, created leveled groups, and developed routines for word study, the information and materials in Chapters 4 through 8 and the Appendixes will guide your instruction. Chapters 4 through 8 explore the characteristics of each particular stage, from the emergent learner through to the advanced reader and writer in the derivational relations stage of spelling development. Each of these chapters covers the research and principles that drive instruction and the most appropriate sequence and instructional pacing.

Activities described in each chapter include concept sorts, word sorts, and games, which will help you focus instruction where it is needed to move students into the next stage of development. These word study activities promise to engage your students, motivate them, and improve their literacy skills. The activities sections have shaded tabs for your convenience, creating a handy classroom resource. New to this edition are additional vocabulary strategies for each developmental level.

Importantly, as you work with the *Common Core State Standards*, you will see how *Words Their Way* supports the Reading Foundational Skills and the Language Standards across all the grades. The depth and breadth of word knowledge developed through *Words Their Way* also supports the Common Core's emphasis on students reading more complex literary and informational texts.

The Appendixes at the back of the book contain most of the assessment instruments described in Chapter 2, as well as word sorts, sound boards, and game templates you will need to get your own word study instruction under way.

Companion Volumes

Additional stage-specific companion volumes provide you with a complete curriculum of reproducible sorts and detailed directions, including:

- *Words Their Way®: Letter and Picture Sorts for Emergent Spellers* (2nd ed.), by Donald R. Bear, Marcia Invernizzi, Francine Johnston, and Shane Templeton
- *Words Their Way®: Word Sorts for Letter Name–Alphabetic Spellers* (2nd ed.), by Francine Johnston, Donald R. Bear, Marcia Invernizzi, and Shane Templeton
- *Words Their Way®: Word Sorts for Within Word Pattern Spellers* (2nd ed.), by Marcia Invernizzi, Francine Johnston, Donald R. Bear, and Shane Templeton
- *Words Their Way®: Word Sorts for Syllables and Affixes Spellers* (2nd ed.), by Francine Johnston, Marcia Invernizzi, Donald R. Bear, and Shane Templeton
- *Words Their Way®: Word Sorts for Derivational Relations Spellers* (2nd ed.), by Shane Templeton, Francine Johnston, Donald R. Bear, and Marcia Invernizzi

Other related volumes are designed to meet the needs of English learners and students in the intermediate and secondary levels:

- *Words Their Way® for PreK–K*, by Francine Johnston, Marcia Invernizzi, Lori Helman, Donald R. Bear, and Shane Templeton
- *Words Their Way® with English Learners: Word Study for Phonics, Vocabulary, and Spelling* (2nd ed.), by Lori Helman, Donald R. Bear, Shane Templeton, Marcia Invernizzi, and Francine Johnston
- *Words Their Way®: Emergent Sorts for Spanish-Speaking English Learners*, by Lori Helman, Donald R. Bear, Marcia Invernizzi, Shane Templeton, and Francine Johnston
- *Words Their Way®: Letter Name–Alphabetic Sorts for Spanish-Speaking English Learners*, by Lori Helman, Donald R. Bear, Marcia Invernizzi, Shane Templeton, and Francine Johnston
- *Words Their Way®: Within Word Pattern Sorts for Spanish-Speaking English Learners*, by Lori Helman, Donald R. Bear, Marcia Invernizzi, Shane Templeton, and Francine Johnston
- *Vocabulary Their Way®: Word Study with Middle and Secondary Students* (2nd ed.), by Shane Templeton, Donald R. Bear, Marcia Invernizzi, Francine Johnston, Kevin Flanigan, Lori Helman, Diana Townsend, and Tisha Hayes
- *Words Their Way® with Struggling Readers: Word Study for Reading, Vocabulary, and Spelling Instruction, Grades 4–12*, by Kevin Flanigan, Latisha Hayes, Shane Templeton, Donald R. Bear, Marcia Invernizzi, and Francine Johnston

Acknowledgments

We would like to thank the reviewers of our manuscript for their careful consideration and comments: Joan Boshart, Crossroads; Jennifer Carlson, Hamline University; Roni Daniel, Roche Ave. Elementary School; Terri L. Lurkins, Highland CUSD5; Elizabeth E. Shriver, Cleveland State University. Colleagues and friends are too numerous to mention here, but those who have in recent years worked with and taught us include Kelly Bruskotter, Sharon Cathey, Shari Dunn, Kevin Flanigan, Michelle Flores, Kristin Gehsmann, Ashley Gotta, Amanda Grotting, Tisha Hayes, Lori Helman, Ryan Ichanberry, Darl Kiernan, Sandra Madura, Kara Moloney, Ann Noel, Leta Rabenstein, Kelly Rubero, Alisa Simeral, David Smith, Regina Smith, Kris Stosic, and Alyson Wilson. We would like to thank the video production team from University of Nevada, Reno, for their excellent work on the video accompanying this book, as well as most of the photos in the book. The team includes Mark Gandolfo, Theresa Danna-Douglas, Maryan Tooker, and Shawn Sariti.

We would also like to thank the following teachers for their classroom-tested activities: Cindy Aldrete-Frazer, Tamara Baren, Margery Beatty, Telia Blackard, Janet Bloodgood, Cindy Booth, Karen Broaddus, Wendy Brown, Janet Brown Watts, Karen Carpenter, Carol Caserta-Henry, Jeradi Cohen, Fran de Maio, Nicole Doner, Allison Dwier-Seldon, Marilyn Edwards, Monica Everson, Ann Fordham, Mary Fowler, Erika Fulmer, Elizabeth Harrison, Esther Heatley, Lisbeth Kling, Pat Love, Rita Loyacono, Barry Mahanes, Carolyn Melchiorre, Colleen Muldoon, Liana Napier, Katherine Preston, Brenda Riebel, Leslie Robertson, Geraldine Robinson, Elizabeth Shuett, Jennifer Sudduth, and Charlotte Tucker.

Finally, a very special "thank you" to the following individuals: Meredith Fossel, who joined us in this new edition to navigate new terrains and ways of presenting word study; program manager Karen Mason and project manager Cynthia DeRocco for support and attention to detail truly above and beyond; Lauren Hill, Rob Leon, and the rest of the MPS North America LLC team; and Max Chuck, our developmental editor for this new edition.

Words Their Way®

Developmental Word Knowledge

For students of all ages and language backgrounds, knowing the ways in which their written language represents the language they speak is the key to literacy. In this sixth edition, we describe how teachers can most effectively guide and support students' learning about the sounds, structure, and meanings of words—crafting our instruction so that our students learn about words *their* way. In addition to demonstrating how a developmental approach to word study best supports students' deep and long-term word learning, this new edition further explores how educators may apply this developmental model as they implement effective and engaging phonics, vocabulary, and spelling instruction from preschool through the middle grades and beyond, and apply best practices for ongoing progress monitoring, response to intervention, and scaffolding instruction for multilingual learners. Whether you are a long-standing companion on this adventure or joining us for the first time, we welcome you on this continuing journey to learn and teach about words *their* way.

The Braid of Literacy

Literacy is like a braid of interwoven threads. The braid begins with the intertwining threads of oral language and stories that are read to children. As children experiment with putting ideas on paper, a writing thread is entwined as well. And all along the way, vocabulary is being learned and developed. As children move into reading, the threads of literacy begin to bond. Students' growing knowledge of spelling or **orthography**—the ways in which letters and letter patterns in words represent sound and meaning—strengthens that bonding. The size of the threads and the braid itself become thicker as orthographic knowledge grows (see Figure 1.1).

During the preschool years, children acquire word knowledge in a fundamentally aural way from the language that surrounds them. Through listening to and talking about everyday events, life experiences, and stories, children develop a speaking vocabulary. As they have opportunities to talk about their everyday experiences, children begin to make sense of their world and to use language to negotiate and describe it. Children also begin to experiment with pen and paper when they have opportunities to observe parents, siblings, and caregivers writing for many purposes. They gradually come to understand the forms and functions of written language. The first written words students learn are usually their own names, followed by those of significant others. Words such as *Mom*, *cat*, and *dog* and phrases like *I love you* represent people, animals, and ideas dear to their lives.

As students grow as readers and writers, the language of books and print becomes a critical component to furthering their literacy development. Vocabulary is learned when purposeful reading, writing, listening, and speaking take place. Even more words can be learned when children explicitly examine printed words to discover consistencies among them and how consistent patterns relate to oral language—to speech sounds and to meaning.

A major aim of this book is to demonstrate how an exploration of spelling—orthography—can lead to lengthening and strengthening of the literacy braid. Teachers must understand the ways in which these threads intertwine to create this bond so that they can direct children's attention to words *their* way.

FIGURE 1.1   Braid of Literacy

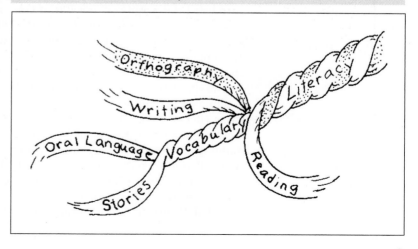

There are similarities in the ways learners of all ages expand their knowledge of the world. It seems that humans have a natural interest in finding order and patterns, comparing and contrasting, and paying attention to what remains the same despite minor variations. Infants learn to recognize Daddy as the same Daddy with or without glasses, with or without a hat or whiskers. Through such daily interactions, we categorize our surroundings. Similarly, our students expand their vocabularies by comparing one concept with another. Gradually, the number of concepts they analyze increases, but the process is still one of comparing and contrasting. They may first call anything with four legs "doggie" until they attend to the features that distinguish dogs, cats, and cows, and later terriers, Labrador retrievers, border collies, and greyhounds. In the process, they learn the vocabulary to label the categories.

FIGURE 1.2   Emma Sorting Words

Word study, as described in this book, occurs in hands-on activities that reflect basic cognitive learning processes: comparing and contrasting by categorizing word features, and then discovering similarities and differences within and between categories. Word features include their sounds, their spelling patterns, and their meaning. For example, by sorting words according to whether they end in a "silent" *e*, as Emma is doing in Figure 1.2, students can discover a consistent pattern: words ending with a "silent" *e* usually have a long vowel sound (ā - *cake*) while those without a final *e* have a short vowel sound (ă - *cat*). Under the guidance of a knowledgeable teacher, the logic of the spelling system is revealed when students sort words into categories. During word study, words and pictures are sorted in routines that require children to examine, discriminate, and make critical judgments about speech sounds, spelling patterns, and meanings.

Children's Spellings: A Window into Developing Word Knowledge

Students have probably been "inventing" their own spelling ever since paper and pencil have been available, but it was not until the early 1970s that Charles Read (1971, 1975) and Carol Chomsky (1971) took a serious look at young children's spelling attempts. Their work introduced the world of literacy to the notion of "invented spelling." Read understood that preschoolers' attempts were not just random approximations of print. To the contrary, his linguistic analysis showed that children's invented spellings provided a window into their developing word knowledge. These inventions revealed a systematic logic to the way some preschoolers selected letters to represent speech sounds.

At about the same time, Edmund Henderson and his colleagues at the University of Virginia had begun to look for similar logic in students' spellings across ages and grade levels (Beers & Henderson, 1977; Henderson & Beers, 1980). Read's findings provided these researchers with the tools they needed to interpret the errors they were studying. Building on Read's discoveries, Henderson discerned an underlying logic to students' errors that changed over time, moving from the spelling of single letters and letter groups or patterns (Henderson, Estes, & Stonecash, 1972) to the spelling of meaning units such as suffixes and word roots. The Virginia spelling studies corroborated and extended Read's findings upward through the grades and resulted in a comprehensive model of developmental word knowledge (Henderson, 1990; Templeton & Bear, 1992; Templeton & Morris, 2000).

Subsequent studies confirmed this developmental model across many groups of students, from preschoolers (Ouellete & Sénéchal, 2008; Templeton & Spivey, 1980) through adults (Bear, Truex, & Barone, 1989; Massengill, 2006; Worthy & Viise, 1996), as well as across socioeconomic levels, dialects, and other alphabetic languages (Bear, Helman, & Woessner, 2009; Cantrell, 2001; He & Wang, 2009; Helman, 2009; Helman & Bear, 2007; Yang, 2005). The power of this model lies in the diagnostic information contained in students' spelling inventions that reveal their current understanding of written words (Invernizzi, Abouzeid, & Gill, 1994). In addition, the analysis of students' spelling has been explored independently by other researchers (e.g., Bahr, Silliman, & Berninger, 2009; Bissex, 1980; Ehri, 1992; Foorman & Petscher, 2010; Holmes & Davis, 2002; Larkin & Snowling, 2008; Nunes & Bryant, 2009; Richgels, 1995, 2001; Treiman, 1993; Treiman, Stothard, & Snowling, 2013; Young, 2007).

Henderson and his students not only studied the development of children's spelling, but also devised an instructional model to support that development. They determined that through an informed analysis of students' spelling attempts, teachers can differentiate and provide timely instruction in phonics, spelling, and vocabulary that is essential to move students forward in reading and writing. We call this efficient and effective instruction **word study.**

Why Is Word Study Important?

Becoming fully literate depends on fast, accurate recognition of words and their meanings in texts, and fast, accurate production of words in writing so that readers and writers can focus their attention on making meaning. This rapid, accurate recognition and production depends on students' written word knowledge—their understanding of phonics and spelling patterns, word parts, and meanings. Planning and implementing a word study curriculum that explicitly teaches students necessary skills, and engages their interest and motivation to learn about words, is a vital aspect of any literacy program. Indeed, how to teach students these basics in an effective manner has sparked controversy among educators for nearly two hundred years (Balmuth, 1992; Carnine, Silbert, Kame'enui, & Tarver, 2009; Mathews, 1967; Schlagal, 2013; Smith, 2002). But helping students learn about words should not be controversial.

Many phonics, spelling, and vocabulary programs are characterized by explicit skill instruction, a systematic scope and sequence, and repeated practice. However, much of the repeated practice consists of drill and memorization, so students have little opportunity to discover spelling patterns, manipulate word concepts, or apply critical thinking skills. Although students need explicit skill instruction within a systematic curriculum, it is equally true that "teaching is not telling" (James, 1899/1958).

Students need hands-on opportunities to manipulate words and features in ways that allow them to generalize beyond isolated, individual examples to entire groups of words that are spelled the same way (Joseph, 2002; Juel & Minden-Cupp, 2000; Templeton, Smith, Moloney, Van Pelt, & Ives, 2009; White, 2005). Excelling at word recognition, spelling, and vocabulary is not just a matter of memorizing isolated rules and definitions. The best way to develop fast and accurate recognition and production of words is to engage in meaningful reading and writing, and to have multiple opportunities to examine those same words and their features in and out of context. The most effective instruction in phonics, spelling, and vocabulary links word study to the texts students are reading, provides a systematic scope and sequence of word features, provides multiple opportunities for hands-on practice and application, and promotes active thinking. Word study teaches students how to look at and analyze words so that they can construct an ever-deepening understanding of how spelling works to represent sound and meaning. We believe that this word study is well worth 10 to 15 minutes of instruction and practice daily (Carlisle, Kelcey, & Berebitsky, 2013).

What Is Word Study?
In this video author Marcia Invernizzi explains why word study is important.

What Is the Purpose of Word Study?

The purpose of word study is twofold: it examines words in order to 1) reveal the logic and consistencies within our written language system, and 2) help students master recognizing, spelling, defining, and using specific words. First, students develop a *general* knowledge of English spelling. Through active exploration, word study teaches students to examine words to discover generalizations about English spelling, such as the role of final silent *e* to mark a long vowel sound. They learn the regularities, patterns, and conventions of English orthography needed to read and spell. This general knowledge reflects what students understand about the nature of our spelling system. Second, word study increases *specific* knowledge of words—the spellings and meanings of individual words.

General knowledge is what we use when we encounter a new word, when we do not know how to spell a word, or when we do not know the meaning of a specific word. The better our general knowledge of the system, the better we are at decoding unfamiliar words, spelling correctly, or guessing the meanings of words. For example, if you know about short vowels and consonants you would have no trouble attempting the word *brash* even if you have never seen or written it before. The spelling is straightforward, like so many single-syllable short vowel words. The general knowledge that words that are similar in spelling are related in meaning, such as *compete* and *competition*, makes it easier to understand the meaning of a word like *competitor*, even if it is unfamiliar. Additional clues offered by context also increase the chances of reading and understanding a word correctly.

To become fully literate, however, we also need specific knowledge about individual words. The word *rain*, for example, might be spelled *rane*, *rain*, or *rayne*; all three spellings are theoretically plausible. However, only specific knowledge allows us to remember the correct spelling. Likewise, only specific knowledge of the spelling of *which* and *witch* makes it possible to know which is which! The relationship between specific knowledge and general knowledge of the system is *reciprocal*—each supports the other. Conrad (2008) expressed this idea in noting that "the transfer between reading and spelling occurs in both directions" (p. 876) and that "the orthographic representations established through practice can be used for both reading and spelling" (p. 869).

What Is the Basis for Developmental Word Study?

Word study evolves from four decades of research exploring developmental aspects of word knowledge with children and adults (Henderson, 1990; Henderson & Beers, 1980; Templeton, 2011; Templeton & Bear, 1992). This line of research has documented the specific kinds of spelling errors that tend to occur in clusters and reflect students' uncertainty over certain recurring spellings or orthographic principles. These "clusters" have been described in terms of (1) errors dealing with the alphabetic match of letters and sounds (FES for *fish*), (2) errors dealing with letter patterns (SNAIK for *snake*) and syllable patterns (POPING for *popping*), and (3) errors dealing with words related in meaning (INVUTATION for *invitation*; a lack of knowledge that *invite* provides the clue to the correct spelling of the second vowel). The same cluster types of errors have been observed among students with learning disabilities and dyslexia (Bear, Negrete, & Cathey, 2012; Sawyer, Lipa-Wade, Kim, Ritenour, & Knight, 1997; Templeton & Ives, 2007; Treiman, 1985; Worthy & Invernizzi, 1989), students who speak in variant dialects (Cantrell, 2001; Dixon, Zhao, & Joshi, 2012; Stever, 1980; Treiman, Goswami, Tincoff, & Leevers, 1997), and students who are learning to read in different alphabetic languages (Bear, Templeton, Helman, & Baren, 2003; Helman, 2004; Helman et al., 2012; Yang, 2005). Longitudinal and cross-grade-level research in developmental spelling has shown that developmental progression occurs for all learners of written English in the same direction, and varies only in the rate of acquisition (Invernizzi & Hayes, 2004; Treiman, Stothard, & Snowling, 2013).

Word study also builds on the history of English spelling. Developmental spelling researchers have examined the three layers of English orthography in the historical evolution of English spelling and students' developmental progression from *alphabet* to *pattern* to *meaning* layers. Figure 1.3 illustrates how the layers of written English are arranged. Each of the three layers of the English spelling system is built on the one before: to the straightforward alphabetic base of Old English was added the more abstract letter patterns in Middle English, and to that layer were added the Greek and Latin meaning units such as prefixes, suffixes, and roots in early Modern English. For mature readers, upper level word study examines interactions among the three layers.

FIGURE 1.3   Three Layers of English Orthography

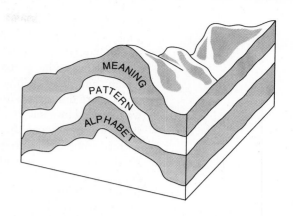

Alphabet

Our spelling system is **alphabetic** because it represents the relationship between letters and sounds. In the word *sat*, each sound is represented by a single letter; we blend the sounds for *s*, *a*, and *t* to read the word *sat*. In the word *chin*, we still hear three sounds, even though there are four letters, because the first two letters, *ch*, function like a single letter, representing a single sound. So we can match letters— sometimes singly, sometimes in pairs—to sounds from left to right and create words. This **alphabetic layer** in English spelling is the first layer of information at work.

Developmental Word Study Instruction
This video introduces the three layers of English.

The alphabetic layer of English orthography was established during the time of Old English, the language spoken and written by the Anglo-Saxons in England between the Germanic invasions of the sixth century B.C.E. and the conquest of England by William of Normandy in 1066 (Lerer, 2007). Old English was remarkably consistent in letter–sound correspondence and used the alphabet to systematically represent speech sounds. The long vowels were pronounced close to the way they are in modern Romance languages today, such as Spanish, French, and Italian (i.e. E is pronounced as long A as in *tres* and I is pronounced as long E as in *Rio*).

The history of the alphabetic layer reflected in the story of Old English is relevant to teachers today because beginners spell like "little Saxons" as they begin to read and write (Henderson, 1981). Armed with only a rudimentary knowledge of the alphabet and letter sounds, beginning spellers of all backgrounds use their alphabet knowledge quite literally. They rely on the sound embedded in the names of the letters to represent the sounds they are trying to represent (Invernizzi, 1992; Read, 1971; Young, 2007). This strategy works quite well for consonants when the names do, in fact, contain the correct corresponding speech sounds (*Bee, Dee, eF, eS*, and so forth). It works less well for letters that have more than one sound (*C: /s/ and /k/*), and it does not work at all for consonants with names that do not contain their corresponding speech sounds (*W: double you; Y: wie;* and *H: aitch*). Short vowel sounds are particularly problematic for novice spellers because there is no single letter that "says" the short vowel sound. As a result, beginning readers choose a letter whose name, when pronounced, sounds and feels closest to the targeted short vowel sound (Beers & Henderson, 1977; Read, 1975). For example, beginning readers often spell the short *e* sound in *bed* with the letter *a* (BAD) and the short *i* sound in *rip* with the letter *e* (REP).

Pattern

Why don't we spell all words in English "the way they sound"—at the alphabetic level, in other words? If we did, words like *cape, bead,* and *light* would look like *cap, bed,* and *lit*—but these spellings, of course, already represent other words. Therefore, the **pattern layer** overlies the alphabetic layer. Because there are 42 to 44 sounds in English and only 26 letters in the alphabet, single sounds are sometimes spelled with more than one letter or are affected by other letters that do not stand for any sounds themselves. When we look beyond single letter–sound match-ups and search for **patterns** that guide the groupings of letters, however, we find surprising consistency (Hanna, Hanna, Hodges, & Rudorf, 1966; Venezky, 1999).

Take, for example, the *ain* in *rain*: we say that the silent *i* is a **vowel marker**, indicating that the preceding vowel letter, *a*, stands for a long vowel sound. The *i* does not stand for a sound itself, but marks the vowel before it as long. The *ai* group of letters follows a pattern: when you have a pair of vowels in a single syllable, this letter grouping forms a pattern that often indicates a long vowel. We refer to this as the "AI pattern" or as the consonant-vowel-vowel-consonant (CVVC) pattern—one of several high-frequency long-vowel patterns. Overall, knowledge about orthographic patterns within words is considerably valuable to students in both their reading and their spelling.

Where did these patterns originate? The simple letter–sound consistency of Old English was overlaid by a massive influx of French words after the Norman Conquest in 1066. Because these words entered the existing language through bilingual Anglo-Norman speakers and writers, some of the French pronunciations and spelling conventions were adopted, too. Old English was thus overlaid with the vocabulary and spelling traditions of the ruling class, the Norman French. This complex interaction of pronunciation change on top of the intermingling of French and English spellings led to a proliferation of different vowel sounds represented by different vowel patterns. The extensive repertoire of vowel patterns today is attributable to this period of history, such as the various pronunciations of the *ea* pattern in words like *bread* and *thread*, *great* and *break*, *meat* and *clean*. It is uncanny that students in this pattern stage of spelling spell like "little Anglo-Normans" when they write *taste* as TAIST or *leave* as LEEVE.

Meaning

The third layer of English orthography is the **meaning layer.** When students learn that groups of letters can represent meaning directly, they will be much less puzzled when encountering unusual spellings. Examples of these units or groups of letters are prefixes, suffixes, and Greek and Latin roots. These units of meaning are called **morphemes**—the smallest units of meaning in a language.

One example of how meaning functions in the spelling system is the prefix *re-*: Whether we hear it pronounced "ree" as in *rethink* or "ruh" as in *remove*, the morpheme spelling stays the same because it directly represents meaning. Why is *sign* spelled with a silent *g*? Because it is related in meaning to *signature*, in which the *g* is pronounced. The letters *s-i-g-n* remain in both words to visually preserve the meaning relationships that these words share. Likewise, the letter sequence *photo* in *photograph*, *photographer*, and *photographic* signals spelling–meaning connections among these words, despite the changes in sounds that the letter *o* represents.

The explosion of knowledge and culture during the Renaissance required a new, expanded vocabulary to accommodate the growth in learning that occurred during this time. Greek and Latin were used by educated people throughout Europe and classical roots had the potential to meet this demand for meaning. Greek roots could be combined (e.g., *autograph* and *autobiography*), and prefixes and suffixes were added to Latin roots (*inspect*, *spectator*, and *spectacular*). So, to the orthographic record of English history was added a third layer of meaning that built new vocabulary out of elements that came from classical Greek and Latin.

The spelling–meaning relations inherent in words brought into English during the Renaissance have important implications for vocabulary instruction today as students move through the intermediate grades and beyond (Templeton 2011/2012, 2012). When students explore how spelling visually preserves meaning relationships among words with the same derivations (e.g., note the second b in *bomb* and *bombard*), they see how closely related spelling is to meaning and vocabulary. The seemingly arbitrary spelling of some words—in which silent letters occur or vowel spellings seem irrational—is in reality central to understanding the meanings of related words. For example, the silent *c* in *muscle* is "sounded" in the related words *muscular* and *musculature*—all of which come from the Latin *musculus*, literally a little mouse (the rippling of a muscle reminded the Romans of the movements of a mouse!). Such words, through their spellings, carry their history and meaning with them (Venezky, 1999; Templeton et al., 2015).

Learning the Layers of English Orthography

Organizing the phonics, spelling, and vocabulary curriculum according to historical layers of alphabet, pattern, and meaning provides a systematic guide for instruction. It places the types of words to be studied in an evolutionary progression that mirrors the development of the orthographic system itself. Anglo-Saxon words, the oldest words in English, are among the easiest to read and the most familiar. Words like *sun, moon, day,* and *night* are high-frequency "earthy" words that populate easy reading materials in the primary grades. Anglo-Saxon words survive in high-frequency prepositions, pronouns, conjunctions, and auxiliary verbs (e.g., *have, was, does*) although the pronunciation is now quite different. More difficult Norman French words of one and two syllables—words like *chance, chamber, royal, guard,* and *conquer*—frequently appear in books suitable for the elementary grades. The less frequent, more academic vocabulary of English—words like *calculate, maximum, cumulus, nucleus, hemisphere, hydraulic,* and *rhombus*—are Latin and Greek in origin and appear most often in student reading selections in the upper elementary grades and beyond.

Alphabet, pattern, and meaning represent three broad principles of written English and form the layered record of orthographic history. As students learn to read and write, they appear to reinvent the system as it was itself invented. As shown in Figure 1.4, beginners invent the spellings of simple words phonetically, just as the Anglo-Saxons did over a thousand years ago. As students become independent readers, they add a second layer by using patterns, much as the Norman French did. Notice in Figure 1.4 the overuse of the silent *e* vowel marker at the ends of all of Antonie's words, much like Geoffrey Chaucer's! Intermediate and advanced readers invent conventions for joining syllables and units of meaning, as was done during the Renaissance when English incorporated a large classical Greek and Latin vocabulary (Henderson, 1990; Templeton, Bear, Invernizzi, & Johnston, 2010). As Figure 1.4 shows, both Julian, age 14, and Queen Elizabeth I in 1600 had to deal with issues of consonant doubling in the middle of words.

In this book, we argue that orthographic knowledge—understanding the ways in which letters and letter patterns in words represent sound and meaning—plays a central role in a comprehensive language arts program that links reading and writing. Word knowledge accumulates as students develop orthographic understandings at the alphabetic, pattern, and meaning levels. This happens when they read and write purposefully and are also provided with explicit, systematic word study instruction by knowledgeable teachers. Word study should give students the experiences they need to progress through and integrate these layers of information.

- For students who are experimenting with the alphabetic match of letters and sounds, teachers can contrast aspects of the writing system that relate directly to the representation of sound. For example, words spelled with short *e* (*bed, leg, net, neck, mess*) are compared with words spelled with short *o* (*hot, rock, top, log, pond*).

FIGURE 1.4 **Comparison of Historical and Students' Development across Three Layers of English Orthography: Alphabet, Pattern, and Meaning**

	Historical Spelling	Students' Spelling-by-Stage
Alphabet	**Anglo-Saxon (Lord's Prayer, 1000)**	**Letter Name–Alphabetic (Tawanda, age 6)**
	WIF (wife)	WIF (wife)
	TODAEG (today)	TUDAE (today)
	HEAFONUM (heaven)	HAFAN (heaven)
Pattern	**Norman French (Chaucer, 1440)**	**Within Word Patterns (Antonie, age 8)**
	YONGE (young)	YUNGE (young)
	SWETE (sweet)	SWETE (sweet)
	ROOTE (root)	ROOTE (root)
	CROPPE (crop)	CROPPE (crop)
Meaning	**Renaissance (Elizabeth I, 1600)**	**Syllables & Meaning (Julian, age 14)**
	DISSCORD (discord)	DISSCORD (discord)
	FOLOWE (follow)	FOLOWE (follow)
	MUSSIKE (music)	MUSSIC (music)

Source: Adapted from "Using Students' Invented Spellings as a Guide for Spelling Instruction That Emphasizes Word Study" by M. Invernizzi, M. Abouzeid, & T. Gill, 1994, *Elementary School Journal, 95*(2), p. 158. Reprinted by permission of The University of Chicago Press.

- For students experimenting with pattern, teachers can contrast patterns as they relate to vowels. For example, words spelled with *ay* (*play, day, tray, way*) are compared to words spelled with *ai* (*wait, rain, chain, maid*).
- For students experimenting with conventions of syllables, affixes (prefixes and suffixes), and other meaning units, teachers can help students see that words with similar meanings are often spelled the same, despite changes in pronunciation. For example, *admiration* is spelled with an *i* in the second syllable because it comes from the word *admire*.

Throughout this text, the foundational skills found in the CCSS and most state core standards are addressed explicitly. The vocabulary standards may be found in the language sections of state standards and at the upper levels include a focus on academic vocabulary instruction.

The Development of Orthographic Knowledge

When we say word study is developmental, we mean that the study of specific word features must match the level of the learner's word knowledge. Word study is not a one-size-fits-all program of instruction that begins in the same place for all students within a grade level. One unique quality of word study, as we describe it, lies in the critical role of differentiating instruction for different levels of word knowledge. Though particular sources of information may predominate at different stages—for example, *alphabetic* for beginning spellers and readers, *syllabic* and *morphemic* for more skilled and proficient readers and spellers—there may also be subtle influences of or interaction with other sources of information (Templeton, 2003). For example, beginning readers and spellers may read and spell certain morphemes such as *-ed*, *-ing*, and *un-* correctly, but instruction will focus primarily on developing their understanding of alphabetic, and later, pattern correspondences in spelling. More focused instruction involving morphemes and their spelling will occur at later stages.

Knowledgeable educators have come to know that word study instruction must match the needs of the child. This construct, called **instructional level,** is a powerful determinant of what may be learned. Simply put, we must teach within each child's zone of understanding (Harré & Moghaddam, 2003; Vygotsky, 1962). To do otherwise results in frustration or boredom and little learning in either case. Just as in learning to play the piano—when students must work through book A, then book B, and then book C—learning to read and spell is a gradual and cumulative process. Word study begins with finding out what each child already knows and starting instruction there.

One of the easiest and most informative ways to know what students need to learn is to look at the way they spell words. Students' efforts to spell provide a direct window into how they think the spelling system works. By interpreting what students do, educators can target a specific student's instructional level and plan word study instruction that this student is ready to learn. Furthermore, by applying basic principles of child development, educators have learned how to engage students in learning about word features in a child-centered, developmentally appropriate way.

When students are instructed within their own zone of understanding or **zone of proximal development (ZPD)**—studying words *their* way—they are able to build on what they already know, to learn what they need to know next, and to move forward. Zone of proximal development was first described by Vygotsky (1962): the "zone" refers to the span between what a learner knows and is able to do independently, and what she is able to do with support and guidance. With explicit instruction and ample experience reading, writing, and examining words, spelling features that were previously omitted or confused become incorporated into an ever-increasing reading and writing vocabulary.

Stages of Spelling Development

As we have described, students move from easier one-to-one correspondences between letters and sounds, to more difficult, abstract relationships between letter patterns and sounds, to even more sophisticated relationships between meaning units as they relate to sound and pattern. Developmental spelling research describes this growth as a continuum or a series of chronologically ordered stages or phases of word knowledge (Ehri, 2005; Nunes & Bryant, 2009; Steffler, 2001; Templeton, 2011). In this book, we use the word *stage* as a metaphor to inform instruction. In reality, as students grow in conceptual knowledge of the three layers of information about English and of specific word features, there is some overlap in the layers and features students understand and use. In fact, as students grow in their understanding of how spelling represents both sound and meaning, they also become more flexible in their application of spelling strategies and they are able to do more than just "sound it out." They may be able to use analogies to other words with similar sounds, patterns, or meanings, or use spelling–meaning connections to figure it out. There is a range of grades during which students pass through these stages, as described in Figure 1.5. You may find that state foundational core standards indicate performance standards suggesting earlier acquisition of the skills and understandings represented by each of these stages.

Stages are marked by broad, qualitative shifts in the types of spelling errors students make as well as changes in the way they read words. It is not the case that students abandon sound once they move to the use of patterns, or abandon patterns once they move to the use of meaning units or **morphology.** Rather, the names of the stages capture the key understandings that distinguish them among the layers of English orthography and among the levels of students' general knowledge of the orthography (Bryant, Nunes, & Bindman, 1997; Ehri, 1997, 2006; Templeton, 2002, 2003). Over the years, the labels used to describe the five stages of spelling development have changed somewhat to reflect what research has revealed about the nature of developmental word knowledge, and to represent most appropriately what occurs at each level.

Because word study is based on students' level of orthographic knowledge, the word study activities presented in this book are arranged by stages of spelling. Knowing each student's stage of spelling determines appropriate word study activities. This chapter presents a brief overview of these stages. As illustrated in Figure 1.5, the Chapters 4 through 8 explore each of these stages in depth. By conducting assessments throughout the year, as described in Chapter 2, teachers can determine the spelling stages of their students and track students' progress and development. An important prerequisite to instruction and assessment is knowing the continuum of orthographic development.

For each stage, students' orthographic knowledge is defined by three functional levels that are useful guides for knowing when to teach what (Invernizzi et al., 1994):

1. What students do correctly—an independent or easy level
2. What students "use but confuse"—an instructional level or zone of proximal development at which instruction is most helpful
3. What is absent in students' spelling—a frustration level in which spelling concepts are too difficult

In Vygotskian terms (1962), we focus on each student's zone of proximal development by determining what students use but confuse. This is where instruction most benefits the student.

FIGURE 1.5 **Spelling and Reading Stages, Grade Levels, and Corresponding Instructional Chapters**

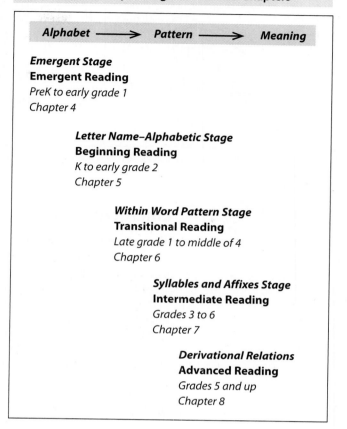

Alphabet $\longrightarrow$ *Pattern* $\longrightarrow$ *Meaning*

Emergent Stage
Emergent Reading
PreK to early grade 1
Chapter 4

Letter Name–Alphabetic Stage
Beginning Reading
K to early grade 2
Chapter 5

Within Word Pattern Stage
Transitional Reading
Late grade 1 to middle of 4
Chapter 6

Syllables and Affixes Stage
Intermediate Reading
Grades 3 to 6
Chapter 7

Derivational Relations
Advanced Reading
Grades 5 and up
Chapter 8

PD **pd** TOOLKIT™
for Words Their Way®

Development of Students
In five different videos, teachers describe the development of their students in each stage.

FIGURE 1.6 Emergent Writing

A. "All the birdies" Haley

B. "Cowboy"

C. CAMERON "Jasmin" JMOE

Source: From dissertation by Janet Bloodgood (1996). Adapted with permission.

Emergent Stage

The **emergent stage** encompasses the writing efforts of children who are not yet reading conventionally and in most cases have not been exposed to formal reading instruction. Emergent writers typically range in age from 2 to 5 years, although anyone not yet reading conventionally is in this stage of development. Emergent writing may range from random marks to legitimate letters that bear a relationship to sound. However, most of the emergent stage is decidedly **prephonetic,** which means there is little if any direct relationship between a character on the page and an individual speech sound.

As we explore in Chapter 4, emergent writing may be divided into a series of steps or landmarks. Children move from producing large scribbles undecipherable from the drawing (as illustrated in Figure 1.6A, Haley's picture of birdies), to using something that looks like scribbles separate from the picture (see Figure 1.6B where the child labeled his drawing to the left as "cowboy"), and on to using letters to represent some sounds in words (Figure 1.6C where Jasmin has been written as JMOE). In between, emergent learners are learning and experimenting with various symbols such as numbers and letter like forms (Cabell, Tortorelli, & Gerde, 2013). Moving from this stage to the next stage hinges on learning the **alphabetic principle:** letters represent sounds in a systematic way, and words can be segmented into sequences of sound from left to right.

FIGURE 1.7 Early Letter Name–Alphabetic Spelling: Ellie's Note to Her Sister, Meg—"When Are You Coming?"

Letter Name–Alphabetic Stage

The **letter name–alphabetic spelling stage** encompasses that period during which students are first formally taught to read, typically during kindergarten and early first grade. Most letter name–alphabetic spellers are between the ages of 4 and 7 years, although a beginning reader at age 55 also can be a letter name–alphabetic speller (Bear, 1989; Massengill, 2006; Viise, 1996). Early in this stage, "letter name" is students' dominant approach to spelling; that is, they use the *names* of the letters as cues to the sounds they want to represent (Read, 1975). In Ellie's early letter name–alphabetic spelling shown in Figure 1.7, she wrote YNRUKM: she used the letter *Y* to represent the /w/ sound at the beginning of the word *when*, because the first sound in the pronounced letter name *Y* ("wie") matches the first sound in the word *when*. The letter name for *N* includes the "en" sound to finish off the word *when*. Ellie used *R* and *U* to represent the entire words *are* and *you*, another early letter name strategy.

As students move through this stage, they learn to segment the individual speech sound or **phonemes** within words and to match an appropriate letter or letter pairs to those sounds. Students in the later part of the letter name–alphabetic stage spell much like the sample in Figure 1.8. Kaitlyn shows mastery of most beginning and ending consonants. She spells many high-frequency words correctly, such as *will*, *love*, *have*, and *you*. What clearly separates her from Ellie's early letter name spelling is her consistent use of vowels. Long vowels, which "say their name," appear in TIM for *time* and HOP for *hope*, but silent letters are not represented. Short vowels are used but confused, as in *miss* spelled as MES and *much* as MICH.

Within Word Pattern Stage

Students entering the **within word pattern spelling stage** can read and spell many words correctly because of their automatic knowledge of letter sounds and short-vowel patterns. This level of orthographic knowledge typically begins as students transition to independent reading toward the end of first grade. It expands for most students throughout second and third grade and into fourth. Although most within word pattern spellers typically range in age from 6 to 9 years, many low-skilled adult readers remain in this stage. Regardless, this period of orthographic development lasts longer than the letter name–alphabetic stage, because the vowel pattern system of English orthography is quite extensive.

The within word pattern stage begins when students move away from the linear, sound-by-sound approach of the letter name–alphabetic spellers and begin to include patterns or chunks of letter sequences and silent vowel markers like final *e*. Within word pattern spellers can think about words in more than one dimension; they study words by sound and pattern simultaneously. As the name of this stage suggests, within word pattern spellers take a closer look at vowel patterns within single-syllable words (Henderson, 1990).

Kim's writing in Figure 1.9 is that of an early within word pattern speller. She spells many short-vowel and high-frequency words correctly, such as *hill*, *had*, *them*, *girl*, and *won*. She also spells some common long-vowel patterns correctly in CVCe words like *time* and *game*. Kim hears the long vowel sound in words like *team*, *goal*, and *throw*, but she selects incorrect patterns, spelling them as TEME, GOWL, and THROWE and she omits the silent *e* in *cones*. These are good examples of how Kim is using but confusing long-vowel patterns.

During the within word pattern stage, students first study the common long-vowel patterns (long *o* can be spelled with *o*-consonant-*e* as in *joke*, *oa* as in *goal*, and *ow* as in *throw*) and then less common patterns such as the VCC pattern in *cold* and *most*. The most difficult patterns are **ambiguous vowels** because the sound is neither long nor short and the same pattern may represent different sounds, such as the *ou* in *mouth*, *cough*, *through*, and *tough*. These less common and ambiguous vowels may persist as misspellings into the late within word pattern stage.

Although the focus of the within word pattern stage is on the pattern layer of English orthography, students must also consider the meaning layer to spell and use **homophones**, words such as *bear* and *bare*, *deer* and *dear*, and *hire* and *higher*. These words sound the same but have different spellings and meanings. Because of this, sound, pattern, and meaning must be considered when spelling. Homophones introduce the spelling–meaning connection that is explored further in the next two stages of spelling development.

FIGURE 1.8   Late Letter Name–Alphabetic Spelling: Kaitlyn's Farewell Note to Her First-Grade Teacher

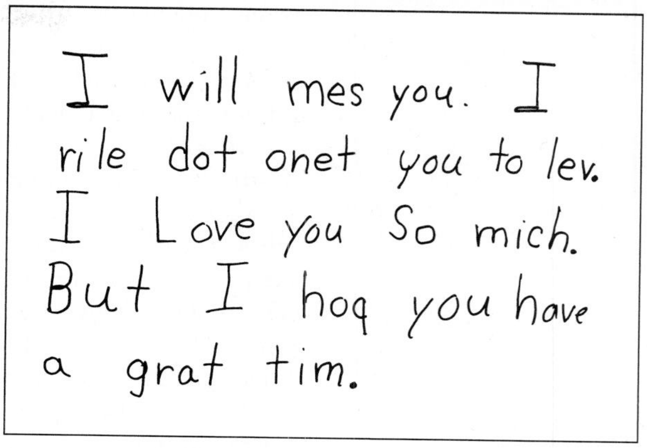

> I will mes you. I ri le dot onet you to lev. I Love you So mich. But I hoq you have a grat tim.

FIGURE 1.9   Early Within Word Pattern Spelling: Kim's Soccer Game

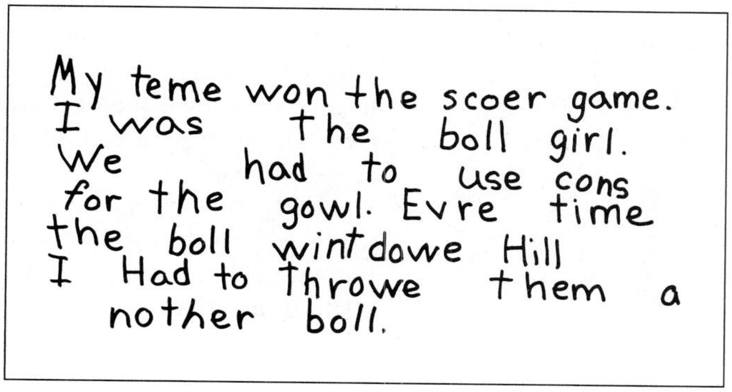

> My teme won the scoer game. I was the boll girl. We had to use cons for the gowl. Evre time the boll wintdowe Hill I Had to Throwe them a nother boll.

Syllables and Affixes Stage

The **syllables and affixes stage** is typically achieved in middle to upper elementary school, when students are expected to spell many words of more than one syllable. This represents a new point in word study when students consider spelling patterns where syllables meet, and meaning units such as affixes (prefixes and suffixes). Students in this fourth stage are most often between 8 and 12 years old, though many adults can also be found in this stage.

In Figure 1.10, a fourth-grader in the early part of the syllables and affixes stage has written about his summer vacation. Xavier spelled most one-syllable short and long vowel words correctly (*went, west, drove, last*). Many of his errors are in two-syllable words and fall at the places where syllables and affixes meet. Xavier does not know the conventions for preserving vowel sounds when adding affixes such as *-ed* and *-ing*. He spelled *stopped* as STOPED and *hiking* as HIKEING. The principle of doubling the consonant to keep the vowel short is used in LITTEL for *little*, but is lacking in his spelling of *summer* as SUMER. Final syllables often give students difficulty because the vowel sound is not clear and may be spelled different ways, as shown in Xavier's spellings of LITTEL for *little* and MOUNTINS for *mountains*.

Toward the end of the syllables and affixes stage, students explore the spelling of affixes that affect the meanings of words—for example, DESLOYAL for *disloyal* and CAREFULL for *careful*. Though studying simple affixes and base words as a decoding strategy begins earlier, studying base words and affixes more closely at this stage helps students construct the foundation for further exploration of word meanings in the next stage, derivational relations. At that stage, students study the spelling–meaning connections of related words (Templeton, 2004). By studying base words and derivational affixes, students learn more about English spelling as they enrich their vocabularies.

FIGURE 1.10 Syllables and Affixes Spelling: Xavier's Account of His Summer Adventures

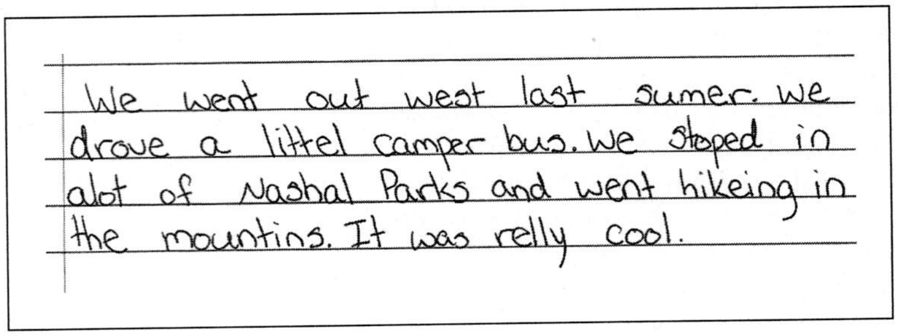

We went out west last sumer. We drove a littel camper bus. We stoped in alot of Nashal Parks and went hikeing in the mountins. It was relly cool.

Derivational Relations Stage

The **derivational relations spelling stage** is the final stage in the developmental model. Some students move into the derivational stage as early as grade 4 or 5, but most derivational relations spellers are found in middle school, high school, and college. This stage continues throughout adulthood, when individuals continue to read and write according to their interests and specialties. This stage of orthographic knowledge is known as *derivational relations* because this is when students examine how many words may be *derived* from base words and word roots. Students discover that the meanings and spellings of meaningful word parts or morphemes remain constant across different but derivationally related words (Henderson & Templeton, 1986; Henry, 1988; Nunes & Bryant, 2009; Schlagal, 2013; Templeton, 2004). Word study in this stage builds on and expands knowledge of a wide vocabulary, including thousands of words of Greek and Latin origin. We refer to this study as **generative** because as students explore and learn about the word formation processes of English they are able to *generate* knowledge of literally thousands of words (Graves, 1986; Harris, Schumaker, & Deshler, 2011; Kirk & Gillon, 2009; Nunes & Bryant, 2006; Templeton, 2012; Templeton et al., 2015).

Early derivational relations spellers like sixth-grader Kaitlyn (Figure 1.11) spell most words correctly. However, some of her errors reflect a lack of knowledge about derivations. For example, *favorite* spelled FAVERITE and *different* spelled DIFFRENT do not reflect their relationship to *favor* and *differ*. Her errors on final suffixes, such as the *-sion* in *division* and the *-ent* in *ingredients* are also very typical of students in this stage.

The logic inherent in this lifelong stage can be summed up as follows: words that are related in meaning are often related in spelling as well, despite changes in sound (Templeton, 1979, 1983, 2004). Spelling–meaning connections provide a powerful way of expanding vocabulary.

FIGURE 1.11   Derivational Relations Spelling: Kaitlyn's Sixth-Grade Math Journal Reflection

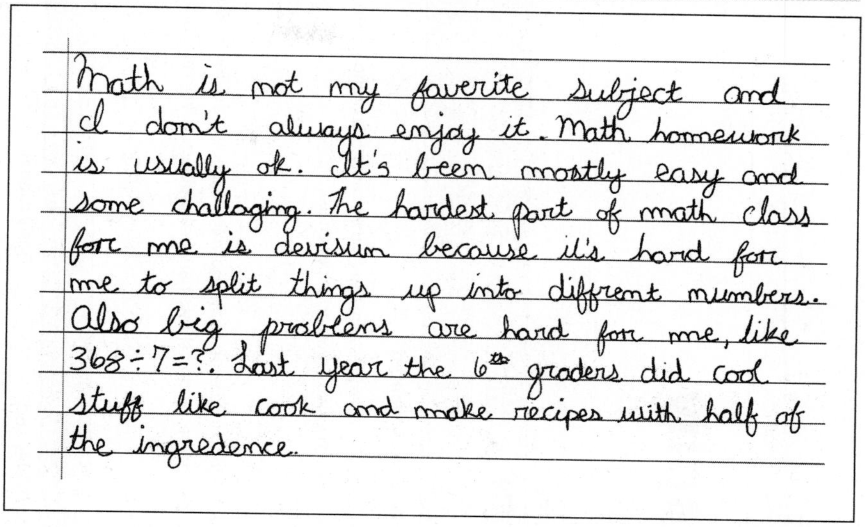

> Math is not my favorite subject and I don't always enjoy it. Math homework is usually ok. It's been mostly easy and some challaging. The hardest part of math class for me is devision because it's hard for me to split things up into diffrent numbers. Also big problems are hard for me, like 368 ÷ 7 = ?. Last year the 6th graders did cool stuff like cook and make recipes with half of the ingredence.

The Synchrony of Literacy Development

The scope and sequence of word study instruction we present in Chapters 4 through 8 is based on research describing the developmental relationship between spelling and reading behaviors. When teachers conduct word study with students, they address learning needs in all areas of literacy because development in one area relates to development in other areas. This harmony in the timing of development has been described as the **synchrony** of reading, writing, and spelling development (Bear, 1991b; Bear & Templeton, 1998). All three advance in stage like progressions that share important conceptual dimensions. Figure 1.12 illustrates the synchrony among reading, writing, and spelling, and presents key examples in the following discussion of each reading stage.

Individuals may vary in their rate of progress through these stages, but most tend to follow the same order of development. The observed synchrony makes it possible to bring together reading, writing, and spelling behaviors to assess and plan differentiated instruction that matches students' developmental pace. The following discussion centers on this overall progression, with an emphasis on the synchronous behaviors of reading and writing with spelling.

Emergent Readers

During the emergent stage, children may undertake reading and writing in earnest, but adults will recognize their efforts as more pretend than real. These students may "read" familiar books from memory using the pictures on each page to cue their recitation of the text. Chall (1983) called this stage of development *prereading* because students are not reading in a conventional sense. Emergent readers may call out the name of a favorite fast food restaurant when they recognize its logo, but they are not systematic in their use of any particular cue.

During the emergent stage, children lack an understanding of the alphabetic principle or show only the beginning of this understanding as they start to learn some letters. Emergent learners gradually acquire directionality as they try to fingerpoint read, and in their writing. By the end of this stage, emergent learners will have learned many letters of the alphabet and they may even include a few letters to represent sounds when they write.

Beginning Readers

Understanding the alphabetic nature of our language is a major hurdle for readers and spellers. The child who writes *light* as LT has made a quantum conceptual leap, having grasped

FIGURE 1.12   The Synchrony of Literacy Development

Layers of the Orthography

ALPHABET/SOUND · PATTERN · MEANING

Reading and Writing Stages:

Emergent	Beginning	Transitional	Intermediate/Advanced
Pretend read	Read aloud; word-by-word, finger-point reading	Approaching fluency, phrasal, some expression in oral reading, emergence of silent reading	Read fluently, with expression. Develop a variety of reading styles. Vocabulary grows with reading experience.
Developing concept of word	Rudimentary—Firm concept of word		
Pretend write	Word-by-word writing; writing moves from a few words to paragraph in length	Approaching fluency, more organization, several paragraphs	Fluent writing, build expression and voice, experience different writing, styles and genre, writing shows personal problem solving and personal reflection.

Spelling Stages:

Examples of spellings:

Word	Emergent → Early	Middle	Late	Letter Name–Alphabetic → Early	Middle	Late	Within Word Pattern → Early	Middle	Late	Syllables and Affixes → Early	Middle	Late	Derivational Relations → Early	Middle	Late
bed	 (scribble)	M3T	E	bd	bad		_bed_								
ship		TFP	S	sp	sep	shep	_ship_								
float		SMT	F	ft	fot	flot	flott	floaut	flote _float_						
train	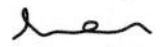	FSMP	G	jn	jan	tan	chran tran	teran traen	trane _train_						
bottle			B	bt	botl	bodol	botel	bottel	botal	botol	_bottle_				
cellar			S	slr	salr	celr	seler	celer	seler			_cellar_			
pleasure			P	pjr	plasr	plager	plejer	pleser	pleser	plesher	plesour	plesure	_pleasure_		
confident										confident	confednet	confadent		_confident_	
opposition										opasishan	opasitian	oposision	oposistian	oposision	_opposition_

that there are systematic matches between sounds and letters that must be made when writing. Early letter name–alphabetic spellers have moved from pretend reading to the beginning of real reading, as they start to use systematic letter–sound matches to identify and store words in memory. Beginning reading is achieved when students have a **concept of word in text**, which is demonstrated by a child's ability to point accurately to a few lines of familiar text—a demonstration of the one-to-one correspondence between what they read and say (Clay, 1979; Morris, Bloodgood, Lomax, & Perney, 2003; Uhry, 1999).

Just as early attempts to spell words are partial, beginning readers initially have limited knowledge of letter sounds as they try to identify words by using the letter sounds they do know. The kinds of reading errors students make during this phase offer insights into what they understand about print. Using context as well as partial consonant cues, a child reading about good things to eat might substitute *candy* or even *cookie* for *cake* in the sentence, "The cake was good." Readers in this stage require support in the form of predictable, memorable texts or books that limit the number and nature of words.

The reading by letter name–alphabetic spellers is often disfluent—that is, choppy and often word-by-word, unless they have read the passage before or are otherwise familiar with it (Bear, 1992). If you ask such spellers to read silently, the best they can do is to whisper. They need to read aloud to vocalize the letter sounds and usually fingerpoint as they read. Chall (1983) described children as being "glued to print" during this stage as they plod along slowly reading words, sometimes letter-by-letter, sound-by-sound.

Transitional Readers

During the transitional stage, students' reading becomes fluent because it is supported by a store of words that can be identified automatically "at first sight." These tend to be words they have read over and over again in meaningful contexts and words with frequently occurring letter patterns such as the consonant-vowel-consonant (CVC) pattern for short-vowel words. However, they "use but confuse" the various long-vowel patterns of English (Invernizzi, 1992).

During this stage, students integrate the knowledge and skills acquired in the previous two stages and they become more flexible in thinking about sound, pattern, and meaning. Advances in word knowledge affect students' writing, too. Their sizable sight word vocabulary allows them to write more quickly and with greater detail. Writing and reading speeds increase significantly from the beginning letter name–alphabetic stage to the transitional within word pattern stage, and over the course of this stage, oral reading is gradually replaced by silent reading as the preferred mode (Bear, 1992; Ehri, 2014; Invernizzi, 1992).

Intermediate and Advanced Readers

The stages of word knowledge that characterize intermediate and advanced readers include *syllables and affixes* and *derivational relations*, as shown in Figure 1.12. Students in these stages have relatively automatic word recognition, leaving their minds free to think as rapidly as they can read. Intermediate students read most texts with good accuracy and speed, both orally and silently. Students learn to become *flexible, strategic readers* and ultimately become *proficient adult readers* (Spear-Swerling & Sternberg, 1997). Reading becomes an ever-more dominant mode of learning information and concepts. Intermediate and advanced readers are usually fluent writers. The content of their writing often displays complex analysis and interpretation, reflecting a more sophisticated, discipline-specific vocabulary. The degree to which they write at this level often depends on the quality of the writing instruction they receive.

Vocabulary and word use play a central role in the connections that intermediate and advanced readers forge between reading and writing. From adolescence on, most of the new vocabulary students learn—except perhaps for slang—comes from reading, and reflects new domains of content-specific knowledge that students explore (Beck, McKeown, & Kucan,

2002; Zwiers, 2008). Studying spelling–meaning connections is central to maximizing this vocabulary growth (Nunes & Bryant, 2006; Templeton, 2004).

Chapter 2 will help you identify your students by the stages of reading, writing, and spelling. You will then know which chapters contain the activities that are most relevant to their development, as shown in Figure 1.5 on page 11.

Teachers often return to Figure 1.13 to examine the integrated model of how reading, writing, and spelling progress in synchrony. In parent–teacher conferences, teachers often refer to Figure 1.13 when they discuss a student's development. They explain to the parent how the child's spelling level corresponds to the characteristics of her reading level, as well as the types of writing we may expect from a child at that particular developmental level.

Words Their Way

Students acquire word knowledge implicitly as they read and write, and explicitly through instruction orchestrated by the teacher. An informed interpretation of students' reading and writing attempts shows us which words they can read and spell, and of those, which they might learn more about. There is more to pacing instruction than plugging students into a sequence of phonics or spelling features. Instructional *pacing* must be synonymous with instructional *placing*. That is, we must fit our instruction to what our students are using but confusing. How do we know what they are using but confusing? A good deal of what students understand about orthography is revealed in their uncorrected writing. Using the spelling inventories described in the next chapter as a guide, you will be able to place students and pace the content of word study.

Figure 1.13 illustrates the theory of developmental word knowledge and shows how word study links reading and writing. To help students explore and learn about words their way, instruction must be sensitive to two fundamental tenets:

1. Students' learning of phonics, spelling, and vocabulary is based on their developmental or instructional level.
2. Students' learning is based on the way they are naturally inclined to learn—through comparing and contrasting word features and discovering consistencies.

When these two tenets are honored, students learn *their* way—building from what is known about words to what is new. Rather than rote memorization activities designed only to ensure repeated mechanical practice, word study encourages exploration and examination of word features that are within a student's stage of literacy development. Word study is active, and by making judgments about words and sorting words according to similar features, students construct their own understandings about how the features work. Engaging instruction and thoughtful practice helps students internalize word features and become automatic in using what they have learned.

To foreshadow the word study instruction to come in this book, Figure 1.14 summarizes the characteristics of each spelling stage, the reading and writing context, and the word study instruction that is appropriate for each stage. After learning in Chapter 2 how to assess the developmental word knowledge of your students, the remaining chapters offer more detail about planning word study instruction for each stage of development. Figure 1.14 can be a reference as you learn more about the developmental stages discussed in Chapters 4 to 7 and later to check for the integration of reading, word study, and writing.

FIGURE 1.13   The Integration of Word Study with Reading and Writing

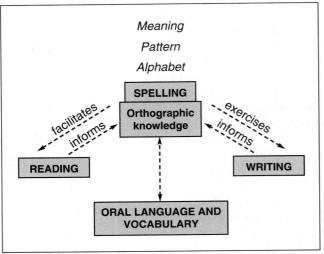

FIGURE 1.14 Developmental Stages, Characteristics, and Word Study Instruction

I. EMERGENT STAGE—CHAPTER 4

Characteristics

1. Scribbles letters and numbers
2. Lacks concept of word
3. Lacks letter–sound correspondence or represents most salient sound with single letters
4. Pretends to read and write

Reading and Writing Activities

1. Read to students and encourage oral language activities
2. Model writing using dictations and charts
3. Encourage pretend reading and writing

Word Study Focus

1. Develop oral language with concept sorts
2. Play with speech sounds to develop phonological awareness
3. Plan activities to learn the alphabet
4. Sort pictures by beginning sound
5. Encourage fingerpoint memory reading of rhymes, dictations, and simple pattern books
6. Encourage invented spelling

II. LETTER NAME–ALPHABETIC STAGE—CHAPTER 5
EARLY LETTER NAME–ALPHABETIC STAGE

Characteristics

1. Represents beginning and ending sounds
2. Uses letter names to invent spellings
3. Has rudimentary or firm concept of word seen in accurate fingerpointing and word knowledge
4. Reads word by word in beginning reading materials

Reading and Writing Activities

1. Read to students and encourage oral language activities
2. Develop concept of word by plenty of reading in predictable books, dictations, and simple rhymes
3. Record and reread individual dictations
4. Label pictures and write in journals regularly

Word Study Focus

1. Collect known words for word bank
2. Sort pictures and words by beginning sounds
3. Study word families that share a common vowel
4. Study beginning consonant blends and digraphs
5. Encourage invented spelling

MIDDLE TO LATE LETTER NAME–ALPHABETIC STAGE

Characteristics

1. Correctly spells initial and final consonants and some blends and digraphs

2. Uses letter names to spell vowel sounds
3. Spells phonetically, representing all salient sounds in a one-to-one, linear fashion
4. Omits most silent letters and preconsonantal nasals in spelling (*bop* or *bup* for *bump*)
5. Fingerpoints accurately and can self-correct when off track
6. Reads aloud slowly in a word-by-word manner

Reading and Writing Activities

1. Read to students
2. Encourage invented spellings in independent writing, but hold students accountable for features and words they have studied
3. Collect two- to three-paragraph dictations that are reread regularly
4. Encourage more expansive writing and consider some simple editing procedures for punctuation and high-frequency words

Word Study Focus

1. Sort pictures and words by different short-vowel word families
2. Sort pictures and words by short-vowel sounds and CVC patterns
3. Continue to examine more difficult consonant blends with pictures and words
4. Study preconsonantal nasals and digraphs at ends of words
5. Sort pictures comparing short- and long-vowel sounds
6. Collect known words for word bank (up to 200)

III. WITHIN WORD PATTERN STAGE—CHAPTER 6

Characteristics

1. Spells most single-syllable short vowel words correctly
2. Spells most beginning consonant digraphs and two-letter consonant blends
3. Attempts to use silent long-vowel markers
4. Reads silently and with more fluency and expression
5. Writes more fluently and in extended fashion
6. Can revise and edit

Reading and Writing Activities

1. Continue to read aloud to students
2. Guide silent reading of simple chapter books
3. Write each day, writers' workshops, conferencing, and publication

Word Study Focus

1. Complete daily activities in word study notebook
2. Sort words by long and short vowel sounds and by common long-vowel patterns

(continued)

FIGURE 1.14 Developmental Stages, Characteristics, and Word Study Instruction (*continued*)

3. Compare words with *r*-influenced vowels
4. Explore less common vowels, diphthongs (*oi, oy*), and other ambiguous vowels (*ou, au, ow, oo*)
5. Examine triple blends and complex consonant units such as *thr, str, dge, tch, ck*
6. Explore homographs and homophones

IV. SYLLABLES AND AFFIXES—CHAPTER 7

Characteristics
1. Spells most single-syllable words correctly
2. Makes errors at syllable juncture and in unaccented syllables
3. Reads with good fluency and expression
4. Reads faster silently than orally
5. Writes responses that are sophisticated and critical

Reading and Writing Activities
1. Plan read-alouds and literature discussions
2. Include self-selected or assigned silent reading of novels from different genres
3. Begin simple note-taking and outlining skills, and work with adjusting reading rates for different purposes
4. Explore reading and writing styles and genres

Word Study Focus
1. Examine plural endings
2. Study compound words
3. Study consonant doubling and inflectional endings
4. Study open and closed syllables and other syllable juncture issues
5. Explore syllable stress and vowel patterns in the accented syllable, especially ambiguous vowels
6. Focus on unaccented syllables such as *er* and *le*
7. Explore unusual consonant blends and digraphs (*qu, ph, gh, gu*)
8. Study base words and affixes
9. Focus on two-syllable homophones and homographs
10. Join spelling and vocabulary studies; link meaning and spelling with grammar and meaning

11. Explore grammar through word study
12. Sort and study common affixes (prefixes and suffixes)
13. Study stress or accent in two-syllable words

V. DERIVATIONAL RELATIONS—CHAPTER 8

Characteristics
1. Has mastered high-frequency words
2. Makes errors on low-frequency multisyllabic words derived from Latin and Greek
3. Reads with good fluency and expression
4. Reads faster silently than orally
5. Writes responses that are sophisticated and critical

Reading and Writing Activities
1. Include silent reading and writing, exploring various genres
2. Develop study skills, including textbook reading, notetaking, adjusting rates, test taking, report writing, and reference work
3. Focus on literary analysis

Word Study Focus
1. Focus on words that students bring to word study from their reading and writing
2. Join spelling and vocabulary studies; link meaning and spelling with grammar and meaning
3. Examine common and then less common roots, prefixes, and suffixes (e.g., *ion*)
4. Examine vowel and consonant alternations in derivationally related pairs
5. Study Greek and Latin word roots and stems
6. Focus on abstract Latin suffixes (*ence/ance; ible/able; ent/ant*)
7. Learn about absorbed or assimilated prefixes
8. Explore etymology, especially in the content areas
9. Examine content-related foreign borrowings

Getting Started

THE ASSESSMENT OF
ORTHOGRAPHIC DEVELOPMENT

In the chapter's opening image, you see four second-grade teachers who have just completed a spelling assessment. They review the data as a team and develop instructional goals and plans for word study in their classrooms. They see how children have progressed and what specific types of word study they want to plan for students in each of their three or four groups.

These teachers know that effective teaching cannot begin until you understand what students already know about words and what they are ready to learn. Likewise, you cannot make instructional adjustments until you evaluate the results of your teaching. This chapter presents an informal assessment process that will enable you to:

1. Informally observe and interpret orthographic knowledge in writing and reading.
2. Select and administer a qualitative spelling inventory.
3. Score and analyze the spelling inventory and identify specific features students need to study.
4. Determine students' developmental stage of word knowledge or **instructional level.**
5. Group students for differentiated instruction.
6. Use supplemental assessments for a wide array of instructional needs.
7. Set goals and monitor students' growth in orthographic knowledge over time.
8. Interpret the orthographic knowledge of your English learners.

Informal Observations to Assess Orthographic Knowledge

There is synchrony in the development of reading, writing, and spelling, and informally observing students' literacy behaviors provides rich information for planning instruction. Using strategies for reading and writing is related to students' increased levels of orthographic knowledge (Sharp et al., 2008). Because of these interactions, we look to what students do as they write and read.

Observe and Interpret Students' Writing

Teachers observe students daily as they write for various purposes. These observations help reveal what students understand about words. The following example demonstrates what you might learn about a kindergartner's literacy development. Sarah called this her "first restaurant review." Although it appears to be a menu, she posted it on the wall the way she had seen reviews posted in restaurants.

What Sarah Wrote	How Sarah Read What She Wrote
1. CRS KAM SAS	First course, clam sauce
2. CRS FESH	Second course, fish
3. CRS SAGATE	Third course, spaghetti
4. CRS POSH POPS	Fourth course, Push Pops

This writing tells a lot about Sarah: she sees a practical use for writing and she enjoys displaying her work. She has a good grasp of how to compose a list and she is even beginning to understand menu planning! When we look for what Sarah knows about spelling, we see that she represents many consonant sounds and some digraphs (the /sh/ in *fish* and *push*), but blends are incomplete (using K in KAM for the *cl* in *clam*). She has placed a vowel in all but one syllable; however, in spelling *fish* as FESH, Sarah confuses *e* and *i*. In the word *course*, spelled as CRS, the letter *r* represents the /r/ and the vowel sound. According to

FIGURE 2.1   Jake's Writing Sample

> My Acident
>
> Last year I scrapped my chian. I was
> shacking and my mom was too. My
> Dad met us at the docters offises. And
> I had to have stiches. Then my Dad
> bout me an ice crem cone. And we
> went home. I didn't go to school the
> nexs day. I was to tird.

PD TOOLKIT™

for Words Their Way®

Qualitative Spelling Checklist

Print this assessment form and make a copy for each student.

the sequence of development presented in Chapter 1, Sarah is considered a letter name–alphabetic speller who would benefit from instruction emphasizing short vowel sounds and the spelling of blends.

In Figure 2.1, we see a writing sample from Jake, an older student. The writing is readable because many words are spelled correctly and the others are close approximations. When we look for what Jake knows, we see that he has mastered most consonant relationships—even the three-letter blend in SCRAPPED—but not the complex *tch* unit in STICHES. Most long and short vowels are spelled correctly, as in *had, have, went, cone, home,* and *day*. When we look for what Jake uses but confuses, we see that he confuses the *-ck* and *-ke* ending in SHACKING for *shaking*. He inserts an unnecessary extra vowel when he spells *chin* as CHIAN but omits some silent vowel markers where they are needed, as with CREM for *cream*. Based on the vowel errors, Jake is considered a within word pattern speller who would benefit from the study of vowel patterns. We will take another look at Jake's word knowledge when we examine his spelling inventory later in this chapter.

Student writings, especially unedited rough drafts, are a gold mine of information about their orthographic knowledge. Many teachers keep a variety of student writing samples to document students' needs and growth over time. The Qualitative Spelling Checklist in Appendix A, and on the PD Toolkit, provides a systematic way to analyze your students' writing samples for specific orthographic features.

Relying entirely on writing samples has drawbacks, however. Some students are anxious about the accuracy of their spelling and will only use words they know how to spell. Others will get help from resources in the room, such as word walls, dictionaries, and the person sitting nearby, and thus their writing may overestimate what they really know. On the other hand, when students concentrate on getting their ideas on paper, they may not pay attention to spelling and make excessive errors. Some students write freely with little concern about accuracy and need to be reminded to use what they know. Daily observations will help you to determine not only student's orthographic knowledge but also their habits and dispositions.

Observe Students' Reading

Important insights into orthographic knowledge can also be made when we observe students' reading. Reading and spelling are related but not mirror images because the processes differ slightly. In reading, words can be recognized with many types of textual supports, so the ability to read words correctly lies a little ahead of students' spelling accuracy (Bear & Templeton, 2000; Templeton & Bear, 2011). For example, within word pattern spellers, who are also transitional readers, read many two-syllable words like *shopping* and *bottle* correctly but may spell those same words as SHOPING and BOTEL.

Spelling is a conservative measure of what students know about words in general, so if students can spell a word, then we know they can read the word. It seldom works the other way around except in the emergent and early letter name stages, in which students might generate spellings they don't know how to read (Invernizzi & Hayes, 2010; Rayner, Foorman, Perfetti, Pesetsky, & Seidenburg, 2001). When students consult reference materials such as a spell checker or dictionary, the spelling task becomes a reading task; we all know the phenomenon of being able to recognize the correct spelling if we just see it.

Like spelling errors, reading errors show us what students are using but confusing when they read, and certain errors can be expected of students in different stages. Teachers who understand students' developmental word knowledge will be in a good position to interpret students' reading errors and to make decisions about the appropriate prompt to use in reading with students (Brown, 2003). A student who substitutes *bunny* for *rabbit* in the sentence "The farmer saw a rabbit" is probably a beginning reader and an early letter name–alphabetic speller. The student uses the picture rather than knowledge about sound–symbol correspondences to generate a logical response. For students in this partial alphabetic phase (Ehri, 2014), drawing attention to the beginning sound can teach them to use their consonant knowledge. The teacher might point to the first letter and say, "Can that word be *bunny?* It starts with an *r.* What would start with *rrrrr?*"

Later in development, assessments of oral reading substitutions show a different level of word knowledge. A transitional reader who substitutes *growled* for *groaned* in "Jason groaned when he missed the ball" is probably attending to several orthographic features of the word. The student appears to use the initial blend *gr*, the vowel *o*, and the *-ed* ending to come up with an approximation that fits the meaning of the sentence. Because this student has vowel knowledge, a teacher might direct the student's attention to the *oa* pattern and ask him to try it again.

Our response to reading errors and our expectations for correcting such errors depend on a number of factors, one of which is knowing where students are developmentally. For example, it is inappropriate to ask students in the early letter name–alphabetic stage to sound out the word *flat* or even to look for a familiar part within the word in the hope that they might use their knowledge of *-at* words by analogy. Emergent and early letter name–alphabetic spellers may be able to use the beginning letters and sounds of words to help but frequently must also turn to context clues to read the words on the page (Adams, 1990; Biemiller, 1970; Johnston, 2000). They simply don't know enough words or patterns to apply analogy. However, students in the latter part of the letter name–alphabetic stage could be expected to sound out *flat* because they know other written words that sound and look the same, and they know something about blends and short vowels. Having students read at their instructional levels means that they can read most words correctly and when they encounter unfamiliar words in text, their orthographic knowledge, combined with context, will usually help them read the words with adequate comprehension. There are parallels between oral reading errors and the types of spelling errors students make but there is not a one-to-one match, for with the use of context, students can read more difficult words than they can spell.

Qualitative Spelling Inventories

Although observations made during writing and reading offer some insight into students' development, assessments should also include an informal qualitative spelling inventory.

Spelling inventories consist of lists of words specially chosen to represent a variety of spelling features at increasing levels of difficulty. The lists are not exhaustive in that they do not test all spelling features; rather, they include orthographic features that are most helpful in identifying a stage and planning instruction. Students take an inventory as they would a spelling test. The results are then analyzed to obtain a general picture of their orthographic development.

PD TOOLKIT™
for Words Their Way®

The Assessment Process
In this video teachers discuss the steps in the assessment process.

The Development of Inventories

The first inventories were developed under the leadership of Edmund Henderson at the University of Virginia. Most of these inventories consist of a list of words sampling a range of spelling features characteristic of each stage (Bear, 1982; Ganske, 1999; Invernizzi, 1992; Invernizzi, Meier, & Juel, 2003; Morris, 1999; Viise, 1994). The same developmental progression has been documented through the use of these inventories with learning disabled students (Invernizzi & Worthy, 1989), students identified as dyslexic (Sawyer, Wade, & Kim, 1999), and functionally literate adults (Worthy & Viise, 1996). Spelling inventories have also

been developed and researched for other alphabetic languages (Ford & Invernizzi, 2009; Gill, 1980; Temple, 1978; Yang, 2005).

Although there are multiple assessment tools that may be used with a broad range of students in preschool, primary, intermediate, and secondary classrooms (see Table 2.4 later in this chapter for examples), in this chapter we start by focusing on the three inventories shown in Table 2.1: the Primary Spelling Inventory (PSI), the Elementary Spelling Inventory (ESI), and the Upper-Level Spelling Inventory (USI). Each can be found in Appendix A, or printed from the website that accompanies this book.

Using Inventories

Spelling inventories are quick and easy to administer and score, and they are reliable and valid measures of what students know about words. Many teachers find these spelling inventories to be the most helpful and easily administered literacy assessments in their repertoires. Using these spelling inventories requires the four basic steps summarized here and discussed in detail in the sections that follow.

1. Select a spelling inventory based on grade level and students' achievement levels. Administer the inventory much as you would a traditional spelling test, but do not let students study the words in advance.
2. Analyze students' spellings using a **feature guide.** This analysis will help you identify what orthographic features students know and what they are ready to study, as well as their approximate stage.
3. Organize groups using a **classroom composite form** and/or the **spelling-by-stage classroom organization chart.** These will help you plan instruction for developmental groups.
4. Monitor overall progress by using the same inventory up to three times a year. Weekly spelling tests and unit spell checks will also help you assess students' mastery of the orthographic features they study.

MONITORING PROGRESS

SELECTING AN INVENTORY. The best guide to selecting an inventory is the grade level of the students you teach. However, you may find that you need an easier or more challenging assessment depending on the range of achievement in your classroom. Table 2.1 is a guide to making your selection. Specific directions are provided in Appendix A for each inventory, but the administration is similar for all of them.

Some teachers begin with the same list for all students but shift to small-group administration of other lists. For example, a second-grade teacher may begin with the Primary Spelling Inventory and decide to continue testing a group of students who spelled most of the words correctly using the Elementary Spelling Inventory. A key point to keep in mind is that students must generate about five errors for you to determine a spelling stage. The three spelling inventories described in this chapter can cover the range of students from primary to high school and college.

TABLE 2.1 *Words Their Way*® Spelling Assessments

Spelling Inventories	Grade Range	Developmental Range
Primary Spelling Inventory (PSI) (p. 315)	K–3	Emergent to late within word pattern
Elementary Spelling Inventory (ESI) (p. 319)	1–6	Letter name to early derivational relations
Upper-Level Spelling Inventory (USI) (p. 322)	5–12	Within word pattern to derivational relations

Primary Spelling Inventory. The Primary Spelling Inventory (PSI) (Appendix A, page 315) consists of a list of 26 words that begins with simple CVC words (*fan, pet*) and ends with inflectional endings (*clapping, riding*). It is recommended for kindergarten through early third grade because it assesses features found from the emergent stage through the within word pattern stage. The PSI has been used widely along with the accompanying feature guide and is a reliable scale of developmental word knowledge. The PSI validity was established using the California Standards Tests (CST) for English Language Arts (ELA) (Sterbinsky, 2007).

For kindergarten students or with other emergent readers, you may only need to call out the first five words. In an early first-grade classroom, call out at least 15 words so that you sample digraphs and blends; use the entire list of 26 words for late first grade, and second and third grades. For students who spell more than 20 words correctly, you should use the Elementary Spelling Inventory.

Elementary Spelling Inventory. The Elementary Spelling Inventory (ESI) (Appendix A, page 319) is a list of 25 increasingly difficult words that begins with *bed* and ends with *opposition*. The ESI can be used in grades 1 through 6 to identify students up to the derivational relations stage. If a school or school system wants to use the same inventory throughout the elementary grades to track growth over time, this inventory is a good choice, but we especially recommend this inventory for grades 3 through 5. By third grade, most students can try to spell all 25 words, but be ready to discontinue testing for any students who are visibly frustrated or misspell five in a row. We have found that this inventory tends to overestimate upper-level spellers so students who spell more than 18 words correctly should be given the Upper-Level Spelling Inventory.

The words on the ESI present a reliable scale of developmental word knowledge. As with the PSI, the validity of the ESI was established using the California Standard Tests (CST) for English Language Arts (ELA) (Sterbinsky, 2007). In this study with 862 students, the relationships between scores on the ESI teachers' stage analysis and standardized reading and spelling test scores were moderate to strong. Using these inventories can be considered a stable measure to screen for developmental levels.

Upper-Level Spelling Inventory. The Upper-Level Spelling Inventory (USI) (Appendix A, page 322) can be used in upper elementary, middle, and high school. The USI is also suitable for assessing the orthographic knowledge of students at college and university levels, as well as adults in general equivalency diploma (GED) programs. List words were chosen because they help identify—more specifically than the ESI—what students in the syllables and affixes and derivational relations stages are doing in their spelling.

The USI is a list of 31 words, arranged in order of difficulty from *switch* to *succession*. The USI is highly reliable; for example, scores of 183 fifth-graders on the USI significantly predicted their scores on the Word Analysis subtest of the CST four months later (Sterbinsky, 2007). With normally achieving students, you can administer the entire list, but stop giving the USI to students who have misspelled five of the first eight words—the words that assess spelling in the within word pattern stage. The teacher should use the ESI with these students to identify within word pattern features that need instruction.

PREPARING STUDENTS FOR THE SPELLING INVENTORY. Unlike weekly spelling tests, these inventories are not used for grading purposes and students should not study the particular words either before or after the inventory is administered. Set aside 20 to 30 minutes to administer an inventory. Ask students to number a paper as they would for a traditional spelling test. For younger children, you may want to prepare papers in advance with one or two numbered columns. (Invariably, a few younger students write across the page from left to right.) Very young children should have an alphabet strip on their desks for reference in case they forget how to form a particular letter. Sometimes it is easier to create a relaxed environment working in small groups, especially with kindergarten and first-grade students. Children who are in second grade and older are usually familiar with spelling tests and can take the inventory as a whole class. If any students appear upset and frustrated, you may assess them individually at another time or use samples of their writing to determine an instructional level with the Qualitative Spelling Checklist.

Students must understand the reason for taking the inventory so they will do their best. They may be anxious, so be direct in your explanation:

> "I am going to ask you to spell some words. You have not studied these words and will not be graded on them. Some of the words may be easy and others may be difficult. Do the best you can. Your work will help me understand how you are learning to read and write and how I can help you."

Teachers often tell students that as long as they try their best in spelling the words, they will earn an A for the assignment. Once these things are explained, most students are able to give the spelling a good effort. You can conduct lessons, such as described in Figure 2.2, to prepare younger students for the assessment or to validate the use of invented spelling during writing. Lessons like these are designed to show students how to sound out words they are unsure of how to spell.

Some students will try to copy if they feel especially concerned about doing well on a test. Creating a relaxed atmosphere with the explanation suggested above can help overcome some of the stress students feel. Arrange seating to minimize the risk of copying or hand out cover sheets. Some teachers give students manila folders to set up right around their papers to create personal workspaces. There will be many opportunities to collect corroborating information,

---

FIGURE 2.2   Model Lesson

To help young students feel more comfortable attempting to spell words, conduct several lessons either in small groups or with the whole class using the theme "How to Spell the Best We Can." You might do this to prepare young students for taking the inventory or to encourage them to invent spellings during writing. If you want students to produce quality writing, they need to be willing to take risks in their spelling. Hesitant writers who labor over spelling or avoid using words they can't spell lose the reward of expressing themselves.

A Discussion to Encourage Invented Spelling

"We're going to do a lot of writing this year. When we want to write a word, and we don't know how to spell it, what might we do?" Student responses usually include:

"Ask the teacher."
"Ask someone."
"Look it up."
"Skip it."

If no one suggests the strategy of listening for sounds, you can tell your students, "Write down all the sounds you hear when you say the word to spell it the best you can."

Spell a Few Words Together

"Who has a word they want to spell?"

Following a lesson on sea life, a student may offer, "Sea turtle."

"That's a great one. Can we keep to the second word, *turtle?*" Assuming they agree, ask students to say the word *turtle*. Encourage them to say it slowly, stretching out the sounds and breaking it into two syllables (*turrr-tlllle*). Model how to listen for the sounds and think about the letters that spell those sounds: "Listen. *T-t-t-turtle*. What's the first sound at the beginning of *turtle?* What letter do we use to spell that /t/ sound?"

"Turtle. *T*."

Write a *T*. Then ask a few students for the next sounds they "hear" and "feel."

Depending on the level of the group, you may generate a range of possible spellings: TL, TRTL, TERDL, and TERTUL.

Finally, talk about what to do if the student can only figure out one or two sounds in a word. "Start with the sound at the beginning. Write the first letter and then draw a line." Here, write *T* with a line.

T _____

Occasionally, a student will be critical about another student's attempt: "That's not the right way to spell it!" Be careful to handle this criticism firmly. You might say, "The important thing is that you have written your word down and you can reread what you have written." Remind students that they are learning; there will be times when they do not know how to spell a word and it is okay to spell it the best they can. Encourage them by saying, "You will see your writing improve the more you write. At the end of the year, you will be surprised by how much more you can write."

so there is no reason to be upset if primary students copy. If it is clear that a student has copied, make a note to this effect after collecting the papers and administer the inventory individually at another time.

ADMINISTER THE INVENTORY. When administering a spelling inventory, call the words aloud by pronouncing each word naturally without drawing out the sounds or breaking them into syllables. Say each word twice and use it in a sentence if context will help students know what word is being called. For example, use *cellar* in a sentence to differentiate it from *seller*. Sentences are provided with the word lists in Appendix A. For most words, however, offering sentences is time-consuming and may even be distracting.

Move around the room as you call the words aloud to monitor students' work and observe their behaviors. Look for words you cannot read due to poor handwriting. Without making students feel that something is wrong, it is appropriate to ask them to rewrite the word or later to read the letters in the words that cannot be deciphered. Students using cursive whose writing is difficult to read can be asked to print.

Occasionally, if there is time, students are asked to take a second try at spelling words about which they may have been unsure. Through this reexamination, students show their willingness to reflect on their work. These notations and successive attempts are additional indicators of the depth of students' orthographic knowledge.

KNOW WHEN TO STOP. As you walk around the room or work with a small group, scan students' papers and watch for misspellings and signs of frustration to determine whether to continue with the list. With younger students who tire quickly, you might stop after the first five words if they do not spell any correctly. For older students in groups, who can usually take an entire inventory in about 20 minutes, it is better to err on the side of too many words than too few. Rather than being singled out to stop, some students may prefer to "save face" by attempting every word called out to the group even when working at a frustration level. In Figure 2.3, you can see that Jake missed more than half the words on the inventory but continued to make good attempts at words that were clearly too difficult for him. However, his six errors in the first 15 words identify him as needing work on vowel patterns, and testing could have been discontinued at that point. Sometimes teachers are required to administer the entire list in order to have a complete set of data for each child. In this case, tell students before you start that the words will become difficult but to do the best they can.

Score and Analyze the Spelling Inventories

After you administer the inventory, collect the papers and set aside time to score and analyze the results. Scoring the inventories is more than marking words

FIGURE 2.3 Jake's Spelling Inventory

Jake		September 8	9/25
1. bed		14. caryes	carries
2. ship		15. martched	marched
3. when		16. showers	shower
4. lump		17. bottel	bottle
5. float		18. faver	favor
6. train		19. rippin	ripen
7. place		20. selar	cellar
8. drive		21. pleascher	pleasure
9. brite	bright	22. forchunate	fortunate
10. shoping	shopping	23. confdant	confident
11. spoyle	spoil	24. sivulise	civilize
12. serving		25. opozishun	opposition
13. chooed	chewed		

right or wrong. Instead, each word has a number of orthographic "features" that are counted separately. For example, a student who spells *when* as WEN knows the correct short vowel and ending consonant and gets points for knowing those features even though the complete spelling is not correct. The feature guides will help you score each word in this manner. This analysis provides *qualitative* information regarding what students know about specific spelling features and what they are ready to study next.

ESTABLISH A POWER SCORE. Begin by marking the words right or wrong. It helps to write the correct spellings beside the misspelled words as was done in the sample of Jake's spelling in Figure 2.3. This step focuses your attention on each word and the parts of the words that were right and wrong (key to the qualitative **feature analysis**). Scoring in this way also makes it easier for other teachers and parents to understand students' papers. Calculate a raw score or *power score* (nine words correct on Jake's paper in Figure 2.3). and refer to Table 2.2 below to get a rough estimate of the student's spelling stage. The table lists the power scores on the three major *Words Their Way*™ inventories in relation to estimated stages and their breakdown by early, middle, or late stage designations. As we can see, Jake's ESI power score of 9 places him in the late within word pattern stage.

SCORE THE FEATURE GUIDES. Feature guides help teachers analyze student errors and confirm the stage designations suggested by the power score. The feature guides that accompany each inventory are included in Appendix A and are found on the PD Toolkit. Jake's spellings are used as an example in Figure 2.4 to guide you in the scoring process. Use the following steps to complete the feature guide. Alternatively, the assessment application on the website allows you to score the inventory electronically.

1. To score by hand, make a copy of the appropriate feature guide for each student and record the date of testing. The spelling features are listed in the second row of the feature guide and follow the developmental sequence observed in research.

2. Look to the right of each word to check off features of the word that are represented correctly. For example, because Jake spelled *bed* correctly, there is a check for the beginning consonant, the final consonant, and the short vowel for a total of three feature points. Jake also gets a point for spelling the word correctly, recorded in the far right column. For the word *bright*, which he spelled as BRITE, he gets a check for the blend but not for the *igh* spelling pattern. Notice on Jake's feature guide in Figure 2.4 how the vowel patterns he substituted have been written in the space beside the vowel feature to show that Jake is

for Words Their Way®

Assessment Application
Use the Online Assessment Application or download scoring guides for the spelling inventories.

TABLE 2.2 **Power Scores and Estimated Stages**

Inventory	Emergent	Letter Name			Within Word Pattern			Syllables & Affixes			Derivational Relations		
		E	*M*	*L*	*E*	*M*	*L*	*E*	*M*	*L*	*E*	*M*	*L*
Primary Spelling Inventory	0	0	1–3	4–6	7–10	11–15	16–19	20–22					
Elementary Spelling Inventory		0	1–2	3–4	5–6	7–8	9–10	11–13	14–16	17–18	19–20	21–26	
Upper-Level Spelling Inventory					1–2	3–6	7–8	9–10	11–15	16–18	19–22	23–25	26–31

FIGURE 2.4 Jake's Feature Guide for the Elementary Spelling Inventory

Student's Name _Jake Fisher_   Teacher _T. Atkinson_   Grade _5_   Date _September_

Words Spelled Correctly: _9/ 25_   Feature Points: _43 / 62_   Total: _52 / 87_

Spelling Stage: _Late Within Word Pattern_

SPELLING STAGES → : EMERGENT (LATE) | LETTER NAME—ALPHABETIC (EARLY, MIDDLE, LATE) | WITHIN WORD PATTERN (EARLY, MIDDLE, LATE) | SYLLABLES AND AFFIXES (EARLY, MIDDLE, LATE) | DERIVATIONAL RELATIONS (EARLY)

Features →	Consonants Initial	Consonants Final	Short Vowels	Digraphs	Blends	Common Long Vowels	Other Vowels	Inflected Endings	Syllable Junctures	Unaccented Final Syllables	Advanced Affixes	Bases or Roots	Feature Points	Words Spelled Correctly
1. bed	b ✓	d ✓	e ✓										3	1
2. ship		p ✓	i ✓	sh ✓									3	1
3. when			e ✓	wh ✓									2	1
4. lump	l ✓		u ✓		mp ✓								3	1
5. float		t ✓			fl ✓	oa ✓							3	1
6. train		n ✓			tr ✓	ai ✓							3	1
7. place					pl ✓	a-e ✓							3	1
8. drive		v ✓			dr ✓	i-e ✓							3	1
9. bright					br ✓	igh i-e							3	1
10. shopping			o ✓	sh ✓				pping					1	
11. spoil					sp ✓		oi oy						2	
12. serving							er ✓	ving ✓					1	
13. chewed				ch ✓			ew oo	ed ✓					2	
14. carries							ar ✓	ies					2	
15. marched				ch ✓			ar ✓	ed ✓						
16. shower				sh ✓			ow ✓			er ✓			3	
17. bottle									tt ✓	le			1	
18. favor									v ✓	or			1	
19. ripen										pen				
20. cellar									ll	ar ✓			1	
21. pleasure											ure	pleas ✓		
22. fortunate							or ✓				ate ✓	fortun	1	
23. confident											ent	confid	2	
24. civilize											ize	civil		
25. opposition											tion	pos		
Totals	7 / 7		5 / 5	6 / 6	7 / 7	4 / 5	5 / 7	3 / 5	2 / 5	2 / 5	1 / 5	1 / 5	43	9

using but confusing these patterns. Every feature in every word is not scored; however, the features sampled are sufficient to identify the stages of spelling.

3. After scoring each word, add the checks in each column and record the total score for that column at the bottom as a ratio of correct responses to total possible features. (Adjust this ratio and the total possible points if you do not have a student spell all of the words.) Notice how Jake scored six out of six under Digraphs, seven out of seven for Blends, and four out of five under Long Vowels. Add the total feature scores across the bottom and the total words spelled correctly. This gives you an overall total score that you can use to rank order students and to compare individual growth over time. If you use the assessment application on the website, it will calculate the total feature scores and the spelling stage for you.

COMMON CONFUSIONS IN SCORING. To ensure consistency in scoring students' spelling, keep the following points in mind when you consider reversals and a few confusing spelling errors.

Reversals. Letter reversals, such as writing *b* as *d*, are not unusual in young spellers, and questions often arise about how to score them. Reversals should be noted, but in the qualitative analysis, reversals should be seen as the letters they were *meant* to represent and not counted as wrong. These might be considered handwriting errors rather than spelling errors. A **static reversal,** such as the *b* written backward in *bed* or the *p* reversed in *ship*, should be counted as correct. There is space in the boxes of the feature analysis to make note of these reversals. Record what the student did, but add the check to give credit for representing the sound. Letter reversals occur with decreasing frequency through the letter name–alphabetic stage.

Confusions can also arise in scoring **kinetic reversals** when the letters are present but out of order. For example, beginning spellers sometimes spell the familiar consonant sounds and then tag on a vowel at the end (e.g., FNA for *fan*). This can be due to repeating each sound in the word *fan* and extracting the short *a* after having already recorded the FN. With students in the early stages of spelling give credit for the consonants and vowels that are present but do not give a point for correct spelling. However, when students reverse letters in vowel patterns, such as spelling *train* as TRIAN or *bright* as BRIHGT, do not give credit for the feature since this suggests they need more work on the pattern.

Other Confusions. There are a few unique errors to consider that can be confusing to score. Early beginning spellers sometimes spell part of the word and then add a random string of letters to make it look longer (e.g., FNWZTY for *fan*). Older students will sometimes add vowel markers where they are not needed (as in FANE for *fan*) or will include two possibilities when in doubt (as in LOOKTED for *looked* or TRAINE for *train*). In these cases, students should get credit for what they represent correctly. In the case of FANE for *fan* or TRAINE for *train*, the student would get credit for the consonants and vowel features but would not get the extra point for spelling the word correctly. In general, give students credit when in doubt and make a note of the strategy they might be using. Such errors offer interesting insights into their developing word knowledge. FANE for *fan* may be incorrect but it represents a more sophisticated attempt than FN since the short vowel is correctly represented.

IDENTIFY FEATURES FOR INSTRUCTION. The completed feature guide can be used to determine a starting place for instruction. Looking across the feature columns from left to right, *instruction should begin at the point where a student first makes two or more errors on a feature.* Consider the totals along the bottom of Jake's feature guide. Ask yourself what he knows and what he is using but confusing. His scores indicate that he has mastery of Consonants and Short Vowels, so he does not need instruction there. Jake only missed one of the Long Vowels (*igh* in *bright*) for a score of 4/5 and this can be considered an acceptable score. However, he missed two of the Other Vowels, so this is the feature that needs attention during instruction.

The features in the columns are presented in a general scope and sequence from beginning consonants to roots. However, there may be times when you vary the order of feature presentation. For example, some students may need more work on short vowels even when they have mastered blends and digraphs. In the upper spelling stages we sometimes see students ready to study a number of features at the same time. In this case, the order will not be as important and this offers more flexibility in grouping.

DETERMINE A DEVELOPMENTAL STAGE. The continuum of features at the top of the feature guide shows gradations for each developmental stage of *early, middle,* and *late.* A student who has learned to spell most of the features relevant to a stage is probably at the end of that stage. Conversely, if a student is beginning to use the key elements of a feature but still has some misspellings from the previous stage, the student is at an early point in that new stage. Tables in each instructional chapter (Chapters 4 to 8) provide additional information about how to determine where students are within each stage. These gradations make assessing orthographic knowledge more precise than simply an overall stage designation, and this precision will be useful in designing a word study curriculum.

Developmental levels should be circled in the shaded bar across the top that lists the stages. For example, Jake spelled all of the Short Vowels and most Long Vowel features correctly, and he also spelled some of the words in the Other Vowels category, so Jake is at least in the middle of the within word pattern stage. This has been circled in the top row. These stage designations can be used to complete the Spelling-by-Stage form described later in this chapter that will help you create instructional groups. Knowing the student's developmental stage is a guide to the instructional chapter for word study. In Jake's case, refer to Chapter 6 for activities.

You do not need to make the discrimination within stages too weighty a decision. When it comes to planning instruction, take a step backward to choose word study activities at a slightly easier level than the stage determination may indicate. It is more effective to introduce students to sorting routines when they are working with familiar features and known words; moreover, it is easier to move students up to a higher group than to move them back to a lower group.

Spelling inventory results should be compared to what we know about students' orthographic knowledge from their reading and writing. Together, reading, writing, and spelling inventories provide a rich collection of information to understand students' knowledge of orthography. Use the Synchrony of Literacy Development model in Figure 1.12 on page 16 by reading from top to bottom across the literacy behaviors of reading, spelling, and writing. Look for corroborating evidence to place students' achievement along the developmental continuum. This model helps to generate expectations for student development using an integrated literacy approach. A student's reading behaviors should be in synchrony with his or her range of writing behaviors.

Referring back to Jake's writing in Figure 2.1, we see similar strengths and weaknesses. His mastery of short vowels and his experimentation with long vowels and other vowels is what we would expect of a student in the middle to late within word pattern stage of spelling. When Jake reads he may confuse words like *choose* and *chose.* These errors in word identification will be addressed in word study when he examines the other vowels. His spelling inventory, writing sample, and reading errors offer supporting evidence that we have identified his developmental stage and the features that need attention.

Some students are out of synchrony in their development, such as the one who is notoriously poor at spelling but is a capable reader. When there is a mismatch between reading and spelling development, you can help improve spelling and obtain synchrony by pinpointing the stage of spelling development and then providing instruction that addresses the student's needs.

Sample Practice

The spelling examples of five students in Figure 2.5 can be used to practice analyzing student spellings and determining a developmental stage if you do not have a class of children to assess or if you want to try analyzing a broad spectrum of responses. Make a copy of the

FIGURE 2.5   Examples of Students' Spelling in September

Spelling Words	Greg (Grade 1)	Jean (Grade 1)	Reba (Grade 2)	Alan (Grade 3)	Mitch (Grade 5)
bed	bd	bed	bed	bed	bed
ship	sp	sep	ship	ship	ship
when	yn	whan	when	when	when
lump	lp	lop	lump	lump	lump
float	fot	flot	flote	flote	float
train		tran	trane	train	train
place		plac	plais	place	place
drive		driv	drive	drive	drive
bright		brit	brite	brigt	bright
shopping		sopng	shopen	shoping	shopping
spoil			spoal	spoale	spoil
serving			serving	serveing	serving
chewed			chud	choued	chewed
carries			cares	carres	carries
marched			marcd	marched	marched
shower				shouer	shower
bottle				bottel	bottle
favor				favir	favor
ripen				ripen	ripen
cellar				seller	celler
pleasure					pleshur
fortunate					forchenet
confident					confedent
civilize					civilize
opposition					oposition

RESULTS:

Greg   Early letter name–alphabetic
Review consonants, study
short vowel word families,
digraphs, and blends

Jean   Middle letter name–alphabetic
Study short vowels

Reba   Middle within word pattern
Study long vowel patterns

Alan   Late within word pattern
Study long vowels and other vowel patterns

Mitch   Middle syllables and affixes
Study syllable juncture and unaccented
final syllables

There is a good chance that the previous
results overestimated his stage. He should
be given the USI since he only missed
five words.

ESI feature guide for each student. Determine both the developmental stage of the speller and the place you would start instruction. After you are finished, check the results at the bottom of the page. Were you close in the stages you selected? If you scored the spelling in terms of the three gradations within a stage, you may find that although your assessment may differ by a stage name, it is possible that the difference is just between the latter part of one stage and the early part of the next. Also compute a power score for each student (number correct) and use the table on page 30 to estimate the stage. Were your results similar?

Group Students for Instruction

Your spelling analysis as discussed in the previous section will pinpoint students' instructional levels and the features that are ripe for instruction. In most classrooms, there will be a range in students' word knowledge. For example, in a second-grade class most students will be in the within word pattern stage but there will also be students in the letter name–alphabetic stage who need to study short vowels and consonant blends, while others may be in the syllables and affixes stage and ready to study two-syllable words. After analyzing students individually, you can create a classroom profile by recording the individual assessment data on a single chart.

We present two ways to record information about the class: the classroom composite to group students by features, and the spelling-by-stage classroom organization chart to group students by developmental levels. These charts show you the instructional groups at a glance. Before we discuss them, however, let's consider the importance of grouping for instruction in word study.

PD **TOOLKIT**™
for Words Their Way®

The Role of the Instructional Coach
In this video an instructional coach meets with three second grade teachers to discuss assessments and plans for teaching word study.

Grouping to Meet Students' Diverse Needs

Grouping for instruction is a challenge for teachers and there are reasons to be suspicious of ability grouping. There may be stigmas associated with grouping and sometimes the lower-ability groups receive inferior instruction (Allington & Cunningham, 2006; Morris, 2008). However, students benefit from differentiated instruction. Experience shows that when students study a particular orthographic feature, it is best if they are in groups with students who are ready to study the same feature. For example, it is difficult to study long-vowel patterns when some of the students in the group still need work on digraphs or blends and may not even be able to read the words that contain the long-vowel patterns. When students are taught at their instructional levels in spelling (even when instruction is below grade level), they will make more progress than with materials that are too difficult for them (Morris, Blanton, Blanton, Nowacek, & Perney, 1995). Chapter 3 offers suggestions about how to manage multiple instructional groups.

Classroom Composite Chart

After administering an inventory and completing a feature guide for each student, transfer the individual scores in the last row of the form to a Classroom Composite Chart (Figure 2.6) to get a sense of the group as a whole. If you use the electronic assessment application on the website, the Classroom Composite Chart will be created automatically. The following steps will help you do this manually.

PD **TOOLKIT**™
for Words Their Way®

Assessment Application
The online Assessment Application will automatically generate a class composite.

1. Begin by stapling each student's spelling test and feature guide together.
2. Sort student papers by the power score (or number of words correct) or by the total feature score, and record students' names from top to bottom on the composite form on the basis of this rank order.
3. Next, record scores from the bottom row of each student's feature guide in the row beside his or her name on the composite chart.
4. Highlight cells in which students are making two or more errors on a particular feature and column. For example, a student who spells all but one of the short vowels correctly

FIGURE 2.6 Classroom Composite Chart

Teacher _____ School _____ Grade _____ Date _____

SPELLING STAGES →

Spelling Stage	Feature	Possible Points
EMERGENT LATE / EARLY — LETTER NAME–ALPHABETIC EARLY	Consonants	7
LETTER NAME–ALPHABETIC MIDDLE	Short Vowels	5
LETTER NAME–ALPHABETIC LATE	Digraphs	6
WITHIN WORD PATTERN EARLY	Blends	7
WITHIN WORD PATTERN MIDDLE	Common Long Vowels	5
WITHIN WORD PATTERN MIDDLE	Other Vowels	7
WITHIN WORD PATTERN LATE	Inflectional Endings	5
SYLLABLES AND AFFIXES EARLY	Syllable Junctures	5
SYLLABLES AND AFFIXES MIDDLE	Unaccented Final Syllables	5
SYLLABLES AND AFFIXES LATE	Advanced Suffixes	5
DERIVATIONAL RELATIONS EARLY	Bases or Roots	5
	Correct Spelling	25
	Total Rank Order	87

Students' Names	Consonants (7)	Short Vowels (5)	Digraphs (6)	Blends (7)	Common Long Vowels (5)	Other Vowels (7)	Inflectional Endings (5)	Syllable Junctures (5)	Unaccented Final Syllables (5)	Advanced Suffixes (5)	Bases or Roots (5)	Correct Spelling (25)	Total Rank Order (87)
1. Stephanie	7	5	6	7	5	7	5	5	5	4	3	23	82
2. Andi	7	5	6	7	5	7	5	4	4	3	2	21	76
3. Henry	7	5	6	7	5	7	5	4	3	3	2	20	74
4. Molly	7	5	6	7	5	7	4	4	3	2	2	20	72
5. Jasmine	7	5	6	7	5	7	3	3	3	2	2	19	69
6. Maria H.	7	5	6	7	5	7	3	3	2	3	2	19	69
7. Mike T.	7	5	6	7	5	6	3	3	2	2	1	17	64
8. Lee	7	5	6	7	5	6	2	2	1	2	1	15	59
9. Beth	7	5	6	7	5	7	2	2	1	1	2	14	59
10. Gabriel	7	5	6	7	5	6	2	2	1	1	2	14	58
11. Yamal	7	5	6	7	4	6	2	2	1	1	0	12	53
12. Elizabeth	7	5	6	7	4	6	2	2	1	0	0	11	51
13. John	7	5	6	7	3	5	2	2	1	1	0	10	49
14. Patty	7	5	6	7	3	5	2	2	1	0	0	11	49
15. Maria R.	7	5	6	7	3	4	2	2	1	0	0	11	48
16. Sarah	7	5	6	7	4	4	2	1	0	1	0	9	46
17. Jared	7	5	6	7	2	3	1	1	1	1	0	9	43
18. William	7	5	6	7	3	3	2	0	1	0	0	8	42
19. Steve	7	5	6	7	3	3	2	1	0	0	0	8	42
20. Anna	7	5	6	6	4	3	1	1	0	0	0	8	41
21. Nicole W.	7	4	6	6	3	3	1	1	0	0	0	8	39
22. Robert	7	5	5	7	3	3	2	0	0	0	0	6	38
23. Celia	7	4	6	6	2	3	1	0	0	0	0	7	36
24. Nicole R.	7	4	5	6	2	3	2	0	0	0	0	7	36
25. Jim	7	5	5	6	2	2	1	0	0	0	0	7	35
26. Mike A.	7	3	4	5	1	0	1	0	0	0	0	4	25
Highlight for instruction*	1	1	1	1	12	13	22	16	15	13	10		

*Highlight students who miss more than 1 on a particular feature; they will benefit from more instruction in that area.

has an adequate understanding of short vowels and is considered to be at an independent level. However, students who misspell two or three of the short vowels need more work on that feature. Highlighted cells indicate a need for sustained instruction on a feature. Do not highlight cells in which students score a zero because this indicates frustration level rather than using but confusing a feature. Focus instead on features in columns to the left of any zero levels that need attention first.

5. **Look for instructional groups.** If you rank order your students when completing the composite chart, you can find clusters of highlighted cells that can be used to assign students to developmental stages and word study groups. For example, the fifth-grade class composite in Figure 2.6 shows that many students fall under the syllables and affixes stage of development because this is where they are making two or more spelling errors (students 3 through 16). John, Maria R., and Patty, who missed more than two words in vowel patterns, might join this group or might go in a lower group, but should be carefully monitored. A smaller group of students falls under the middle-to-late within word pattern stage (students 17 through 25), and should begin word study by looking at single-syllable word patterns for long vowels and then other vowel patterns. One student (Mike) needs individualized help, beginning with short vowels as well as digraphs and blends. At the upper end of the class composite are two children who fall into the derivational relations stage. However, we suggest that any students who score more than 18 or better on the ESI be re-assessed with the USI to gather more information about particular features to study.

Spelling-by-Stage Classroom Organization Chart

When you know students' developmental stages, you can also form groups with the Spelling-by-Stage Classroom Organization Chart (see Figure 2.7). Many teachers find this easier to use than a class composite when planning groups. Refer to the stage circled in the shaded bar with the developmental stages on each student's feature guide. Students' names are recorded underneath a spelling stage on the chart, differentiating among those who are early, middle, or late. (To determine early, middle, and late designations, refer to each chapter for further information.) Once the names are entered, begin to look for groups. In each of the classroom examples in Figure 2.7, three or four groups have been circled.

You can see different ways to organize word study instruction in the three classroom profiles presented in Figure 2.7. The first profile is of a first-grade class with many emergent spellers. The four circled groups suggested for this class are also the teacher's reading groups.

In the third- and sixth-grade examples, you can see where teachers have used arrows to reconsider the group placement of a few students. Inventory results are considered along with other observations of students' reading or writing. The arrows indicate students who might be placed slightly higher or lower as the groups take shape. Some of the group placement decisions are also based on social and psychological factors related to self-esteem, leadership, and behavior dynamics.

The teacher in the sixth-grade classroom could consider running two groups at the upper levels or combining them as one group. The three students in the letter name–alphabetic stage will need special attention because they are significantly behind for sixth graders. Ideally, these students will have additional instruction with a literacy specialist or in a tutoring program to review and practice activities that are appropriate for the letter name–alphabetic spelling stage.

Factors to Consider when Organizing Groups

The Classroom Composite Chart and the Spelling-by-Stage Classroom Organization Chart help to determine word study groups for instruction. While students within a class work on different features and with different words, they can still work side by side during many of the follow-up word study routines that occur after the initial small-group discussion. Different schemes for managing class, group, and individual word study are discussed in Chapter 3.

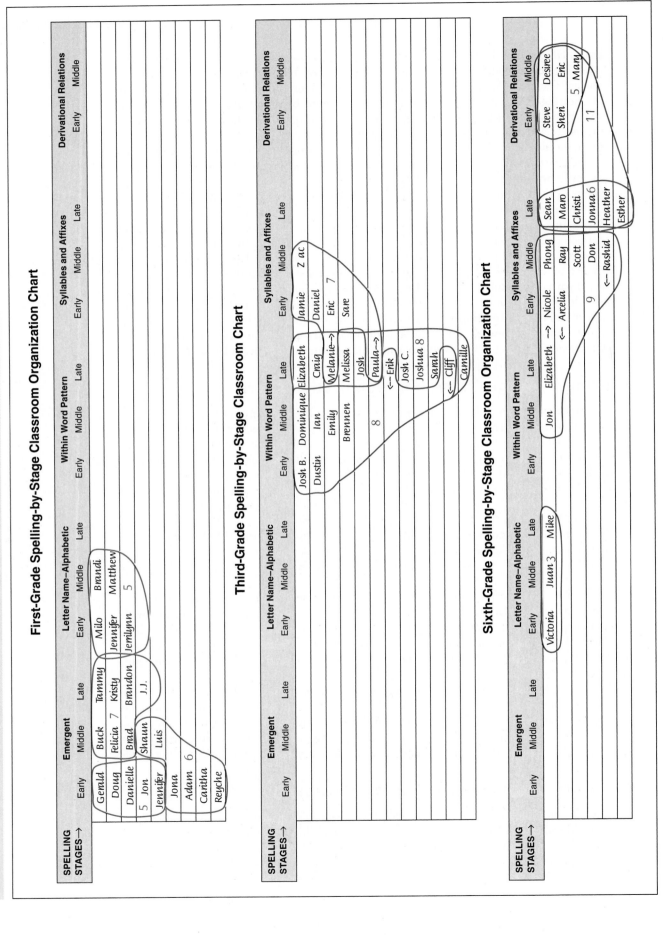

FIGURE 2.7 Examples of Spelling-by-Stage Classroom Organization Charts

First-Grade Spelling-by-Stage Classroom Organization Chart

Third-Grade Spelling-by-Stage Classroom Chart

Sixth-Grade Spelling-by-Stage Classroom Organization Chart

If there is a wide range of achievement some students may not be placed exactly at their developmental stages. Although you will certainly try to accommodate them, your best spellers are not likely to be negatively affected with grade-level word study activities that might be a bit easy for them. However, your less able spellers will probably suffer if they are working at a frustration level in which they will not make progress, so group your neediest students as close as possible to their instructional level.

In many classrooms, there are students at each end of the developmental continuum who, in terms of word study and orthographic development, are outliers. For example, Zac, in the third-grade class in Figure 2.7, is the only student in the middle syllables and affixes stage and it is impractical to place him in a group by himself. He has been placed in the closest group for instruction. However, you might accommodate Zac by asking him to work with a different, more difficult set of words sharing the same features that the early syllables and affixes spellers are studying, such as harder words with open and closed syllables. Less advanced students, such as Jon in the sixth-grade example in Figure 2.7, may work with partners who can help them read and sort the group's words, such as one-syllable words with long-vowel patterns. English language learners also benefit from sorting with partners who can clarify word pronunciations and meanings.

Interpreting feature guides, determining stages, and then creating and monitoring groups involves ongoing assessment, observations, and teacher judgment. It cannot be reduced to a simple formula. Be assured that over time you will gain expertise and satisfaction in being able to accurately identify and meet the instructional needs of your students.

Other Assessments

There are other assessments and forms useful as supplements or alternatives to the Primary, Elementary, or Upper-Level Spelling Inventories. For example the Emergent Class Record and the Kindergarten Spelling Inventory are appropriate for young students. Some teachers may want to have data for reporting grade-level achievement and will find the McGuffey Spelling Inventory useful. Other teachers prefer to have a single, continuous feature inventory that can be used across all grade levels such as Viise's Word Feature Inventory. Finally, Spell Checks and Goal Setting Forms can help teachers closely monitor progress. The alternate assessments described in this section and listed in Table 2.3 can meet all of these needs. These assessments can be found online to print out for use in your classroom.

PD **TOOLKIT**™
for Words Their Way®

Assessment of Students
In a video for each stage, teachers describe their assessment results and students' yearly growth.

TABLE 2.3 **Alternative Assessments**

Spelling Inventories	Grade Range	Developmental Range
Qualitative Spelling Checklist	K–8	All stages
Emergent Class Record	Pre K–K	Emergent to letter name–alphabetic
Kindergarten Spelling Inventory (KSI)	Pre K–K	Emergent to early letter name–alphabetic
McGuffey Spelling Inventory (QWIK)	1–8	All stages
Viise's Word Feature Inventory (WFI)	K–12+	Letter name to derivational relations
Spell Checks	K–12	Early letter name–alphabetic to early derivational relations
Goal-Setting/Progress Monitoring Charts	K–12	Early letter name–alphabetic to early derivational relations

Qualitative Spelling Checklist

When you look at students' writing in their journals or in the first drafts of their reports and stories, you can use the Qualitative Spelling Checklist (page 312 in Appendix A) to verify what types of orthographic features students have mastered, what types of features they are using but confusing, and the degree to which they are applying their spelling knowledge in actual writing. Through a series of 20 questions, you check off the student's progress through the stages. Consider what features are used consistently, often, or not at all. The checklist is set up to be used at three different points during the school year and can serve as a record of progress over time. Collecting a variety of writing samples across the curricular areas is a great way to verify students' application and transfer of their word study instruction.

Emergent Class Record

The Emergent Class Record is used to assess daily writing or spelling inventory results of pre K children, kindergarten students, or other emergent spellers. Making a copy of the PSI feature guide for each student may seem like a waste of paper when at most they will only score a few initial and final consonants. The Emergent Class Record can be used as an alternative with the entire class represented on one form. It captures the prephonetic writing progression (from random marks to letters) that is missing from the other feature guides and covers the range from emergent through letter name–alphabetic spelling that is expected in many kindergarten classes at the beginning of the year. Other emergent assessments are described in Chapter 4 and are available to print from the website.

Kindergarten Spelling Inventory

The Kindergarten Spelling Inventory (KSI) has been used widely with thousands of children as part of Virginia's Phonological Assessment and Literacy Screening (PALS) (Invernizzi, Juel, Swank, & Meier, 2006). Carefully chosen after extensive research, each of five three-phoneme words is scored for the number of phonemes represented in a student's spelling. A feature guide is provided, but unlike the feature guides described so far, students get credit for identifying phonemes and representing those sounds with phonetically logical letters, even if those letters are actually incorrect. As a result, the KSI is a reliable measure of phonemic awareness development, letter–sound correspondences, and the gradual development of conventional spelling (Invernizzi, Justice, Landrum, & Booker, 2005). KSI scores in kindergarten predict children's end-of-year reading standards scores as much as three years later (Invernizzi, Juel, Swank, & Meier, 2008).

McGuffey Spelling Inventory

The McGuffey Qualitative Inventory of Word Knowledge (QIWK) (Schlagal, 1992) is useful for conducting individual testing and for obtaining grade-level information. The inventory spans grades 1 through 8, with 20 to 30 words in each level. After administering the grade-level list, use the list from the previous grade level with students who fall below 50 percent and use the list from the next higher grade level for students who score above 90 percent to determine an instructional spelling level (Morris, Blanton, Blanton, & Perney, 1995; Morris et al., 1986).

The McGuffey Inventory is especially useful when you want to report spelling achievement in terms of grade levels. In addition, the words in these lists present plenty of opportunities to observe a student's spelling across a variety of features. For example, for teachers wanting to obtain a fuller assessment of prefixes, suffixes, and roots, Levels 5 and 6 offer a larger number of derivational words with prefixes and suffixes to analyze. Because a feature guide has not been developed for the McGuffey Inventory, you must analyze errors yourself to determine which features and patterns students know, and which they are using but confusing.

Viise's Word Feature Inventory

The Word Feature Inventory (WFI) developed by Neva Viise is another qualitative inventory (Viise, 1996; Worthy & Viise, 1996). The WFI is divided into four achievement levels corresponding to four of the five stages of developmental word knowledge: letter name–alphabetic, within word pattern, syllables and affixes, and derivational relations. The words on each level are divided into groups of five, each subgroup probing the student's treatment of a specific word feature such as short vowel, consonant blend, long-vowel pattern, and so on. As with the PSI, ESI, and USI, an assessment of students' spellings of the words on this list will indicate the features that have already been mastered and pinpoint the level at which instruction must begin. The WFI is a continuous measure and can be used across all grade levels.

Set Goals and Monitor Student Growth over Time

Monitoring students' progress in response to instruction has gained importance in the last few years. Brief, ongoing assessment alerts us to the need for adjusting the content and pacing of our instruction to meet student needs, and arranging additional instruction for students who may need extra help meeting long-term goals.

Use a Variety of Assessments to Monitor Growth

Teachers have been monitoring their students' progress for years through weekly spelling tests that provide immediate feedback regarding students' short-term retention of specific words they have studied. But few teachers consider long-term retention, the generalization of the spelling patterns students have learned relative to words they may not have studied, or the application of students' orthographic word knowledge in their writing. We offer several ways you can monitor progress in orthographic development in the short and long terms.

MONITORING PROGRESS

WEEKLY SPELLING TESTS AND UNIT TESTS. We recommend weekly tests at most grade levels as a way to monitor mastery of the studied features, and to send a message to students and parents alike that students are accountable for learning to spell the words they have sorted and worked with in various activities all week. Students will usually be successful on these weekly tests when they are appropriately placed for instruction. If they are incorrectly spelling more than a few words, it may mean that you need to adjust your instruction. They may either need to spend more time on a feature, or they are not ready to study the feature and should work on easier patterns first. You may also want to periodically give a review test or unit test—without asking students to study in advance—to check for retention. Simply select a sample of words from previous lessons and call them aloud as you would for any spelling test or use the prepared spell checks on the PDToolkit and in the *Words Their Way* supplements.

SPELLING INVENTORIES. Students may be given the same spelling inventory up to three times during the year to assess progress and to determine whether changes need to be made in groups or instructional focus. You can even use the same paper several times if you fold back previous results and ask students to record their latest effort in the next column. Figure 2.8 shows Benny's spelling inventory results at three different times during the first-grade year recorded on the same form. He has made noticeable progress during the year,

FIGURE 2.8 Samples of Benny's Spelling Errors at Three Times in First Grade

	September	January	May
1. fan	FNA	fan	fane
2. pet	PT	pat	pet
3. dig	DKG	deg	dig
4. hope	HOP	hop	hope
5. wait	YAT	wat	wayt
6. sled	SD	sed	sled
7. stick	SK	stek	stike
8. shine	HIN	shin	shine

moving from early letter name–alphabetic spelling to the within word pattern stage. However, don't expect such dramatic progress in one year beyond the primary grades. Some students will take two years to master the within word pattern stage. Therefore, teachers in upper elementary, middle school, and high school may find that using an inventory only at the beginning and end of the year is sufficient.

We recommend using the same spelling inventory each time so that you can compare progress on the same words. In Benny's inventory results, we can track the qualitative changes in his spelling over time. Don't be too surprised if students sometimes spell a word correctly one time and later spell the same word incorrectly. Because students are sometimes inventing a spelling for a word that they do not have stored in memory, they may invent it correctly one time and not the next. Or they might master short vowel sound matches but later use but confuse silent vowel markers as Benny did in his spelling of *fan* as FANE.

Remember that you should not have students directly study the words in the inventory, although the words may naturally show up in word study activities that you plan. If students study the list in advance, assessment results will be inflated and you will lose valuable diagnostic information. Using the same inventory more than three times a year may also familiarize students with the words enough to inflate the results. In between administrations of the spelling inventories, use the spell checks described next to monitor progress within and across stages.

SPELL CHECKS. Spell checks are mini-inventories that can be used over shorter periods of time than spelling inventories to monitor students' generalization of specific features over and beyond what they may have demonstrated on weekly spelling tests. Spell checks serve several purposes: (1) to fine-tune placement, (2) as a pretest for a feature or unit of study before instruction to determine what students already know, (3) as a posttest after instruction to determine what students have learned, and (4) as a delayed posttest administered several weeks after instruction to determine what students have retained over time.

Like inventories, spell checks are organized by sequential groups of phonics features and spelling patterns, but each spell check includes more features and more words for each feature within a stage. Because spell checks are more thorough, they can be used to confirm the stage designation and placement determined by the spelling inventories. If students misspell only one or two words in a feature category on the inventory, you may want to do some further assessment using the spell checks. In Jake's case, we might want to gather some more information about his knowledge of less common long-vowel patterns because he misspelled *bright*. If Jake were to spell at least eight (out of ten) words correctly on the spell check for less common long-vowel patterns, you would have additional assurance that he is ready to move on to the study of *r*-influenced vowels, the next set of features in the scope and sequence toward the latter part of the within word pattern stage.

Spell checks can also be used as pretests to confirm the appropriateness of the next unit of instruction. Jake might be given a pretest on *r*-influenced vowels, in which a score of 30 to 70 percent would suggest that he is using but confusing this feature, making it an area ripe for instruction.

Spell checks are also used to monitor progress and refine the focus and pacing of instruction for individuals or small groups. Figure 2.9 shows Omar's spell checks for short vowels and preconsonantal nasal sounds (the *m*'s and *n*'s that come before consonants at the end of words). The first is a pretest on which he scored 30 percent. The second, using a different form on which he scored 90 percent, was given after he had spent several weeks working on that

FIGURE 2.9   Omar's Spell Checks for Preconsonantal Nasals

Oct 10		Nov 7	Nov 29	
1. rug	rung	1. bring	1. rung	
2. lamp		2. camp	2. lamp	
3. prin	print	3. hunt	3. print	
4. theng	think	4. blend	4. thingk	think
5. limp		5. wink	5. limp	
6. stup	stump	6. tent	6. stup	stump
7. send		7. thank	7. send	
8. plat	plant	8. dup	dump	8. plant	
9. lag	long	9. sang	9. long	
10. jok	junk	10. hand	10. junk	
3/10 30%		9/10 90%	8/10 80%	

FIGURE 2.10 **Omar's Goal-Setting/Progress Monitoring Chart**

10. Spell short vowels with preconsonantal nasals *Pretest* 3/10 30%	ing ✓ ang ✓ ong ✓ ung ✓ amp ✓✓ ump XX imp ✓ ant ✓ int ✓ ent ✓ unt ✓ and ✓ end ✓✓ ank ✓ ink ✓X unk ✓
Criterion Met ✓	Spell Check 10 Form A 11/7 90% Form B 11/29 80%

feature in his word sorts. Several weeks later, his teacher assessed his retention of this feature by administering another form of the same spell check. Although Omar misspelled two words in the delayed posttest, eight out of ten words spelled correctly is still a good indication of mastery. His teacher recorded all these scores on the progress monitoring chart for late letter name–alphabetic spellers (Figure 2.10). If Omar had scored less than 80 percent on the delayed posttest, some targeted review would be needed. In his case, it appears that the *ump* pattern is a problem and words like *jump* and *stump* might be compared to words like *cup* and *pup* in which there is no preconsonantal nasal.

Develop Expectations for Student Progress

Although it true that all students do not develop at the same rate despite the very best instruction, it helps to articulate end-of-grade expectations in terms of stages of development (see Table 2.4). You should know the typical range of development within grade levels so that you can provide additional instruction and intervention for students who lag below that range. You should also know where students must be (at the very least) at the end of the year if they are to succeed in subsequent grades and meet standards in reading and writing.

Goal-Setting/Progress Monitoring Charts

The stage expectations listed by grade level in the right-hand column of Table 2.4 are long-term, basic goals. Generally speaking, long-term goals reflect your basic expectations for what stage your students must be in to succeed in the next grade level. In contrast, short-term goals indicate the features necessary to study and learn to reach the basic long-term stage goal

TABLE 2.4 **Spelling Stage Expectations by Grade Levels**

Grade Level	Typical Spelling Stage Ranges Within Grade	End-of-Year Spelling Stage
PreK	Early/Middle emergent–Middle/Late emergent	Middle emergent
K	Emergent–Letter name–alphabetic	Middle letter name–alphabetic
1	Late emergent–Within word pattern	Early within word pattern
2	Late letter name–Early syllables & affixes	Late within word pattern
3	Within word pattern–Syllables & affixes	Early syllables & affixes
4	Within word pattern–Syllables & affixes	Middle syllables & affixes
5	Syllables & affixes–Derivational relations	Late syllables & affixes
6 +	Syllables & affixes–Derivational relations	Derivational relations

(Flanigan et al., 2011). The goal-setting/progress monitoring charts make explicit what must specifically be learned to reach the ultimate long-term goal.

Goal-setting/monitoring charts can be used to track student progress and to guide your conferences with specialists, parents, and students from early letter name to late syllables and affixes. (Charts are not provided beyond the early derivational relations stage because mastery continues throughout adulthood.) Use the results from one of the inventories to determine which chart is most appropriate. As shown in Figure 2.10, Omar's teacher has checked off each feature Omar used correctly. Omar is making good progress; he could identify most short vowels in September and spelled them correctly in CVC words, and words with blends and digraphs, and in words with preconsonantal nasals by November. Progress monitoring charts help students define a set of goals that are within reach, within their zone of proximal development.

Older students should understand exactly what they need to learn to become stronger readers and writers, and it can motivate them to be involved in their own short-term goal setting. We recommend that you meet with them individually to share the results of the inventory or spell checks and set goals together. Then students can keep a record of their own weekly assignments, tests, and spell checks to chart their own progress. This is especially helpful for students who are struggling with reading, writing, and spelling and may feel overwhelmed with all they need to learn. It may not be important for them to remember the name of the stage they are in or their numerical power scores, but it's reassuring for them to hear the specifics of what features they already know and what features they need to learn next to move forward.

Changing Groups in Response to Progress

Groups should be fluid. If students are frustrated or not challenged by the activities, then they should be placed in a different group. Use the progress monitoring assessments to refine your groups. When considering whether a student should be moved to a group studying more advanced features, seek multiple pieces of evidence.

1. First, look at the student's spelling samples from the spelling inventories and the spell checks. Consider both the power scores and the feature scores.
2. Next, look at several uncorrected writing samples using the qualitative checklists. If students are ready to be moved they should be correctly applying the features they have studied in their independent, unedited writing. The goal-setting/progress monitoring charts should confirm these sources of evidence.
3. Finally, look at the big picture, the synchrony of literacy development. Table 2.5 shows the concordance of developmental spelling stages with reading stages and approximate levels of reading achievement. If you want to move a student from a late letter name word study group to an early within word pattern group, look to see if the student can read at least at a first-grade level. Orthographic knowledge develops in synchrony with reading and writing.

In Table 2.5 we present a concordance of spelling and reading stages across the grade levels. The text levels represent the most current systems used to level texts. The lexile levels (Lexile Framework for Reading, 2013) reflect broad ranges using the new "stretch" ranges presented in the Common Core State Standards, though other forms of text complexity should be considered. The letters draw on the levels found in *Guided Reading Levels* (Fountas & Pinnell, 2001), and the numbers reflect DRA levels (Beaver & Carter, 2003) and approximate similar numeric leveling systems used by other publishers such as Rigby and National Geographic. The grade levels are general ranges and averages; the actual match will vary. The single grade-level designations are mid-year approximations. For example, this table says that by mid-year, most third graders are in the early syllables and affixes stage and are early intermediate readers. When spelling and reading development is out of synchrony, this often indicates that there has been a mismatch of instruction (Invernizzi & Hayes, 2010).

Sharing Progress with Parents and Other Teachers

Spelling inventories, spell checks, and goal-setting/progress monitoring charts are valuable artifacts to add to students' portfolios and use in parent conferences to discuss individual

TABLE 2.5 Concordance of Spelling and Reading Stages across Grade Levels

Grade Level*	Spelling Stage	Reading Phase	Reading Stage	Book Levels		
				Lexiles*	Letters	Numbers
PreK–K	Early emergent–early letter name	Pre-alphabetic	Early to early emergent	NA	A–B	1–2
K–Early 1st	Early letter name	Partial alphabetic	Early beginning	NA	C	3–4
1st	Middle letter name	Partial alphabetic	Middle beginning	NA	D, E	4–8
1st–Early 2nd	Late letter name	Full alphabetic	Late beginning	200–400	F, G	10–12
Late 1st–Early 2nd	Early within word pattern	Full alphabetic	Early transitional		H, I	14–16
2nd	Middle within word pattern	Consolidated alphabetic	Middle transitional	400–600	J, K	18–20
2nd–Early 3rd	Late within word pattern	Consolidated	Late transitional		L, M	24–28
3rd	Early syllables & affixes	Consolidated	Early intermediate	500–820	N, O, P	30–36
4th	Middle syllables & affixes	Automatic	Middle intermediate	600–900	Q, R, S	40
5th	Middle syllables & affixes to early derivational relations	Automatic	Intermediate to advanced	740–1010	T, U, V	50
6th	Late syllables & affixes to middle derivational relations	Automatic	Intermediate to advanced	800–1015	W, X, Y	60
7th	Early to middle derivational relations	Automatic	Early to middle advanced	925–1185	W, X, Y, Z	70
8th	Middle derivational relations	Automatic	Middle advanced to advanced	1000+	Z & up	80+

* Approximations lexile levels based on Common Core State Standards for English, Language Arts, Appendix A (Additional Information), NGA and CCSSO, 2012.

needs and progress. Benny's parents should be able to appreciate the growth he has made over his first-grade year, as shown in Figure 2.8. It reassures parents to see their child's earlier invented spellings give way to greater accuracy in writing. In looking at the end-of-grade expectations chart in Table 2.4, we see that Benny is right on target as he finishes first grade entering into the within word pattern stage of development.

Unlike some literacy skills, spelling results are visible, and with a little explanation parents can understand how you are using spelling errors to plan instruction. Parents who are accustomed to seeing their children bring home lists of spelling words taken from thematic units and content materials are sometimes a little dismayed when they see word lists designed for their children's developmental level. In one case, second graders were given words like *butterfly*, *chrysalis*, and *caterpillar* to memorize for a test each week. When their third-grade teacher designed word study based on a spelling inventory, the parents thought the words (*drew*, *flew*, *blow*, *snow*) were too easy and that their children were not being challenged enough. The teacher responded by explaining the spelling inventory and showing parents the results—the students consistently used but confused long *o* and long *u* patterns. The parents then understood and appreciated that the teacher was teaching their children *how to spell* and not just assigning them words to memorize and forget.

In many schools, literacy specialists meet with teachers in grade-level meetings to review assessment results, discuss grouping, and plan for word study instruction. Many schools use spelling inventory results as universal screening tools to help identify students who need intervention services. Spell checks and goal-setting/progress monitoring charts are then used to gauge how well students respond to classroom instruction and additional interventions. The end-of-grade-level expectations chart in Table 2.4 can be useful in this regard. Often, spelling inventories are administered at all grade levels and each year the results are put in students' permanent records and serve as an important part of the school's cumulative literacy assessment. Next year's teachers and specialists have access to these records and can use them to place students and plan instruction.

Parents and Word Study
Learn how word study is part of a family literacy program in this video.

Assessing the Spelling Development of English Learners

To obtain a complete understanding of the word knowledge of students who are learning English, explore their literacy knowledge in their primary or first language. A spelling inventory in students' spoken language can indicate their literacy levels in the primary language and more specifically, show which orthographic features they already understand. *Words Their Way*™ *with English Learners* discusses spelling development, assessment, and instruction for English learners in depth (Helman, Bear, Templeton, Invernizzi, & Johnston, 2012) and also provides inventories in several languages.

By assessing their orthographic knowledge using the assessments described in this chapter, teachers can observe whether English learners are applying the rules of phonology and orthography from the written form of their primary language to English, or vice-versa (Helman, 2004, 2010). Bilingual learners rely on knowledge of their primary language to spell words in a second language (Fashola, Drum, Mayer, & Kang, 1996; Nathenson-Mejia, 1989; Shen & Bear, 2000; Yang, 2005; Zutell & Allan, 1988). For example, Spanish speakers take the 22 sounds of Spanish and match them to the roughly 44 sounds of English, making some logical substitutions along the way.

How a Literacy Leader Facilitates Word Study
In a two-part video, a team of second-grade teachers discuss assessments, set goals and plan instruction.

Predictable Spelling Confusions

Because students are expected to learn the orthography of English, it is useful to administer one of the inventories from Table 2.1 to see what they know and are ready to learn. The responses will also reveal some of the predictable confusions students may make. Bear et al. (2003) have identified which English consonant sounds are problematic for Spanish speakers, who make a variety of substitutions that can be traced to the influence of Spanish on their spelling. Examples include spelling *that* as DAT and *ship* as CHAP because the digraphs /th/ and /sh/ do not exist in Spanish. Because the silent *h* in Spanish can be spelled with a *j*, *hot* may be spelled JAT. Spellers use the nearest equivalents in their attempts to spell English. Short *a, e, i,* and *u* do not occur in Spanish, and the sound we call short *o* is spelled with the letter *a.* We can expect many confusions about how to represent these short vowel sounds such as using *A* for the short *o* in *hot.*

The spelling sample of a second grader in Figure 2.11 shows how a student's spoken Spanish can affect her English spelling. Several of Rosa's attempts follow the logical substitutions that are seen from English-speaking students in the letter name–alphabetic stage; that is, SHEP for *ship* and WAN for *when.* Other errors make good sense in relation to Spanish letter–sound correspondences. For example, given the pronunciation of *a* as /ah/ in Spanish, her spelling of SHAPEN for *shopping* is understandable. She replaces the *ch* in *chewed* with *sh* (SHOD). Rosa is also trying to find a spelling for the long *i,* shown by her use of AY in two of her spellings (bright as BRAYT and ripen as RAYPN). The long *i*—when elongated—really sounds like two vowels ("eye-ee"—a diphthong). Rosa is using the *y,* pronounced as a long *e* in Spanish, to spell the second half of the vowel combination.

The Influences of Students' Primary Languages

As Rosa's spelling illustrates, English learners' spellings efforts are logical and interesting. As you listen to the speech and oral reading of English language learners, notice the influences of their first languages on pronunciation and look for spelling errors that may be explained by a primary language or dialect. For example, one teacher learned about the influence of different East Indian dialects when she noticed confusions of /p/ for *f* and /sh/ for *s.* Another teacher noted her Korean students consistently confusing *r* for *l* and vice-versa. In spoken Korean, /r/ and /l/ are not different sounds and are represented with the same letter in Hangul, the Korean writing system (Yang, 2005).

Through observing English learners' native languages, teachers can better understand the literacy development in English. Look in each of the instructional chapters for specific guidance on the interrelatedness of students' home languages and English.

Conclusion

Looking at a child's spelling gives us a window into that child's word knowledge, the information he or she uses to read and write words. The word *assessment* comes from the Latin word *assidere*—"to sit beside." Spend some time sitting beside your students and looking through the window that their spellings provide and use inventories to assess what they know about how words work.

A summary of the developmental sequence can be found inside the front cover, and each of the instructional chapters for this book offers detailed information about the stage, the features to study, and activities to enhance instruction. Remember that the inventories only sample the most common features. At each stage, there is a considerable body of knowledge that students should master before they move on to the next stage. Keep your fingers on the pulse of development by monitoring progress over time using the spell checks and the goal-setting/progress monitoring tools discussed in this chapter and available from the website. And always keep in mind the synchrony of literacy development—the heart of planning instruction—the topic for Chapter 3.

FIGURE 2.11
Rosa's Spelling

1. bed	bed
2. ship	shep
3. when	wan
4. lump	lamp
5. float	flowt
6. train	trayn
7. place	pleays
8. drive	kids
9. bright	brayt
10. shopping	shapen
11. spoil	spoyo
12. serving	sorven
13. chewed	shod
14. carries	cares
15. marched	marsh
16. shower	showar
17. cattle	cadoto
18. favor	fayvr
19. ripen	raypn
20. cellar	sallar

Organizing for Word Study

PRINCIPLES AND PRACTICES

Once you determine the developmental level of each of your students, as described in Chapter 2, you are ready to organize your classroom for word study. In this chapter, we will describe the basic activities for word study, how to lead thoughtful word study discussions, how to create and organize materials, and how to set up weekly routines that facilitate effective and efficient word study. We will address related issues such as expectations for editing and grading, before ending with a review of guiding principles of word study and a table of resources. To illustrate the details that make up this chapter, let's first visit the classroom of Mrs. Zimmerman as she introduces a group of her students to *r*-influenced vowels.

Earlier in the year, Mrs. Zimmerman assessed her third-grade students and divided them into three instructional groups for word study. On most Mondays, she meets with each group for about 15 to 20 minutes to go over the words and help her students make discoveries and reach conclusions about the particular group of words she has chosen. After getting her students started on independent reading and journal writing, Mrs. Zimmerman calls her first group to a table. She has a set of words cards laid out on a table. She begins by saying, "Let's go over these words to be sure everyone knows how to read them and what they mean." After discussing *mare,* which Julio defines as a "mother horse," she picks up *bear* and *bare* and reads both. "Who remembers what words like these are called? That's right, they're homophones." She holds up *bear* and asks who knows what it means.

Classroom Organization Across the Grades
In this video fundamental word study activities and weekly schedules are introduced.

"It's an animal and I saw one last summer when we went camping," offers Shannon.

"What about this *bare*?" asks Mrs. Zimmerman, as she holds up the word. Rayshad explains that it means "having no hair, like being bald."

"Any other ideas?" asks Mrs. Zimmerman, to which Jessie adds, "You might go barefooted, without shoes."

Other examples are given and then Mrs. Zimmerman continues, "There is another set of homophones here. Can anyone find them?" Mason finds *hair* and *hare* and again they talk about the meaning of each. They recall that they have heard the word *hare* in the story *The Hare and the Tortoise,* which they read during a unit on fables.

Mrs. Zimmerman now moves into the heart of the lesson by using an open-ended question to get students thinking and observing, "What do you notice about our words for this week?" Rachel points out that all the words have A's and Samuel adds that they also have Rs. "What else?" Mrs. Zimmerman probes, "Tell me more." Tiffany identifies the patterns of AR and AIR and Belle adds that there are also words with ARE. Mrs. Zimmerman responds, "So you are using your eyes to see how they are alike. What do your ears tell you? Julio?" Julio says that he can hear /ar/ and /air/. Mrs. Zimmerman affirms, "Yes, I hear those also. Does anyone hear any other sounds?

Mrs. Zimmerman then begins a teacher-directed sort by setting up categories. "Let's sort our words by sounds. I am going to put *cart* here as one of our key words and *care* over here for the other. Listen to the sounds in each: *caaarrrt, caaarrrre.*" Then she picks up and reads the word *farm.* "Will this go with *cart* or *care*? *Farm* and *cart* sound alike in the middle so we will put *farm* under *cart.* How about *chair*? Does it sound like *cart* or *care* in the middle?" After sorting several more words, Mrs. Zimmerman hands out the rest of the word cards and calls on students to read and sort each word by its vowel sound. After sorting all the words, the students read down each column to verify that the words all have the same sound in the middle. The final sort by sound looks like Figure 3.1.

Next, Mrs. Zimmerman directs her students' attention to the spelling patterns: "When you look at these words what do you notice about all the words in each column?" Lisa replies that they all have an *a* and *r* in them. "Does

FIGURE 3.1
Mrs. Zimmerman's Sound Sort

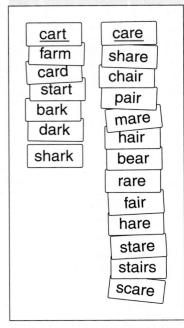

everyone see that pattern? What else?" she prompts. William volunteers that under *care*, there is an *e* at the end or an *i* in the middle. "Shall we put these words into two separate categories by spelling pattern?" asks Mrs. Zimmerman. "What should we use as headers?" The students agree to keep *care* as one header and to use *chair* for the other, and these words are underlined. Mrs. Zimmerman passes out the word cards and students take turns placing each word under *care* or *chair* after reading it aloud.

"I have an oddball!" calls out Tan, and she places the word *bear* off to the right.

"Ahh," says Mrs. Zimmerman. "Why is it an oddball?"

"It is the only "air" sound spelled with an *EA*," explains Tan.

After sorting the words by pattern as shown in Figure 3.2, they read down each column of words to verify that they all have the same sound as well as the same pattern. Mrs. Zimmerman then asks her students if the patterns remind them of other words they have studied. Brian points out that *ai* and *a* with an *e* on the end are patterns that go with long *a*. "Are these long *a* words?" probes Mrs. Zimmerman. "Listen: *caaaare, chaaair.*" The children agree that they can hear the sound of /a/ in those words. "What do you notice about the *a* in *cart*?" asks Mrs. Zimmerman. This time there is some discussion as students come to the conclusion that they cannot even hear a vowel! Mrs. Zimmerman tells the students that over the next few weeks they will look at more words with an *r* after the vowel and they should watch how the *r* influences the sound of vowels. To end the lesson, Mrs. Zimmerman asks students to reflect on what they have learned and she records their summary: The sound "air" can be spelled two ways—*air* and *are*.

Before they return to their seats, Mrs. Zimmerman gives each student a handout for sorting independently. She reminds them to draw colored lines down the back to mark their set of words and then underline the key words before cutting them apart. They are to sort first by sound (naming each word quietly as they sort) and then by pattern as they did in their final group sort. Two volunteers agree to illustrate the homophones for the class homophone dictionary.

After Mrs. Zimmerman meets with another word study group, she quickly checks in with each student in the first group to look at his or her sort. As she moves around the room, she asks individual students to read a column of words and explain how they are alike. On Tuesday, she will ask all her students to sort their words once more and then to write the words by categories in word study notebooks along with a sentence or two about what they have learned. On other days, they will work with partners to sort again and to find more words from the books they are reading that fit the same sounds and/or patterns. On Friday, Mrs. Zimmerman assesses all three groups at one time by calling out a word in turn for each group to spell.

This classroom vignette illustrates several key principles of developmental word study:

FIGURE 3.2   Mrs. Zimmerman's Pattern Sort

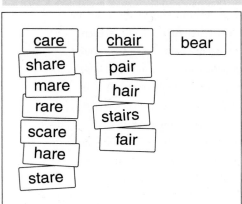

1. *A step backward is a step forward.* Students in this group had already studied the fairly consistent *ar* sound in words like *car* and *star*. In this sort, those sounds are reviewed and a new sound is introduced that is spelled with two different patterns.

2. *Use words students can read.* Mrs. Zimmerman began this lesson by going over the words, reading and discussing their meanings.

3. *Sort by sound and pattern.* Mrs. Zimmerman began by comparing two sounds before leading a visual sort in which spelling patterns were compared. Even when students sort by pattern it is important for them to "say it" as they "lay it."

4. *Don't hide exceptions.* In this sort, the word *bear* was included as an **oddball**, a word that has the same sound but a different spelling pattern. Words like *pear* and *wear* might have been included as well. These so-called exceptions reveal that there is a small subset of words with the /air/ sound spelled with an *ear* pattern.

5. *Teaching is not telling.* Mrs. Zimmerman is careful to use open-ended questions so that students have the opportunity to draw their own conclusions about the set of words. She expects her students to do the thinking for themselves with guidance from her as needed. ●

The Role of Word Sorting

Throughout this book you will see many examples of games and activities, but the simple process of sorting words into categories, like the word sort described in Mrs. Zimmerman's class, is the heart of word study. Categorizing is a fundamental way that humans make sense of the world. It allows us to find order and similarities among various objects, events, ideas, and words that we encounter. When students sort words, they engage in the active process of searching, comparing, contrasting, and analyzing. Word sorts help students organize what they know about words and form generalizations that they can then apply to new words they encounter in their reading or spell in their writing (Gillet & Kita, 1979; Henderson, 1990).

for Words Their Way®

For each stage, there are videos of word sort lessons and activities.

Because sorting is such a powerful way to help students make sense of words, we will take some time here to discuss it in depth. We recommend this same categorization routine for students in all stages studying a variety of word features. At first, emergent and beginning readers learn to pay attention to sounds at the beginnings of words by sorting pictures (Figure 3.3). By the time they are transitional readers, enjoying their first *Frog and Toad* books (by A. Lobel), students benefit from sorting written words by vowel sounds and vowel patterns. In later grades, students enhance their spelling and vocabulary through sorting words by prefixes and suffixes. In middle school and high school, students sort words by Greek and Latin roots that share common meanings. As children progress in word knowledge, they learn how to look at and think about words in different ways.

Teaching New Word Knowledge through Sorting

Word sorting offers the best of both constructivist learning and teacher-directed instruction. Begin by "stacking the deck" with words that can be contrasted by sound, pattern, or meaning. During sorting, Mrs. Zimmerman's students will discover generalizations about how the English spelling system works. Over the next few weeks, they will continue to explore *r*-influenced vowels through a series of sorts and will discover that *r* often "robs" the vowel of the sounds we normally associate with it. Rather than simply memorizing 20 words each week for a spelling test, students have the opportunity to construct their own word knowledge that they can apply to reading and writing. Through sorting, students acquire and integrate new word knowledge that is extended and refined through the activities we describe. In addition to learning how to spell, read, understand, and use new words, students develop productive habits of mind (Marzano, 1992).

FIGURE 3.3   Beginning Sound Sort

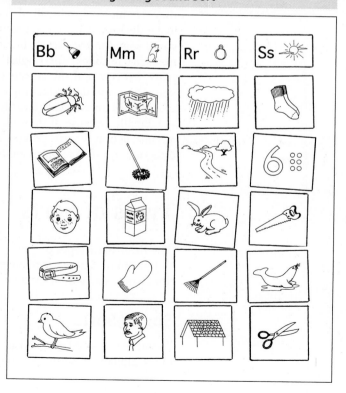

Teaching Phonics through Sorting

One central goal of word study is to teach students how to spell and decode new words and to improve their word recognition speed in general. To accomplish this goal, we teach students how to examine words to learn the regularities that exist in the spelling system. Picture sorts and word sorts are designed to help students learn how and where to look at and listen to words.

Picture and word sorting differ from other phonics approaches in some important ways. First, word sorts are interesting and fun for students because they are hands-on and manipulative. The process of sorting requires students to pay attention to words and to make logical decisions as they place each one in a column. Consider the ancient proverb: "I hear and I forget, I see and I remember, I do and I understand." Word sorts help students learn by doing (Morris, 2013).

Second, students work with words or the names of pictures that they can already pronounce. In this way, processing words from the known to the unknown while sorting through a set of cards, children concentrate on analyzing the sounds or patterns within each word. This is not possible if students cannot first name the words. Because learning to spell involves associating the spelling of words and their pronunciations, it is important that children know and can already pronounce most of the words to be sorted.

A third way in which sorting differs from some other phonics approaches is that sorting is analytic, whereas many phonics programs take a synthetic approach. In both approaches, students are taught letter–sound correspondences. However, in a **synthetic phonics** approach, students are taught the letter-sound correspondences and then expected to sound out words phoneme by phoneme. This can make reading tedious and can detract from meaning and engagement. An **analytic phonics** approach uses known words; students are asked to examine their parts listening for sounds, looking for patterns, or thinking about meaning. Analytic phonics supports the synthetic skills necessary to decode new words when reading and to encode words when writing.

A fourth way in which sorting differs from most phonics and spelling programs is that sorting does not rely on memorizing or reciting rules prior to understanding the underlying principles. During sorting, students determine similarities and differences among features as they use higher-level critical thinking skills to make categorical judgments. When students make decisions about whether the middle vowel sound in *cat* sounds more like the medial vowel sound in *map* or *top*, independent analysis and judgment are required. Memorization *is* necessary to master the English spelling system. One simply must remember that the animal is spelled *bear* and the adjective is spelled *bare*, but memorization is easier when served by knowledge and understanding of the principles of English spelling. Likewise, rules are useful mnemonics for concepts already understood.

Finally, because of the simplicity of sorting routines, teachers find it easier to differentiate instruction among groups of learners. Sorting is infinitely adaptable and the process of categorizing word features lends itself to cooperative learning.

Types of Sorts

The three basic types of sorts reflect the three layers of English orthography: sound, pattern, and meaning. There are many variations of these sorts that students can do under your direction, with a partner, or by themselves for additional practice.

Sound Sorts

Sound is the first layer of English orthography that students must negotiate to make sense of the alphabetic nature of English spelling. At different points in development, students sort words by rhyme, initial sounds, consonant blends or digraphs, rhyming word families, or vowel sounds. Advanced spellers may sort by unaccented syllables, the number of syllables, and syllable stress.

Pictures are naturally suited for sound sorts: the picture begs to be named, yet there is no printed form of the word for reference. As students sort each picture, they must pay attention to the sounds or **phonemes** contained in the word. Picture sorting is particularly suited for students who are still developing phonemic awareness and do not have extensive reading vocabularies. Students say the names of the pictures as they place under the letters and **key pictures** associated with the initial sound. Refer to Figure 3.3. For variety, small objects can be used instead of pictures, like a penny, pencil, and pin for sorting by beginning /p/ sound. English learners will need extra time and support to learn the names of the objects and pictures before sorting them by sound. Printed words, too, can be sorted for sound, as Mrs. Zimmerman did using the key words *cart* and *care*. Because sound is the first aspect of a word that a speller has for reference, sound sorts are very important. For example, only after the long *a* in *tape* is identified can the speller consider which of several spelling patterns might be used. (Is it *taip* or *tape*?) Not all word sorts involve a sound contrast, but many do.

for **English Learners**

Pattern Sorts

Students use the printed form of the word to sort by visual patterns or letter sequences. Letter name–alphabetic spellers sort words into word families (*hat, rat, pat* versus *ran, fan, tan*). Students in the within word pattern stage sort their words into groups by vowel patterns (*wait, train, mail, pain* versus *plate, take, blame*). More advanced spellers will sort by the pattern of consonants and vowels at the syllable juncture (*button, pillow, ribbon* versus *window, public, basket*) or by patterns of constancy and change across derivationally related words (e.g., *divine–divinity, mental–mentality*).

Pattern sorts often follow a sound sort as we saw in the lesson with Mrs. Zimmerman. The words under *care* were subdivided into two pattern groups: words spelled with *air* and words spelled with *are*. Because certain patterns go with certain sound categories, students must be taught first to listen for the sound and then to consider alternative ways to spell that sound.

Sometimes a new feature is best introduced with a pattern sort to reveal a related sound difference. Consider the words in Figure 3.4 that have been sorted by the final *ch* or *tch* pattern. The final sound in all the words is the same, so a sound sort would not help to differentiate their spellings. However, now that the words are sorted by the final consonant patterns, read down each column to see if you notice anything about the vowel sounds within each column. What did you discover? The *tch* pattern is associated with the short vowel sound whereas *ch* is associated with the long vowel sound. Exceptions are *rich* and *such*, which are moved to the oddball category. The visual patterns of words are best remembered when associated with categories of sound.

Word sorts with printed word cards are the mainstay of pattern sorts and are useful for all students who have a functional sight word vocabulary. **Key words** containing the pattern under study may be underlined or bolded (as in Figure 3.6) to label each category. Students sort word cards by matching the pattern in each word to the pattern in the key word at the top of the column. **Headers** are used to highlight the recurring pattern (as shown in Figure 3.6, where *tch* and *ch* label the feature of interest). Students can sometimes create their own headers as part of the word sorting lesson to summarize a generalization. Because it is easier to sort words by visual pattern, students can lose sight of the fact that certain patterns go with certain sounds. Sometimes mixing a few pictures in with a stack of word cards challenges students to be vigilant in their word analysis.

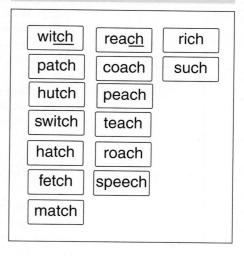

FIGURE 3.4   Word Sort by Final *ch* and *tch* Patterns

wi**tch**	rea**ch**	rich
pa**tch**	coa**ch**	such
hu**tch**	pea**ch**	
swi**tch**	tea**ch**	
ha**tch**	roa**ch**	
fe**tch**	spee**ch**	
ma**tch**		

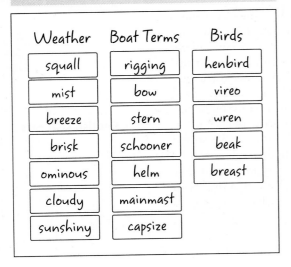

FIGURE 3.5 Concept Sort Based on *Stuart Little*

Weather	Boat Terms	Birds
squall	rigging	henbird
mist	bow	vireo
breeze	stern	wren
brisk	schooner	beak
ominous	helm	breast
cloudy	mainmast	
sunshiny	capsize	

for **English Learners**

Meaning Sorts

Sometimes the focus of a sort is on meaning. The two major types of **meaning sorts** are concept sorts and meaning sorts related to spelling.

CONCEPT SORTS. Sorting objects, pictures, or words by concepts or meaning is a good way to link vocabulary instruction to students' conceptual understanding. Concept sorts are appropriate for all ages and stages of word knowledge, and should be used regularly in the content areas. Pictures of mammals, mathematical formulas, geometric shapes, or social studies vocabulary words all can be sorted for greater understanding. The creative possibilities for using concept sorts are endless. As writing tools, they can be used to organize ideas before composing. Concept sorts are even useful for teaching grammar when words are sorted by parts of speech.

You can use concept sorts for assessing and building background knowledge before embarking on a new unit of study. For example, a science unit on states of matter might begin by having students categorize the following words into groups that go together: *steam, wood, air, ice cube, rain, metal, glue, paint, plastic, smoke, milk,* and *fog.* Discussing the reasons behind their conceptual groupings will be the most revealing. Revisit the sort as the unit progresses to review and assess core concepts and vocabulary. Having students categorize examples under the key words *solid, liquid,* and *gas* will help them sort out the essential characteristics for each state of matter. Concept sorts are effective for dealing with new words in novels, too. While reading *Stuart Little* (by E. B. White), a group of Mrs. Birckhead's third-graders sorted some of the vocabulary they encountered, as shown in Figure 3.5.

Concept picture sorts are particularly beneficial for English learners. Without knowing the English labels, they can sort pictures of a dog, a cat, a duck, and so on into an animal category. These can be contrasted with pictures of a flower, a tree, a cornfield, a pumpkin, and so on—all examples of plants. English vocabulary is learned as students repeat the sort, naming each picture and category with help from a teacher or peer.

SPELLING–MEANING SORTS. Students see that meaning influences the spelling of words when they first encounter soundalike **homophone** pairs like *by* and *buy* or *to* and *too.* Students enjoy homophones because they are interesting, and it makes sense that words with different meanings take different spelling patterns. When you teach homophones through word sorting, students expand their vocabularies and learn about spelling patterns at the same time, as demonstrated by the discussion of *bear* and *bare* in Mrs. Zimmerman's class. **Homographs** are words that are spelled the same but pronounced differently, depending on part of speech: We *record* our sorts so that we have an ongoing *record* of them. By sorting homographs into grammatical categories by part of speech, students enrich their vocabularies while learning how to pay attention to syllable stress.

Advanced spellers learn how words that are related in meaning often share similar spellings. This spelling–meaning connection in derivationally related words provides a rich arena for meaning sorts that build on Greek and Latin elements. Spellers who are learning derivational relations will sort words by similarities in roots and stems such as the *spect* in *spectator, spectacle, inspect,* and *spectacular* versus the *port* in *transport, import, portable,* and *port-o-john.*

A Continuum of Support when Introducing Sorts

Instruction in word study, as in comprehension and other areas of the curriculum, should follow a gradual release model (Fisher & Frey, 2008) that begins with teacher modeling and explicit explanations (Duffy, 2009), moves to guided practice, and then proceeds to independent work. Each week, students get a new set of words to work with and you need to decide how best to introduce those words so that students are led to form generalizations about how a feature works. Introductory lessons can range from teacher-directed sorts to student-centered sorts done independently. Which level of support you select depends on several factors:

1. How familiar students are with the sorting process
2. Whether a new feature is being introduced
3. The amount of time available for sorting
4. How well students can work independently

Different levels of support are summarized in Table 3.1 and described in the following subsections, but the infinite variations of these allow you to adapt word sorting to your own tastes and situation. Open-ended questions that require students to do their own thinking and form their own generalizations are used at all levels, but you should always be ready to model your own thinking when they are unable to articulate a generalization.

Mrs. Zimmerman chose a teacher-directed sort to introduce the new feature of *r*-influenced vowels in the vignette at the beginning of this chapter. Such a lesson can take 20 minutes or more. The next week when she gives them words with *er*, *ear*, and *eer*, she might ask students to sort the words on their own before coming to the group because she knows that they are experienced sorters who will be thinking about sounds and patterns as they sort. She may only need five to ten minutes of group time in which the students quickly re-sort their words, check the sort, and reflect on what they discovered.

Teacher-Directed Closed Sorts

The highest level of support and explicit instruction is offered in teacher-directed **closed sorts**. Define the categories in advance using key words and/or headers and make it clear how to conduct the sort (Gillet & Kita, 1979). For example, in a beginning sound phonics sort, isolate the beginning sound to be taught and make an explicit connection to the letter that represents it using a key word to designate the category. You might think aloud like this: "*Shhhhhoe, shhhhhell*. I hear the same sound at the beginning of *shoe* and *shell*, so I am going to put the picture of the shell under *shoe*. They both begin with /sh/, the sound made by the letters *s–h*."

After modeling several words this way, gradually release the task to the students' control as they finish the sort under your supervision. After sorting, students discuss the characteristics of the words in each column and develop a generalization based on the selected feature. Students may then sort independently or collaboratively in pairs under your guidance. This practice is carefully monitored and corrective feedback is provided.

The teacher-directed sort is the most commonly used approach to introduce a new sort to a group, providing a model of direct instruction that is explicit and systematic, yet sensitive to individual variation. The teacher-directed lesson plan includes three components: demonstrate and sort, check and reflect, and extend.

DEMONSTRATE AND SORT. There are four steps to introducing the sort using key pictures or words.

1. *Review the words.* Look over the words or pictures for items that are potentially difficult to identify or that may be unfamiliar to students. Give names of pictures as needed. ("This is a picture of a yard.") Students should already be able to read most of the words in a sort but any words students cannot identify should be set aside until later. Help students define unfamiliar words and words with multiple meanings, and use them in sentences. ("Does anyone know what a *hutch* is? It is a kind of wooden cage up on legs. Pet rabbits often live in hutches.") You might keep dictionaries handy and ask students to look up selected words and report back to the group. ("A hutch is a pen for animals but also a piece of furniture.") Supply pictures when possible to develop new meanings and revisit vocabulary throughout the week. Your English learners will especially benefit from picture dictionaries and a vocabulary discussion.

for **English Learners**

TABLE 3.1 Continuum of Support for Introducing Word Sorts

	FOR NOVICE SORTERS OR TO INTRODUCE NEW FEATURES		FOR EXPERIENCED SORTERS OR TO ASSESS	
	Teacher-Directed Closed Sort	*Teacher-Directed Guess My Category*	*Student-Centered Closed Sort*	*Student-Centered Open Sort*
Materials	One set of words for group to focus on using a pocket chart, overhead, interactive whiteboard, or other method. Students bring their own set of words to the group or are given a set at the end of group work to take back to their seats to cut apart and sort.		Students get their own set of words with key words and/or headers.	Students get their own set of words with no key words or headers.
Introduce the Sort	Read through all the words and talk about any that students might not know. Introduce each category with a header and a key word and explicitly describe the features students are to look for.	Read through the words and talk about any that are unfamiliar. Set up the categories with key words but do not describe the feature or put up headers.	Read through the words and talk about any that are unfamiliar. Students can also do this on their own, putting aside any words they don't know to discuss and sort later.	Students work on their own to read through words and put aside any words they don't know.
Sorting	Demonstrate how to sort two or three words in each category and describe explicitly why each word goes there. Students help to complete the sort and justify their placements.	Model by sorting several words in each category but do not explain the reasons. Students are then invited to try sorting the rest of the words.	Students use headers and key words to set up categories and sort independently.	Students determine categories and sort their own words. They explain to you or each other why they sorted as they did.
Check and Reflect	Model how to check the columns and create a generalization with student help. Be ready to model as needed to summarize what the sort has revealed. Sort again at this point if time allows to reinforce the features and reflect once more.	Ask students to describe the features in each category and then check each column. Create a generalization with students' help. Supply headers at this point or label key words.	Call group together or check in individually for students to describe the features and talk about any unfamiliar words. Everyone checks.	"Close" the sort. Establish key words so everyone sorts the same way. Check and talk once more about generalizations. Supply or label headers.
Sort Individually	Students sort their own set of words in the group under your supervision or at their seats. Monitor, remind students to check, and ask each student to state generalizations.	Students sort their own set of words using the key words and headers in the group or independently. Monitor and check in during or after students sort.		

2. *Establish the categories.* Use open-ended questions such as "What do you notice about these words?" or "How might we sort these words?" to get students thinking about categories. If you stacked the deck with words that share common patterns or sounds and your students are familiar with categorizing, they should notice common features fairly quickly. If not, then define the categories for them. Introduce letter cards, key pictures, key words, or headers with pattern cues to indicate the categories. If you are working with sounds, you can emphasize or elongate them by stretching them out. If you are working with patterns, you can think aloud as you point out the spelling pattern. If you are working with syllables, affixes, or derivational relations, you can explicitly point out the unit you are using to compare and contrast.

3. *Model several words into each category and explain why you are sorting.* "We are going to listen for the vowel sound in the middle of these words and decide if they sound like *map* or like *duck*. I'll do a few first. Here is a rug. *Ruuuuug, uuuug, uuuuuuh.* Notice how I peel off the sounds before and after the vowel to make it easier to hear the vowel in the middle. *Rug* has the 'uh' sound (/ŭ/) in the middle, so I'll put it under *duck, uuuuck, uuuuh.* Here is a flag. *Flaaaaag, aaaag, aaaa.* I'll put *flag* under *maaaap. Flag* and *map* both have the /ă/ sound in the middle; the /ă/ sound is made by the vowel letter *a.*"

4. *Turn the task over to students to finish the sort.* Display the rest of the pictures or words, pass them out, or continue to hold them up one at a time. Students can take turns and enjoy the anticipation of turning over a word in the stack. Students should name the picture or read the word aloud and then place it in a category, explaining why it goes there. If students make a mistake at the very beginning, correct it immediately. Simply say: "*Sack* would go under *map*. Its middle sound is /ă/." Then model how to segment the phonemes to isolate the medial vowel: /s/–/ă/–/k/.

Sorting Short -*e* -*o* and -*u* with Initial Blends
Watch how Ms. Kiernan sorts with her students.

Check and Reflect

You may ask students to sort their own set of words cooperatively or independently under your supervision. Unless your students are in the last two levels of word knowledge (syllables and affixes or derivational relations), ask them to name each word or picture aloud as they sort. If someone does not know what to call a picture, tell the student immediately. If someone cannot read a word, lay the card aside to consider later. Model how to check the sort by reading down each column to listen for sound or look for the pattern. Oddballs may be discussed at this point and you may move to the reflection portion of the lesson.

During this second, repeated sort, do not correct your students, but when they are through, have them name the words or pictures in each column to check themselves. When students make mistakes it is sometimes useful to find out why they sorted a picture or word in a particular way. Simply asking, "Why did you put that there?" can provide further insight into a student's word knowledge. If mistakes are made during the second sort, your students will learn more if you guide them to finding and correcting the mistake on their own. You might say, "I see one word in this column that doesn't fit."

After checking their work, students reflect on why they sorted the way they did. It is important to have students verbalize what the words or pictures in each column have in common. The best way to initiate such a discussion is to say, "What do you notice about the words in each column?" Guide them to consider sound, pattern, and meaning with questions such as, "How are the sounds in these words alike? What kind of pattern do you notice? Are any of these words similar in meaning?" Avoid telling rules, but help students shape their ideas into generalizations, such as, "All of these words have the letter *u* in the middle and make the 'uh' sound," or "The words with an *e* on the end have the /ā/ sound in the middle." Be sure to talk about why the oddballs are placed in another category and return to any words that students were not able to read. With the generalization or "big idea" now stated they may be able to apply it to the decoding of unfamiliar words. During the reflection part of the lesson, students are asked to declare their knowledge about sound, pattern, and meaning.

EXTEND. After the group demonstration, sorting, and reflection, students participate in a number of activities at centers, with partners, as seatwork, and for homework to reinforce and extend their understanding. They continue to sort a number of times individually and with partners for several days. They hunt for similar words, draw and label pictures, add to word charts, complete word study notebooks, and play games. Extensions are described in more detail later in this chapter.

Guess My Category: A Teacher-Directed Sort

When students are comfortable with sorts, you can introduce any new area of study with a collection of objects, words, or pictures in a variation of the teacher-directed sort called Guess My Category. After reviewing the words, set up key words or pictures as in a closed sort but do not offer any explanation of the categories. Rather, it is your students' job to develop hypotheses about how the things in each category are alike. Begin by sorting two or three pictures or words into each group. When you pick up the next picture or word, invite someone to guess where it will go. Continue doing this until all the pictures or words have been sorted. Try to keep the students who have caught on to the attributes of interest from telling the others until the end. Look at the words below sorted under the key words *dead*, *street*, and *reach*. Can you guess the categories and decide where to sort *speak*, *bread*, and *sweet*?

dead	street	reach
head	queen	dream
breath	trees	beach

After sorting, check the sort, and guide a reflection as you would for the teacher-directed sort above. Students get their own words to sort and are assigned follow-up activities to do throughout the week.

Guess My Category is particularly useful in small groups for exploring content-specific vocabulary while also stimulating creative thinking. Give small groups sets of words, pictures, or objects that might be grouped in various ways; ask each group to come up with its own categories. Allow them to have a miscellaneous designation for those things that do not fit the categories they establish. After the groups are finished working, let them visit each other's sorts and try to guess the categories that were used. For example, pictures of animals might be sorted into groups according to body covering, habitat, or number of legs.

FIGURE 3.6 Closed Sort Handout for *tch* and *ch* Patterns with Headers and Key Words

tch	ch	
witch	**teach**	catch
coach	each	patch
hutch	rich	switch
much	hatch	reach
fetch	much	match
peach	screech	sketch

Student-Centered Sorts

As students become sorting pros, student-centered sorts increase the cognitive demand and can reduce the amount of teacher-directed group time. In many classrooms, students are given their words for the week on Monday morning, and they sort their words independently in anticipation of the categories they will be sorting later in teacher-directed groups. The handout for a closed sort, such as the example in Figure 3.6, provides the headers and key words students need to complete the sort on their own. They have some support, but must still read each word and think about sounds and patterns as they make their own decisions about where to sort. Remind students to watch out for oddballs. Oddballs present an enjoyable challenge for students that forces them to test the hypotheses they form about the words.

The student-centered **open sort** is really our favorite, demanding the highest level of independent effort and thought because students are not given any clues to the categories or features—only a set of words to sort. Open sorts are often the most satisfying for students as well because they present a puzzle to solve. Distribute a handout that has no headers or key words, such as Figure 3.7, and ask students to create their own categories. (If you are using prepared sorts that come with headers and key words, as in Figure 3.6, cut off the headers and key words to save for later.) Students can be asked to compare their categories with a partner to begin the reflection part of the lesson and come up with their own generalizations before sharing with the larger group.

Even with student-centered sorts you should still meet with the students individually or in a group to discuss the sort and check it for accuracy as described previously. In the case of an open sort, you may find that some students have sorted the words in ways that do not reveal a generalization or the "big idea." For example, your students may sort the words in Figure 3.7 by the number of letters, by rhyming words, or by beginning consonants (with a blend or no blend). After acknowledging that the words could be sorted that way, you should "close the sort" by agreeing on categories. At this point you might give students the headers and key words that were cut off the handout, or have students create their own headers as a way for them to summarize the features as part of the reflection process. In the final sort (see Figure 3.4 on page 53), the *tch* and *ch* endings have been underlined to identify both key words and headers. The same headers should be used each time students sort.

Student-centered sorts are diagnostic in nature because they reveal what students know when they work independently. Open sorts provide opportunities for students to test their own hypotheses and they often come up with unexpected ways to organize words. These open sorts are interesting to observe and to discover what students already understand or misunderstand. Some of the most productive discussions about orthography come when students explain *why* they sorted the way they did in an open sort.

Teacher Talk and Student Reflection

Peter Johnston has written extensively about how the language teachers use with students can position them as problem solvers or passive recipients (2004, 2012). Word study, as we describe it, offers valuable opportunities for students to be actively involved in making discoveries about the spelling system and developing vocabulary—but only if teachers facilitate group discussions that foster thoughtful interactions (Gehsmann, Millwood, & Bear, 2012). Ganske and Jocius (2013) reported that teachers they observed often relied on a traditional initiate/respond/evaluate format during word study lessons. The teacher *initiates* a question to which he or she knows the answer, the student *responds*, and the teacher *evaluates* the response as right or wrong. Such interactions are more like interrogations dominated by the teacher than discussions in which students practice higher-level thinking skills and learn from each other.

Student reflection and discussion are critical parts of word study instruction, but teachers must carefully consider how it is done. The language we use when we talk with students has a powerful influence on their understanding and can cultivate a sense of self-efficacy and problem solving. Asking open-ended questions such as, "What do you notice about these words?" suggests there are multiple aspects of words worth considering and that there is no one right answer. When students are writing and ask how to spell a word, asking, "Do you know another word that has a similar sound at the beginning?" conveys the message that they can figure it out for themselves (Johnston, 2004). Table 3.2 presents examples of teacher talk that encourages students to use language in problem solving, to reason and reflect, and to apply their growing word knowledge to other words.

Try to frame your response to their answers in ways that avoid judgment and will further the discussion. Instead of saying "Right" or "Good job," try, "Who agrees? Why?" or "Who can add to that?" When you say, "I like your ideas" or "Who can add to Todd's comment?"

FIGURE 3.7 Open Sort Handout for *tch* and *ch* Patterns

witch	teach	catch
coach	each	patch
hutch	rich	switch
much	hatch	reach
fetch	much	match
peach	screech	sketch

TABLE 3.2   Questions to Guide Critical Thinking during Word Study

Problem Solving	Reflection	Application & Transfer
What do you notice about these words? Remember to use your ears and your eyes as you examine them.	What can you tell us about these words now that we have sorted them? How are they alike?	Let's go back to these words we were not sure about earlier. Can we read them now? Can we figure out what they mean?
How are they alike? How are they different from this set over here? Tell me more.	Why did you put this word here?	What if we changed that prefix to another prefix? What would the word mean then?
Where in the word do you find the ___ (sound, spelling patterns, root)? Who can add to that?	What did we learn from this sort to be a better reader or speller?	If you're not sure how to spell a word, how would you know which pattern to use? What would be your best bet? Why?
How else could you figure that out? Does anyone have a different idea?	In your reading, which pattern do you see more frequently? Which pattern has the most words in your column? The fewest?	If you weren't sure what a word meant, what could you do to figure it out?
What are some ways we could figure out the meaning of that word? How could we check?	How did you figure that out?	Can you think of other words that have the same root or base word?
Which part of the word are you sure about? Which part are you not sure about? What do the rest of you think?	Tell me how your sorting went. What words were difficult? What were you sure of/unsure of? What problems did you come across in your sort?	One of the things people do when they aren't sure about a word is think of another word they know that has a similar base word or root. Let's try it. Let's say you don't know the meaning of *recital*. What other word might you think of that you do know?
Can you divide the word into parts? What is the base word? Are there any prefixes or suffixes?	What word parts did you use? Do the word parts give you information about the word's meaning?	What other word can you think of that has the same _____ (sound, pattern, root)?
How are you planning to go about this word sort?	Write down an observation about these words.	Let's try making some new words with these word parts. Let's see if we can guess the meaning.
Do you all agree? Why or why not? Any more ideas?	Do you think this will apply to other words like this?	How or when could you use this word?

Source: Based on Palmer, J., and Invernizzi, M. (2014). *Not This, But That: No More Phonics and Spelling Worksheets*. Portsmouth, NH: Heinemann.

you are giving students credit for their thinking rather than congratulating them on coming up with the answer you wanted to hear.

Questions such as these can help you get meaningful conversations about words going in your classroom and help to cultivate strategies for problem solving and reflection. Include talk about position, frequency, and related words. Some spelling patterns are found at the ends of words (like the *oy* in *toy* and *enjoy*) and others in the middle (like the *oi* in *soil* or *choice*). By asking students to reflect on where certain patterns occur within words, you can lead students to consider position as they learn to read and spell. Frequency of occurrence is also worthy of reflection. For example, word hunts will reveal that words ending in *er* are much more common than words ending in *or* or *ar*. Once students are clued into the frequency of certain spelling patterns, they can apply this insight by using a "best bet" approach to spelling and reading unfamiliar words. Reflecting on related words will extend students' insights to other words—a major goal of word study. Words with similar roots and affixes are related in both spelling and meaning. For example, the word *cover* is related to *discover, uncover, recover, discovery, recovery,* and so on. Such is the generative nature of word study.

Extensions and Follow-Up Routines

After an introductory sort, assign students a variety of follow-up activities designed to reinforce generalizations and their memory of words, build speed and accuracy, and connect to reading and writing. Ideally, such activities develop productive habits of looking for and thinking about word attributes, while at the same time providing individual practice and experience manipulating and categorizing words. All of these activities can and should be introduced to the whole class through modeling before assigning them to be completed independently.

Repeated Sorts

To become fluent readers and writers, students must achieve automaticity in reading (Samuels, 1988), the fast and accurate recognition of words in context, and automaticity in writing to produce fast and accurate spellings. The words they encounter in context and use in writing are made of the same sounds, patterns, and meaning units they examine out of context in word study. One of the best ways to achieve automaticity in word recognition and spelling is to repeat a picture or word sort over several days. In Mrs. Zimmerman's class, students sort individually after the group lesson, again on Tuesday, and then on Wednesday with partners. They eagerly participate in timed or speed sorts and they are expected to take their words home to sort several days a week for homework. All this adds up to sorting the same words six to eight times throughout the week.

Buddy Sorts

Students love to work cooperatively. In a buddy sort, they work together to read the words or name the pictures in each column, place the words into categories, check the sort, and then talk to each other about the generalization covered by the sort. The sorting can take place in tandem, side by side with two sets of words, or alternating turns with one set of words. Buddy sorts can provide support for students who are not sure of how to name pictures (often the case for English learners) or read words. Two sorts that work well with buddies are blind sorts and blind writing sorts.

for **English Learners**

Blind Sorts

In a **blind sort**, headers or key words are used to establish categories, but then the teacher or a partner shuffles the word cards and calls each word aloud without showing it. The student indicates the correct category by pointing to or naming the header. The response is checked and corrected immediately when the printed word is revealed and put in place. Buddies can switch roles (reader or sorter) after going through the whole set of words or they can switch roles word by word. This sort is important for students who need to attend less to visual patterns and more to the sounds. Sometimes, you can use a blind sort as a way to introduce a sort when sound is particularly important, as in the study of short vowels. Note, however, that blind sorts do not present a challenge when sound is not an issue, as in the study of prefixes or root words.

Writing Sorts

Writing words as a study technique for spelling is well established. Undoubtedly the motoric act reinforces the memory for associating letters and patterns with sounds and meanings. However, the practice of assigning students to write words five or more times is of little value because it can become mindless copying. Where there is no thinking, there is no learning. Writing words into categories demands that students attend to the sounds or patterns of letters and think about how those characteristics correspond with the key word or header at the top of the column.

FIGURE 3.8 Word Study Notebook

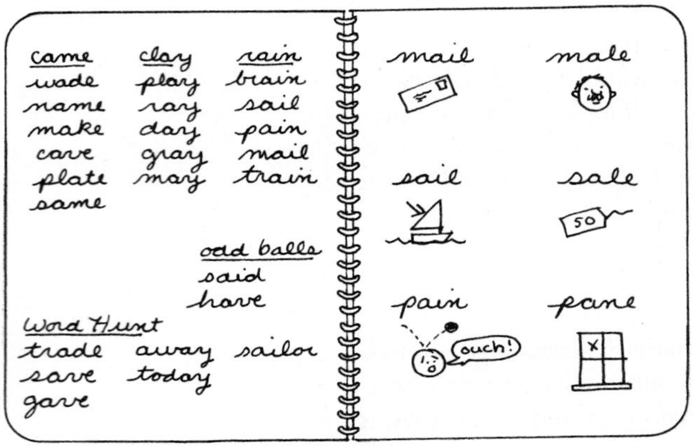

Start a **writing sort** by writing headers or key words for each category at the top of a paper. Students can record a sort that they complete with word cards or by turning over one word at a time from their collection and writing it under the correct header. Figure 3.8 shows how the words from a long *a* sort have been written under the key words *came*, *clay*, and *rain*. Students can also be asked to write a reflection about what they have learned from the sort.

Blind Writing Sorts

A combination of the blind sort and writing sort, a **blind writing sort** requires students to write each word in the correct category before seeing the word. In a blind writing sort, students must rely on the sounds they hear in the word as well as their memory for the letters associated with them, cued by the key word at the top of the column. This is what spelling is all about. Blind writing sorts are an established weekly routine in many classrooms once students have had the chance to practice the sort several times. Some teachers conduct them in a group using the document camera or interactive whiteboard, saying the word aloud and letting the students write it before they reveal the word for checking. Blind writing sorts done with a buddy or for homework are a good way to prepare for a weekly test by identifying which words need more attention. Partners take turns calling the words aloud for each other to write. It is important to immediately show the word to check the spelling and placement after each word is written. Writing sorts are also an instructionally sound way to construct spelling tests. Key words are written and then students write and sort the words as they are called.

Speed Sorts

Students are highly motivated to practice their sorts to prepare for **speed sorts**. The easiest way to do speed sorts is a quick whole-class activity. Display a timer (laying a tablet or phone with a timer on a document camera is one way) or simply call the seconds aloud from the classroom clock. Students set up their headers, shuffle the rest of their words, then hold up the words to signal that they are ready (students in different groups will have different words). When you say "go," everyone begins to sort. As they finish, students record their times. After checking, the speed sort can be repeated immediately as well as on other days so students can attempt to beat their own times. To encourage accurate sorting, seconds may be added for incorrectly placed words.

Students can also be paired to time each other using a stopwatch and chart their progress over time. Partners then check for correctness using an answer sheet. We do not recommend pitting students against each other in a competitive mode, however; instead, students should compare their speeds with their own earlier speeds and work toward individual improvement.

Word Hunts

Students do not automatically see the relationship between spelling words and reading words. Word hunts help them make this important connection. In **word hunts**, students hunt through their reading and writing for words that are additional examples of the sound, pattern, or meaning unit they are studying and can develop an understanding of how many other words have the same feature. For example, they see many short *a* words, or that *le* is much more common at the ends of words than *el*. Some patterns are found in virtually every text again and again, whereas others are harder to find; thus, word hunts are more appropriate for some features than others. Before students are expected to do word hunts, you should model the activity.

MODELING AND RECORDING WORD HUNTS. Start with a portion of text projected onto a whiteboard, a big book, or simply a book being used for instruction. Working line by line, demonstrate how to locate words that fit the categories under study and how to record those words into categories. Then, assign students to look in familiar texts for other words that contain the same features. Add these words to written sorts under the corresponding key word. See Figure 3.8 for words added to the long *a* categories at the bottom of the notebook page. Ask the students to use familiar books or already-read portions of the books they are currently reading so they do not confuse skimming for words with reading for meaning.

Figure 3.9 shows an example of a word hunt conducted on a retelling of *The Three Billy Goats Gruff* by a group of students in Mrs. Fitzgerald's third-grade class. After working with the long *o* and short *o* in word study, students found more words that she underlined. Then, they organized the words by sound and patterns and recorded them in their word study notebooks. Three words, including *gobble*, were added to the short *o* column. *Groaned* and *goat* were added to the *oa* column, *home* to the *o*–consonant–*e* column, and *meadow* was added to the *ow* column. A new pattern of open, single long *o* spellings was discovered with *so*, *go*, and *over*. Students debated where to put *too* and *who* before classifying them as oddballs.

This word hunt in *The Three Billy Goats Gruff* retelling added more examples for students to consider and created new categories. Word hunts connect word study to other literacy contexts and can also extend the reach to more difficult vocabulary such as *meadow* and *gobble*. With these words, students are able to generalize the pattern within one-syllable words to two-syllable words. Word hunts thus provide a step up in word power.

CONDUCTING WORD HUNTS. Word hunts can be conducted in small groups, with partners, or individually for seatwork or homework. Figure 3.10 shows students gathered around a large sheet of paper on which key words have been written. Students skim and scan pages of books that they have already read, looking for words that match the key words according to the feature under study. Discussion may ensue as to whether a word contains the spelling feature in question and sometimes students consult the dictionary, particularly to resolve questions of stress, syllabication, or meaning.

When conducting word hunts with emergent to beginning readers, have students scan texts that are guaranteed to contain the phonics features targeted in their search. Many core reading programs provide **phonics** or **decodable readers**, which are simple books organized around specific phonics features that repeat in the text. Other publishers offer phonics readers such as the *Ready Readers* by Pearson Learning Group or the *Learn to Read* series by Starfall. Phonics readers can also be downloaded from websites such as Reading A-Z. Although such controlled texts may not be the heart of your reading program, they offer beginning readers a chance to put into practice what they are learning about words and to see many words that work the same way. Simple poems and jingles such as those in *I Saw You in the Bathtub, And Other Folk Rhymes* (Schwartz & Hoff, 1991) also contain recurring sounds and patterns in their rhyme scheme.

FIGURE 3.9 Word Hunt in Story Summary

> The Three Billy Goats
>
> The goats had to go over a bridge to get to the meadow on the hill. By the bridge lived an old troll. One day Little Billy Goat Gruff started over the bridge. Trip trap Trip trap went his feet. "Who is on my bridge?" the troll roared in his great big voice. Little goat said, "Oh, it is only I, the little billy goat. I must go over the bridge to get to the meadow on the hill." "You can not cross over my bridge. I will eat you up," roared the troll. "Oh, don't eat me," said the little goat. "I am too little."

FIGURE 3.10 Cooperative Group Word Hunt

Brainstorming

Although word hunts in text can extend the number of examples to consider, students may also supply additional examples through brainstorming. Brainstorming might be considered a word hunt through one's own memory. You may want to ask for more words that rhyme with *cat*, words that describe people ending in *er*, or words that have *spir* as a root. Word hunts in current reading materials are not always productive when it comes to some features. For example, it is unlikely that a word hunt would turn up many words with the Latin root *spir*, but students may be able to brainstorm derived words they already know, such as *inspire* or *perspire*. Words brainstormed by students can be added to established categories listed on the board, a chart, or a word study notebook.

Brainstorming can also be used to introduce a sort. You might ask students for words that have particular sounds, patterns, or roots and write them on the board. You can then write words in categories as they are given, as in a Guess My Category sort, or categories might be determined by discussion. These words can be transferred to word study sheets for weekly word sorting routines. After one student raised a question about why the word *sleeve* had an *e* on the end when it already had the *ee* pattern, Mrs. Zimmerman asked her students to think of other words that ended in either *ve* or *v*. After listing their brainstormed words on the board, students sorted them into two groups—those that had a long vowel sound and needed the *e* to mark the vowel (*stove*, *alive*, *cave*) and those that did not (*give*, *love*, *achieve*). Students could think of no words that ended in plain *v*, and they concluded that an *e* always came after *v*, whether it was needed to mark the vowel or not.

Draw and Label/Cut and Paste

Draw and label is a good activity at a variety of levels to demonstrate the meanings of words. See the second page of the word study notebook in Figure 3.8 (page 62) for an example. Multiple meanings for words like *block* can be illustrated (e.g., as a toy, a section of a neighborhood, and a sports play). Homophones like *bear* and *bare* are made more memorable through drawings, and creating an ongoing class homophone book, as shown in Figure 3.11, is a popular activity. Even advanced spellers in the derivational relations stage enjoy drawing pictures to illustrate the meanings of words like *spectacles*, *spectators*, and *inspector*.

Drawing pictures of additional words that start with a particular sound is a good activity for emergent and letter name–alphabet spellers. Provide paper that is divided into columns headed by a key letter (see Figure 3.12) so that students can see where to draw, how big to draw, and how many to draw. It helps to begin by asking students to brainstorm other words before assigning them the drawing task. They might even look through alphabet books for ideas. After drawing pictures under the appropriate key letter, ask students to label the picture–spelling as best they can. Hold students accountable for spelling the initial sound correctly, but encourage them to try the rest of the word as well.

A variation of draw and label, the **cut and paste activity** is like a word hunt using pictures instead of written words, making it appropriate for emergent and letter name–alphabetic spellers. Students hunt through old catalogs and magazines for pictures beginning with a certain sound and then cut out the pictures to paste them in the appropriate column.

Many teachers have their students paste words or pictures from a sort into the correct categories as a culminating activity. When using pictures, the

FIGURE 3.11 **Class Homophone Book**

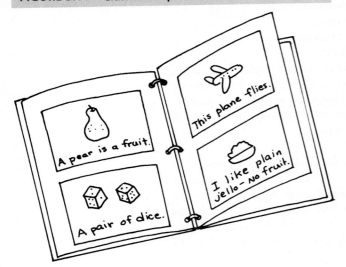

FIGURE 3.12 **Draw and Label Activity**

students are expected to label them spelling as best they can; the results can be used for assessment. See an example in Figure 3.13.

Alternative Sorts

Skilled reading requires attention to many aspects of written words simultaneously. Some students have a hard time attending flexibly to multiple features of words, often focusing exclusively on either sound or the visual patterns. These students often lack the insight that words represent more than just pronunciations; they have a difficult time grasping the idea that words have both meaning and sound (Cartwright, 2010). To lessen this difficulty, students can be challenged to sort their words a different way as an added activity. For example, they might sort pictures by living and nonliving things, whether you would find them inside or outside, whether you could hold them in your hand, or things people can make or not make. Words intended for a short vowel sort might also be sorted by blends at the beginning or end. Other alternative categories are parts of speech, or words that show action or objects. You might suggest an alternative sort based on the words in the sort, or students might simply be asked to select as many words as possible that are related to a semantic category (e.g., shoes, socks and slippers are things you wear on your feet). It is not necessary to come up with categories that include all the words. The important thing is to teach children how to think more flexibly about word features, including sound, pattern, and meaning, and to allow ample time to discuss their insights. This kind of flexible thinking about words will improve spelling, word identification, decoding, and comprehension (Cartwright, 2008). The *Words Their Way* supplements and the PDToolkit include a number of concept sorts to use to show students' flexibility in sorting.

FIGURE 3.13   Paste and Label the Pictures

Games and Other Activities

At the end of each chapter that follows and throughout the PDToolkit, you will find a number of games and other activities that provide additional practice with words and generalizations for each stage of spelling. Classrooms are busy places and there is not much time for games, but most of these are designed to move quickly in cooperative settings. You can use games during the week to reinforce a particular sort and keep them available over time to provide review.

Now that we have described the rationale for sorting, provided directions for introducing and discussing sorts, and demonstrated a variety of ways to sort, we will focus next on how to prepare sorts.

Guidelines for Preparing Word Sorts

After identifying spelling stages and grouping students for instruction, as described in Chapter 2, you must decide on what orthographic features to study and prepare collections of words or pictures for sorting. The particular feature you choose to study should be based on what you see students using but confusing on an inventory or in their writing. No matter what the feature is, when preparing word lists for sorting, collect sets of words that offer a contrast between at least two sounds, patterns, or meaning categories. Compare *b* to *s*, compare long *o* patterns such as *oa*, *o-e*, and *ow*, or compare words with different prefixes. By carefully setting

up contrasts in a collection of words, you are stacking the deck so that students can make discoveries and form generalizations as they sort.

Resources for Sorts and Words

Chapters 4 through 8 have guidelines for features to study at each stage and Appendix D has a collection of sample sorts for different stages that can give you ideas about the kinds of contrasts to set up. The *Words Their Way®* companion books provide a complete curriculum for each stage, with prepared sorts and assessments for each unit. (See a list of these and other resources at the end of this chapter.) However, there are also times when you may want to modify existing sorts or create your own. Only you can be sure of what words your students can already read and thus use for sorting. It is unlikely that any prepared collection of sorts or sequence of study will be just right for your students. Pictures can be found in Appendix C, and Appendix E has extensive word lists that you might use to create your own sorts. Additional resources can be used for determining features to study and finding words:

- Word lists can be found in *The Reading Teacher's Book of Lists* (Fry & Kress, 2006), *The Spelling Teacher's Book of Lists* (Phenix, 1996), and *The Spelling List and Word Study Resource Book* (Fresch & Wheaton, 2004).
- Special dictionaries such as the *Scholastic Rhyming Dictionary* (Young, 2007) list words by rhymes and vowel patterns. Regular dictionaries are good for finding words with such beginning features as blends, digraphs, and prefixes. Use online dictionaries to search for internal spelling patterns such as vowel digraphs or root words. To search for an internal pattern, you usually use an asterisk or a question mark before or after the pattern. Using a question mark as in "??ar?" or "?ar??" would yield five-letter words with *ar* in the middle. Using an asterisk, as in "*ar*," would yield all the words in the dictionary with *ar* in them.
- Some websites have excellent vocabulary enrichment activities such as a "Word of the Day" with information about the origins and use of different words. Take some time to explore sites such as YourDictionary, Etymonline, WordCentral, Wordnik, Vocabulary .com, AllWords, and OneLook.
- The spelling features introduced across grade levels in basal phonics and spelling programs generally follow the same progression of orthographic features outlined in this textbook (e.g., Templeton & Bear, 2011). One difference, however, is that some basal phonics or spelling programs present only one sound or spelling pattern at a time in lists that offer no contrasts. For example, one unit may be on words ending with the /ch/ phoneme spelled with the *tch* pattern (*patch, itch, fetch*, etc.). Without a contrast such as the one shown in Figure 3.4, students are not able to discover that the spelling of the final sound (*tch* or *ch*) is related to the medial vowel sound.

Making Sorts Harder or Easier

Students in different stages and with different levels of skill will be more successful when sorts are developed with certain factors in mind. The difficulty of sorts can be adjusted in several ways:

- You may use fewer words with English learners if students do not know the vocabulary. In such instances, limit the words you use when introducing a new sort. They may be learning new vocabulary at the same time they are learning to pronounce the words. Gradually introduce a few new words each day so that students can focus on both the sort and the new vocabulary. Concept sorting with these same words gives more exposure to the new vocabulary.
- The more contrasts that a sort provides, the more challenging it will be. If students are young or inexperienced, starting with two categories is a good idea. As they become adept at sorting, step up to three categories and then four. Even after working with four categories or more, however, you may want to go back to fewer categories when you introduce a new unit of study.

- The difficulty of the sort also depends on the contrasts you choose. For example, it is easier to compare the sounds for /b/ and /s/ than for /b/ and /p/ because the letter names *b* and *s* are made in different parts of the mouth. Likewise, it is easier for students to learn the short sound for *i* when it is contrasted with the short sound of *a* or *o* than with *e*. Start with obvious contrasts before moving to finer distinctions.
- The level of difficulty can be increased or decreased by the actual words you choose as examples within each category. For example, adding words with blends and digraphs (*black, chest, trunk*) to a short vowel sort can make those words more challenging than simple words like *tap* and *set*. Ideally, students should be able to read all of the words in a word sort. In reality, however, this may not always be the case. The more unfamiliar words in a given sort, the more difficult that sort will be. This caveat applies to both being able to read the word and knowing what the word means. A fifth-grader studying derivational relations will need easier words to study than a tenth-grader in that same stage, simply because the fifth-grader will have a more limited vocabulary. If there are unfamiliar words in a sort, try to place them toward the end of the deck so that known words are the first to be sorted. Unfamiliar words can be set aside, but revisit them later and encourage your students to compare the new spelling with the known words already sorted in the columns to arrive at a pronunciation.
- Including a miscellaneous or oddball column with "exception" words that do not fit the targeted letter–sound or pattern feature can increase the difficulty of a sort.

Oddballs

Words that are at odds with the consistencies within each category will inevitably turn up in word hunts and should be deliberately included in teacher-developed sorts. These words go into a miscellaneous category known as Oddballs, rather than exceptions or irregular words. The word *work*, for example, would be an oddball in a sort with other *r*-influenced *o* words like *fork, corn,* and *sport,* but it fits a small—but regular—category of words that start with *wor*: *world, worm, worse,* and *word*. Oddballs are sometimes high-frequency words such as *have, said, was,* and *again*. Such words become memorable from repeated usage, but are also memorable because they are odd. They stand out in the crowd. Such words should be included in the sorts you prepare, but not too many. One to three oddballs per sort are plenty, so that they do not overshadow the regularity you want students to discover.

The oddball category is also where students may place words if they are simply not sure about the sound they hear in the word. This often happens when students say words differently due to dialectical or regional pronunciations that vary from the "standard" pronunciation. For example, one student in Wise County, Virginia, pronounced the word *vein* as *vine* and was correct in placing *vein* in the oddball column as opposed to the long *a* group. To this student, the word *vein* was a long *i*. Sometimes students detect subtle variations that adults may miss. Students often put words like *mail* and *sail* in a different sound category than *maid, wait,* and *paid,* because the long *a* sound is slightly different before liquid consonants like *r* and *l*. *Mail* may sound more like /mā-əl/.

Preparing Your Sorts for Cutting and Storing

Word study does not require a great monetary investment because the basic materials are already available in most classrooms. Access to a copier and plenty of unlined paper will get you well on your way.

SORTS FOR STUDENTS. Copies of prepared word sheets or picture sheets as shown in Figure 3.14 are available in the *Words Their Way* supplements for each stage listed on page 88. They can also be created by hand using the templates and pictures in this book, the Create Your Own feature in the PDToolkit, or by using the tables format on your computer and setting all margins at 0 inches. You may want to have the handouts ready first thing Monday morning so the sorts can be cut apart and ready for group activities, or you may want to pass the word sheets

FIGURE 3.14   Sample Word Study Handouts

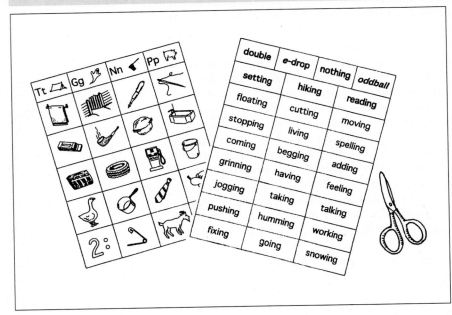

out after the group time and assign students to cut them apart at their seats.

Show students how to use markers or crayons to draw three vertical lines down the backside of their paper or scribble over it quickly to distinguish their word cards from others in case they should end up on the floor or get mixed up in some way (students use different colors). Older students may initial their words or mark them in some other unique way. Next, model how to cut words apart efficiently using three long vertical cuts before stacking them and cutting them horizontally. Eliminate the borders by enlarging the sort about 10 percent before copying to reduce cutting time and paper waste. The words or pictures can be stored in an envelope or plastic bag that is reused each week. Sometimes the cut-up words and pictures are kept for review, sometimes they are pasted into a notebook or onto paper, and sometimes they may be simply discarded. Take the time to teach these marking and cutting routines explicitly so that students complete them quickly and independently.

With younger students or when cutting is too time-consuming, you may want to have prepared sets of pictures and words already cut for sorting. Make sets of pictures by copying the pictures in Appendix C onto card stock that is quite durable; laminating and coloring the pictures is optional. One or more sets of these pictures can be stored by beginning sounds or by vowel sounds, in library pockets or in envelopes. They can then be used for small-group work or for individual sorting assignments. For example, you may find that you have one student who needs work on digraphs. You can pull out a set of *ch* and *sh* pictures, mix them together, and then challenge the student to sort them into columns using the pocket as a header. The sound boards in Appendix B can be copied, cut apart, and used to label the picture sets. Resource teachers who have limited time to work with students often create word card sets that can be stored in envelopes and reused from year to year.

Some teachers make manila sorting folders for seats or centers as shown in Figure 3.15. File folders are divided into columns with key words or pictures for headers glued in place. Words or pictures for sorting are stored in the folder in library pockets or plastic bags and students sort directly on the folder. You may want to avoid laminating as it makes the sorting surface slippery, unless you anticipate heavy use. Once the folders are developed, you can individualize word study fairly easily by pulling out the folders that target the exact needs of your students.

SORTS FOR TEACHER MODELING. For group time you will need your own set of words that students can see as you direct a sort. In small groups, you may simply use the same cut-out words students have as you model on a table or rug. For larger groups you may want to model sorts using an overhead projector (make a transparency of the handout and cut it apart), or enlarge the pictures or word cards to use in a pocket chart. Advances in technology make it possible to sort easily with document cameras, interactive whiteboards, and interactive tables. The possibilities are exciting to consider for word sort activities, which lend themselves to electronic applications.

DIGITAL SORTING ACTIVITIES. Digital sorts for each stage are available online at the *Words Their Way* PD Toolkit, as shown in Figure 3.16, and sorts and word lists in

Appendices D and E can be used with a variety of software to create eSorts (Zucker & Invernizzi, 2008). You can introduce students to sorts using an interactive whiteboard, and then students can repeat the sorts with paper copies, computers or handheld devices. The *Words Their Way* Word Study in Action program also includes developmental sorts for the interactive whiteboard (Bear et al., 2012).

CHOOSING APPLICATIONS FOR WORD STUDY. The digital world of phonics, spelling, and vocabulary instruction is a fast-growing area, but should be selected and used with attention to whether they are developmentally appropriate. With the myriad of new applications and software available for students, it is important to have in mind guidelines for choosing word study applications. Some applications are attractive and fun to play but may not be a proper fit for students. These questions can guide you in selecting the appropriate digital word study to use with your students:

1. Is the application or game instructive for students at this time? Is it developmentally appropriate?
2. Can students read the words or name the pictures?
3. Can they complete the activity quickly with high accuracy?
4. Are students asked to think about words and generalizations?
5. Are students given feedback that will help them understand errors they might make?
6. Does the learning generalize to similar patterns and in different contexts, including their writing?

There are engaging applications to reinforce the alphabet, songs, rhyming, and letter-sound correspondence but often the software does not provide actual instruction for students who need it. Many applications have a poor mix of tasks that do not properly guide students, and often emphasize rote memorization without deeper examinations or reflection. You might add directions to the activities that correct for any deficiencies. For example, remind students to say the words aloud, and ask them to write the words into categories in their word study notebooks.

There are many applications that can be used for word study extensions – create a puzzle: *Stick Around;* explain your sort: *3D Avitar, Doceri,* and *EducCreations;* make a word map: *Popplet;*

FIGURE 3.15   Henry Sorts Independently Using a File Folder

PD TOOLKIT™
for Words Their Way®

Many of the word sorts can be played online in practice and test modes. You can also create your own.

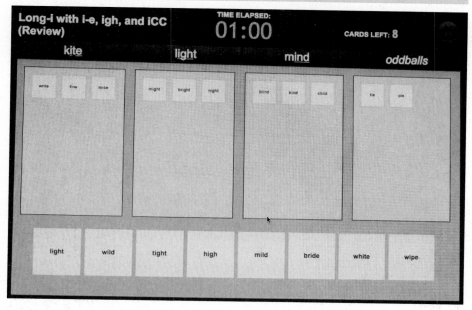

FIGURE 3.16   Word Sorting on the *Words Their Way* PDToolkit

Long-i with i-e, igh, and iCC (Review)

TIME ELAPSED: 01:00   CARDS LEFT: 8

kite	light	mind	oddballs
write fine mice	might bright night	blind kind child	tie pie

light   wild   tight   high   mild   bride   white   wipe

FIGURE 3.17 Follow-the-Path Game for Initial Consonants

Ball starts with a B.

sentence writing: *Explain Everything*, spelling and word meaning practice: *Spelling City, Quizlet, My Spelling Test Spelling Notebook* and *Notability*.

Preparing Word Study Games for Extension and Practice

Games appeal to children, encouraging them to practice in more depth and apply what they have learned in new situations. Games can be left out for several weeks after a related sort to provide review. This book contains many ideas for creating games, and you will want to begin making these to supplement the basic word or picture sorts as you have time. Look for generic games in the activity section of each chapter first, as many of them can be used with a variety of word features you will study across the year. For example, the Follow-the-Path game being played by the boys in Figure 3.17 can be laminated before labeling the spaces so that new letters can be substituted as they become the focus of study. Label the spaces with a washable overhead projector pen. Over time you can create more specific games. See Appendix F for templates and spinner directions.

Preparing Your Room

Classroom space is needed for group work, individual work, and partner work. Separate areas for word sorting and discussion are needed to convene a group on the floor or at tables in one part of the classroom while other students continue to work at their desks or in other areas of the room. Individual sorting and partner work can be done just about anywhere but some teachers set up centers or workstations for sorting or playing games. A stopwatch is needed for speed sorts and can be placed in a word study center. Many teachers also post chart-sized sound boards in this area. Table 3.3 summarizes what you might need, depending on the age and range of developmental word knowledge in your classroom.

TABLE 3.3 Word Study Materials

From the Supply Room	From the Bookstore	From the Copy Room	Digital Resources
Scissors	Alphabet books and word books	Copy paper for sorts	Digital timer
Card stock	Phonics readers	Photocopied picture cards	Online access to PDToolkit
Word study notebooks	Dictionaries	Photocopied word cards	Access to online dictionaries
Manila folders	Homophone books	Student sound boards	Applications for spelling and phonics activities and games
Game board materials such as spinners and dice	Etymological dictionary	Photocopied game templates	
Stopwatches	Word histories	Poster sound boards	
Library pockets			
Chart paper			

Implementation of Word Study Instruction

What does a word study classroom look like? How can you differentiate instruction within a heterogeneous classroom? How much time does it take? What exactly do students do on different days? Ganske and Jocius (2013) concluded that lack of time certainly influenced the lack of extended discussions in the classrooms they observed, but how do you find time? These questions and more about organizing for word study are answered in the sections that follow.

Managing Word Study in the Classroom

Once you have prepared your word sorts and introduced your students to basic sorting procedures, it is time to set up a weekly schedule and develop predictable routines. When scheduling word study in your classroom, consider the following:

- *Develop a familiar weekly routine with daily activities.* Routines will save you planning time, ease transitions, and make the most of the instructional time you devote to word study. We describe several weekly schedules to give you ideas about how to create your own schedules. Include homework routines as well. When parents know what to expect every evening, they are more likely to see that the work gets done.
- *Schedule time for group work with the teacher.* Students at the same developmental level should work with you for directed word study. During this time, model new sorts, guide practice sorts, and lead discussions that help students develop and test hypotheses and reach conclusions. Chapter 2 offers assessment-driven guidelines on grouping students for instruction.
- *Plan time for students to sort independently and with partners.* Students need time to sort through words on their own and make decisions about their attributes. Build this independent work into seatwork and center activities. Word study also lends itself nicely to many cooperative activities. Working together in pairs and in groups allows students to learn from each other.
- *Keep it short.* Word study should be a regular part of daily language arts, but it need not take up a great deal of time. Teacher-led introductory lessons take the most time, but subsequent activities take little time and do not require a lot of supervision once students understand the routines. Try a quick word hunt through already-read pages following a guided reading lesson—search for and share words from the reading that fit the features. Word study extensions can fit easily into odd bits of time during the day. Students can play spelling games right before lunch or sort their words one more time before they pack up to go home.

Scheduling Time for Word Study

It is essential that you find time in your day for word study at all grade levels because orthographic knowledge promotes fluent reading and writing and vocabulary knowledge—critical goals for academic success. In this section, we present five types of word study schedules for different structures and grade levels.

As you develop a word study schedule, consider the ways students are situated around the room, and try to use the entire room. At all grade levels it's nice to have an area where you can meet with a small group, often called a circle area. Word study stations or centers can be scattered around the room, and seatwork takes place at students' seats. Some teachers conduct word study lessons as part of their reading groups. Other teachers work with two to three separate word study groups and may rotate their students from small-group time with the teacher to individual seatwork and workstation or center times. Still others use a block of time that incorporates differentiated word study. Some teachers meet individually with students in a largely independent workshop routine. In all settings, focus the word study on active inquiry and problem solving, in which students are engaged in their own learning.

PD **TOOLKIT**™
for Words Their Way®

Classroom Organization
Teachers describe their classroom routines for different stages in five videos. Look for related materials for each video.

You can create and post a schedule for students to follow that you review at the beginning of the day. Table 3.4 illustrates one type of schedule in which reading and word study groups are integrated into 25-minute sessions in a circle–seat–center rotation. This is a common configuration in grades 1 to 3. In another schedule, in which the teacher focuses only on word study, the circle–seat–center rotation is the same but the time periods are only 15 to 20 minutes.

Notice also in Table 3.4 that there is a brief period for students to assess their learning and activity level before moving to another activity. In the primary grades these evaluation and break periods are maybe two to three minutes and may include singing a song or a movement activity. But over time, these periods may include some discussion using the questions below. Betty Lee, a *Washington Post* Teacher of the Year, used the following questions with first-grade students as they got ready to rotate in the circle–seat–center configuration, and she posted them on the wall for reference:

1. *Did you finish your work?* This first question asks students to think about the nature and complexity of the task.
2. *Did you do the best you could?* This question asks students to look at themselves to see if they were ready to complete the task, and to consider their level of engagement.
3. *What did you do when you were through?* This third question is designed for students to think about what they might do if they complete an assignment early.

Over the first several weeks of school develop a number of activities students can do when they are through, including going to the class library or their desks to find a book to read independently.

In the intermediate and secondary grades, students may stay in small groups a whole period, and the teacher may travel among the groups to pose similar questions for self-reflection. Some of the questions in Table 3.2 might be used for this. In the intermediate grades, students may complete contracts or self-assessment forms instead of having a whole-class meeting. Often in these grades students have plenty of projects to work on once the assigned word study or vocabulary activities are completed.

WORD STUDY AS AN INTEGRATED PART OF THE READING GROUP. Because orthographic knowledge, spelling, and reading development are so closely aligned, it makes good sense for word study instruction to occur as an extension of the reading group whenever

---

TABLE 3.4 Circle–Seat–Center Schedule

		9:00—9:25	9:25—9:30	9:30—9:55	9:55—10:00	10:00—10:25	
Whole-Class Review of Schedule & Activities	Group 1	Circle	Evaluation and Break	Seat	Evaluation and Break	Center	Evaluation and Break
	Group 2	Center		Circle		Seat	
	Group 3	Seat		Center		Circle	Whole-Class Activities

possible. Small-group periods can integrate reading, word study, and spelling instruction as you move quite seamlessly from the reading lesson into word study by asking students to look back through certain pages to find words that contain the feature you are about to introduce. For example, after a shared reading of *The Cat on the Mat* (by B. Wildsmith), go back and find words in the *at* family as a way to introduce a sort. After reading a chapter in *Frindle* (by A. Clements), ask students to find words that end in *ed* as an introduction to a unit on inflectional endings. This is the time when you may spend 10 minutes on reading and 15 minutes to introduce a new word study sort and have your students repeat the sort under your supervision. On subsequent days, you may only spend three to five minutes on word study and the rest on reading. The word study would be completed as individual or partner extension activities that are completed in centers or at students' seats, or for homework. This organizational setup is efficient and integrates word study into the total reading and language arts program.

SEPARATE WORD STUDY GROUPS IN A CIRCLE–SEAT–CENTER ROTATION. Table 3.4 shows a plan that works well if your word study groups are separate from the reading groups. Introduce a new sort during **circle time** to a group of students who are at the same developmental level. Half of the remaining students work independently or in buddy pairs for **seatwork**, while the other half work at stations for **center time**. After about 15 to 20 minutes, the groups rotate. Students at the centers join you at the circle table, students who were working at their seats go to the centers, and students who had been with you return to their seats to work independently or with buddies. Counting transition time, three word study groups rotate through all three instructional formats in about an hour. A second, slightly longer rotation occurs also for reading groups. This organization scheme works well in schools in which the entire morning is devoted to reading and language arts. Of course, if you have classroom assistants or aides they can have their own circle time or supervise students at seats or centers. These push-in teachers may include language specialists and Title I teachers, and may make it possible to have four groups.

WORD STUDY BLOCK. Some teachers set aside a separate word study block on Mondays to meet with each developmental group and then schedule a short follow-up each day of the week. All students may cut and sort their words at the same time, but the words they sort and the word features they categorize are different. Across the week, during this block of time, students will engage in different follow-up activities each day. This organizational plan works well for teachers who prefer everyone to be doing the same thing at the same time, yet allows for differentiation of instruction within the word study block.

INDIVIDUALIZED WORD STUDY IN INTERVENTION SETTINGS. Resource teachers who work with small groups of students identified with special needs may have only short sessions with mixed-ability groups, making it challenging to implement word sorts. However, these are usually the very students who need differentiated word study the most! In these settings we recommend that you have appropriate sorts selected and cut out in advance. Form groups when possible, but give individual students the pockets of prepared picture or word cards or word study folders, described earlier, to use independently as you circulate to talk about words, check sorts, and lead students to make generalizations. Students might complete follow-up activities under your supervision on some days of the week, or they might take their sorts back to the regular classroom setting and engage in the same activities as their classmates using their own word cards.

Intervention
There are several videos in which teachers and an administrator talk about word study interventions.

INDIVIDUALIZED STUDENT CONTRACTS IN UPPER ELEMENTARY, MIDDLE SCHOOLS, AND HIGH SCHOOLS. Reading and the English language arts are often taught in a readers' workshop environment in the upper grades, in which students may be reading self-selected books as part of literature circles (Daniels, 2002) or book clubs (Raphael, Pardo, Highfield, & McMahon, 2013). The workshop environment allows you to meet with groups and individuals to give direct instruction in word study and provide feedback as necessary.

One- or two-week contracts are particularly useful at the secondary level. Students contract in advance to complete a certain amount of work in different areas and to turn in that

work by a certain date. Figure 3.18 shows a sample student contract that reflects the importance of activities that examine word meanings. Student contracts "spell out" exactly what is expected in terms of assignments and how much they have to do to earn various grades. The feature of study may be determined by the goal-setting charts described in Chapter 2.

Weekly Schedules

An important decision involves scheduling word study activities over the course of a week to assure adequate practice time. In the following section, we describe several possible schedules but encourage you to adapt these to your own setting. In the examples, all of the teachers begin with a small-group word study lesson.

Schedules for Students Working with Picture Sorts

Betty Lee, introduced her emergent to letter name–alphabetic spellers to picture sorts at circle time while other students worked at centers or at their seats. She organized the word study activities into a five-day schedule, as summarized in Table 3.5. This schedule can be modified to three days and we recommend an abbreviated schedule when you review initial consonants

---

FIGURE 3.18   Sample Student Work Contract

WORD STUDY CONTRACT

Name _____   Date _____

Feature of Study _____

Directions: Select activities to earn up to 100 points toward your word study grade. Complete all written work in your word study notebook and turn in along with this contract for final grading.

Required Activities

____ Sort, record, and reflect (30 pts)   ____ Work with a partner to complete at least one spelling activity.

Partner signs here: _____

Explore Spelling (10 pts each)

____ Repeat sort 2 times   ____ Sort a different way and record

____ Blind sort with partner   ____ Word hunt (find at least 5 words)

____ Blind writing sort with partner   ____ Speed sorts

____ Play a game with partner   Record times: _____

Explore Meaning (20 pts each—select at least one)

____ Define 7 words   ____ Brainstorm or hunt for additional words

____ Use 7 words in sentences   ____ Report etymologies for 7 words

____ Illustrate 7 words   ____ Make up new words and define them

____ Create a comic strip using 5 words   ____ Create your own game

____ Complete a word tree or root web   ____ Other

Total Points _____   Test Grade _____

TABLE 3.5 **Schedules for Word Study with Pictures**

Betty Lee's 5-Day Schedule

Monday	Tuesday	Wednesday	Thursday	Friday
Introduce picture sort in circle time and re-sort for seatwork	Re-sort in circle time Draw and label for seatwork	Re-sort, paste, and label for seatwork	Word hunts in circle or center time	Games and activities in centers (continue into the next week)
3-Day Schedule				
Introduce picture sort in circle time and re-sort for seatwork	Re-sort and Word Hunt in circle time Draw and label for seatwork	Re-sort, paste, and label for seatwork Games in centers		

at the beginning of first grade, or for moving through the large number of blends and digraphs at a steady pace.

Figure 3.19 shows an individual pocket folder used to keep materials organized and guide students to the daily routines. Students can keep their cut-out pictures in the envelope until they are pasted down or discarded. Each folder has a **sound board** (one of three sound charts that can be found in Appendix B) to use as a reference and a record of progress. Students simply color the boxes lightly with crayon to indicate which sounds they have worked with.

MONDAY—PICTURE SORT. Ideally, the choice of initial sounds is based upon what students are reading. You may start by finding words in the text that begin with particular letters as described in the Whole-to-Part Plan in Chapter 4. In small groups, model a picture sort with a letter as a header to help students develop a strong association between the beginning sound of a word and the letter or letters that represent it. Each picture is named and compared with the key picture to listen for sounds that are the same. The sort might be repeated several times in the circle as a group or with partners. During their center or seat time, students do the same picture sort again on their own or with a partner.

FIGURE 3.19 **Pocket Folder for Organizing Materials**

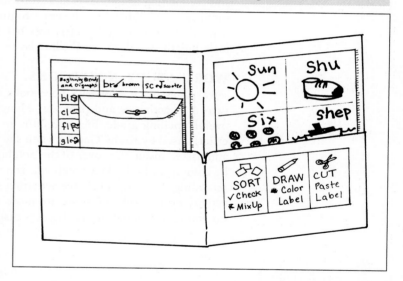

TUESDAY—DRAW AND LABEL. Students sort again and then extend the feature through drawing and labeling activities that ask them to think of other words that have the same beginning sound, as in Figure 3.12 on page 64. Encourage students to write as much of the word as they can, using developmental spelling to label their drawing. Assess these spellings to judge student progress in hearing and representing sounds.

WEDNESDAY—CUT AND PASTE. After re-sorting, students can paste the picture sort into categories and label them. Or, they can look through old catalogs and magazines for pictures that begin with a particular sound. These pictures are cut out, pasted into categories or into an alphabet book (as described in Activity 4.25 in Chapter 4), and labeled.

THURSDAY—WORD AND PICTURE HUNTS. Under your direction, students reread nursery rhymes and jingles, and look for words that begin with the same sounds they have been categorizing all week. You can then add the words to a chart. Students can also go for word hunts in alphabet books or picture dictionaries as a circle or center activity. Keep a variety on hand to teach students rudimentary research skills. Their findings can be recorded as an additional draw and label activity.

FRIDAY—GAME DAY AND ASSESSMENT. Introduce new games and activities related to the sort and then keep them available for several weeks in centers. Children delight in the opportunity to play board or card games and other fun activities for further practice. Assessment at this level is primarily informal as the teacher watches for automaticity and accuracy during sorting and how well students label pictures or use initial sounds in writing.

MONITORING PROGRESS

Schedule for Students Working with Word Sorts

The next schedule works well for children who are readers and able to spell entire words. This can be students in the middle to late letter name–alphabetic stage all the way up to derivational relations, so this is the basic schedule for most teachers. Sorting words in a variety of contexts and completing assignments in a word study (WS) notebook comprise most of the schedule summarized in Table 3.6. The exact routines you do each day throughout the week may vary depending on time and preferences but we do recommend re-sorting for several days and including the blind sort on Wednesday or Thursday for students working with vowel patterns.

WORD STUDY NOTEBOOKS. Composition books with stiff cardboard covers and sewn pages make good WS notebooks that last all year. They provide a built-in, orderly record of activities and progress. Many teachers grade the WS notebooks as part of an overall spelling grade. Figure 3.20 is an example of the kinds of expectations and grading criteria used by Kathy Gankse when she taught fourth grade. This chart can be reproduced and pasted inside the cover of the notebook. Possible assignments such as the following can be completed in the WS notebook. You may want to distinguish required activities, such as recording the sort, and choice activities, such as draw and label. There is no need to do each activity every week and some are more valuable at times than others. Other ideas for WS notebooks are noted in the chapters that follow.

TABLE 3.6   **Suggested Schedule for Students Who Sort Words**

Monday	Tuesday	Wednesday	Thursday	Friday
Introduce sort and supervise individual sort	Re-sort Record sort and reflect First speed sort	Re-sort Blind sort WS notebook assignments	Re-sort Word hunt Second speed sort	Assessment and games (Games continue into the next week as seat or center activities)
Homework: Re-sort	Homework: Re-sort and writing sort	Homework: Blind sort	Homework: Re-sort and blind writing sort	

- *Writing sorts.* Students record the words into the same categories developed during hands-on sorting using the same key words or headers. You can also ask students to write a reflection that summarizes the generalization or the big idea about this word sort.
- *Select five to ten words to draw and label.* Even older students enjoy the opportunity to illustrate words with simple drawings that reveal their meanings. Ask students to illustrate homophones like *bear* and *bare* and the multiple meanings of homonyms like *park* or *yard*.
- *Word operations.* Students change a letter (or letters) of a selected word to make new words. Initial letters, or orthographic units, might be substituted to create lists of words that rhyme. For example, starting with the word *black*, a student might substitute other consonant blends or digraphs to generate *stack*, *quack*, *track*, *shack*, and so on. Students studying more complex words might substitute prefixes, suffixes, or roots—for example, using *graph* to generate *autograph*, *biography*, *photograph*, and *photography*.
- *Select five words to use in sentences.* Meaning and usage are important as students begin to study homophones, inflected words (*ride*, *rides*, *riding*), and roots and suffixes. Challenge students to use two or more words from their sort, especially derivationally related words. (I will need new *spectacles* to *inspect* the *spectacular* new *specimens*.)
- *Record words from word hunts in trade books and response journals.* Students add new words from their reading and writing to the written sorts in their WS notebooks.
- *Record times from speed sorts.* When students are timed early in the week and then again after repeated sorting, they are likely to show improvement.
- *Record a blind writing sort.* Led by a partner or the teacher, a blind writing sort is a good preparation for a final spelling assessment.

FIGURE 3.20 Expectations for Word Study Notebooks

Word Study Notebooks

Weekly activities for this WS notebook include:
1. Record your Sort and Reflection
2. Draw and label six words
3. Make up sentences with five words
4. Record words from Word Hunt
5. Record times for Speed Sorts

You are expected to:
1. Use correct spelling of assigned words
2. Use complete sentences
3. Use your best handwriting
4. Make good use of word study time

You will be evaluated in this manner:
★ Excellent work
✓ Good work but could be improved
R You need to redo this assignment

MONDAY—INTRODUCE THE SORT. Words are introduced and sorted according to one of the levels of support described in Table 3.1 on page 56. Many teachers like to keep each group's attention on one set of word cards used for modeling and guided practice. Then, students sort their own words individually in the group, at their seats, and for homework. Repeat this procedure with the next group, focusing on a different feature. Each group has different words, depending on the students' stage of development. After meeting with a second and third group, circulate around the room to check in with students sorting at their desks.

If you do not want to take a large block of time on Monday to do all the introductory small-group sorts, spread them across the week by meeting with one group a day on Monday, Tuesday, and Wednesday, with each group's independent work operating on an "offset" schedule (see Table 3.7). In such a schedule, students with the least ability get the most practice, but everyone does similar activities by Thursday and Friday. An alternative is to give all groups a five-day schedule but begin and end on different days of the week.

TUESDAY—PRACTICE THE SORT, INITIAL SPEED SORT, AND WRITING SORT. Students sort again, usually at their seats. Encourage students to "say it and lay it." That means that they read the words as they sort. Circulate through the classroom and ask students to read the words and explain their thinking in preparation for writing a reflection. If more support is needed, students can bring their words to sort under your supervision in a brief session or as part of a guided reading group. Assign students a writing sort for seatwork or for homework. Speed sorts might also be planned for Tuesday. Students are sure to show improvement when they do a speed sort later in the week.

TABLE 3.7   "Offset" Weekly Plan

	Day 1	Day 2	Day 3	Day 4	Day 5
Lowest Group	Meet with teacher	Re-sort Record sort	Blind sort WS notebook	Re-sort Word hunt	Testing and games
Middle Group	Sort independently	Meet with teacher Record sort	Blind sort WS notebook	Re-sort Word hunt	Testing and games
Highest Group		Sort independently	Meet with teacher Record sort	Re-sort Word hunt	Testing and games or blind sort and test on next day

for Words Their Way®

Weekly Schedules and Classroom Activities with Students in the Syllables and Affixes Stage
Ms. Bruskotter describes how her 5th graders use a blind sort and other routines to work with their words.

WEDNESDAY—BLIND SORTS AND WRITING SORTS. Students work in pairs to do blind sorts. After each partner has had a turn to lead the sort, the pair might do a blind writing sort in which partners take turns calling words aloud for the other to write into categories. This can also be a homework assignment.

THURSDAY—SECOND SPEED SORT AND WORD HUNTS. Thursday is a good day to sort for speed as students try to beat their times from earlier in the week. Conduct word hunts in groups, with partners, or individually. All students in the class can be engaged at the same time by convening in their respective groups. Circulate from group to group to comment and listen in on students' discussions. Ask group members to provide reasons for the agreed word groupings. Afterward, students record words from the hunt in their WS notebooks. For homework that night, students can find additional examples to add to their notebooks from the books they are reading at home.

FRIDAY—GAMES AND ASSESSMENT. Although games can be played any time, Fridays might be when new games are introduced. Games from previous weeks provide ongoing review and you need not provide a game for every sort. Students pair up with partners or join small groups according to their developmental levels during center time or a designated word study time.

You can use a traditional spelling test format for assessment. If you have two or three groups, simply call one word in turn for each group. This may sound confusing, but students will recognize the words they have studied over the week and rarely lose track. It is not necessary to call out every word studied during the week; 10 words is probably enough. Many teachers call out some bonus or transfer words that were not among the original list to see whether students can generalize the orthographic principles to new words. In this way, the generalization is emphasized, as opposed to rote memorization of a given list of words. You might prompt students in the case where two or more patterns are possible by saying something like, "If you know how to spell *train* then you can spell *brain*." It is particularly effective to conduct the spelling test as a writing sort, having students write each word as it is called out into the category where it belongs. Award one point for correct category placement and one point for correct spelling.

Some teachers are expected to assign grades for spelling, or spelling may be averaged into a language arts or writing grade. Ideally, such a grade should include more than an average of Friday test scores. Figure 3.21 offers a more holistic assessment using a form that can be adapted for different grade levels. You may wish to add a section for students to rate themselves. The form in the illustration might be used with students in upper elementary grades who can be expected to spell most words correctly.

Organizing for Word Study 79

FIGURE 3.21 Grading Form for Word Study

NAME _____   GRADING PERIOD _____

	Excellent Effort	Good Effort	Needs Improvement
Weekly Word Study			
Word sorts			
Word study notebook			
Partner work			
Final tests			
Editing Written Work			
Spells most words right			
Finds misspelled words to correct			
Assists others in editing work			
Uses a variety of resources to correct spelling			
A = Excellent work in most areas B = Good work in most areas C = Needs improvement in most areas			
Recommended Grade _____			
Comments:			

Friday completes the cycle for the week. If students have been appropriately placed and engaged in a variety of activities throughout the week, they should score well on the Friday test (90 percent or better). Results of the Friday test and observations made during the week influence your plans for the next week. If scores are low, you need to consider why this is so. Was the feature too difficult? Were the words selected too difficult? Did the students get enough practice? Should you revisit the feature? Group membership may also change depending on a given student's success.

Scheduling for Students in the Middle and Secondary Grades

Because middle and secondary English classes are not usually as heterogeneous as elementary classrooms, students are more likely to have similar word study needs. Still, the typical middle or secondary English teacher plans instruction for students in at least two different stages of word knowledge. If you work with students reading below grade level in middle school or high school, we recommend *Words Their Way® with Struggling Readers: Word Study for Reading, Vocabulary, and Spelling Instruction, Grades 4–12* (Flanigan, Hayes, Templeton, Bear, Invernizzi, & Johnston, 2011) as a resource to help you organize and carry out word study.

Students in middle and high school sometimes change classes every 50 minutes, or if the school uses block scheduling, every 1 hour and 40 minutes. Either way, the constraints of periods or blocks limit the way word study is conducted. Some teachers find that a two-week cycle works well. Students have more time to work with a set of words and word hunts can go on for days instead of taking time on a particular day. One way to organize word study instruction in secondary classrooms is by using contracts or individualized assignment plans, as described previously. However, you must still find time to meet with students to introduce new sorts, provide corrective feedback, and discuss generalizations either individually or in groups (Templeton et al., 2015).

If students are in the late syllables and affixes stage or the derivational relations stage, it is less important for them to physically sort word cards, although students at this level still enjoy the hands-on sorting. Instead, sorts can be conducted in writing, using a worksheet format in which students write the words listed at the top or bottom of the sheet into the appropriate category. Other word study activities may also be conducted as paper-and-pencil tasks and organized in a word study section of a three-ring binder.

In middle and high school, work with content teachers to coordinate vocabulary instruction so that domain-specific vocabulary can be intertwined in the English vocabulary instruction (Bear et al., 2014). Generative vocabulary processes should also continue to be addressed, incorporating the Greek and Latin roots and affixes that occur across all disciplines as well as those that occur primarily in specific content areas (Templeton et al., 2015). At least quarterly, teachers might meet to share the key vocabulary and concepts, as well as roots and affixes, that will be taught. By sharing responsibility for teaching vocabulary, the number of exposures to words that students encounter enhances their vocabulary. This deepens their knowledge of words and their understanding of nuances in vocabulary.

Word Study Homework and Parental Expectations

Classrooms are busy places and many teachers find it difficult to devote a lot of time to word study but homework can provide valuable additional practice. A letter such as the one shown in Figure 3.22 is a good way to encourage parents to become involved in their children's spelling homework. A checklist such as the one in Figure 3.23 can be sent home with an extra copy of the words for the week stored in an envelope or plastic zip bag. You might allow students to choose two or three activities, and more options can be added to the checklist occasionally, such as using a small number of words in sentences. Parents are typically firm believers in the importance of spelling because it is such a visible sign of literacy. Unfortunately, developmental or invented spelling is often misunderstood and parents unfairly associate the acceptance of developmental spelling with lack of instruction and an "anything goes" expectation regarding spelling. Communicate clearly to parents that their children will be held accountable for what they have been taught. Homework assignments help them see what is being taught in phonics and spelling.

Getting Started with Word Study

For students who are not familiar with the process of sorting and for teachers who are hesitant about implementing a brand new organizational scheme, we offer some recommendations about how to gradually transition into fully differentiated word study.

1. *Begin with the whole group and teach the routines.* Start with one to three weeks of whole-class sorts that will be relatively easy for everyone in the class. Use a teacher-directed closed sort for maximum support so you can model and offer explicit directions. Teach students the basic routines that you want them to use throughout the week. Role-play buddy activities such as blind sorts or writing sorts by having students observe as you partner with a student, demonstrating how to lead the sort and take turns. Show students how to cut words out quickly and neatly.

FIGURE 3.22   Parent Letter

Dear Parents,

Your child will be bringing home a collection of spelling words weekly that have been introduced in class. Each night of the week your child is expected to do a different activity to ensure
that these words and the spelling principles they represent are mastered. These activities have
been modeled and practiced in school, so your child can teach you how to do them.

Monday   Remind your child to *sort the words* into categories like the ones we did in school.
Your child should read each word aloud during this activity. Ask your child to explain to you
why the words are sorted in a particular way—what does the sort reveal about spelling in general? Ask your child to sort them a second time as fast as possible. You may want to time them.

Tuesday   Do a *blind sort* with your child. Lay down a word from each category as a header
and then read the rest of the words aloud. Your child must indicate where the word goes without seeing it. Lay it down and let your child move it if he or she is wrong. Repeat if your child
makes more than one error.

Wednesday   Assist your child in doing a *word hunt,* looking in a book they have already read
for words that have the same sound, pattern, or both. Try to find two or three for each category.

Thursday   Do a *writing sort* to prepare for the Friday test. As you call out the words in a random order your child should write them in categories. Call out any words your child misspells a
second or even third time.

Thank you for your support. Together we can help your child make valuable progress!

Sincerely,

2. *Teach students how to talk about the sorts.* You need to show students how to think about
   words, how to reflect, and how to form generalizations that summarize their new learning. If students have trouble responding to your open-ended questions, model your own
   thinking with phrases like "I notice that…" or "I learned that…." Ask students to begin
   their reflections the same way and give them the language to formulate statements until
   they can do it for themselves. ("This week we learned about how two-syllable words
   sometimes have double letters in the middle and short vowel sounds in the first syllable.")
   Ask students to turn and talk to a partner before sharing in the group to increase verbal
   interactions.

3. *Begin to differentiate.* Once routines are
   well established, begin to work with two
   and then three groups of students. Because
   students in the lowest group need the most
   help, create that group first as the other
   students continue to work together. Then
   split that group. Observe how students sort,
   how they do on spell checks, and how they
   work together to modify groups as needed.

4. *Introduce student-centered sorts.* With experience students gain skill and independence,
   which makes it easier for you to manage
   the groups in a more timely fashion or to
   move to the offset schedule in Table 3.7
   on page 78. Model how to do open sorts
   by thinking aloud as you sort before you
   assign them to students.

FIGURE 3.23   Word Study Homework Checklist

Word Study at Home   Name _____

Check off the activities you complete and return this to your teacher.

_____ Sort the words into the same categories you did in school.

_____ Write the words into categories.

_____ Blind sort with someone at home.

_____ Write the words into categories as someone calls them aloud.

_____ Hunt for more words that fit the categories and write them here:

Parent's Signature _____

Shari Dunn and Tamara Baren suggest introducing the sorting process to young students by using objects or pictures, beginning with just two categories in a closed concept sort (such as animals/not animals, or animals/birds). Objects with obvious attributes will be easier for young students to sort than abstract sounds. Also, teach routines that students will be using such as draw and label or cut and paste. When they are familiar with the sorting process, introduce sound sorts such as two rhyming categories or two initial sounds.

Integrating Word Study into Reading, Writing, and the Language Arts Curriculum

The weekly schedules described in this chapter provide examples of how to integrate spelling instruction into the language arts classroom, implementing routines that are central to both reading and writing. Students return again and again to trade books they have already read to analyze the reading vocabulary. Poetry lessons might begin with reference to a word study lesson on syllable stress. In a writing lesson, students might discuss comparative adjectives from a previous word study lesson that focused on words ending in *er*. During a lesson on parts of speech, students can be asked to sort their week's spelling words into categories of nouns, verbs, and adjectives. Whatever scheduling scheme you choose, your sequence of activities must fit comfortably within your reading/writing/language arts block of instruction.

The features and strategies that students learn during word study should also be applied to decoding strategies during reading and to spelling strategies during writing. If students get stuck on a word while reading, prompt them with a word study cue. For example, remind them to look for the vowel pattern or to break a word into syllables. Point out the similarity between the orthographic features in a particular word and the spelling features they have been sorting. The more frequently you make such connections between word study and decoding strategies, the more often your students will use them. This is equally true for writing—many teachers use the features students are categorizing during word study for targeted proofreading.

Teachers and parents often complain that students get perfect scores on their spelling tests only to misspell those same words in their writing assignments the following week. To ensure transfer of the big ideas gained during word study, students must be engaged in activities that specifically require them to apply their growing word knowledge through wide reading and writing. Using techniques such as the following promotes the connection between reading, writing, and word study.

GENERALIZE TO NEW WORDS. Words that students cannot read when a sort is first introduced can be used after sorting to apply a generalization, so set those aside to return to later. After working with a feature (such as the *r*-influenced vowels that Mrs. Zimmerman had her students sort), display additional words that have the same phonics or spelling feature so that students can apply what they have learned to reading additional words (e.g., *flare, blare, snare, flair, lair*). This might be presented in sentences such as, "The cougar retreated to its lair." Do the same thing with spelling unfamiliar words. Ask students to attempt *start, sharp,* or *smart*. In the case of the /air/ sound there are two possible spellings, so begin with a clue such as, "You know how to spell *care*, so how would you spell *dare*?"

DICTATED OR SILLY SENTENCES. Select several words from the weekly word sort and dictate a sentence for the student to write. For example, following an *at* and *an* rhyming family word sort, letter name spellers might be asked to write, "The fat cat sat in the tan van" (Johnston, Invernizzi, Juel, & Lewis-Wagner, 2009). Derivational spellers might be asked to write, "The competitor competed in the competition," following a sort involving derivational pairs in which they examined how vowel sounds are altered when adding suffixes as in the change in vowel sounds from the long *e* in *compete* to the altered sounds of the *e* in *competitor* and *competition*.

RELATIONS AMONG RELATED RELATIVES. Provide a word root such as *divide* and ask students to write related words like *division, divisive, divisor,* or *dividend*. Interesting discussions about students' thinking as they spelled these related words are likely to follow, including lots of talk about the meaning as well as about sound and spelling patterns.

COVER AND CONNECT. Write a word on the board and demonstrate how to cover up word parts, saying the remaining portion and then connecting that segment with the rest of the word when it is uncovered (O'Connor, 2007). The parts that are covered vary according to developmental stage of word knowledge. For letter name–alphabetic spellers, consonant digraphs, consonant blends, or the short-vowel rhyming family can be covered and then connected (e.g., *fl-at*). For within word pattern spellers, long-vowel patterns can be covered and connected to the remaining consonant blends or digraphs (e.g., *sn-ake*). For syllables and affixes spellers, prefixes and suffixes can be covered and connected to base words, or syllables can be covered and connected one to the next (e.g., *re-read-ing; in-ter-est-ing*). When students encounter a word they don't know in their reading, they can be prompted to use this cover and connect strategy for decoding.

WORD WALLS. Word walls have become a staple in many primary classrooms. They are a useful resource for learning a relatively small set of words and can supplement systematic developmental word study. Word walls as originally conceived by Pat Cunningham (2000, 2013) are a display of alphabetically-ordered, high-utility words that grows cumulatively across the school year. We provide a list of high-frequency words on page 366 but select words based on your students' needs. Cunningham recommends that five words needed for reading and writing be added each week, and students should engage in activities that help secure those words in memory—chanting the letters, writing the words several times, and playing games (like Bingo) with the words. If you want to hold students responsible for using the word wall, then you need to add words gradually, plan quick daily activities, model using it, and review the wall regularly. We recommend that word walls for beginning readers provide separate column headers for consonant digraphs, like CH for *chick*, SH for *shoe*.

Word walls should not look the same at all grade levels. In kindergarten, they should begin with student's names and then several high-frequency words might be added each week such as *the, can,* and *like* —words that students often use in their writing and see in their reading. By second grade, students should have mastered many of the most common words but other words like *because,* or homophones like *their, there,* and *they're,* are good candidates for a word wall. You can easily find out which words students have already mastered by asking them to spell them. The list in Appendix E has high-frequency words ordered by the first hundred, second hundred, and third hundred.

WORD DISPLAYS. Besides word walls there are other kinds of word displays that serve various purposes. Charts of word families, syllable types, Latin roots, content vocabulary, word hunt results, and other word displays posted around the room announce to students, parents, and visitors that words are valued and celebrated. Word displays call attention to the richness and power of a versatile vocabulary and provide a ready reference for writing. See Figure 3.24 for more ideas.

Resources such as *The Reading Teacher's Book of Lists* (Fry & Kress, 2006) will give you more ideas about interesting categories of words, but it is important that students are involved as much as possible in the creation of such lists for them to be useful and meaningful. For example, in the activity Said is Dead, students help brainstorm lists of words (e.g., *shouted, jeered, whispered, lisped*) to use in their writing instead of that overworked verb (*said*). In addition, be mindful of referring to such displays on a regular basis

FIGURE 3.24 Word Displays

- Spelling demons (relevant, unparalleled)
- Onomatopoeia words (boo-hoo, cockadoodledoo)
- Sophisticated synonyms (tell = explain, enumerate, explicate, justify, illustrate)
- Oxymorons (*plastic silverware*)
- Multiple meanings (*bat, run, draw*)
- Brand names that now represent a generic product (*Kleenex* for tissue)
- Homophones and homographs (due/dew, wind/wind)
- Collective nouns (*batch of brownies, gaggle of geese*)
- Acronyms (LASER, SCUBA)
- Eponyms (Louis Pasteur—*pasteurization*)
- Spanish–English cognates (*content–contento*)
- Palindromes (*mom*)
- Idioms (*pulling your leg*)
- Puns (*an artist who could really draw a crowd*)
- Similes (*smiling like an angel*)
- Alliteration (*big bad Bruce*)

if you want students to benefit from them. Continue to add to such lists to keep them fresh in students' minds and when you add a new word, go back over the list of previous words.

Selecting Written Word Study Activities: A Caveat Regarding Tradition

There are many long-standing activities associated with spelling that teachers often assign their students, such as writing words five times, listing them in alphabetical order, and copying definitions from the dictionary. Assignments like these do not fulfill the purpose of spelling instruction, which is not only to learn the spellings of particular words but also to understand generalizations about the spelling system itself and to cultivate a curiosity about words. Writing a word five times is a rote, meaningless, and ineffective activity (Templeton & Morris, 2000), whereas writing words into categories requires recognizing common spelling features and using judgment and critical thinking. Writing words in alphabetical order may teach alphabetization, but it will not teach anything about spelling patterns. (Alphabetizing words might be assigned occasionally as a separate dictionary skill, but students will be more successful at it when they can first sort their word cards into alphabetical order before writing them.)

Students do need to associate meanings with the words they are studying so it is reasonable to ask them to discuss or look up the meanings of a few words they do not know or to find additional meanings for words, but asking students to write out the definitions of long lists of words whose meanings they already know is boring and not likely to encourage dictionary use or a curiosity about words.

Writing words in sentences can also be overdone. You might ask students to choose 5 words (out of 20 to 25) each week to write sentences in their word study notebooks. For example, students like the challenge of using two or more in the same sentence. This is a more reasonable assignment than writing 20 isolated sentences with the weekly spelling list. Many teachers employ sentence writing to work on handwriting, punctuation, and grammar (see the expectations in Figure 3.20 on page 77). Writing sentences is also more useful for some features than others. For example, sentences will help students show that they understand homophones or the tenses of verb forms when studying inflectional endings such as *ed* and *ing*.

Be wary of other traditional assignments that take up time and may even be fun, but have little value in teaching children about spelling. Activities such as Hangman, word searches, and acrostics may keep students busy, but they impart little or no information about the English spelling system. While it is exciting to see the interest generated for the yearly spelling bee broadcast on national television, it is still the case that spelling bees reward children who are already good spellers and quickly eliminate the children who need practice the most.

Word study can be fun, but make good use of the time available and do not overdo it. Remember that word study activities should be short in duration so that students can devote most of their attention and time to reading and writing for meaningful purposes.

Spelling Expectations

Invented spelling, or spelling "as best you can," frees students to write even before they can read during the emergent stage, and they should be free to make spelling approximations when writing rough drafts at all levels. The Common Core State Standards encourage this and refer to this process as "phonetic spelling." Invented spelling, or as we like to call it, **developmental spelling**, also offers you diagnostic information about what students know and what they need to learn. But that does not mean that you do not hold students accountable for accurate spelling. Knowing where students are in terms of development level and considering which word features they have studied enables you to set reasonable expectations for accuracy and editing. For example, you can expect third-grade students in the within word pattern stage to spell words like *jet, flip,* and *must,* but it is unreasonable to expect them to handle multisyllabic words like *leprechaun* or *celebration.* Just as students are gradually held more and more accountable for conventions of writing such as commas and semicolons, so, too, are they gradually held more accountable for spelling accuracy.

A study by Clarke (1988) found that first-graders who were encouraged to use invented developmental spellings wrote more and could spell as well at the end of the year as first-graders who had been told how to spell the words before writing. The National Reading Panel report (2000), and more recently, a comprehensive review of research on spelling instruction (Graham & Santangelo, 2014), also underscored the importance of encouraging students to apply their knowledge of letter–sound relationships in their writing. This suggests that students are not marred by their own invented developmental spellings, nor do they persevere with errors over time. However, unless you communicate that correct spelling is valued, students may develop careless habits.

Many teachers wonder when they should make the shift from allowing students to write in invented developmental spelling to demanding correctness. The answer is "from the start." You must hold students accountable for what they have been taught; what they have not been taught can be politely ignored. For example, if a student has been taught consonant sound-to-letter correspondences, you would expect the student to spell those sounds correctly, as in PGS LK MD (*Pigs like mud*). However, if the student has not yet been taught the short vowel sounds needed in *pigs* and *mud*, these attempts should be allowed to stand as is. Because the sequence for phonics and spelling instruction is cumulative and progresses linearly from easier features such as individual letter sounds to harder features such as Latin-derived *tion*, *sion*, and *cian* endings, there will always be some features that have not yet been taught. Thus, students (and adults) will always invent a spelling for what they do not yet know.

PROOFREADING FOR SPELLING. While students might be encouraged to spell as best they can when they compose rough drafts, daily journal entries, or observation notes for a science experiment, there are times when writing products should be spelled as accurately as possible, especially in the upper grades. Proofreading involves identifying misspelled words, so it is not an easy task for younger students who are still spelling many words incorrectly. Proofreading needs to be handled judiciously in the lower grades and can be adjusted for students' development. After identification, the errors need to be corrected using a variety of spelling strategies (Turbil, 2000). Students need to be explicitly taught how to execute this complex skill, not simply told to proofread. You can use your own or a student's writing samples (with permission) that contain errors to model the ideas in Figure 3.25. Subsequent chapters have additional information about what spelling strategies and resources are appropriate for each stage, including the development of dictionary skills.

FIGURE 3.25 Proofreading Tips

- Focus only on spelling. Don't expect students to edit for punctuation, spelling, and word choice all at the same time. Have students reread with just spelling in mind as one step of the editing process.
- Reread carefully for errors. It is often hard to proofread one's own work because it is so familiar that we may not pay careful attention to the printed words. The key is to focus attention on spelling and this can be done by reading aloud, pointing to each word with a pencil, reading each line backward, or getting someone else to read it for you, such as an assigned editing buddy. Waiting a few days to reread also seems to help.
- Give students tools such as colored pencils in blue or green (rather than red) to use for correcting, circling, or underling misspelled words. This way you can monitor their corrections and even talk with them about the strategies they used.
- Keep the task manageable. You might assign students to find and correct a certain number of errors so that they do not feel overwhelmed. Five might be reasonable for students who are still misspelling a large percentage. Or you might ask students to look for errors related to the feature they are currently studying, such as long vowels or inflected endings.
- Teach students to use resources such as a word wall or dictionaries to correct misspellings. A simple spelling dictionary is a list of words arranged alphabetically and may be only a few pages long. This is much easier to use as it does not have definitions or other information typically found in a dictionary.
- Teach students to use spellcheck as part of a word processing application.
- Sometimes we want a final draft to be absolutely perfect, especially if it will be published in a classroom collection, school newspaper, or other permanent place. This is the point at which teachers, parents, or other reliable sources should serve as the final copyeditor.

Principles of Word Study Instruction

A number of basic principles guide the kind of word study described in *Words Their Way*® (you were introduced to some of these at the beginning of the chapter as they related to Mrs. Zimmerman's class). Many of these principles set word study apart from other approaches to the teaching of phonics, spelling, or vocabulary.

LOOK FOR WHAT STUDENTS USE BUT CONFUSE. Students cannot learn things they do not already know something about. This is the underlying principle of Vygotsky's (1962) zone of proximal development (ZPD) and the motivating force behind the assessment described in Chapter 2. By analyzing invented developmental spellings, a ZPD may be identified and instruction can be planned to address features the students are using but confusing instead of those they totally neglect (Invernizzi et al., 1994). Take your cue from the students to teach developmentally.

A STEP BACKWARD IS A STEP FORWARD. Once you have identified students' stages of developmental word knowledge and the orthographic features under negotiation, take a step backward and build a firm foundation. Then, in setting up your categories, contrast something new with something that is already known. It is important to begin word study activities where students will experience success. For example, students in the within word pattern stage who are ready to examine long vowel patterns begin by sorting words by short vowel sounds, which are familiar, and long-vowel sounds, which are being introduced for the first time. Then they move quickly to sorting by pattern. A step backward is the first step forward in word study instruction.

USE WORDS STUDENTS CAN READ. It is much easier to analyze words students can already pronounce. Known words come from any and all sources that students can read: language experience stories, recent readings, poems, and phonics readers. As much as possible, choose words to sort that students can read out of context. Put any aside they cannot read to examine later.

FIGURE 3.26   Doubling Sort: Comparing Words That "Do" with Words That "Don't"

COMPARE WORDS THAT "DO" WITH WORDS THAT "DON'T." To learn what a Chesapeake Bay retriever looks like, you have to see a poodle or a bulldog, not another Chesapeake Bay retriever. What something *is* is also defined by what it is *not*; contrasts are essential to students' building of categories. Students' spelling errors suggest what contrasts will help them sort out their confusions. For example, a student who is spelling *stopping* as STOPING will benefit from a sort in which words with consonants that are doubled before adding *ing* are contrasted with those that do not take doubled letters, as in Figure 3.26.

BEGIN WITH OBVIOUS CONTRASTS. When students start studying a new feature, choose key words or pictures that are distinctive. For example, when students first examine initial consonants, do not begin by contrasting *m* with *n*, which are both nasals and visually similar. It is better to begin by contrasting *m* with something totally different at first—*s*, for example—before working toward finer distinctions as these categorizations become quite automatic. Move from general, gross differences to more specific discriminations.

SORT BY SOUND AND PATTERN. Students examine words by how they sound and how they are spelled. Both sound and visual pattern are part of students' orthographic knowledge. Too often, students focus on visual patterns at the expense of how words are alike in sound. The following sort illustrates the way students move from a sound sort (by hard and soft *g*) to a visual pattern sort (by final *dge*, *ge*, and *g*). See what you can discover from this sort. (Hint: pay attention to the vowel sounds.)

First Sort by Sound of g		Second Sort by Pattern		
Soft	*Hard*	*dge*	*ge*	*g*
edge	bag	edge	cage	bag
cage	twig	judge	huge	twig
huge	slug	badge	stage	slug
judge	drug	lodge	page	flag
stage	leg			drug
badge	flag			leg
page				
lodge				

DON'T HIDE EXCEPTIONS. Exceptions arise when students make generalizations. Do not hide these exceptions. By placing so-called irregular words in a miscellaneous or oddball category, new categories of consistency sometimes emerge. For example, in looking at long vowel patterns, students find exceptions like *give*, *have*, and *love*, yet it is no coincidence that they all have a *ve*. They form a small but consistent pattern of their own. True exceptions do occur (e.g., *was*, *women*, *laugh*) and become memorable by virtue of their rarity.

AVOID RULES. Rules with many exceptions are disheartening and teach students nothing. They may have heard the long vowel rule, "When two vowels go walking, the first one does the talking," but this rule does not apply in phonetically regular words like *boot* or *soil*. Learning about English spelling requires students to consider sound and pattern simultaneously to discover consistencies in the orthography. This requires both reflection and continued practice. Students discover consistencies and make generalizations for themselves. Your job is to stack the deck and structure categorization tasks to make these consistencies explicit and to instill in students the habit of looking at words, asking questions, and searching for order. Rules are useful mnemonics if you already understand the underlying concepts at work. They are the icing on the cake of knowledge. But memorizing rules is not the way students make sense of how words work. Rules are no substitute for experience.

WORK FOR AUTOMATICITY. Accuracy in sorting is not enough—accuracy *and* ease are the ultimate indicators of mastery. Acquiring automaticity in sorting and recognizing orthographic patterns leads to the fluency necessary for proficient reading and writing. Your students will move from hesitancy to fluency in their sorting. Keep sorting until they do.

RETURN TO MEANINGFUL TEXTS. After sorting, students need to return to meaningful texts to hunt for other examples to add to the sorts. These hunts extend their analysis to more words and more difficult vocabulary. For example, after sorting one-syllable words into categories labeled *cat*, *drain*, and *snake*, a student added *tadpole*, *complain*, and *relate*. Through a simple word hunt, this child extended the pattern-to-sound consistency in one-syllable words to stressed syllables in two-syllable words.

These principles of word study boil down to one golden rule of word study instruction: *Teaching Is Not Telling* (James, 1958). In word study, students examine, manipulate, and categorize words. In order for this to happen, you must create a systematic program of word study, guided by an informed interpretation of spelling errors and other literacy behaviors. This is a teacher-directed, student-centered approach to vocabulary growth and spelling development. The next five chapters will show you exactly how to provide effective word study instruction for students at different stages of development.

RESOURCES FOR IMPLEMENTING WORD STUDY *in Your Classroom*

Throughout this text you will see references to the PDToolkit for *Words Their Way*®, which includes video, sample word sorts and games, and a Create Your Own feature. Companion books listed below offer additional resources for teachers.

PDToolkit for *Words Their Way*®

PDToolkit for *Words Their Way*®, the website that accompanies this text, prepares you for word study by examining successful classroom instruction—from assessment to organization to implementation across grade levels. You'll hear teachers explain the process, watch students master skills, and see how a successful word study approach is established and managed.

Words Their Way® *with English Learners: Word Study for Phonics, Vocabulary, and Spelling*, Second Edition, by L. Helman, D. R. Bear, S. Templeton, M. Invernizzi, and F. Johnston

Based on the same research and developmental model, this companion volume focuses on using word study to enhance literacy learning for English learners.

Words Their Way for PreK–K Learners by F. Johnston, M. Invernizzi, L. Helman, D. Bear, and S. Templeton

The literacy diet for PreK and K is presented in detail in separate chapters. Foundations of word study for each aspect are presented with ample activities for the classroom. The PDToolkit includes activities and materials as well as videos for Emergent and Letter Name word study.

Words Their Way with Struggling Readers: Word Study for Reading, Vocabulary and Spelling Instruction, Grades 4–12, by K. Flanigan, L. Hayes, S. Templeton, D. R. Bear, M. Invernizzi, and F. Johnston

The needs of struggling readers in grades 4 to 8 are discussed with an emphasis on developmental instruction and presentation of reading and vocabulary activities for success in disciplinary studies. Numerous schedules for classroom organization are presented.

Vocabulary Their Way: Word Study with Middle and Secondary Students, Second Edition, by S. Templeton, D. R. Bear, M. Invernizzi, F. Johnston, K. Flanigan, D. Townsend, L. Helman, and L. Hayes

Support for discipline-specific instruction in the middle and secondary grades that addresses context-based instruction, word-specific instruction, and generative vocabulary/morphology instruction. Subject matter areas include English Language Arts, Social Studies, Mathematics, Science, and Art/Music/Physical Education/Career and Technical Education.

Each of the following stage-specific companion volumes provides reproducible sorts and detailed directions for the teacher. You'll find extensive background notes about the features of study and step-by-step directions on how to guide the sorting lesson. Organizational tips and follow-up activities extend lessons through weekly routines.

Words Their Way®: *Letter and Picture Sorts for Emergent Spellers*, Second Edition, by D. R. Bear, M. Invernizzi, F. Johnston, and S. Templeton

Teachers in pre K through grade 1 will find ready-made sorts as well as rhymes and jingles for emergent readers.

Words Their Way®: *Word Sorts for Letter Name–Alphabetic Spellers*, Second Edition, by F. Johnston, D. R. Bear, M. Invernizzi, and S. Templeton

Primarily for students in kindergarten through grade 3, the 50 blackline masters include picture sorts for beginning consonants and for digraphs and blends, word families with pictures and words, and word sorts for short vowels.

Words Their Way®: Word Sorts for Within Word Pattern Spellers, Second Edition, by M. Invernizzi, F. Johnston, D. R. Bear, and S. Templeton

Words Their Way®: Word Sorts for Syllables and Affixes Spellers, Second Edition, by F. Johnston, M. Invernizzi, D. R. Bear, and S. Templeton

Words Their Way®: Word Sorts for Derivational Relations Spellers, Second Edition, by S. Templeton, F. Johnston, D. R. Bear, and M. Invernizzi

Helman, L., Bear, D. R., Invernizzi, M., Templeton, S., Johnston, F. (2011). Words their way: Emergent sorts for Spanish-speaking English learners. Boston: Allyn & Bacon.

Helman, L., Bear, D. R., Invernizzi, M., Templeton, S., Johnston, F. (2009). Words their way letter name-alphabetic sorts for Spanish-speaking English learners. Boston: Allyn & Bacon.

Helman, L., Bear, D. R., Invernizzi, M., Templeton, S., & Johnston, F. (2014). Words their way: Within word pattern sorts for Spanish-speaking English learners. Boston: Allyn & Bacon.

Teachers of grades 1 through 4 will find 50 reproducible sorts that cover the many vowel patterns as well as other features such as complex consonants.

This text includes 56 sorts for syllables and affixes spellers in grades 3 to 8. Prefixes and suffixes are introduced.

Teachers of grades 5 to 12 will find 60 upper-level word sorts that help students build their vocabulary as well as spelling skills. Lots of additional words are provided to modify or create new sorts.

Spanish speakers learning to read English benefit from word study that clarifies some of the contrasts between English and Spanish spelling. These supplements contain sorts and games with directions and assessments that explore the first three stages of English spelling development.

chapter 4

Word Study for Learners in the Emergent Stage

This chapter describes the literacy development that occurs during the emergent stage, a period in which young children imitate and experiment with the forms and functions of print: directionality, the distinctive features of print, the predictability of text, and how all of these correlate with oral language. The emergent stage lies at the beginning of a lifetime of learning about written language. Emergent children do not read or spell conventionally and they score 0 on spelling inventories like those in Chapter 2 because they have only very tenuous understandings of how units of speech and units of print are related. Nevertheless, children are developing remarkable insights into written language, and with the help of caregivers and teachers they learn a great deal. Before we go into a thorough description of the emergent stage, we will visit a kindergarten classroom in mid-year.

During a unit about pets, Mrs. Smith shares a big book, *Cat on the Mat*, by Brian Wildsmith. This simple patterned book opens with a cat sitting contentedly on a mat, but on each subsequent page bigger and bigger animals join as the cat becomes increasingly agitated. When an elephant joins, the cat hisses and all the animals run away. Mrs. Smith introduces the book by pointing to the cover and asking, "Where is the cat?" Several children sing out, "on the rug." Then she says, "Let's look at the title here." As she reads she point to each word. "It says, Cat on the…" and she pauses while several children say, "on the rug." "Hmmm," says Mrs. Smith. "The picture does look like a rug but this word (pointing to *Mat*) starts with *M* and *r-r-r-r*ug would start with *R*. What else could this be? I will give you a clue: it rhymes with cat. Listen, *Cat on the Mmmmmat*. We use mats at rest time, don't we?"

After asking the children what they think the book will be about she says, "Let's read and find out what happens." She points to the words in the single sentence for each two-page spread and by the third sentence the children are catching on to the pattern and saying the name of the new animal. She pauses before the elephant appears and asks for predictions about what the next animal might be and why they think it might be that animal. On a second reading the children can all join in and read along chorally. Mrs. Smith takes the time to ask about how the cat is feeling about sharing the mat with so many animals. The children suggest *mad* but she introduces several new vocabulary words (*upset*, *angry*, and *furious*) and uses them to describe the cat's growing discontentment leading up to the hiss.

In this fashion, Mrs. Smith shares a predictable book with her children that they can easily memorize and read along with her. In the process she draws her students' attention to letters and sounds and models pointing to words as she reads. She also finds an opportunity to introduce some new vocabulary. After enjoying the big book version, she plans a number of follow-up activities to further develop emergent literacy skills.

On the next day the story is reread and the cat's feelings are described again with the target vocabulary words. Mrs. Smith defines the words (*upset* is when you are feeling unhappy and bothered). She asks the children what would make them feel upset. "Would you feel upset getting the birthday present you've always wanted?" "Would you feel upset if someone threw water on you?" "Would that make you feel furious?" "What else would make you furious?" Drake says, "I felt furious when my brother broke my toy." Discussions like these continue over several days so the children hear and use the words in different ways.

Mrs. Smith has created a chart with the lines of patterned text. She has also written them on sentence strips and placed them in order in a pocket chart. After the children have read the sentences chorally on the chart, Mrs. Smith passes out the strips. As a group they put the sentences back in order by comparing them to the chart. Then Mrs. Smith calls on volunteers to read sentences from the pocket chart and she observes carefully to see which children are beginning to point accurately to the words as they recite. On another day word cards for the animals are

FIGURE 4.1   **Pointing with** *Cat on the Mat*

held up one by one as volunteers come up to match the words to the chart or sentence strips. When Abby matches *cow* to *cat* Mrs. Smith says, "Yes they both start with *C* but look at the other letters. What do you hear at the end of *cat*?" She makes sure the book, chart, strips, and words are left out where everyone can practice freely with them during the day.

Most of the children in Mrs. Smith's class are ready to study initial consonants and she pulls a small group to do a picture sort. She begins by holding up the letter *M* and asks the group to find a word in the story that begins with that letter. They quickly find *mat* at the end of every sentence. She repeats with *C*. The children find *cat* and then *cow*. Mrs. Smith then brings out a collection of pictures that start with *M* and *C* and puts up a picture of a *cat* and a *mat* as headers in a pocket chart. After naming all the pictures, she models how to sort: "Here is a mouse. Listen to the first sound *mmmmm*ouse. *Mouse* starts like *mat* so I will put it under *M*." After modeling several she invites the children to take turns sorting the rest. This sort is repeated, and on subsequent days the children have a number of opportunities to sort on their own, to hunt for more pictures in alphabet books and magazines beginning with *M* and *C*, and to draw and label pictures with those sounds. After the children compare the sounds in several ways, the pictures are combined with *d* (dog) and *s* (sat) for a four-category sort as shown in the opening picture of this chapter. The children work with all four letters and sounds for several days before moving on to a new contrast. ●

Mrs. Smith uses a core book as the basis for teaching a variety of emergent literacy skills in a developmentally appropriate fashion, starting with a whole text and working down to the parts (sentences, words, letters, and sounds). Children practice reading five lines of the text to develop a concept of word in text. The five lines are written on individual sentence strips and children match the lines to their recitation of the lines. Children then focus on the words *mat* and *cat* to study beginning consonant sounds /*m*/ and /*c*/, and they sort pictures that begin with these sounds.

From Speech to Print: Matching Units of Speech to Print

Learning to read and spell is a process of matching oral and written language at three different levels: (1) the discourse level, at which the text is organized into phrases and sentences, (2) the sentence level of words within sentences, and (3) the word level of sounds and letters within words and syllables. For someone learning to read, mismatches occur because of the fixed nature of print versus the flowing stream of speech it represents.

The Discourse Level

In oral language, the *discourse level* includes the specific situation or context in which language is used and shared (Gee, 2005). It includes the "musical" level of language, usually consisting of sentences or phrases. Within these phrases, speakers produce and listeners hear elements of **prosody** such as expression, intonation contours, and tone of voice, all of which communicate ideas and emotions. For example, a rising note at the end of a statement often indicates a question; precise, clipped words in a brusque tone may suggest irritation or anger.

Oral language is a direct form of communication accompanied by gestures and facial expressions that take place in a shared context, whereas *written language* is an indirect form of communication and must contain complete, freestanding messages to make meaning clear. Punctuation and word choice are often the reader's only cues to the emotions and intent of the writer. In addition, written language tends to be more formal and carefully constructed, using literacy devices such as "happily ever after" to cue the reader. When children learn to read, they must match the prosody of their oral language to these more formal structures of written language.

The Word Level

A second level of structures that children must negotiate is the unit called *words*. In print, words are clearly set off with spaces between a string of letters. In speech, words are not distinct; there is no clear, separable unit in speech that equates perfectly to individual words. For example, the phrase "once upon a time" represents a single idea composed of four words and five syllables. Because of this, when children try to match their speech to print, they often miss the mark, as Lee does in her elephant story in Figure 4.5 (page 97). It takes exposure, explanation, and practice, as well as alphabet knowledge, to match words in speech to written words (Flanigan, 2006; Morris, 1980; Roberts, 1992; Uhry & Shepart, 1999; Uhry, 2002) which is why early childhood teachers should point to words as they read from charts or big books.

Sounds in Words

Sounds and letters make up the third level of analysis. In learning to read, children must segment the speech sounds or **phonemes** within words and match them to the letters in print. In speech, the phonemes (consonants and vowels) are interconnected and cannot be easily separated (Liberman & Shankweiler, 1991). Yet letters of the alphabet and individual speech sounds must be understood as discrete units that match in systematic ways in order to master reading and spelling English. This understanding is called the **alphabetic principle**.

Characteristics of the Emergent Stage of Reading and Spelling

Some emergent children may have well-developed language skills and know a great deal about stories and books; others may not. However, a certain level of proficiency in oral language is not a prerequisite for learning the alphabet or seeing printed words tracked in correspondence to speech. To withhold these essential components of the learning-to-read process would put them in double jeopardy. Besides putting them behind in language and story development, they also would be behind in acquiring the alphabetic principle. Children can develop oral language, learn about stories, *and* learn about words, sounds, and the alphabet simultaneously as teachers model reading and writing and encourage children to imitate and experiment.

Emergent Reading

Can children in the emergent stage read? Yes, but not in a conventional way. The emergent child's reading is best described as pretend reading or reading from memory, and both are valuable practices for movement into literacy. **Pretend reading** is basically a paraphrase or spontaneous retelling at the discourse level that children produce while turning the pages of a familiar book. In pretend reading, children pace their retelling to match the sequence of pictures and orchestrate dialogue and the voice and cadence of written language (Sulzby, 1986).

Memory reading is more exacting than pretend reading. Without knowing any better, it might *sound* as though a child was reading. It involves an accurate recitation of the text accompanied by pointing to the print in some fashion. Reading from memory helps children coordinate spoken language with print at the level of words, sounds, and letters. Emergent children's attempts to touch individual words while reading from memory are initially quite inconsistent and vague. Children gradually acquire **directionality**, realizing that they should move left to right, top to bottom, and end up on the last word on the page. However, the units that come in between are a blur until the systematic relationship between letters and sounds is understood. The ability to fingerpoint or track accurately to words in print while reading from memory is a phenomenon called **concept of word in text (COW-T)**. It is a watershed event that separates the emergent reader from the letter name–alphabetic beginning reader (Flanigan, 2007; Henderson, 1981; Morris, 1992, 1993).

When children lack a COW-T, word boundaries are also missing in their writing, even if some phoneme–grapheme correspondences have been made. Note how the words all run together in Figure 4.2. However, words gradually begin to evolve as distinct entities with their boundaries defined by beginning and ending sounds as fingerpointing becomes more exact. Children's early letter name–alphabetic writing provides evidence of this understanding, as illustrated in Figure 4.3.

Emergent readers are in what Ehri (1997) calls the **prealphabetic phase** of reading. They may learn to identify a few words, such as their names and the names of friends and family. They might also identify signs in their environment, but their strategy is to look for nonalphabetic cues such as the shape and color of a stop sign. They may identify a large retail store because it starts with a big red *K*, but they are not systematic in their selection of any particular cue. During the emergent stage, children lack an understanding of the alphabetic principle or show only the beginning of this understanding even as they begin to notice letters. On entering preschool, Lee realized that other children's names on their cubbies had some of the same letters that were

FIGURE 4.2 **Late Emergent Writing without Word Boundaries**

"I like housekeeping"

FIGURE 4.3 **Early Letter Name–Alphabetic Spelling with Word Boundaries**

"I like housekeeping"

in her name. Perplexed and somewhat annoyed, she pointed to one of the letters. "Hey, that's MY letter!" she insisted. Children in the emergent stage also begin to see some letters from their names in environmental print. Walking around the grocery store, Lee pointed to the box of Cheer detergent and said, "Look, Mommy! There's my name!" Lee's special relationship with the letters in her name is a living embodiment of the prealphabetic strategy.

Emergent Writing

Like emergent reading, early emergent writing is largely pretend. Regardless of most children's cultural backgrounds or where they live, this pretend writing occurs spontaneously wherever writing is encouraged, modeled, and incorporated into play (Ferreiro & Teberosky, 1982). The child's first task as a writer is to discover that scribbling can represent something and, thereafter, to differentiate drawing from writing and pictorial representation from oral communication. The child must come to realize that a drawing of a flower does not actually say "flower." Writing is necessary to communicate the complete message. Children in the early phases of the emergent stage experiment with symbolic forms while they are learning important concepts about print. The top row of Figure 4.4 presents a progression of drawings and their accompanying utterances.

There are many similarities between infant talk and emergent writing. When babies learn to talk, they do not begin by speaking in phonemes first, followed by syllables, words, and finally phrases. In fact, it is quite the opposite. They begin by cooing in discourse, prosodic contours that approximate the music of their mother tongue. Likewise, children begin to write by approximating the broader contours of the writing system; they start with the linear arrangement of print (Ferreiro & Teberosky, 1982; Puranik, Lonigan, & Kim, 2011). This kind of pretend writing has been called **mock linear** (Clay, 1975; Harste, Woodward, & Burke, 1984). However, unlike learning to talk, which evolves naturally, children must be taught to read and write.

PD TOOLKIT™
for Words Their Way®

Early Childhood Writing
Watch a preschooler write about butterflies using mock linear writing.

FIGURE 4.4   The Evolution of Emergent Writing

Random Marks	**Representational Drawing**	**Drawing Distinct from Writing**
	"This is my sister."	"A flower for my Mom."
Mock Linear or Letterlike	**Symbol Salad**	**Partial Phonetic**
"A note for Daddy."	"Macaroni"	"cat" / "baby" / "I love you"

The bottom row of Figure 4.4 shows the movement from mock linear writing to real writing that uses letters to represent speech sounds. When children begin to represent speech sounds with letters of the alphabet, they are well on their way to acquiring the alphabetic principle, the foundation of the English writing system (Liberman, Shankweiler, & Liberman, 1986). Once children attain the alphabetic principle, they are no longer emergent learners.

As children develop across the emergent stage, there are dramatic changes that can be characterized as early, middle, and late emergent behaviors, as summarized in Table 4.1.

EARLY. In the early emergent stage, children learn to hold a pencil, marker, or crayon and to make marks on paper (or windows, walls, or floors). These marks are best described as scribbles that lack directionality and may not serve a communicative function. Sometime during this early emergent stage, scribbles evolve into more representational drawings and children learn that print is distinct from drawing.

MIDDLE. In the middle emergent stage, children begin to approximate the most global contours of the writing system: the top-to-bottom linear arrangement. They experiment with letterlike forms that resemble the separate circles and lines of manuscript writing or the connected loops of cursive. The child may identify his or her efforts as "writing" and announce that it is a "note for Daddy," as shown in Figure 4.4. Parents may be challenged at this point when children come to them with their pretend writing and say, "Read this to me, Mommy" or "What does this say?" What is exciting and significant is that young children recognize that print carries a message that can be read by others. As letters of the alphabet and numbers are learned, they begin to show up in letter strings or a "symbol salad," as in the spelling of *macaroni* in Figure 4.4.

LATE. By the late emergent stage, children are beginning to use letters to represent speech sounds in a systematic way, as shown in the last box in Figure 4.4. This marks the acquisition of the alphabetic principle. These partial representations of sounds, or **phonetic** spellings, represent four critical insights and skills:

1. To produce a spelling, children must know some letters—not all, but enough to get started.
2. They must attend to the sounds or phonemes within spoken words and syllables.

TABLE 4.1   **Characteristics of Emergent Spelling**

	What Students Do Correctly	What Students Use but Confuse	What Is Absent
Early Emergent	Mark on the page Hold the writing implement	Drawing and scribbling for writing	Letters Directionality
Middle Emergent	Linear movement across page Clear distinction between writing and drawing Letterlike forms	Letters and numbers Letter strings Directionality	Phonemic awareness Sound–symbol correspondences
Late Emergent SKP for *housekeeping* D for *duck*	Consistent directionality Use of letters Some letter–sound matches	Substitutions of letters that sound, feel, and look alike: *B/P, D/B* Salient phonemes	Complete sound–symbol correspondence Spacing between words Consistent representation of beginning and final sounds in single syllable words.

3. They must know that letters represent speech sounds. Again, they do not have to know all of the letter sounds; indeed, if they know the names of the letters, they might use those as substitutes.

4. They must know how to form or write some of the letters they know.

Beginning to Match Sounds to Letters

To create a spelling, children must be able to isolate individual sounds in the word and apply their knowledge of letter names, or **phonics**, the systematic correspondence between letters and sounds. Initially, children are only able to discern the most prominent sound in a word or syllable, which they may represent with just one letter: *K* for *cat*, *S* for *mouse*, *B* for *baby*. The last box in Figure 4.4 shows some of these partial spellings.

Emergent children rely on the feel of their mouths as they analyze the speech stream. Say the phrase "once upon a time" aloud while paying attention to what your tongue and lips are doing. The tongue touches another part of the mouth only for the /s/ sound of *once*, the /n/ sound of *upon*, and the /t/ sound of *time*. The lips touch each other twice: for the /p/ sound in the middle of *upon* and for the /m/ sound at the end of *time*. It is not surprising, therefore, that Lee wrote "once upon a time" as 1SPNTM in Figure 4.5. Late emergent spellers pay attention to those tangible points of an utterance in which one part of the mouth touches another, or to the most forcefully articulated sounds that make the most vibration or receive the most stress. If some letters are known, they will be matched to these prominent sounds.

Figure 4.5 illustrates Lee's phonemic analysis of words and phrases in her elephant story relative to her knowledge of the alphabet and letter sounds. The phonemes represented by letters are always the most prominent sounds, but the most prominent are not always at the beginnings of words; she spelled *went* as T and *him* as M. Lee is not yet able to isolate every phoneme and her spellings reflect this partial awareness as in F for *fair* or TM for *time*. Notice her confusion with word boundaries and how she tries to mark them with periods. As children begin to achieve a concept of word, they become better able to pay attention to sounds that correspond to the beginnings and ends of word units. When letter names are coordinated with word boundaries in a consistent fashion, the child is no longer an emergent speller. Spelling that honors word boundaries consistently is spelling in the early part of the next stage, the letter name–alphabetic stage.

FIGURE 4.5 Lee's Elephant Story

1spntm	Once upon a time
Lft. T. f	the elephant went to the fair.
pplsm. et. sk	The people saw him eating strawberry cake.
nobDSMg	And nobody saw him again.
Vn	The end

The Context for Early Literacy Learning

To make progress in the emergent stage, learners need lots of teacher-scaffolded experiences with reading and writing for real purposes. These experiences should progress from modeling and explanation by the teacher, to guided practice, and then to independent practice by the child in a gradual release model (Duffy, 2009; Fisher and Frey, 2008; Pearson & Gallagher, 1983):

1. *Modeling and explanation*: Beginning in preschool, look for opportunities to introduce new vocabulary, identify rhyming words, talk about letters and sounds, write for children, and point to words in enlarged text as they read.
2. *Guided practice*: Ask children to sort pictures by beginning sounds, clap the syllables in words, recite poems and songs from memory, and add a question mark to a sentence, all under close supervision.
3. *Independent practice*: The most important condition for emergent literacy to blossom is the opportunity to practice, and children's approximations must be encouraged and celebrated. After modeling and guided practice, children can then be expected to produce rhyming words, sort pictures by beginning sounds, write letters in attempts to spell, and fingerpoint read short memorable selections of text.

Teaching children letters of the alphabet and the sounds they represent is absolutely essential during the emergent stage, but children do not have to get them all straight before they begin to read and write. Pretend writing and pretend reading come first, and as they evolve, real reading and real writing will follow.

Support Emergent Writing

The mere act of leaving one's mark on paper has been called the "fundamental graphic act" (Gibson & Yonas, 1968)—an irresistible act of self-fulfillment. Young children will write, or pretend to write, well before they learn to read, provided they are encouraged to do so. The trick in developmental literacy instruction is how to give that encouragement. As the teacher, you should provide immediate and ready access to implements of writing (markers, crayons, pencils, chalk) and model how to use them. Children can write in centers:

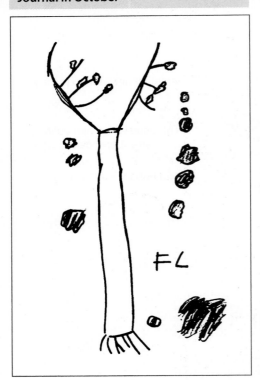

FIGURE 4.6 Kaitlyn's Kindergarten Journal in October

- A grocery store play area where grocery lists are drawn and labeled
- A restaurant where menus are offered and orders are written
- A block center with cardboard shapes for making signs
- A writing center with a variety of paper, alphabet stamps, markers, and pictures cut from magazines

You could also give children journals and encourage them to write in them. Figures 4.4 and 4.5 show samples of Lee's daily preschool journal entries. For many young writers, their first efforts may be drawings accompanied by labels such as Kaitlyn's kindergarten journal entry in Figure 4.6. In addition, writing extensions to other literacy activities and thematic studies can be modeled and encouraged. Children might record their observations of seeds growing, write about a field trip, or record a prediction. Expect these efforts to range from scribbles to partial phonetic writing, as shown in Figure 4.4.

As described in the gradual release model, it is critical that teachers write *for* and *with* children to demonstrate and explain the forms and functions of print. This can take place as they record students' ideas in child dictations or during interactive writing when they make the writing process explicit by talking aloud about how to spell, punctuate and compose (Aram & Biron, 2004; Button, Johnson & Furgerson, 1996). Outfitted and supported accordingly, writing will happen well before children can spell conventionally or properly compose (Chomsky, 1970; McGee & Richgels, 2012; Strickland & Morrow, 1989).

In a developmental framework for early writing, what matters is engaging children in the process as the first step and as an incentive for learning more about the process. Cabell, Tortorelli, and Gerde (2013) describe the developmental learning trajectory for students' early writing as well as corresponding goals based on where they are developmentally. Using this framework, teachers can interpret children's writing and then provide the appropriate instruction to move to the next level. For example, children at the drawing and scribbling level will need instruction that walks them through the process of including letters in their writing. Children who already include letters and letterlike forms, but without a connection to speech sounds, will need instruction to use letters to represent the most prominent sounds. Teachers should help children who already write letters to represent one sound to focus on and represent both beginning and ending sounds of spoken words.

Support Emergent Reading

There are two kinds of reading formats for emergent learners: *reading to* students, which includes interactive read-alouds with children's literature, and *reading with* students. **Interactive read-alouds** (Barrentine, 1996) promote oral language discussions around vocabulary, ideas, and concepts related to the content and genre of a book as teachers read aloud to children. During **shared reading** (Holdaway, 1979) teachers read *with* students from enlarged texts like big books and charts on which children can see the print and join in chorally on rereadings. Both formats involve lots of modeling by the teacher and provide a supportive social context with opportunities to talk about the forms and functions of print. However, shared reading, in which students' attention is directed to enlarged print, is particularly powerful for cultivating awareness of important aspects of how print works. Teachers can use **print referencing** (Justice & Sofka, 2010), such as where to begin to read on the page, or demonstrate left-to-right directionality and the return sweep at the end of each line—conventions of written language known as **concepts about print (CAP)**. Of course, all the talk and demonstration in the world will not substitute for hands-on practice, so early literacy instruction includes lots of guided practice with fingerpointing to familiar texts as Mrs. Smith did with *Cat on the Mat*. In the process, pretend or memory reading gradually moves children towards conventional reading.

The reading materials best suited for shared reading with emergent readers include simple predictable books, familiar nursery rhymes, poems, songs, jump rope jingles, and children's own talk written down. Familiarity with songs and rhymes helps bridge the gap between speech and print and cultivates the sense that what can be sung or recited can be written or read. Recording students' own language in the form of picture captions and dictations also nurtures the notion that print is talk written down. The ownership that comes with having one's own experiences recorded in print is a powerful incentive to explore the world of written language.

Although children in the emergent stage are heavily supported by memory in their first efforts to read, these attempts are nonetheless valuable. The best way to create a reader is to make reading happen, even if it is just pretend. Useful techniques for fostering early literacy development include the **whole-to-part model** (McCracken & McCracken, 1995) used by Mrs. Smith in the opening vignette. The whole-to-part model begins with the shared reading of familiar rhymes and jingles (whole texts). Then follow-up activities move to the parts (sentences, words, letters, and sounds) as children rebuild the text with sentence strips in pocket charts, and match word cards to individual words on the sentence strips as an explicit way to direct attention to words in print. The smallest parts involve sorting pictures and words by beginning sounds to draw attention to letter–sound correspondences.

PD pd **TOOLKIT**™
for Words Their Way®

Whole Class Reading and Picture Sort and **Small Group Reading and Sorting** Watch how Ms Smith supports young readers and focuses attention on five lines from a predictable book.

The Literacy Diet for the Emergent Stage

Through reading and writing activities, word study instruction for the emergent reader must aim toward the development of six fundamental components that constitute a comprehensive "diet" for early literacy learning and instruction (Invernizzi, 2002):

1. Oral language, concepts, and vocabulary
2. Phonological awareness (PA)
3. Alphabet knowledge
4. Letter–sound knowledge
5. Concepts about print (CAP)
6. Concept of word in text (COW-T)

If all components are addressed on a daily basis, no matter how far along the emergent continuum a child may be, conventional reading and writing should inevitably follow. At the same time, Common Core State Standards (CCSS) will be met. In the sections that follow, each component is described with teaching tips. The literacy diet and activities are covered more thoroughly for early childhood educators in *Words Their Way for PreK–K* (Johnston, Invernizzi, Helman, Bear, & Templeton, 2015).

Oral Language, Concepts, and Vocabulary

Most children have an oral vocabulary of 13,000 words by the time they enter kindergarten (Justice, 2006), and have mastered the basic subject–verb–object word order of the English language. But children come to school with widely varying language experiences (Biemiller & Slonim, 2001). In a classic study, researchers estimated that by 3 years of age, some children had heard 3 million more words than other children, and by the time they enter school, some children have heard 30 million more words than others (Hart & Risley, 1995).

A well-developed vocabulary is an essential part of school success and explicit instruction is needed (Biemiller, 2001, 2004). To help children develop the deep and wide vocabulary knowledge they will need to succeed in their future academic studies, vocabulary and language learning must become an integral part of all aspects of the early childhood classroom. There are many strategies to build a language-rich environment that will support students' vocabularies, advancing oral language, and concept development. Here we describe how daily classroom interactions can be a context for word learning—how to get children talking and using language, how to use read-alouds, and how to develop big ideas and language through concept sorts. Activities 4.1 through 4.7 at the end of the chapter provide more ideas.

CLASSROOM INTERACTIONS FOR LANGUAGE DEVELOPMENT. Adults should engage children in conversation at every opportunity and consciously use language that includes new vocabulary and complex sentences. Sit with them at snack time, at lunchtime, and on the playground, and ask them questions that will engage them in conversations. At the same time, children need many opportunities to talk with each other. Peer interactions are particularly important for children with less language skill because they benefit from conversation with children who have better language skills (Mashburn, Justice, Downer, & Pianta, 2009). This is also true for children who are learning English.

SOPHISTICATED SYNONYMS. Be on the lookout for, gradually teach, and consistently use more sophisticated synonyms for the common language of everyday routines as well as for topical interests. For example, children can be asked to *distribute* or *allocate* materials. During discussions, encourage *participants* to *contribute* and *elaborate* their ideas and those of others. Children may be asked to *assemble adjacent to* the wall, and then to *proceed* in an *orderly* fashion. Lane and Allen (2010) describe how a kindergarten teacher begins the year by asking the "weather watcher" to report to the class using terms such as *sunny,* *cloudy*, or *warm* but she gradually introduces new terms—the appointed "meteorologist" is expected to *observe* the weather *conditions* and report the *forecast* using words such as *overcast*, *brisk*, or *frigid*.

LANGUAGE IN CENTERS. Centers provide a stimulus for new vocabulary and concept development. Sand is *gritty* and *moist* and can be *sifted* with *sieves*. In the block center, encourage children to *construct*, *erect*, and *dismantle* their creations. McGee and Richgels (2012) suggest keeping a list of words posted in centers as a reminder of vocabulary to use with students. Add to the lists as more words occur to you and save them from year to year.

Targeting Vocabulary in Read-Alouds

Books expose children to new words and more complex sentence structures, and they provide background and conceptual knowledge that children may not have experienced first-hand. Read from a variety of genres and select storybooks that offer rich language and themes appropriate for young children. For example, nonfiction about seasons, weather, transportation, and how seeds grow provides new vocabulary and develops background information, especially when read for units of study. Folktales offer strong plots that help children develop a sense of story and poetry offers rhyme and playful language.

Reading aloud to children exposes them to a wide range of new words, but teachers also need to develop the meanings of particular words in more depth to ensure vocabulary growth. When new words are introduced with a simple explanation, children should be asked to repeat them and say them in phrases and sentences. After reading about how a little bear *hustled* after his mother (*Blueberries for Sal* by Robert McCloskey), you might pause briefly to draw attention to the word and then follow up later with more discussion: "*Hustle* means to walk very quickly. Say the word *hustle*. Would you hustle to catch the bus? Would you hustle to bed? Would you hustle fast or hustle slow? Tell your partner how you would fill in this sentence: I hustled to _____." Beck, McKeown, and Kucan (2002, 2008) describe how to plan repeated exposure to words in different contexts to help children learn the meanings and uses of new vocabulary words. For example, you might urge the children to hustle as they line up to go inside.

SELECTING WORDS. Review books to select vocabulary to develop. It is easy and tempting to simply look for hard words, but the most difficult examples may not be the words children are most likely to retain and use on their own. Four criteria are important in selecting target words: (1) utility, (2) concreteness, (3) repetition in text, and (4) relatedness to themes or topics of study.

Utility. When thinking about utility, consider words that can be used regularly in the classroom or words that will show up in other books. For example, the book *Corduroy* by Don Freeman includes "amazing, admiring, and enormous." After focusing on these words during the read-aloud, make a point of using them in other contexts. Instead of saying, "I like the drawing you did," substitute with "I admire your drawing. The colors are amazing and that house is enormous!"

Concreteness. Concrete words are more likely to be illustrated in the story (such as the *elevator* in *Corduroy*). Many denote concepts that children can act out, like *hustled*. Abstract words like *imagined* will take more work to develop.

Repetition in Text. Also consider words that are used more than once in the story, because these will offer repeated exposure in a meaningful context. The word *hustled* occurs several times in *Blueberries for Sal* (McCloskey, 1948).

Thematic or Topical Relatedness. When considering thematic or topical relatedness, choose words that can be clustered in a semantic category (Whitehurst, 1979). The words *buds*, *blooms*, and *blossoms* all relate to the growing seeds motif in *The Tree* (A First Discovery Book). From the same book, other concrete selections that form clusters for repetition include *seed*, *roots*, and *sapling*.

INTERACTIVE READING. Reading to children should be an interactive process that stimulates lots of responses from children who ask questions and provide comments such as pointing out things they notice in the illustrations (Barrentine, 1996). Ideas for planning and conducting an interactive read-aloud with a focus on vocabulary development can be found in Activity 4.1. Such read-alouds take additional time to implement because you want children to have the opportunity to engage in a lot of oral language. At the same time, excessive interruptions can disrupt the flow of the text, so it is important to strike a balance between stopping and reading. Sometimes you may want to read a book with few, if any, interruptions and sometimes you may use a second reading to focus on words and invite responses. To increase opportunities to talk, you might want to use the "turn and talk" technique described in the activity section. Children talk with assigned partners to answer a question, share a response, or make a prediction. Turn and talk techniques multiply the opportunities for individuals to articulate their own ideas and are especially beneficial for children who are shy or learning to speak English.

EXPERIENCES AND EXTENSIONS. Reading aloud to children provides virtual experiences that can stimulate oral language and vocabulary learning, but real experiences with cooking, science experiments, special visitors, classroom pets, and field trips are particularly engaging and provide direct opportunities for verbal interactions. These experiences will be particularly important for English learners, but the immediacy of real life is engaging for all young children. It is easy to think that experiences and conversations just happen, and to a certain extent they do, but *planned* experiences with careful attention to vocabulary, language, and concepts are more likely to be fruitful (Neuman & Roskos, 2012). Even better, combining read-alouds with experiences supports the necessary repetition of targeted vocabulary and promotes linkages that facilitate learning. Because it is important for children to encounter new words and concepts in different contexts, planning experiences that promote vocabulary learning and help maintain that vocabulary over time is critical.

Let's say you conduct a series of read-alouds on animals that make good pets, and you decide to get a hamster for the classroom. Some of the concepts and vocabulary that you can develop and sustain include *hamster, male, female, habitat, nutrition, diet, exercise, bedding, gnaw,* and *nocturnal.* These words represent conceptual understandings you can develop about hamsters that children can then use in their daily conversations about hamsters.

Use the same criteria outlined earlier to select words: utility, concreteness, opportunities for repetition, and relatedness. An experience like caring for a classroom pet can lead to lots of reading and writing activities as well. You might create labels with the students' help for the *cage, water bottle, exercise ball,* and so on. Children might dictate their observations and insights about hamsters in the language experience approach described beginning on page 117 or participate in an interactive writing activity described on page 139. In addition, you might ask children to illustrate and write about hamsters in their own journals.

Planned Extensions. Follow-up activities to a read-aloud offer opportunities for children to interact with peers and apply their understanding of concepts and vocabulary through cooperative learning formats or centers (Wasik, Bond, & Hindman, 2006). Reread favorites and then always keep the books available so children can pick them up during free time to explore on their own.

Retellings and Dramatic Play. Prompting children to retell what they heard in the read-aloud encourages them to use new words and more complex sentence constructions in hands-on, engaging activities (Ward, 2009). Retellings should be modeled for students: "When you have a chance to look at this book on your own, try to retell the story. Watch how I do that by looking at the pictures." Proceed to retell the story using the pictures and your memory of the words.

An intervention known as **dialogic reading** is a well-researched approach to reading aloud that is designed to stimulate oral language and dialogue while enhancing students' ability to retell stories (Doyle & Bramwell, 2006; Whitehurst, Arnold, Epstein, Angell, Smith, & Fischel, 1994). Studies of dialogic reading have demonstrated growth in expressive and receptive language when used by parents and teachers of at-risk preschoolers (Justice & Pullen, 2003; NELP, 2008). Instructional guidelines to enhance students' ability to retell stories through questioning, modeling, and recitation are described in Activity 4.2 at the end of this chapter. You might find that they are even happier to do a retelling when they can record themselves and listen to it afterward.

Use dramatic play to act out stories or parts of stories under adult direction to get lots of children actively involved as actors or audience. Brainstorm with children about which characters are needed and what each one will do, and then walk through the dramatization by posing questions and prompting oral responses. You can also stimulate retellings by supplying props like puppets, flannel board cutouts, objects used in the story (such as three bowls for the three bears), or plastic figures. Stick puppets are easy to make by simply copying pictures of characters or objects from the book, adding some color, cutting around them, and gluing them to popsicle sticks. After modeling the use of props or puppets as a group activity, they can be placed in a center or made available during free time.

CONCEPT SORTS. The human mind appears to work by using compare-and-contrast categorization to develop concepts and relationships among objects and attributes. By recognizing similarities among items, it is possible to create groups or categories according to meaningful associations, the foundation of critical thinking (Gillet & Kita, 1979). The ability to categorize demonstrates maturing hierarchical and associative thinking, but needs to be coupled with conversation about why and how objects and pictures are being categorized (Carpenter, 2010). **Concept sorts** can be used at all levels of development as children categorize objects, pictures, words, or phrases.

Concept sorts can develop deeper understanding about words and how they relate to other words within a semantic field. For example, most 5-year-olds know about tables, chairs, sofas, beds, ovens, refrigerators, microwaves, and blenders, but in their minds, these may be all undifferentiated "things in a house." Teachers can help to expand students' understanding of "things in a house" by introducing two different conceptual categories—*furniture* (tables, chairs, sofas, and beds) and *appliances* (refrigerators, ovens, microwaves, and blenders). Discussion can focus on how appliances are different from furniture, such as the fact that appliances require "electricity" and need to be plugged into "receptacles." Basic concept development tasks are a surprisingly simple way to expand students' word knowledge, and they are also a good way to engage English learners and get them involved in verbal interactions (Bear & Helman, 2004).

You can use concept sorts to extend interactive read-alouds and provide additional exposure to new vocabulary. For example, after listening to Ruth Heller's book *Chickens Aren't the Only Ones*, provide children with picture cards to sort into groups of birds, mammals, and reptiles. In this way, they build on a simple conceptual understanding of where eggs come from to include other attributes of the animal kingdom. Concept sorts based on daily life experiences and information gleaned from books develop and expand students' understandings of their world and the language to talk about it. For example, during a unit on animals, you can introduce children to a concept sort such as the one shown in Figure 4.7.

The concept sorts described in the activities section of this chapter are all variations on the theme of categorization tasks. In addition to basic sorting, concept development activities are generally followed by draw-and-label or cut-and-paste procedures, as described in Chapter 3. As always, we recommend having children write at every possible opportunity during or following the concept sorts. For example, as a culminating activity for a unit on animals, one kindergarten teacher helped her children create their own books in which they drew pictures of their favorite animals. When asked to label these pictures or write briefly about the animals, her children's efforts ranged from random letters to readable approximations such as "I LIK THE LINS N TGRS."

To provide additional practice saying and hearing new words, encourage children to name the pictures as they sort and to justify their placements as they describe their categories ("Why did you put a bear with the wild animals?"). If the pictures used in concept sorts reflect words that are new to students, they need to be explicitly taught. It is important to talk about

for Words Their Way®

Work and Play, Clothes and Body Parts, Creatures, and Transportation
Four prepared concept sorts are ready to print.

FIGURE 4.7   **Concept Sort for Wild Animals and Pets**

for **English Learners**

MONITORING
PROGRESS

the meanings of words and use them it repeatedly each time they appear in sorting. It might be an opportune time to discuss the meaning of *claw* or *hoof* when sorting pictures of birds and animals. English learners may need to learn the names of more common objects, like *bird* or *cow*.

ASSESSING AND MONITORING VOCABULARY GROWTH. Use instructional activities that extend interactive read-alouds, such as retellings and concept sorts, to measure progress in students' vocabulary growth. Note increases in word use or tally the number of ideas, facts, or concepts children express when retelling or explaining the sort. Retell assessments are authentic, valid, and reliable means of assessing understanding (Fuchs, Fuchs, & Maxwell, 1988). Noting the number of objects, pictures, or items correctly sorted into conceptual categories also yields a reliable means of assessing depth of receptive vocabulary (Ward, 2009). Other developmentally appropriate ways of assessing receptive vocabulary growth in emergent learners include pointing to pictures that answer direct questions (e.g., "Which picture is the veterinarian?") or answering sets of yes/no questions (e.g., "Is an acorn a seed?" "Do plants grow from seeds?" "Do all seeds look the same?").

Phonological Awareness

The ability to pay attention to, identify, and reflect on various sound segments of speech is known as **phonological awareness (PA)**. It is the umbrella term for a range of understandings about speech sounds, including syllables, rhyme, and a sense of alliteration. **Phonemic awareness** is a subcategory of phonological awareness and refers to the ability to identify and reflect on the smallest units of sound: individual phonemes. The ability to segment *sit* or *thick* into three sounds (/s/-/i/-/t/ or /th/-/i/-/ck/) is an example of phonemic awareness. Children can hear and use individual phonemes easily at a tacit level—they can talk and can understand when others talk to them. But it is not easy to bring tacit, subconscious awareness of abstract individual phonemes to the surface to be examined consciously and explicitly.

Phonological awareness and phonemic awareness are widely identified as critical understandings needed to progress in literacy (Ball & Blachman, 1988; Ehri & Roberts, 2006; National Reading Panel, 2000). This is because children need a certain amount of phonemic awareness to grasp the alphabetic nature of English; understanding beginning sounds will get them started. Thereafter, phonemic awareness, word recognition, decoding, and spelling continue to develop in a symbiotic fashion. Growth in one area stimulates growth in another (Ehri, 2006; Morris et al., 2003; Perfetti, Beck, Bell, & Hughes, 1987).

Phonological awareness develops gradually over time and progresses from a sensitivity to big chunks of speech sounds, such as syllables and rhyme, to smaller parts of speech sounds, such as individual phonemes (Pufpaff, 2009; Pullen & Justice, 2003; Ziegler & Goswami, 2005). Early emergent learners might participate in phonological awareness activities that focus attention on syllables and rhyming words, whereas middle emergent learners may also easily grasp alliteration by sorting pictures that begin with the same sound. Find opportunities throughout the day to talk about a variety of speech units—have children line up by the number of syllables in their own name or listen for the beginning sound in the title of a book. As you draw children's attention to units of sound, familiarize them with terms such as *word*, *rhyme*, *syllable*, and *beginning sound*.

Using a variety of instructional strategies that are identified as successful and effective, phonological awareness activities can be engaging whole-group language activities that benefit all students (Blachman, 1994, 2000; Lundberg, Frost, & Peterson, 1988; Smith, Simmons, & Kame'enui, 1995). These activities need not be conducted as isolated tasks, nor do they need to take up a lot of time. According to some estimates, an entire year of phonemic awareness instruction need not exceed 20 hours (Armbruster, Lehr, & Osborn, 2001). The activity section of this chapter has many suggestions, and additional resources are listed in Resource Connections below.

RESOURCE CONNECTIONS

Resources for Teaching Phonological Awareness

Adams, M. J., Foorman, B. A., Lundberg, I., & Beeler, T. (1998). *Phonemic awareness in young children.* Baltimore, MD: Paul H. Brookes.

Blevins, W. (1997). *Phonemic awareness activities for early reading success.* New York: Scholastic.

Ericson, L., & Juliebo, M. F. (1998). *The phonological awareness handbook for kindergarten and primary teachers.* Newark, DE: International Reading Association.

Fitzpatrick, J. (1998). *Phonemic awareness: Playing with sounds to strengthen beginning reading skills.* Cypress, CA: Creative Teaching Press.

Opitz, M. F. (2000). *Rhymes and reasons: Literature and language play for phonological awareness.* Portsmouth, NH: Heinemann.

Yopp, H. K., & Yopp, R. E. (2000). *Oo-pples and boo-noo-noos.* Portsmouth, NH: Heinemann.

Children achieve partial phonemic awareness at the very end of the emergent phase of literacy development when they can isolate consonant sounds at the beginnings (and sometimes ends) of words and syllables. They develop full phonemic awareness during the letter name–alphabetic stage as they learn to separate all the sounds in a word, including blends and medial vowels (/s/-/t/-/ĕ/-/p/). We can see the development of phonemic awareness in children's spelling of *slide* as it moves from partial (S or SD) to developing (SID or SLD) to full (SLID). The following sections discuss different aspects of phonological awareness. You can find related activities for each in the activity section (4.8 to 4.19) at the end of the chapter, and at the PALS website of the University of Virginia.

SYLLABLES AND WORDS. Young children are concrete thinkers, so it is not surprising that they associate the length of a word with the size of its referent. Although *caterpillar* is a fairly long word, it refers to a relatively small insect, and so young children may think the word *caterpillar* is smaller than the word *cat*, because cats are bigger than caterpillars (Papandropoulou & Sinclair, 1974; Templeton & Spivey, 1980). This is no "small" confusion because to learn to read it is necessary to pay attention to the word's sound independently of its meaning.

Building phonological sensitivity in young children is complicated by the fact that words are made up of more than one syllable. A first step in leading children to an awareness of spoken words as a unit is to take two concrete "short" words and make them into one "long" *compound word* (e.g., *snow*, *man*, *snowman*). Although the emphasis in building phonological sensitivity is on the sounds of words, there can be a productive interplay between sound and meaning.

for Words Their Way®

Learning About Rhyme
Watch how Jackie introduces rhyme to preschoolers. Prepared rhyme sorts are available.

RHYMES, JINGLES, AND SONGS. Rhyme awareness activities are an easy, natural way for children to play with words and to begin to focus on speech sounds. Songs, jingles, nursery rhymes, and poems fill students' ears with the sounds of rhyme. Many children develop a sense of rhyme easily, whereas others need more structured activities that draw their attention specifically to rhyming words. The first step is to talk about the rhyming words in favorite and familiar books, songs, and poems. Some lend themselves to an activity in which you simply pause and let the children supply the second rhyming word in a couplet. A picture book such as *Is Your Mama a Llama?* by Deborah Guarina or *"I Can't," said the Ant* by Polly Cameron have illustrations and clues to help children name the rhyme. Some other favorite rhyming books are listed in the activities section at the end of this chapter.

You can follow rhyming book read-alouds with picture sorts for rhymes. For example, an extension to *"I Can't," said the Ant* is matching pictures of objects named in the book with other rhyming pictures. To make it easier for beginners, lay out just two pictures that rhyme along with one that does not. This odd-one-out setup, shown in Figure 4.8, enables children to identify more readily the two rhyming pictures.

FIGURE 4.8 Odd-One-Out with Rhyming Words

Songs are naturally full of rhythm and rhyme and hold great appeal for children. Several songs recorded by Raffi, a popular singer and songwriter for children, are particularly well suited for language play. For example, rhyme features prominently in the song "Willoughby Wallaby Woo" from the collection *Singable Songs for the Very Young*. The song features a rhyme starting with *W* for everyone's name and can be easily adapted for the children in your class. Sing the initiating phrase, changing the first letter of a name to *W* ("Willoughby Wallaby Wackie"), then children sing the next phrase, naming the appropriate classmate ("An elephant sat on Jackie"). You can pass a stuffed elephant to the child to add to the fun. Change the song to focus on alliteration by holding up a particular letter to insert in front of every word. *B*, for example, results in "Billaby Ballaby Boo," and *F* produces "Fillaby Fallaby Foo."

English learners may not understand rhyming in English. In Spanish, for example, rhyming focuses on the stress and vowels in words of more than one syllable, whereas in English rhyming focuses more on one-syllable word endings. Expect that developing a sense of rhyme in English may take a little longer to master for English learners than native speakers.

for **English Learners**

As children become more adept at listening for rhymes, they can play a variety of sorting and matching games. Traditional games such as Bingo, Lotto, and Concentration, in which picture cards are matched to other picture cards that rhyme, are always winners.

ALLITERATION AND BEGINNING SOUNDS. Children must become aware that speech can be divided into smaller segments of sound—phonemic awareness—before they will advance in literacy. They must also learn some of the terminology used to talk about these sounds. Without this knowledge, instruction in phonics will have little success. Children have no trouble hearing sounds, but directions such as "Listen for the first sound" may mystify them. In response to the question, "What sound does *cow* start with?" one puzzled child tentatively replied, "Moo?" Without a stable concept of word in text, "first sound" is a relative notion. Use phonological awareness activities at the emergent level to help children attend to sounds, and learn to label and categorize these sounds in various ways.

Activities that play with **alliteration** focus students' attention on the beginning sounds. Start with ABC books such as *Dr. Seuss's ABC*, which celebrates alliteration in the famous Seuss style. Play beginning-sound games with puppets or stuffed animals. Use games such as I Spy or I'm Thinking of Something to accentuate the initial sound. "This thing I'm thinking of begins with *mmmmm*. This thing is small and gray. It is an animal." As the children respond "mouse" or "mole," ask them to exaggerate the beginning sound. As children become proficient at playing this game, they create their own riddles.

Alliteration is further developed as children sort pictures by beginning sound under a corresponding letter, an activity that will be described in detail shortly. At this point, oral language activities designed to teach phonemic awareness cross over into learning letter–sound correspondences, or phonics.

ASSESSING AND MONITORING PHONOLOGICAL AWARENESS. You can find a collection of assessments that cover different aspects of phonological awareness at the PD Toolkit: syllable, rhyme, and phonemic awareness of initial consonants (alliteration). In general, a score of 80 percent is considered sufficient mastery of a task.

Phonological awareness tasks similar to these have been scientifically validated by Invernizzi and her colleagues, with thousands of children screened in Virginia with Phonological Awareness Literacy Screening (PALS) assessments at the preschool and kindergarten levels (Invernizzi et al., 2006). Monitoring the development of phonological awareness during kindergarten helps to identify children who need additional instruction.

PD **pd** TOOLKIT™

for Words Their Way®

Syllable Sort, Rhyme Identification, Beginning Sounds, and Alliteration These and other assessments for the emergent stage are ready to print.

MONITORING
PROGRESS

Alphabet Knowledge

Among the reading readiness skills that are traditionally studied, letter naming appears to be the strongest predictor of later reading success (NELP, 2008; Snow, Burns, & Griffin, 1998). There is a great deal to learn about the alphabet. Letters have names, a set sequence, sounds, and upper- and lowercase forms. They must be written in particular ways, and directional orientation is vital. In the three-dimensional world, a chair is a chair whether you approach it from the front or the back, from the left or the right. Not so with letters: A *b* is a *b* and a *d* is a *d*. Print is one of the few things in life in which direction makes a difference and young children lack this directionality. They also confuse letters that share visual features: *S* may be mistaken for *Z*, *E* for *F*, *h* for *n*, and so forth (Clay, 1975; Ehri & Roberts, 2006). In addition, children must learn to recognize the distinguishing but stable characteristics of letters across different fonts, sizes, shapes, and textures, as shown in Figure 4.9. Children form an abstract concept of *B* from seeing such variations and encountering *B* in many contexts.

FIGURE 4.9 **Different Print Styles**

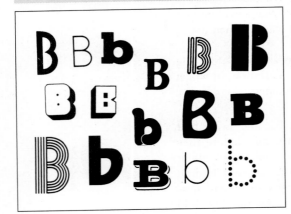

Learning the names of the letters is an important first step toward learning the sounds associated with the letters. Most of the letters have names that include a sound commonly associated with it and can serve as mnemonic devices for remembering the sounds (Huang, Tortorelli & Invernizzi, 2014; Kim, Petscher, Foorman, & Zhou, 2010). *B* (bee), *K* (kay), and *Z* (zee) have their sounds at the beginnings of their names, whereas *F* (eff), *L* (ell), and *S* (ess) have their sounds at the end. The names of the vowels are their long sounds. Only *H* (aitch), *W* (doubleyou), and the consonant *Y* (wie) have no sound association, and not surprisingly these letters are often the most difficult to learn. Letter names serve as the first reference point many children use when writing and explain some of the interesting invented spellings they create during the letter name–alphabetic stage, discussed more in the next chapter.

Most mainstream middle-class children take five years to acquire all this alphabet knowledge at home and in preschool. Magnetic letters on the refrigerator door, alphabetic puzzles, and commercial alphabet games are staples in many middle-class homes (Adams, 1990). There is also an increasingly broad range of apps many parents use to develop alphabet and letter–sound knowledge. Truly advantaged children also have attentive parents at the kitchen table, modeling letter formation and speech segmentation as they encourage their child to write a grocery list or a note to Grandma; others have less preparation. The best way to share five years of accumulated alphabet knowledge with children who have not had these experiences is to teach it directly, in as naturalistic, fun, and game like a manner as possible (Delpit, 1988).

for Words Their Way®

Font Sorts
Ready to use font sorts with directions are available for emergent learners.

TEACHING THE ALPHABET. The alphabet is learned the same way that concepts and words for concepts are learned—through actively exploring the relationships between letter names, the sounds of the letter names, their visual characteristics, and the motor movement involved in their formation. Alphabet games and activities are designed to develop all aspects of alphabet knowledge, including letter naming, letter recognition (both uppercase and lowercase), letter writing, and letter sounds. Many alphabet activities begin with the child's name—building it with letter tiles, cutting it out of play dough, or matching it letter for letter with a second set. Writing or copying their own names and the names of other family members or friends is alluring to emergent writers, making a great introduction to the alphabet as well as to writing. Letters take on personalities: *M* is Manuel's letter and *T* is Tonisha's letter.

The following list provides some general routines for teaching children about the forms and functions of the alphabet. See the Activities 4.20–4.30 at the end of this chapter for more detail, as well as games that include traditional formats like Bingo and Concentration.

- Teach the letter sequence by singing the alphabet song daily until children know it by heart. In addition, point to the letters as they sing and then give children a copy of the alphabet strip so they can practice pointing and finding letters as they are named.
- Share alphabet books with students, pointing out the capital and lowercase forms and naming the pictures that begin with a letter. Children typically learn capital letters first, but by kindergarten lowercase letters are needed; teach them together along with the sounds associated with them.
- Make alphabet books available for children to explore on their own but model for children how to use them independently: "Here is the capital *B* and the lowercase *b*. *Bear* and *bowl* begin with *b*." (See a list of alphabet books in the activity section.)
- Children's names provide a meaningful context for studying specific letters (Cunningham, 2005). Studying a name each day is a more appropriate pace than letter of the week in kindergarten classrooms (see Activity 4.23). Children should use their names to participate in daily activities, such as signing in each day for attendance and lunch choices, or signing up for centers or popular tasks like feeding the fish. Start by providing preprinted name cards but move toward expecting children to write out their names.

- Point out letters on signs, in book titles, on charts, and all around the school. The modern world is full of letters, but you need to draw students' attention to them and name them. When you read and write with children there are endless opportunities to talk about letters; this helps them understand the many functions letters serve.
- Create an alphabet center where children have access to puzzles and games that change on a regular basis. Also, provide an alphabet strip and a variety of writing implements (markers, chalk, rubber stamps) and surfaces (paper, card stock, chalkboards, whiteboards, Magna Doodles, etc.) to encourage children to write and form their letters. Handwriting is an important and often neglected component of early literacy instruction (Graham, Harris, & Fink, 2000). Teach children how to write the letters and provide various ways to create letters out of clay, pipe cleaners, or cookie dough. Have children trace textured letters, make letters in trays filled with sand, or glue down rice, pasta, or beans in the shapes of letters. When teaching letter formation, be consistent about spatial matters such as where to start and directionality. Have children vocalize these movements as they form their letters (e.g., "up, down, up, down" for *M*; "around" for *O*) and also repeat the letter names as they trace them.

ASSESSING AND MONITORING GROWTH IN ALPHABET KNOWLEDGE. Use a variety of tasks to determine how much instruction is needed for learning letters. Ask children to point to and recite the letters in order as a first step. Watch how they handle *LMNOP*—because of the way these letters are sung in the alphabet song, sometimes they become one letter! Present upper- and lowercase letters in random order to assess letter recognition; alphabet recognition assessments are included on the PDToolkit website. You can easily assess letter production by calling out letters, in or out of order, for children to write. According to research conducted with hundreds of thousands of kindergartners in Virginia, kindergartners are able to recognize and name an average of 20 lowercase letters, presented in random order in the fall of the year and nearly all of them by the end of kindergarten (Invernizzi et al., 2006). Longitudinal research suggests that kindergarten children who name fewer than 12 lowercase letters in the fall of the year would benefit from additional instruction to prevent falling further behind. Alphabet learning is easy to monitor; assess children regularly to plan instruction for those who are not making progress.

MONITORING
PROGRESS

Letter–Sound Knowledge and Phonics

During the emergent stage, children learn their letters, develop phonemic awareness, and begin to make connections between letters and sounds as they come to understand the alphabetic principle in spelling. Toward the end of the emergent stage, many children will begin producing partial phonetic spellings that contain one or two letters for each syllable (see Figure 4.3, page 94). Sorting pictures by beginning sounds secures these tentative efforts and moves children along in acquiring more knowledge of letter–sound correspondences through a game like, manipulative phonics activity.

Letters such as *M* and *S* are appropriate for students' first consonant contrast because both letters have **continuant** sounds that can be isolated and elongated without undue distortion (*mmmmoon* and *sssssun*). The sounds also feel very different in the mouth during **articulation**, which makes it easier for children to judge the categories while sorting. The sound for *B* (/b/) cannot be elongated or isolated without adding a vowel to it (*buh*), but it is still fairly easy to learn, perhaps because it has a distinctive feel as the lips press together and also because it is one of the earliest consonantal phonemes acquired during oral language development (Pense & Justice, 2008). However, contrasting *B* and *P* in an early sort is confusing because they are both articulated or produced the same way (Purcell, 2002). The only difference is that the /b/ sound causes the vocal cords to vibrate whereas /p/ does not. Try placing two fingers on your larynx and feel the difference in **voiced** /b/ and **unvoiced** /p/ as you say *bay* and *pay*.

Table 4.2 shows a pronunciation chart of consonants. Read across each row saying the sound of the letter (i.e., /p/, /b/, /m/) to see how those sounds share the same place of articulation (i.e., lips together). Compare the voiced and unvoiced pairs such as /f/ and /v/ or /t/ and /d/.

TABLE 4.2 Pronunciation Chart of Consonant Sounds

Unvoiced	Voiced	Nasals	Other	Place of Articulation
p	b	m		lips together
wh	w			lips rounded
f	v			teeth and lips
th (thin)	th (the)			tip of tongue and teeth
t	d	n	l	tip of tongue and roof of mouth
s	z			tongue and roof of mouth
sh			y	sides of tongue and teeth
ch	j		r	sides of tongue and roof of mouth
k	g	ng		back of tongue and throat
h				no articulation—breathy sound

Notice how the nasal sounds of /m/, /n/, and /ng/ pass through the nose rather than the mouth. As teachers, learning about articulation may seem unnecessarily complicated, but it explains so many of the interesting things children do in their invented spellings during the emergent and letter name–alphabetic stages. Use the chart to see the logic in the invented spelling JP for *chip*, VN for *fan*, and PD for *pet*. In each case, the substitutions vary only because one is voiced and the other is unvoiced. Otherwise, they are articulated exactly the same way. Knowing about articulation helps you make decisions about setting up picture sorts. The letters in any row will feel very much alike and are best not contrasted in the very first letter–sound sorts. Remember the principle of word study highlighted in Chapter 3—begin with obvious contrasts!

English learners are often unfamiliar with many of the sounds of English and will substitute sounds and letters closest to their primary languages and alphabets. They will not articulate some sounds at first, but their substitutions are logical. For example, Spanish speakers may use the letter *v* to represent the /b/ sound because these sounds are the same in Spanish. The logic behind the misspellings of English learners was discussed in Chapter 2, and more detail will be provided in Chapter 5.

for **English Learners**

GUIDELINES FOR BEGINNING SOUND PICTURE SORTS. There are a number of factors to keep in mind when organizing sorts for beginning letter sounds.

- *Start with meaningful text.* Choose several sounds to contrast that represent key words from a familiar rhyme, patterned book (such as C and M from *Cat on the Mat*), or dictation.
- *Make sorts easier or harder as needed.* Start with two obvious contrasts and then add one or two for up to four categories. Look for fast and accurate picture sorting before moving on. Be ready to drop back to fewer categories if a child has difficulty.
- *Use a key picture and a letter as headers.* Using a key picture and a letter as a header helps children associate the letter and the sound. The headers may be letters or words selected from familiar text. Suggestions for key pictures are on the sound boards in Appendix B. Whatever key word you select, be consistent and use the same one every time.
- *Begin with teacher-directed sorts.* Discuss both the sound and the letter name, and model the placement of two or three pictures in each category. Be explicit about why you sort the way you do. Say, for example, "Map, mmmmap, mmmat. *Map* and *mat* start with the same sound. I will put map under the letter *M*." Over time, as children catch on to what it is you want them to do, you can use fewer directives. The opening photo on page 90 shows how a sort would look after sorting. You can find pictures for sorting in Appendix C; these can be enlarged for group modeling.

- *Use sets of pictures that are easy to name and sort.* Introduce the picture names to be sure that children know what to call them. Use easily identified pictures that do not start with consonant blends or digraphs. Single-syllable words are better than two-syllable words because they have fewer sounds that need attention.
- *Correct mistakes on the first sort but allow errors to wait on subsequent sorts.* Show children how to check their sorts by naming the pictures down the columns, emphasizing the beginning sounds. Then ask if there are any pictures that need to be changed. Tell children to check their own work using the same process and praise them when they find their own errors. If they do not, prompt them by saying, "There is a picture in this row that needs to be changed. Can you find it?"
- *Vary the group sorting.* Start by putting out all the pictures face-up and let children choose one that they feel confident in naming and sorting correctly. Ask them to name the picture and the letter by saying, "_____ begins with the _____ sound and goes under the letter _____." Another time, pass out the pictures and call on children to come up and sort the card they were given. Then turn the pictures face-down in a stack or spread them out on the floor and let children turn over the picture they will sort. Children enjoy the anticipation of not knowing which picture they will get.
- *Plan plenty of time for individual practice.* After group modeling and discussion, put sets of pictures in centers or create copies of picture sets for children to cut apart for more sorting. Create sheets of pictures for sorting by copying pictures from this book, cutting them apart, and pasting them in a mixed-up fashion on a template.
- *Plan follow-up activities.* Cut-and-paste, draw-and-label, and word hunts through familiar chart stories, nursery rhymes, or little books are helpful follow-up activities. They require children to recognize, or recall, the same beginning sounds and to judge whether they fit the category.
- *Encourage pretend writing and invented spelling.* In the process of inventing spellings, children exercise their developing phonics knowledge in a meaningful activity (Clarke, 1988; NRP, 2000; Snow et al., 1998). To get children started, demonstrate how to use letters to represent sounds as you write with children during interactive writing (see the Morning Message described in Activity 4.38). Asking children to label their drawings or to write just a sentence about something is a good way to get writing started (see Figure 4.6).

ASSESSING AND MONITORING GROWTH IN LETTER–SOUND KNOWLEDGE. There are several ways to assess students' abilities to match beginning consonant sounds to the appropriate letters. The first step is observing children to see how quickly and accurately they sort. Then monitor children's daily writing efforts using invented spelling for ongoing and authentic assessment. The Emergent Class Record found on the PDToolkit helps you analyze children's writing across the emergent stage. There is also a Beginning Consonant Sounds and Letters assessment on the website that asks children to circle a picture that begins with a given letter. A simple five-word spelling assessment such as the Kindergarten Spelling Inventory (KSI), also found on the website, is particularly appropriate for late emergent spellers. You might also call out five of the words on the Primary Spelling Inventory described in Chapter 2.

Assess children formally at least three times a year, and informally all the time using daily writing. For children receiving additional instructional interventions, we recommend more frequent monitoring to gauge their progress (Invernizzi, 2009). Longitudinal research indicates that kindergarten children should be aware that letters are associated with speech sounds and be able to provide at least four letter sounds in the fall of the year and at least 20 letter sounds in the spring (Invernizzi et al., 2005) in order to succeed without additional instruction or intervention. On average, kindergartners can accurately produce 14 letter sounds in the fall and nearly all of them in the spring (Invernizzi et al., 2014).

Concepts about Print (CAP)

Children are surrounded by print on signs, package labels, magazines, computers, and television, even on the clothes they wear; however, children need adults to talk about the purposes print serves and the special ways in which the visual forms of print are organized.

PD TOOLKIT™
for Words Their Way®

Beginning Sounds: Alliteration, Assessment of Beginning Consonant Sounds and Letters and **Kindergarten Spelling Inventory**
These three emergent assessment tools are ready to use.

MONITORING
PROGRESS

For example, when you print the words to "Where Is Thumbkin?" on chart paper and point to them as the children sing along, you are helping them understand concepts of print. It happens when you stop to point out the X in the exit sign and explain what it means. It happens when you show a book cover and remind children that they have heard other stories written and illustrated by Tomie dePaola. The key is to be conscious of the many ways we use print and to "think aloud" as we draw children's attention to it in explicit ways. Justice and Ezell (2004) call this **print referencing**.

PRINT REFERENCING. When you use a print referencing style during shared read-alouds, such as naming and pointing out letters or asking questions about print and pointing to words as they read, children show growth on measures of concepts about print, letter recognition, and name writing (Justice, Kaderavek, Fan, Sofka, & Hunt, 2009). Reading with children during interactive or shared reading and writing with children during interactive writing and as you take dictations, provides abundant opportunities to develop concepts about print. Table 4.3 provides a list of the functions and forms of print and offers examples of print referencing that you might use.

TABLE 4.3 CAP and Print Referencing Examples

Functions of Print	Print Referencing During Reading and Writing
Print is speech written down and once written down it does not change	I'm going to write down what you say and then we can read it back.
Print is different from illustrations	You look at the picture while I read what it says over here.
Print carries a message	Here are the words to "Humpty Dumpty." Can you find the box that says "scissors"?
Print serves many purposes	Here is the recipe for cookies. Let's read and find out what ingredients we need.

Forms of Print	Print Referencing During Reading and Writing
Book-handling skills—Start with the cover and turn from front to back	Let's look at the cover of the book to see what it is about.
Directionality—Print is oriented left to right with a return sweep and top to bottom	This is the top of the page where I will start reading. Then I will go to the next line. Show me where to go next.
Language related to units of print—Letters (capital and lowercase), numbers, words, sentences, lines	There are four letters in this word. Let's name them. The first letter is a capital because it is a person's name.
Language related to books—Title, author, illustrator, title page, dedication, poem, song, beginning, end	We have read another book by this author. Where do we look for the author's name?
Language related to phonological sensitivity—Syllable, sound, beginning and ending sound	This is a long word. Let's clap the syllables in *caterpillar*. Can this word be *rug*? What is the first sound in *rug*?
Punctuation and special print—Periods, question marks, exclamation marks, quotation marks, bold print, italics	Listen to how I read this sentence. It ends with an exclamation point so I want it to make it sound exciting.
Concept of word—Words are composed of a string of letters; words are separated by spaces	Watch while I point to the words in this sentence. We need to leave a space here before we write the next word.
Word identification—Words can be identified in different contexts	Here is the word *cat*. Can you find the word again on this page? What will you look for?

Source: Adapted from Justice et al., 2009.

Reference specific print forms and functions during tasks that encourage children to write their own names, such as sign-up procedures. When you incorporate print into dramatic play centers such as restaurants, doctors' offices, and so on, children use writing as they pretend to be waiters writing down a dinner order, doctors writing a prescription, and the like. In the process, they learn that print takes many forms and serves many functions. You can find some specific activities (4.35 to 4.38) at the end of this chapter.

ASSESSING AND MONITORING GROWTH IN CAP. Marie Clay (1985) first developed a formal protocol for assessing concepts about print using a series of questions while sharing a book with a child. Many variations of this exist; in fact, state and local standards for early literacy may include a checklist of questions regarding children's development in CAP. You can also see concepts about print in children's efforts to write their names. Their efforts, which may range from scribbles to letter-like forms mixed with numbers to recognizable signatures, can predict later literacy achievement (Welsch, Sullivan, & Justice, 2003). We provide several assessments on the PDToolkit that help you interpret name writing and other writing. There is also a Concepts about Print sort and a checklist to use as you share a book. Concepts about print can be informally assessed all the time as you read and write with children by posing questions such as "Who can point to a capital letter *D*?" or "What do we put at the end of a sentence?"

Concept of Word in Text (COW-T)

The ultimate concept about print is achieving a concept of word in text (COW-T)—the ability to fingerpoint or track accurately to printed words in text while reading from memory. Reaching this milestone depends on a student's ability to isolate the beginning consonant sounds of spoken words and knowledge of letter–sound correspondences—skills that help the beginning reader find words on the page. Incorporating concept of word activities into daily literacy practice not only strengthens students' speech-to-print matching, but it also solidifies their alphabet knowledge, emerging phonemic awareness, and knowledge of words in print. Prior to achieving a concept of word in text, emergent children, as well as emergent adults, have great difficulty identifying individual phonemes within words (Morais, Cary, Alegria, & Bertelson, 1979). There is an interaction between alphabetic knowledge, the ability to match speech to print, and phonemic awareness (Flanigan, 2007; Morris et al., 2003; Tunmer, 1991). However, achieving a concept of word in text is not an all-or-nothing affair—there is a developmental continuum.

The concept of word continuum includes *developing*, *rudimentary*, and *firm* levels. During the emergent stage, learners move from the developing level to a rudimentary concept of word. Children with a firm concept of word in text are letter name–alphabetic spellers, described in the next chapter. To determine where your children are on the concept of word continuum, examine the accuracy of their fingerpoint reading to memorized rhymes and jingles, their ease with identifying words in context, and their ability to remember words in isolation that were viewed previously in context (Blackwell-Bullock, Invernizzi, Drake, & Howell, 2009; Flanigan, 2007; Morris, 1993).

DEVELOPING COW-T. Children who are just developing a COW-T will have some orientation to the page, moving from the top to the bottom and linearly side to side (but perhaps not from left to right). What they point to on the page as they recite does not coincide with printed word units at all. The pre-literate child may point in a rhythmic approximation of the memorized text with little attention to word boundaries.

Through your demonstrations, students' fingerpointing behaviors change. Left-to-right movement becomes habitualized. As they note white spaces, children begin to track rhythmically across the text, pointing to words for each stressed beat. For example, when tracking the traditional five-word ditty, "Sam, Sam, the baker man," they may point four times: Sam/Sam/the-baker/man, as if keeping time on a drum. An article (*the*, *a*, *an*) may be treated as part of the noun that follows it.

RUDIMENTARY COW-T. As children become aware that print has something to do with sound units such as syllables, their fingerpointing becomes more precise and changes from a gross rhythm to a closer match. This rudimentary COW-T works well for one-syllable words, but not so well for words of two or more syllables. When they track "Sam, Sam, the baker man," they may now point six times: Sam/Sam/the/ba/ker/man. When they pronounce /ker/, the second syllable of *baker*, they point to the next word, *man*. Figure 4.10 illustrates the phenomenon of getting off track on two-syllable words.

As children learn the alphabet and the sounds associated with the letters, beginning sounds anchor their fingerpointing more directly to the memorized recitation. They realize that when they say the word *man*, they need to have their finger on a word beginning with an *m*. If they do not, then they must start again. These self-corrections mark the transition to a full COW-T where children point accurately. Figure 4.11 shows the progression of fingerpointing accuracy in relation to writing development during the emergent to early letter name–alphabetic stage of word knowledge. Children with a rudimentary COW-T will begin to remember a few written words. This is a sign that these children are on their way to becoming the beginning readers or the early letter name–alphabetic spellers described in the next chapter.

FINGERPOINT READING AND TRACKING WORDS. The best way for children to move from a developing to a rudimentary COW-T is to have them point to the words as they reread memorized text and to draw their attention to letters and sounds when they get off track. These texts might be picture captions, dictated experience stories, poems, songs, simple patterned books, or excerpts from a favorite story printed on sentence strips or chart paper. Rhythmic texts are particularly appealing to use when children are developing a COW-T but may throw them off in their tracking. Eventually moving to less rhythmic, less predictable texts may be in order (Cathey, 1991). Once these texts become familiar, encourage children to read them from memory, pointing to each word as it they say it. In this way, children learn how to find the words on the page—an important prerequisite to acquiring a sight vocabulary.

PICTURE CAPTIONS. One of the best ways to help children make connections between speech and print is to record what they say in a dictation and then to read it back. Picture captions are quick and easy forms of dictation.

- First, have the children draw a picture, such as their favorite toy or Halloween costume, and encourage them to include as much detail as possible.

FIGURE 4.10 Trying to Match Voice to Print

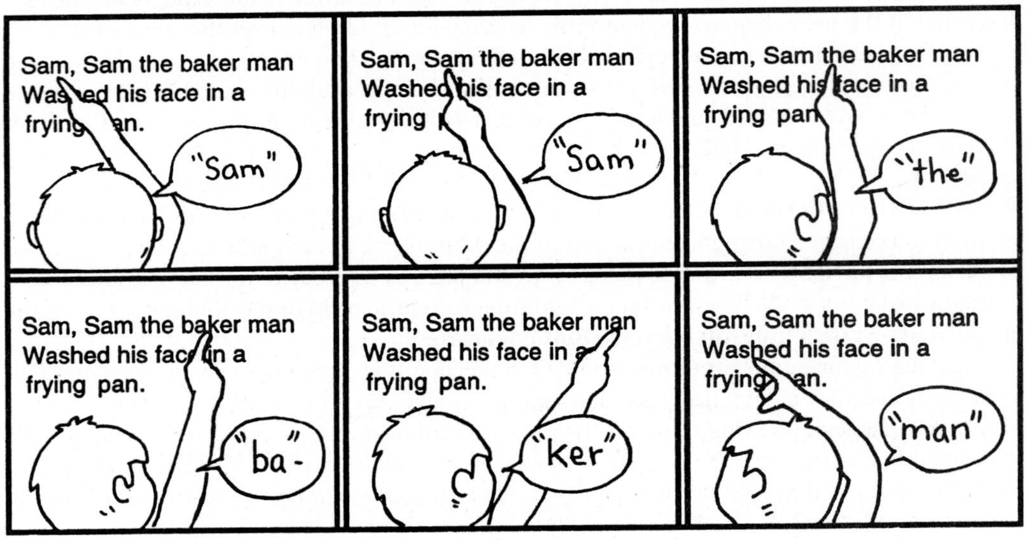

FIGURE 4.11 **Voice-to-Print Match in Relation to Spelling Development**

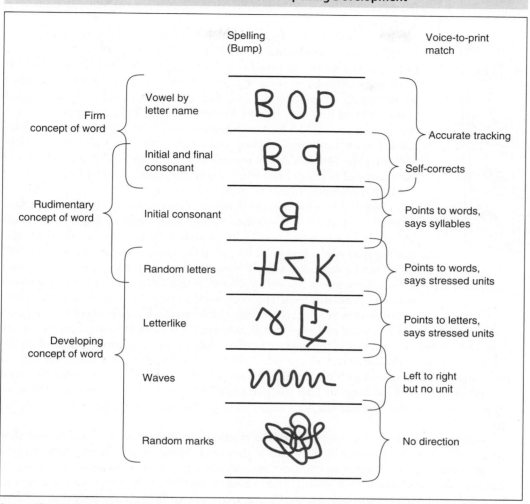

Spelling (Bump)

Voice-to-print match

Concept of word	Spelling type	Voice-to-print match
Firm concept of word	Vowel by letter name	Accurate tracking
	Initial and final consonant	Self-corrects
Rudimentary concept of word	Initial consonant	Points to words, says syllables
Developing concept of word	Random letters	Points to words, says stressed units
	Letterlike	Points to letters, says stressed units
	Waves	Left to right but no unit
	Random marks	No direction

Source: Gill (1992). Focus on research: Development of word knowledge as it relates to reading, spelling, and instruction. *Language Arts*, *69*, 6, 444–453. Adapted with permission.

- While they are finishing their drawings, walk around and ask each child to tell something about his or her picture. Choose a simple phrase or sentence from the description and write it verbatim beneath the picture (see Figure 4.12). Say each word as you write it, drawing attention to the sounds and letters and involving the child when appropriate with questions such as, "What sound do you hear first?"
- Read the caption by pointing to each word. Ask the child to read along with you and then to read it alone while pointing. Later, the child may attempt to reread the caption to a buddy.

Like picture captions, spoken or dictated accounts of students' experiences also help them link speech to print. This approach is traditionally referred to as the **language experience approach (LEA)**, and is described in more detail beginning on page 117.

RHYMES FOR READING. Familiar rhymes, songs, or jingles are easily memorized passages that children can use to model and practice

FIGURE 4.12 **Drawing with Dictated Caption**

This is a firetruck going to the house.

FIGURE 4.13 Rhymes for Reading

There was a little turtle.

He lived in a box.

He swam in the water.

He climbed on a rock.

fingerpointing in a shared reading format. This activity meets many of the common core state standards (CCSS Foundational Skills 1, 1.a–d, 2, 3, 3.a–c, 4).

It is important for children to first learn the rhyme, song, or jingle "by heart," because developing a COW-T is all about matching oral speech to print. It helps to use pictures for prompts, as shown in Figure 4.13. To teach your children to memorize the rhyme, point to each picture frame while singing or reciting the line that goes with it, repeating as needed. Some children may only be able to memorize two lines, whereas others can handle four or six. The Resource Connections box below has some printed resources for traditional rhymes and jingles. They can also be found by searching the Internet. Many nursery rhymes, songs, and jump rope jingles are illustrated in *Words Their Way*®: *Letter and Picture Sorts for Emergent Spellers* (Bear, Invernizzi, Johnston, & Templeton, 2010).

Once children memorize the rhyme, introduce it on chart paper printed in text large enough for everyone to see. Model how to fingerpoint "read" and invite children to "read" with you chorally (in unison) or using echo reading (you read a line, then they read the same line again, fingerpointing). If you used a song, it is time to slow it down and read it at this point. After at least three passes (modeling, choral, echo), call on children to fingerpoint read independently, touching each word as they say it. After several rounds of fingerpoint reading, see whether children can identify one or two targeted words per line. Point to a word and ask, "What's this word?" If a child doesn't know the word, show him or her how to start at the beginning of the line to reread or **voice point** up to the word in question. Alternatively, you can ask children to find a word in a particular line by providing a beginning sound: "I'm thinking of a word in this line that starts just like the word *ball*. What word am I thinking of? Can you point to it? How did you know that was the word I was thinking of? Yes! *Box* and *ball* both begin with the /b/ sound. They both begin with the letter *b!*"

Later, give children their own copy of the rhyme on a single sheet of paper so that they can get more practice pointing to the words as they read chorally and individually. You might also give them sentence strips to cut apart and rebuild the text, or individual word cards to match to the same words in context. When children have their own copies of the rhyme, they can highlight or underline the words you ask them to find. Add words that children remember without having to voice point to their beginning sound sorts. A detailed whole-to-part, five-day lesson plan for teaching a concept of word in text using memorable rhymes or jingles is described in Activity 4.39. Learners with limited English will benefit from practicing fingerpointing using materials in their primary languages. Rhymes and jingles in Spanish can be found in *Words Their Way*®: *Emergent Sorts for Spanish-Speaking English Learners* (Helman,

RESOURCE CONNECTIONS

Resources for Traditional Rhymes and Jingles

Cole, J. (1989). *Anna Banana: 101 jump-rope rhymes*. New York: Scholastic.

Cole, J., & Calmenson, S. (1990). *Miss Mary Mack and other children's street rhymes*. Illustrated by Alan Tiegreen. New York: Morrouno.

Ratisseau, S. (2014) *Jumping Joy: A book about jump rope rhymes*. Seattle, WA: Laughing Elephant

Schwartz, A. (1989). *I saw you in the bathtub*. New York: HarperCollins.

Sierra, J., & Sweet, M. (2005). *Schoolyard rhymes: Kids' own rhymes for rope jumping, hand clapping, ball bouncing, and just plain fun*. New York: Knopf.

Bear, Invernizzi, Templeton, & Johnston, 2009) and *Words Their Way®: Letter Name–Alphabetic Sorts for Spanish-Speaking English Learners* (Helman, Bear, Invernizzi, Templeton, & Johnston, 2009).

ASSESSING AND MONITORING GROWTH IN COW-T. You can easily assess concept of word in text by asking children to point to individual words in a familiar piece of text, such as a nursery rhyme or jump rope jingle. "One, Two, Buckle My Shoe" or "Humpty Dumpty" work well because they have words of more than one syllable. Observe how children point to words on the page, using the descriptors in Figure 4.11. After several rounds of fingerpoint reading, ask children to name the words that you point to in context or more randomly, as described previously, and observe their strategies. Do they reread an entire line and count up the memorized words to identify it? Or do they identify it immediately? Ask, "How did you find that word?" or "How did you know that word?" Children who can tell you that a word starts with a *w* are using developing letter–sound knowledge to track words in text. This is a necessary precursor to acquiring sight words, which is discussed in the next chapter. The COW-T assessment at the PDToolkit uses "Humpty Dumpty" to monitor progress toward achieving a COW-T.

The Language Experience Approach (LEA)

The five components of emergent literacy development—vocabulary, language, and concept development; phonological awareness; alphabet and letter–sound knowledge; concepts about print; and developing a COW-T—are all highly intercorrelated. One way to develop and integrate all of these components is through language-rich, hands-on experiences that engage students' attention and help them connect these abstract, decontextualized school-acquired concepts to everyday life. Teachers can write down accounts of these experiences and use them to develop emergent word knowledge, meeting many of the Common Core State Standards for Kindergarten (CCSS Foundational Skills 1,1.a-d, 2, 2.d, 3.a-c, Language 1, 1.a, 1.f, 2, 2.a-d).

The language experience approach (LEA) was developed by Stauffer (1980) and refined by Allen (1976) and others (Hall, 1980; Henderson, 1981; Nessel & Jones, 1981; Labbi, Eakle, & Montero, 2002). LEA is based on the premise that what you say can be written and what you write can be read. The motivation and engagement that results from using students' self-generated language has revitalized an interest in LEA, especially for emergent learners and for children learning English as another language (Dorr, 2006). Experience is the best teacher!

Field trips, cooking activities, playground events, and class pets provide opportunities for shared experiences in which new vocabulary and the students' own language abounds. Observations and comments can then be written next to each student's name during a group dictation, as shown in Figure 4.14, or children can dictate individual accounts. In an activity described by McCabe (1996) called "Tell a story to get a story," the teacher tells a simple two-to-three-sentence story and then asks the children if they know a similar story: "Has anything like that happened to you?" Children tell their own stories, which the teacher records as dictations.

Students' own language should be recorded as closely as possible so that they will be able to read it back. The child should approve any grammar corrections with prompts like, "Good idea, can we say it this way?" When the dictation is completed, it should be read and reread many times. With this format, attention to words and their boundaries can be highlighted in a meaningful context. For example, a child may be

FIGURE 4.14 Dictated Language Experience Chart

> The Fire Station
> Amanda said, "We went to the fire station yesterday."
> Jason said, "We rode on a big orange bus."
> Clint said, "I liked the ladder truck. It was huge!"
> D. J. said, "The firemen told us how to be safe."
> Beth said, "Firemen wear big boots and a mask."

asked to locate his or her own name in the group dictation or to find a word that starts with the same letter as his or her own name. Each child should get a personal copy of the dictation to practice fingerpointing while reading together chorally and from memory. These copies can be collected into a notebook called a *personal reader* (described in more detail in the next chapter). You can cut up a second copy of the dictation into sentence strips or individual words to match back to the original.

The steps for LEA whole-to-part teaching are as follows:

1. Plan a hands-on experience such as a simple science experiment or feeding a baby animal. Exchange thoughts and observations orally with the students. Introduce and use new vocabulary, then suggest writing down their ideas, calling on one child at a time.
2. Have the children dictate a narrative account of the experience and their observations while you record their statements on a chart—one statement per line for emergent learners. While writing, include print referencing. Shape the dictation into a coherent account as needed. For example, ask a child to hold an idea until later if it comes too early in a sequence of events.
3. Have children reread the dictated account several times chorally until it becomes very familiar. Then they get their own copy of the dictation to illustrate and practice voice pointing.
4. Use the dictation to develop concepts and vocabulary, alphabet knowledge, letter–sound correspondences, print concepts, and a concept of word in print.

Children in the late emergent stage with a rudimentary COW-T can begin to select words to include in a word bank of known words. Word banks are described in the next chapter.

WORD STUDY *Routines and Management*

The research in emergent literacy suggests that a comprehensive approach to instruction and early intervention is the most effective procedure (Pressley, 2006). A comprehensive approach includes attention to the six components of the emergent literacy "diet" described in this chapter. These essential components can be integrated into major organizational time units during which you *Read To*, *Read With*, *Write With*, do *Word Study*, and *Talk With* (RRWWT) children. During *read to* time, you read aloud literature that offers exposure to new vocabulary and literary language. During *read with* time, children engage in shared reading and rereading of familiar texts. When you model how to write by stretching out the sounds in words and matching them to letters, you are *writing with* children, who will, in turn, write for themselves. *Word study* includes direct instruction in phonological awareness, the alphabet, and letter sounds. Finally, a comprehensive program provides children with ample opportunities to *talk with* you and their peers about the books and experiences they have shared.

Combining these activities into a cohesive RRWWT routine is important so that the activities and materials flow together in a logical way and serve multiple purposes. Recall how Mrs. Smith introduced an engaging core book and used it to draw attention to letters and sounds, to highlight vocabulary, to offer children practice tracking familiar text, and to sort pictures by rhyme and beginning sounds. *Words Their Way*®: *Letter and Picture Sorts for Emergent Spellers* (Bear et al., 2010) offers examples of how these components can be integrated and provides prepared sorts as well as rhymes and jingles for reading.

Emergent Literacy Daily Management Plan

The daily management of emergent literacy instruction should include whole groups, small groups, and literacy centers, as outlined in Table 4.4. For example, in the video of Mrs. Smith with a whole group you can see her model fingerpoint reading and other concepts about print for the whole group, and then call a small group to introduce a picture sort of initial sounds

TABLE 4.4   **Emergent Literacy Plan**

Whole-Group Activities	Small-Group/Circle Time Differentiated Activities	Seat/Center Differentiated Activities
"Read To": Read-alouds for thematic units and vocabulary work Introduce concept sorts	Concept sorts Retelling and dramatization	Practice concept sorts Retell using picture books, puppets, etc.
"Read With": Shared reading of big books, rhymes, songs, dictations Memorize "whole" texts such as nursery rhymes and jingles	Reread familiar texts until memorized "Parts"—Work with sentence strips, word cards, etc.	Partner or individual work with sentences and words
"Word Study": Sing and recite alphabet Share alphabet and language play books Name of the Day	Introduce differentiated sorts: rhyme, font, initial consonants	Practice sorts Letter and sound hunts Games and puzzles for rhyme, alphabet, initial consonants
"Write With": Modeled and interactive writing Morning Message	Language experience dictations	Picture captions Draw and label Journal writing

Note: "Talk With" happens throughout all the activities.

that children later practiced independently. Working from a whole text, then with sentences, words, letters, and sounds, is known as the whole-to-part framework.

Whole-group activities emphasize reading to and with students, teacher modeling, listening, and vocabulary development. Print referencing opportunities arise with whole-group instruction. Read-alouds serve many purposes and you can plan two or more whole-group sessions during the day for emergent children where they listen to read-alouds from a variety of genres, including information books related to thematic studies, alphabet books, and books with language play such as rhyme. Use whole-group time to sing songs while pointing to the words, practice the alphabet song, model writing, and introduce shared reading activities designed to facilitate CAP and COW-T. This is where the "whole" of a whole-to-part model takes place, with some attention to the parts.

Children can participate actively under close supervision while in small groups or during circle time. This is when to implement differentiated instruction according to assessed needs. You can form small groups initially based on alphabet knowledge and phonological awareness but also on concept of word (developing vs. rudimentary). For example, some children will need to focus on alphabet recognition and look for letters in familiar texts, whereas children who already know their letters and have a rudimentary COW-T may be ready to acquire some sight words from repeated readings of familiar text. The small group is where the "parts" of the whole-to-part lesson format are addressed in depth, such as rhyming picture sorts or picture sorts for beginning sounds.

Independent work provides additional practice. Once children are introduced to activities and sorts in small groups, they can work independently, with partners, in centers, or at their seats. Betty Lee's word study routines described in Chapter 3 are designed for independent work. Games and puzzles, such as described in the activities section in this chapter, should be first introduced and modeled in groups and then placed in centers. Writing can be an independent activity as children work in journals or draw and label pictures based on sorts.

RESOURCES FOR IMPLEMENTING WORD STUDY *in Your Classroom*

There are a number of materials available to help you implement word study with children in the emergent stage:

1. *Words Their Way for PreK–K* (Johnston et al., 2015) offers a more thorough coverage of the literacy diet described in this chapter, as well as more activities and lesson plans. It is recommended for early childhood teachers working with children in the emergent and letter name–alphabetic stages.

2. Pictures to create sound sorts for rhyme and initial sounds can be found in Appendix C and can be used with the template on page 400 to create your own sorts. See the directions and lists of rhyming pictures on pages 333 and 334.

3. Assessments, prepared sorts, prepared games, and game templates are available on the website. Under the tab for Additional Resources, look for the List of Available Images to give you ideas about picture names to type into the Create Your Own application found under Sorts and Games or download the file of pictures and move images into your own templates.

4. *Words Their Way®: Letter and Picture Sorts for Emergent Spellers* (Bear et al., 2010) offers a complete curriculum of sorts including concept sorts, rhyme sorts, alphabet font sorts, and beginning consonant sorts. There are also 34 reading selections—ready-to-print illustrated copies of short rhymes and jingles to use for developing concept of word.

5. *Words Their Way®: Emergent Sorts for Spanish-Speaking English Learners* (Helman et al., 2009) provides many prepared sorts to develop concepts and vocabulary as well as sound sorts with different contrasts.

6. Websites to support emergent literacy learning: *PALS* website at the University of Virginia *Webbing into Literacy* Curry School of Education, *Reading Rockets*.

ACTIVITIES for the Emergent Stage

This section provides specific activities arranged by the six components of early literacy. Within each, the activities are roughly in order of increasing difficulty. However, concept sorts do not have to precede sound awareness, which in turn must precede alphabet. In reality, these develop simultaneously and constitute the "literacy diet" during the emergent years, with many activities that cut across the categories. Some of the games are generic to all stages of developmental word knowledge as indicated by the Adaptable for Other Stages symbol used throughout the book. Common Core State Standards for Kindergarten are listed with each activity.

Oral Language, Concepts, and Vocabulary

Activities include read-alouds, retellings, and concept sorts.

4.1 Using Interactive Read-Alouds to Develop Vocabulary

Books provide the best exposure to new vocabulary for young children, but simply reading to them is not enough. You need to draw attention to words and plan ways to ensure that new words are acquired and used. (CCSS Language 1.d, 1.f, 4, 4.a, 5, 5.c, 5.d, 6)

PROCEDURES

1. Select a book with rich language that is age-appropriate for your listeners. Preview the book, looking for new vocabulary and conceptual understandings that will extend students' background knowledge. For example, rural or small-town children might not be familiar with the escalator mentioned in *Corduroy* by Don Freeman. Select three to five words based on (1) utility, (2) concreteness, (3) repetition, and (4) relatedness to themes or topics of study. Prepare child-friendly definitions. (You might occasionally model using a picture dictionary, and even use it yourself to develop definitions, but dictionaries often do not provide clear examples or explanations.)

2. Introduce the book by reading the title and naming the author and illustrator. Look at the cover and at least the first few pages to elicit a prediction ("What do you think this book will be about?") and to set a purpose for reading. Build background knowledge as needed and try to introduce the target words conversationally, perhaps pointing to a picture or supplying a brief definition. Ask the children to listen for the words as you read.

3. Make the read-aloud interactive by inviting comments and questions from the children during reading. Encourage them to connect with the characters and theme ("Have you ever worn overalls like Corduroy's?"). Expand on children's brief utterances ("lost button") with complete sentences to model more complex language ("Yes, Corduroy had lost a button but he did not realize it."). Point out the targeted words when they occur in context and have children say the words with you.

4. After reading, invite children to respond to the story in personal ways and then revisit the targeted words as you model their use, pose questions, and elicit children's responses. Use the new words in questions about the story and ask children to use them in sentences, act them out, or find other applications for them to engage the children. ("Why do you think Corduroy admired the furniture in the store?" "What is something that you admire?" "Turn to your partner and use the word *admire* in a sentence.")

4.2 PEER—Retellings through Dialogic Reading

In this activity, described as "dialogic reading" (Whitehurst et al., 1994), children learn how to talk about and retell a storybook. With your guidance and prompting they talk about a familiar book. Gradually give the children more responsibility for retelling the story until they can do so with little or no assistance. Parents can be trained in this technique and you can send books home that have been read and discussed in school. Adults can use the PEER sequence (Morgan & Meier, 2008) to stimulate oral language and help the child become the storyteller. (CCSS Language 1, 1.b, 1.d, 1.e, 1.f, 6)

PROCEDURES Begin by reading a book aloud and then follow up with small-group or individual rereadings before engaging in a prompted discussion. Repeat the prompt sequence several times using the PEER guidelines:

P Prompt the child to say something about the book using open-ended questions. (Point to a picture of a mouse and say, "What is he doing?" The child says, "Running.")

E Evaluate the child's response. ("That's right!")

E Expand the response by rephrasing or adding information to it. ("The mouse is running away from the cat.")

R Repeat the prompt and ask the child to expand on it. ("What is the mouse doing?" The child says, "He is running away from the cat.")

Use additional prompts such as the following to stimulate talk:

1. Ask what, when, where, why, and how questions.
2. Leave a blank at the end of a sentence for the children to fill in.
3. Ask children to retell what has happened so far or to retell the ending.
4. Ask children to describe what they see happening in pictures.
5. Ask children to make connections with their own experiences.

4.3 Turn and Talk

A good way to increase the opportunities for oral interaction and vocabulary use in your classroom is to ask children to turn and talk to an assigned partner during a discussion. Rather than calling on one child, everyone has a chance to respond to a question, to share an experience, to make a prediction, to summarize, and so on. Turn and talk is a good way to encourage children who might be reluctant to speak in front of the whole group. This includes English learners as well as shy or less verbal students. (CCSS Language 1.d, 1.f, 5.c, 6)

PROCEDURES

1. Model your expectations for "turn and talk" with another adult. Demonstrate how both partners need a chance to speak and suggest ways to encourage a reluctant talker. ("Tell me what you think. It's your turn now" or "You go first this time.") You can also ask two children who do a particularly good job together to model for the rest of the group. Children should not move about during turn and talk but instead turn "knee to knee and eye to eye" and talk softly so they do not disturb others.

2. Select partners before the read-aloud or other shared experience begins. You may allow children to pick their own partners on the way to the group and then sit down together. Or you may select partners, taking into consideration childrens' language competence and confidence. A more verbal child may provide a model for a less verbal child, but he or she might also dominate the conversation, so watch to see how pairs work out and be ready to intervene with suggestions about ways to give the less verbal child an equal opportunity. Use the same partners for a week or longer to save organizational time.

3. Bring turn and talk time to a close by offering a countdown warning. One way to do this is to silently hold up five fingers and then lower each finger in turn. As children notice, they should imitate you down to the final fist when everyone should be done talking. How much time you allow will vary, but bring turn and talk time to a close before children lose their focus and get off the assigned topic.

4. As partners talk to each other, listen in to monitor their conversations. When the group is back together you might call on one or two children to report what they talked about. Because less verbal or shy children have had a chance to rehearse their ideas, they should be better able to speak before a larger group after turn and talk time.

4.4 Paste the Pasta and Other Concrete Concept Sorts

Categorizing pasta by size, shape, and color is a good hands-on activity that introduces the idea of sorting to young children. Many early childhood curricula include the study of pattern, but being able to categorize by particular attributes must come first. It is difficult for young children to stay focused on a single attribute of interest. They may begin sorting by color and then switch to shape in midstream. They will need many activities of this kind, sorting real, concrete objects that have different features. (CCSS Language 1.b, 1.d, 1.f, 5.a, 5.b, 5.c, 5.d, 6)

FIGURE 4.15   Paste the Pasta

MATERIALS You need three to six types of pasta of various sizes and shapes. You may wish to use pasta of various colors or you can dye your own by shaking the pasta in a jar with a tablespoon of alcohol and a few drops of food coloring, then lay it out on newspaper to dry. If you dye your own, make sure that any one color encompasses a variety of shapes and sizes. Two or three colors are enough. Children can sort onto paper divided into columns, as shown in Figure 4.15, or simply into piles.

PROCEDURES

1. Prepare a mixture of the dried pasta and give each child a handful and a sorting paper.

2. Begin with an open sort, in which you invite the children to come up with their own way of grouping. This gives you an opportunity to evaluate which children understand attribute sorting and which need more guidance. Ask the children to share their ideas and show their groups. Discuss the different features or attributes by which they can sort.

3. Ask children to re-sort using a category different from their first one. You might end this activity by letting the children glue the pasta onto their sorting sheets by categories and then labeling their chosen sorts.

VARIATIONS There is no end to the concrete things you can sort with your children as you explore the different features that define your categories, as in the following suggestions.

Children—male/female, hair color, eye color, age, favorite color
Shoes—sandals/sneakers, right/left, tie/Velcro/buckle/slip-on
Clothing—mittens/gloves, types of headwear, short-sleeved tops/long-sleeved tops, coats with or without hoods, coats that button or zip
Buttons—two holes/four holes/no holes, shape, color, size
Bottle caps—size, color, plastic/metal, plain/printed, ribbed/smooth
Blocks—shape, color, size, length
Toys—size, color, purpose, plastic/wood/metal
Food—sweet/sour/bitter/salty, fruits/vegetables/grains, healthy/not healthy

4.5 Concept Books and Concept Sorts

Simple concept books designed for young children make great beginnings for concept sorts. Examples include *Is It Red? Is It Yellow? Is It Blue?* and other books by Tana Hoban, and *My Very First Book of Shapes* by Eric Carle. Topics include shapes, colors, textures, positions, types of clothing, animals, opposites, and so on. (CCSS Language 1, 1.b, 1.d, 1.e, 1.f, 5.a, 5.b, 5.c, 5.d, 6)

PROCEDURES

1. Because concept books have little text, engage children in discussing what they see and supplying appropriate labels. "This is a book about colors. Here is a picture of a toy dump truck. What color is the dump truck? Yes, the dump truck is red. Now it's your turn. Tell me what you see here."

2. Collect objects or pictures of objects that can be used for sorting. In the case of colors, you can probably find real objects around the room such as books, markers, toys, and so on. Explain to the children that they are going to help you sort the objects by color. Use complete sentences to model: "Here is a red ball. I will put the ball with the other things that are red." After sorting, help children make generalizations such as "How are all these things alike? Yes, all the things in this category are red."

3. Make labels for each category of your sort with help from the students: "I am going to write *red* on this card to label this category. Listen, *rrrr-ed*. What letter do I need to write down first?"

4. Put sorts where children can use them on their own and encourage them to talk as they sort. Children can look for more pictures in magazines or catalogs that fit the categories or they can draw pictures, cut them out, and paste them into categories. Encourage them to label their own sorts with invented spellings.

VARIATIONS You can develop other concept sorts along the same lines. The following list of categories represents opposites or antonyms that are frequently confused by young children and can be better understood through sorting.

- Real/imaginary
- Smooth/rough
- Big/little
- Hard/soft

Of course, any book can be the starting point for a concept sort. In the next chapter, we describe a food sort based on *Gregory the Terrible Eater* by Marjorie Sharmat.

4.6 All My Friends Photograph Sort

Another example of an open-ended sort involves guessing each other's categories. (CCSS Language 1.b, 1.d, 1.f, 5, 5.a, 5.b, 6)

MATERIALS Take digital pictures of your students and create a composite so that they are all on one page. Each small group gets a set of pictures to cut apart and sort. The children also need a sheet of construction paper to divide into columns for sorting.

PROCEDURES Brainstorm with the children some of the ways that the pictures might be grouped (hair length, hair color, clothing, boys/girls, facial expressions). Have children work in groups to sort by these or other categories they discover. After pasting their pictures into the columns on their paper, each group can hold up their effort and ask the others in the class to guess their categories. The category labels or key words should then be written on the papers.

VARIATIONS Children can sort photographs from home according to places (inside/outside, home/vacation), number of people in the photograph (adults, sisters, brothers), number of animals in the photograph, seasons (by clothing, outside trees/plants), age of people in the photograph, and so forth. As children learn to recognize their classmates' names, have them match the names to the pictures.

4.7 Transportation Unit

Teachers of young children often organize their curriculum into thematic units of study. Such units frequently lend themselves to concept sorts, which review and extend the understandings central to the unit goals. The following example uses a transportation theme. (CCSS Language 1.b, 1.c, 1.d, 1.f, 5.a, 5.b, 5.c, 5.d, 6)

MATERIALS You need a collection of toy vehicles (planes, boats, cars, and trucks) or pictures of vehicles (a prepared picture sort is on the PDToolkit website). Books featuring transportation, such as *My Truck Is Stuck* by Kevin Lewis, can introduce the sort.

FIGURE 4.16   Transportation Draw and Label

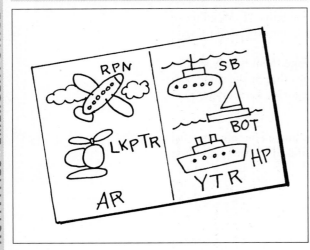

PROCEDURES

1. Lay out the pictures on the floor or table and invite the children to think of which ones might go together. Encourage them to think up a variety of possibilities that will divide everything into only two or three categories. This is an open sort because the children are providing the categories.
2. After each suggestion, sort the vehicles by the identified attributes, talking about the categories and how things are sorted: "A truck has wheels so I will put it with the car and the bicycle." Record the ideas for different sorts on a chart or chalkboard. Some possibilities include plastic/metal, big/little, old/new, one color/many colors, windows/no windows, wheels/no wheels, and land/air/water.
3. After exploring this open sort thoroughly, have the children select the category they like the best. They can then be given construction paper to label their categories and draw or cut out pictures for each. As always, encourage them to label the pictures and the categories with invented spelling, as shown in Figure 4.16.

Phonological Awareness (PA)

Phonological awareness consists of an array of understandings about speech sounds that includes a sensitivity to syllables, rhyme, alliteration, and phonemes. Syllables, rhyme, and alliteration are the best places to start with emergent learners and many activities for developing these are included here. The Morning Message (Activity 4.38) and Start with Children's Names (Activity 4.23) also include phonological awareness instruction in the context of reading and writing.

4.8 Two for One! Long Words, Short Words

Emergent learners have difficulty separating the sound structure of a spoken word from its meaning. One way to sensitize children to the phonological aspects of words is to build compound words. The following activity focuses on the concept that some words are long and some are short, and the difference between long and short words has nothing to do with the size of the referent. (CCSS Foundational Skills 2)

MATERIALS Consult the list of compound words in Appendix E. Pick concrete, two-syllable compound words that you can easily illustrate. The words *bedroom, blackbird, cowboy, doorbell, fingernail, fireman, football, doghouse, lipstick, mailman, pancake, raincoat, sandbox, snowman,* and *snowball* are good choices for starters. Pictures for many of the words can be found in Appendix C.

PROCEDURES
1. Take a picture of snow and another picture of a man. After discussing the meaning of each word separately, place the two pictures side by side and ask children to say each word in succession: "snow-man." Talk about how the one word, *snowman,* is made of two words, *snow* plus *man.*
2. Replace the two separate pictures of snow and a man with one picture of a snowman and discuss again how the word *snowman* is made up of two words: *snow* and *man.* However, because a *snowman* might not be "as big" as a real man, it is necessary to take this exercise one step further to develop the idea of word size in terms of sound as opposed to meaning.
3. Hold up the picture of snow and ask children to clap as they say the word *snow.* Next, hold up the picture of the man and ask the children to clap as they say the word *man.* Finally, hold up the picture of the snowman and ask the children to clap for each word in *snowman.*
4. Discuss how the word *snowman* is longer than either the word *snow* or the word *man* because *snowman* has two claps, whereas *snow* and *man* have only one! *Snowman* has more claps, so it is a longer word.

VARIATIONS Hold up the printed word *snow* and compare it to the printed word *snowman.* Count the letters and talk about which word has more letters. Say, "I'm going to say two short words and you tell me what long word those two short words make. Ready? *Bed* (pause) *room.* What longer word do those two smaller words make? Yes, they make the word *bedroom!* Let's clap out the syllables in *bedroom* (clap, clap). Ready for another one?" Repeat with other concrete words.

4.9 Whose Name Is Longer? Let's Clap to Find Out!

Once children develop sensitivity to syllables through clapping out compound words, move on to clapping out the syllables in everyone's names. Tie this in with Activity 4.23 (Start with Children's Names). (CCSS Foundational Skills 2, 2.b)

PROCEDURES Choose two children whose first names differ in the number of syllables. Say each name and have your children clap to each syllable as they pronounce it. "Whose name is longer? Which name has more claps? *Shamika* has three claps; *Charles* has only one." Go around the classroom clapping out the syllables in everyone's name. Have children move into groups by the number of claps in their names.

4.10 Rhyme in Children's Books

Filling children's heads with rhyme is one of the easiest and most natural ways to focus their attention on the sounds of the English language. Books written with rhyme provide one way to do this. As you read and reread these books aloud, pause to allow the children to guess the rhyming word. *I Can't, Said the Ant* is an old favorite that invites child participation, with each line cued by an illustration. (CCSS Foundational Skills 2.a, Language 6)

Here are some more of our favorites:

- Bluemie, E. (2012). *How do you wokka-wokka?* Somerville, MA: Candlewick.
- Cameron, P. (1961). *I can't, said the ant*. New York: Putnam Publishing.
- Crews, D. (1986). *Ten black dots*. New York: Greenwillow.
- Degan, B. (1983). *Jamberry*. New York: Harper.
- Dewdney, A. (2005). *Llama Llama red pajama*. New York: Viking Juvenile. Look for more books in this series, including *Llama Llama mad at Mama* (2007), *Llama Llama misses Mama* (2009), and *Llama Llama time to share* (2012).
- Guarina, D. (1989). *Is your mama a llama?* Illustrated by Steven Kellogg. New York: Scholastic.
- Raffi. (1999). *Down by the bay*. New York: Crown Books. Look for other titles by Raffi.
- Rinker, S. D. (2011). *Goodnight, goodnight, construction site*. San Francisco, CA: Chronicle Books.
- Seuss, Dr. (1965). *Hop on pop*. New York: Random House. Also see *There's a wocket in my pocket* and *Fox in socks*.
- Shaw, N. E. (1997). *Sheep in a jeep*. Boston, MA: Houghton Mifflin. Look for other books in this series, including *Sheep out to eat* (1995).
- Slate, J. (1996). *Mrs. Bindergarten gets ready for kindergarten*. New York: Scholastic.
- Wilson, K. (2002). *Bear snores on*. New York: Little Simon. Look for more titles in this series, including *Bear wants more* (2003), *Bear's new friend* (2006), and *Bear says thanks* (2012).
- Wilson, S. (2003). *Nap in a lap*. New York: Henry Holt.
- Wood, A. (1995). *Silly Sally went to town*. Boston, MA: Houghton Mifflin Harcourt.

4.11 Match and Sort Rhyming Pictures

After reading rhyming books aloud, follow up with an activity in which the children sort or match rhyming pictures. (CCSS Foundational Skills 2)

MATERIALS Three rhyming picture sorts are ready to print from the PDToolkit website. Appendix C in this book contains pictures grouped by initial sounds and by vowels. These can be copied, colored lightly, and glued to cards to make sets for sorting. The lists on pages 333 and 334 will help you find rhyming sets. You can create sets of matching pairs or sets of three or more pictures that can be sorted by rhyme.

PROCEDURES Display a set of pictures and model how to sort them by rhyme. Say something like, "Let's look for rhyming words. *Boat* rhymes with *coat*, so I will put it with the picture of the coat. Can you find two pictures that rhyme?" To make it easier for beginners, put out three pictures at a time: two pictures that rhyme and one that does not. Name the pictures and ask children to find the two that rhyme: "Listen. *Boat, train, coat*. Which pictures rhyme?" After sorting pictures as a group, put the pictures in a center for child to match on their own or create a rhyming sort handout so that each child can have his or her own sort.

4.12 Rhyming Books as a Starting Point to Invent Rhymes

Making up your own rhymes is quite an accomplishment and it is likely to come after the ability to identify rhymes. Younger children need support to create rhymes, and a good place to start is pure nonsense. Jan Slepian and Ann Seidler's *The Hungry Thing* (2001) tells of a creature who comes to town begging for food but has trouble pronouncing what he wants; *shmancakes* (pancakes), *feetloaf* (meatloaf), and *hookies* (cookies) are among his requests. Only a small boy can figure out what he wants. (CCSS Foundational Skills 2, Language 6)

PROCEDURES After reading the book, children can act it out. As each takes the part of the Hungry Thing, they must come up with a rhyming word for the food they want, such as *moughnut*, *bandwich*, or *smello*. The story continues in *The Hungry Thing Returns*.

VARIATIONS No one was a greater master of nonsense than Dr. Seuss. *There's a Wocket in My Pocket* (1974) takes readers on a tour of a young boy's home in which all kinds of odd creatures have taken up residence. There is a *woset* in his closet, a *zlock* behind the clock, and a *nink* in the sink. After reading this to a group, ask children to imagine what animal would live in their cubby, under the rug, or in the lunchroom. Their efforts should rhyme, to be sure, but anything will do: a *rubby*, *snubby*, or *frubby* might all live in a cubby.

4.13 Making Up Rhymes

Children who need more explicit instruction in rhyme will benefit from making up rhymes. (CCSS Foundational Skills 2a)

MATERIALS Pictures of rhyming objects such as *rose*, *nose*, *hose*, and *toes* (see the list of rhyming pictures at the beginning of Appendix C).

PROCEDURES

1. Introduce a rhyming element. Ask your children to say *ose*. Explain that you are going to make words that have *ose* in them. Hold up a picture of a *rose* and ask children to say the word *rose* and listen for the *ose* at the end. Emphasize the rhyme in a whole word. Say *rrr-ooose*, emphasizing the *ose*.
2. Hold up a picture of a *nose*. Ask your children to tell you what it is. Tell them that *n-ose* has *ose* in it. Hold up other pictures (*hose* and *toes*) and ask if they can hear the *ose* at the end.
3. Ask children if they can tell what sound is the same in *rose*, *nose*, *hose*, and *toes*. Emphasize the *ose* at the end of each word makes them rhyme.
4. Ask children to brainstorm other words that rhyme with rose: *goes*, *chose*, and *blows*, for example. Make other rhymes in a similar fashion.

4.14 Use Songs to Develop a Sense of Rhyme and Alliteration

Earlier, we mentioned how appropriate works by the singer/songwriter Raffi are for young students. Teaching these songs by Raffi, some of which are available in books, can lead to inventive fun with rhymes and sounds. (CCSS Foundational Skills 2, Language 6)

"Apples and Bananas" (from *One Light, One Sun*)
"Spider on the Floor" (from *Singable Songs for the Very Young*)
"Down by the Bay" (also available from *Singable Songs for the Very Young*)

Another song that features names, rhyme, and alliteration is "The Name Game," originally sung by Shirley Ellis. It has apparently passed into the oral tradition of many neighborhoods and may be known by some children in your class. Sing the song over and over, substituting the name of a different child on every round, as in the following two examples:

Sam Sam Bo Bam, Banana Fanna Bo Fam, Fee Fi Mo Mam, Sam!
Kaitlyn Kaitlyn Bo Baitlyn, Banana Fanna Bo Faitlyn, Fee Fi Mo Maitlyn, Kaitlyn!

Encourage children to share with you any playground songs and chants they might already know. Generations of children have made up variations of "Miss Mary Mack" and a new generation with a taste for rap is creating a whole new repertoire. You can take an active role in teaching these jingles to your students—or letting them teach you! Write them down to become reading material.

4.15 Rhyming Bingo

You can adapt bingo to many features. (CCSS Foundational Skills 2)

Rhyming Bingo
This game is ready to use and print.

MATERIALS Prepare enough Bingo game boards for the number of children who will participate (small groups of three to five children are ideal). An appropriate game board size for young children is a 3-by-3 array; for older students, the game board can be expanded to a 4-by-4 or 5-by-5 array. Copy sets of pictures from Appendix C and form rhyming groups such as those listed on pages 333 and 334. Paste all but one of each rhyming group in the spaces on the game boards and then laminate them for durability. Each game board must be arranged differently.

Prepare a complementary set of cards on which you paste the remaining picture from each rhyming group. These will become the deck from which rhyming words are called aloud during the game. You will need some kind of marker to cover the squares on the game board. These may be as simple as two-inch squares of construction paper, plastic chips, bottle caps, or pennies.

PROCEDURES
1. Give each child a game board and markers to cover spaces.
2. You, or a designated child, act as the caller, who turns over cards from the deck and calls out the name of the picture.
3. Each child searches the game board for a picture that rhymes with the one that has been called out. Children cover a match with a marker to claim the space.
4. The winner is the first child to cover a row in any direction or the first child to fill his or her entire board.

4.16 Rhyming Concentration

This game for two or three children is played like traditional Concentration or the more current Memory game. (CCSS Foundational Skills 2)

MATERIALS Assemble a collection of six to ten rhyming pairs from the pictures in Appendix C. Paste the pictures on cards and laminate for durability. Be sure the pictures do not show through from the backside.

PROCEDURES Shuffle the pictures and then lay them face-down in rows. Children take turns flipping over two pictures at a time. If the two pictures rhyme, the child keeps the cards to hold to the end of the game. A child who makes a match gets another turn. The winner is the child who has the most matches at the end of the game.

VARIATIONS This can be adapted to use with beginning sounds. Put letters on one set of cards and paste a picture of something that begins with that letter on another.

4.17 Pamela Pig Likes Pencils: Beginning Sounds and Alliteration

Sensitivity to beginning consonant sounds is essential for children to move out of the emergent phase and begin to learn to read, and alliteration is a good way to get started. (Alliteration is the occurrence of two or more words having the same beginning sound.) The following activity helps children focus their attention on beginning consonant sounds in sequences of

Adaptable for Other Stages

ACTIVITIES | EMERGENT STAGE

spoken words. You might introduce this by reading *A My Name Is Alice*, by Jane Bayer and illustrated by Steven Kellogg. (CCSS Foundational Skills 2)

MATERIALS You will need a variety of animal puppets that can be named with matching beginning consonant sounds, such as Bob Bear, Donald Dog, Cass Cat, or Pamela Pig. Try to pick names and animals beginning with just one single consonant sound—not a blend or consonant digraph. Although Charles starts with the letter *C*, it doesn't start with the initial *c* sound (/s/ or /k/); it sounds with a /ch/ sound instead. You want both the name and the animal to have the same beginning sound. Puppets may be store-bought, but they can also be simple pictures of an animal like a bear or a cat cut out and fastened to the end of a stick to hold up.

PROCEDURES

1. Hold up your puppet and introduce it. Emphasize the beginning consonant sound as you introduce the name and the animal name. Say something like, "This is Pamela. She is a pig named Pamela. We call her Pamela Pig."

2. Explain that Pamela Pig like things that start with the same sound as her name, /p/. So Pamela likes *pencil*s because *pencil*s start with the /p/ sound just like *Pamela* and *pig*.

3. Display various pictures (see Appendix C) or objects, some of which start with a /p/ sound (*pen, paper, paint, pan, pin, pear*) and some of which don't. Pick two at a time (one that starts with a /p/ sound and one that doesn't) and ask, "Which one would Pamela Pig pick?"

VARIATION Have children brainstorm other things that Pamela Pig would like. They may volunteer such things as parties, plays, or parks. Have children jump rope to the familiar jump rope jingle that plays on alliteration: "Chant (initial sound) my name is (child's name) and my friend's name is (name). We live in (place) and we sell (item)."

4.18 It's in the Bag—A Phoneme Blending Game

MATERIALS You will need a paper bag (gift bags are attractive) and an assortment of small objects collected from around the classroom, from outside, or from home: chalk, pen, paper clip, tack, key, rock, stick, and so on. You might use a puppet to add interest. (CCSS Foundational Skills 2, 2.c, 2.d)

PROCEDURES Lay out a dozen or so objects and name them with the students, explaining that you will use them to play a game, and then introduce the puppet. The puppet will name an object in the bag, saying it very slowly (by syllables: *pa-per-clip*, or phonemes: *rrr-oooo-ck*), and the children will guess what it is saying. Let children take turns using the puppet to practice saying words slowly.

VARIATIONS Use objects or pictures related to a topic of study. For example, if you are teaching a unit on animals, you could put toy animals or pictures of farm animals in the bag. This can be a sensory activity by letting children reach into the bag, figure out an object by touch, and then say it slowly for the other children to guess. Objects that begin with the same beginning sounds can also be put into the bag to sort.

4.19 Incorporate Phonological Skills into Daily Activities

Teachers of emergent children can incorporate sound play into many daily activities and routines. (CCSS Foundational Skills 2, 2.a, 2.b, 2.c, 2.d)

1. Lining up, taking attendance, or calling children to a group: Call each student's name and then lead the class in clapping the syllables in the name. Announce that everyone whose name has two syllables can line up, then one syllable, three, and so on. Say each student's name slowly as it is called. Make up a rhyme for each child's name that starts with a sound of interest: Billy Willy, Mary Wary, Shanee Wanee, and so on. Substitute the first letter in everyone's name with the same letter: Will, Wary, Wanee, Wustin, and so on.

2. During read-alouds: Pause to let children fill in a rhyming word, especially on a second or third reading. If they have trouble, say the first sound for them with a clue: "It rhymes with cat and starts with *m*." Draw attention to a long word by repeating it and clapping the syllables: "That's a big word! Let's clap the syllables: *hip-po-pot-a-mus*, five syllables!" You can also pause while reading and say a key word very slowly before asking the children to repeat it fast: "The next day his dad picked him up in a red… *jeeeep*. What's that? A jeep, right." Point to the letters as you do this.

Alphabet Knowledge

The following activities are designed to develop all aspects of alphabet knowledge, including letter recognition (both uppercase and lowercase), letter naming, letter writing, and letter sounds. You may notice that these activities address more than one letter at a time: In kindergarten, one letter per week is much too slow a pace and it does not address the needs of children who come to school already knowing their letters.

4.20 The Alphabet Song and Tracking Activities

Every early childhood classroom should have an alphabet strip or chart at eye level. Too often these strips are put up out of the children's reach. The best locations for the strips are desktops or tabletops for easy reference. Use the following activities to make active use of these charts. (CCSS Foundational Skills 1.a,1.d)

MATERIALS Use commercial or teacher-made alphabet strips for both wall display and for individual students.

PROCEDURES
1. Learn the ABC song to the tune of "Twinkle, Twinkle, Little Star." Sing it many times.
2. Model, pointing to each letter as the song is sung or the letters are chanted. Then ask the children to fingerpoint to the letters as they sing or chant.
3. Play "find the letter" by naming a letter for children to touch on their strip. Ask them to name the letter that comes before or after the target letter.
4. When children know about half of the alphabet, they can work on putting a set of letter cards, tiles, or linking letters in alphabetical order. Use uppercase or lowercase letters, or pair the two (see Figure 4.17). Keep an ABC strip or chart nearby as a ready reference.

FIGURE 4.17   **Alphabet Link Letters**

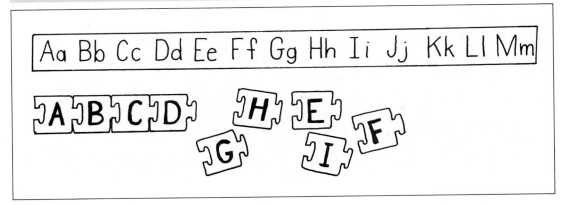

4.21 Share Alphabet Books

Share alphabet books with a group as you would other good literature and plan follow-up activities when appropriate. (CCSS Foundational Skills 1.d, 2, 3.a)

MATERIALS Some books are suitable for toddlers and merely require naming a letter and a single accompanying picture, such as *Eric Carle's ABC* (2007). Others, such as Graeme Base's *Animalia*, will keep even upper elementary children engaged as they try to name all the items that are hidden in the illustrations. Look for alphabet books such as the ones listed here to draw attention to beginning sounds through alliteration.

- Base, G. (1986). *Animalia*. New York: Harry Abrams.
- Bayer, J. (1984). *A My Name Is Alice*. Illustrated by Steven Kellogg. New York: Dial.
- Berenstain, S., & Berenstain, J. (1971). *The Berenstain's B Book*. New York: Random House.
- Cole, J. (1993). *Six Sick Sheep: 101 Tongue Twisters*. New York: Morrow.
- Seuss, Dr. (1963). *Dr. Seuss's ABC*. New York: Random House.

Many ABC books can be incorporated into thematic units, such as Jerry Pallotta's ABC books featuring insects and animals, or Mary Azarian's *A Farmer's Alphabet*. Some alphabet books present special puzzles, such as Jan Garten's *The Alphabet Tale*. Invite children to predict the upcoming animal by showing just the tip of its tail on the preceding page. Following is a list of some outstanding ABC books for school-age children but there are many more.

- Azarian, M. (1981). *A Farmer's Alphabet*. Boston, MA: David Godine.
- Baker, K. (2010) *LMNO Peas*. San Diego, CA: Beach Lane Books.
- Ernst, L. C. (1996). *The Letters Are Lost*. New York: Scholastic.
- Fain, K. (1993). *Handsigns: A Sign Language Alphabet*. New York: Scholastic.
- Falls, C. B. (1923). *ABC Book*. New York: Doubleday.
- Folsom, M. (2005). *Q Is for Duck: An Alphabet Guessing Game*. San Anselmo, CA: Sandpiper.
- Gág, W. (1933). *The ABC Bunny*. Hand lettered by Howard Gág. New York: Coward-McCann.
- Hague, K. (1984). *Alphabears: An ABC Book*. Illustrated by Michael Hague. New York: Holt, Rinehart & Winston.
- Horenstein, H. (1999). *Arf! Beg! Catch! Dogs from A to Z*. New York: Scholastic.
- Jay, A. (2005). *ABC: A Child's First Alphabet Book*. New York: Dutton Juvenile.
- McPhail, D. (1989). *David McPhail's Animals A to Z*. New York: Scholastic.
- Musgrove, M. (1976). *Ashanti to Zulu: African Traditions*. Illustrated by Leo and Diane Dillon. New York: Dial.
- Pallotta, J. (1989). *The Yucky Reptile Alphabet Book*. Illustrated by Ralph Masiello. New York: Bantam Doubleday, Dell. (There are many more in this series, such as *The Dinosaur Alphabet Book*.)
- Shannon, G. (1996). *Tomorrow's Alphabet*. Illustrated by Donald Crews. New York: Greenwillow.
- Sobel, J. (2006). *B is for Bulldozer*. New York: HMH Books for Young Readers.
- Tyron, L. (1991) *Albert's Alphabet*. New York: Atheneum.
- Zuckerman, A. (2009). *Creature ABC*. San Francisco, CA: Chronicle Books.

PROCEDURES

1. Discuss the pattern of the books, solve the puzzle, and talk about the words that begin with each letter as you go through the books a second time.
2. Focus on alliteration by repeating tongue twisters and creating a list of words for a particular letter. Brainstorm other words that begin with that letter and write them under the letter on chart paper or an interactive whiteboard.
3. Make individual or class alphabet books. You can pick a theme or pattern for the book. Refer to the alphabet books you have read for ideas. One idea is a noun–verb format; for example, ants attack, bees buzz, cats catch, and dogs doze.
4. Look up a particular letter you are studying in several alphabet books or a picture dictionary to find other things that begin with that sound. This is an excellent introduction to using resource books.

FIGURE 4.18 *Chicka Chicka Boom Boom* **Board**

4.22 Chicka Chicka Boom Boom Sort

Martin and Archambault's *Chicka Chicka Boom Boom* (1989) is a great favorite and provides a wonderful way to move from children's books to alphabet recognition. Letters can be sorted by capitals and lowercase and by beginning sounds (see Figure 4.18). Some teachers create a large coconut tree on the side of a metal filing cabinet so that children can act out the story and match uppercase and lowercase forms using magnetic letters. (CCSS Foundational Skills 1.d, 2)

4.23 Start with Children's Names

Names are an ideal point from which to begin studying alphabet letters because children are naturally interested in their own names and their friends' names. We like the idea of a "name of the day" (Cunningham, 2009) better than a "letter of the week," because more letters are covered in less time. (CCSS Foundational Skills 1, 1.a, 1.b, 1.d, 2, 2.b, 2.e)

MATERIALS Prepare a card for each child on which his or her name is written in neatly executed block letters. Put all the names in a box or gift bag. Have additional blank cards ready to be cut apart as described. A pocket chart is handy for displaying the letters.

PROCEDURES

1. Each day, with great fanfare, draw a name—it becomes the name of the day. Begin with an open-ended question: "What do you notice about this name?" Children will respond in all sorts of ways depending on what they know about letters: "It's a short name." "It has three letters." "It starts like Taneesh's name." "It has an *o* in the middle."

2. Next, children chant or echo the letters in the name as you point to each one. A cheer, led by you, is lots of fun:

Teacher: "Give me a *T*."	Children: "*T*"
Teacher: "Give me an *O*."	Children: "*O*"
Teacher: "Give me an *M*."	Children: "*M*"
Teacher: "What have we got?"	Children: "*Tom*!"

3. On another card, write the student's name as the children recite the letters again. Then cut the letters apart and hand out the letters to children in the group. Challenge the children to put the letters back in order to spell the name correctly in a pocket chart or on a chalkboard ledge. After several repetitions, put the cut-up letters into an envelope with the child's name and picture on the outside. Add the envelope to the name puzzle collection. Children love to pull out their friends' names to put together.

4. All of the children in the group should attempt to write the featured name on individual whiteboards, chalkboards, or pieces of paper. This is an opportunity to offer some handwriting instruction, as you model for the students. Discuss the details of direction and movement of letter formation as the children imitate your motions.

5. Each day, add the featured name to a display of all the names that have come before. Compare the names with sorting activities:
   - Sort the names by the number of letters or syllables.
   - Sort the names that share particular letters; for example, find all the names with an *e* in them.
   - Sort the names that belong to boys and girls.
   - Sort the names by alphabetical order.

VARIATIONS Create a permanent display of the names and encourage children to practice writing their own and their friends' names. If you have a writing center, you might put all the names on index cards in a box for reference. Encourage children to reproduce names not only by copying the names with pencils, chalk, and markers, but also with rubber stamps, foam cutout letters, link letters, or letter tiles. The names display is an important reference tool during writing time.

4.24 One Child's Name

Learning the letters in one name is a good starting point for children in the early emergent stage. Use the following approach: Spell out a child's name with letter cards, tiles, foam, or plastic letters using both uppercase and lowercase. Spell it with uppercase letters in the first row and ask the child to match lowercase letters in the row below, as shown in Figure 4.19. Ask children to touch and name each letter. Scramble the top row and repeat. Play Concentration with the set of uppercase and lowercase letters needed to spell a child's name. (CCSS Foundational Skills 1.a, 1.b, 1.d)

FIGURE 4.19   Brandon's Name Puzzle

4.25 Alphabet Scrapbook

MATERIALS Prepare a book for each child by stapling together blank sheets of paper. (Seven sheets of paper folded and stapled in the middle is enough for one letter per page.) Children can use this book in a variety of ways (see Figure 4.20). (CCSS Foundational Skills 1.d, 3.a, 3.c, 1.a, 2.d)

PROCEDURES

1. Have children practice writing uppercase and lowercase forms of the letter on each page.
2. Have children cut out letters in different fonts or styles from magazines and newspapers and paste them into their scrapbooks.
3. Have children draw and label pictures and other things that begin with that letter sound.
4. Have children cut and paste magazine pictures onto the corresponding letter page. These pictures can be labeled, too.
5. Have children add sight words as they are learned to create a personal dictionary.

FIGURE 4.20   Alphabet Scrapbook

4.26 Alphabet Eggs

MATERIALS Create a simple set of puzzles designed to practice pairing uppercase and lowercase letters. On poster board, draw and cut out enough four-inch egg shapes for each letter in the alphabet. Write an uppercase letter on the upper half and the matching lowercase letter on the lower portion (see Figure 4.21). Cut the eggs in half using a zigzag line. Make each zigzag slightly different so the activity is self-checking. Children should say the letters to themselves and put the eggs back together by matching the uppercase and lowercase form. (CCSS Foundational Skills 1.d)

VARIATIONS There are many other shapes that can be cut in half for matching. For example, use pumpkin shapes in October, or heart shapes in February. There is no end to matching possibilities. Acorn caps can be matched to bottoms, balls to baseball gloves, frogs to lily pads,

PD **pd** TOOLKIT™
for Words Their Way®

Alphabet Eggs Matching
This game is ready to use and print.

ACTIVITIES | EMERGENT STAGE

FIGURE 4.21 Alphabet Eggs

and so on. You can also create matching sets to pair letters and a picture that starts with that letter, rhyming words, contractions, homophones, and so on.

4.27 Alphabet Concentration

This game works just like Concentration with rhyming words, as described in Activity 4.15. Create cards with uppercase and lowercase forms of the letters written on one side, using both familiar and not-so-familiar letters. Be sure they cannot be seen from the backside. Do not try this with all 26 letters at once, or it may take a long time to complete; eight to ten pairs are probably enough. (CCSS Foundational Skills 1.d)

VARIATIONS To introduce this game or to make it easier, play it with the cards face-up. As children learn the letter sounds, matching consonant letters to pictures that begin with that letter sound can change the focus of this game.

Adaptable for Other Stages

4.28 Letter Spin

This fast-paced game helps children practice upper- and lowercase letter recognition. (CCSS Foundational Skills 1.d)

MATERIALS Make a spinner with six to eight spaces, and label each space with a capital letter. If you laminate the spinner before labeling, you can reuse it with other letters. Print the letters with a grease pencil or non permanent overhead transparency pen. Write the lowercase letters on small cards, creating five or six cards for each letter (see Figure 4.22). See Appendix F for tips on making a spinner.

PD TOOLKIT™
for Words Their Way®

Alphabet Spin
Print the template for game.

FIGURE 4.22 Letter Spin Game

PROCEDURES

1. Lay out all of the lowercase cards face-up.
2. Each student, in turn, spins and lands on an uppercase letter. The child then picks up one card that has the corresponding lowercase form, orally identifying the letter.
3. Play continues until all the letter cards have been picked up.
4. The child with the most cards when the game ends is the winner.

VARIATIONS Ask children to name and write the uppercase and lowercase forms of the letter after each turn. You can adapt this game to any feature that involves matching—letters to sounds, rhymes, vowel patterns, and so on.

4.29 Alphabet Cereal Sort

MATERIALS For this sorting activity, you need a box of alphabet cereal—enough to give each child a handful. Prepare a sorting board for each child by dividing a paper into 26 squares. Label each square with an uppercase or lowercase letter. Other three-dimensional letters would work just as well as cereal. (CCSS Foundational Skills 1.d)

PROCEDURES

1. Allow the children to work individually or in teams to sort their own cereal onto their papers (see Figure 4.23).
2. Allow children to discard (or eat) broken or deformed letters.
3. After the children finish, they can count the number of letters in each category (e.g., *A*=8, *B*=4). This could become a graphing activity.
4. Finally, eat the cereal! (Or glue it down.)

VARIATIONS Have the children spell their names or other words using the cereal.

4.30 Font Sorts

Children need to see a variety of print styles or fonts to identify their ABCs in different contexts. Draw children's attention to different letter forms wherever you encounter them. Environmental print is especially rich in creative lettering styles. Encourage children to bring in samples from home—like the big letters on a bag of dog food or cereal—and create a display on a bulletin board or in a class big book. (CCSS Foundational Skills 1.d)

MATERIALS Cut out different styles of letters from newspapers, catalogs, magazines, and other print sources. You can also search your computer fonts and print out letters in a large size. Cut the letters apart, mount them on small cards, and laminate for durability. Sample font sorts can be found at the PDToolkit. Use both capitals and lowercase, but avoid cursive styles for now (see Figure 4.24).

PROCEDURES After modeling the sort with a group of students, place the materials in a center where the children can work independently. Avoid putting out too many different letters at one time—four or five are probably enough, with 8 to 12 variations for each.

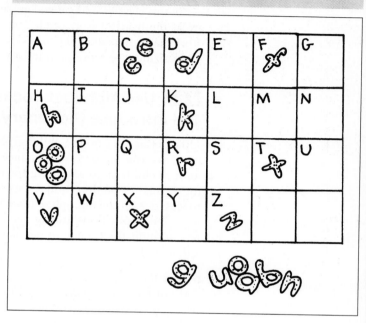

FIGURE 4.23   Cereal Sort

FIGURE 4.24   Sorting Letters with Different Print Styles

VARIATIONS If you created alphabet scrapbooks (Activity 4.25), children can paste in samples of different lettering styles.

Letter–Sound Knowledge

Specific guidelines for creating and using picture sorting for initial sounds are described earlier in this chapter, and general guidelines are presented in Chapter 3. Picture and word sorts are at the heart of word study and the procedures are revisited throughout this book. Use other games and activities to review beginning sounds after children have already practiced categorizing targeted sounds in basic picture sorting activities.

4.31 Use Alphabet Books to Enhance Beginning Sounds and Introduce Dictionary Skills

Alphabet books can be a child's first introduction to reference materials such as dictionaries. They can be used to introduce an initial sound or they can be a resource for a word hunt as children go searching for more words that start with targeted letters. Watch out for the choices authors and artists sometimes make, however. The *C* page may have words that start with the digraph *ch* (*chair*), hard *c* (*cat*), and soft *c* (*cymbals*), which may be confusing. Children will eventually need to sort out these confusions, but not at this time. It's best to limit the *C* page to just hard *C* exemplars for starters. (CCSS Foundational Skills 1.d, 2, 3.a)

MATERIALS A variety of alphabet books (see list in Activity 4.21), picture dictionaries, and word books. The *Busy Bee Kids Printables* website has an ABC book you can download and print, and you may find others.

PROCEDURES
1. Before you start studying individual sounds, see if children can find different letters amongst letters placed in alphabetical order, as on an alphabet strip. Once children can recite the alphabet in order, select a letter and challenge them to name the letters that follow, in order. Even young children first learning the alphabet and beginning sounds are ready to use the most basic of dictionary skills—alphabetic order.
2. When studying a particular beginning sound, pass out alphabet books to pairs of children and ask them to find a letter and report what is pictured there. Begin by naming the letter, pointing to where it falls in the alphabet, and deciding where in the books to look—in the first, middle, or last part. Otherwise, children may start at the beginning and look through the entire book to get to Z!
3. Create a chart of words or pictures that children find beginning with a particular letter.
4. Read the list to children several times to emphasize the beginning sound and challenge them to find more words over the next week or so. This will reinforce the idea that there are many words that begin with a particular letter.

VARIATIONS Picture dictionaries and wordbooks such as those by Richard Scarry or Roger Priddy, in which pictures are thematically arranged and labeled with words, are another resource that young children enjoy. They are an excellent way to encourage vocabulary growth as adults and young children take turns pointing, questioning ("What's that?"), and naming the colorful pictures on the pages. However, young children may ignore the printed labels unless they are pointed out. Challenge children to look through such books on a word hunt for things that start with a particular letter. For example, if you look on the body parts page of such a book you will find several words that start with *H*—*hand*, *head*, and *hair*. Show children how to use the printed word as a clue in addition to naming and listening for the beginning sound.

4.32 Soundline

This center activity is a good way to review the beginning consonant matches children learned in the picture sorts. (CCSS Foundational Skills 1.d, 2.d, 3.a)

MATERIALS You will need heavy string or a piece of rope and wooden clothespins. Write uppercase and lowercase letters on the top of the clothespins. Glue a picture beginning with each letter on a square of tagboard and laminate. Prepare two or three for each letter that has been studied.

FIGURE 4.25 Soundline

PROCEDURES Introduce this as a group activity before putting it in a center where children can do it independently. Children match the picture card to the clothespin and hang it on the rope (see Figure 4.25). Add new letters and sounds as children learn them.

4.33 Letter Spin for Sounds

This is a good game to review up to eight beginning sounds at a time. It is a variation of the letter spin described in Activity 4.28. (CCSS Foundational Skills 1.d, 2.d, 3.a)

MATERIALS You will need a spinner divided into four to eight sections and labeled with beginning letters to review; you can use a large cube, like a die, instead of a spinner. You will need a collection of picture cards that correspond with the letters, with at least four pictures for each letter. Follow the procedures for the letter spin activity.

PROCEDURES
1. Lay out all the pictures face-up.
2. Two to four children take turns using the spinner, selecting one picture that begins with the sound indicated by the spinner. After selecting, the student's turn is over and the next child spins. If there are no more pictures for a sound, the child must pass.
3. Play continues until all of the pictures are gone. The winner is the one with the most pictures at the end.

4.34 Initial Consonant Follow-the-Path Game

This game is simple enough that even preschoolers can learn the rules and use it to practice a variety of features. You will see this game adapted in many ways in Chapters 5 and 6. (CCSS Foundational Skills 1.d, 2.d, 3.a)

Adaptable for Other Stages ● ● ● ● ●

MATERIALS Copy the two halves of a follow-the-path game board, found in Appendix F and on the website. Keep the game in a folder that can be easily stored: paste each half on the inside of a manila folder (colored ones are nice) leaving a slight gap between the two sides in the middle (so the folder can still fold). Add some color and interest with stickers or cutout pictures to create a theme such as "Trip to the Pizza Parlor" or "Adventures in Space." Label each space on the path with one of the letters you want to review, using both uppercase and lowercase forms (see Figure 4.26); sets of three to six letter sounds work best. Reproduce a set of picture cards that correspond to the letters. Copy them on card stock or glue cutout pictures to cards. You will need two to four game pieces to move around the board; flat ones, like bottle caps or plastic disks, store well. Keep the pictures and playing pieces in a labeled plastic zip-top bag inside the folder.

PROCEDURES
1. Turn the picture cards face-down in a stack.
2. Each child draws a picture in turn and moves his or her playing piece to the next space on the path that is marked by the corresponding beginning consonant.
3. The winner is the first to arrive at the destination.

FIGURE 4.26 Follow-the-Path Game

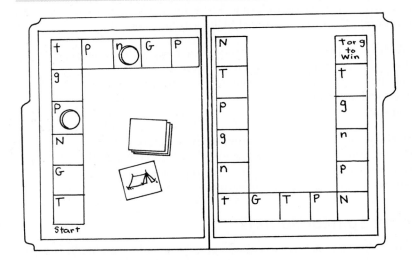

PD TOOLKIT™

for Words Their Way®

Follow the Path Game
A variety of games can be played in the emergent stage using the blank Follow the Path template, which is available to download and print.

Adaptable
for Other Stages
● ● ● ● ●

VARIATIONS Place pictures in each space for a "Follow-the-Pictures" game. Children roll a die or spin a spinner marked with letters to move to the appropriate space.

Concepts about Print (CAP)

Concepts about print are best learned in the context of reading and writing. Put songs that you sing, poems and jingles that you learn, and portions of longer books with catchy memorable refrains (such as "I'll huff and I'll puff and I'll blow your house down") on charts for easy reference. Use them for print referencing and to develop concept of word.

4.35 Who Can Find?

This works best with a big book, chart story, or poem you have read several times. It can also be used after creating a dictation or other writing. (CCSS Foundational Skills 1.d, 3.a, Language 2, 2.b)

PROCEDURES
1. After reading a piece of text several times, ask children questions about conventions of print such as, "Who can find a period? Who can find a capital *A*? Who can find the last word in the first sentence? Who can find the title? Who can find a word that rhymes with *can*?"
2. Call children forward to point to the features of print you name. It is easy to differentiate this activity for children at various points of development so that it offers just the right challenge. Ask some children to find letters, and ask others to find words.

4.36 Explore the World of Logos

Children can learn to "read" their environment in the prealphabetic or logographic stage in which they use shapes, colors, and logos to distinguish words. Draw students' attention to these forms of print to emphasize the many functions print serves and the different forms it can take. (CCSS Language 2, Foundational Skills 1, 1.a, 3.c)

MATERIALS Collect commercial labels and logos from cereal boxes, advertisements, signs, and so on. Encourage children to bring in examples from home. Mount these on card stock.

PROCEDURES

1. Hold up an example, such as the label on a fast food bag, and ask children if they can "read" it. Talk about what it says and where it came from.
2. Create a sentence strip for a pocket chart printed with: "I can read _____." Insert the logo in the empty space.
3. Put these in a center for children to use on their own after introducing it in a group.

4.37 What Were You Saying?

Many concepts about print can be directly taught by writing in speech bubbles—especially speech bubbles connected to students' own pictures. (CCSS Foundational Skills 1, 1.a, 1.b, 3.c, Language 2)

MATERIALS You will need a digital camera to take photos of your students. If you don't have a digital camera, find pictures of children engaged in an activity such as kicking a ball to a friend or licking an ice cream cone.

PROCEDURES

1. Print or project a picture that shows children. Ask questions to engage your children in recounting the event.
2. Draw a speech bubble coming out of one child's mouth. Explain that the pictures only *show* what is happening, but you can *write* what the child actually said in the speech bubble. Prompt by saying something like, "What do you think she is saying in this picture?"
3. Write down what the children say in the speech bubble (see Figure 4.27). You can reference various aspects of print, such as letter–sound matches, capitals, and punctuation.
4. Read what it says in the speech bubble while pointing to individual words. Point out once again that the picture *shows* what happened, but the writing in the speech bubble tells what was actually *said*. Ask individual children to come up and read their own speech bubbles.

FIGURE 4.27 Using Speech Bubbles to Teach Concepts about Print

VARIATIONS Read comic strips, comic books, and children's books that feature speech bubbles, such as one of the following.

- Peggy Rathman's *10 Minutes till Bedtime* (1999) and *Goodnight Gorilla* (1994). New York: Scholastic.
- Susan Meddaught's *Martha Speaks* (1992). Boston: Houghton Mifflin.
- Mo Willems's *Don't Let the Pigeon Drive the Bus* (2003), *Knuffle Bunny* (2004), and their sequels. New York: Hyperion Books.
- Easy to read comics known as TOON books. New York: RAW Junior, LLC.

4.38 Interactive Writing and Morning Message

The act of writing with children offers you the opportunity to model the use of the alphabet, phonemic segmentation, letter–sound matching, concept of word, and conventions such as capitalization and punctuation, all in the context of a meaningful group activity. As you write on the chalkboard, chart paper, or an interactive whiteboard, children see their own ideas expressed in oral language transformed into print, allowing many opportunities for print referencing. See Table 4.3 on page 112 for ideas about things to point out. During interactive writing, children share the pen and are invited to come forward to add a letter, a word, or a period. Such writing can take place any time of the day and for any reason; for example, to list class rules, make a shopping list, record observations from a field trip, create a new version of a familiar text, or list questions for a classroom visitor.

Morning Message is a favorite form of group writing in which you and your children compose sentences that report on daily home and school events that are important to the class. Each morning, talk with the entire group to discover bits of news that can be part of the morning message. In preschool or early kindergarten, this may be only one sentence. Keep a lively pace and be sure all children are engaged. (CCSS Foundational Skills 1, 1.a-d, 2, 2.d, 3.a-c, Language 1, 1.a, 1.f, 2, 2.a-d)

MATERIALS It is important that everyone can see the print. Many teachers use a large sheet of chart paper, markers, and white tape for covering mistakes. To involve students, give each one a lap-sized whiteboard, chalkboard, or clipboard so they can participate in listening for sounds, handwriting, and the use of punctuation.

PROCEDURES
1. Chat with children informally, sharing news from home or the classroom. This is a time for generating lots of talk so do not rush through this step too quickly.
2. Select a piece of news to record in the form of a single sentence such as, "We will go to PE." Recite the sentence together with the children to decide how many words it contains, holding up one finger for each word. Then draw a line for each word on the board or chart (see Figure 4.28).
3. Repeat each word, emphasizing the sounds as they are written, and invite the group to make suggestions about what letters are needed: "The first word we need to write is *we*. *Wwwwwweeeeee*. What letter do we need for the first sound in *wwweee*?" A child might suggest the letter *Y*. "The name of the letter *Y* does start with that sound. Does anyone

FIGURE 4.28   Morning Message

have another idea?" Every letter in every word need not be discussed at length. Focus on what is appropriate for the developmental level of your students.

4. Let children take turns coming forward to write, usually just one child per letter or word at this level. You can do the writing in the beginning, but as children learn to write their letters you can share the pen. Use white tape to cover any mistakes made on paper. Model and talk about concepts about print such as left to right, return sweep, capitalization, punctuation, and letter formation. Clap the syllables in longer words, spelling one syllable at a time.

5. After the sentence is completed, read it aloud to the group, touching each word, and then have the children read with you. If your sentence contains a two- or three-syllable word, touch it for every syllable, helping children see how it works. Invite children to come forward and fingerpoint as they read.

6. Repeat steps 2 to 5 for another sentence. Keep in mind children's attention span when deciding how many sentences to write. One sentence may be enough at the beginning.

VARIATIONS Leave up the morning message all day and encourage children to read it on their own. You might want to use it for some activities in the next section, such as Cut-Up Sentences, Be the Sentence, or for the whole-to-part lessons. You can send home a collection of all the morning messages for a week on Friday as a summary of class news that most children will be able to proudly read from memory to their parents.

Concept of Word in Text (COW-T)

When children are learning about letters and sounds at the same time or they are fingerpoint reading from memory, there is a complementary process at work. Learning one gives logic and purpose to learning the other. Fingerpoint reading familiar rhymes and pattern books followed by deliberate attention to words in and out of context is the best way to achieve a COW-T.

4.39 The Concept of Word Whole-to-Part Five-Day Lesson Framework

You can use the following five-day format with any kind of text—language experience dictations, poems, rhymes, jingles, songs, or parts of a simple patterned book. The key is to limit the text to no more than two to eight lines that children can memorize after repeated readings. The procedures move from introducing a whole text to the parts. Activities on days 2 to 5 can vary, depending on the skill of your children and the time you have. (CCSS Foundational Skills 1, 1.a-d, 2, 3, 3.a-c, 4)

MATERIALS You will need chart paper, a pocket chart, sentence strips, envelopes, and word cards. Record the text on chart paper using print large enough for all to see and/or prepare two sets of sentence strips with individual lines from the text. Have word cards ready to record selected words. In addition, photocopy or type several lines from the text to give children their own single-sheet copy. Glue these into personal readers made from newsprint or blank white paper stapled together as described in the next chapter. Leave out the chart, sentence strips, and word cards for children to use independently as a center activity after they have been introduced in the group.

PROCEDURES

Day 1. Introduce the whole text.

1. Have children memorize a rhyme, poem, song, or jingle or a patterned refrain from a storybook introduced during shared reading. Use simple pictures if possible to help them

memorize the lines by heart, as shown in Figure 4.13 (page 116). If children have difficulty memorizing four or five lines, cut back to two.

2. Next, introduce the printed text on chart paper or a pocket chart—one sentence per line. Model how to read the text by using your finger or pointer to touch every word as you say it. Talk about how you are starting with the first *word* on the left and touching each *word* in the *sentence* as you say it. Touch multisyllabic words several times and explain why.

3. Ask the children to read each sentence exactly as you do after you have read it (echo reading). Then invite the children to say it with you (chorally) as you point to each word; this is the third reading.

4. Ask individual children to come up and recite as much of it as you think they are capable of while pointing to each word. Be prepared to guide as needed to ensure accurate pointing.

Day 2. Work with the parts (sentences).

1. Review the text from day 1 by repeating steps 3 and 4 above.

2. Hand out sentence strips and ask children to find which sentence it matches in the pocket chart and place it there. Discuss how they knew it was the same—prompt for specifics like "starts with" or "the word…." Rebuild the text with and without a model for reference. Simple pictures like those in Figure 4.13 can help children get the sentence strips in order.

3. Pass out individual copies of the rhyme. Read this together as every child tracks the print. Glue it into their personal readers.

4. Pair children with a buddy and have them practice reading the rhyme to each other while fingerpointing. Ask the non reading buddy to make sure his or her partner is saying and pointing to each word. Have each partner read twice.

Day 3. Work with the parts (words).

1. Repeat steps 4 and 5 from day 1 above.

2. Pass out individual word cards for each sentence and have children come up and find a word and place it on top of its match in the pocket chart. Discuss how they knew it was the same word. (Prompt for letters and beginning sounds.)

3. Pass out the sentence strips along with envelopes containing that particular sentence cut up into individual words. Have children rebuild the sentence word by word.

4. See Cut-Up Sentences (Activity 4.40) and Be the Sentence (Activity 4.41).

Day 4. Work with the parts (letters and sounds).

1. Use the chart copy or pocket chart to reread the text and then say, "I'm thinking of a word in this line that starts with the same sound as _____. What word am I thinking of? How did you know?" Or ask children to find words.

2. Have children reread their own copies. Name words (or letters for children still learning the alphabet) for them to find and talk about how they found it (what letter or sounds they used.) They can highlight or underline the words you ask them to find. Children can also call out words for each other to find.

3. Select two to four letter sounds to use as the basis for the picture sorting activity described on page 110. Repeat the sort over the next few days and complete extensions.

Day 5. Review the whole and assess the parts.

1. Have the children reread the text using the chart or personal copies. Select words for a word bank, described in the next chapter.

2. Have children illustrate their rhymes in their personal readers as a reward for all their hard work.

3. Assess children using the guidelines described on pages 115 and 117. Ask individual children to read the rhyme as they point to the words. Observe how accurately they track and whether they self-correct when they get off track. Point to a few words for a child to name, or hold up word cards in isolation to name.

4. Periodically have children reread charts done throughout the year and all the pages in their personal readers. Personal readers can go home so children can share their developing skills. Be sure that parents understand that they will read from memory but should try to touch each word as they read.

4.40 Cut-Up Sentences

The spaces between words are not always obvious to emergent students, so cutting sentences into words is a concrete way to show this. (CCSS Foundational Skills 1, 1.a-d, 2, 3, 3.a-c, 4)

MATERIALS Write a sentence from a familiar piece of text on a sentence strip. Sentences should come from a familiar book or a poem the group has read together. A pocket chart is handy to hold the sentences. Prepare a second copy to cut into words.

PROCEDURES

1. Gather a small group of children with similar needs and read the sentence several times, pointing to the words.

2. Then cut the sentence into words, snipping off each word as you read it aloud. Explain to the group that you need their help to rebuild the sentence because the words are all mixed up. Pass out the words to children in the group and then, pointing to the words in an intact copy of the sentence, ask who has each word as they are named from left to right.

3. Give children clues about how to find the words in order to rebuild the sentence: "What letter would you expect to see at the beginning of *swam?*" The child holding the word should come forward and display the word under the target word for comparison, checking each letter before leaving it in place.

4. Give each child a copy of the sentence strip and scissors. Under your guidance, have them cut off each word as it is named and then help them to reassemble the sentence. The words can be pasted down under a drawing done by the child or put into an envelope with the sentence written on the outside (see Figure 4.29). These can be sent home with the students.

5. Leave the word cards and model sentence strip with a pocket chart in a center for children to practice in their spare time.

FIGURE 4.29 Cut-Up Sentences

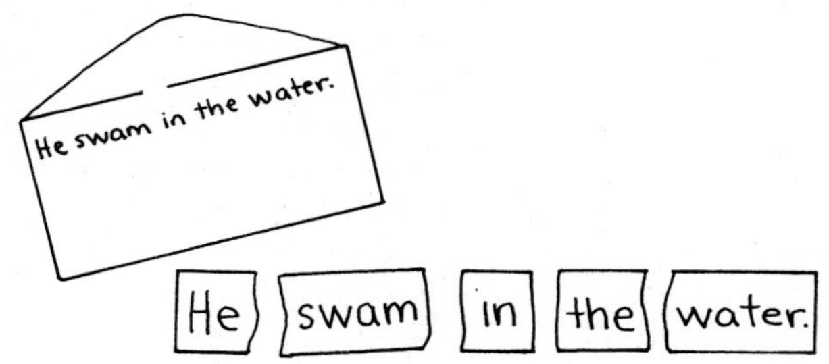

4.41 Be the Sentence

Children can also rebuild familiar sentences by pretending to be the words themselves. Write a familiar sentence on a chart or on the board. Start with short sentences such as "Today is Monday" or "I love you." Then write each word from the sentence on a large card. Give each word to a student, naming it for him or her. "Stephanie, you are the word *Monday*. Lorenzo, you are the word *is*." Ask the children to work together to arrange themselves into the sentence. Have another child read the sentence to check the direction and order. Try this again with another group of children and then leave the words out for children to work with on their own. (CCSS Foundational Skills 1, 1.a-d, 2, 3, 3.a-c, 4)

4.42 Stand Up and Be Counted

As children build a repertoire of known songs, nursery rhymes, and jump rope jingles, post them around the room and use them for oral concept of word activities that integrate phonological awareness with concept of word in print. (CCSS Foundational Skills 1, 1.a-d, 2, 3, 3.a-c, 4)

MATERIALS You will need a memorized nursery rhyme or jump rope jingle posted on the wall at an appropriate level. Be sure there is some floor space for everyone to sit in a circle.

PROCEDURES
1. Sitting in a circle, recall the nursery rhyme or jump rope jingle and recite it as you point to the written copy on the wall or chart.
2. Go around the circle, having children stand up for each word in the nursery rhyme. One child will stand up for *Hey*, another for *Diddle*, and a third for the next *Diddle*, and so on. Watch to see whether two children stand up for a two-syllable word like *Diddle* or *over*.
3. After everyone is finished standing up for each word, have everyone sit down, and say, "I think we made some mistakes. Did anyone notice?" Some children will notice. Ask them to explain.
4. Say to the students, "Yes, two people stood up for the word *over* but *over* is one word. It has two syllables, but it means one thing—over (motion with your hands jumping over something). Let's clap the word *over*. See? *Over* has two claps, but it's only one word. Go to the chart or wall poster and point out the word *over*. (You might note that it starts with an *o*.)
5. Repeat the exercise.

VARIATIONS Have children recite a sentence or rhyme and add a Lego or Unifix cube for each word as it is recited. Count the cubes (words). Compare sentences or lines. Ask the students, "Which sentence is longer? How can you tell?" (Longer sentences have more words—Legos or Unifix cubes.)

The word study activities for the emergent stage promote concept and vocabulary development, awareness of sounds, concepts about print and of word, and the alphabetic principle. These activities spring from and return to children's books and are extended through writing. Once children achieve a concept of word in print and can segment speech and represent beginning and ending consonant sounds in their spelling, they are no longer emergent but beginning readers. This is also when they move into the next stage of spelling, the letter name–alphabetic stage. Word study for the letter name–alphabetic speller/beginning reader is described in Chapter 5.

Word Study for Beginners in the Letter Name–Alphabetic Stage

The letter name–alphabetic stage of literacy development is a period of beginnings. Students begin to read and write in a conventional way. That is, they begin to learn words and actually read text, and their writing becomes readable to themselves and others. However, this period of literacy development needs careful scaffolding because students know how to read and write only a small number of words. The reading materials and activities you choose should provide contextual support. In word study, the earliest sorts are pictures; later, students work with words in families and words known immediately by sight. In the following discussion of reading and writing development and instruction, we look closely at the support teachers provide and the way word knowledge develops during this stage. However, before we examine this stage of word knowledge and provide guidelines for word study instruction, let us visit the first-grade classroom of Mr. Richard Perez.

During the first weeks of school, Mr. Perez observed his first graders as they participated in reading and writing activities, and he used the PSI inventory described in Chapter 2 to collect samples of their spelling for analysis. The efforts of three students are shown in Table 5.1. Like most first-grade teachers, Mr. Perez has a range of abilities in his classroom, so he manages three instructional groups for reading and word study, and uses students' spellings as a guide to plan phonics instruction. Some days he uses part of small-group time for teacher-directed word study.

Cynthia is a typical student in the early letter name–alphabetic group who writes slowly, often needing help sounding out a word and still confusing some consonants such as y and w and d and t. Her spelling is limited primarily to consonants with few vowels. Cynthia has memorized jingles, such as *Five Little Monkeys Jumping on the Bed*, but sometimes gets off track when she tries to point to the words as she reads.

Deciding to take a step back with this group, Mr. Perez plans a quick review of beginning sounds. Every three days, he introduces a set of four initial consonants, such as b, m, r, and s. After modeling the picture sort and practicing it in the group, he gives each student a handout of pictures to be cut apart for individual sorting practice, as shown in Figure 5.1(A). The next day, the students sort the pictures again and Mr. Perez observes how quickly and accurately they work. During seatwork time or center time, the students draw and label pictures beginning with those sounds, paste and label pictures, and do word hunts (follow-up routines described in Chapter 3).

TABLE 5.1   Spellings of Three First-Graders

Word	Cynthia	Tony	Maria
fan	FN	fan	fan
pet	PD	Pat	pet
dig	DK	dkg	deg
wait	YAT	Wat	wat
sled	SD	Sd	slad
stick	SK	Sek	stik
shine	CIN	Sin	shin

Each day when Mr. Perez meets with Cynthia's group, they read chart stories, jingles, and books with predictable texts. To help the students in this group develop a sight vocabulary, Mr. Perez has a **word bank** for each student. To create the word bank, he took the words the students could quickly identify from their reading and wrote them on small cards for their collections. The students add new words several times a week and review their words on their own or with classroom volunteers.

Tony is part of a large group in the middle letter name–alphabetic stage who has beginning and ending consonants under good control but shows little accuracy when spelling digraphs and blends, as shown in Table 5.1. He is using but confusing vowels in some words. Tony points to the words as he reads *Five Little Monkeys* and immediately self-corrects on the rare occasion he gets off track with words that have more than one syllable, such as *jumping* and *mama*.

Mr. Perez has Tony's group work with picture sorts of digraphs (*sh, ch, th,* and *wh*) for several weeks and then begins the study of same-vowel word families such as *op, ot,* and *og*. Mr. Perez takes 10 to 15 minutes during group time to introduce new word families. The students then receive their own set of words, shown in Figure 5.1(B), to cut apart for sorting. They work alone and with partners to practice the sort, writing and illustrating the words, and then play follow-up games.

Maria represents a third group of students in the late letter name–alphabet stage who correctly spell single consonants, as well as many digraphs and blends, as shown in Table 5.1. This group also uses some short vowels accurately. Maria can read some leveled books independently and is quickly accumulating a large sight vocabulary simply from doing lots of reading.

Mr. Perez reviews different-vowel word families for several weeks, making an effort to include words with digraphs and blends, but he soon discovers that the word family sorts are too easy and decides to move to the study of short vowels in nonrhyming words. Each Monday, he introduces a collection of words that can be sorted by short vowels into three or four sets. This group also receives a handout of words, as shown in 5.1(C), to cut apart and use for sorting. They learn to work in pairs for buddy sorts, writing sorts, word hunts, and games on other days of the week. ●

FIGURE 5.1 **Word Study Handouts for Letter Name–Alphabetic Spellers in Three Different Instructional Groups**

A. Beginning Consonant Sort

Bb 🐷	Mm 🐞	Rr ⭕	Ss ☀

B. Word Family Sort

pot	dog	cot	hop
log	frog	top	jog
mop	dot	hot	pop

C. Short Vowel Sort

pig 🐷	cup ☕	*oddball*
zip	bit	but
big	jug	pin
tub	rip	will
him	cut	rub
hum	win	fun
six	nut	run
put	did	gum

Literacy Development of Students in the Letter Name–Alphabetic Stage

for Words Their Way®

Development of Students in The Letter Name-Alphabetic Stage
Ms. Kiernan, a first grade teacher, describes the development of her students over the school year in this video.

Many components of the literacy diet described for the emergent stage continue to develop during the letter name–alphabetic stage. Vocabulary, oral language, and concepts grow throughout all the stages described in this book, but phonological awareness and concept of word in text will reach maturity. At the beginning of this stage, students may only segment and represent the most prominent beginning and final consonant sounds, demonstrating only partial phonemic awareness. By the end of the stage, they have full phonemic awareness and are able to isolate the elusive vowels and to pull apart the tightly meshed blends. As they learn to segment these sounds, they also learn the letter correspondences that represent them, including initial and final consonants, digraphs, blends, and short vowels. A new component becomes critical during the letter name–alphabetic stage—acquiring a reading vocabulary of **sight words** that can be recognized automatically in any context. It is fast and ever-growing word recognition that fuels fluency and comprehension.

Reading

During the letter name–alphabetic stage, students transition from depending on simple, **predictable** reading materials they read with support from shared reading and their memory for language, to less predictable beginning reading materials. With less predictable materials they must rely on an expanding sight vocabulary and the ability to figure out unfamiliar words using a variety of decoding strategies. This transition in reading material should be accompanied by word study instruction that continues to develop letter–sound correspondences.

CONCEPT OF WORD IN TEXT. Students who are solidly in the letter name–alphabetic stage of spelling have acquired a **concept of word in text**—the ability to track or fingerpoint read a memorized text without getting off track on a two-syllable word. There are two levels of concept of word in text: rudimentary and firm (Blackwell-Bullock & Invernizzi, 2012; Flanigan, 2006, 2007; Morris, 1981; Morris, Bloodgood, Lomax, & Perney, 2003).

Rudimentary. Students with a rudimentary concept of word can point to and track the words of a memorized text using their knowledge of consonants as clues to word boundaries. However, they may get off track with two-syllable words, and when they are asked to find words in what they read, they are slow and hesitant. They may **voice point** by returning to the beginning of the sentence or line to get a running start with memory as a support to read and locate the requested word. Students with a rudimentary concept of word are able to learn a few sight words from familiar stories and short dictations that they have reread several times. In word study, students with a rudimentary concept of word are in the early part of the letter name–alphabetic stage; they need to review beginning consonants and then study blends and digraphs along with same-vowel word families. With a rudimentary concept of word, students' sight vocabulary grows slowly, so most word study is done with picture sorting.

Firm. Students with a firm concept of word can fingerpoint read accurately, and if they get off track they can quickly correct themselves without voice pointing or starting over. When asked to find words in the text, students can identify them immediately or nearly immediately. They can acquire many sight words after several rereadings of familiar text. Students with a firm concept of word are ready to study different-vowel word families and then examine individual short vowels and the consonant-vowel-consonant pattern (CVC) for short vowels, including short vowel words containing beginning and ending consonant blends. With an expanding sight word vocabulary, sorts rely more on words than pictures to support word identification.

SIGHT WORD LEARNING. We define *sight words* as any words that are stored completely enough in memory to be recognized automatically and consistently in and out of context. A large store of sight words makes it possible to read fluently and to devote attention to comprehension rather than to figuring out unknown words. It also provides a corpus of known words from which students can discover generalizations about how the spelling system works. However, beginning readers do not recognize many words by sight and what they remember about words may be incomplete. As **partial alphabetic** readers (Ehri, 2000), they know something about consonants, but they lack the vowel knowledge needed to sound out words or easily store words in memory. In a familiar rhyming book, like *Five Little Monkeys Jumping on the Bed* by Eileen Christelow, they can point to the words using their memory for the rhyming pattern and their knowledge of beginning sounds /f/, /l/, /m/, /j/, and /b/. The word *monkeys* might be recognized out of context by virtue of several letters in the word (*m-k* or *m-y* perhaps). In another context, however, these partial phonetic cues alone will not suffice. *Monkeys* might be confused with *Mike* or *many*.

The term *sight words* is often confused with **high-frequency words**, which are the most commonly occurring words in print (i.e., *was, the, can, these*). A list of Fry's top 300 high-frequency words can be found in Appendix E. It is important to understand that though a reader's store of sight words will include many high-frequency words, it is not limited to those words; any word can be a sight word.

Another common misunderstanding about sight words is that they are phonetically irregular words children cannot sound out and therefore must be learned in a different way, as unanalyzed wholes or "by sight." Although there are some high-frequency words that lack dependable letter–sound correspondences (*of* = /uv/ and *was* = /wuz/), most words are more regular than not, especially in the consonant features that are most likely to be partially understood. For example, the high-frequency word *from* is 75 percent regular; only the *o* in the middle is irregular. There is no evidence that readers learn these words in a different way, but like all word learning at this stage, repetition in and out of context, along with word study, helps secure these words in memory.

READING FLUENCY. All beginning readers read slowly, except when they are reading well-memorized texts, and they are often described as word-by-word readers (Bear, 1989, 1991b). They do not have enough sight words to permit fluent reading and their reading rates may be painfully slow. For example, a beginning reader may read as slowly as 30 words per minute, depending on the familiarity, difficulty, and genre of the text (Invernizzi & Tortorelli, 2013). Although fluency is an important goal of learning to read, we find the current focus on getting beginning readers to "read fast" a disturbing trend. Chall called the first stage of reading the "glued to print" stage (1983). Beginning readers need to pay careful attention to the words on the page if they are going to store words fully in memory to build their sight vocabularies.

Most beginning readers point to words when they read, and they read aloud to themselves. This helps them to keep their place and to buy processing time. While they hold the words they have just read in memory, they read the next word, giving them time to fit the words together into a phrase. If you visit a first grade classroom during "sustained silent reading" (SSR) or during "drop everything and read" (DEAR), you are likely to hear a steady hum of voices. Fingerpointing, dysfluency, and reading aloud to oneself are natural reading behaviors to expect among beginning readers.

Writing

There is a similar pattern of dysfluency in beginning writing because students often write words slowly, sound by sound (Bear, 1991a). In the emergent stage of development, writers are often unable to later read what they have written because they lack or have limited letter-to-sound correspondences. Students in the letter name–alphabetic stage can usually read what they write depending on how completely they spell, and their writing is generally readable to anyone who understands the logic of their letter name strategy.

A first-grader shares her thoughts about winter in the example shown in Figure 5.2. Ellie represents most beginning and ending single consonants, as in her spelling of LK for *like* and WR for *wear*, but the sn blend in *snow*, spelled SO, is incomplete. Many vowels are missing, although she does include some that "say their name" as in MAK for *make* and SO for *snow*. She substitutes *a* for short *i* in *mittens* and *i* for short *o* in *hot*. Notice how she uses the letter *h* to represent the *ch* digraph in *chocolate* (spelled HIKLT) because the name of the letter (*aitch*) has the sound she is trying to represent. Correctly spelled words like *Mom* and *the* are probably sight words for Ellie.

During this stage you should continue to model writing for a variety of purposes, while using print referencing to develop concepts about print as described in Chapter 4. Interactive writing and recording students' individual or group dictations are fertile opportunities for print referencing as well as drawing students' attention to sound and letter correspondences. At the same time, students need to write for themselves as they spell "as best they can." Journal writing, letters to friends, observations, predictions before reading, and written responses after reading provide authentic reasons to learn about letters and sounds.

In the early phases of the letter name–alphabetic stage, you may sometimes dictate sentences for students to write. This removes the burden of trying to remember what they were trying to write so students can concentrate on writing for sounds and using the phonics features they have been learning in word study. For example, Tony's group might be asked to write, "Put the top on the hot pot.'" Asking students to simply copy sentences is of little value. It is the hard work of transcribing speech into print that exercises phonemic awareness and students' growing understanding of the orthography.

FIGURE 5.2   Ellie Writes about Winter

I LK WNT. I MAK a SOMN in the SO I WR MATS. Mom Mask Me hit hiklt

I like winter. I make a snowman in the snow. I wear mittens. Mom makes me hot chocolate.

Vocabulary Learning

Children's vocabularies continue to grow with exposure to and participation in oral language. The quality and quantity of vocabulary growth depends on the richness and frequency of verbal interactions with peers and adults. It is very important for you to be mindful and systematic about teaching students new words in the early childhood years, as a way to close the tremendous oral vocabulary gap that exists between children who come from literate homes and those who do not (Biemiller, 2005). Talking about the meanings of words or doing lots of reading helps, but not enough to enhance the vocabulary learning of those students who need it the most (Beck, McKeown, & Kucan, 2013). Observations of kindergarten and first-grade classrooms reveal that the current focus on teaching phonics in high-risk settings has resulted in measurable progress in decoding skills, but without attention to vocabulary these students are still at risk in later grades when knowing word meanings is critical for comprehension (Juel, Biancarosa, Coker, & Deffes, 2003).

There are many ways you can enhance vocabulary development in young students. Reading aloud continues to provide a rich source of new vocabulary as well as complex sentence structures. Highlight and discuss several words from a read-aloud throughout the week. Interactive read-alouds, "turn and talk," retellings, dramatizations of stories, and other suggestions from Chapter 4, continue to play an important role in stimulating oral language and encouraging the use of new vocabulary. In this chapter, we highlight several strategies and the activity section features creative dramatics, think-pair-share, and anchored word instruction (Juel et al., 2003).

SOPHISTICATED SYNONYMS. Opportunities exist throughout the day for you to model sophisticated words for familiar concepts as a way to promote vocabulary growth. Lane and Allen (2010) describe how a kindergarten teacher began the year by asking the "weather watcher" to report to the group using terms such as *sunny*, *cloudy*, or *warm*. However, as the teacher introduced new terms over several months, the appointed "meteorologist" was expected to *observe* the weather *conditions* and report their *forecast* with terms such as *brisk*, *frigid*, or *overcast*. Lane and Allen suggest that teachers look for, gradually teach, and consistently use synonyms for the common language of everyday routines. Students can be asked to *distribute*, *replenish*, *dispense*, or *allocate* materials. During group discussions *participants* are encouraged to *contribute*, *articulate*, *verbalize*, and *elaborate* their ideas. The class can be asked to *queue up adjacent to* or *parallel* to the wall and *proceed* in an *orderly* fashion. Students are complimented for being *amiable*, *agreeable*, *courteous*, *proficient*, *gracious*, and *considerate*. Rather than "dumbing down" our language to children, we should consciously elevate our language and provide appropriate explanations, repeated exposure, and opportunities for them to use that same language.

ENRICH SIMPLE TEXT. Most beginning readers and writers are not able to grow their vocabularies through their own reading because the simple predictable texts they use for reading instruction rarely include words whose meanings they do not know. However, you can infuse more vocabulary as you discuss the story and illustrations using alternative words. For example, *The Cat Sat on the Mat* by Brian Wildsmith, described in Chapter 4, is written with very simple, predictable language. However, the cat experiences a range of emotions, from *contented* to *uneasy* to *agitated* to *furious*, as more and more animals gather on the mat. Part of your discussion should focus on how the cat feels, offering the opportunity for you to introduce many synonyms for *happy*, *sad*, and *mad*—the words children are likely to suggest. Discussing illustrations will especially benefit English learners, who rely on the illustrations to understand much of the story. You might even look up some of the synonyms in their home language. *Content* and *furious* turn out to be *contento* and *furioso* in Spanish! Studying **cognates** (words descended from the same ancestral root) is addressed more in later chapters but it can begin in the early stages as well.

CONCEPT SORTS. Use objects, pictures, and known words in concept sorts to expand children's vocabulary and to encourage rich verbal interactions. For example, after reading about and discussing concepts related to weather, students can sort pictures of mittens, sandals, sunscreen, jackets, and galoshes under the headings of *sun*, *rain*, and *snow*. You should model and use the language of comparison/contrast: "warmer than, cooler than, not as hot as," and so forth. This explicit attention to language helps students "unpack" what they tacitly know about the concepts underlying the labels, and becomes part of their own discussions about words and concepts. Students can sort words and pictures multiple times over several days. They sort in multiple categories—you can see this when they contrast things they like with those they do not like, animals that live in the water or on land, and so on. Concept sorts for English learners are particularly worthwhile because objects (such as plastic animals) or pictures can be sorted into categories without needing to know the English terms. At the same time, English-speaking partners can supply unknown words and, while talking about the sort, students practice using and hearing the vocabulary they hear from you and their classmates. In a weather concept sort with English learners, there are several concepts students sort into pairs to practice the new vocabulary. English learners in Kristen Polanski's classroom talk about relationships they observe, as when an English learner who speaks Hmong as her primary language reports that moon and sun are a pair for "when the sun go down and the moon come up." Vocabulary is learned best when it is used many times in phrases and sentences (CCSS, 2010). Concept sorts are included in the activity section that follows.

Orthographic Development in the Letter Name–Alphabetic Stage

Students in the letter name–alphabetic stage provide a wonderful example of how learners construct knowledge in an attempt to make sense of the world of print. Without prior knowledge of how to spell words, children carefully analyze the sound system more consciously than do adults, and they make surprisingly fine distinctions about the ways sounds and words are formed in the mouth. They match the phonemes they can segment to the letter names of the alphabet in ways that may seem curious and random to the uninformed adult.

Letter Names

Letters have both sounds and names, and students in the letter name–alphabetic stage use their knowledge of names of the letters in the alphabet to spell phonetically or alphabetically. For example, students in the early part of this stage are likely to spell the word *jeep* as GP, selecting *g* as the first letter because of its name ("gee"). According to letter name logic, there is no need to add the vowel because it is already part of the letter name for *g*. Sometimes early letter name–alphabetic spellers do include vowels, especially when they spell long vowels that "say their name," as Ellie did when she spelled *snow* as SO. This phenomenon accounts for the reason the stage is called *letter name–alphabetic*. Spellers in this group operate in the first layer of English—the alphabetic layer.

A few letter names do not cue students to the sounds they represent. For example, the letter name for *w* is "double u" and the name for *h* is "aitch." Neither offers a clue to the sound it represents. However, when you say the name of the letter *y* you can feel your lips moving to make the shape of the /w/ sound and the name for *h* does end with the /ch/ sound. Consequently, early letter name–alphabetic spellers may spell *witch* as YH. Read through the letter names in Table 5.2 to see what they offer students in terms of sound matches. Most consonants offer a clue to the sound they represent either at the beginning ("bee") or the end ("ef") of the letter name.

Letter Sounds

Children need to learn not only letter *names*, but also letter *sounds* to help them grasp the **alphabetic principle**, the insight that individual speech sounds can be represented by letters of the alphabet. Children appear to learn the letter sounds for letters that include the sound in their names (*b*, *d*, *f*) more easily than letters whose names have no relationship to their sound (*w*, *y*, *h*). Letters that are associated with more than one sound (*c*, *g*, and all the vowels) or letters that share a sound with another letter (*k*, *c*, *s*, *g*, *j*) require more instructional time and attention (Huang, Tortorelli, & Invernizzi, 2014). Children who demonstrate greater degrees of phonological awareness are more likely to learn and retain letter sounds (Piasta & Wagner, 2010). The initial sounds associated with letters should be examined, compared and contrasted, and sorted in distributed cycles of review that include attention to letter names, letter sounds, and letter formation (Jones, Clark, & Reutzel, 2013).

TABLE 5.2 **Names of the Letters of the Alphabet**

A	ay	H	aitch	O	oh	V	vee
B	bee	I	ie	P	pee	W	doubleyoo
C	see	J	jay	Q	kyoo	X	ecks
D	dee	K	kay	R	are	Y	wie
E	ee	L	el	S	es	Z	zee
F	ef	M	em	T	tee		
G	gee	N	en	U	yoo		

During the early part of the letter name–alphabetic stage, when students have only partial phonemic awareness, spelling efforts may be limited to the most prominent sounds in syllables, usually the beginning and ending consonants. As phonemic awareness improves in the middle part of this stage, students' spellings gradually include a vowel in each stressed syllable, and they spell short vowels by matching the way they articulate the letter names of the vowels (discussed more later in this chapter). By the end of the letter name–alphabetic stage, students have learned how to spell many words with short vowels correctly and with full phonemic awareness they also spell blends. Table 5.3 summarizes characteristics of the letter name–alphabetic stage.

How Consonant Sounds Are Articulated in the Mouth

Knowing something about phonetics (the science of sounds) will help you understand and appreciate what young students do as they attempt to represent sounds with letters. When they spell, letter name–alphabetic students rely not only on what they hear in the letter names, but also on how the letters are articulated, or formed in the mouth. For example, when students try to spell the *dr* in *drive*, they are misled in their spelling by the similarity between

---

TABLE 5.3 Characteristics of Letter Name–Alphabetic Spelling

	What Students Do Correctly	What Students Use but Confuse	What Is Absent
Early Letter Name–Alphabetic B, BD for *bed* S, SP for *ship* YN for *when* L, LP for *lump* FOT for *float* G, J, GF, JF, or GV for *drive*	Partial phonemic awareness Represent prominent sounds, usually beginning consonants Directionality Use most letters of the alphabet Partial spelling of consonant blends and digraphs Spell some known sight words correctly: *the, is*	Letter name–sound matches Consonants based on manner and point of articulation (*j/dr, b/p*) Concept of word is rudimentary; gets off track on two-syllable words Spaces between words	Most vowels Complete blends and digraphs
Middle Letter Name–Alphabetic BAD for *bed* SEP or SHEP for *ship* LOP for *lump* FOT for *float* GRIV for *drive*	Developing phonemic awareness All of the above plus: Spell beginning and ending consonants Spell frequently occurring short vowel words: *cat, dog* Concept of word is fully developed	Short vowels by place of articulation Consonant blends and digraphs	Silent letters Preconsonantal nasals
Late Letter Name–Alphabetic *bed ship lump* STEK for *stick* FLOT for *float* DRIV for *drive* BAKR for *baker*	Full phonemic awareness All of the above plus: Spell many short vowels and most consonant blends and digraphs Spell many sight words, including some containing frequently occurring long vowel words: *like, come*	Some short vowels still confused Substitutions of common short vowels for ambiguous vowels: COT for *caught* Preconsonantal nasals Affricate blends (*dr, tr*)	Most long vowel markers or silent vowels Vowels in unstressed syllables

dr and *jr*, and they may spell *drive* as JRV. Say "drive" and "jrive." Do they sound and feel alike? Linguists call these sounds **affricates**, which are formed by forcing air through a small closure at the roof of the mouth to create a feeling of friction (*fric*tion, *affric*atives—see the meaning connection?). English has several other letters and letter combinations that create the affricate sound and these are often substituted for each other: *j, g, ch, dr, tr,* and the letter name for *h* (aitch). Try saying "jip / chip," and then "trip / drip" several times to feel the similarity and help you understand why young students confuse these affricates.

The voiced and unvoiced consonant pairs discussed in Chapter 4 and listed in Table 4.2 account for other confusions experienced by letter name–alphabetic spellers. They may spell *brave* as BRAF or *oven* as OFN. Both *v* and *f* are articulated in exactly the same place on the lips, but one is **voiced** and the other is **unvoiced**. When phonemes are voiced, the vocal cords vibrate. You can feel the difference in the first sound of *van* compared to *fan*. One implication for instruction is that students in the letter name–alphabetic stage benefit from saying the words aloud as they are sorting so that they can feel the sound differences. Another implication is that when you first teach these sounds, avoid contrasting voiced and unvoiced pairs: *b/p, d/t, g/k, z/s, v/f,* and *j/ch* (Purcell, 2002), as suggested by the sixth principle described in Chapter 3, "begin with obvious contrasts." Only when most consonant sounds are mastered should students focus attention on these finer distinctions. This is especially true for English learners, who may not have one of the contrasting sounds in their primary language.

When talking about letter sounds with students, it is important to realize that some are rather difficult to say in isolation. Try to say the sound for *b*. What vowels did you attach to the *b*? If you said the letter name ("bee"), then you used the long *e* vowel. If you said "buh," the sound associated with *b*, you attached the **schwa** sound (/ə/ = "uh"). Now try to say a /b/ sound without a vowel. Try to whisper *b* and cut your breath short in a whisper. The whisper is as close as you come to separating the vowel from the consonant sound. Consonant sounds that cannot be held like these are known as **stop consonants** (*b, d, g, k, p, t*). Other consonants, known as **continuants** (*f, l, m, n, r, s, v, z*), can be said slowly without adding a vowel. You may find there are times when saying the sound in isolation draws attention to the feature of interest, but asking students to say "D says duh, duh, duh" is not the goal of word sort lessons. D says "duh" only in words like *duck* and *dump*; it says "dee" in words like *deal* or *deed*. The goal of word study is to extrapolate the sound of D across many different exemplars.

Vowels in the Letter Name–Alphabetic Stage

Vowels pose special problems for letter name–alphabetic spellers, who rely on the names of letters and how sounds feel in the mouth. Try saying the word *lip*. You can feel the initial consonant as your tongue curls up toward your palate and you can feel the final consonant as it explodes past your lips, but did you feel the vowel? Unlike consonants—articulated by tongue, teeth, lips, and palate—vowels are determined by more subtle variations in the shape of the mouth. In addition, they are tightly wedded to the consonants around them.

The major difference in the medial vowel sounds is described linguistically as **tense** and **lax**. The vocal cords are tense when producing the **long** *a* sound (*ate*), but relax a bit in producing the **short** *a* sound (*at*). The vowels we call "long" are no longer in duration than short vowels; the terms are holdovers from Classical Latin. Although these terms may not be the most accurate terms linguistically, they are more common than *tense* and *lax* and teachers understand each other when they are used. The simplest way to talk about vowels is probably the best. Descriptions like "the sound in the middle" may suffice to draw students' attention to the vowels at first, but students have no trouble learning *long vowel* and *short vowel*; such terms make word study discussions easier.

HOW VOWELS ARE ARTICULATED IN THE MOUTH. Through the letter name–alphabetic stage, students become adept at fully segmenting words into phonemes, including the medial vowel, and they use the alphabetic principle to represent each sound with a letter. Long vowels say their letter name, so the letter choices are obvious. Students spell *line* as LIN, *rain* as RAN, and *boat* as BOT. Perhaps what is most interesting about the letter name–alphabetic

FIGURE 5.3   **Vowels in the Mouth**

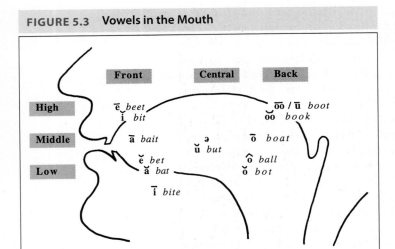

stage is the way students spell the short vowels. They turn to the names of the letters, but find no clear letter–sound matches for the short vowel sounds. For example, there is no letter name that says the short *i* sound in *bit* or the "uh" sound in *cup*. Very early letter name–alphabetic spellers might use *f* ("ef") or *s* ("ess") for short *e* because the letters name start with the short *e* sound. Spellers throughout the letter name–alphabetic stage use their knowledge of the alphabet to find the letter name closest to the place of **articulation** of the short vowel sound they are trying to write.

You may have never analyzed sounds at this level, so let's take a moment to consider the vowels, and where and how sounds are made in the vocal tract. In Figure 5.3, the vowels are placed to mimic the general area where you can feel their place of articulation. Vowels are subtly differentiated by the shape of the mouth, the openness of the jaw, and the position of the tongue when a word is said. They are all voiced because it is impossible to articulate a vowel sound without vibrating the vocal cords. Compare the vowels in this figure by saying the following words in sequence several times and trying to identify where the vowel sound is produced:

beet	bit	bait	bet	bat	bite
but	bot	ball	boat	book	boot

Do you feel how producing the vowels moves from high in the front of the oral cavity (*beet*) to low in the oral cavity (*bite*) to the back of the oral cavity (*bot*), down the front, back, and up (*boot*)? Also contrast the way your lips feel when you say the rounded vowel in *boot* with the high front vowel sounds in *beet* or *bit*.

The way a word is pronounced may vary by dialect. For example, many people say *caught* and *cot* the same way. Some rhyme *roof* with *hoof* while others rhyme *roof* with *poof*. Although these dialectical differences do not interfere with learning to spell, being aware of these differences when students sort and talk about words enhances word study. Everyone speaks a dialect, but we all learn to read and write the same orthography.

A LETTER NAME STRATEGY TO SPELL SHORT VOWELS. Students in the letter name–alphabetic stage use their knowledge of letter names and the feel of the vowels as they are produced in the vocal tract to spell *bed* as BAD. Without being consciously aware that they are doing this, letter name–alphabetic students spell short vowels with the letter name closest in articulation to that short vowel. There are five letter names from which to choose: *a, e, i, o,* and *u.* How would an alphabetic speller spell the word *bed*? What letter name is closest to the short *e* sound in *bed*? Try saying *bed/bead* and *bed/bait* to compare how the short vowel sounds and the long vowels or letter names feel in your mouth. Repeat the pairs several times and pay attention to how your mouth is shaped. The short *e* sound is closer in place of articulation to the long *a* or letter name for *a* than it is to the letter name for *e*. Students might spell *ship* as SHEP for a similar reason—the short *i* sound is closer to the letter name for *e* than the letter name for *i*. (If you look at Figure 5.3, you will see how short *i* and long *e* are both high front vowels, whereas the long *i* is a low front vowel.) Short *a* poses little problem for spellers because the letter name for *a* is already close in place of articulation. This is a good reason to teach it first. However, because short *e* is close to short *a*, these pairs are not good contrasts for first introducing short vowel sounds. Table 5.4 will help you remember how the letter names of vowels are substituted for the short vowel sounds beginning readers try to spell. The amazing thing about these letter name substitutions for short vowels is that they are so predictable. Read (1975) found that nearly all students go through a period when they substitute the short vowels with other letter names closest in articulation.

Systematic word study helps students in the letter name–alphabetic stage learn to spell short vowel words correctly. They see that short vowels follow a specific pattern—a consonant-vowel-consonant (CVC) pattern. Regardless of how many consonant letters are on either side of the single vowel (*cat*, *clap*, *clack*, or *strap*), one vowel letter in the middle signals the short vowel sound. The CVC pattern is introduced in the late letter name–alphabetic stage and is contrasted with long vowel patterns in the within word pattern stage.

Sometimes students in the letter name–alphabetic stage may spell *bent*, *bet*, *bat*, and *bait* the same way as BAT. But letter name–alphabetic spellers are also readers, and when they reread their own spelling of *bait* as *bat*, a word that they know spells something else, they experience disequilibrium (Bissex, 1980). This forces them to find other ways to spell a word like *bait*, perhaps as BATE. When students are able to spell basic short vowel patterns and also begin to experiment with long vowel patterns, they have entered the next spelling stage: the within word pattern.

TABLE 5.4	**Letter Substitutions for Short Vowels**

Spelling Attempt	Logical Vowel Substitution
BAT for *bat*	None, short *a* is close to *a*
BAT for *bet*	*a* for short *e*
BET for *bit*	*e* for short *i*
PIT for *pot*	*i* for short *o*
POT for *put*	*o* for short *u*

Other Orthographic Features

In addition to short vowels, students work through four other features during the letter name–alphabetic stage: (1) consonant digraphs, (2) consonant blends, (3) preconsonantal nasals, and (4) influences on the vowel from certain surrounding consonants.

CONSONANT DIGRAPHS AND BLENDS. Letter name–alphabetic spellers take some time to learn the consonant units known as digraphs and blends. A **digraph** is composed of two letters that represent a single sound. Digraphs are generally easier than blends because they only require segmenting and attending to a single phoneme. The digraphs studied in this stage include the bold letters in **th**in, **fi**sh, ea**ch**, and **wh**en. They can come at the beginning or end of words.

The digraph *th* actually represents two different sounds that are the same in articulation but different in voicing. The *th* in *bath* and *thin* is unvoiced while the *th* in *bathe* and *then* is voiced. Most children (and adults) ignore this difference—if they are aware of it at all. However, English learners may need to have the differences discussed. Listen as they try to pronounce words with *th* and offer help as needed.

A consonant **blend** is slightly different. A blend is a spelling unit (sometimes called a *consonant cluster*) of two or three consonants that retain their identity. Each sound in a blend can be heard, but they are tightly bound and not easily segmented into individual phonemes, making blends difficult for students to spell accurately. This is why the *t* in the *st* blend may be omitted in *stick*, as in the spellings SEK or SEC. In English, blends can occur at the beginning or end of syllables, as shown by the bold letters in the following words: **bl**ack, **cl**ap, **tr**ap, ju**st**, li**sp**, and ma**sk**. If you have trouble remembering these terms it may help to know that *blend* begins and ends with the blends *bl* and *nd*, while *digraph* ends with *ph* (a digraph representing the /f/ sound studied in later stages).

PRECONSONANTAL NASALS. Some final blends are especially difficult, deserving special mention. The nasal sounds associated with *m*, *n*, and *ng* are made by air passing through the nasal cavity in the mouth. Nasals that come right before a final consonant, such as the *n* in *pink*, are known as **preconsonantal nasals**. Try saying *bad*, *ban*, and then *band* or *bang* as you pay attention to the sounds. You cannot feel the *n* in *band* because it passes out through the nose on the way to the *d*, but it is definitely there! Preconsonantal nasals are often omitted by spellers during the letter name–alphabetic stage (*pink* may be spelled PEK and *jump* may be spelled JOP). When students begin to spell words with preconsonantal nasals correctly, they are usually at the end of the letter name–alphabetic stage, having achieved full phonemic awareness.

CONSONANT INFLUENCES ON THE VOWEL. The letters *r*, *w*, and *l* influence the vowel sounds they follow. For example, the vowel sounds in words like *bar*, *ball*, and *saw* are not the same as the short vowel sounds in *bat* and *fast* even though they have the CVC pattern. The consonant sounds /r/ and /l/ are known in linguistics as **liquids** because they roll around in the mouth and have vowel-like qualities. Both can change the pronunciation of the vowel they follow. These spellings are often known as *r*-**influenced** (or *r*-controlled) and *l*-influenced (or *l*-controlled). The *w* also has an effect on vowels that follow it in words such as *want*, *was*, *wash*, *word*, and *war*.

It can be difficult to spell *r*-influenced vowels by sound alone. For example, *fur*, *her*, and *sir* have the same vowel sound (represented as /ər/) yet are spelled three different ways. In addition, it is impossible to isolate a vowel from the *r* that follows in words like these. The *r*-influenced vowels that follow a CVC pattern (*car*, *for*) are examined during the late letter name–alphabetic stage and can be compared with short vowels in word sorts. Students might also contrast consonant blends with an *r* (*fr*, *tr*, *gr*) and *r*-influenced vowels (e.g., *from/form*, *grill/girl*, *tarp/trap*) as a way to compare exactly where the *r* falls.

Spelling Strategies in the Letter Name–Alphabetic Stage

Young writers do not know how spell many words from memory, so if we want them to express their ideas in writing we need to encourage them to use invented spelling or developmental spelling. Children at the letter name–alphabetic stage benefit from the phonemic analysis and letter–sound matching involved in figuring out a word as they write independently. This active analysis and application of growing skills is much more beneficial than simply being given the spelling (Clarke, 1988). In addition, waiting for someone to come by and give them a word can slow down their production. In general, avoid providing the spelling for words for students in this beginning stage as they write; instead, encourage them to spell "as best they can." You can make exceptions. For example, if children write about a specific topic, like autumn, you can brainstorm and post a word bank of special words they could use, such as *leaves*, *cool*, *falling*, and *down*. Such a word bank can often help reluctant writers get started, but beware of an overreliance on copying.

Frequently model how to break words into syllables and slowly stretch out the sounds to match to a letter. Do this during interactive writing and other times when you write for and with students, but select words that have regular letter sound matches (e.g., *flat* but not *laugh*) to model. Look for ideas about introducing invented spelling to students on page 28 in Chapter 2. Also model and teach students how to use resources in the room such as their sound boards, word banks, word walls, or other word displays around the room. Parents need to understand the rationale behind invented spelling, so be ready to communicate with them about the value of letting children spell as best they can.

What about children who won't invent? Sometimes you have students who resist spelling as best they can and are anxious that every word is spelled correctly. While we want students to develop a spelling conscience, or a desire to spell correctly, such over-concern at this point in their development will likely severely limit what they can write about as well as the practice they get when they try to figure out words. For example, one of the authors had a first-grader, T.J., who spelled every word correctly using beautiful handwriting. But T.J. wrote almost the same thing in his journal every day. It was a cause for celebration when T.J began to misspell as he took risks and wrote about a wider variety of topics.

Briefly talk with students about their spelling in independent work and nudge them to apply what they have learned. For example, Sabina wrote about playing with her sister: "I like to PLA WIT mi STR." Her teacher complimented her on spelling "like" correctly and asked how she knew it. Sabina replied that she had used the word wall. The teacher then pointed to *with* and said, "Here's a word that is almost correct. Listen to the end of the word 'with.' Do you hear that special sound that needs two letters? It is the sound you hear at the beginning of *thumb* (referring to a sound board with digraphs). You sorted words with TH several weeks ago. Can you fix that word?" In this way, the teacher held Sabina accountable and helped her apply what she knew. Other words (*play* as PLA and *sister* as SSTR) were left as Sabina's best efforts based on her current word knowledge.

It is too early to ask students in the letter name–alphabetic stage to look up words in a standard dictionary that they need for writing, but we recommend that you keep a dictionary handy and occasionally model how you use one. This is a good time to introduce students to the delights of age-appropriate picture dictionaries and wordbooks where they might find labeled pictures arranged thematically as a source of ideas for writing. Refer to Activity 5.15 for ideas about how to teach beginning dictionary skills and a list of resources.

Word Study Instruction for the Letter Name–Alphabetic Stage

This section starts with a discussion of how to support beginning readers as they acquire a concept of word in text and build a sight word vocabulary. In the whole-to-part model we propose, students learn to read big books, poems, and jingles at the same time they study letter–sound correspondences through picture and word sorts. This **analytic phonics** approach begins with whole words that are broken into letters and sounds that students can compare and examine. **Synthetic phonics** has a different sequence. Students are taught vowel sounds (usually short vowels) along with consonants in isolation, and then are expected to blend those sounds to decode words as they read in text that is controlled by phonic regularity. We believe an analytic approach to phonics represents an easier and more engaging entry into the world of reading. Although students are taught to sound out words, this is not the starting point for the phonics instruction we recommend. Learning to blend letters and sounds together is addressed in the study of word families and short vowels (see Activities 5.22 and 5.23 for examples). Be assured that all the phonics features are covered in a systematic way.

Reading Instruction

Beginning reading should focus on solidifying a concept of word in text so that students can begin to amass a sight word vocabulary as quickly as possible. Think of acquiring sight words as establishing an orthographic lexicon, a mental dictionary of known written words organized by spelling patterns. It is best to acquire sight words by reading and rereading familiar texts and by analyzing known words out of context, in word study. Through rereading, students see the same words over and over again, thereby increasing the number of words they can recognize automatically.

The more words students can recognize automatically, the greater the opportunity for making generalizations across words in their word sorts. The result is a general increase in word knowledge. But what students know about particular words during the letter name–alphabetic stage may only be partial. For example, as they read, early letter name–alphabetic spellers may substitute *leopard* for *lion* in a story about big cats at the zoo. Those errors indicate that they are attending to beginning letters for cues. This is also evident in the way they spell during this time—they might spell *lion* as LN. Ehri (2000) has described these readers as "partial alphabetic," because their letter–sound knowledge is not automatic or complete and they use only partial letter–sound cues (usually consonant cues) to identify and spell words. Partial information is not enough to ensure fast and accurate word recognition. Instead, letter name–alphabetic spellers need support to make reading happen.

SUPPORT READING. Without a large sight vocabulary beginning readers cannot read very much without some kind of support. Support can come from two sources: the text and the teacher. Predictable text has repetitive patterns, rhyme, and simple language that make it memorable when students have recited or sung it, or read or heard it, many times. Texts are also easy to read when the words are about an event students experienced first-hand, as in individual and group dictations created using the language experience approach (LEA) described in the last chapter (also see Activity 5.9). Your support comes from shared reading strategies such as reading the text aloud and then encouraging students to read in unison (**choral reading**) or immediately after you read (**echo reading**). Or you might provide a book introduction (Clay, 1991) that uses the language of the text and anticipates difficult words and concepts.

Tension lies between these two forms of support. The more predictable a text is, the less your support is needed. Conversely, the less support provided from recurring elements of text, the more scaffolding is required from you. During the letter name–alphabetic stage, students move from reading primarily predictable books to texts that are more controlled in terms of high frequency words and decodability (Mesmer, Cunningham, & Heibert, 2012). As students develop a sight vocabulary and letter–sound knowledge, they need less support.

SIGHT WORD LEARNING. Acquiring a sight vocabulary is critical to becoming a fluent reader, but progress is slow during the early letter name–alphabetic period and students need repeated exposure to words to fully store them in memory. Taking words they first encounter in context and examining them out of context makes a difference in how well students learn those words (Ehri & Wilce, 1980), and how many words they learn over time (Johnston, 1998, 2000). Other things influence word learning such as repeated exposure and the nature of the words themselves. For example, words that have concrete referents (e.g., nouns and adjectives like *moon* or *green*) or that are easily visualized (e.g., action verbs like *run*) are easier to learn than abstract prepositions, articles, or adverbs (such as *from* or *when*), which have no meaning by themselves (Mesmer et al., 2012). Chapter 4 provides details for examining words through in-text and out-of-text activities in whole-to-part activities. Students can be actively involved in the process of determining which words they want to learn through the use of word banks.

Word Banks. Lifting words out of context and writing them on small cards to make a **word bank** is an effective way to build a reading vocabulary or sight word vocabulary. Word banks are collections of known words gathered from the texts that students have been reading and rereading, to be reviewed in isolation (Stauffer, 1980). Why do students need to review words they already know? The answer is they do not know them the same way more mature readers do; they know them only partially and tentatively. Letter name–alphabetic students may confuse *ran* and *run*, *stop* and *ship*, *lost* and *little* because they have them stored partially in memory as *r_n*, *s_p* or *l_t*. They may read *gingerbread* correctly every time because it is the only long word they know that starts with *g*, but when you ask them to spell it (GRBRD) you get a better idea of what they really know about the word.

The words in a word bank come from many sources that students read and reread: predictable books, preprimer readers, leveled books, poems, and individual and group dictations. By using words from familiar readings and numbering the stories and rhymes to correspond to word cards, you can encourage students to return to the primary source to find a forgotten word and to match the word bank card to its counterpart in print. Regularly reviewing word bank words encourages students to look more thoroughly at words and to note individual letter–sound correspondences. As they study initial sounds through picture sorts, ask students to find words in their word banks that start with those same sounds. This helps them make connections between the pictures they sort and the words they read. Later in the letter name–alphabetic stage, the word bank becomes a source of known words to be used in word sorts.

Word banks take extra work but are well worth the effort, particularly for students early in this stage who are not making good progress in reading. They motivate students because they offer tangible evidence of growing word knowledge (Johnston, 1998). When the word bank contains between 150 and 200 words and the student is at the end of the letter name–alphabetic stage, the word bank can be discontinued. If you find it overwhelming to manage individual word banks, an alternative is to have one collection that students in a reading group share. More guidelines for word banks and other sight word activities can be found in the activities at the end of this chapter.

Personal Readers. Collect copies of familiar rhymes and jingles, group or individual dictations, or selected passages from books that children have read in a **personal reader** (Bear, Caserta-Henry, & Venner, 2004); see Figure 5.4. Students are enormously proud of their personal readers and they reread the selections many times before taking them home to read some more. Personal readers are an ideal place for students to collect words for their word banks. They can simply underline the words they know best and these words can then be transferred to small cards. A number can be written on each word card that matches the numbered stories.

FIGURE 5.4   Personal Reader with Word Bank

In Figure 5.4, the student's word bank is a plastic bag that can be stored in the personal reader; little leveled books fit inside the front pocket. In addition, a small soundboard (see Appendix B) of consonant sounds is included for reference in word study and writing. The personal reader might also contain a page that lists the words in the student's word bank.

Sequence and Pacing of Word Study

Converging evidence from research (NRP, 2000) has established that children need systematic phonics instruction, but there is disagreement about the nature of that instruction and the exact sequence. Our recommended sequence, outlined in Table 5.5, is based on research in children's spelling over several decades, which has revealed the developmental order in which phonics features are typically mastered. This is one reason we call this book *Words Their Way*. Initially, students use beginning consonants in their writing, so this is the place to begin word study in the early letter name–alphabetic stage. As their ability to segment phonemes becomes more complete later in the stage, they begin to use but confuse short vowels and consonant blends. This is the time to study those features.

Although there is a predictable pattern of development, the exact sequence and pace is not the same for every student because they progress at different rates. (See the three columns in Table 5.5 for ideas about how to modify the pace.) However, there is no time to waste—you must set as fast a pace as possible during the letter name–alphabetic stage because success in beginning reading depends on learning the basic phonics elements that are covered in this stage. Pacing should be tied to ongoing assessment to determine whether instruction is effective. We discuss progress monitoring for this stage on pages 170 and 171.

Placing students in the early, middle, or late parts of this stage using the spelling inventory depends primarily on how well they spell short vowels. If students do not attempt vowels, they are in the early part of the stage. If they use but confuse vowels, perhaps getting one or two correct on an inventory, they are in the middle of the stage. If they spell half or more of the short vowels on an inventory, they are in the late letter name–alphabetic stage. If students are spelling most short vowels, as well as most digraphs and blends, they are ready to move to studying long vowels in the within word pattern stage, in which short vowels are reviewed as long vowels are introduced. Table 5.3 helps you identify whether students are in the early, middle, or late part of the stage.

TABLE 5.5   Pacing and Sequence Guide for Letter Name–Alphabetic Spellers

	Introductory Pace	Moderate Pace	Advanced Pace or Review
Early Letter Name–Alphabetic			
Picture Sorts for Initial Consonants*	Contrast two sounds that are very different in place of articulation, such as /m/ and /s/. Contrast up to four sounds when students are able. A suggested sequence is: 1. *b m r s* 2. *t g n p* 3. *c h f d* 4. *l k j w* 5. *y z v*	Review all initial consonants sounds (four at a time) and then, as needed, contrast easily confused consonants: w/y/; g/j; c/s; b/p; d/t	Review initial consonant sounds only as needed. Use progress monitoring spell checks to determine which consonants need attention.
Picture and Word Sorts for Same-Vowel Word Families	Start out slowly, spending as much as one week on a set: at; an/ad; ap/ag; op/ot/og; un/ut/ug; ip/ig/ill; op/ot/og; et/eg/en	Use the same sequence but move more quickly once students catch on to how word families work	Use progress monitoring to determine which families need attention.
Picture Sorts for Digraphs	s/h/sh; c/j/ch; h/sh/ch; t/th; th/wh; sh/ch/wh/th	s/h/sh; sh/ch/h; th/wh; wh/sh/ch/th	wh/sh/ch/th
Pictures Sorts for Blends	Contrast single sound to blends first (e.g., s/t/st or s/p/sp) then compare blends (sp/sk/sm; sc/sn/sw; p/l/pl; pl/sl/bl; cr/cl/fr/fl; bl/br/gr/gl; pr/tr/dr; k/wh/; qu/tw)	*s*-blends; *l*-blends; *r*-blends	*r*-blends others as needed
Middle Letter Name–Alphabetic			
Word Sorts for Mixed-Vowel Word Families	at/ot/it/; an/un/in; ad/ed/ab/ob; ill/ell/all; ag/eg/ig/og/ug; ick/ack/ock/uck; ish/ash/ush	an/un/in; ag/eg/ig/og/ug; ill/ell/all; ick/ack/ock/uck; ish/ash/ush	Use progress monitoring spell checks to determine which families need attention
Picture Sorts for Short Vowels	a/o; i/u; e/o; e/i/o/u	a/o; i/u; e/i/o/u Combine with word sorts	Skip unless needed
Late Letter Name–Alphabetic			
Word Sorts with Short Vowels in CVC Words	a/o; i/u; e/i/o/u with easy words	a/o; i/u; e/i/o/u with easy words	a/e/i/o/u with harder words
Word Sorts for Short Vowels with Blends and Digraphs	Ex: **dr**op trip di**sh**	Ex: **dr**ag da**sh** **sl**ed	Use progress monitoring to determine what needs attention
Word Sorts for Preconsonantal Nasals	rag/rang; lip/limp; win/wind; ram/rap/ramp; sad/sand/sank; ng/mp; nt/nd/nk	rag/ran/rang; win/wig/wing; ng/mp; nt/nd/nk	ng/mp; nt/nd/nk as needed
Word Sorts for *R*-Influenced	a/ar o/or	a/ar o/or	Move on to next stage

*When using picture sorts, add words if students can read them. Do not use words students cannot read.

The Study of Consonant Sounds

Word study in the early letter name–alphabetic stage begins with picture sorts to focus students' attention on initial consonant sounds. Picture sorts help students continue to develop their phonemic awareness as they isolate beginning sounds and learn to pull apart consonant blends.

You can find pictures for sorts in Appendix C and prepared sorts on PDToolkit and in the other books in the *Words Their Way*® series. Chapter 3 identified follow-up activities, such as draw and label or cut and paste, and many of the games described for beginning consonants in Chapter 4 can be easily adapted for this stage. There are also games on PDToolkit that are ready to print and use.

INITIAL CONSONANTS. Mr. Perez, whom we met at the beginning of this chapter, was wise in deciding to take a step back to firm up Cynthia's understandings of consonants. Many students benefit from a fast-paced review of consonants at the beginning of first grade to secure tentative letter–sound matches. There is no particular order to the sequence of beginning sounds, but we recommend starting with frequently occurring initial consonants, in which the contrasts or differences are clear both visually and phonologically. You might find that the sequence listed in Table 5.5 is effective for a review, but bear in mind that some beginning sounds are easier than others, depending on the relationship of the sound to the letter name. Because of this, some contrasts will take more time than others.

Figure 5.5 is an example of a sort that started with pictures and then included sight words from the students' word banks. Chapter 4 offers suggestions for how to plan and carry out picture sorts for initial sounds and the activity section has suggestions for further practice. You can include picture sorts with initially occurring short vowels here as a way to introduce those letter–sound correspondences.

Some students may still be confused with certain letter sounds based on letter name mix-ups (e.g., *y* and *w*) or voiced and unvoiced pairs (e.g., *b* and *p*), and therefore benefit from specific word study activities that contrast those pairs. In particular, English learners benefit from word study that addresses confusions that arise because of sounds that are missing or that are different in their native language. Picture sorts can clarify beginning consonant sounds in English that may not exist in other languages like those sounds described in Table 5.7. For example, Spanish speakers may sort a series of pictures that begin with /j/ or /h/ to clarify the differences in these sounds in English, but which do not occur in Spanish. For Chinese speakers, it helps to spend time studying nasal sounds to compare /n/ and /ng/. Spanish speakers also benefit from studying *s*-blends, a combination that does not exist in Spanish. Arabic speakers may sort pictures that begin with a voiced /g/ as in *goat* and a voiceless /k/ as in *coat* (Helman , Bear, Invernizzi, Templeton, & Johnston, 2009, 2011).

Beginning consonants are reviewed and ending consonants are targeted in same-vowel word families. Most students do not need to study ending consonant sounds with picture sorts, perhaps because once they develop the phonemic awareness to attend to final sounds, they transfer their knowledge of letter–sound matches to spell those final consonants as well. Some students may have a few problems even when they know most consonant matches, but do not hesitate to move on if they are beginning to represent vowels in their invented spellings. English learners whose native language does not have many ending consonants may need more sorts with final consonant sounds.

After students know their consonant sounds, they are ready to learn about consonant digraphs and blends. The goal is to not only master letter–sound correspondences, but also to help students see these two-letter combinations as single orthographic units in the CVC pattern.

for Words Their Way®

Images for Picture Sorts
Use this resource to make picture sorts that can be printed or played online.

for **English Learners**

FIGURE 5.5   Initial Consonant Picture and Word Sort

DIGRAPHS. Digraphs are introduced before blends because there is only one phoneme to deal with, but most students are ready to study both at about the same time. The consonant digraphs to study in the letter name stage are *ch*, *sh*, *th*, and *wh*. (We do not include *ph* at this point because there are few words that beginning readers will encounter that begin with *ph*.) There are several things to keep in mind when setting up picture sorting contrasts for digraphs. First, consider the confusion students show in their spelling attempts. Some students substitute *j* for *ch*, as they spell words like *chin* as JN, or they may confuse the letter name of *h* (aitch) with *ch* and spell *chin* as HN. Consider a contrast to study *ch* that compares pictures that start with *ch* with single consonants, such as *h*. You can compare *th* to single *t*, *sh* to single *s*, and *ch* to single *c*. However, it is difficult to sort pictures by *w* and *wh* because many words beginning with *wh* do not have a distinctive sound. (Which witch was which?) Compare *wh* to *th*, *sh*, and *ch* in a culminating digraph sort. Add known words to picture sorts, as shown in Figure 5.5; include question words starting with *wh* (*who*, *what*, *when*, and *why*). Table 5.5 contains a suggested sequence and possible contrasts for studying digraphs. Digraphs are revisited in the study of word families and short vowels in both initial and final positions.

BLENDS. You can group beginning consonant blends into three major and one minor categories as follows:

> *s*-blends: *sc*, *sk*, *sl*, *sn*, *sm*, *sp*, *st*, *sw*
> *l*-blends: *bl*, *cl*, *fl*, *gl*, *pl*, *sl*
> *r*-blends: *br*, *cr*, *dr*, *fr*, *gr*, *pr*, *tr*
> Blends with /w/: *qu*, *tw*

The easiest group to learn seems to be the *s*-blends, because *s* is a continuant that you can hold without distorting the sound (*sssss*). Blends with the "slippery" *l* or *r* are the hardest because some are confused with affricatives such as *j*. In *qu*, the *u* is acting as a consonant representing the /w/ sound. Three-letter blends (*spr*, *str*, *squ*, *thr*, *shr*) are less common and not studied until the within word pattern stage.

To study initial consonant blends, begin with picture sorts that contrast a single initial consonant with its blend. This is the problem for spellers such as Tony, who spell *stick* as SEK. To help Tony listen for the sounds in the blend, contrast *st* with pictures that begin with *s*. After studying several blends in this fashion, pick up the pace and introduce other blends in groups; see Table 5.5 for suggestions. Once students catch on to how blends work and learn to segment and blend the individual sounds in a consonant blend, they may move quickly through a sequence of study or even skip some contrasts altogether. The procedures and routines for studying digraphs and blends using picture sorts are the same as for other beginning sound sorts, as described in Chapter 4.

Students in the early part of the letter name–alphabetic stage do not need to master consonant blends and digraphs completely because they will be revisited throughout the stage by studying word families and short vowels. Research by Johnston (2003) and others shows that blends, digraphs, and short vowels all begin to appear in students' spelling about the same time, so there should be some interplay among these features in the instructional sequence, as shown in Table 5.5. Consonant blends and digraphs that create an affricate sound (*trip*, **drip**, *chip*) take longer to master because their sounds are so similar.

Final consonant blends (*last*, *lisp*, *task*, *left*, *kept*, *felt*, *shelf*, and *help*) are not studied with pictures, due to a lack of examples, but should be included toward the end of the stage in the study of short vowel words. Other ending blends that include an *r*, like *rd*, *rt*, and *rp*, in words like *bird*, *art*, or *chirp*, are studied with *r*-influenced vowels.

Preconsonantal nasals, a particular type of final blend that includes *mp*, *nt*, *nd*, and *nk*, are also studied at the end of the letter name stage. We add the digraph *ng* as well, which may be studied in word families, as there are many words spelled with *ang*, *ing*, *ong*, or *ung*. Appendix E has lists of words by families that include words with preconsonantal nasals among them. Many students find this feature particularly difficult and will need explicit routines for making words with and without the nasal, changing *rag* into *rang* or *hug* into *hung*, for example. The building, blending, and extending exercises described in Activity 5.22 can be adapted for this.

The Study of Short Vowels

Once letter name–alphabetic spellers have a solid, if not complete, mastery of beginning and ending consonant sounds, they are ready to study medial short vowels. Students need full phonemic awareness to isolate the elusive vowel, but if vowels are still missing or used only occasionally in their spelling, start the study with word families as Mr. Perez did with his middle group. Once students are using (though still confusing) short vowels consistently, ask them to compare short vowels in word sorts that examine the CVC pattern across a variety of vowels, as Mr. Perez did with his highest group. Appendix D contains lists of words spelled with short vowels which you can use to create handouts similar to those used by Mr. Perez in Figure 5.1(C). Appendix D also has suggested sorts, and prepared games and more sorts are on the website and in *Words Their Way®: Word Sorts for Letter Name–Alphabetic Spellers*.

for Words Their Way®

Look for word family sorts to print or use online.

WORD FAMILIES. Word families, which are sometimes called **phonograms**, consist of groups of rhyming words like *cat*, *mat*, *sat*, and *bat* that are spelled similarly. They offer an easy and appealing way to introduce vowels early in this stage. This supports students in their first efforts to analyze the vowel because the vowel and the ending letter(s) are presented as a chunk or pattern called a **rime** (e.g., the *at* in *cat* and *mat*). What comes before the vowel is the **onset**. Examples of onset-rime breaks are *m-an*, *bl-and*, *m-at*, and *th-at*. It is easier and more natural for students to divide words into onsets and rimes than divide them into individual phonemes (Goswami, 2008; Treiman, 1985).

Studying word families makes sense for several other reasons. First, 37 rimes can be used to generate 500 different words that students encounter in primary reading materials (Wylie & Durrell, 1970). In addition, these same rimes are familiar chunks in thousands of multisyllabic words: the *an* chunk can be found in *canyon*, *fantastic*, and *incandescent*. Second, vowel sounds are more stable within families than across families (Adams, 1990; Wylie & Durrell, 1970). For example, the word *dog* is often presented as a short *o* word in phonics programs, but in some regions of the United States, it is pronounced more like *dawg*. If you say it that way, then you probably pronounce *fog* as *fawg*, *frog* as *frawg*, and *log* as *lawg*. When studying word families, the actual pronunciation of the short vowel does not matter, it is the *og* chunk that is examined and compared.

SAME-VOWEL WORD FAMILIES. Knowing that students in the early letter name stage have trouble with the medial vowel, it is a good idea to compare word families that share the same vowel before contrasting different vowels. This supports students' first efforts to read and spell those words. What they really must attend to are the beginning and ending consonants in order to sort and spell the words. Studying same-vowel word families reviews those features. In sorting words like *mat* and *man*, for example, students must focus on the final consonant more than any other phoneme. Nevertheless, the phonological awareness of the rime unit (e.g., *-at,-an*) lays the foundation for future vowel study as students begin to look inside the word for common features.

There is no particular order for studying word families, but a good choice is to start with short *a* families (*at, an, ad, ap, ag*) because these words abound in early reading materials, and students are likely to already know several words from these families by sight. In addition, short *a* is the least likely short vowel to be confused when students try to make matches based on letter names and place of articulation. Compare other same-vowel word families in a similar way (*in, it, ip* or *ot, op, og*, etc.).

MIXED-VOWEL WORD FAMILIES. Move quickly to compare different vowel families. The difference between *top*, *tip*, and *tap* lies in the medial vowel, and it is through such contrasts that students are forced to listen to the vowel sound itself and look carefully at the vowel in the middle of a word. Students in the middle letter name stage should be ready to study mixed-vowel word families. Include words with blends and digraphs after they have been studied with picture sorts. For example, the *ag* family can be expanded to include *flag*, *brag*, *drag*, *shag*, and *snag*.

FIGURE 5.6 **Same-Vowel Word Family Sort with Pictures**

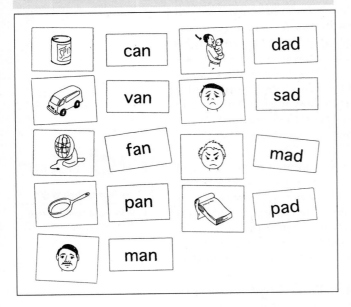

Table 5.5 suggests contrasts and a sequence for studying word families under three possible pacing guides. However, it is just a suggestion for planning your own course of study. Consider the words that your students know as sight words, and the kinds of words they encounter in their reading. If you are reading a story with lots of short *u* words, then study a few short *u* families.

Introducing Same-Vowel Word Families with Pictures. Apply the following procedure when introducing a word family sort with pictures (see Figure 5.6).

1. Start with just the pictures for a rhyming sort. (See the list of rhyming short vowel pictures at the beginning of Appendix C.) Use pictures as headers for each column (e.g., *can* and *dad*) and then pick up another picture. Say to students, "*Van.* Does *van* rhyme with *can* or *dad—van, can: van, dad?* I will put it under the *can.*" Model several and then have students help you finish the sort. Name all the pictures in each column and talk about how they rhyme.

2. Now lay out the word cards. Name a header such as *can* and say, "Who can find the word *can?* What letters would you look for at the beginning and end?" Repeat for *dad,* and then ask students to find the word for each picture.

After all the words are sorted and matched to the pictures, read down each column. Ask the students how the words are alike; they should note that they all end with the same two letters. Explain that the words are in the same family (the *an* family or *ad* family) and they all rhyme.

3. Remove the words and shuffle them. Give them out to the students to match to the pictures again. Read each column and then remove the pictures to see whether the students can use just the initial sound and the rime to read each word in the column.

4. Give students their own set of pictures and words to sort for seatwork. Follow up with other word family activities such as Build, Blend, and Extend, described in Activity 5.22.

Introducing Mixed-Vowel Word Families with Words. Word cards without pictures are used to compare mixed-vowels in word families such as *ig, ag,* and *og.* Students should already know how to read several words in each family.

1. Begin by laying down a known word as a header for each family. Choose words you are sure the students can read, such as *big, dog,* and *bag.* Explain that the rest of the words are to be sorted under one of these headers.

2. Pick up another word such as *frog* and say, "I am going to put this word under *dog* because it ends in *o* and *g.*" Then read the words: "Listen: *dog, frog.*" Continue to model one or two words in each category, always *sorting first* and then reading down, starting with the header.

3. Ask students to sort the next word. They should sort first and then read from the top of each column to help them identify the new word. They are not expected to sound out the word first and then sort. Instead, their sense of rhyme will support them as they read the new word, by simply changing the first sound of a word they already know. The final sort might look like the following:

big	dog	bag
dig	frog	wag
pig	hog	rag
wig	fog	flag
	log	tag

4. After all of the words are sorted, read down each column and lead a discussion to focus students' attention on the common features (sounds and letters): "How are the words in this column alike?" After giving students a chance to discuss what they notice about the words, summarize by explaining that the words in each column are in the same family because of the two ending letters and sounds that rhyme.

5. Provide students with individual sorts. Conclude as in the previous sort with follow-up activities.

Guidelines for Word Families. As you study word families, keep these thoughts in mind.

- When studying word families, it is appropriate to modify one of the principles of word study described in Chapter 3, "Use words students can read." When working with word families, students probably cannot read *all* the words initially. However, because the words are in rhyming families, students are supported with pictures and with headers that are familiar. Students sort visually by the rime spelling first, and then read unknown words by blending different onsets with the header rime.

- *Include words with digraphs and blends once they are introduced.* Studying the *ack* family can grow a lot when you include *black, clack, track, shack, quack, stack, snack,* and *crack.*

- *Supply supplemental reading materials that feature word families.* With the publication of research about onsets and rimes, and renewed interest in word families, there has been a flood of reading materials for students that feature a particular family or short vowel. Some of these little books are engaging and well-written, offering students support in the form of patterned or rhyming text. Other books are contrived and nonsensical, as in "Nan and Dan sat in the pan." Use well-written books as a starting point or as a follow-up for word study, and students can use the books to go on word hunts for additional words that follow the same phonics features. However, choose books carefully; text featuring sentences such as "The tan man ran the van" make reading into an exercise in word calling rather than comprehension. Although some phonics readers are better than others, they shouldn't constitute the sole reading materials used at this level.

- *Plan follow-up activities.* There are lots of activities and games to use when studying word families. Follow-ups to sorting include re-sorting, blind sorts, and writing sorts, as described in Chapter 3. Board games designed to study beginning sounds can be adapted to word families. Activities like Build, Blend, and Extend; Sound Wheels; Flip Charts; and Show Me are favorites and are included in this chapter's activities. From this point on, expect students to spell the words they sort correctly; you can administer short spelling tests to assess their mastery and include dictated sentences that feature a family (e.g., "The frog sat on a log in the fog"). Use **word study notebooks** to record writing sorts and the results of word hunts or brainstorming sessions.

- *Set a fast pace.* Studying word families can take a long time if you feel compelled to study every family in a thorough fashion, but this should not be the case. See Table 5.5 for ideas about how to modify the pace. Although students may still make errors in spelling short vowels, many quickly pick up the notion that words that sound alike probably share similar rimes and are spelled alike. They will also be able to use this knowledge to figure out new words by analogy; for example, noting the *and* in *stand*, they quickly decode it.

THE STUDY OF SHORT VOWELS IN THE CVC PATTERN. Once students are spelling about half of the short vowel words correctly on a spelling inventory and working with mixed-vowel word families easily and accurately, they are ready to study short vowels in nonrhyming words outside of word families. This asks them to look at words in a new way, not as two units with various rimes (*m-ad, fl-ag, tr-ack*), but as three units with the same CVC pattern (*m-a-d, fl-a-g, tr-a-ck*), one vowel surrounded by consonants. This ability to see words as patterns is the key feature of the next stage, the within word pattern stage. While studying short vowels, students come to see that CVC is the basic pattern for all short vowels across variations that include VC (e.g., *at*), CCVC (e.g., *flat*), CVCC (e.g., *fast*), and CCVCC (e.g., *blast*).

FIGURE 5.7   Short Vowel Sort across Families

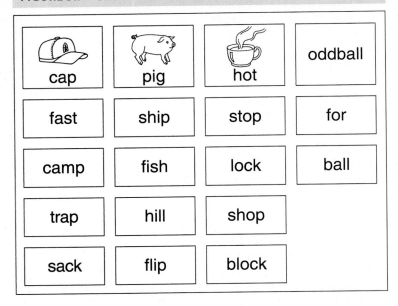

cap	pig	hot	oddball
fast	ship	stop	for
camp	fish	lock	ball
trap	hill	shop	
sack	flip	block	

Word Sorting to Compare Two or More Short Vowels. Use the following procedure for a teacher-directed short vowel sort.

1. Make a collection of word cards that features two or more short vowels to model on a tabletop, pocket chart, overhead projector, or document camera,.

2. Begin by laying down a known word as a key word for each vowel. Read each word and isolate the vowel: "Here is the word *cap*. Listen: *cap, ap, /ă/. Cap* has the short *a* sound in the middle. Let's listen for other words that have the same vowel sound in the middle." Repeat for each category. See Figure 5.7.

3. Pick up a new word such as *fast* and say, "I am going to put this word under *cap*. Listen: *ca-a-ap, f-a-a-ast*. They have the same vowel sound in the middle." Continue to model one or two words in each category, reading each new word and comparing it to the key word. Hold up an oddball, like *for* or *was*. Ask students if they hear the same vowel sound in the middle. Model how to place it in the oddball category because it does not have the same vowel sound. Ask your students to help finish the sort. They should read each word and then sort it. Once the words are sorted, read down each column to check and discuss how the words are alike in sound and spelling. If students cannot read a word put it aside to revisit later. See Figure 5.7 for the final sort.

4. After all the words are sorted, read down each column to check and then discuss the common features: "How are the words in each column alike? How are the oddballs different? What is odd about them?" Help students identify the CVC pattern by labeling the units in *cap, pig,* and *hot*. Point out that *hill* and *trap* are also CVC words because *ll* and *tr* are consonant units on each side of the single vowel. At this point revisit any unknown words. Ask the students to put each in the correct column and sound it out.

5. Reread the words in each column and then lead the students in sorting a second time. Leave mistakes to the end and check them by reading down the columns.

6. Give students their own set of words to sort at their seats, with partners, or for homework.

7. Because it is easy to sort the words visually by attending to the vowel letters, the blind sort described in Chapter 3 is important as a follow-up activity. One partner reads each word aloud while the other partner indicates where it goes without seeing the word. Model this first in a small group and then let partners work together.

If students are still making some errors in the spelling of digraphs and blends, which is likely, include words with those features in the short vowel sorts. At this time, they have many more sight words that contain beginning and ending consonant digraphs and blends. You might even plan a two-way sort as shown in Figure 5.8—first by vowel sounds and second by digraphs or blends. This encourages flexibility in word analysis, a desirable trait (Sharp, Sinatra, & Reynolds, 2008). Consider doing a third sort, perhaps sorting by action words (e.g., *crash, drag, trim*) versus things (e.g., *crumb, truck, crib*); take time to discuss words that could be used as both, depending on context (e.g., "We will trim the tree."; "We added trim to the valentine."). Cartwright (2006, 2008) argues that having students think about words by different attributes builds cognitive flexibility, an important component of reading comprehension. Discussing the different meanings and uses of words also makes students aware of the multiple meanings or *polysemy* of words, an important aspect of vocabulary development (Templeton et al., 2015).

Guidelines for Short Vowels. As you study short vowels in CVC words, keep these points in mind:

- When studying short vowels, plan contrasts that are distinct from each other. We recommend that students first compare short *a* to short *i* or short *o*. Do not compare short *a* to short *e*, or short *e* to short *i*, until later as those are the very sounds students are most likely to confuse.

- You can sort most short vowels using with printed words, but you can also use pictures to focus students' attention on the vowel sounds. Use pictures for column headers, such as the sound board for vowels in Appendix B; Appendix C contains pictures for sorting. Consider what words your students already know from familiar texts and word banks as you select words for sorts.

- This is a good time to establish the **oddball**, or miscellaneous category, to accommodate variations in dialect and spelling. Some students may hear a short *o* in *lost*, but others will hear a sound closer to "aw." Some students hear a different vowel in *pin* and *pen*, but others consider them homophones. Rather than forcing students to doubt their own ear, the oddball category offers an alternative and acknowledges that not everyone speaks the same way, nor does spelling always match pronunciation. Good words to use for oddballs in this stage are high-frequency words students may already know as sight words, such as *for, put, was,* and *what. Was* will be odd in a short *a* sort despite its CVC spelling because it doesn't have the short *a* sound. Other oddballs have a short vowel sound but are spelled in unusual ways (e.g., *laugh, head*). You can find examples in the word lists in Appendix E.

- Plan word hunts and other follow-ups. It is fairly easy to find words with short vowels in just about any beginning reading material because they are, by their nature, common in English. Encourage students to look for two-syllable words with a CVC syllable, such as *funny* or *kitten*.

- Pacing is important. Be prepared to spend some time on short vowels, as they pose special problems for young spellers and can persist as problems beyond first grade. Start with simple three-letter words that include many of the words studied in word families (e.g., *bag, can, pat*) but then move to more complex words with blends and digraphs at the beginning and end (e.g., *brag, than, path*). However, short vowels will be reviewed when they are compared to long vowels in the next stage, so do not expect complete mastery.

R-INFLUENCED VOWELS. Words like *car* and *for* look as though they follow the CVC pattern, but they do not have the short sounds of *a* or *o*. Instead, the vowel sounds are subsumed by the *r* that follows and are known as r-*influenced vowels* (or r-*controlled vowels*). Do not expect students to segment a vowel sound separately from the *r* but instead teach *ar* and *or* as patterns or chunks. Because words spelled with *ar* and *or* are common in beginning reading materials, it is worthwhile to introduce them at the end of this stage. The *r*-influenced vowels form a major subcategory of vowels that will be examined more extensively during the next stage. Below is a sort that compares the *r*-influenced *o* sounds with short-*o*. Read down each column so you can hear the difference. What is odd about *word* and *work*? How are they different from the other *r* words? How are they similar to each other?

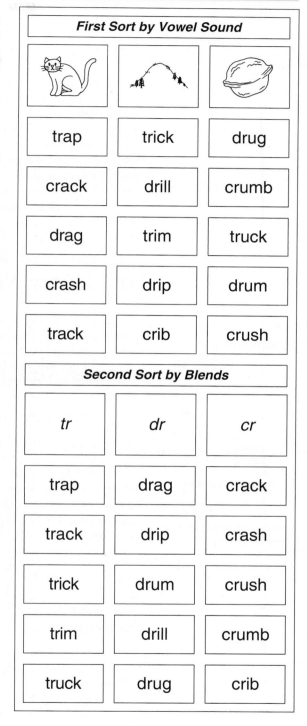

FIGURE 5.8   Two-way Sort by Vowel and Blends

First Sort by Vowel Sound		
trap	trick	drug
crack	drill	crumb
drag	trim	truck
crash	drip	drum
track	crib	crush

Second Sort by Blends		
tr	*dr*	*cr*
trap	drag	crack
track	drip	crash
trick	drum	crush
trim	drill	crumb
truck	drug	crib

o	or	*Oddballs*
fox	for	word
shop	sort	work
spot	fort	
trot	horn	

This chapter has presented examples of teacher-directed sorts or closed sorts—the teacher selects the words and leads a group sorting activity accompanied by a discussion of the features of interest. We recommend teacher-directed sorts when you introduce a new feature such as word families or short vowels. Offer clear explanations when introducing a new feature but gradually release responsibility to students who can sort independently as long as they can read the words as suggested in Table 3.1. Open sorts, as described in Chapter 3, ask students to establish their own categories and offer you diagnostic information that will help to determine how much students understand about the orthography.

Assess and Monitor Progress in the Letter Name–Alphabetic Stage

MONITORING PROGRESS

It is critical that you monitor student progress in attaining a firm concept of word (COW) in text, and the fundamental phonics/spelling features that support the automatic recognition of a basic reading vocabulary, or sight words. Without these attaining these fundamentals, students will not progress in reading. Assess students regularly to determine whether they need more practice or are ready to move on.

Assess and Monitor Progress in Concept of Word

PD pd TOOLKIT™

for Words Their Way®

Humpty Dumpty, Humpty Dumpty Word Recognition and Concept of Word in Text Recording Form
These forms will guide you in assessing concept of word.

Students in the letter name–alphabetic stage move from a rudimentary to a firm concept of word in text in the early part of this stage. Without a firm concept of word in text, students' sight word development will be delayed. Chapter 4 presents a detailed assessment for monitoring COW; the same procedures are appropriate in this stage, with one addition. Not only should students be pointing accurately to words in familiar text without getting off track on two-syllable words, but they should also be acquiring some sight words. The ultimate litmus of a firm concept of word in text is a student's ability to identify some words seen previously in context when shown in isolation, in a randomized list. So, to the assessment procedures we described in Chapter 4 we add a procedure for assessing word recognition in isolation.

Assess and Monitor Progress in Phonemic Awareness, Phonics, and Spelling

Phonemic awareness, phonics, and spelling are all highly related; therefore, frequent spelling assessments scored by features are an easy way to monitor student progress. You can administer the spelling feature inventories described in Chapter 2 several times a year to track progress. As shown in Table 5.6, Zack began the year as an early letter name speller, often omitting vowels and blends, which suggested that his phonemic awareness was only partial. By January, he was in the middle letter name stage, including a vowel in each word and spelling many vowels, blends, and digraphs correctly. He had full phonemic awareness, fully segmenting each word into sounds. By May, his correct spelling of short vowels as well as his use of silent *e* showed that he was transitioning into the within word pattern stage. Zack made solid progress over the course of the year in phonemic awareness, phonics, and spelling.

Ongoing assessment can be as simple as observing how quickly and accurately students sort pictures, or you can have students paste the pictures they have sorted into categories and

TABLE 5.6   **Zack's Spelling Progress across the First Grade Year**

	September	February	May
fan	✓	✓	✓
pet	PAT	✓	✓
dig	DK	deg	✓
rob	✓	✓	✓
hope	HOP	hop	✓
wait	YAT	wat	Wate
gum	GM	✓	✓
sled	SLD	slad	✓
stick	STK	stik	✓
shine	SIN	shin	✓
dream	GREM	drem	Dreme
blade	BAD	blad	✓
coach	KOH	coh	Coche
fright	FRIT	frit	Frite

label them. Weekly assessment in the middle to late part of this stage may involve a brief spelling test of five to ten words. In addition, we provide a series of spell checks on the PD Toolkit for letter name–alphabetic spellers. We recommend that you use these as a pretest before introducing a feature, and after spending a few weeks or so on a feature you can use them as a post-test. Progress monitoring or goal-setting forms are also available.

Assess and Monitor Progress in Sight Word Development

Once students achieve a firm concept of word in text, they should remember some words that they have seen in context, out of context. While students cannot be expected to remember all of the words they have read in context, they should be able "pick up" a handful of words after several readings to add to their sight vocabularies. Frequently assessing students' word recognition in isolation should provide the feedback you need to determine whether or not to back up or move forward in reading levels, spelling features, or instructional support. If students are not progressing, make sure they receive texts that they can read successfully.

The easiest way to monitor progress in sight word development is to keep track of the number of known words in students' word banks. The number of known words, or sight words, should grow steadily across the early mid to late letter name–alphabetic phase when students are given regular opportunities to select and review words out of context that they have read in context. You will know that a student is developing a solid sight word vocabulary when his or her word bank exceeds 200 known words.

You can also note progress in sight word development as students are able to read increasingly difficult levels of reading materials with less support in the form of shared reading. By the middle to late letter name–alphabetic stage, less predictable reading materials require young readers to carefully focus on print and rely more on word recognition and less on memory of the language. Use running records to monitor word recognition accuracy in context (Clay, 2009).

You should constantly assess and adjust your instruction to match the individual needs of your students. The responsibility is on us as teachers to make sure our students are progressing. We are the first responders!

Word Study with English Learners in the Letter Name–Alphabetic Stage

for **English Learners**

In general, most other languages do not have as many single consonants or blends as we do in English. English learners may need more time to master these sounds because they will have to learn how to hear and pronounce the sounds, segment the sounds, and learn the letter correspondences. In Table 5.7 you can see the sounds that English learners may omit or mispronounce.

TABLE 5.7 **Consonant Confusions for English Learners**

Sound	Potential Confusion
b	The voiced *b* is confused with the unvoiced *p* and is difficult in final position.
c	Is often confused with hard *g*. Many languages do not have a hard *c*.
d	Is confused with /th/ in Spanish, so *dog* may be pronounced /thŏg/.
f	Is confused with *v*, especially in Arabic. In Japanese it is confused with /h/.
g	The hard *g* sound may be confused with *k* by speakers of Arabic, French, or Swahili.
h	Is silent in Spanish and in Chinese it sounds more like /kh/ as in *loch*.
j	May be confused with *h* in Spanish and may also be pronounced /ch/.
k	May be confused with hard *g* by Spanish speakers.
l	May be confused with *r*. Final *l* may be especially difficult.
m	May be dropped at the ends of words.
n	Is difficult for speakers of Chinese, especially at the ends of words. May be confused with *l*.
p	Is easily confused with its voiced mate *b*.
r	Is rolled in Spanish and may be spelled with *w*. It is confused with *l* in many Asian languages.
s	Is difficult to perceive in final position.
sh	Is a sound that does not exist in many languages and is confused with *ch*, *g*, and *j*.
s-blends	Blends in Spanish such as *st*, *sk*, and *sp* are separate syllables that begin with *e* as in *es-pañol*.
t	Is confused with the voiced sound of *d* by Spanish speakers and not pronounced at the ends of words.
v	May be confused with *b* in Spanish and Korean. It does not exist in many languages.
w	Is a letter that does not exist in many languages and may be confused with *v*.
y	May sound more like /ch/ in Spanish.
z	May be confused with *s* and not voiced in Spanish.

For example, Spanish-speaking students may confuse words that begin with *d* and *th*, pronouncing *dog* with a *th* sound, more like "thog." *Jump* may be pronounced "chump." It is important to create sorts that make these comparisons clear (*d* and *th* or *j* and *ch*) once the other beginning sounds are established. Refer to *Words Their Way® with English Learners*, *Words Their Way®: Emergent Sorts for Spanish-Speaking English Learners*, and *Words Their Way®: Letter Name–Alphabetic Sorts for Spanish-Speaking English Learners* (Helman et al., 2012) for additional sorts to help students learn these distinctions.

Only a handful of consonants occur in the final position in Spanish (*d, n, l, r, s, z*), so it is common for English learners to omit the ending consonant sounds in words like *hard*, which may be spelled HAR. Final consonant picture sorts may be needed to bring attention to these sounds. Sorting words by rhyme or word families like *bag, rag, tag* can also be more of a challenge for English learners. Contrasts in which the vowel and the final consonant differ (*at, op, un*) are a better starting place. In Spanish, the *s*-blends work differently. In many Spanish words, the *sp* blend is split between two syllables. The *s* is given a vowel (*es*) and *p* starts the second syllable, as in *Es-pañol*.

Still, there are many consonants shared by Spanish and English (*b, d, f, g, k, l, m, n, p, r, s, t, w, y*), and Spanish-speaking students can begin studying consonants with these. Spanish picture sorts can be found can be found in the toolkit for *Words Their Way for English Learners* (Helman et al., 2012) under both the Emergent and Letter Name categories and in *Palabras a Su Paso: El Estudio de Palabras en Acción* (Pearson Schools, 2013). Explain the different sounds in English and Spanish, and acknowledge students' confusion as logical. Because students might not be able to name the pictures, you might pair them with an English-speaking partner who can supply the English names.

As with consonants, other languages do not have as many vowel sounds as we do in English. Spanish has only one short vowel sound (short *o*), and it is spelled with the letter *a* as in *gracias*. Expect students to substitute vowels in their own language that are close in point of articulation for these short English vowels when they say and spell English words. Short *e* may be pronounced like the long *a* (*pet* as PAIT), short *i* like the long *e* (*tip* as TEEP), and short *a* and short *u* like the short *o* (*cat* and *cut* as *cot*) (Helman et al., 2012). See Chapter 6 for more information about vowel confusions for students learning English.

WORD STUDY *Routines and Management*

The letter name–alphabetic stage easily spans kindergarten through second grade. A handful of students in third grade and even a few students in the upper elementary grades will still need to work on the features that characterize this stage. English learners of any age can be in this stage. It may be tempting to rush through, but word study in the letter name–alphabetic stage helps to build a solid foundation for the study of long vowels and other vowel patterns in the next stage.

A balanced literacy program includes Read To, Read With, Write With, Word Study, and Talk With activities (RRWWT). During *read to* time, teachers read aloud literature that offers exposure to new vocabulary and literary language. During *read with* time, students meet in large groups for shared reading and small groups for instructional-level reading. Teachers model how to compose ideas and spell words as they *write with* students, who, in turn, write for themselves. *Word study* includes direct instruction in letter–sound correspondences, phonics, and spelling patterns. Finally, a comprehensive program provides students with ample opportunities to *talk with* teachers and peers about the books and experiences they have shared. Whole-group read-alouds continue to be the best place to focus on vocabulary, but you should look for other opportunities throughout the day to highlight new vocabulary words. Concept sorts can be developed for science, social studies, and math.

To differentiate instruction, you need small groups. In first-grade classrooms, teachers like Mr. Perez often find that reading groups and word study groups are virtually the

same. Word sorts can be introduced as part of the reading group. Students practice the sorts for seatwork and in centers with partners or individually once they learn the routines. Other teachers have a separate word study time, meeting with small groups initially to introduce a sort, but then expecting follow-up routines to be done independently or with partners.

Word study during the letter name–alphabetic stage begins with picture sorts for initial sounds, and ends with word sorts for short vowels in nonrhyming words. During this transition, there are various routines and generic activities to help students explore study features in depth (see Chapter 3). Betty Lee's schedule is particularly appropriate in the early letter name–alphabetic stage for students who are doing picture sorts and keeping their materials in two-pocket folders. Later in the stage when students are sorting words, other routines that involve writing sorts in word study notebooks are more effective. Table 5.8 summarizes routines for this stage. Games and activities are described in detail in the section that follows.

Pacing is important. There are many blends and many word families, and if every one were studied for a week, it could take many months. You might want to create two- or three-day cycles. For example, you might introduce two word families on Monday, another two on Wednesday, and then combine them for several days. Be ready to pick up the pace by combining a number of blends or families into one sort (up to four or five) or by omitting some features. The progress monitoring assessments provided on the PDToolkit help you to know what students can do. Ultimately, your own observations dictate the pace that is appropriate for your students. Table 5.5 offers three pacing guides that you may use to identify shortcuts for achieving students or more in-depth study for struggling students.

TABLE 5.8 **Sample Weekly Schedules for Word Study in the Letter Name–Alphabetic Stage**

	Picture Sorting	Word Sorting
Day 1	Small-group sort: Demonstrate, sort and check, reflect	Small-group sort: Demonstrate, sort and check, reflect
Day 2	Seatwork or center: Repeat the sort, check	Seatwork or center: Repeat the sort, check, write the sort in word study notebook
Day 3	Seatwork: Repeat the sort, draw and label	Seatwork, partner work: blind sort, writing sort, word study notebook extensions
Day 4	Small group or seatwork: Repeat the sort, word or picture hunts in magazines, ABC books, and familiar texts	Seatwork: Repeat the sort Small group: Word hunt in familiar texts
Day 5	Assessment and games, paste and label pictures used for sorting during the week	Assessment and games
	Homework: Students take pictures home to sort again and hunt for more pictures that begin with the sound	Homework throughout the week: Repeat the sort, blind sort, writing sort, word hunts

RESOURCES FOR IMPLEMENTING WORD STUDY *in Your Classroom*

Several sources are available to help you implement word study with students in the letter name–alphabetic stage.

1. The pictures in Appendix C and word lists in Appendix E, as well as suggested sorts in Appendix D, are available for use with the templates in Appendix F to create your own picture sorts.

2. Prepared sorts, spell checks, and games are available on the PDToolkit for *Words Their Way*. A Create Your Own feature allows you to create your own sorts. You can also print game board templates and use the words or images from your sorts with the games. Look for "List of Available Images for Create Your Own" under the Additional Resources tab to find what pictures can be selected.

3. *Words Their Way for PreK–K* provides a comprehensive description of word study and other literacy activities for the emergent and letter name stage: oral language, vocabulary, and concept development, alphabet recognition and production, phonological awareness, concepts about print and writing, concept of word in text, and word study for phonics and spelling.

4. *Words Their Way®: Word Sorts for Letter Name–Alphabetic Spellers* provides a complete curriculum of sorts beginning with a review of initial consonants, picture sorts for blends and digraphs, word family sorts, and short vowel sorts. Spell checks are supplied for each of the units.

5. *Words Their Way®: Letter Name–Alphabetic Sorts for Spanish-Speaking English Learners* provides different contrasts and additional practice.

ACTIVITIES for the Letter Name–Alphabetic Stage

In this section, specific activities for students in the letter name–alphabetic stage are organized into the following categories:

1. Vocabulary activities
2. Phonemic awareness activities
3. Development and use of personal readers and word banks
4. Dictionary
5. Study of initial consonant sounds
6. Study of word families
7. Study of short vowels

Some of the games and activities are adaptable, using a variety of features at different stages. These are indicated by the Adaptable for Other Stages icon. Common Core State Standards for Foundational Skills and Language are listed for kindergarten and first grade.

Adaptable for Other Stages

● ● ● ● ●

Vocabulary Activities

These activities are designed to help students develop their oral vocabularies. The vocabulary activities in Chapter 4 are also relevant here (Activities 4.1 to 4.7).

5.1 Anchored Vocabulary Instruction

Printing words on cards that are the focus of vocabulary instruction during a read-aloud is a way to anchor the meaning of the word to its sounds and spelling (Juel et al., 2003). These vocabulary cards will also serve as a reminder to review the words over time and in different contexts. (CCSS Foundational Skills (K–1st) 3, Language (K–1st) 5, 6)

MATERIALS Children's books to read aloud and a supply of 2-by-6-inch (or larger) cards. Print words neatly with markers.

PROCEDURES

1. Preview a book that you plan to read aloud and select a few words whose meanings may not be known to all of your students. Focus on words that are important to the meaning of the story but are also words that are likely to come up again in other stories. Juel et al. (2003) provide the examples of *pond, mill,* and *haystack* from *Rosie's Walk* (by P. Hutchins) as words urban children would probably not know. Write the words you select on cards in neat block letters.

2. Before reading the story, introduce the words. You might begin by asking students if they can supply a definition and then back that up with your own. At times you might model using a picture dictionary to look up the meaning of a word. If a concrete word like *haystack* is in the story, show a picture of a haystack. You can supply your own picture, photo, or bring in concrete objects. Even a quick sketch can help and might be added to the card. Always try to use "kid-friendly" definitions with accessible language. For example, a new word like *community* may be defined as a "neighborhood" or *vacant* as "empty." As students develop decoding skills, you might begin by asking them to figure a word out before telling them. Students in the late letter name stage, for example, would probably be able to read *mill* or *pond* but might not know exactly what they are.

3. To help anchor the word in memory, point to the word as you say it slowly, stretching out the sounds as you touch the letters, and then have the students repeat it with you. You might point out the beginning or ending sound, the length and number of phonemes or syllables, or other letter–sound characteristics of the word, depending on what your students might need. For example, students whose home language is Spanish might have a hard time with double *l*s at the end of a word like *mill*, because that combination (*ll*) has a different letter–sound correspondence in Spanish. You could point out the double *l*s in *mill* and have the students say it with you, emphasizing the final sound. Students are not expected to learn these as reading vocabulary, but Juel's research shows that seeing the words can help students remember them as meaning vocabulary.

4. When you come to the word during the read-aloud, hold up the card and briefly draw attention to it to remind students of its meaning and letter–sound properties. Ask someone to point to the word on the book page.

5. After reading, go through the word cards once more and ask students to say each word, define it, and perhaps use the word in a sentence that also recalls events in the story. For example, you might hold up *pond* and say, "Who can tell me where the fox got all wet? Yes, he fell in the pond." Ask questions that use the words, such as "Would you rather land in a pond or in a haystack? Tell me why."

6. Add new word cards to a growing set to be reviewed over time. Keep them handy to pull out when you have a few minutes to spare and go through them. It is this continued exposure that will assure that the words are retained over time. If students use the words or notice the anchored words in new contexts, make it a cause for great celebration. You can be deliberate in selecting new read-alouds with these same words, such as *The Little Red Hen*, in which the hen takes grain to the mill, or *The Small Small Pond* by Denise Fleming.

5.2 Think-Pair-Share

In Chapter 4, we described "turn and talk" (Activity 4.3 in Chapter 4) as a way to give more students the opportunity to engage in oral language and use new vocabulary. Instead of calling on one student to talk, all students are asked to talk with a partner. "Turn and talk" can be used with all ages but think-pair-share is a variation that provides more "think time" and ends with the opportunity to share ideas in the larger group. Both activities give less verbal children and English learners a chance to articulate their ideas in a less threatening situation. (CCSS Language (K–1st) 5, 6)

PROCEDURES

1. *Think.* During a read-aloud or discussion, instead of raising hands to answer questions, make predictions, share experiences, define words, or use words in sentences, ask students to think of their own response for a few moments.
2. *Pair.* Students then turn and talk to a partner or discuss in small groups. You can assign partners or groups in advance and have them stay together for a week or more. Students can also count off to form groups. Observe the pairs or groups to make sure all students are participating.
3. *Share.* After everyone has had a chance to talk, call on individuals or groups to report back to the larger group. By listening in on the groups, you might identify ideas or examples that seem particularly worthwhile.

5.3 Books and Concept Sorts

Books make great beginnings for concept sorts. As an example to get you started, *Gregory the Terrible Eater* by Marjorie Sharmat tells the story of a young goat who wants to eat real food while his parents constantly urge him to eat "junk food." In this case, the goats' favorite foods really are junk from the local dump: tires, tin cans, old rags, and so on. (CCSS Language (K–1st) 5, 5.a, 6)

MATERIALS You will need a copy of the book to read aloud. Collect real objects or pictures of items suggested by the story; for example, fruits, vegetables, newspaper, shoelaces, spaghetti, and pieces of clothing.

PROCEDURES

1. After enjoying this story together, introduce the students to a concept sort. Gather the students on the rug around a large table or pocket chart, and challenge them to group the items by the things Gregory likes and the things he dislikes. Encourage them to talk about the items in complete sentences such as, "Carrots are real food that Gregory likes."
2. After deciding where everything should go, ask the students to describe how the things in that category are alike. Decide on a key word or descriptive phrase that will label each category. *Real food* and *junk food* are obvious choices, but your students might be more inventive. As you print the selected key words on cards, model writing for the students. Say each word slowly and talk about the sounds you hear in the words and the letters you need to spell them. You might give all of the students in the group a card and ask them to label one of the individual items using invented spelling.
3. Plan time for individual sorting. Keep the items and key word cards available so that students will be free to redo the sort on their own or with a partner at another time, perhaps during free time or center time. Encourage them to talk as they sort.
4. Follow the sorting with draw-and-label or cut-and-paste activities. This may be done as a group activity, in which case a section of a bulletin board or a large sheet of paper is divided into two sections and labeled with the key words. If students work independently, give each student a sheet of paper folded into two sections. Ask the students to draw items, or give them a collection of magazines or catalogs to search for pictures to cut out and paste into the correct category (seed catalogs are great for fruits and vegetables). Again, encourage students use invented spelling to label the pictures.

EXTENSIONS *Gregory the Terrible Eater* serves as an excellent introduction to studying healthy eating. The same pictures the students have drawn or cut out can serve as the beginning pictures for categories such as meats, grains, fruits and vegetables, and dairy products.

VARIATIONS Other books can also be used as the starting point for concept sorts of many kinds, as in the following:

- *Noisy Nora* by Rosemary Wells. Sort pictures that suggest noisy activities or objects with pictures that suggest quiet activities or objects.
- *Town Mouse, Country Mouse* by Jan Brett and various authors. Sort pictures of things you would see in the country and things you would see in the city.

- *Alexander and the Wind-Up Mouse* by Leo Lionni. Sort pictures of real animals and toys or imaginary animals.
- *Amos and Boris* by William Steig. Sort pictures of things that Amos would see on the land and things that Boris would see in the ocean.

5.4 Thematic Unit on Animals as a Starting Point for Concept Sorts

Creatures
This concept sort is a great way to introduce a unit of study on animals.

Teachers of young students often organize their curriculum into thematic units of study. Such units frequently lend themselves to concept sorts, which review and extend the understandings central to the goals of the unit. Studying animals particularly lends itself to concept sorts and can be used as a way of introducing a unit. (CCSS Language (K–1st) 5, 5.a, 5.b, 6)

MATERIALS Plastic animals or animal pictures.

PROCEDURES Lay out the collection of animals and ask students to think of ways that they can be grouped together. Such an open sort will result in many different categories based on attributes of color, number of legs, fur or feather coat, and so on. A lively discussion will arise as students discover that some animals can go in unexpected categories.

The direction you eventually want this activity to go depends on the unit goal. If you are studying animal habitats, then you will eventually guide the students to sorting the animals by the places they live. If you are studying classes of animals, then the students must eventually learn to sort them into mammals, fish, amphibians, and birds. If you are focusing on the food chain, your categories may be carnivores, herbivores, and omnivores.

5.5 Creative Dramatics

Creative dramatics is a way to encourage students' self-expression as well as vocabulary development (Honig & Shin, 2001; Mages, 2008; Lobo & Winsler, 2006). Students enjoy reciting what they hear and appreciate the rhythm of language as they act out memorable scenes from familiar stories. In creative dramatics, props are not necessary but add to the fun. For example, after hearing the story *Caps for Sale* (by E. Slobodkina) students walk around the room singing, "Caps for sale, caps for sale. Red and white and blue and green. The finest caps you've ever seen." Students can also act out the part of the story when the monkeys steal the caps from the peddler after he falls asleep under a tree and then mimic the peddler with "Chi, chi, chi, chi." (CCSS Language (K) 1, 1.f, 5.d, 6, (1st) 1, 1.j, 5, 6)

MATERIALS Many picture books can work, as well as classic folk tales. There are a number of anthologies to consider including:

De Las Casas, D. (2011). *Tell along tales!: Playing with participation stories*. Santa Barbara, CA: Libraries Unlimited.

Siks, G. B. (1958). *Creative dramatics: An art for children*. New York: Harper & Row, Publishers.

Ward, W. (1981). *Stories to dramatize* (Reprint ed.). Anchorage, KY: The Children's Theatre Press.

PROCEDURES
1. After they listen to a story, ask students to select a character and think about how that particular character acts, like crawling on all fours and roaring like a lion as in *Leo the Lion* or stirring a pot of food after hearing a version of *Stone Soup*.
2. Reread a short scene and have three or four students act out the scene with its movement and a few of its lines. Props are not typically used, and everyone is given a chance to participate.

3. Ask the students who were watching to comment on what they liked and how they might improve the next time.

4. Have another three or four students try the same scene.

EXTENSIONS Prepare copies of key lines from the scene in 26-point text that students place in their personal readers to reread, as in Figure 5.9. Note in the figure how Kari has underlined words for her word bank and also how she has recorded her rereadings with tick marks. Have students draw pictures of the scene they dramatized and bring the stories they have written to the group to dramatize a scene.

FIGURE 5.9 Caps for Sale

<u>Caps</u> for <u>sale</u>
Caps for sale
<u>Red</u> and <u>white</u> and blue and green
The <u>finest</u> caps <u>you</u> have ever seen.

Caps for sale
Caps for sale
Red and white and blue and green
The finest caps you have ever seen.

‖‖ ‖‖ ‖‖ ‖‖

5.6 Acting Out Meanings

Young children love any type of movement activity. As they encounter new words through read-alouds and your use of sophisticated words (see page 151), take advantage of opportunities to act out words so your students can develop understanding. (CCSS Language (K) 1, 1.f, 5.d, 6, (1st) 1, 1.j, 5, 5.d, 6)

MATERIALS Any children's picture book can work, but choose a picture book that lends itself to action. Morales' *Niño Wrestles the World* or Knutson's *Love and Roast Chicken* are two excellent examples.

PROCEDURES

1. After reading *Love and Roast Chicken: A Trickster Tale from the Andes Mountains* (Knutson) aloud, discuss the meaning of the word *scurried*. You might demonstrate the terms *scurry, scramble, dash,* or *hustle*.

2. Invite the students to do these actions. In so doing, you are supporting their developing awareness of the shades of meaning, or nuances, among these words. Common verbs such as *march, stroll,* or *walk* are good starting points because they are the easiest for students to distinguish.

EXTENSIONS

1. Try acting out adjectives, which are just a bit more challenging. Begin with frequently occurring ones like *happy, sad, tiny,* and *enormous*, and invite students to demonstrate them through facial expressions and body movement. This is particularly effective with English learners.

2. Explore antonyms in the same way. Begin by sharing concept books such as Eric Carle's *Opposites* or Tana Hoban's *Exactly the Opposite*, both of which feature colorful illustrations. Then engage students in acting out antonyms as they follow along with your discussion and modeling. You might play "Simon Says" using directives such as, "Simon says walk **fast**. Simon says walk **slow**. Simon says put your hand **over** your head. Simon says put your hand **under** your chin." Other action-filled multicultural choices might include:

Brown, M. (2013). *Marisol McDonald and the clash bash: Marisol McDonald y la fiesta sin egual*. New York: Lee and Low. (Latino; bilingual; story)

Look, L. (2004). *Uncle Peter's amazing Chinese wedding*. New York: Atheneum. (Asian; story)

McKissack, P. (1986). *Flossie and the fox*. New York: Dial. (African American; folktale)

Rodgers, G. (2014). *Chufki rabbit's big bad bellyache: A trickster tale*. EI Paso, TX: Cinco Puntos Press. (Native American/American Indian; folktale)

Roth, S. L., & Abouraya, K.L. (2012). *Hands around the library: Protecting Egypt's treasured books*. New York: Dial. (Middle Eastern; nonfiction)

Woodson, J. (2012). *Each kindness*. New York: Nancy Paulsen Books. (African American; story)

Phonemic Awareness

Phonemic awareness continues to develop from partial to full across the letter name–alphabetic stage. Students' developing awareness is exercised by sorting pictures and words for sounds—first for single consonants, then for blends, followed by onset and rime in word families, and finally all the sounds in short vowel sorts. Routines such as interactive writing and morning message, described in Activities 4.39 and 4.40 in Chapter 4, should continue in this stage, providing you with the opportunity to model phonemic segmentation as you stretch out the sounds in words to write. Students will get this same practice as they write with invented spelling for many different purposes. For this reason we do not suggest many separate phonemic awareness activities here. However, students who need extra help developing full phonemic awareness will benefit from the following activity using sound boxes.

5.7 Beginning-Middle-End: Find Phonemes in Sound Boxes

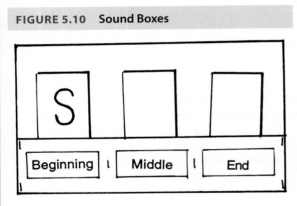

FIGURE 5.10 Sound Boxes

Originally developed by Elkonin (1973), sound boxes serve as a concrete way to demonstrate how words are made of smaller pieces of sound. The following variation is a song the teacher and children sing as they try to find the location of each sound in the word. (CCSS Foundational Skills (K) 2.d, (1st) 2.c, 2.d)

MATERIALS You will need large letter cards and a three-pocket holder, such as the one shown in Figure 5.10.

PROCEDURES
1. Place the letters needed to spell a three-letter word in the pocket backwards so the children cannot see the letters. Announce a CVC word, such as *sun*. Choose words from a familiar book, poem, or dictation when possible. Words that start with continuant sounds such as /m/, /s/, or /f/ work well because they can be said slowly.

2. Sing the song to the tune of "Are You Sleeping, Brother John?"

   Beginning, middle, end; beginning, middle, end.
   Where is the sound? Where is the sound?
   Where's the ssss in sun? Where's the ssss in sun?
   Let's find out. Let's find out.

3. Children take turns coming forward to pick the position and check by turning the letter card.

5.8 Push It Say It

This activity is a good way to teach students how to blend sounds as they move letter tiles or little cards around, as shown in Figure 5.11. Throughout the letter name stage, students learn to manipulate the sounds in words by exchanging one letter for another to make a new word. This skill will eventually help them sound out or decode unfamiliar words as they read by blending sounds and word parts together. (CCSS Foundational Skills (K) 2.c, 2.d, (1st) 2.b, 2.c, 2.d)

MATERIALS You will need a large set of tiles or cards containing the letters of the alphabet, the consonant digraphs, and rimes for word families (such as *at, ill, ock*) for modeling and smaller sets so students can work along with you. Model with the cards on a desktop with a small group or prepare magnetized cards to use on a board.

PROCEDURES

1. Choose the rime card that matches the sort you are about to do or the features from a previous sort that need reviewing. If you are working with the *at* and *an* families, cut out these rime cards as well as an assortment of beginning sounds such as *f*, *m*, and *r*. Two or three rime cards and two or three consonant cards are enough for one lesson. Continuant consonants such as *f*, *m*, and *r* are easier to elongate than the stop consonants (*b*, *t*, *g*) so start with these. Students will need practice with all the consonants eventually.

2. First, identify the rimes as the *at* or *an* family, and have your students repeat them after you. Next, push a beginning letter such as the *f* card up while saying "f-f-f-f." Then, push the *an* card up while saying "an." Say the word *fan* as you push the cards together, as shown in Figure 5.11.

3. Tell your students that you can take the *an* away and change the word to *fat*. Push the *f* card up a little further while saying "f-f-f-f." then push the *at* card up next to it while saying "at." Then say *fat* as you push them together.

4. After modeling this procedure, ask your students to push and say *fan* with their own cards. Ask them how they might change *fan* into *fat*. Repeat with one or two other beginning sounds to change *fan* into *man*, *man* into *ran*, and *ran* into *rat*, and so on.

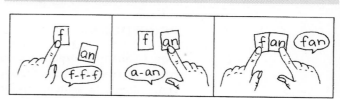

FIGURE 5.11   **Push It Say It**

EXTENSIONS

1. Add consonant blends and digraphs as they are studied. Note that digraphs such as *sh*, are written on *one* card (not separated into a *s* card and an *h* card), while blends should be on separate cards. Follow the same procedures above, using the digraphs and blends and exchanging different-vowel rimes. Model how to change *ship* into *shop*, *shop* into *chop*, *chop* into *chip*, using digraphs or *top* into *stop* into *slop* using blends.

2. The "Push It Say It" routine for medial vowel, CVC words is slightly different for the non-rhyming words because you will use a separate vowel card and push three or four cards. Change *pat* to *pet*, *pet* to *pit*, *pit* to *pot*, *pot* to *hot*, *hot* to *hit*, and son on.

Development and Use of Personal Readers and Word Banks

Personal readers are collections of dictations and other short pieces of text that serve many purposes, helping students develop a concept of word and concepts about print as well as a sight vocabulary. Word banks take words out of context for close study and enhance sight word learning.

5.9   Collecting Individual Dictations and Group Experience Stories

Recording students' individual or group dictations as they talk about personal or group experiences is a key feature of the language experience approach, or LEA (Stauffer, 1980). The text created makes especially good reading material for beginning readers because it is inherently familiar and easy to remember. It is ideal to have every student in a group contribute a sentence, but dictations need to be kept to a reasonable length to be sure beginning readers can read them back. This activity is described on page 117. Here we offer a description of using group dictations across a four-day sequence to collect words for a word bank. This can be accomplished in fewer days with smaller groups. (CCSS Foundational Skills (K) 1, 1.a, 1.b, 1.c, 1.d, 3.a, 3.c, 4, (1st) 1, 1.a, 3, 3.g, Language (K) 1.f, (1st) 1.j)

MATERIALS You will need chart paper, an overhead projector, a computer, or another way to record dictation so that students can observe you write. You will also need to make copies of the dictation for each student. See the section above on page 161 for further directions in how to develop and use personal readers.

PROCEDURES

Day 1. Share an experience and collect dictations, as described in Chapter 4. When it is complete, read the entire dictation as you point to the words. Then have students repeat after you, sentence by sentence using echo reading, as you point to each word. Reread it again as the students read along with you in a choral reading fashion.

Before day 2, make a copy of the dictation for each student in the group. Computers make it easy to create these copies. Select a font that has the type of letters easily recognized by young readers (Geneva or Comic Sans MS work well) and enlarge it as much as possible. It is also easy to make copies by writing neatly in your best manuscript handwriting.

Day 2. Reread dictations and underline known words.
1. Choral read the original dictation and then again as students follow along on their own copies, pointing to words as they read. Call on individual students to read a sentence.
2. Once students can read the dictation successfully, ask them to underline known words to harvest for their word bank, as described in Activity 5.11. Point to the underlined words randomly to make sure they know the words they underline. Students might make an illustration to go with the dictation.

Day 3. Choral read and harvest known words.
Students can work together or individually to read the dictation again. Make word cards for underlined words that are recognized accurately and quickly.

Day 4 and On. Choral read and review new word cards.
1. Have students continue to reread their dictations, review the words in their word banks, and complete their pictures.
2. Start a new dictation or story cycle when students can read the previous dictation with good accuracy and modest fluency.
3. Include personal readers in reading intervention plans. We like to see students using their personal readers in targeted interventions with the literacy specialist and Title I teachers. Students have additional opportunities to reread their entries to promote fluency, for phonics instruction, and the development of a sight vocabulary. Make an extra copy of the entries, share digital copies, and have the personal readers accessible to students when they meet with their teachers. Students also take the personal readers home, or access their personal readers online where they reread the stories, review their word banks, and sort words and pictures (Bear et al., 2004; Johnston, Invernizzi, Juel, & Lewis-Wagner, 2009).

EXTENSIONS

for **English Learners**

1. Bilingual entries in the personal readers are particularly useful during the early part of the letter name–alphabetic stage (Helman et al., 2012). These bilingual stories are written in both the first and second languages. Initially, dictations are just one or two sentences long. A school aide or parent can help with the translations. Shari Dunn and her students developed bilingual class readers that included students' individual pages about pets and other themes, like weather and health.
2. Develop digital personal readers that include digital photographs to accompany the students' dictations.

3. Incorporate software into the dictation process. Use voice recognition, drawing, and animation software in the dictation process to help students create their own language experience stories (Labbo, Eakle, & Montero, 2002).
4. Extend your language experience dictations into student-generated writing by using an author's computer chair (Labbo, 2004).

5.10 Support Reading with Rhymes and Pattern Stories

Rhymes and jingles and predictable patterned texts make good reading materials because they provide support for beginning readers and can then be used to harvest known words for word banks. (See Activity 4.39 in Chapter 4 for a complete guide to the whole-to-part lesson plan and supporting activities.)

MATERIALS Find a rhyme, jingle, song, or predictable story that students will find memorable and readable. You can focus on one major pattern or verse, such as the refrain in *The Gingerbread Man*. Find a big book, make a chart, or project a copy of the text electronically for group work, and make copies of the rhymes and patterns for students' personal readers.

PROCEDURES

Day 1. Introduce and read the text.
1. Talk about the title and cover and look at the pictures (if applicable) with the students.
2. Read the rhyme or story while fingerpointing the text. Read fluently and with expression, but not too fast. Stop periodically to discuss and enjoy the story.
3. Reread the text and invite students to choral or echo read the entire text if it is short; or read parts of the text.
4. Decide which parts of the text will be compiled for personal readers. Type the text onto a single page that can be duplicated for each student. Number and date this entry.

Days 2, 3, and 4. Reread the rhyme or story and harvest words for word banks as described in Activity 5.11. Use the same procedures described in Activity 5.9 for dictations as follow-ups for rhymes and predictable text. Write sentences from the text can on sentence strips, and have students work to rebuild the text in a pocket chart as described in Activities 4.40 and 4.41 in Chapter 4. In Figure 5.9, you see a sample of a rhyme adapted from the story *Caps for Sale* (by E. Slobodkina). Kari has underlined a number of words to harvest for her word bank. In addition, Kari has made a tick mark each time she reread the rhyme.

5.11 Harvesting Words for Word Banks

Students need to have a stock of sight words that they can read with ease. These can be harvested from books, familiar rhymes, or dictations, and stored in a word bank to be reviewed over time. Although word bank words are traditionally chosen by the students, you can encourage young readers to include high-frequency words (*will, this, want*) that they need to learn, or words containing the spelling features being examined during word study. Favorite words are those that interest the reader (*dinosaur, chocolate, birthday*); these longer concrete nouns may be more memorable to the student than the high-frequency words! The following activities help students develop and maintain a word bank. (CCSS Foundational Skills (K) 3.c, 3.d, (1st) 3.g)

MATERIALS You will need copies of personal readers, dictations, familiar books, and so on. Prepare a collection of blank word cards. Tagboard and index cards can be cut to a size that is large enough to hold easily, yet small enough so that students can work with them on a desktop when sorting (4 by 1.5 inches is about right). You can also create a sheet of words for a particular story or poem read by a group of students. Reproduce and cut apart the sheets and the words, which you can hand out as students identify them.

Have students store their words in envelopes, plastic bags, small margarine containers, or small gift bags. Plastic and metal index card file boxes work well—words can be sorted with dividers. You can start with plastic bags for the first 50 words and then move to a box.

PROCEDURES Harvesting words may vary depending on the sources:

1. *From personal readers.* If students have an individual copy of dictations, jingles, parts of stories, and so on, simply ask them to underline the words they know. Many students will be tempted to underline every word, but over time they will begin to understand the procedure and realize they need to be selective and underline only words they really know. Suggesting that they scan through the text backwards can help some students find known words more accurately. You, your assistant, or a classroom volunteer can point to the underlined words in a random fashion to check whether the student can indeed name the word quickly (without rereading the sentence in which it occurs). Write known words on word cards. Writing the word for the student will ensure that it is neat and accurate. Ask the student to spell it aloud as you or another adult writes, to focus their attention on all the letters. On each card write the number of the page in the personal reader. This makes it possible for students to go back and use context clues to name the word if they forget it. Then ask students to write their initials on the back of each card in case words get mixed up during word bank activities.

2. *From familiar books.* Students can also collect sight words independently from books they have read. Select words from the book that seem useful or interesting, write them on cards and store them in a library pocket in the back of the book. After reading the text, teach students to read through the words in the pocket to see which ones they know at sight. Have students write the words they know onto their own cards and place them in their word banks. They can match unknown words back to their counterparts in the text.

3. *From any text.* The easiest procedure for harvesting words is to simply ask the students to point to words in a book or from a chart that they would like to put in their word bank. After several words are written on cards, you or a helper can hold up the words to check for recognition.

TIPS To ensure that unknown words do not enter students' word banks, develop a short-term word bank for words that students recognize from the latest stories and dictations stored inside their personal readers (see Figure 5.4). Periodically, work with students in small groups to have them read through the words in their short-term word banks. Words they know from memory go into the permanent word bank.

Create a group word bank to use instead of or in addition to individual word banks. The group agrees on the words to add (with some gentle prodding by you to add high-frequency words that will show up in other stories) and the words can be reviewed in the group. Also make them available for individuals or partners to use in the word bank activities described in Activities 5.12–5.13.

5.12 The Grand Sort with Word Bank Words

Have students review the word bank regularly as an important way to secure those words in memory as sight words. In this sort, students simply go through their word cards, say the words they know and put them in one pile, and place the unknown words to the side. Have students try to move quickly reading through the pile. The words students put in the "I know" pile are words you and they can use in other sorts. Reading through their words banks is a common activity with your supervision in circle time, with a partner or classroom volunteer, or independently.

You can discard the unknown words, but this can be a touchy point for some students who are hesitant to throw away words. There is no harm in letting a few temporarily unknown words remain, but working with a lot of unknown words makes students' work hesitant, prone to errors, and frustrating. Students in the early letter name–alphabetic stage do not have the word knowledge they need to sound out many unknown words, so you should show them how to figure out an unknown word by using context. Referring to the number on the card,

PD TOOLKIT™

for Words Their Way®

Weekly Schedules and Activities In The Letter Name-Alphabetic Stage
Watch children in first grade read in their personal readers as a seatwork activity.

the students return to their personal reader to find the word and figure it out with context. Because this procedure can be time-consuming, it is important that only a small percentage of words in a word bank are unknown. (CCSS Foundational Skills (K) 3.c, 3.d, (1st) 3.g)

5.13 Reviewing Word Bank Words

There are other ways to review and work with words in the word bank. (CCSS Foundational Skills (K) 3.c, 3.d, (1st) 3.g)

1. *Pickup.* Lay out a collection of five to ten words face-up. Words that the student does not know or frequently confuses are good candidates. Someone calls out the words randomly for the student to find and pick up. This simple activity requires the student to use at least partial alphabetic cues to find the words, but does not require him or her to sound out the word.

2. *I Am Thinking Of.* This activity is similar to Pickup, but the student is given clues instead of words: "I am thinking of a word that rhymes with *pet*" or "I am thinking of a word that starts like *play*."

3. *Concentration.* Make a second set of words and play this classic game as described in Activity 4.16 in Chapter 4. Work with no more than ten sets of words at a time so that the activity moves quickly.

4. *Word Hunts.* Have students look through their word banks for words that have a particular feature; for example, words that start with *t*, words that end in *m*, or words that have an *o* in them.

5. *Alphabetize Words.* Make and laminate a large alphabet strip up to six feet long. Students place their words under the beginning letter. Sort pictures by beginning sounds as well.

6. *Build sentences.* When students have nouns and verbs included in their word banks, they can start to build sentences. It's fun to add the names of friends and family to their word bank so they can build sentences like "Devon can run." During writing time, encourage students to use their word banks as a resource for words they might want to use. Sentence starter frames such as "I like to…" might get them started if they can't think of anything to write about.

7. *Sort words.* Once students have 50 or more words in their word banks, they can use them to sort in various ways: by conceptual groups (animals, people, things we do, etc.), by beginning sounds, by alphabetical order, etc.

5.14 Read It, Find It

This simple and fun game for two players reinforces the identification of words. (CCSS Foundational Skills (K) 3.c, 3.d, (1st) 3.g)

MATERIALS You will need 30 pennies, or as many pennies as there are words on the game board. Prepare a game board by creating a 5 by 5 or 6 by 6 grid. Write each word into one of the spaces on the grid. Prepare a set of word cards that have the same words as those on the board and place them face-down. It is okay if some words repeat. You can take words from word banks or from previous word sorts.

Adaptable for Other Stages
● ● ● ● ●

PROCEDURES

1. One player flips a penny for heads or tails position. Each player chooses 15 pennies. One player will be heads and turns all his or her pennies to the heads side. The other will be tails and turns the pennies to the tails side.

2. The player who did not flip begins by taking a card from the pile and reading it. The player then finds the word on the board and covers it with a penny. If the player cannot read the word or reads it incorrectly, he or she cannot cover the word. The game proceeds as each player draws one card per turn.

3. The first player to cover 15 words, using up all his or her pennies, is the winner.

Dictionary Skills in the Letter Name–Alphabetic Stage

Children can begin to use simple dictionaries and learn some basic skills, even in kindergarten and first grade.

5.15 Alphabetical Order

Alphabetical order is a skill that students in this stage can begin to master once they know their letters. Begin with activities that students can complete with relative ease. You may want to demonstrate in whole class and then guide facilitated practice in differentiated groups. (CCSS Foundational Skills (K) 2.a, 3.a)

- Develop flexibility with the alphabet. Help children learn to recite the alphabet in order starting at any point and going forward.
- Ask students to quickly find a letter on an alphabet strip to develop a sense of where letters fall in sequence; before M or after M is a good starting point.
- Keep a collection of alphabet books handy and ask students to find a page for a particular letter or beginning sound, and to look for pictures of other things that begin with that sound. Get them to think about where to look in the book—beginning, middle, or end to find the letter.
- Ask students to find words on a word wall. As a partner center activity, students call out words for each other.
- Look for opportunities to order words alphabetically: students' first names, color words, pictures with their names printed on them.
- Students with at least 50 words enjoy using index card boxes with alphabet dividers to organize their word bank words in by the first letter.
- At first have students use alphabet strips as a guide. These strips can a size that fit on their desks, or they can be large strips on the floor. Have students place their word bank words beside the letters, and have them use pictures in the same way.
- Once large numbers of words end up under the same letter, introduce the idea of ordering them by the second letter. Model how to do this as you add words to a word wall where you will need to go to even the third or fourth letter to alphabetize words like *them*, *then*, and *they*.

5.16 Picture Dictionaries and Illustrated Word Books

When you teach young children, keep a simple dictionary handy and occasionally model how to look up words. Letter name–alphabetic spellers can begin to use these resources as well. Below are some ideas about how to use picture dictionaries along with a list of dictionaries and word books for young children.

- *Word books* are wonderfully illustrated collections of words that are fun for browsing but can also be used for word hunts and to get ideas for writing. In Richard Scarry's *Best Word Book Ever* you can find words arranged thematically, usually in the form of labeled pictures. Others like *My First Dictionary by DK* are arranged alphabetically with each word illustrated.
- Students studying beginning blends and digraphs often find words that begin with those sounds. They would find *chair*, *change*, *chicken*, *choose* and *chopstick* in *Curious George's Dictionary*.
- In addition, picture dictionaries can be used to for vocabulary development. Because he is so active and expressive, Curious George can be used to vividly illustrate words such as *afraid*, *before*, *curious*, *peek*, and *scamper* and each entry word is accompanied by a sentence defining that word. Suggestions for supporting young children's exploration

Dictionaries for Beginning Readers

Richard Scarry's Best Picture Dictionary Ever (1998)

Richard Scarry's Best Word Book Ever (1999)

Richard Scarry's Best First Book Ever! (1979)

Scholastic First Picture Dictionary (2009)

My First 1000 Words (2005)

My First Dictionary DK (2012)

The Cat in the Hat Beginner Book Dictionary (1964)

Curious George's Dictionary (2008)

The American Heritage Picture Dictionary (2006)

of this dictionary and engagements with print more generally are provided in the dictionary's Foreword (Templeton, 2008).

- Websites such as Enchanted Learning have simple alphabet books and picture dictionaries to download and print (see Resource Connections above for a list of dictionaries.)

Study of Initial Consonant Sounds

A number of activities or games in Chapter 4 are appropriate for students in the letter name–alphabetic stage who are working to master single consonants, digraphs, and blends: Soundline (4.32), Letter Spin for Sounds (4.33), and Initial Consonant Follow-the-Path Game (4.34). Concentration is another adaptable game. Any two pictures that begin with the same sound(s) make a match that can be claimed.

5.17 Sound Boards

MATERIALS Sound boards are references for letter–sound features (beginning consonants, digraphs and blends, and vowels); you can find examples in Appendix B. They provide a key word and picture for each letter–sound match, helping students internalize the associations. (CCSS Foundational Skills (K) 3.a, (1st) 3.a)

PROCEDURES Place a copy of the sound boards at the front of students' writing folders or personal readers. These boards make it easy for students to find letters to stand for the sounds they want to use. Tape reduced copies of relevant sound boards to students' desks; you can also post charts of various letter–sound features. Recently, the new technology of chart printers has made it possible to take the individual sound boards and enlarge them to poster size. Add a little color and display them in a prominent place for reference. Keep sound boards in students' word study folders (see Figure 3.19) to serve as a record of progress. Students can lightly color the letters they have studied. Use sound boards to generate more words to add to a word family. Write the family rime on a small card and slide it down beside the beginning sounds. In Figure 5.12, the word family *ack* has been expanded by adding many different blends and digraphs.

5.18 Hunting for Words and Pictures

Word hunts, described in Chapter 3, are conducted several different ways and at different times in the letter name–alphabetic stage. (CCSS Foundational Skills (K) 2, 3)

Adaptable for Other Stages
● ● ○ ● ○

FIGURE 5.12 **Expanding a Word Family Using a Sound Board**

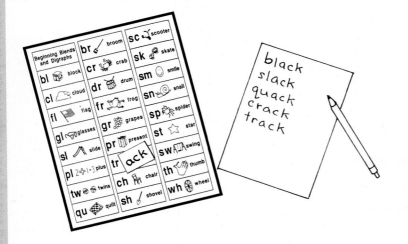

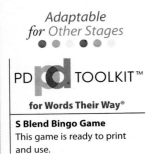

Adaptable for Other Stages

● ● ● ● ●

PD **pd** TOOLKIT™

for Words Their Way®

S Blend Bingo Game
This game is ready to print and use.

1. **Picture Hunts:** In the early letter name–alphabetic stage, students can hunt for pictures that correspond to beginning sounds in magazines or catalogs, and paste them onto individual papers, onto group charts, or into alphabet scrapbooks. To save time, you, an aide, or a student helper can rip out pages on which there are pictures that contain the feature being hunted. Have students label the pictures they find by spelling as best they can. Students can also hunt for pictures in alphabet books and record their findings as drawings.

2. **Word Hunts:** Students can also search for words that begin with the particular initial consonants, blends, or digraphs in familiar reading materials such as their personal readers or by going through their own word banks. Once they begin studying vowels, picture and word hunts will help them attend to those medial sounds and letters. Note that hunting for additional word family words can be challenging for certain families unless you have books that have been specially written, but words with most short vowels should be plentiful in the materials they are reading (short-*u* words can be harder to find than the others).

At first students will need to be supervised as they work in small groups to find words and you, an aide, or a helper can serve as a scribe to record their findings. By the late letter name–alphabetic stage, students can work independently and record results of word hunts in word study notebooks.

5.19 Initial Sound Bingo

In this version of Bingo, students discriminate among the initial sounds. This is another activity that can be adapted to single consonant, blends, digraphs, and word families. (CCSS Foundational Skills (K) 3.a, (1st) 3.a)

MATERIALS Make Bingo cards with 9 or 16 squares. In each square, write a letter(s) that features the sounds students have been studying in sorts. Figure 5.13 shows a game prepared to review the *s*-blends. Note that each card must be different. You also need markers (bottle caps. pennies, or squares of paper work well) and picture cards to match sounds.

PROCEDURES Work with small groups of two to four students. Give each student a Bingo card and markers. Have students take turns drawing a card from the stack and calling out the picture name. Students place a marker on the corresponding square. Play continues until someone gets Bingo (three or four in a row) or the board is filled.

5.20 Gruff Drops Troll at Bridge

This is a special version of the basic follow-the-path game, described in Activity 4.34 in Chapter 4, that reinforces *r*-blends. This game was developed after reading Paul Galdone's *The Three Billy Goats Gruff*, which was part of a class study of books about monsters. Many of the books yielded a great crop of consonant-plus-*r* words such as *growl*, *groan*, and *fright*. (CCSS Foundational Skills (K–1st) 3.a)

FIGURE 5.13 **Blend Bingo Boards**

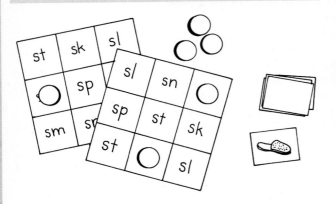

FIGURE 5.14   Game Board for Gruff Drops Troll at Bridge

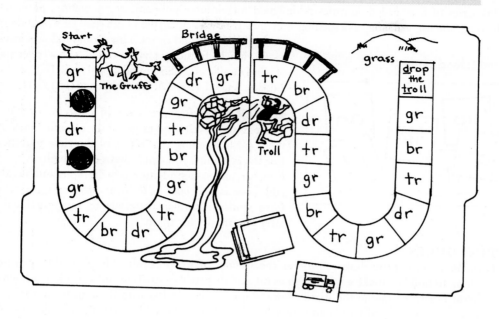

MATERIALS Prepare a game path filled in with *r*-blend combinations, as shown in Figure 5.14 (or whatever features you want to review). Add some artwork to create a theme. You will also need markers and pictures. Follow-the-path templates and directions for preparing the boards can be found in Appendix F.

PROCEDURES Each student selects a marker. Students turn over picture cards and move the marker to the correct space. In this game, the winner drops the troll from the bridge by turning up a picture that begins with *dr* (for *drop*) or *tr* (for *troll*) for the last space.

5.21 Match!

In this game, similar to the game of Slap Jack, students look for pairs that match by beginning sounds. (CCSS Foundational Skills (K–1st) 3.a)

MATERIALS Create a set of cards that feature pictures with four to eight different beginning sounds. Include at least four pictures for each sound. Pictures can be copied from Appendix C, glued on card stock, and laminated.

PROCEDURES Each student has half the deck of pictures. Students turn a picture card face-up from their deck at the same time. If the pictures begin with the same sound, the first person to recognize and say "Match!" gets the pair. If the pictures do not match, another set is turned over until a match occurs. There can be penalties for calling out "Match" carelessly, such as losing a turn.

The Study of Word Families

Once students begin studying word families, they are expected to read and spell the words they sort. Many word games can be adapted, such as Match! (Activity 5.21). Some activities are especially designed to enhance students' understandings of how families work.

PD **Toolkit**™
for Words Their Way®

Gruff Drops Troll At Bridge
Print this game for students to review blends.

Adaptable for Other Stages
● ● ● ● ●

ACTIVITIES | LETTER NAME–ALPHABETIC STAGE

5.22 Build, Blend, and Extend

This series of teacher-led activities is designed to reinforce phoneme segmentation, phoneme blending, and using analogy as a spelling strategy ("If I can spell *cat*, then I can spell *fat*") as students work with onsets and rimes. This should follow sorting lessons in which students have worked with a collection of word families. (CCSS Foundational Skills (K) 2.a, 2.c, 2.d, 2.e, 3.a, 3.d, (1st) 3.a, 3.b, Language (1st) 2.e)

FIGURE 5.15   Build, Blend, and Extend Cards

MATERIALS Prepare a set of cards to use in a pocket chart. Write the targeted onsets and rimes on these cards, keeping the letters of the rime together. For the *at* family, you would have cards with *at*, *b*, *c*, *f*, *h*, *m*, *p*, *r*, and *s*. As students study digraphs and blends, add those as well, such as *th*, *ch*, and *fl*; see Figure 5.15. Give students similar materials to use individually after you model for them.

PROCEDURES

1. *Building.* This procedure reinforces the *spelling* of word families. Explain that you are going to build or make a word such as *bag* and display two cards (*b* and *ag*). Then ask what letter needs to change the word to *rag*. Replace the *b* in *bag* with the *r* to make the new word. Model several words and then have students build additional words that you call out: *sag*, *tag*, and *brag*.
2. *Blending.* This activity reinforces the *reading* of word families. It is similar to building except that you start by displaying a word the students all know, such as *cat*, and then substitute a different beginning letter. Model how to blend the new onset with the familiar rime to read the word: "*Mmmmmm, aaaaaaat, mat*. The new word is *mat*." Ask students to use the two parts of the onset and rime to sound out the word just it was modeled.
3. *Extending.* During the extending part of this activity, find words that are not included in the sort to demonstrate to students that they can read and spell many more words once they know how to spell several words in a family. You may wish to demonstrate using unusual words like *vat* or challenging words with digraphs and blends such as *chat*, *flat*, or *scat*.

VARIATIONS

1. Students work with small cards at their seats as you lead the activity, or ask students to write the words on paper, small whiteboards, or chalkboards.
2. Add more digraphs and blends as they are studied. There are many words you can make with families such as *ack* and *ick*.
3. For the study of short vowels and the CVC pattern, the vowel is separated from the rime (*at* is cut apart into *a* and *t*).

5.23 Word Family Wheels and Flip Charts

Wheels and flip charts are fun for students to play with independently or with partners. Use the wheels and flip charts to reinforce blending the onset with the rime to read words in word families they have sorted. (CCSS Foundational Skills (K) 2.a, 2.c, 2.d, 2.e, 3.a, 3.d, (1st) 3.a, 3.b, Language (1st) 2.e)

PROCEDURES To make word family wheels, follow these three steps.

1. Cut two 6-inch circles from tagboard. Cut a wedge from one circle, as shown in Figure 5.16, and write the vowel and ending consonants or rime to the right of it. Make a round hole in the center.
2. On the second tagboard circle, write beginning sounds that form words with that family. For example, the *op* family can be formed with *b*, *c*, *h*, *l*, *m*, *p*, *s*, *t*, *ch*, *sh*, *cl*, and *st*. Space the letters evenly around the outside edge so that only one at a time will show through the "window" wedge.

for Words Their Way®

Word Family Wheels, Flip Books, Show Me, and **Slide-A-Word**
Download and print these four games for students to use at school and home.

3. Cut a slit in the middle of the second circle. Put the circle with the wedge on top of the other circle. Push a brass fastener through the round hole and the slit. Flatten the fastener, making sure the top circle can turn.

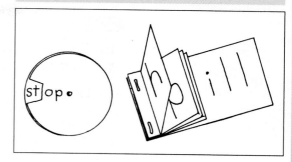

FIGURE 5.16   Word Family Wheel and Flip Book

Use the following steps to make flip books:

1. Use a piece of tagboard or lightweight cardboard for the base of the flip book. Write the family or rime on the right half of the base.
2. Cut blank pieces of paper that are half the width of the base piece and staple to the left side of the base. Write beginning sounds or onsets on each one. Have students draw a picture on the backside of the pages to illustrate the word.

5.24 Show Me

This activity is a favorite with teachers who are teaching word families and short vowels. (CCSS Foundational Skills (K) 2.a, 2.c, 2.d, 2.e, 3.a, 3.d, (1st) 3.a, 3.b, Language (1st) 2.e)

**FIGURE 5.17
Show Me Game**

MATERIALS Make each student an individual three-pocket folder to hold letter cards. To make the folder, cut paper into approximately 7-by-5-inch rectangles. Fold up a 1-inch section along the 7-inch side, and then fold the whole thing into overlapping thirds. Staple at the edges to make three pockets (see Figure 5.17). Cut additional paper into 1.5-by-4-inch cards to make 14 for each student. Print letters on the top half of each card, making sure the entire letter is visible when inserted in the pocket. A useful assortment of letters for this activity includes the five short vowels and *b, d, f, g, m, n, p, r*, and *t*. Too many consonants can be hard to manage.

PROCEDURES Each student gets a folder and an assortment of letter cards. When you or student helper call out a word, the students put the necessary letters in the spaces and fold up their pockets. When "Show me" is announced, all students open their pocket folders at once for you to see.

VARIATIONS Start with words having the same families, such as *bad, sad*, or *mad*, in which the students focus primarily on changing the initial consonants. Move on to a different family and different vowels. For example, you could follow this sequence: *mad, mat, hat, hot, pot, pet*. Add cards with digraphs or blends to spell words such as *sh-i-p* or *f-a-st*.

5.25 Word Maker

Students match blends and digraphs with word families to make words. (CCSS Foundational Skills (K) 2.a, 2.c, 2.d, 2.e, 3.a, 3.d, (1st) 3.a, 3.b, Language (1st) 2.e)

MATERIALS Create a collection of cards that have onsets on one half (single consonants, blends, and digraphs) and common short vowel rimes on the other, such as *at, an, it, ig*, and so on (similar to the cards shown in Figure 5.15). For students in the later letter name–alphabetic stage, include rimes with ending blends, digraphs, and preconsonantal nasals, such as *ish, ang, ast, amp*, and *all*.

PROCEDURES

1. Each student begins by drawing five cards from the deck. With the five cards face-up, each student tries to create words, as shown in Figure 5.15.
2. Once the students have made one or two words from their first five cards, they begin taking turns drawing cards from the deck. Every time they make a word, they can draw two more cards. If they cannot make a word, they draw one card.
3. Play continues until all the letter cards are used up. The player with the most words is the winner.

FIGURE 5.18
Cube for Roll the Dice Game

VARIATIONS Have students work independently with the word maker cards to generate and record as many words as possible.

5.26 Roll the Dice

This game for two to four players reinforces word families. (CCSS Foundational Skills (K) 2.a, 2.c, 2.d, 2.e, 3.a, 3.d, (1st) 3.a, 3.b, Language (1st) 2.e)

MATERIALS You need a cube on which to write four to six contrasting word families, (e.g., *an*, *ap*, *ag*, and *at*). One side can be labeled "Lose a Turn," and "Roll Again" (see Figure 5.18). You will also need a blackboard, paper, chart board, or Smartboard for recording words.

PROCEDURES The first player rolls the die. If it lands on a word family, the student must come up with a word for that family and record it on the chalkboard or paper. Students keep their own lists and can use a word only once, although someone else may have used it. If a player is stumped or lands on Lose a Turn, the die is passed to the next person. The person who records the most words at the end of the allotted time wins.

VARIATIONS Play with two teams for a relay. The first person of each team rolls the die and writes a word on the board. The player hands the die to the next player and goes to the end of the line. No word can be repeated by either team. This game can also be used with blends, digraphs, and vowel patterns.

FIGURE 5.19 **Game Board for Word Families**

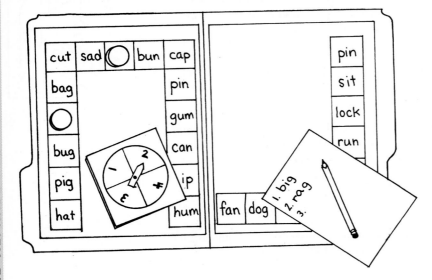

5.27 Rhyming Families

Use this is variation of the follow-the-path game to reinforce word families. (CCSS Foundational Skills (K) 2.a, 2.c, 2.d, 2.e, 3.a, (1st) 3.a, 3.b, Language (1st) 2.e)

MATERIALS Prepare a game board as shown in Figure 5.19. You will also need a single die or a spinner, pieces to move around the board, pencils, and paper for each player. Directions for making game boards and spinners as well as game board templates are in Appendix F. Write a word from each word family you have been studying in each space on the board. You can also write in special directions such as Roll Again, Go Back Two Spaces, and Write Two Words.

PROCEDURES The object is to make new words to rhyme with words on the game board that differ from the other players' words.

1. Spin to determine who goes first. The first player spins and moves the number of places indicated on the spinner. The player reads the word in the space where he or she lands. All players write a rhyming word by changing the initial letter(s). Players number their words as they go. Play continues until someone reaches the end of the path.
2. Beginning with the player who reaches the end first, each player reads the first word on his or her list. Players who have a word that is different from anyone else's gets to circle that word. Continue until all words have been compared.

3. Each circle is worth one point; the player who reaches the end first receives two extra points. The student with the most points wins the game.

VARIATIONS Label each space on the game board with the rime of a family you have studied (*at, an, ad, ack*). Use no more than five different rimes and repeat them around the path. Prepare a set of cards that have pictures corresponding to the families. Students move around the board by selecting a picture and moving to the space it matches. For example, a student who has a picture of a hat would move to the next space with *at* written on it.

5.28 Go Fish

This version of the classic game can be used as a review of word families. (CCSS Foundational Skills (K) 2.a, 2.c, 2.d, 2.e, 3.a, 3.d, (1st) 3.a, 3.b, Language (1st) 2.e)

Adaptable for Other Stages
● ● ○ ● ● ○

MATERIALS Create a deck of 32 cards with four words from eight different word families written on them (e.g., *that, bat, fat,* and *hat*). Write each word at the top left of the card so that the words are visible when held in the hand, as shown in Figure 5.20.

FIGURE 5.20 **Playing Cards for Go Fish**

PROCEDURES
1. Deal five cards to each player and place the remainder in the middle as a draw pile.
2. The first player asks any other player for a match to a card in his or her hand: "Do you have any words that rhyme with *hat*?" If the player receives a matching card or cards, he or she may ask for another rhyming word. If the other player does not have the card requested, he or she tells the first player to "Go fish," which means that the first player must draw a card from the "fish pond." The first player's turn is over when he or she can no longer make a match.
3. Once a player has a set of four rhyming words, they can lay the set down. Play continues until one player runs out of cards. Award points to the first person to go out and to the person who has the most sets of cards.

VARIATIONS Go Fish can be adapted for beginning sounds and blends using pictures.

PD **pd** TOOLKIT™
for Words Their Way®

Word Family Go Fish and **Hopping Frog Game** This card game and board game are ready to print and use. Hopping Frog Game is also available as a blank template.

Study of Short Vowels

After short vowels have been explored through word sorts and weekly routines, games can provide additional practice.

5.29 Hopping Frog Game

This game is for two to four players to review the five short vowels. (CCSS Foundational Skills (K) 2.d, 2.e, 3.a, 3.d, (1st) 3.b)

Adaptable for Other Stages
● ● ○ ● ● ○

MATERIALS Create a game board like the one shown in Figure 5.21. Cut green circle lily pads for each space and write CVC words students have used in word sorts on each one (e.g., *pin, get, hot, bad, leg, run, bug, wish*). You will need four frog markers (in different colors) or some other playing pieces. The spinner is marked into five sections, with a vowel in each one. Add pictures to cue the sound: *a,* apple; *e,* ten; *i,* fish; *o,* frog; *u,* sun. See Appendix F for directions on how to make a spinner.

PROCEDURES Each student selects a marker. Players take turns spinning and moving their markers to the first word that matches the vowel sound on which they land (e.g., *e, get*). They

FIGURE 5.21 **Frog Marker and Hopping Frog Game**

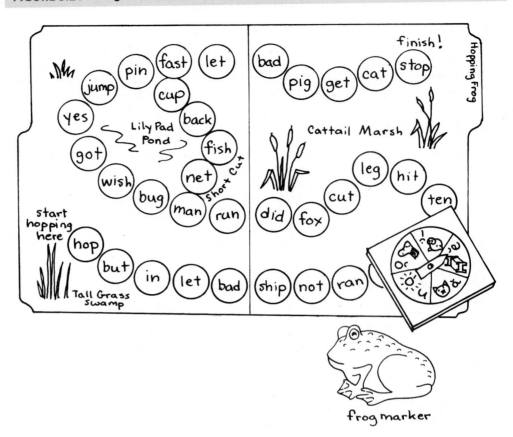

frog marker

then pronounce this word and must say another word with the same vowel sound to stay on that space. The next player then spins and plays. The first player who can finish the course and hop a frog off the board wins.

VARIATIONS Label the spaces with *a, e, i, o,* or *u*. Make a collection of short vowel pictures on tagboard using the short vowel pictures in Appendix C. It is important that the pictures do not show through the card. On several additional cards write commands such as Skip a Turn, Go Back Two Spaces, and Move Ahead Three Spaces. The players move around the board by turning over a picture and moving their playing piece to the next free space on the board that has the corresponding short vowel.

5.30 **Making-Words-with-Cubes Game**

Adaptable for Other Stages
● ● ● ● ●

Short vowel words are built with letter cubes in this game. It can be used for other vowels as well. (CCSS Foundational Skills (K) 2.d, 2.e, 3.a, 3.d, (1st) 3.b)

MATERIALS Letter cubes can be found in commercial games or made from blank wooden cubes. Write all the vowels on one cube to be sure that a vowel always lands face up. (The sixth side can be a star that indicates that the player can select the vowel.) Put a variety of consonants on five or six other cubes. (You can write pairs like *qu* and *ck* together.) The students need a sand clock or timer, paper and pencil, and a record sheet such as the one shown in Figure 5.22.

PROCEDURES

1. In pairs, students take turns being the player and the recorder. The recorder writes the words made by the player.

2. A player shakes the cubes, spills them out onto the table, and then starts the timer. Whatever letters land face-up are used to make words. The word maker moves the cubes to create words and spells them to the recorder. The cubes can then be moved around to make more words. Ignore errors at this point. Write the words in columns by the number of letters in the words.

3. When the time ends, the students review the words and check for accuracy. Score words by counting the total number of letters used. Students soon realize that the bigger the words they make, the greater their score.

FIGURE 5.22   Making-Words-with-Cubes Game

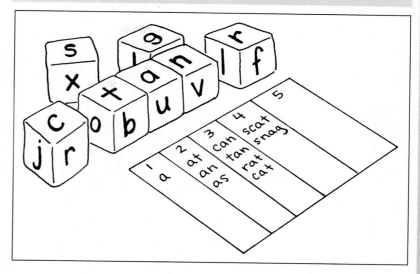

VARIATIONS Students in the within word pattern stage should work with two vowel cubes. On a second cube, write vowel markers such as *e* (put two or three), *a, i,* and *o.* By this time, students may be able to use multiplication to total the letters (e.g., 4 three-letter words is 12).

5.31 Follow-the-Pictures Spelling Game

This variation of the basic follow-the-path game works as a follow-up to word sorts for short vowel words. (CCSS Foundational Skills (K) 2.d, 2.e, 3.a, 3.d, (1st) 3, 3.b)

*Adaptable
for Other Stages*
● ● ● ● ●

MATERIALS Copy pictures from Appendix C for medial short vowels, then cut apart and paste them onto a follow-the-path template that you copy from Appendix F. You may need to adjust the size to fit. Use two to five short vowels at a time. You will also need playing pieces to move along the path and a spinner or single die. In some spaces you can write Roll Again, Go Back Two Spaces, and other directives. Include an answer card on which all the words are written in the same order they are pasted on the board to settle any arguments about spelling.

PROCEDURES Students take turns spinning for a number. Before they can move to the space indicated by the spinner, they must correctly spell the word pictured. If they cannot spell the word, they must stay where they are for that turn. The student who reaches the end first is the winner.

VARIATIONS Paste pictures on the game board. Use long vowel pictures for students in the within word pattern stage.

5.32 Slide-a-Word

Ask students to list and then read all the CVC words they are able to generate using a slider, as seen in Figure 5.23. As different short vowels are studied, the central vowel letter can be changed. (CCSS Foundational Skills (K) 2.d, 2.e, 3.a, 3.d, (1st) 3.b)

MATERIALS Supplies include tagboard or poster board, ruler, marker, single-edge razor blade, and scissors. Cut a piece of tagboard or poster board into 8.5-by-2.5-inch strips. Using the razor, cut a pair of horizontal slits on each end 1.5 inches apart. Write a vowel in the center. Cut two 12-by-1.5-inch strips for each slider. Thread them through the slits at each end

FIGURE 5.23 **Slider for Slide-a-Word**

and print a variety of consonants, blends, or digraphs in the spaces as they appear through the slits. Turn the strips over and print additional beginning and ending sounds on the back.

PROCEDURES Students slide the strips to generate as many words as they can, listing each word as they find it.

5.33 Put in an *m* or *n*: Preconsonantal Nasals

The difference between *rag* and *rang* is real but it is subtle, so these contrasts can help learners understand how the preconsonantal nasals work. (CCSS Foundational Skills (K) 2.d, 2.e, 3.a, 3.d, (1st) 3.a, 3.b)

MATERIALS Create word pairs like the ones listed below on word cards.

rag	rang	rig	ring	sag	sang	tag	tang
cap	camp	rap	ramp	trap	tramp	bag	bang
dig	ding	pup	pump	hag	hang	lip	limp
rug	rung	gag	gang	bet	bent	wig	wing
sprig	spring	pin	ping	hug	hung	lap	lamp
swig	swing						

PROCEDURES Three or four students can play. Shuffle and deal all the word cards. Have players look for pairs (e.g., *rag/rang* or *cap/camp*) in their hands and lay them down before play begins. Students then take turns laying down a word from their hand. The student who has the match to the pair takes the card, matches it to the word in his or her hand, reads the words aloud, and adds the two cards to his or her pile. The student with the most cards is the winner.

Word Study for Transitional Learners in the Within Word Pattern Stage

O rthographic development and word study instruction during the within word pattern spelling stage helps students build on their knowledge of the sound layer of English orthography as they begin to explore the pattern layer. Before we discuss development, let's visit the classroom of Ms. Watanabe, a second-grade teacher working with a group of eight students in the early part of this stage of development.

On Monday morning, after meeting briefly with a reading group to share responses to *Fox and His Friends* by James Marshall, Ms. Watanabe takes time to introduce a word sort. She has prepared a word study sheet, like the one in Figure 6.1, and has written the words on index cards that she will use to model the sort in a pocket chart. The students have already studied the common long *a* patterns (CVCe in *cake*, CVV in *say*, and CVVC in *chain*), and this sort will introduce long *e* patterns. Notice in this lesson how she guides the discussion so that students are led to make discoveries and connect with a previous sort.

Ms. Watanabe begins by saying, "Let's read these words together." As she reads each of the words, Ms. Watanabe places it randomly at the bottom of her pocket chart. There is some discussion of the homograph *read* when Jason points out that it can be read two ways. They agree for now to pronounce it as "reed." She then says to the group, "Turn and talk to your partner about the sounds and patterns in these words. What do you notice when you use your ears and eyes?" After a few minutes she calls on several students to share. Troy explains that they all have *e*'s in them and Ms. Watanabe responds with, "Tell me more." The group continues discussing the sounds and the fact that some words have one *e*, two *e*'s or an *e* and an *a*.

Ms. Watanabe continues: "Let's start with a sound sort listening for long and short vowels." She puts up pictures of a web and a queen as headers for the sounds they are to listen for: "We'll place all the words with short *e* in the middle under this picture of a web. We'll put words with the long *e* sound under this picture of a queen. Let's place words that do not fit either under the oddball column." She places a blank word card on the right side of the pocket chart to make a third column. "Jean, get us started. Where would you put this word?"

Jean places the word *bed* underneath the picture of the web while she says, "Web. Bed."

"Jean, why did you put *bed* under the web?"

"Because they sound alike in the middle. They both say 'eh' in the middle."

"Thank you! David, where would this word go?" Ms. Watanabe hands David the word *team*. David takes the word card and talks himself through the task as he has seen Ms. Watanabe model: "Team, web. . . Team, queen. *Team* has a long *e* sound." He places the word *team* underneath the picture of the queen.

Further into the sort, the students struggle with the vowel sound in the word *been* but agree it does not really sound like short *e* so they put it in the oddball column. After all the words are sorted, Ms. Watanabe and the students check each category by reading the words from top to bottom. Then Ms. Watanabe begins the reflection part of the lesson with the question, "How are the words in each column alike?"

FIGURE 6.1   Long *e* and Short *e* Word Study Sheet

🕸️	🧑	Long E Short E Sort 1
web	queen	team
seat	bed	seen
yes	jeep	read
meal	tree	leg
treat	bell	sheep
jet	cream	seed
eat	been	feel

FIGURE 6.2   **Long *e* and Short *e* Pattern Sort**

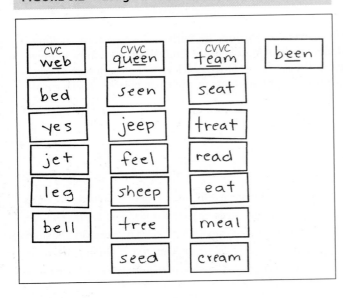

David notes that the words under the picture of the web all have one *e*. Jean points out that the words in the second column all have two vowels. This leads to Ms. Watanabe's next question: "Do you see some words in the second column that look alike or are spelled alike?" Ms. Watanabe invites Tomas to come up, and he quickly pulls out all the words spelled with *ee* and puts them in a new column, leaving behind the words spelled with *ea*. Once more, Ms. Watanabe asks the students how the words in each column are alike. She helps them come to the conclusion that short *e* is spelled with a single *e*, whereas long *e* is spelled with two vowels—either *ee* or *ea* (refer to the final sort in Figure 6.2). Ms. Watanabe wants the students to make connections with a previous sort, when she introduced the use of initials C (for consonant) and V (for vowels) to talk about the patterns; she asks, "These words with *ee* and *ea* remind me of a long-*a* pattern we labeled CVVC. Does anyone else notice that?"

The children think for a few moments then Troy begins waving his hand. "Both of these columns have the CVVC pattern!" said Troy. Ms. Watanabe asks him to explain and he adds that the words have two vowels in the middle just like the *ai* pattern. "Do the rest of you agree with Troy? Could we say that another way?" asks Ms. Watanabe. Sylvia responds by saying, "Long-*e* has two different CVVC patterns—*ea* and *ee*."

Ms. Watanabe continues with, "And what about the short-*e* words?" The students agree that they have the CVC pattern—just like short-*a*. After labeling the headers with C and V to show the patterns, they revisit the oddball word *been* to talk about how it has the CVVC pattern but not the long-*e* sound.

Ms. Watanabe ends the lesson by giving each student a copy of the word study sheet in Figure 6.1. Under her direction, the students underline the patterns in the key words and label them with C and V to use as headers. The students return to their seats, cut apart the words, and sort them independently while Ms. Watanabe checks in with another group. Later, Ms. Watanabe moves among the students and asks them, "Why did you put these words together?" This prompt gets individual students to reflect again on the categories and explain why they sorted as they did. Students store their word cards in plastic bags to sort throughout the week. The next day they will sort again, and Ms. Watanabe will watch to see how accurately and easily they sort. Later they will write the sort in their word study notebooks, work with partners to do a blind sort and a writing sort, and go on a word hunt for more words that have the same vowel sounds and patterns. ●

Literacy Development of Students in the Within Word Pattern Stage

The within word pattern stage is a transitional stage of literacy development between the beginning stage when students' reading and writing are quite labored, and the intermediate stage when they can read and write a variety of genres more fluently. We think of transitional readers as the "Wright Brothers" of reading: they have taken flight but have limited elevation in their reading, and it does not take much to bring them down to frustration level or to cause them to be less fluent in their reading. You may find transitional students in the middle-to-late part of first grade, but most are in second- and third-grade classrooms. You will also find struggling readers in middle school and high school who are in this stage (Flanigan, Hayes, Templeton, Bear, Invernizzi, & Johnston, 2011).

Reading in the Within Word Pattern Stage

Transitional readers read most single-syllable words accurately when they read at their instructional level, and they also read many two- and three-syllable words when there is enough contextual support. During this stage, students move from the **full alphabetic phase** to the **consolidated alphabetic phase** (Ehri, 2000), in which they begin to recognize patterns and chunks to analyze unfamiliar words. Instead of processing a word like *chest* as four or five letters to match to sounds (*ch-e-s-t*), they process it as two chunks (*ch-est*). This enables them to decode and store words more readily and their sight word vocabulary grows quickly. This, in turn, enables them to read in phrases and with greater expression (Templeton & Bear, 2011). Most fingerpointing characteristics from the beginning stage disappear, and transitional readers read orally at rates of over 60 words per minute (Bear, 1992; Bear & Cathey, 1989; Morris, 2013; Morris et al., 2013; Huang, Tortorelli, & Invernizzi, 2014). All of these factors account for a transitional reader's increasing fluency compared to the dysfluent, word-by-word reading in the beginning stage of literacy.

Students generally read out loud at the beginning of the transitional period, but by the end they can manage substantial periods of silent reading during Drop Everything and Read (DEAR) or Sustained Silent Reading (SSR). They can read independently without support and this makes it possible to use reading group time to share reactions to a selection. Transitional readers can discuss text in greater depth than they did as beginning readers, partly because what they read is longer and more complex.

Books for transitional readers cover a wide range of levels, from late first-/early second- through third-grade materials. In the early part of this stage, transitional readers read and reread familiar text from several sources—core reading programs, picture books, and favorite poems. They can read beginning chapter books such as the *Frog and Toad* books (by A. Lobel) and the *Henry and Mudge* books (by C. Rylant). By the end of this stage, students can read easy chapter books such as *The Time Warp Trio* series (by J. Scieska), the *Encyclopedia Brown* series (by D. Sobol), or the *Magic Tree House* series (by M. P. Osbourne). Transitional readers also explore different genres, and informational text is more accessible. For example, they read informational books from the *Let's Find Out* and *I Can Read* series, and magazines such as *Ranger Rick*.

Lots of reading experience is crucial during this stage. Students should read **instructional-** and **independent-level** materials for at least 30 minutes each day (Halladay, 2012). They need this practice to propel them into the next stage; otherwise, they will stagnate as readers and writers. You can promote fluent and expressive reading, which is an important goal during this stage (Rasinski, 2010), with repeated and timed repeated readings (Samuels, 1979), reader's theater, and poetry readings. However, fluent, expressive reading relies on automatic word recognition and extensive word knowledge (Bear, 1989). Simply trying to increase reading rates without building the underlying word knowledge is a shortsighted goal.

Writing in the Within Word Pattern Stage

Just like reading, writing also becomes more fluent during this period because students know how to automatically spell many words. They write with greater speed and less conscious attention (Bear, 1991a; Nagy, Berninger, Abbott, Vaughan, & Vermeulen, 2003). This added fluency gives transitional writers more time to concentrate on ideas, which may account

FIGURE 6.3   Yolanda's Squirrel Story

Twelve year old Chistine was glad it was Fially Satarday alltow she loved school Epspshelly math she loved taking her pet Squrrle Nuts to the park even more.

(Nuts runs away and)

Christine orginizes a search. She looked evrywhere. Christine climbd a tree Nuts wasnt there.

(Nuts returns and the next day)

Christine and Nuts woke up they went down stairs and there breakfeast was ready it was all difrent kinds of pancake animals.

(Later)

Christine thought Nuts ran away but he didn't because Nuts went tawa difrent park. Christine serches the howl park.

(The story ends with Christine)

niting a sweter for Nuts the colors where red, white and blue.

for the greater sophistication in the way they express their ideas. Cognitively, they compose with a better sense of the reader's background knowledge and with a greater complexity in the story line or informational piece.

Excerpts of Yolanda's two-and-a-half-page, single-spaced story about a squirrel named Nuts (see Figure 6.3) show how much students know about written language and spelling in the later part of the within word pattern stage. Yolanda, a second-grader, has a rich language base and she writes with a strong voice. In terms of orthographic knowledge, Yolanda spells most long vowel patterns and *r*-influenced words correctly (*woke, search*). But her word knowledge is not stable, as seen in her later spelling of *searches* as SERCHES and her overgeneralization of patterns (BREAK-FEAST for *breakfast* and HOWL for *whole*). Later in the story, Yolanda spelled *thought* as TOOUGHT but then went back and wrote in an *h*. She also confuses homophones (*there/ their*). Yolanda is a late within word pattern speller who should be placed in a word study group in which students are studying diphthongs and ambiguous vowels.

Vocabulary Learning

Estimates vary, but students in the early grades can, on average, add 10 to 15 new words a week to their oral vocabularies (Biemiller, 2005). During the transitional stage of literacy, you need to take an active and deliberate role in making sure this vocabulary growth happens for all students. You can make words interesting in many ways and in so doing help students become "wordsmiths"—children who are curious about words, their sounds, meanings, and usage. This type of attitude toward words raises students' **word consciousness** or word awareness, which is a critical aspect of vocabulary growth (Blachowicz & Fisher, 2009; Lubliner & Scott, 2008; Scott, Skobel, & Wells, 2008; Stahl & Nagy, 2006).

Do not confuse vocabulary instruction with spelling or phonics instruction (Gehsmann & Templeton, 2011/2012, 2013). When we refer to vocabulary we are referring to *meaning* and *concepts*. We have observed that sometimes teachers assign spelling words in elementary classrooms that are really vocabulary words (e.g., *butterfly, chrysalis, antenna*). Although students in the within word pattern stage can read and learn the meanings of many multisyllabic words (*glimmer, strategy, gesture*), they should not be expected to spell those words. This difference reflects the slant of development in word learning during the elementary years; the words students may read and study for meaning are more complex than those they study in spelling. For example, with context you can probably identify the partially spelled word in this sentence, "The caterpillar changes into a butterfly during the time it spends in the c-r-s-lis." However, spelling *chrysalis* is a challenge for even adult spellers. Spelling a word is more exact than reading a word, as every letter must be represented accurately.

There are many ways you can help students develop a deeper, richer oral vocabulary. Use sophisticated language in daily interactions (see Chapter 5, page 151), and develop the habit of commenting on and making observations about words throughout the day. Read-alouds, word sorts, and concept sorts provide opportunities to discuss new words and focus on multiple meanings. Students in this stage should start using a dictionary as a reference tool and begin studying common prefixes and suffixes and how they affect the meaning of the base words to which they attach.

READ-ALOUDS. Good children's literature is the best starting place for vocabulary learning and is a much richer source than television or adult daily conversation (Hayes & Ahrens, 1988). Picture books and chapter books are full of new, rich vocabulary that is wrapped in complex sentences. Context is the key to unpacking the meanings of new words from read-alouds, and with your help, students can develop that skill to learn the meanings of new words. During and after listening to books read aloud, encourage students to talk about what they heard. Use the think-pair-share strategy described in Activity 5.2 to maximize the opportunity for everyone to use oral language.

When learning new vocabulary during this stage, students benefit from repeated exposure to words and from seeing the words in print as they hear them (Beck, McKeown, & Kucan, 2013; Rosenthal & Ehri, 2008). To help students, record the words on cards, charts, and webs; post them for everyone to see; and refer to them as a reminder to use them in conversation throughout the day. It takes many exposures, over several weeks and in multiple contexts for students to learn a new word, so be deliberate when using new words and encouraging students to use them as well. Refer back to the last chapter for anchored vocabulary instruction in Activity 5.1 (Juel, Biancarosa, Coker, & Deffes, 2003).

WORD SORTS AND VOCABULARY. Always take the time to read through words in a spelling sort to be sure students know the meanings. Most of the words will be familiar ones, unless students are English learners, but there are still opportunities to explore the meaning layer of English, most specifically in the case of homophones and homonyms.

Students will encounter many **homophones** during this stage; these words that sound the same but are spelled differently provide rich fodder for vocabulary development. Why is *thrown*, the verb, spelled with an *ow*? Because the vowel-consonant-*e* pattern is already taken for the noun *throne*—the chair occupied by kings and queens. The spelling pattern reflects the different meaning! Share with students that we spell these words differently *because they mean different things!* This insight provides a fun and interesting approach to both spelling and vocabulary instruction.

Create an ongoing collection, such as a Homophone Pear/Pair Tree, as a whole-class activity in second- or third-grade classrooms that goes on all year long. When students discover a homophone pair, ask them to write it on a pear shape and then add it to the branch of a tree posted on a bulletin board. This encourages students to always be on the lookout for homophones. They will truly become wordsmiths as they collect hundreds of homophones, such as the ones on page 375 in Appendix E. Usually there is one homophone in a pair that is familiar (*bear*), while the other one (*bare*) is what Beck and colleagues (2013) call a Tier 2 word. These are words that students can use in multiple contexts and are part of the *general academic* vocabulary that students need to acquire throughout the school years (Templeton et al., 2015). As teachers, we can never *rest* until we *wrest* every ounce of meaning from word study!

English is also rich in **homonyms**—words that are spelled the same but have different meanings (*park* the car or play in the *park*). There are also **homographs**—words spelled alike but pronounced differently (*read*). Look for these words in word sorts and take the time to explore the multiple meanings through discussion, illustration, and examples in sentences. Consider a simple homonym like *block*—something you build with, something you run around in the neighborhood, something you might do during a soccer game, and a portion of time.

Polysemous words and phrases share meaning in their origin, like *bed*, a place for sleeping and the place where a stream runs, or the two meanings of *head*, a part of the body or the chief of an organization. Native speakers and English learners alike benefit from spending time reviewing the many meanings of words. Be sure to point out how context helps to determine which meaning should be taken into account.

CONCEPT SORTS. Studying subjects such as math, science, and social studies expose students to many new ideas and vocabulary that they can explore through concept sorts. In Activity 6.1, we describe a concept sort with math terms related to addition (*plus, combine, increase*) and subtraction (*take away, difference, decrease*) and also offer other examples. To prepare concept sorts, preview the vocabulary in textbooks or other curricular materials looking for the key terms, and then write them on cards or sorting templates like the one in Appendix F. Work with students to brainstorm words on a particular topic (e.g., words related to outer space, government words, or key vocabulary words from other content areas) that can then be sorted into categories.

Plan a concept sort for the beginning of a study unit as an informal assessment of background knowledge. Begin by going over the words to be sure students can read them and are familiar with the meanings of the words (they will develop deeper understanding with repeated exposure). Students can sort the words as an **open sort** either individually or with a partner. This enables you to see what students know about a topic and get a sense of the difficulty of the reading. Similarly, at the end of a study unit, ask students to complete the sort again and add related words to show what they learned.

DICTIONARIES. All kinds of dictionaries and thesauruses are important resources for within word pattern stage students. Students in the beginning of this stage can start using dictionaries to check word meanings. This does not mean students should be assigned to look up ten definitions to fulfill a seatwork or homework requirement—a strategy sure to make them dislike dictionaries. Instead, use a dictionary as a resource during reading groups, class discussions, word study lessons, and content area study to answer questions and provide information. For example, the dictionary can help students understand what *vent* means in the sentence "Josh had to vent when he got outside with his friends."

The best way to encourage dictionary use in your classroom is to keep dictionaries handy and use them often to look up definitions, to check spellings, or to answer questions such as, "Do many words begin with QU?" Model for students how interesting and informative dictionaries can be and show them how they are organized. Once students have some skill using alphabetical order and guide words, take turns assigning a student each day to be the dictionary "meister" responsible for looking up any word that the class is curious about. Or, when introducing a new sort, ask students to each look up one word and report what they found out, particularly the multiple meanings of homonyms like *drive*, or *fudge*. Children's dictionaries are most appropriate for second to fourth grade, where you will find most within word pattern spellers. Modern dictionaries, such as the *Merriam-Webster Children's Dictionary* published by DK, are visual feasts that invite students to browse. See Activities 6.7 and 6.8 for resources and ideas about teaching dictionary skills. Over the course of this stage, build a word reference area in your class library that includes thesauruses, various dictionaries (like rhyming dictionaries), Spanish and other language dictionaries, and books of antonyms, synonyms, and homophones. While students' spelling focuses on the single-syllable word patterns, students can use these references to learn more about the meaning of two- and three-syllable words.

BASIC MORPHOLOGY: PREFIXES AND SUFFIXES. Students learn to spell prefixes and suffixes in the next stage—syllables and affixes. However, they are taught simple affixes as meaning vocabulary beginning in late first and early second grade, when most students are developmentally in the within word pattern stage of spelling. Some prefixes and suffixes are included at the primary level in the Common Core State Standards adopted by most states (2010). Understanding how simple affixes combine with base words lays the foundation for more extensive exploration in forming words later on. But words with affixes are explored first as vocabulary words that students encounter during reading and content studies. They should not be treated as spelling words until students know how to spell the base words on which they are built.

The most common prefixes in the English language are *un-* (meaning "not"), *re-* ("again"), *in-* ("not"), and *dis-* ("not"), and account for about 58 percent of all prefixes (White, Sowell, & Yanagihara, 1989). Some state standards mandate studying the prefixes *un-* and *re-* as well as the suffixes *-ly*, *-ful*, and *-y*, and the comparatives *-er/-est* in second grade. Use frequently occurring and easily understood words to walk students through a discussion of, for example, *small/smaller/smallest* versus *tall/taller/tallest* to learn how suffixes are added to a base word to change the meaning. Beginning with the base word *care*, talk about being *careful* and watching over a baby brother or sister *carefully*. Appendix E has lists of words with prefixes and suffixes.

Orthographic Development in the Within Word Pattern Stage

Students in the within word pattern stage use but confuse vowel patterns (Invernizzi, Abouzeid, & Gill, 1994). They no longer spell *boat* sound by sound to produce BOT but as BOTE, BOWT, BOOT, or even BOAT as they experiment with the possible patterns for the long-*o* sound. When spellers begin including silent letters, they are ripe for instruction in long vowel patterns. In Eduardo's early within word pattern writing in Figure 6.4, we see that he knows a good deal about short vowels, spelling *with*, *pick*, *on*, *it*, and *up* correctly and *blanket* as BLANCKET. But Eduardo is experimenting with long vowel patterns, as in PLAED for *played* and TOOTHE for *tooth*.

Table 6.1 summarizes students' orthographic development across the within word pattern stage. Short vowels, blends, and digraphs are nearly mastered and should only require some review. Their phonemic awareness is well developed and they should be able to isolate the vowel sounds in the middle of words. However, learning the various ways the sounds within those words can be spelled with patterns is the challenge—and accounts for the name selected to label this stage.

PD **pd** **TOOLKIT**™
for Words Their Way®

Development Of Students In The Within Word Pattern Stage
In this video, Ms. Flores gives an overview of the literacy development of students in the within word pattern stage.

The Pattern Layer

Students in this stage explore the **pattern layer** of English spelling. This requires a higher degree of abstract thinking because they face two tasks at once. They must not only isolate the phonemes to determine the sounds they need to represent, but must also choose from a variety of patterns that represent the same phoneme, which usually involves silent letters as part of the vowel spelling (*cute*, *through suit*) or special consonant patterns (*lodge*, *itch*). There are several reasons why the same phoneme may be spelled with different patterns.

- *How words are spelled may depend on their histories and origins.* English has been enriched with vocabulary from many different languages over hundreds of years and has also imported diverse vowel sounds and spelling patterns. In addition, certain patterns represent sounds that have changed over the centuries. For example, *igh*, as in *knight*, once sounded quite different from long-*i* (the word was pronounced *k-n-ict* in early Middle English). Over time, pronunciation is simplified but spelling tends to stay the same. Therefore, one vowel sound may be spelled many different ways (Vallins, 1954).

- *How vowel sounds are spelled may depend on their position within a word.* Comparing words such as *say* and *rain* reveals that, in single-syllable words, long-*a* is usually spelled *ay* at the end of a word (but rarely in the middle) and often *ai* in the middle (but never at the end). Similarly, *oy* and *ew* usually occur at the ends of words or syllables whereas *oi*, *ui*, and *ou* occur in the middle of words.

| FIGURE 6.4 | Eduardo's Tooth Story |

> My toothe came
> Owt beckus I plaed tugwoure
> with a blancket with botes on it
> and the tooth fairy
> came tw pick it up.

TABLE 6.1 Characteristics of Within Word Pattern Spelling

	What Students Do Correctly	What Students Use but Confuse	What Is Absent
Early Within Word Pattern			
ship, when, jump ROBE for rob FLOTE for float TRANE for train BRITE for bright	Consonants, blends, digraphs Preconsonantal nasals Short vowels in CVC words r-Influenced CVC words: car, for Spell known sight words	Silent letters in long vowel patterns -k, -ck, and -ke endings: SMOCK for smoke, PEKE for peak Substitutions of short vowels for ambiguous vowels: COT for caught	Vowels in unaccented syllables: FLOWR for flower Consonant doubling: SHOPING for shopping e-Drop: DRIVEING for driving
Middle Within Word Pattern			
float, train FRITE for fright TABUL for table	All of the above plus: Common long vowel patterns (CVCe, CVVC) -k, -ck, and -ke endings	Less common and ambiguous vowel patterns -ed and other common inflections: MARCHT for marched, BATID for batted	Consonant doubling e-Drop
Late Within Word Pattern			
bright SPOYLE for spoil CHOOD for chewed SURVING for serving	All of the above plus: Long vowel patterns in one-syllable words r-Influenced vowel patterns	Ambiguous vowels Complex consonant units: SWICH for switch, SMUGE for smudge Vowels in unaccented syllables: COLER for color	Consonant doubling Changing y to i: CAREES for carries

- *How vowel sounds are spelled may depend on sounds next to them.* Examining words such as *ridge* and *cage* reveals that the /j/ sound is usually spelled *dge* when it follows a short vowel and *ge* when it follows a long vowel.
- *How vowel words are spelled may depend on the meaning of the word.* Although the long vowel sound in /pān/ may be spelled *a*-consonant-*e* or *ai*, the appropriate spelling is determined by *meaning*. Are you writing about the glass in a window (pane) or extreme discomfort (pain)? The meaning carries with it a consistent spelling: the /sāl/ on a boat is always spelled *sail*; the /sāl/ where products are sold is always spelled *sale*. For homophones like these, we hang our memory for spelling on a meaning hook.

The Complexities of English Vowels

Studying vowel patterns characterizes much of the word study during the within word pattern stage. Short vowels pose a problem for letter name–alphabetic spellers because they do not match a letter name. However, once students learn to associate the five common short vowel sounds with *a, e, i, o,* and *u*, the relationship is usually one letter to one sound. In contrast, mastering other vowels is challenging due to the following factors.

1. There are many more vowel sounds than there are letters to represent them. Each designated vowel, including *y*, represents more than one sound. Listen to the sound of *a* in these words: *hat, car, war, saw, father, play*. To spell so many sounds, vowels are often paired (e.g., the *ai* as a long-*a* in *rain*, or *au* for the sound in *caught*), or a second vowel or

consonant is used to mark or signal a particular sound. The silent *e* in *came*, the *y* in *play*, and the *w* in *saw* are all silent **vowel markers**.

2. Not only are there more vowel sounds than vowels, most of those sounds are spelled a number of different ways, as indicated in Table 6.2. However, some spelling patterns are far more likely to occur than others. For example, there are more instances of the *a*-consonant-*e* pattern (VCe) for the long-*a* sound in the middle of a syllable than for any of the other patterns. It is important to know that there just aren't that many words in which long-*a* is spelled *ei*, as in *eight*.

3. In addition to short and long vowels, there are **"other" vowel** sounds, all of which are spelled with various patterns. These include *r*-influenced vowels (*car*, *sir*, *earn*), **diphthongs** that blend two vowel sounds (*brown*, *toy*), and **ambiguous vowels** that are neither long nor short (*caught*, *chalk*, *straw*, *thought*). These other vowel patterns involve either a second vowel, or the vowel is influenced by a consonant letter that has some vowel-like qualities, such as *l*, *r*, or *w* (*bald*, *bird*, *crowd*).

4. English is a language of multiple dialects, and the dialect differences are noticeable in the pronunciations of vowels. In some regions of the United States, the long-*i* sound in a word like *pie* is really more of a vowel diphthong as in *pi*-e (can you hear both a long-*i* and a bit of a long-*e* at the end?). *House* may be pronounced more like *hoose* in some areas, and *roof* may sound like *ruff*. Sometimes the final *r* in *r*-controlled vowels is dropped, as in Boston where you "pahk the cah" (*park the car*). In other regions, a final *r* is added to words, as in the "hollers" (hollows) of southwest Virginia. Such regional dialects add color and interest to the language, but some teachers worry about how speakers of such dialects will learn to spell if they cannot pronounce words "correctly." Rest assured that these students will learn to associate certain letter patterns with their own pronunciations

TABLE 6.2 **Vowel Patterns**

Long Vowels		Other Vowels	
Common and Less Common Long Vowels		**Consonant-Influenced Vowels**	**Diphthongs and Ambiguous Vowels**
Common long-*a* patterns:	*a-e* (cave), *ai* (rain), *ay* (play)	*r*-Influenced vowels	$\overline{oo}$ (moon) and $\breve{oo}$ (book)
Less common:	*ei* (eight), *ey* (prey)	*a* with *r*: ar (car), are (care), air (fair)	oy (boy), oi (boil)
Common long-*e* patterns:	*ee* (green), *ea* (team), *e* (me)	*o* with *r*: or (for), ore (store), our (pour), oar (board)	ow (brown), ou (cloud)
Less common:	*ie* (chief), *e-e* (theme)	*e* with *r*: er (her), eer (deer), ear (dear), ear (learn)	aw (crawl), au (caught)
Common long-*i* patterns:	*i-e* (tribe), *igh* (sight), *y* (fly)	*i* with *r*: ir (shirt), ire (fire)	o (dog)
Less common:	*i* followed by *nd* or *ld* (mind, child)	*u* with *r*: ur (burn), ure (cure)	
Common long-*o* patterns:	*o-e* (home), *oa* (float), *ow* (grow)	A *w* influences vowels that follow: *wa* (wash, warn), *wo* (won, word)	
Less common:	*o* followed by two consonants (cold, most, jolt)	An *l* influences the *a* as heard in *al* (tall, talk).	
Common long-*u* patterns:	*u-e* (flute), *oo* (moon), *ew* (blew)		
Less common:	*ue* (blue), *ui* (suit)		

and will also, over time, learn the sound patterns of Standard American English (Cantrell, 2001). The value of word sorting over more inflexible phonics programs is that students can sort according to their own pronunciations, and a miscellaneous or oddball column can be used for variant pronunciations.

5. Many words in English do not match even one of the patterns listed in Table 6.2. These words are sometimes called "exceptions to the rule." We prefer to put them in the miscellaneous or **oddball** category. When students study words in the within word pattern stage, the oddball category will get a lot of use. Sometimes these words are true exceptions (*was*, *build*, and *been*); at other times they are not exceptions, but rather part of a little known category. One little-known category is illustrated in *dance*, *prince*, and *fence*—because of the final *e*, the words may look like they should have long vowel patterns. But in these words, the *e* is there to signal or mark the "soft" /s/ sound of *c* (consider the alternative: *danc*, *princ*, and *fenc*). Do not ignore the exceptions; in fact, deliberately include a few such words in your sorts. They become memorable as deviations from the common patterns.

6. English vowels pose special challenges for English learners as they compare vowels in their primary language with English. Students find that some vowels in English are not made in their languages, and that the vowels may not be spelled the same ways. English learners' strategies in this stage are discussed later in more depth.

Despite the complexity of vowel spellings, by the end of the within word pattern stage, students who have experienced systematic word study have a good understanding of vowel patterns in one-syllable words. This knowledge is required to examine the way syllables are joined during the next stage of development, the syllables and affixes stage. For example, when students understand the patterns in words like *bet* and *beat*, they are ready to understand why *betting* has two *t*s and *beating* has only one.

The Influence of Consonants on Vowels

In English, vowel patterns often consist of two vowels, one of which signals or marks a particular sound for the other vowel. Common examples are the silent *e* in words such as *bake* and *green*; however, consonants are also vowel markers, such as the *gh* in *night* and *sigh*, which signals the long-*i* sound. Students who associate the CVC pattern with short vowels may be puzzled by *saw*, *joy*, *hall*, or *car*. In those words, *w*, *y*, and *l* no longer act as consonants but take on vowel-like qualities. The consonant sound of *l* is lost in a word like *talk*—it has become part of the vowel sound, which is neither long nor short. When *w* precedes *a*, *ar*, and *or* the vowel takes on a different sound, as in *wand*, *war*, and *word*. These words may look like they are exceptions, but they are, in fact, simply additional patterns that are very regular. This is why it is important to learn patterns that relate to sound and meaning as opposed to memorizing rules. The influence of *r* is particularly common and deserves further discussion.

THE *R*-INFLUENCED VOWELS. As our friend Neva Viise says, "*R* is a robber!" The presence of an *r* following a vowel robs the sound from the vowel before it. The terms **r-influenced** or **r-controlled** both refer to this situation. Listen to the sound of *a* in *car*—it sounds quite different from short *a* in *cap*. The influence of *r* in *er*, *ir*, and *ur* makes them indistinguishable in some cases (*herd*, *bird*, *curd*). Even long vowel sounds before the robber *r* are pronounced differently than the same vowels preceding other consonants (*pair* versus *pain*). Young students sometimes confuse *r*-blends with *r*-influenced vowels, as in the spelling of *girl* as GRIL or *bird* as BRID. They can hear an *r* but are not sure of its location.

Triple Blends, Silent Initial Consonants, and Other Complex Consonants

There are several other consonant issues that pose challenges for within word pattern spellers who already know basic beginning and ending consonant blends and digraphs. For example, three-letter blends and digraphs often require further study: *spr* (*spring*), *thr* (*throw*), *squ* (*square*), *scr* (*scream*), *shr* (*shred*), *sch* (*school*), *spl* (*splash*), and *str* (*string*). Because words that contain these triplets have a variety of vowel patterns, they are specifically studied toward the end of the stage but you can include them in sorts throughout the stage when appropriate. There are also several silent consonants to study in one-syllable words: *kn* (*knife*), *wr* (*wrong*), and *gn* (*gnaw*).

Another pattern of special interest is related to vowel sounds. Based on Venezky's (1970) work, Henderson (1990) called these **complex consonant patterns**. For example, students in the within word pattern stage can examine words that end in *ck* (*kick*), *tch* (*catch*), and *dge* (*ledge*). Contrasting these pairs helps students make interesting discoveries. Say the following word pairs and listen to the vowel sounds.

ta**ck**	ta**ke**	fe**tch**	pea**ch**	fu**dge**	hu**ge**
lick	like	notch	roach	badge	cage
rack	rake	patch	poach	ledge	siege
smock	smoke	sketch	reach	ridge	page

What do you notice about the vowel sounds in the *ck*, *tch*, and *dge* patterns? What about the vowel sounds in the *ke*, *ch*, and *ge* patterns? By now you've probably figured out that *ck* (*tack*), *tch* (*fetch*), and *dge* (*fudge*) are associated with short vowel sounds, whereas *ke* (*take*), *ch* (*peach*), and *ge* (*huge*) are associated with long vowel sounds.

The consonants *g* and *c* have two different sounds that are determined by the vowel that follows them. When *g* and *c* are followed by *a, o,* and *u*, they have a "hard" sound, as in *gate* and *cake*. When they are followed by *i, e,* or *y*, they have a "soft" sound (/s/ or /j/) as in *ginger* or *cent*. (*C* is more regular than *g* because the *g* is hard in many words like *girl* and *gill*.) Similarly, words ending in *ce* (*dance*), *ge* (*edge*), *ve* (*leave*), and *se* (*sense*) have a silent-*e* associated with the consonant rather than the vowel. These patterns illustrate that how sounds are spelled often depends on other sounds next to them.

Homophones, Homographs, and Other Features

Homophones will inevitably turn up when students study vowel patterns and you can include them in the word sorts you plan even at the beginning of this stage. However, we also recommend an intensive look at homophones at the end of this stage. At this point, students know most of the vowel patterns and are ready to focus on the meanings of the words. The different spellings of homophones (*Mary/marry/merry*) and the different pronunciations of homographs (*wind* up string, listen to the *wind*) may at first seem confusing, but they reflect the historical origins and may even make reading easier and meaning clearer (cf., Taft, 1991; Templeton, 1992).

Pairs of homographs and homophones sometimes differ grammatically as well as semantically. For example, when you discuss the homophones *read* and *red*, it makes sense to talk about the past tense of the verb *to read* and the color word *red*. Take the opportunity to explore the interaction of sound, pattern, and meaning of irregular or "strong" verbs. Many of these verbs differ by vowel sounds (*drink/drank*), spelling patterns (*pay/paid*), or both (*sweep, swept*). Studying contractions presents students with a new series of features to examine that are rooted in the pattern and meaning layers of the orthography. For example, we examine meaning when we compare *its* and *it's* or *we're* and *were*.

Spelling Strategies

Students in the within word pattern stage have a growing store of known words they can spell accurately, including many high frequency words, but there are still many words they don't know how to spell. Accept students' best spelling efforts but make it clear that they are also accountable for spelling word features they have formally studied, and that they should use a variety of strategies to spell words they do not know.

ENCOURAGE STUDENTS TO TRY A WORD SEVERAL WAYS. Teach students to attempt spelling a word before they ask for help, and offer positive feedback on what they try. Australians Parry & Hornsby (1988) described this popular strategy as "have-a-go," and various forms have been developed. See Activity 6.6 for an example and procedures.

USE POSTED RESOURCES IN THE ROOM. Model for students how to use a word wall (described in Chapter 3), calendar, number and color charts, homophone charts, and other word sources displayed in the classroom. Modeling the use of these resources as you write for students is essential if you want them to use the resources for themselves. For example, if you write the sentence "Today is the first day of October," remind students that the name of the month is on the calendar. Or if you need to spell "through," identify it as a word wall word and model how you first listen to the beginning sound and then check out the words under T. Challenge students to master words that they use frequently to wean them from the word wall.

USE SPELLING DICTIONARIES TO LOOK UP WORDS. Spelling dictionaries or personal dictionaries are simply alphabetic lists of words (without definitions) commonly needed by young writers. This can be as simple as a blank book made by folding several sheets of paper (put two or three letters on each page). You can also download printable versions, or buy commercially prepared books like those listed below. These usually have one or two pages for each letter with a list of the most common words as well as space for students to add more words.

- *My Dictionary*, available from Sunshine Books International (65 pages), also has words organized thematically
- *My Word Book*, published by Primary Concepts (35 pages)
- *Words I Use When I Write* (different grade levels), available from Educators Publishing Service

Add words from the word walls to spelling dictionaries as they are introduced. Students might also request words that they want to use in their writing on a regular basis. Model for students how to use a spelling dictionary by narrowing down the beginning sound and first letter before thinking about where in the alphabet that letter would be—the beginning, middle, or end. Personal dictionary words can also be organized thematically by colors, food, action words, word wall words, and content area words that students might need for writing about a topic of study.

REMIND STUDENTS WHAT THEY KNOW. Students often forget to use what they already know to figure out something new. Here are reminders to use when students ask you how to spell a word, or during conferencing when you see they have made a mistake.

Use rhymes to make analogies. One easy way to encourage students to puzzle out the spelling of a new word on their own is to ask them if they know how to spell another word that rhymes. For example, if a student is unsure of how to spell the name of the country *Spain* ask her if she knows how to spell *rain, drain,* or *brain.* Of course, not all words that rhyme are spelled the same (e.g., *mane* also rhymes with *Spain*), but thinking of a known rhyming word will work more times than not. Prompt students by saying something like, "if you know how to spell *night,* then you can spell *slight.*"

Use word chunks. Encourage students to get down chunks of the word that they are sure of first, then tackle the next part. Getting down the initial consonant chunk, whether it is a single consonant, a blend, or a digraph, leaves the vowel and what follows as the chunk to ponder.

Use the "best bet" strategy. While sorting and studying vowel patterns, students will notice that one pattern invariably has more examples than another. For example, there are always more long-*u* words spelled *u-consonant-e* than long-*u* words spelled with *ui*. Prompt students to think about the most common pattern they know first, and then use some of the other strategies such as thinking of rhyming words they know.

Word Study Instruction for the Within Word Pattern Stage

Carefully planned word sorts are a systematic way to guide students' mastery of the complexities of vowel and consonant patterns in the within word pattern stage. Principles of instruction were previously outlined in Chapter 2 but here we highlight five that are particularly applicable to this stage:

- *Use words students can read.* Be sensitive to the difficulty of words in the sort and make sure students can read most of them easily. Words starting with consonant blends, like **blame** or **frame**, are harder than words starting with single consonants like *came* or **name** even though they share the same CVCe spelling pattern. If there are words that students cannot read set them aside and revisit them later in the sort when they can apply what they have learned to sound out the word.

- *Look for what students use but confuse.* A spelling inventory will give you a good idea of what students know and what they are ready to learn. However, it is also important to look in your students' personal writing and reading materials for words to include in sorts. The words students can already read and spell are still useful when they are looking for patterns across words to form generalizations.

- *Sort by sound and pattern.* Plan sorts that first ask students to contrast vowels by how they sound. Long vowels should be first introduced by comparing them to their corresponding short vowel sounds, as Ms. Watanabe did in the vignette at the beginning of this chapter. Sound sorts are important because sound is the first clue that spellers have to use and because certain patterns go with certain vowel sounds. You can use long and short vowel pictures for sound sorts, but most sound sorts at this stage are done with words. Consider using pictures as the column headers for your initial sound sort. After sorting by sound, sort by sight—look for the visual orthographic spelling patterns used to spell each sound category.

- *Avoid teaching rules—instead, have students find reliable patterns.* Traditionally, students were taught rules about silent-*e* and jingles like "when two vowels go walking the first one does the talking." However, rules are often unreliable. For example, the rule about two vowels works for *oa* and *ai* in *boat* and *rain*, but does not work for *oy* or *oi* in *boy* or *join*, yet *oy* and *oi* are regular spelling patterns (Johnston, 2001). We prefer to talk about patterns rather than rules. The time to talk about rules is when students have already observed a pattern, can think of examples that fit the pattern, and understand the pattern as demonstrated in their reflections. Consider rules as useful mnemonics for something already understood; they are not for teaching.

- *Don't hide exceptions.* Include two or three oddball words in sorts when appropriate. For example, include *love* and *some* in a long-*o* sort, which look as though they fit the CVCe pattern but whose vowel sounds are not long. However, don't overdo it. Too many oddballs placed in a sort can make it difficult for students to find the pattern. The best oddballs are high-frequency words like *done* or *come* that students already know how to read. High-frequency words (both regular and irregular) are listed in Appendix E and marked with asterisks in the word lists. Help students see that even the oddballs are *mostly* correct in terms of sound–spelling correspondences; it is often the vowel sound or spelling that is "odd." Students enjoy the challenge of finding the oddballs in a sort and the oddballs often serve as the real test of whether students are sorting carefully.

Ready-made sorts are available to print.

The Word Study Lesson Plan in the Within Word Pattern Stage

Word sorts often begin as a teacher-directed activity and then offer individual practice throughout the week. Most sorts will follow the standard format presented in Chapter 3 and are reviewed here.

1. *Demonstrate the sort.* When starting a sort, go over the words with students to be sure they can read the words and talk briefly about the meanings of unfamiliar words or multiple meanings of polysemous words like *park* or *train*. If there are more than a few words whose meanings students do not know, which is often the case for English learners, continue to talk about the meanings throughout the week. After going over the words, begin the sort with an open-ended question such as, "What do you notice about these words?"

   As described in Chapter 3 there are many ways to introduce a sort. In a **teacher-directed** or **closed sort**, some teachers set up the categories with **key pictures** or **key words**, as Ms. Watanabe did with short-*e* and long-*e*. Other teachers like to establish the key words as part of the group discussion with students, then highlighted. Teacher-directed closed sorts are helpful when students are new to sorting or when they start studying a new feature. Once students understand the process, use open sorts to require more analytic thinking and encourage discovery. Ask students look for their own categories and then explain why they sorted the way they did. After sorting, lead a discussion to focus students' attention on the distinguishing features. See Table 3.2, Questions to Guide Critical Thinking during Word Study, on page 60.

2. *Check and reflect.* After completing a sort, read down each column to listen for sounds or look for patterns and reflect on what the sort reveals. Asking students, "How are these words alike?" is a good question to get started on the reflection part of a lesson. If students do not come up with the insights needed to understand the feature, be ready to model your own thinking and the language students need to talk about words. You might say, "When I look at all the words in this column, I notice that the vowel sound is long and the pattern is consonant-vowel-vowel-consonant." A sort is successful when students sort accurately and quickly, and can discuss why they sorted as they did. If students seem just to mimic other students, you can ask them to say it another way or ask, "What else did you notice about the words we sorted?" When there are errors in the sort, offer gentle hints such as, "One word in this column does not sound (or look) right. Can you find it?"

3. *Extend: Students work independently across the week.* After a group sort, it is important for students to work independently or with partners using their own sets of words. Some teachers create reusable sorts in manila folders with the key words or pictures at the top and the words stored in a plastic bag inside the folder. Figure 6.5 shows a student isolating the long-*e* sound in *leaf* before placing it in the column with the picture of the feet at the top. Saying the words aloud and comparing them in this way is a necessary strategy when students begin a sort. Word study is extended through activities that students complete at their seats, in word study notebooks, at a word study center, or at home. **Word hunts** in previously read material provide opportunities for students to make connections between what they are learning in word study and the words they read in books (page 62 in Chapter 3). Often students will find more difficult two-or-three syllable examples of a feature they have been studying in one-syllable words. For example, they might find *retreat*, *ordeal*, or *creature* as examples of the long-*e* sound spelled with an *ea*. Word hunts help students generalize what they are studying to other words. We recommend **blind sorts** at this stage, in which students sort words by sound as a partner reads them aloud, because students must not only distinguish the vowel sound but also associate it with a visual orthographic pattern. Do not assign blind sorts until after students have already had plenty of opportunities to sort and discuss the words. Games are an enjoyable way to practice reading the words and thinking about their patterns. Many games are described in the activities section at the end of this chapter, or can be adapted from games in the previous chapter.

FIGURE 6.5   Long Vowel Sorts: Student Sorts by Sound

The three examples of introductory lessons that follow can serve as models for most of the sorts used in this stage.

Picture Sorts to Contrast Long and Short Vowels

Students in the early part of the within word pattern stage who still have problems distinguishing between spoken short and long vowel sounds benefit from a picture sort. Picture sorts develop phonemic awareness and focus attention on the sound without the support of the printed word. Use picture sorts for just one day and then follow up with word sorts. (CCSS Foundational Skills (1st) 2.c)

1. Use a prepared sort or select 10 to 14 pictures for one short vowel and its corresponding long vowel from the picture sets that come with this book. Arrange them in a template that students can later sort on their own or paste them on index cards for a group sort. Prepare headers such as "Short u" and "Long u" and decide on a picture that will be a key word. Headers such as *cup* and *tube* are good, are used in many sorts, and can be found on a sound board in Appendix B.

2. Set up the headers and explain to the students that they will be listening to the vowel sound in the middle of each word that names the pictures. Some words have the short-*u* sound, as in *cup*. (Isolate the vowel by peeling off the initial consonant and then the final consonant: cup, up, u). Some words will have the long-*u* sound, as in *tube* (tube, ube, o͞o).

3. Model several pictures: "Here is a cube. Listen to the vowel: c-yo͞o-b. Will I put that under *cup* or *tube*? Yes, *cube* has the long vowel sound in the middle just like *tube*. They both have the /o͞o/ sound in the middle." (Note that there is a slight difference between the long-*u* in *tube* (/o͞o/) and *cube* (/yo͞o/). The long-*u* sound seldom really "says its name" ("yo͞o"), except in a few words like *cube, mule, use,* and *huge*. Adults tend to lump these variations together, but children can sometimes be more sensitive to the differences. They could be sorted into a different category but students should understand that both are long-*u* and both have the /o͞o/ sound.)

4. Have students sort the remaining pictures. Then check the sort by naming the pictures in each column and ask the students why they sorted as they did.

5. Give the students their own set of pictures to sort and observe them to see how accurately they sort. Do not expect students to spell these words because they have not been working with the printed forms.

Teacher-Directed Two-Step Sort for Long Vowels

One basic procedure is a two-step sort that begins with sound and moves to pattern. The following example is similar to the sort done by Ms. Watanabe, but contrasts short-*a* and long-*a* sounds and patterns. This teacher-directed sort starts with one set of words that everyone uses, after which students use their own sets at their seats. (CCSS Foundational Skills (1st) 2.c, 3.c, (2nd) 3.a, 3.b)

1. Use a prepared sort or create your own sort for students. You can find prepared sorts in Appendix D, on the *Words Their Way PDToolkit*, in the *Words Their Way* supplement, and in *Word Study in Action* materials for this stage.

   To create your own sorts, use the word lists for this stage in Appendix E and select about seven short-*a* words, seven long-*a* words that are spelled with the CVVC pattern (*rain, pail*), and seven with the CVCe pattern (*cake, tape*). Include one or two oddballs that do not fit the expected sound or pattern (e.g., *was* or *said*). Use short-*a* and long-*a* pictures (e.g., *cat* and *cake*) as sound headers. Prepare word cards or write the words randomly on a word study handout template for students to cut apart.

2. Introduce the sort by reading the words together and talking about any whose meaning may be unclear. If there are homophones like *tale* and *tail*, talk about what each means. Invite students to make observations about the words: "What do you notice?"

3. Introduce the *cat* and *cake* key words for the sound sort. Say, "Listen to the vowel sound in the middle of *cat*. What vowel sound do you hear? *Cat* has a short-*a*." Repeat with *cake*.

PD **pd** TOOLKIT™

for Words Their Way®

Vowel sorts are available to download and print or sort online.

Then model how to sort a few words by the sound of the vowel in the middle and then ask the students to help you finish the sort. Warn them that there are a few oddballs with neither a short nor long vowel sound and challenge students to be on the lookout for them. As they are identified, set the oddballs off to the side. Read all the words in each column to check them and verify that they all have the same sound.

4. After discussing the two sound categories, ask students to look for patterns in the long-*a* column and separate them into two subcategories. Talk about how the words in each column have different spelling patterns and why the oddballs do not fit. Help students see that the words with a silent-*e* fit the CVCe pattern: a consonant, a vowel, another consonant, and the silent-*e*. Repeat for the CVVC pattern and contrast with the CVC words in the short vowel category. Decide on key words for new headers from among the word cards and underline them or add labels for CVC, CVCe, and CVVC.

5. Keep the headers in place and scramble the words to sort a second time. Do not make any corrections until the end. Check each column by reading the words and review how the words in each column are alike by sound and by pattern. If a mistake has been made, ask the students to find it. Talk about why the oddballs don't fit and review the homophones once more. The final categories will look something like the following sort.

CVC	CVCe	CVVC	
cat	*cake*	*rain*	was
gas	game	tail	said
back	lake	chain	
has	cape	paint	
camp	tale	pain	
tack	trade	train	

6. Students need their own sheet of words to cut apart and sort. Remind students to scribble on the back or draw three stripes in a color they can recognize if they lose a word card. Some teachers ask older students to quickly initial each word card instead. Identify the headers and ask students to sort words while you observe. After sorting, check and reflect, and then ask students to shuffle the words and store them for activities on subsequent days.

Open Sorts

After students are familiar with listening for vowel sounds and looking for the patterns, challenge them with open-ended sorts. The open sort starts with everyone sorting their own set of words. Remind students to mark the back with an assigned color or their initials so the words don't get mixed up. (CCSS FS (1st) 2.c, (2nd) 3.b, (3rd) 3)

1. Use a prepared sort, or select about 20 words that are spelled with *ir* (*bird*), *ire* (*fire*), or *ier* (*drier*). Look for words that your students should already know how to read. You may also include one or two oddballs that have the same sound but not the same spelling pattern or vice versa (e.g., *fur* and *their*). Write the words randomly on a word study handout template for students to cut apart.

2. Introduce the sort by reading the words together and talking about any whose meaning may be unclear or words that have multiple meanings. Then ask, "Can you figure out how to sort these words?" Invite students to make observations, discover the categories, and find the oddballs. Call on different students to describe the rationale for their sorts. Accept all reasonable categories but come to an agreement about whether to sort by sounds or patterns or both.

3. Close the sort. Agree on key words and underline them to use as headers. Then ask all the students to sort the same way. The categories will look something like the following

sort. Discuss the categories and oddballs with open-ended questions such as, "What do you notice about the words in each column?" Ask students to identify the homophones (*fir* and *fur*) and define or use them in sentences. See if anyone can find a word that has two meanings; for example, the word *flier* can refer to a person who flies an airplane or a printed ad.

bird		**fire**	**drier**	
fir	swirl	wire	pliers	fur
first	chirp	tire	flier	their
dirt	skirt	hire	crier	
third	twirl			
birth	stir			
shirt	firm			

4. Help students summarize what they learned from the sort. Play What If. Ask students, "What if you were going to write the word *conspire* (a new word not included in the sort, but one that follows the same pattern)? How would you figure out how to spell it? What information that you learned from this sort might be helpful?" Shuffle and store the words for sorting activities on subsequent days.

Sequence and Pacing of Word Study in the Within Word Pattern Stage

The sequence of word study in the within word pattern stage begins by taking a step back with a review of short vowel sounds as they are compared with long vowel sounds in CVCe words. If students have not completely mastered short vowels they have another chance to study them in a different context. Then the focus shifts to other common and less-common long vowel patterns and *r*-influenced vowel patterns. Ambiguous vowels and complex consonant patterns are studied toward the end of the stage.

EARLY, MIDDLE, OR LATE PLACEMENT. Identifying whether students are in the early, middle, or late part of the stage (see Table 6.1, page 206) will help you target where in the sequence of features to begin word study instruction. After administering a spelling inventory, consider your students' scores in the different categories of vowels.

Early. In the early within word pattern stage, students know blends and digraphs and spell most short vowels correctly. They often experiment with silent letters that mark long vowels. The final silent-*e* is the most common pattern and the most likely to turn up first. Students might use it but confuse it when spelling short vowels (*job* as JOBE) or long vowel patterns (FLOTE for *float*). If students spell fewer than two of the CVCe long vowels correctly, they are probably in the early part of the stage.

Middle. By the middle of this stage, students are spelling the vowels with the CVCe pattern correctly but still make mistakes on the less-common long vowel patterns as well as other vowels such as *r*-influenced vowels and ambiguous vowels.

Late. By the end of this stage, students will have mastered the long vowel patterns but will be making a few errors in the other vowels—*r*-influenced and ambiguous. They may also be missing some of the complex consonants studied in the late within word pattern stage.

PACING. Table 6.3 suggests contrasts and a sequence of word study under three possible pacing guides in the early, middle, and late part of this stage. You can adjust pacing by adding more categories to a single sort (up to four or five) or by dropping back to fewer categories when students are confused. Because there is a lot to cover in this stage, two years is not too long to address the range of features for students of average achievement.

Pacing depends on several factors: developmental level, grade level, and rate of progress. For early within word pattern spellers in late first- or early second-grade, we recommend an introductory pace. Start with some picture sorts to focus attention on the different short and long vowel sounds and then study the common CVCe pattern across four long vowels (the CVCe pattern is not studied among long-*e* words because the CVCe pattern is rare in one-syllable words). During this introductory pace, students may be using word study notebooks for the first time and learning new sorting routines.

If you teach students beyond the primary grades who are still in the early part of this stage, there is a greater sense of urgency to catch them up with peers. The moderate pace is a good place to start, but monitor progress through observation and assessments to determine whether to go faster or slower. The first few vowels may take more time than those studied later. Students in the middle within word pattern stage might benefit from the fast pace outlined in the last column of Table 6.3: a quick review of long vowels before going on to *r*-influenced and ambiguous vowels.

Many teachers are expected to use their school district's adopted phonics or spelling program and/or their district's core reading program. Although these published programs may follow a developmental sequence similar to the one in Table 6.3, they often set a pace that is too fast for low-achieving students and do not supply enough practice to master the features. To differentiate instruction at students' developmental levels, you must monitor progress and adjust the lessons by adding extra sorts for students who need a slower pace or skip some sorts to increase the pace when possible.

Keep in mind that studying vowel patterns in single-syllable words lays a critical foundation for studying two-syllable words in the next stage and cannot be shortchanged. Perhaps 25 percent of the adult population in the United States is stunted at this point of literacy proficiency. Even community college and university students who are poor spellers benefit from beginning their word study by reviewing vowel sounds and their spelling patterns (Massengill, 2006). It is important to take a step back and conduct word study activities that help students cement their knowledge of vowel patterns in single-syllable words to get a running start as they study two-syllable words. For many of these students, the fast pace in the third column of Table 6.3 may be appropriate.

The Study of High-Frequency Words

A few spelling programs feature high-frequency or high-utility words. The authors of these programs argue that spelling instruction should focus on a small core of words students need the most, such as *said, because, there, they're, friend,* and *again,* and because such words are irregular they simply must be memorized. Unfortunately, this narrow view of word study ignores the relationship between reading and spelling, and it offers students no opportunity to form generalizations that can extend to reading and spelling of thousands of unstudied words.

There are high-frequency words that do not follow common spelling patterns, and they should be included in within word pattern sorts as oddballs. For example, *said* is usually examined with other words that have the *ai* pattern, such as *paid, faint,* and *wait.* It becomes memorable because it stands alone in contrast to the many words that work as the pattern would suggest. Most students are likely to spell it correctly because they have seen it so often when they read. Note that most of the top 300 most-frequently occurring words in Appendix E (Dolch, 1942; Fry, 1980; Zeno, Ivens, Millard, & Duvvuri, 1996) are covered by the end of the within word pattern stage. See page 366 for a list of high-frequency words compiled by Fry.

However, some words in English remain problematic for young writers. There are also some words that students need to write frequently in the lower grades that are not included in the weekly lessons designed to meet their developmental needs. An example is *because,* which occurs often in the writings of first-graders. Many teachers accept students' inventions for such words (BECUZ, BECALZ, BECAWS), but some teachers grow tired of and concerned

TABLE 6.3 **Pacing and Sequence Guide for Within Word Pattern**

Slow Introductory Pace	Moderate Pace	Advanced Pace or Review
Use easy words with few blends or digraphs.	Use oddballs and some words with blends and digraphs.	Use more words spelled with blends and digraphs, oddballs and more infrequent patterns.
Early Within Word Pattern—Common and Less Common Long Vowels		
Long and short vowels in picture and word sorts	Short *a*, *a-e*	*a-e, ai, ay*
Short *a*, *a-e*	Short *i*, *i-e*	*ai, ay, ei, ey*
Short *i*, *i-e*	Short *o*, *o-e*	*o-e, oa, ow*
Short *o*, *o-e*	Short *u*, *u-e*	*u-e, ui, oo, ew*
Short *u*, *u-e*	Combine all CVC vs. CVCe	*ee, ea, ie*
Combine all CVC vs. CVCe	Final *-k, -ck, -ke*	*i-e, igh, y*
Final *-k, -ck, -ke*	*a-e, ai, ay*	VCC in *ol, os, il, in*
Short *a*, *a-e*, *ai*	*o-e, oa, ow*	
Short *o*, *o-e*, *oa*	*u-e, ui, oo, ew*	
Short *u*, *u-e*, *oo*, *ui*	*e, ee, ea*	
Short *e*, *ee*, *ea*	*i-e, igh, y*	
Review CVVC across all vowels	Review CVVC across vowels	
Short *a*, *a-e*, *ai*, *ay*	VCC in *ol, il, in*	
Short *o*, *o-e*, *oa*, *ow*		
Short *u*, *u-e*, *ew*, *ue*		
Short *i*, *i-e*, *igh*, *y*		
VCC in *il, in, ol, os*		
Middle Within Word Pattern—*r*-Influenced Vowels		
Short *a*, *o*, *ar*, *or*	*ar, are, air*	*ar, are, air, w+ar*
Short *i, e, u ir, er, ur*	*er, ear, eer*	*er, ear, eer*
r-Blends, *ar, ir, or*	*ir, ire, ier*	*ir, ire, ier*
a-e, are, air	*or, ore, oar, w+or*	*or, ore, oar, w+or*
er, ere, eer, ear	*ur, ure, ur-e*	*ur, ure, ur-e*
i-e, ire, ier	*ar, or, w+ar, w+or*	
o-e, oar, ore, oor		
ur, ure, ur-e, ea		
or, ur, ir		
w+or, w+ar		
Late Within Word Pattern—Diphthongs and Other Ambiguous Vowels		
Long *o, oi, oy*	*oi, oy*	*oi, oy, ou, ow*
oo (*boot, book*)	*aw, au*	*al, au, aw, w+a*
Short *o, ou, ow*	*wa, al, ou*	
oi, oy, ou, ow	*ou, ow*	
Short *a, al, aw*		
al, au, aw		
Review *ow, ew, aw*		

(continued)

TABLE 6.3 Pacing and Sequence Guide for Within Word Pattern *(continued)*

Slow Introductory Pace	Moderate Pace	Advanced Pace or Review
Complex Consonants		
kn, wr, gn	*kn, wr, gn*	*shr, thr, str, squ*
sh, shr, th, thr	*thr, shr, squ*	Hard/soft *g* and *c*
scr, str, spr	*scr, str, spr, spl*	*dge, ge, tch, ch*
spl, squ	Hard/soft *g* and *c*	
Hard/soft *c* and *g*	*dge, ge*	
dge, ge	*ch, tch*	
ch, tch	*ce, se, ve, ze*	
ce, se, ve, ge		
Miscellaneous		
Contractions	Contractions	
Plurals	Plurals	
Homophones	Homophones	
Irregular vowels		

about such errors, especially beyond the primary grades. Although we feel confident that such errors will be worked out over time with developmentally paced instruction, sometimes there are good reasons to address them sooner.

Some teachers study about five high-frequency words a week as part of the word wall activities described in Chapter 3 (Cunningham, 2012). An alternative is to have a week-long unit of high-frequency words several times a year. In either case, studying high-frequency words should not replace developmental word study by features, but rather should supplement such study. Choose just a few words that consist of the highly functional words seen in your students' writing. The words should not be too far ahead of your students' developmental levels. Post words that students need for short periods, of time such as *Thanksgiving, leprechaun,* and *tyrannosaurus,* for easy reference; however, such words are not appropriate for students who are still learning to spell one-syllable words.

The following guidelines will help you plan the study of high-frequency words.

1. Select six to 10 words for one week of each nine-week period, for a total of 24 to 40 words a year. (Short weeks of two to three days might be good for these.) A list for a second-grade class might include *know, friend, again, our, went, would,* and *once.* Students can take part in the selection by choosing words they have difficulty spelling or by choosing words from your master list. Post a cumulative list of these words in alphabetical order in the room for reference, with the understanding that students are expected to spell those words correctly in all their written work once they have been studied. Create individual student copies of these words in alphabetical order; add to the list as words accumulate. Students may place the individual lists in their writing workshop folders or in a section of their word study notebooks.

2. Develop routines, such as the following, to help students examine and study the words carefully.

   • *Introduction and discussion.* As you write words on the board, the students copy them on their own paper in a column. (Be sure that everyone copies correctly!) Then lead a discussion about each word. "What part of this word do you *already* know how to spell?"

"What part of this word might be hard to remember and why?" (For *friend*, focus on the fact that it has a silent-*i*.) "What might help you remember how to spell this word?" (Students might note that it ends with *end*.)

- *Self-corrected test method.* After the words are written and discussed, have students fold their paper over so that the list is covered. Call the words aloud while the students write them again; students then check their own work by unfolding the paper to compare what they copied to what they spelled. Have students rewrite any words spelled incorrectly. The self-corrected test method to support memorization has been well researched (Horn, 1954; Templeton & Morris, 2000).
- *Self-study method.* The self-study method is a long-standing activity that appears in most published spelling programs. This process can be used independently after students are taught the steps: (1) look at the word and say it; (2) cover the word; (3) write the word; (4) check the word; and (5) write the word again if it is spelled incorrectly.
- *Practice test.* Call out and have students spell each word, and then immediately check it by looking at the chart posted in the room. Students become familiar with using the chart as a reference and can call the words to each other in pairs or small groups, or you may lead the practice test.
- *Final test.* Cover the chart, and have students spell the words as you call out each one. Because the number of words is kept low, the chance of 100 percent success is high. Once students are tested they are responsible for those words from then on. You will undoubtedly need to remind students often to reread a piece of written work to check for the posted words in the editing stage. Students will have about eight weeks to work at getting any problematic words under control; any word that continues to be a problem can reappear on the next list.

Assess and Monitor Progress in the Within Word Pattern Stage

By the end of second grade, most students should be well into the middle of the within word pattern stage or beyond. Students who are not should be getting carefully planned systematic word study in supplemental interventions. There are several ways to monitor students' progress in the within word pattern stage.

Weekly Spelling Tests

In this stage, we recommend weekly spelling tests as a way to both monitor progress and to make students accountable for their learning. Select ten words from the sort and call them out in a traditional way. Many teachers also call out one or two transfer words—words that fit the features but that were not included in the sort. Prompt students to use analogy by saying something like, "If you know how to spell *rain*, then you can spell *stain*." When students are appropriately placed they should score 90 to 100 percent on these weekly assessments. If they do not, you should reconsider the placement or pacing of instruction. Also consider whether students are getting enough practice with the words across a week. We also recommend designing your weekly spelling test as a **blind writing sort**, having students sort the words as they write them. This rewards the kind of thinking about sound, pattern, and meaning that is the whole point of word study. Give one point for the correct spelling and a second point for the correct grouping.

Unit Assessments and Goal Setting

Teachers often observe that students study for weekly tests and then forget the words when they need them for real writing (Gill & Scharer, 1996; Graham et al., 2008; Schlagal, 2013).

MONITORING
PROGRESS

PD **TOOLKIT**™
for Words Their Way®

**Within Word Pattern Spell
Checks** and **Within Word
Pattern Monitoring Chart**
These assessment tools and
goal setting forms are ready to
download and print.

For this reason, we recommend periodic unit spell checks to determine whether the words and features are retained over time. Spell checks have been developed for each of the major units of study and can be found on the website and in *Words Their Way®: Word Sorts for Within Word Pattern Spellers*. You can easily create your own spell checks to use every three to six weeks by selecting words from the word sorts to assess retention of studied words and perhaps including additional transfer words to see whether students can apply their growing knowledge of sounds and patterns to unstudied words. Use these spell checks to monitor progress and fine-tune your instructional pacing. Depending on results, you may find you need to drop back to a slower pace or ratchet up to a quicker pace, as suggested in Table 6.3.

Students in the within word pattern stage can be involved in setting their own goals, using the forms described in Chapter 2 and available at the website. This is especially beneficial for older students who struggle with spelling and need to see their own progress.

Word Study with English Learners in the Within Word Pattern Stage

When planning word study with English learners it is important to know something about their native languages and what literacy experiences they have had. Students who are literate in their first language may spell the sounds they hear in English with the letter–sound correspondences they know from their first language, or if the sounds do not exist they will substitute close approximations. Knowing something about students' native languages and writing systems is helpful so you can guide comparisons and understand the difficulties English learners face.

Teaching Vowels to English Learners

for English Learners

As hard as vowels are for English-speaking students, they can be truly challenging for English learners because many vowel sounds in English do not exist in other languages (Bear, Templeton, Helman, & Baren, 2003; Helman, 2004). Let's use Spanish as an example because it is the second most commonly spoken language in the United States. Unlike English, Spanish vowels have only one sound for each letter. Some are the same as English, but others are different. For example, *o* and *u* represent long-*o* and long-*u*, as in *uno*. However, *i* represents the long-*e* sound (*amigo*) or *si* and *e* represents a sound that is close to long-*a* (*tres*, /trās/). The letter *a* is the only vowel in Spanish that is close to a short vowel sound in English: "ah" (/ö/) as in the vowel in *hot*. Table 6.4 shows some of the spelling errors students who are literate in Spanish might make, such as spelling *job* as JAB.

For students who have learned to spell in Spanish there will be some predictable confusion with long vowels, such as using *e* for long-*a* (LEK for *lake*). Students literate in Spanish expect each vowel sound to be represented. What English speakers think of as a single long vowel is actually sometimes pronounced as a diphthong or glide, as in "pi-ee" (*pie*) or "lay-eek" (*lake*)—depending on one's dialect. Spanish speakers may be more sensitive to these glides and attempt to spell both of the vowel sounds they hear. For example, when you pronounce the English long-*i* slowly, you can feel and hear how the long-*i* is a combination of the bottom vowel "ah" and the "ee" formed at the top of the mouth. The "ah" sound in English may be spelled with a short -*o*, but in Spanish, this sound is spelled with an *a* and the long-*e* sound is spelled with an i, so *pie* might be spelled PAI and *night* as NAIT. SSee Table 6.4 for more examples.

Other Romance languages, such as French, also represent long-*a* with *e* (*tres*) and long-*e* with *i (merci)*. Four to five hundred years ago, English strayed from the original continental pronunciation of vowels and has, over time, changed or dropped the pronunciation of one vowel in combinations such as *ai*, *oa*, *ea*, or *ui*, so that the second vowel is now silent.

TABLE 6.4 **Vowels in Spanish and Predictable Spelling Errors**

Letters	Comparable Sound in Spanish	Spanish Examples	Possible Spelling Errors in English
a	/ō/ "ah"	*papa, madre, casa*	*job* as JAB
e	/ā/ "ay"	*tres*	*lake* as LEK or LEIK
i	/ē/ "ee"	*si, mi, amigo*	*reach* as RICH
ai	/ī/ "eye"	*aire*	*night* as NAIT
o	/ō/ "oh"	*uno, loco*	*float* as FLOT or FLOUT
u	/ū/ "oo" (never "yoo")	*uno, tu, mucho*	*tune* as TUN

Source: Adapted from *Words Their Way® with English Learners: Word Study for Phonics, Vocabulary, and Spelling Instruction* (2nd ed.), by Lori Helman, Donald R. Bear, Shane Templeton, Marcie Invernizzi, and Francine Johnston. Boston: Pearson/Allyn & Bacon.

Strategies for Teaching and Assessing English for English Learners

Some English learners can memorize many words, but their strategies for spelling unknown words often indicate that their orthographic knowledge could be deeper. For example, a student memorized the spelling of *rain* but continued to spell unknown long-*a* words with an *e* (*train* as TREN), using the Spanish spelling of the long-*a* sound as in Table 6.4. The spelling errors in uncorrected writing and spelling inventories described in Chapter 2 reveal what word knowledge English learners bring to the task of reading and writing English.

There may be times when you want to assess students' spelling development in their primary languages. Inventories for Spanish, Chinese, and Korean are available in *Words Their Way® with English Learners*. These inventories will help you find out what students know about their own written language. The more literate students are in their first language, the more information there is to transfer to learning to read in English (Proctor, August, Carlo, & Snow, 2006).

Word sorting lessons are an explicit way to draw English learners' attention to both the similarities and differences between languages in terms of sounds and spelling, as well as helping build vocabulary. The following suggestions can enhance the effectiveness of your word study with English learners:

- Search online resources to learn about similarities and differences in the sound and spelling systems of languages spoken by your students.
- Use concrete, highly imageable words that can easily be visualized, drawn, or acted out—concrete nouns, imageable adjectives, action verbs. These words will be easier to learn than prepositions, conjunctions, or helping verbs.
- Discuss the meanings of the words in the introductory lesson and review throughout the week as needed. Act out words when appropriate and supply photographs or drawings to develop meaning. Students can illustrate words in their word study notebooks or add a small drawing or definition to the word cards to remind them of meaning (see Figure 6.6).

FIGURE 6.6 **Simple Drawings Help English Learners Associate Meaning with Spelling**

- Reduce the number of words in a sort so students will not be overwhelmed with too many new vocabulary words. Spend extra time reading the words in columns aloud as students check their sorts.
- Pair words and pictures when possible. Long and short vowel pictures are included in the pictures that come with this book; more images can be downloaded from the Internet (e.g., Google images).
- Pair English learners with native English speakers who can supply pronunciations during partner sorts.
- Model careful pronunciation but do not be overly concerned if English learners do not master the correct pronunciations.

For further information on these recommendations, refer to *Words Their Way*® *with English Learners.*

WORD STUDY *Routines and Management*

The within word pattern stage easily spans a number of grade levels, usually from first to fourth grade and beyond that for struggling students. A typical third-grade class will have students in the middle and late within word pattern stage, as well as students in the next stage, syllables and affixes. Differentiation occurs when students meet in small groups in which sorts are introduced and discussed under your guidance. However, after that, everyone can engage in the same weekly routines described in Chapter 3 (blind sorts, writing sorts, word hunts, speed sorts, homework). Table 3.6 (page 58 in Chapter 3) shows a weekly schedule for students in the within word pattern stage, and Table 3.7 (page 59 in Chapter 3) offers a variation on this. Once students learn the schedule and the routines they can work independently, with partners, or in small groups on most days of the week, freeing you to meet with instructional-level reading groups. As in the letter name–alphabetic stage, you might find that reading groups are usually the same as the word study groups.

Vocabulary instruction is usually not differentiated unless it involves words from the weekly sort or words that turn up in reading groups. Instead, vocabulary instruction usually takes place in whole-group settings, during read-alouds, and during content area instruction.

PD TOOLKIT™

for Words Their Way®

Weekly Schedules And Classroom Activities With Students In The Within Word Pattern Stage

Watch Ms. Flores lead students in word study activities throughout the week.

MONITORING PROGRESS

Word Study Notebooks in the Within Word Pattern Stage

A word study notebook is an essential tool in the within word pattern stage, and provides an organizational structure and documentation of student work. It is used across the week for a number of activities (see Chapter 3) and students should have ready access to it throughout the day. Ask students to bring their notebook to small-group sessions, along with reading materials and response journals or logs. We recommend using sturdy stitched composition notebooks with a hard marbleized cover and dividing them into several sections set off with a tab or sticky note.

1. Students record their weekly sort, word hunt, and other phonics or spelling activities in the word study section. Ask them to summarize what they learn from their sorts in their own words, as Araceli has done in Figure 6.7 She has numbered each column and written a generalization for each, such as "*Climb* is the same as *bind, wind,* and *hind.*" These written reflections help you assess students' progress.
2. Students record words from their reading or from content area instruction in the vocabulary section. For example, when reading *Stuart Little* encourage students to make lists of boat terms (*rigging, bow, stern*) or weather-related words (*squall, breeze, mist*). These words can be shared and then combined and sorted into semantic categories or added, where possible, to the spelling sorts (e.g., add *breeze* to a long-*e* category of *ee* patterns). Students

FIGURE 6.7	**A Page from Araceli's Word Study Notebook**

Araceli
10/22

I that say his name

shine	climb	sky	right	wind
bite		try	slight	find
slide		my	sigh	blind
slime	2	3	night	hind
spine				
1			4	
				5

1. This word Say i by the e at the end.

2. Climb is the same as bind, wind, and hind.

3. a i tarn's into an y.

4. The i is with gh we can not hear it.

5. This word all got an i-n-d.

might create a science web on pandas, make a list of concepts related to immigration, or compare and contrast geometric terms.

3. A third section might be an ongoing list of homophones, homographs, and polysemous (multiple meaning) words, with sentences or pictures to illustrate the different meanings of the words.

Word Hunts

To help students see the connection between word study and reading, ask them to go through what they have recently read to find words that fit the particular sound or pattern they are studying. The common vowel patterns turn up frequently in most reading materials, but you may also find decodable text or phonics readers that focus on a particular pattern useful for word hunts. Although word sorts are usually limited to one-syllable words in this stage, two- and three-syllable words are welcome additions in a word hunt (e.g., *ai* in *rainbow* or *painted*). Such words often extend generalizations into more difficult vocabulary as well as offer opportunities for applying knowledge of vowel patterns to the decoding of longer words in texts. Record word hunt results on charts and/or in word study notebooks. In addition, challenge students to always be on the lookout for new words that they might add to earlier sorts. In this way, sounds and patterns are constantly revisited.

Homework

In Figure 3.24 in Chapter 3, there is a letter for parents describing homework routines for each day of the week. These routines are especially appropriate for within word pattern spellers for whom homework will provide much needed extra practice. You can send home a checklist, such as the one in Figure 3.22 (Chapter 3), with an extra copy of the words for the week; place everything in an envelope or plastic zip bag. Allow students to choose two or three activities, and more options can be added to the checklist occasionally, such as using a small number of words in sentences.

RESOURCES FOR IMPLEMENTING WORD STUDY *in Your Classroom*

There are a number of materials available to help you implement word study with students in the within word pattern stage.

- Suggested sorts in Appendix D can be used with the template on page 401, and the word lists in Appendix E can be used to create your own sorts.
- Prepared sorts, spell checks, and games are available on the PDToolkit. With the Create Your Own feature you can make your own sorts.

- *Words Their Way®: Word Sorts for Within Word Pattern Spellers* provides a complete curriculum of sorts divided into ten units. The spell checks that are supplied for each unit can be used for pretesting to better identify what students are ready to study and for post-testing to monitor progress.

ACTIVITIES for the Within Word Pattern Stage

Several vocabulary activities are described first in this section followed by some dictionary activities. The remaining games and activities are designed to extend and reinforce spelling sorts. Common Core State Standards for Foundational Skills and Language are listed for grades 1, 2, and 3.

Vocabulary Activities

Refer back to vocabulary activities in Chapter 5 (5.1 to 5.5) that are also appropriate for this stage.

6.1 Concept Sort for Math

Concept sorts are an excellent way for students to work with vocabulary related to units of study. In this example, students categorize terms related to addition and subtraction that they are likely to encounter in word problems. (CCSS Language (1st) 5.a, 5.c, (3rd) 6)

Adaptable for Other Stages
● ● ● ● ●

MATERIALS Prepare a set of word cards with the terms to sort on the front and sample word problems on the back using the terms. For example, "*Take away*. If I have three books and you *take away* two how many will I have?" If you want students to work with these terms individually, use a blank template and write the terms in the boxes in random order. Set off the headers in bold or underline.

PROCEDURES
1. Remind students that there are many words that mean the same thing as "add" and "subtract" and that these words will show up in written word problems.
2. Set up the headers Add and Subtract. Introduce each new term in a simple problem sentence. "*Lost*. I had 10 pencils and I *lost* three so how many do I have left?" Or "*Difference*.

What is the *difference* between six goals and three goals? Do I add or subtract to get the answer?"

3. Continue to sort all the terms, discussing where the terms should go and why. The final sort will look something like the following set of lists. Put the words in a student activity center for students to sort independently or give students their own sheets to cut apart and sort.

add +		subtract –	
and	plus	minus	difference
in all	more	take away	leave/left
combine	sum	lost	less
increase	join	decrease	delete
together		fewer	reduce

4. Challenge students to write their own word problems using the terms.

VARIATIONS You can add terms for multiplication and division. Many content area terms and concepts can be sorted in a similar manner. Simply write words into a template or onto cards, draw a simple figure, or use an online search engine to find pictures and images you can download. Use both pictures and words when appropriate. Here are more examples:

- Geometric shapes: quadrilaterals, hexagons, right triangle, equilateral triangle
- Open and closed figures
- Objects that will or will not be attracted to a magnet
- Food groups: protein, fruits, vegetables
- Parts of speech: nouns, verbs, adjectives, adverbs (see Figure 6.8)
- Animals by carnivores, herbivores, or omnivores; mammals, birds, reptiles, and amphibians
- Things we can and cannot recycle
- States of matter: solids, liquids, and gas
- Simple machines: lever, pulley, wedge, inclined plane, wheel, screw
- Fact and opinion statements
- Habitats and the plants and animals that live there
- Equivalent fractions
- Objects you would or would not see used by settlers or Native Americans of the Old West

FIGURE 6.8 Sorting Words by Part of Speech

6.2 Semantic Brainstorms

This small-group activity focuses on the meanings of the words and serves as a great activity for content studies. (CCSS Language (1st) 5.a, 5.c, 6, (2nd) 6, (3rd) 6)

PROCEDURES

1. Choose a topic related to an area of study. Start with easy, familiar topics such as sports (or countries, animal life, clothes, furniture, or modes of transportation).
2. Have students brainstorm related words and then record them using chart paper or an interactive whiteboard.
3. Ask students to share their findings and see whether they can come up with subcategories from their brainstorming. Categories can be circled by color or written over into columns.

VARIATIONS Look in magazines, newspapers, and catalogs. Circle words that express feelings, colors, people's names, or parts of speech. Use organizing software to record these brainstorms electronically, to be moved about on an interactive white board; use software for drawing graphics the same way. You can record student responses within circles and rectangles using the drawing toolbar in PowerPoint software.

FIGURE 6.9   Honey Bee Semantic Sort

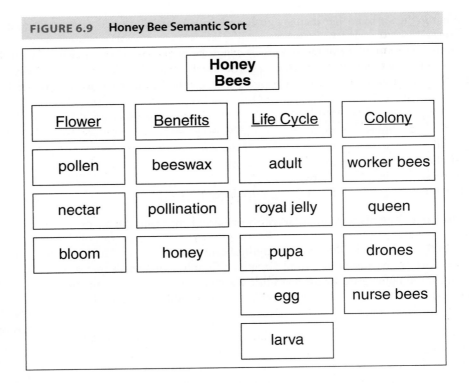

6.3   Semantic Sorts

Students work with content-related words to compare and contrast. In Figure 6.9, terms related to bees have been sorted into categories. (CCSS Language (1st) 5.a, 5.c, 6, (2nd) 6, (3rd) 6)

PROCEDURES
1. Look through a chapter or unit in a textbook and make a list of the key terms; they are often listed at the end of a unit. Make word cards for the words or fill in a template such as the one in appendix F.
2. Have students work alone or with partners to sort the words in an open sort, establishing their own categories. Then bring everyone together to compare and defend their groupings.
3. When doing a sort to introduce a unit of study, do not evaluate student groupings as right or wrong. Let disagreements or errors be the basis for questions to be answered with further study. For example, students might logically put royal jelly under "benefits" of honeybees. Rather than telling them where it should go, say something like, "I see that there is some disagreement about where to put royal jelly. As we read about honeybees we will pay special attention to this term."
4. Have students sort words again after a unit of study is finished. They can copy the sorts into word study notebooks in a separate section for that content area, and be used as one way to evaluate student learning.

6.4   Shades of Meaning

This small-group activity focuses on the nuances of meaning among words in the same semantic category. It is useful for nurturing word consciousness in writing as well as reading. The activity focuses on the discussion and not on whether the order is right or wrong. (CCSS Language (1st) 5.a, 5.c, 5.9, 6, (2nd) 5.b, 6, (3rd) 5.c, 6)

PROCEDURES

1. Choose a vocabulary word that is essential to understanding a particular book or topic of study. For example, you might choose *stampede* from Scieszka's *The Good, the Bad, and the Goofy*, because this term describes so much of the action in this book.
2. Come up with other words that are similar to a stampede (noun): a *charge, rush, flight, mad dash*, and so on. Students can also contribute words.
3. Have students place the words along a continuum of strength (*move, rush, flight, mad dash, charge, stampede*) and then discuss the reasoning for their arrangement. Students might say that a *charge* is more forceful than a *rush*, or a *stampede* is even stronger than a *charge*.

6.5 "Said Is Dead" and "Good-Bye Good"

As students increase their writing fluency their word choices should reflect a more extensive and vivid vocabulary. These two activities are frequently used across the grades to help students add spice to their writing. (CCSS Language (1st) 5.a, 5.d, 6, (2nd) 5.b, 6, (3rd) 3.a, 6)

MATERIALS You will need a thesaurus for every small group, as well as chart paper, a projector, and models of either exemplary or tired writing. Some teachers use chart paper cut in the shape of a headstone. You can find prepared posters of "Said Is dead" and other word lists online but it is better to have students create their own and add to them.

PROCEDURES

1. Begin with a piece of writing (a student sample or something that you create) and project it for all to see. Look through the selection for overused words, such as the verb *said* or the adjective *good*. Then project a piece of literature with a variety of words for contrast.
2. Create a vocabulary chart that students may use for their own writing and brainstorm other words to use in place of said or good. Students can refer to a thesaurus for related words. Post the chart where students can refer to it and continue to add to it over time. A brief list of words developed by students to replace *said* might include the following:

yelled	declared	laughed	ordered	scolded
remarked	screamed	blurted	demanded	argued
exclaimed	cried	boasted	requested	whispered
chuckled	explained	asked	muttered	suggested

Another list to replace *good* might include the following:

fantastic	awesome	wonderful	lovely	superb
cool	joyful	fabulous	super	excellent
exciting	terrific	perfect	beautiful	pleasant
marvelous	enjoyable	great	honorable	compassionate

Spelling Strategies and Dictionary Skills

6.6 Have-a-Go Sheets

Asking students to try spelling a word several ways is an important strategy since identifying the vowel sound and then thinking of different possible patterns is one of the key goals of instruction in the within word pattern stage. (CCSS Language (1st) 2.e. (2nd) 2.d, (3rd) 2.f)

MATERIALS Prepare blank forms like the one in Figure 6.10. While these forms are not necessary—students can write the word in the margin of their paper or on a scrap of paper—they help when first introducing the strategy to students. Keeping a special form in a writing folder can serve as a reminder and also a record of a student's efforts.

FIGURE 6.10   Have-a-Go Sheet

Source: Based on Parry, J., & Hornsby, D. (1988). *Write On: A Conference Approach to Writing*. Portsmouth, NH: Heinemann.

PROCEDURES

1. Students can use the Have-a-Go sheets any time they are writing, and keep them in their writing folders. However, the sheets might be used specifically when students are editing pieces that will be taken to a finished state.
2. Expect students to make two attempts to spell a word they need and consider which one might "look right." Only then can they go to you to ask for help.
3. You can then see where the students need assistance, compliment them on what they figured out, and make suggestions about what else is needed, or even confirm that they got it right! Figure 6.10 contains examples of the kinds of feedback you can use.

6.7   Dictionary Skills for Within Word Pattern Spellers

During the within word pattern stage, students can learn some essential dictionary skills and begin to use simplified dictionaries to look up the meanings of words. (CCSS L (2nd) 4.e, (3rd) 4.d)

MATERIALS You will need beginning dictionaries or elementary dictionaries that are best for students first learning to look up words. These look like traditional dictionaries but include the most common words with brief entries. However, they are not as limited as the picture dictionaries described in Chapter 5. If you do not have sets available in your classroom check with your school librarian, who might have sets that you can borrow. We recommend the following:

> DK *Children's Illustrated Dictionary* (2009)
> *Merriam-Webster Children's Dictionary*
> *Scholastic Dictionary of Spelling*

PROCEDURES

1. Teach alphabetical order up to the second or third letter. Occasionally ask students to put their word sort for the week into alphabetical order before copying it down in their word study notebooks. To start, supply students with an alphabet strip to use as a guide and only require alphabetizing by the first letter. Next, take away the strip and then move on to using the second and even third letter to put words in order.
2. To help with dictionary searches, divide up the alphabet into early, middle, and late sections so students develop a sense of where a letter appears in the alphabetical sequence.

Divide an alphabet strip into thirds then model how to think about where a letter falls (e.g., "The letter N come close to M so I know it is in the middle"). You can ask students to sort their weekly words into thirds by setting up headers such as A–G, H–R, and S–Z.

3. Teach students to use guide words. Once students can alphabetize to two or three places, you can introduce the guide words at the top of the dictionary page that will help them narrow down the location of a word. Begin with lots of modeling and think-alouds as you do this using your own dictionary.

4. Teach students how to interpret definitions. Project a page of a dictionary and point out the bolded entries and the kinds of information they can find. Of particular interest at the within word pattern stage are the multiple meanings of even simple words like *beat*, *track*, or *lodge*. When introducing the words in the sort for the week you might ask several students to look up the definition(s) of selected words and to be ready to report to the group on their findings.

5. Model at every opportunity. You may find that a beginning dictionary is somewhat limited and you need to use a more advanced dictionary. Think out loud as you use the dictionary: "If I want to look up *contagious* I first need to figure out the first few letters—*con*—I think that would be C-O-N. C comes early in the alphabet so I will open the dictionary to the beginning and flip to the C pages. Now to find some C-O words using the guide words at the top of the page. . . ."

6.8 Dictionary Scavenger Hunts and How Many Turns

As you teach basic dictionary skills, you can conduct scavenger hunt type activities for just a few moments each day by asking students to get out dictionaries and find words as quickly as possible. Students can also do this in small groups or with partners, taking turns naming words to find and keep track of the time or the number of pages they turn. (CCSS Language (2nd) 4.e, (3rd) 4.d)

MATERIALS Students should all have similar dictionaries appropriate for primary or elementary grades.

PROCEDURES

1. Call out a word and write it for all to see. When appropriate, prompt students to consider the first and second letter (start with single consonants), to think about where to look in the dictionary (early middle late), and to use guidewords.

2. Challenge students to count the number of times they need to turn a page to find the word. De-emphasize competition, but winners might be allowed to call out the next word.

There are many games available for this stage to download and print. Some are ready to use and others come as blank templates.

Spelling Games and Activities

Many games from the previous chapter can be used with the features covered in this stage. Look for *Match, Go Fish, Making Words With Cubes,* and *Follow the Path Spelling Game.* The Adaptable for Other Stages logo in each chapter indicates games that work for a variety of features and stages.

6.9 Word-O or Word Operations

Students can complete this activity in their word study notebooks. It is especially appropriate for the within word pattern stage because it shows students how analogy can help them spell. (CCSS Language (1st) 2.d, (2nd) 2.d, (3rd) 2.f)

PROCEDURES Give students a word (such as *cart*) and then ask them to add, drop, or change one or two letters at a time to create a new word. Typically consonants, blends, and digraphs are exchanged at the beginning (*part, chart, smart*) or the end (*card*), but vowels can

FIGURE 6.11   Train Station Game: Long Vowel Patterns

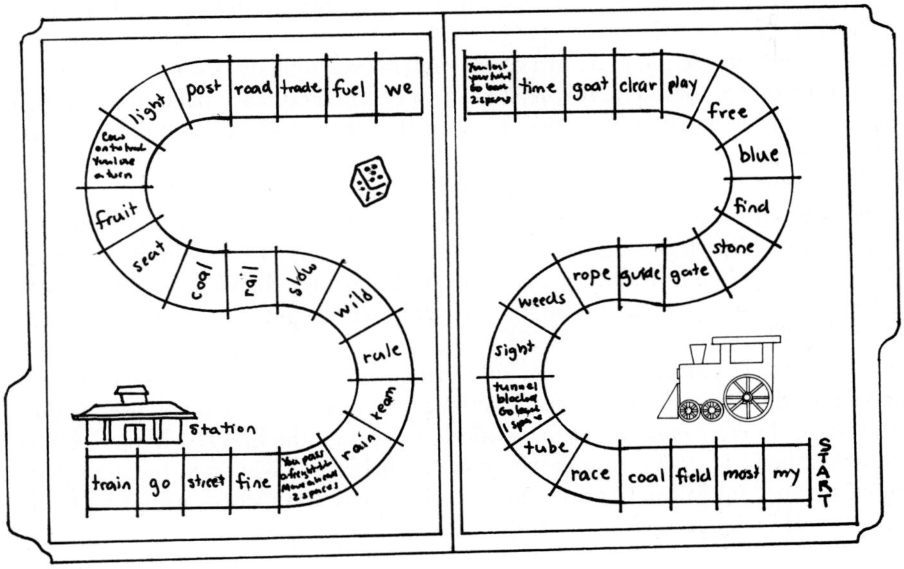

also be exchanged (*green, groan, grain*). Model this activity and show students how to use sound boards, as in Appendix B, for ideas. Challenge students to see how many words they can form. Here is an example starting with the word *space*:

space	pace	place	lace	race	trace			
track	rack	crack	clack	lack	slack	sack	Mack	
mask	ask	task	bask					
base	vase	case						
cast	last							
lass	glass	grass	brass					
brash	trash	crash	cash					

6.10 Train Station Game

Use this board game to emphasize automaticity with common long vowels. (CCSS Language (1st) 2.c, 3.c, (2nd) 3.a, 3.b, (3rd) 2.f, 3)

Adaptable for Other Stages

MATERIALS Use a basic follow-the-path board found in Appendix F, decorated as in Figure 6.11. Write in words that students have studied in word sorts as well as words that share the same feature. Incorporate four special squares into the game board: (1) Cow on the track. Lose 1 turn. (2) You pass a freight train. Move ahead 2 spaces. (3) Tunnel blocked. Go back 1 space. (4) You lost your ticket. Go back 2 spaces.

PROCEDURES This game can be played with up to four students. Each student selects a game piece. The first student then spins or rolls the die and moves the appropriate number of spaces. Students pronounce the word they land on and identify the vowel. If students have studied the long vowel pattern within each long vowel, ask them to say the pattern. For example, "*Nail* is a long-*a* with a CVVC pattern." In addition, students must say another word containing the same vowel sound to stay on that space. Play continues in this fashion until someone reaches the station.

VARIATIONS Divide a spinner into five sections and label each with a vowel. Students move to the next word with the vowel sound they spin.

6.11 Turkey Feathers

In this game, two players compare patterns across a single long vowel. (CCSS Language (1st) 2.c, 3.c, (2nd) 3.a, 3.b, (3rd) 2.f, 3)

MATERIALS You will need two paper or cardboard turkeys without tail feathers (see Figure 6.12), 10 construction paper feathers, and at least 20 word cards representing the long vowel (e.g., for long-*a*: *a-e*, *ai*, and *ay*).

PROCEDURES

1. One player shuffles and deals five cards and five feathers to each player. The remaining cards are placed face-down for the draw pile.
2. Each player puts down pairs that match by pattern. For example, *cake/lane* is a pair, but *pain/lane* is not. Each time a pair is laid down, the player puts one feather on his or her turkey.
3. The dealer goes first, saying a word from his or her hand, and asks if the second player has a card with the same pattern.
4. If the second player has a matching pattern, the first player gets the card and lays down the pair and a feather; if not, the first player draws a card. If the player draws a card that matches any word in his or her hand, the pair can be discarded, and a feather is earned. The next player proceeds in the same manner.
5. The player using all five feathers first wins. If a player uses all the cards before earning five feathers, the player must draw a card before the other player's turn.

FIGURE 6.12 **Turkey Feathers: Comparing Vowel Patterns**

*Adaptable
for Other Stages*
● ● ○ ● ●

Turkey Feathers and **The Racetrack Game**
These games are ready to print.

6.12 The Racetrack Game

Darrell Morris (1982) developed this game, which has become a classic. It can be used for any vowel pattern and serves as a good review of the many patterns for the different vowels. (CCSS Language (1st) 2.c, 3.c, (2nd) 3.a, 3.b, (3rd) 2.f, 3)

MATERIALS This game, for two to four players, is played on an oval race track divided into 20 to 30 spaces, which you can find in Appendix F and on the website (see Figure 6.13 for an example). Different words following particular patterns are written into each space, except for a star drawn in two spaces. For example, you can use *night, light, tie, kite, like, my, fly, wish,* and *dig* on a game designed to practice patterns for long- and short-*i*. Prepare a collection of 40 to 50 cards that share the same patterns. A number spinner or a single die is used to move players around the track.

PROCEDURES

1. Designate one player as the dealer, who shuffles the word cards and deals six to each player; the remaining cards are turned face-down to become the deck. Playing pieces are moved according to the number on the spinner or die.
2. When players land on a space, they read the word and then look for words in their hands that have the same pattern. For example, a player who lands on *night* may pull *sign* and *right* to put in his or her point pile. If players move to a space with a star, they dispose of any oddballs they might have (such as *give*) or choose their own pattern.
3. Any cards played are replaced by drawing from the deck. A player who has no match for the pattern must draw a card anyway.
4. The game is over when there are no more cards to play. The winner is the player who has put down the most word cards.

*Adaptable
for Other Stages*
● ● ○ ● ●

ACTIVITIES | WITHIN WORD PATTERN STAGE

FIGURE 6.13 Racetrack Games Are Popular, Easy to Make, and Simple to Play

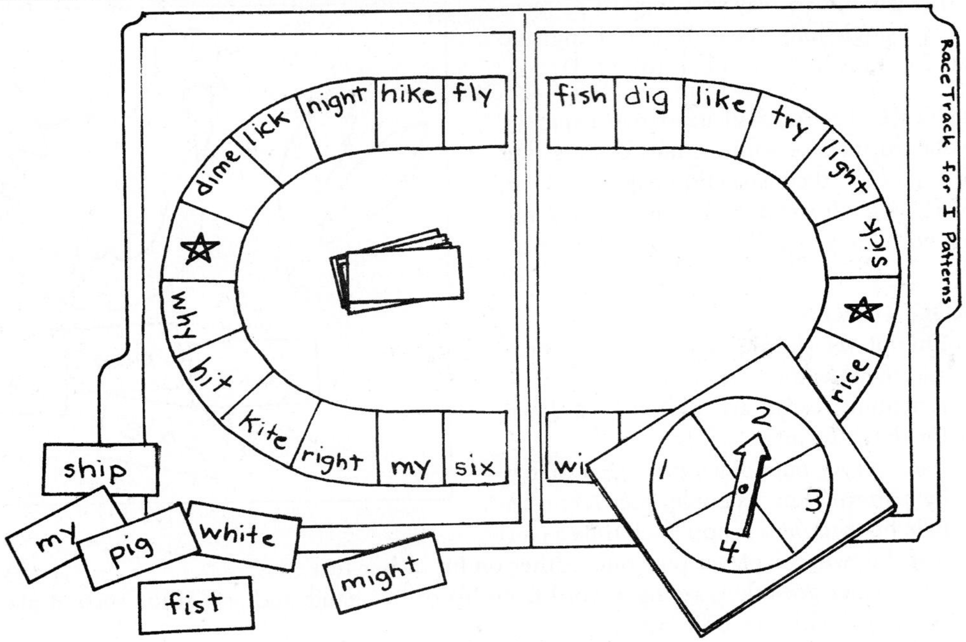

6.13 The Spelling Game

This game for two to four players can be used for any feature and is easily changed from week to week by simply replacing the word cards. (CCSS Language (1st) 2.c, 3.c, (2nd) 3.a, 3.b, (3rd) 2.f, 3)

MATERIALS Use a follow-the-path game board, but leave the spaces blank, except for several spaces where you may write directions such as Go Back 3 Spaces, Lose a Turn, and Go Ahead 2 Spaces. Add playing pieces and a spinner or die. Students use their own collections of words for the week.

PROCEDURES
1. Students each roll the die or spin the spinner. Whoever has the highest number will start and play proceeds clockwise.
2. The second player draws from the face-down stack of word cards. The player says the word to the first player, who must spell the word aloud. If players spell correctly, they can spin or roll to move around the path. Players who misspell the word cannot move.
3. The winner is the first one to get to the end of the path by landing on the space.

VARIATIONS Use this game with word families, short vowels, and multisyllabic words, as well as the many one-syllable words explored in the within word pattern stage. You can also ask students to spell words on a dry erase board before claiming their space.

6.14 "I'm Out"

This card game is a favorite for two to five players; three is optimal. (CCSS Language (1st) 2.c, 3.c, (2nd) 3.a, 3.b, (3rd) 2.f, 3)

MATERIALS Prepare a set of 20 to 30 cards from a study unit, such as words with *a, a-e, ay,* and *ai.* Write the words at the top of cards for easy visibility as students fan them out in their hands. Students can also simply use the words they cut out for sorting.

Adaptable for Other Stages

Adaptable for Other Stages

PROCEDURES

1. Select one student to be the dealer, who deals all the cards so that each player gets the same number. The person to the right of the dealer begins.
2. The first player places a card down, reads the word, and designates the vowel pattern to be followed—for example, *rain–ai*.
3. The next player must place a card down with the *ai* pattern and read it aloud. A player who does not have a word with the *ai* pattern or reads a word incorrectly must pass.
4. Play continues around the circle until all of the players are out of the designated pattern.
5. The player who played the last pattern card begins the new round. This player chooses a different card, places it in the middle, and declares what vowel pattern is to be followed.
6. The object of the game is to be the first player to play every card in his or her hand.

6.15 Vowel Spin

Players spin for a feature (vowel sounds or vowel pattern) and remove pictures or words from their game boards that match the feature. (CCSS Language (1st) 2.c, 3.c, (2nd) 3.a, 3.b, (3rd) 2.f, 3)

Adaptable
for Other Stages
● ● ○ ● ○

MATERIALS Make game boards divided like Tic-Tac-Toe, as shown in Figure 6.14. The game can be played without the board by simply laying out the word cards in a three-by-three array. Make 30 or more word cards or picture cards that correspond to the feature students have been studying. You will also need a spinner divided into three to six sections and labeled with the vowel sounds or patterns to be practiced. You can find directions for making a spinner in Appendix F.

PROCEDURES

1. Put the cards in a deck face-down. Players draw nine cards and turn them face-up on their boards or in a three-by-three array.
2. The first player spins and removes the picture or word cards that fit the sound or pattern indicated by the spinner. The cards go into the player's point pile. That same player draws

enough cards from the deck to replace the gaps on the playing board before play moves to the next player.

3. Play continues until a player is out of cards and there are no more to be drawn as replacements. The player who has the most cards in his or her point pile wins.

VARIATIONS Players prepare boards as described, but turn a winning card face-down as in a tic-tac-toe game instead of removing it. The winner is the first player to turn down three in a row. Blackout is a longer version, where players must turn over all their cards to win. A large die (one-inch square) can be made instead of a spinner. Use sticky dots to label the sides with the different features.

PD **pd** TOOLKIT™

for Words Their Way®

Concentration
There are several prepared concentration games for long and short A, I and O.

*Adaptable
for Other Stages*
● ● ● ● ●

6.16 Vowel Concentration

This game is played the traditional way, but students look for pairs of words with the same sound and pattern. (CCSS Language (1st) 2.c, 3.c, (2nd) 3.a, 3.b, (3rd) 2.f, 3)

MATERIALS Prepare a set of word cards for a particular vowel pattern. Students can use the set of words they cut out for the week but they should not be able to read the word through the back of the card. Remove oddballs since they are not likely to make a pair.

PROCEDURES
1. Players turn all the words face-down in a rectangular array.
2. The first player turns over two word cards. If they have the same vowel sound and pattern (such as *fort* and *north*), the player keeps both cards and adds them to the point pile. The player can take another turn before play passes to the next player.
3. The game ends when all matches have been made. The winner is the player with the most word cards in the point pile.

FIGURE 6.15   Board Game for *Sheep in a Jeep*

6.17 Sheep in a Jeep Game

Students should be familiar with *Sheep in a Jeep* (by N. Shaw, illustrated by M. Apple). In this game, players examine the *ee* and *ea* patterns. (CCSS Language (1st) 2.c, 3.c, (2nd) 3.a, 3.b, (3rd) 2.f, 3)

FIGURE 6.16 Word Jeopardy Game

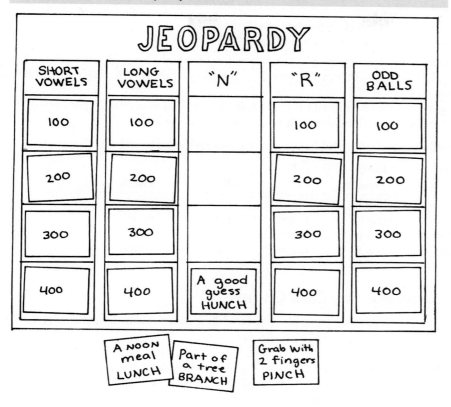

MATERIALS Prepare a game board using a follow-the-path template, as shown in Figure 6.15. Write long-*e* words from the book as well as other words with the same patterns in each space. You will need a spinner with numbers 1 through 4 (see directions for spinners in Appendix F), playing pieces to move around the board, and a pencil and small piece of paper for each player.

PROCEDURES One player spins and moves that number of spaces on the board. The player reads the word on the space and "adds a sheep to the jeep" by saying or writing a word that rhymes with that word. A player who reads the word incorrectly must move back a space. Players alternate turns. The first player to the finish wins.

6.18 Jeopardy Game

In this game, four or five students recall and spell words that follow a particular pattern; for example, the final *ch* pattern. (CCSS L (1st) 2.c, 3.c (2nd) 3.a, 3.b (3rd) 2.f, 3)

MATERIALS Divide a poster board into 5-by-5-inch sections, as shown in Figure 6.16, and place clue cards in each space. The side of each card facing down holds a clue about a word in that category (with the answer); the side facing up shows an amount (100 to 400).

PROCEDURES

1. One player is the moderator or game host. The others roll a die to determine who goes first.
2. The game begins when the first player picks a category and an amount for the moderator to read ("I'll take short vowels for 100"). The moderator reads the clue and the

Adaptable for Other Stages
● ● ● ● ●

player must respond by phrasing a question and spelling the word, as in the following example.

Moderator: When struck, it produces fire.

Player: What is a match? *M-a-t-c-h*.

3. If the answer is correct, the player receives the card and chooses another clue. (A player can only have two consecutive turns.) If the player misses, the player to the left may answer.

4. The game continues until all the clue cards are read and won or left unanswered. Players add their points, and the one with the highest amount wins.

The following words could be used for a game reviewing *ch* and *tch*.

Short Vowels	Long Vowels	N	R	Oddballs
stitch	beach	bench	march	much
watch	teach	lunch	perch	such
sketch	roach	branch	porch	rich
witch	coach	pinch	torch	which

6.19 Vowel Rummy Card Game

Up to four students practice grouping short and long vowel words by pattern. (CCSS Language (1st) 2.c, 3.c, (2nd) 3.a, 3.b, (3rd) 2.f, 3)

Adaptable for Other Stages
● ● ● ● ●

MATERIALS You need 35 to 45 cards. A good starting combination is five cards for each short vowel in the CVC pattern for a total of 25 cards, plus five cards for each long vowel in the CVCe pattern (except for long-*e* because there are so few words in that category) for a total of 20 more cards. You can also include wild cards.

PROCEDURES

1. Five cards are dealt to each player and the rest are turned face-down in a deck. Players look in their hands for pairs, three of a kind, four of a kind, or five of a kind.

2. Each player has one chance to discard unwanted cards and draw up to four new cards from the deck to keep a hand of five cards. For example, a player might be dealt *bone, rope, that, wet, rake*. This player may want to discard *that, wet*, and *rake*, and draw three other cards to possibly create a better hand.

3. The possible combinations are one pair (*that, camp*); two pairs (*that, camp, bone, rope*); three of a kind (*bone, rope, rode*); four of a kind (*bone, rope, rode, smoke*); three of a kind plus a pair (*bone, rope, rode, hat, rat*); or five of a kind.

4. Players lay down their hands to determine the winner of the round. The winner is determined in this order: Five of a kind (this beats everything), four of a kind, three of a kind plus a pair, two pairs, three of a kind, and finally one pair. In the case of a tie, players can draw from the deck until one player comes up with a card that breaks the tie.

5. Play continues by dealing another set of cards to the players. The player who wins the most rounds is the winner.

6.20 Declare Your Category!

This game for two to five players (three is optimal) works best with students who have some experience playing games. In this game, players guess the first player's category. (CCSS Language (1st) 2.c, 3.c, (2nd) 3.a, 3.b, (3rd) 2.f, 3)

MATERIALS Create a deck of 45 word cards with a variety of vowels and vowel patterns. Make at least four cards with any one pattern.

PROCEDURES

1. Seven cards are dealt to each player and the remainder are placed face-down in a deck. Players lay out their seven cards face-up.

2. The first player turns up a key card from the deck (e.g., *home*) and looks for a word in his or her hand to match in some way. It might have the same sound and/or spelling pattern (either *o-e* or VCe); for example, *soap, bone,* or *gave.* The match is laid down for all to see and the player announces, "Guess my category." Play moves to the next person, who must search his or her hand for a similar match. Players can pass when they wish. The player who started the category keeps the sorting strategy a secret. Play keeps going until the last player to put a card down declares the category.

3. If the person who set up the category does not think the next player has put down an acceptable card, he or she can send a card back and give that player another chance. Mistakes are discussed at the end of each round.

4. The player who plays the last card has to declare the category to win and keep all the cards. If the player is wrong, the previous player gets a chance to declare the category.

5. At the end of each round, students are dealt enough cards to get them back to seven. The winner of the round turns up a card from the pile and makes up the next category.

6. Play continues until the deck is empty. The player with the most cards wins.

VARIATIONS Add wild cards to the pile to change categories in midstream. The person who establishes a new category must guess the original category correctly. This player becomes the new judge: "Your category was by words with long-*o* and the silent-*e*. I am putting down my wild card and laying down *loan*. Guess my category." The rules of the game can be expanded to include semantic (e.g., types of birds) and grammatical (e.g., nouns) categories.

6.21 Word Categories

This is a fast moving game for three to five players that reviews vowels as players brainstorm words that match a given pattern. Players only earn points when their word is different from everyone else's. (CCSS Language (1st) 2.d, (2nd) 2.9, 2.e, (3rd) 2.f)

MATERIALS Players will need a timer, pencils, and enough game cards for every player. See a completed sample in Figure 6.17. Blank forms can be found at the PDToolkit.

PROCEDURES

1. The game is played in three rounds. Each player has a Categories game card.

2. Set the timer for one minute (adjust as needed). All players quickly fill in the first column of their answer sheet, adding beginning sounds to the given patterns to create a word. Answers must be real words.

3. Scoring: Players take turns reading their answers aloud for each number. Players circle answers that do *not* match any other player's answer and earn one point for each. Record the score at the bottom of the column of the answer sheet as shown in Figure 6.17.

4. Reset the timer to start the second, and then third, round. Students continue playing, filling in the next column with new answers.

5. Winning the game: After three rounds, players total the three scores on their answer sheets. The player with the highest score is the winner.

6. Challenging another player's answers: While answers are read, other players may challenge their acceptability. In this case, they can consult the dictionary to determine whether or not the word is real.

FIGURE 6.17 Word Categories E Patterns

Word Categories: E patterns					
Round 1		**Round 2**		**Round 3**	
1	n et	1	sl ed	1	b eg
2	t en	2	n eck	2	ch est
3	s ell	3	dr ess	3	b ent
4	m e	4	fr ee	4	f etch
5	s eed	5	t ea	5	sl eek
6	sw eet	6	een	6	st eer
7	p eek	7	wh eel	7	breeze
8	l eak	8	sp ear	8	cl ear
9	wh eat	9	r ead	9	bl each
10	st eam	10	s eal	10	th ief
Points	**3**		**2**		**4** ⑨

6.22 Word Study Uno

This game is a version of the popular card game for three to four players created by Rita Loyacono. (CCSS Language (1st) 2.c, 3.c, (2nd) 3.a, 3.b, (3rd) 2.f, 3)

Adaptable for Other Stages
● ● ● ● ● ●

MATERIALS Create a set of at least 27 word cards by writing words in the upper left corners of tagboard rectangles or blank cards. Include the patterns that you have been studying. For example, if students are studying long-*o* patterns, create word cards that have *o-e*, *oa*, and *ow* combinations. Also create four Wild cards and two of each of the following cards:

Skip *o-e*	Draw 2 *o-e*
Skip *ow*	Draw 2 *ow*
Skip *oa*	Draw 2 *oa*

PROCEDURES

1. Deal five cards to each player. The remaining cards are placed in a deck face-down and the top card is turned face-up to start the discard pile.
2. Players take turns playing cards that match the pattern of the face-up card or play one of the special cards (Skip, Draw 2, Wild). For example, if the beginning card is *boat*, the first player could put down *soap*, *road*, or *goat*, or play a special card. The Skip card indicates that the next player loses a turn. The Draw 2 card forces the next player to pick two cards from the pile without playing any cards.
3. Skip and Draw 2 cards indicate the next pattern that must be played. When a Wild card is played, the player can select the category. A player who cannot put down a card must draw from the pile, and if the draw matches the pattern of the face-up card, it can be played.
4. A player who has only one card remaining must yell, "Uno." If the player forgets, another player can tell the player with one card to draw another card.
5. The first player to run out of cards wins the game.

6.23 Homophone Win, Lose, or Draw

Four or more students work in teams to draw and guess each other's words in a game that resembles charades; a list of homophones can be found in Appendix E. (CCSS Language (2nd) 5, (3rd) 5, (4th) 1.g, 5, (5th) 5)

PROCEDURES

1. Write homophone pairs on cards and shuffle.
2. Students divide into two equal teams, and one player from each team is selected as the artist for that round. The artist must draw a picture representing a given homophone, which requires understanding a homophone's spelling and meaning.
3. A card is pulled from the deck and shown simultaneously to the artists for both teams. As the artists draw, their teammates call out possible answers. When the correct word is offered, the artist calls on that team to spell both words in the pair.
4. A point is awarded to the team that provides the correct information first. The artist then chooses the next artist and play proceeds in the same fashion.

6.24 Homophone Rummy

This activity is suitable for two to six students. The object of the game is to get the most homophone pairs. (CCSS Language (2nd) 5, (3rd) 5, (4th) 1.g, 5, (5th) 5)

MATERIALS Prepare several decks of homophone pairs (52 cards, 26 pairs); a list of homophones can be found in Appendix E. Select words your students are familiar with. Write the words in the upper left corner of the cards, as shown in Figure 6.18.

PROCEDURES

1. Players are dealt seven cards and begin the game by checking their hands for already existing pairs. Pairs can be laid down in front of the player, who must give the meaning for each word or use it in a sentence that makes the meaning clear.

2. The remainder of the deck is placed in a central location and the first card is turned face-up beside it to form a discard pile.

3. The person on the left of the dealer goes first. Each player draws from either the deck or the discard pile. Any new pairs are laid down and defined. The player must then discard one card to end the turn. *Note*: If a card is taken from the discard pile, all the cards below are also taken and the top card must be used to make a pair.

4. A player can be challenged by another player who disagrees with the definitions. The person who challenges looks up the words in the dictionary. Whoever is right gets to keep the pair.

5. The game is over when one player has no cards left. That person yells, "Rummy!" Then the pairs are counted up to determine the winner.

FIGURE 6.18   Homophone Rummy

6.25   Hink Pinks

Hink Pinks is a traditional language game that involves a riddle answered by a pair of rhyming words; for example, "What do you call a chubby kitty or an obese feline? (*fat cat*). What do you call an angry father? (*mad dad*). What do you call a plastic pond? (*fake lake*)." Hinky Pinky usually demands two-syllable rhymes: What is a bloody tale? (*gory story*), whereas Hinkety Pinkety requires three-syllable answers: What is the White House? (*presidents' residence*). You can find lots more examples by searching online. Visual hink pinks are featured in the book *One Sun: A Book of Terse Verse*, by Bruce McMillan. (CCSS Language (4th) 5, (5th) 5)

FIGURE 6.19   Hink Pinks

PROCEDURES

1. Share examples of hink pinks and discuss the structure of the language or read *One Sun* with your students and talk about the riddles and photographs.

2. Brainstorm objects and possible adjectives that rhyme; for example, *pink/sink, bear/lair, sled/bed*. When students understand the concept, have them work in small groups or individually to think of their own hink pinks.

3. Challenge students to draw a picture to illustrate their hink pink (see Figure 6.19) or to write a riddle. These can be exchanged with a classmate.

whale pail

sad Dad

chapter 7

Word Study for Intermediate Readers and Writers

THE SYLLABLES AND AFFIXES STAGE

Beginning in second or third grade for many students, and in fourth grade for most, cognitive and language growth supports movement into the syllables and affixes stage of word knowledge. Although students have been reading and writing words of more than one syllable for some time, it is during this stage that they systematically study the generalizations that govern how syllables are joined. And though they might have studied how **affixes** (both **prefixes** such as *re-* or *un-* and **suffixes** such as *-ing* or *-ly*) affect word meaning, it is during this stage that students also look at how suffixes might affect the spelling of the base word. Examining how affixes and base words combine supports students learning how to figure out the meaning of many longer, unfamiliar words they encounter in their reading.

Many teachers find that there is much about the English writing system or **orthography** at this stage that is new to them as well as to their students. Your own curiosity about words and a willingness to dig deeper into the way words work will enable you to learn right along with your students. This chapter and supporting material will help you facilitate students' word explorations to help them discover the patterns of sound, spelling, and meaning that link thousands of words. This knowledge will help them read, write, and spell more effectively.

Before we talk in detail about the features of study in this stage, let's visit Sharon Radcliffe's fourth-grade classroom in mid-year. Ms. Radcliffe has a range of abilities in her classroom that are evident in both reading levels and spelling inventory results. She has a large group of 14 students who fall into the syllables and affixes stage, four students in the late within word pattern stage, and five students who are in derivational relations. She makes time to meet with each group several times a week for systematic word study while the other groups work independently. In the following vignette, Ms. Radcliffe meets with her syllable and affixes group at the front of the room for a 20-minute lesson while the rest of the students find comfortable places to read and discuss in the Book Club format (Raphael, Pardo, Highfield, & McMahon 2013). The syllables and affixes students are studying the final syllable (*ar/er/or*) that poses a challenge for spellers because it is pronounced the same, /ər/, across the different spellings.

Ms. Radcliffe begins her word study lesson using a directed spelling thinking activity (Zutell, 1996). She asks her students to spell three words, *dollar*, *faster*, and *actor*, as a way to stimulate discussion and set a purpose for the sort. Ms. Radcliffe asks students to tell how they spelled each word, encouraging a variety of answers, which include *doller*, *dollor*, *dollar*, *faster*, *acter*, and *actor*. Ms. Radcliffe then thinks out loud, "Hmmm . . . This is very interesting. We agree on how to spell the first syllable of each word, but we don't always agree about how to spell the final syllable. What makes this part hard?" Jason volunteers that the words sound the same at the end. "Do the rest of you agree?" Ms. Radcliffe asks and then adds, "Let's find out if this is true for other words as well."

Ms. Radcliffe has made a copy of the weekly word sheet and cut it apart to sort on the document camera. She selects several words for discussion whose meaning might not be clear (e.g., *blister* and *mayor*) and reviews the meanings of *lunar* and *solar* from their recent science unit. Next she asks, "How might we sort these words?" She takes several suggestions that include sorting by vowel patterns and when Sara suggests that they sort by the last two letters she responds, "Let's try that since we agreed that was the hard part of the word."

Ms. Radcliffe removes all the words except *dollar*, *faster*, and *actor*, which she underlines to use as key words for the sort. She then displays each word in turn, calling on a student to read it and tell her where to place it (the final sort is shown in Figure 7.1). To check the sort they read down each column to be sure they all have the same sound at the end. Ms. Radcliffe then asks the students, "What do you notice about these words now that we have sorted them?" Several students offer ideas and together they summarize by saying, "When we hear /ər/, the sound will not help us spell it, so we will have to concentrate on remembering whether it is spelled *er*, *or*, or *ar*."

Ms. Radcliffe hands out copies of the word sort and goes over the students' word study assignments for the week. She reminds them, "Cut apart and sort the words and then write the word sort in your word study notebooks."

While they work at their seats, Ms. Radcliffe meets with a different, developmental group to get their weekly sort started. On other days, students work independently by doing a blind sort with a partner, sorting at home, and hunting for additional words in trade books. On Friday, Ms. Radcliffe gives them a spelling test of 10 words, but she also calls the group together to compile a list of the words they were able to find in their word hunts. This extensive list will be used to introduce the following week's lesson, in which students will discover that *er* is the most common way to spell the final sound, that it is always used to spell comparative adjectives (*faster*, *smaller*, *longer*), and that *er* and *or* are often used to spell agents or people who do things (*teacher*, *worker*, *author*, *sailor*).

Ms. Radcliffe's lesson promotes two key ideas of this stage. First, it demonstrates to students how much they already know about spelling a particular word—spelling is not an all-or-nothing affair. Usually they will get most of the word correct, and teachers need to remind and reassure students about this. Second, it demonstrates to students what they need to focus on when they look at a word. Because they already know most of the word, they need to attend to the part that is still challenging. ●

FIGURE 7.1 Final *ar/er/or* Word Sort

dollar	faster	actor
sugar	blister	doctor
grammar	jogger	tractor
solar	speaker	motor
lunar	skater	favor
collar	cleaner	editor
	poster	mayor
	freezer	author
	dreamer	
	bigger	

Literacy Development of Students in the Syllables and Affixes Stage

Students in the syllables and affixes stage of word knowledge are what Henderson (1990) called *intermediate readers*—students who are not yet mature or advanced readers. Reading skill during this stage of development can, on average, span six reading levels, from the third-grade level to the eighth-grade level.

Reading in the Syllables and Affixes Stage

The intermediate and middle school years are a time of expanding reading interests and fine-tuning of reading strategies. Students will be expected to read textbooks and other informational texts as classroom instruction shifts to a greater emphasis on content or disciplinary studies, a key focus in core standards. In previous developmental stages, the challenges posed by reading stem mostly from students' ability to identify words as they read about familiar topics. At the intermediate level, background knowledge and vocabulary become critical elements in comprehension as students explore new genres and topics.

During the syllables and affixes stage, students learn to look at words in a new way, not as single-syllable units with CVC, CVVC, or other vowel patterns, but as two or more units of sound and often of meaning as well. Breaking words into two or more syllabic units is a more sophisticated decoding strategy than the phonics instruction typically offered in the primary grades using consonants, blends, digraphs, and vowel patterns—elements that students master in the within word pattern stage. In the syllables and affixes stage, students operate within Ehri's **consolidated alphabetic phase** (2005, 2014) where they use larger chunks to decode, spell, and store words in memory. For example, a word like *unhappy* can be analyzed as three syllabic chunks (*un-hap-py*) or two **morphemic** chunks (*un-happy*). Word study in the syllables and affixes stage helps students learn where these syllable and morphemic breaks occur in words so that they can use the appropriate chunks to read, spell, and determine the meanings of polysyllabic words.

Students in the intermediate stage read with greater fluency than at the transitional stage. They have many words stored in memory for automatic retrieval and they are learning how to use syllabic and morphemic chunks to quickly and accurately figure out unfamiliar words. This ease of word identification and attention to punctuation help them read with phrasing and expression. By the end of this stage students may read up to 140 words per minute in narrative texts (Hasbrouck & Tindal, 2006) and even faster while reading silently (Morris, 2013).

Writing in the Syllables and Affixes Stage

Intermediate writers become increasingly confident and fluent in their writing and are able to work on longer pieces over many days. The ability to automatically spell most of the words they need for writing allows them to focus more attention on the meaning they are trying to convey. You are likely to hear "voice" in their writing and they are more aware of their audience. Intermediate writers can be expected to revise their written work and to edit it for spelling and punctuation accuracy.

Lexi's essay on the changes she would make to the Lincoln Middle School cafeteria exudes middle school bravado (see Figure 7.2). She touched on all things cool: sound systems, student choice, hamburgers and fries, and celebrities—all of which were sure to bring her the recognition she craved as "manager of the year." At the time, Lexi was a sixth-grader in the later part of the syllables and affixes stage. She spelled *manager* correctly and incorrectly (MANAGAR) in the same essay and also confused the **unaccented final syllables** in other words, such as *radical* (RADACLE) and *music* (MUSICK). Vowel patterns in **accented syllables** were still not firm (AWSOME for *awesome*), and she was uncertain about the double consonants within base words containing an affix (INSTALATION for *installation*). Once these syllable and affix issues were firmed up, Lexi was poised to study the **spelling–meaning connections** of the next stage of development—derivational relations—and to discover the reason DECESION is spelled with an *i* instead of an *e* (because it comes from the word *decide*).

FIGURE 7.2   Lexi's Middle School Essay

If I could be the manager of the cafeteria at Lincoln Middle School I would make some awsome changes. The instalation of a sound system would be my first decesion. The kids could rotate bringing there own choice of musick. Then I would make radacle changes in the menu like we'd have hamburgers and fries and no rootine school menues. Then I'd send an invatation to Miley Cyrus to join us for lunch. If she accepts I'd get the Best Manager of the Year Award!

Vocabulary Learning in the Syllables and Affixes Stage

In this stage of literacy development, students' reading becomes the primary source of new vocabulary as they encounter more and more words in text whose meanings they do not know. This is especially true in disciplinary studies beyond third grade, such as science and social studies as students read information books and textbooks. However, learning words from context cannot be left to chance; you need to take an active role in making sure that students' vocabularies are growing steadily. Understanding academic vocabulary is essential to success in school (Townsend Filippini, Collins, & Biancarosa, 2012) and some ways to teach this are presented in this chapter. *Vocabulary Their Way* (Templeton et al., 2015) provides more detail on teaching **academic vocabulary**, with entire chapters dedicated to content-specific domains including English language arts and mathematics.

Students must be taught vocabulary directly at all levels, but particularly **general academic** and **domain-specific vocabulary** needed in the upper grades (Farstrup & Samuels, 2008; Hiebert, 2005; Nagy & Townsend, 2012; Pearson, Hiebert, & Kamil, 2007; Zweirs, 2008). Core standards often refer to three tiers of vocabulary. After basic tier 1 words, tier 2 corresponds

roughly to general academic vocabulary and tier 3 is akin to domain-specific academic vocabulary (see Beck, McKeown, & Kucan, 2013). These words are often multisyllabic and at first, may be a challenge to pronounce, especially for students in the previous stage and in the beginning of this intermediate stage of reading. For example, students in this stage may struggle to read *analysis*, *analyze*, or *analyst*. The change in accent or stress of polysyllabic words is something they are learning and which will come later in spelling.

Your own enthusiasm and curiosity about words is likely to enhance students' **word consciousness**—they develop a favorable attitude toward words and are curious about words and word learning (Blachowicz & Fisher, 2009; Lubliner & Scott, 2008; Scott, Skobel, & Wells, 2008; Stahl & Nagy, 2006; Templeton et al., 2015). Look for books about language to read to your students such as *Miss Alaineous: A Vocabulary Disaster* by Debra Frasier, *The Boy Who Loved Words* by Roni Schotter, *Frindle* by Andrew Clements, and *The Phantom Tollbooth* by Norton Juster.

Many textbook authors try to provide a rich context to support new vocabulary and often highlight important new terms for the reader. Students also need to learn the strategy of breaking words into morphemic parts (prefixes, suffixes, and base words) so that they can grow confidently and competently into independent word learners. Adams (1990) best emphasized this importance:

> Learning from context is a very important component of vocabulary acquisition. But this means of learning is available only to the extent that children bother to process the spelling—the orthographic structure—of the unknown words they encounter. Where they skip over an unknown word without attending to it, and often readers do, no learning can occur. (p. 150)

MORPHEMIC ANALYSIS. One of your most important responsibilities for word study instruction at this stage is to engage students in examining how important word elements—prefixes, suffixes, and base words—combine. This **morphemic analysis** is a powerful tool for vocabulary development and figuring out unfamiliar words during reading. Students' knowledge of morphology is related to reading comprehension and disciplinary knowledge and achievement (Carlisle, 2010; Nagy, 2007; Nagy, Berninger, & Abbott, 2006; Townsend et al., 2013).

You can show students directly how to apply this knowledge by modeling the following strategy for analyzing unfamiliar words that they cannot identify in their reading.

1. Examine the word for meaningful parts—base word, prefixes, or suffixes.
   - If there is a prefix or a suffix, take it off so you can find the base.
   - Look at the base to see if you know it or if you can think of a related word (a word that has the same base).
   - Reassemble the word, thinking about the meaning contributed by the base, the suffix, and then the prefix. This should give you a more specific idea of what the word is.
2. Try out the meaning in the sentence; check if it makes sense in the context of the sentence and the larger context of the text that you are reading.
3. If the word still does not make sense and is critical to the meaning of the overall passage, look it up in the dictionary.
4. Record the new word on a chart or in a word study notebook to be reviewed over time.

Let's take a look at how Ms. Radcliffe models this process for students, beginning with a familiar word and then extending the lesson to an unfamiliar word.

"I've underlined one of the words in this sentence: *They had to* redo *the programs after they were printed with a spelling error.* What does *redo* mean? Yes, Chloe?"

"When you have to do something over again?"

"Okay! So you already had done something once, right?"

"Now, let's cover up this first part that we call a prefix [covers *re*]. What we have left is the base word *do*. Now, let's look at some other words."

Ms. Radcliffe writes the words *join*, *tell*, and *write* on the board; then she writes the prefix *re-* in front of each base word as she pronounces the new word. "When we join the prefix *re-* to each base word, what happens? Can you tell me what these words now mean? We are going to be doing these things again—we can *rejoin* a group, *retell* a story, *rewrite* a paper." She then asks the students what they think the prefix *re-* means. After a brief discussion, she asks a student to look up the prefix in the dictionary to check their definitions.

Ms. Radcliffe's next step is to model this strategy with a word she is fairly certain the students do not yet know. She shows the following sentence on the overhead:

> As they got closer to the front of the line, her friends had to <u>reassure</u> Hannah that the Big Thunder roller coaster ride was safe.

"Okay," Ms. Radcliffe proceeds, "I've underlined this word [pointing to *reassure*]. Any ideas what this word is?" Most students shake their heads; Kaitlyn frowns as she slowly pronounces "REE–sure." "Good try, Kaitlyn," Ms. Radcliffe responds. "You're trying to pronounce it, but it doesn't sound like a word we've heard before. What about the beginning of the word, though? Could that be the prefix we've just been thinking about? Now look for the base word."

This prompt works for the students and they start trying to pronounce the base, *assure*, without the prefix *re-*. "Right," Ms. Radcliffe encourages. "You've taken off the prefix, *re-*, and are trying to figure out the base word. Any ideas?" Though a couple of students are pronouncing *assure* correctly, they are uncertain about its meaning.

Ms. Radcliffe continues: "Well, we know that, whatever *assure* means, the prefix *re-* means it's being done again! Let's look back at the sentence. Do you think Hannah can't wait to go on the roller coaster—or is she getting worried?" After some discussion with the students, Ms. Radcliffe talks about the base word, *assure*, and explains that Hannah's friends had probably already talked with her about how there had never been any accidents, and had helped Hannah to feel more confident—*assured* her—that Big Thunder was safe. (Most students are nodding their heads now, saying things such as "Oh, yeah, I've heard that word before.") As Hannah and her friends got closer to actually going on the roller coaster, however, they had to assure her again—*reassure* her. Ms. Radcliffe asks students to check the dictionary definition to confirm the meaning of the word (to remove doubts or fears).

Ms. Radcliffe summarizes: "Many times, by looking carefully at a word you don't know—looking for any prefixes, suffixes, and thinking about the base—you can get pretty close to the actual meaning of the word. Then ask yourself if this meaning makes sense in the sentence and text that you're reading." ●

It is critical to model and reinforce this strategic approach to analyzing unfamiliar words in text. Students need plenty of opportunities to try it out under your guidance (Baumann et al., 2003). Encourage students to talk about their ideas as they apply the process so that you can encourage, facilitate, and redirect as necessary. Morphemic analysis will become one of the most effective means of developing and extending students' vocabulary knowledge. It is also important to model what to do when the process does not yield an appropriate meaning for the unfamiliar word (e.g., analyzing *repel* into *re* + *pel* is not much help)—students should consult a dictionary.

DICTIONARIES. It is important to have unabridged dictionaries and online dictionaries, as well as dictionaries that are published specifically for intermediate students, available in the classroom. The *American Heritage Children's Dictionary* (grades 4 to 6) and the *American Heritage Student's Dictionary* (grades 5 to 9) are two dictionaries that are helpful at this stage. Attractive in format, they present definitions, word histories, and usage information in student-friendly language.

Dictionaries are crucial for distinguishing alternative meaning of words and then determining the appropriate one. For example, based on Robyn Montana Turner's biography of Faith Ringgold, Ms. Radcliffe focuses on the word *enhancing* in the sentence "Faith Ringgold decided to use cloth frames as a way of enhancing her art." Pronouncing the word does not seem to help because it is not in the students' speaking/listening vocabularies, and breaking the word into parts does not help. Ms. Radcliffe talks about the context in which the word occurs; it may narrow the possibilities somewhat, but possible meanings suggested by the context include "protecting" or "showing." This is definitely a situation in which the dictionary is useful and you can model strategies for looking up words.

Ms. Radcliffe underlines the word *enhancing* and explains that, to check the meaning of this word in the dictionary, they need to look up the base word, *enhance*. Reminding the students that they may need to watch out for changes in spelling when they are trying to figure out the base word for an unfamiliar word, she notes that the *e* is dropped when the *-ing* is added. Looking up a base word also helps to highlight the spelling of other forms of the word.

The students find that the dictionary definition for *enhance* is "to make greater, as in value, beauty, or reputation." Ms. Radcliffe has the students return to the sentence in the text and discuss which of these features they believe Faith Ringgold had in mind when she decided to use cloth frames. The students agree that, in the context of the sentence and the overall text, Faith Ringgold probably wanted to make her quilts more "beautiful."

Dictionaries can also provide helpful information about the history of a word and make explicit the interrelationships among words in the same meaning "families." Discussing dictionary entries illustrates how one word's entry can include information about words related in spelling and meaning; for example, the entry for *enhance* includes *enhancement*. Sections labeled "Usage Notes," "Synonyms," and "Word History" provide important information about the appropriateness of particular words and subtle but important differences among their meanings. Some entries contain stories that explain spellings and deepen understanding of important terms. See Activity 7.5 for ideas about teaching students how to use the dictionary.

WORD SORTS AND VOCABULARY. The word sorts you use to teach spelling generalizations likely contain words whose meanings should also be explored, perhaps briefly, as Ms. Radcliffe did with *blister* and *mayor*. As part of your introductory routine, ask a student to look up a word and be ready to report to the group its meaning or multiple meanings. This is a good way to encourage regular dictionary use for an authentic reason. Avoid assigning students to look up long lists of words; instead, have students select several words each week to look up in the dictionary and then record definitions or other information (parts of speech, origins, etc.). Word study notebook routines can include illustrating five or more words or using them in sentences to demonstrate their meanings. You can assign words to students and then teach them how to share what they learned in either small groups or as a class activity.

DOMAIN-SPECIFIC VOCABULARY INSTRUCTION. Domain-specific academic vocabulary is used in disciplinary studies and includes specialized vocabulary that has a specific meaning, like the term *square root* in mathematics, *perpendicular* in geometry, and *democratic process* in social studies. Words from specific domains or content areas become increasingly important as students move through the grades. You will find these words in your district and state standards, and the curricula for the different subject areas. If there is a required textbook for a particular content area, it will usually reflect the important concepts and the domain-specific vocabulary that represent those concepts (usually bolded in text). In the next section we discuss criteria that *you* will want to apply when selecting vocabulary. Once you select words, use the following steps with engaging activities.

1. Activate background knowledge. Find out what students already know about the word, and remind them of related terms they may already know. For example, if you chose *solar*, you can explore their understanding of the terms *solar heat*, *solar system*, *solar eclipse*, and so on.
2. Explain the meaning of the word, how it is used, and its relationship to other words that share similar meanings: *solarium*, *solar energy*, and so on.

3. Use graphic organizers, charts, or diagrams as needed to portray relationships among the words.

4. Discuss examples and non-examples. In the case of *solar*, important non-examples would relate to other words that share a similar spelling but have a different meaning: *sole*, *solitude*, *solitary*, *solidify*, and so on.

A number of graphic organizer formats developed over the years have proven effective in helping engage students with new and/or difficult concepts that lead to understanding and deeper knowledge (Blachowicz & Fisher, 2009; Diamond & Gutlohn, 2006; Robb, 1999; Stahl & Nagy, 2006; Templeton et al., 2015). One key to the effectiveness of graphic organizers is their visual presentation of the relationships among target vocabulary and related concepts. Two examples provided in the activity section of this chapter are *semantic maps* and *concept* (or *word*) *maps*. Discussion is critical when using graphic organizers in the classroom. As Stahl and Nagy (2006) observe, "The graphs and procedures are no more than structures to explain to students what particular words mean. It is the explanation, the talk, that is important" (p. 96).

It is important to remember that most reading vocabulary encountered in content areas is developmentally ahead of spelling vocabulary. You can add two-syllable words from a science unit on volcanoes (e.g., *mantle*, *pressure*, *pumice*, and *lava*) to sorts featuring syllable patterns and accent, but other words (e.g., *teutonic*) are not appropriate spelling words for students in the syllables and affixes stage. Words with complex Greek and Latin word parts are studied in the next stage, derivational relations.

GENERAL ACADEMIC VOCABULARY INSTRUCTION. **General academic vocabulary** is ubiquitous in the language used across all disciplines (Coxhead, 2000; Gardner & Davies, 2013), and students' knowledge of general academic vocabulary is related to school success (Townsend et al., 2012). Can you imagine any textbook without these general academic words: *however*, *analysis*, *comparison*, *establish*, *major*, *response*, or *structure*? General academic vocabulary is often the mortar that holds domain-specific vocabulary and concepts together, but the words are often difficult to define in isolation. Instead of trying to define words like *nevertheless*, *however*, *similar*, or *likewise*, use such terms repeatedly in meaningful contexts ("Let's look at how these ideas are similar, or alike"). Help students understand what functions the words serve—what the words ask readers to do (Flanigan, Templeton, & Hayes, 2012). For example, students may know that *establish* is a synonym for *set up* or *show*, but presenting this word in phrases helps students understand the nuances of meaning: to *establish an argument* is a more formal presentation of ideas than *to set up* or *show* an argument. There are other phrases that add depth to students' understanding of *establish*; for example, *establish the truth*, *establishment of the state of Israel*, and *established custom*.

Text structures that compare and contrast, sequence, examine cause and effect, pose a problem, and/or present a resolution have their own general academic vocabulary associated with them. Take an excerpt from a text and model for students how to locate general academic vocabulary. You may want to begin with the lists prepared by Coxhead (2000; available online at www.victoria.ac.nz/lals/resources/academicwordlist/), or Gardner & Davies (2013), to show them general academic vocabulary and how these words and phrases function to hold text together. After this modeling, ask students to work with partners to locate general academic vocabulary, create class charts of these words and phrases, and record these collections in their vocabulary notebooks. They can share their lists with the class and discuss how the general academic vocabulary indicates a particular text structure; for example, phrases like *in contrast*, *on the other hand*, *likewise*, and *along the same lines* indicate a compare and contrast–type text structure.

Another way to familiarize students with the meaning of general academic vocabulary is to increase their exposure to related words or words that come from the same word family. By using dictionaries and other resources, students can find numerous related words that will clarify meanings. For example, when you look up *analyze* in a dictionary or an online source (e.g., OneLook), you find many members of the *analysis* word family including *analyzed*, *analyzing*, *analysis*, *analyst*, *analytic*, *analytical*, *analytically*, *analyses*, *psychoanalyst*, *microanalysis*, and

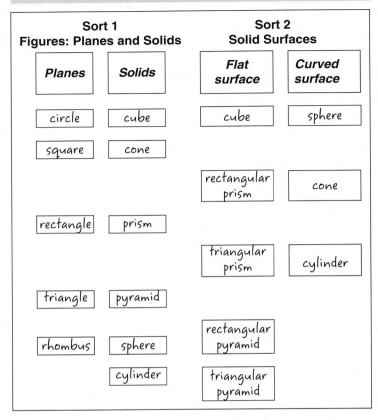

self-analysis. Students can work in pairs to discuss the meaning of a few of these words and develop sentences to share with their classmates. In the next stage of development, students examine the Greek origin of words that begin with *ana-* to find that it is derived from "a loosening," or "breaking up," and possibly find other words. For now, learning this word family in its various contexts, and being comfortable with reading, writing, and talking about what the word *analyze* means is ideal. Furthermore, during this syllables and affixes stage, students may examine this word family for the meaning of different suffixes; for example, *-ed, -ly, -ic, -al*. These exercises increase students' exposure to general academic vocabulary in different contexts.

CONCEPT SORTS AND DISCIPLINARY LEARNING. The growing focus on disciplinary area instruction in the intermediate grades (CCSS, 2010) provides opportunities to use the concept sorts described in earlier chapters. In order for new vocabulary to "stick," students need multiple exposures to those words in multiple contexts (Beck, McKeown, & Kucan, 2002). Concept sorts provide that exposure and help students form relationships between words and their ideas.

Figure 7.3 presents a concept sort developed by a fourth-grade math teacher to introduce the exploration of planes and solids. The teacher gave students a collection of word cards and asked them to work with a partner to discuss what they understood about the terms and to sort them into one of the two categories: planes and solids. Then the students came together as a whole class to share. In this fashion, understandings and misunderstandings were brought to the fore and the teacher got a good sense of the level and depth of students' background knowledge of these terms. You can also ask students to match words to pictures or objects. At the end of a unit, use concept sorts to review or assess the vocabulary.

Some students may argue that some of the solids could go in both categories; for example, a cone and a cylinder both have a flat surface as well as a curved surface. They may wish to create a separate category for them. Later in the unit, the math teacher introduced a second sort of solid figures to fine-tune students' understanding.

WHICH WORDS TO TEACH?. A common lament is that there are "so many words, so little time." Although most of your students' vocabularies grow through wide reading and discussion about that reading, you are still responsible for selecting words for students to tackle. Publishers of the textbooks, eBooks, and other curricular resources that you may be required to use have already selected and highlighted vocabulary and, while that is helpful, you still have a bit of work to do. The following questions will guide your decisions about which "target" or "key" vocabulary words to select, and how to will address them (Templeton et al., 2015).

• *Which words are critical to address <u>in depth</u> before moving into the unit/selection?* What are the words that represent major concepts and for which students need to develop a deep understanding? Introduce and develop these at the beginning of the unit and before the reading, as well as during and after.

- *Which words are critical to address <u>only briefly</u> before moving into the unit/selection?* Students must know these words for the specific reading assignment, but do not require a deep understanding. Mention these words and provide brief definitions.
- *Which words are critical but might lend themselves to students' problem solving during their reading?* These words are important but students may figure them out through morphemic analysis and/or help from the context. Follow up on these words after the reading.

Orthographic Development in the Syllables and Affixes Stage

In previous chapters, systematic word study was limited to vowel and consonant patterns within single-syllable words to build a foundation for the polysyllabic words of intermediate word study, in much the same way that basic math facts build a foundation for long division. Once students have this foundation, they are ready to begin studying polysyllabic words. Lexi's writing sample (Figure 7.2) shows that students in this stage spell most words correctly, making their writing quite readable, but they continue to make more advanced spelling errors.

Table 7.1 provides a summary of what students know, what they use but confuse, and what is still missing in the early, middle, and late syllables and affixes stage. In the early part of this stage, students may still be confused with less common or ambiguous vowel patterns, as in the spelling of CRALL for *crawl*. However, for the most part students know how to spell single-syllable words correctly and are ready to study the conventions involved in adding endings such as *-ing*. Spellings such as SHOPING and AMAZZING show us that students know how to spell the *-ing* suffix but lack knowledge about the doubling rule where syllables join. Examining inflected words with *-ing* endings is a good introduction to studying two-syllable words and the conventions that govern spelling where syllables meet—the **syllable juncture**.

PD TOOLKIT™
for Words Their Way®

Assessment of Students in the Syllables and Affixes Stage
You can learn more about spelling and word study during this stage in this video on assessment.

TABLE 7.1 **Characteristics of Syllables and Affixes Spelling**

	What Students Do Correctly	What Students Use but Confuse	What Is Absent
Early Syllables and Affixes CRALL for *crawl* SHOPING *for shopping* AMAZZING for *amazing* BOTEL for *bottle* KEPER or KEPPER *for keeper*	Blends, digraphs, short vowels Vowel patterns in one-syllable words Complex consonant units in one-syllable words Spell high frequency words correctly	Ambiguous vowels Consonant doubling and *e*-drop Syllable juncture: open- and closed-syllable patterns	Few things are completely missing Occasional deletion of reduced syllables
Middle Syllables and Affixes SELLER for *cellar* DAMIGE for *damage* PERAIDING for *parading*	All of the above plus: Doubling and *e*-drop with inflectional endings Syllable juncture: open- and closed-syllable patterns	Vowel patterns in accented syllables Unaccented final syllables	Few things are completely missing Doubled consonant for absorbed prefixes
Late Syllables and Affixes *parading* *cattle, cellar* CONFEDENT for *confident*	All of the above plus: Vowel patterns in accented syllables Unaccented final syllables	Some suffixes and prefixes Reduced vowels in unaccented syllables	Few things are completely missing Doubled consonant for absorbed prefixes

Syllable juncture problems can also be seen in the "used but confused" doubled letters in KEPPER for *keeper* and the lack thereof in BOTEL for *bottle*.

The syllables and affixes stage represents a new point in word analysis because there is more than one syllable to consider and each syllable may present a spelling problem. For example, students might spell the long vowel in the accented second syllable of *parading* with the *ai* pattern, as in PARAIDING. More likely, however, they will have problems with unaccented final syllables, such as BOTTEL for *bottle* and DAMIGE for *damage*. As the name of the stage suggests, in addition to syllables, students grapple with meaning units such as prefixes and suffixes (known collectively as *affixes*) and begin to study base words as morphemes or meaning units that must retain their spellings when affixes are added. In KEPER for *keeper*, the student may be relying on sound rather than knowledge of the word *keep*. In the sections that follow we describe the major features for instruction in the syllables and affixes stage.

Base Words and Inflectional Endings/Suffixes

One category of suffixes is **inflectional endings**, such as *-s*, *-ed*, and *-ing*, that change the number and tense of the base word but do not change its meaning or part of speech. These endings also include the comparative forms *-er* and *-est*. Although inflectional endings have been examined in oral language since the preschool years, studying them in spelling introduces students to base words and suffixes as well as the rules that govern spelling changes. Probably the most common suffix students learned earlier is the plural, adding *-s* even when the sound it represents varies, as in *cats* (/s/) and *dogs* (/z/). However, plurals deserve to be addressed systematically in this stage to cover additional issues.

- Add *-es* when words end in *ch*, *sh*, *ss*, *s*, and *x*. When *-es* is added to a word, students can usually "hear" the difference because it adds another syllable to the word (*dish* becomes *dish-es*, unlike *spoons*).
- Change the *y* at the end of a word to *i* before adding *-es* when the word ends in a consonant + *y* (*baby* to *babies*) but not when it ends in a vowel + *y* (*monkeys*).
- Words may change spelling and pronunciation in the plural form. Some words with final *f* or *fe* change the *f* to *v* and add *es* (*wife* to *wives*, *wolf* to *wolves*). Other words take a new form (*goose* to *geese* and *mouse* to *mice*). And some words remain the same (*fish*, *sheep*, *deer*).

FIGURE 7.4	Adding Inflectional Endings to Base Words

Sort 1		Sort 2		
resting	jogging	CVVC	CVCC	CVC
reading	running	reading	resting	jogging
feeding	shopping	feeding	walking	running
walking	winning	sleeping	jumping	shopping
sleeping	planning	waiting	smelling	winning
jumping	skipping	raining	dressing	planning
waiting	sobbing			skipping
smelling	hugging			sobbing
dressing	snapping			snapping

One of the major challenges students face when adding *-ed* or *-ing* is whether to double the final letter of the base word. The basic doubling rule is that when a suffix beginning with a vowel is added to a base word containing a single vowel followed by a single consonant (e.g., *shop*), double the final consonant (e.g., *shopping*, *shopped*). This can be simplified as the one-one-one rule: one syllable, one vowel, one consonant—double. There are some exceptions such as words that end with *x* and *w*, which never double (*taxing*, *showed*), but the doubling rule is worth learning and has implications for syllable junctures, as described shortly. It takes time, however, for students to develop a firm understanding of it.

Rather than teaching rules, we suggest a series of word sorts that will allow students to discover the many principles at work.

TABLE 7.2	Changes to Base Words When Adding Inflectional Endings or Other Suffixes That Start with a Vowel		

Base Words	+ *ING*	+ *ED*	+ *S*
1. CVVC, CVCC Ex: *look, walk*	No change Ex: *looking, walking*	No change Ex: *looked, walked*	No change Ex: *looks, walks*
2. CVC* Ex: *bat*	Double final letter Ex: *batting*	Double final letter Ex: *batted, batter*	No change Ex: *bats*
3. CVCe** Ex: *skate*	Drop final *e* Ex: *skating*	Drop final *-e* Ex: *skated, skater*	No change Ex: *skates*
4. Words that end in a consonant + *y* Ex: *cry*	No change Ex: *crying*	Change *y* to *i* Ex: *cried, crier*	Change *y* to *i* and add *es* Ex: *cries*
5. Words that end in a vowel + *y* Ex: *play*	No change Ex: *playing*	No change Ex: *played, player*	No change Ex: *plays*
6. Two-syllable words accented on second syllable Ex: *admit, invite, apply, destroy*	Follow rules for 1–5 Ex: *admitting, inviting, applying, destroying*	Follow rules for 1–5 Ex: *admitted, invited, applied, destroyed, destroyer*	Follow rules for 1–5 Ex: *admits, invites, applies, destroys*
7. Words that end in a *c* Ex: *mimic*	Add a *k* Ex: *mimicking*	Add a *k* Ex: *mimicked*	No change Ex: *mimics*

*Words ending in *x* and *w* do not double (e.g., *boxed, chewed*). Words that end in *ck* avoid having to double a final *k* (*blocked, blocking*).

**Words that end in *ve* avoid having to double a final *v* (*loved, loving*).

In Sort 1 of Figure 7.4, the students first sorted by words that double and those that do not, and then were asked to underline the base word. In Sort 2, sorting by the vowel pattern in the base word helped students discover that there are two conditions when the ending is simply added (CVVC words like *read* and CVCC words like *rest*) whereas only CVC words need to double. This will help clear up the confusion of *smelling* and *dressing*, words that students may initially place in the doubled column.

Table 7.2 summarizes the conditions that govern adding inflectional endings. The rules can get quite complicated, but when planning instruction, begin with the most common in the early syllables and affixes stage (numbers 1–5) and expect to reinforce these throughout the intermediate grades and even beyond in the case of two- and three-syllable words (where rules apply only if the final syllable is accented). Remember that it will take time for students to master these generalizations, and they should know the spellings of the base words before you ask them to think about how to add suffixes that require changing the base word.

Compound Words

When students explore **compound words**, they learn different things. First, they learn how a word like *sun* can combine in different ways to form new words, as shown in the concept map in Figure 7.5. This is an introduction to the combinatorial features of English words in building vocabulary. Second, studying compound words lays the foundation for explicit attention to syllables: compound words often comprise two smaller words, each of which is a single syllable. Third, students reinforce their knowledge of the spellings of many high-frequency,

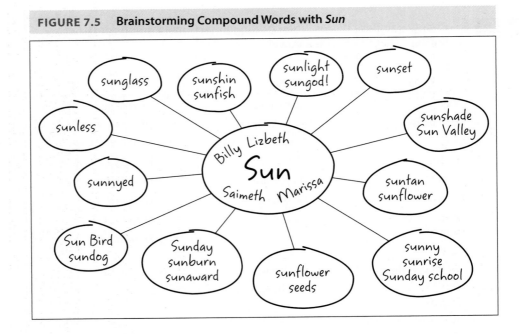

FIGURE 7.5   Brainstorming Compound Words with *Sun*

high-utility words in English that are compound words *(someone, anything)*. Look at Activity 7.4 on page 266 for specific ideas, such as illustrating words and brainstorming words that share the same base.

Open and Closed Syllables and Syllable Patterns

Why is *Tigger*, the name of the tiger from *Winnie the Pooh*, spelled with two *g*s? How do you pronounce *Caddie Woodlawn*? Answering these questions depends on whether the first syllable in the word is open or a closed. **Open syllables** (CV) end with a long vowel sound: *tiger, Katy, reason*. **Closed syllables** (CVC) contain a short vowel sound that is usually "closed" by two consonants: *Tigger, Caddie, rack*et.

Students are first introduced to the basics of open and closed syllables when they examine what happens when *-ed* and *-ing* are added to short and long vowel pattern words. If they write about how a rabbit moves along the ground *(hopping)* and do not double the *p*, they wind up with an entirely different meaning *(hoping)*. The same confusion occurs in words like *riding* and *ridding* or *griped* and *gripped*. As Henderson (1985) explained, "The core principle of syllable juncture is that of doubling consonants to mark the short English vowel" (p. 65). Students learn that when they do not know whether to double the consonants at the juncture of syllables, they should listen to the vowel sound in the first syllable. If they hear a long vowel sound, the syllable is open and will not end with a consonant *(hu-man)*. If they hear a short vowel sound, the odds are likely that the syllable is closed with an extra consonant *(mam-mal)*. Knowing whether to double develops first through examining base words plus inflectional suffixes, and is later applied *within* base words. Because the vowel in the first syllable of *Tigger* is short, the *g* is doubled; because the vowel in the first syllable of *tiger* is long, the *g* is not doubled.

Another way of describing what happens where syllables meet is through **syllable juncture patterns**, as shown in Table 7.3. For example, *hopping, Tigger,* and *stripping* illustrate the VCCV syllable juncture pattern for closed syllables; *hoping, tiger,* and *striping* illustrate the V/CV syllable juncture pattern for open syllables. These patterns are the most frequent. The third pattern, the closed VC/V pattern, with only a single consonant at the juncture after a short vowel *(nev-er, pan-ic)* occurs less frequently. The fourth pattern, the closed VCCCV pattern, includes words that have a consonant digraph or blend at the syllable juncture that cannot be separated *(ath-lete, hun-dred)*. In the VV pattern, each vowel contributes a

PD TOOLKIT™

for Words Their Way®

Syllable Juncture in VCV and VVCV Patterns
Ms. Bruskotter meets with a small group of students in two sessions to study open and closed syllables.

TABLE 7.3 Syllable Juncture Patterns

Pattern	Type	Examples
VC/CV	Closed	*skipping, button, rubber* (doublets)
		chapter, window, garden (two different consonants)
V/CV	Open	*lazy, coma, beacon*
VC/V	Closed	*river, robin, cover*
VCC/CV	Closed	*father, athlete, pumpkin*
VC/CCV		*pilgrim, instant, complain*
VV	Open	*create, riot, liar*

sound—the word is usually divided after the first long vowel sound (*cre-ate, li-on*) so it is another example of an open syllable.

Figure 7.6 shows a two-step sort that you can use to introduce syllable juncture patterns. Begin by sorting three to four words into each column in a Guess My Category activity (see page 58 in Chapter 3). Ask students to help you sort the rest of the words as shown in Sort 1. After sorting, ask students how the words in each column are alike. Explore further by asking if anyone noticed the vowel sounds and where the words were "divided" when you pronounced them. After completing this first sort, the words in the second column can be sorted further by those that have different consonants at the juncture and those that have the same, as shown in Sort 2.

FIGURE 7.6 Introducing Syllable Juncture Patterns

Sort 1		Sort 2	
VC/C	**VCCV**	**Different**	**Same**
baby	contest	contest	dinner
human	dinner	basket	summer
basic	basket	dentist	kitten
bacon	summer	winter	
music	dentist		
silent	winter		
	kitten		

Review Vowel Patterns in Two-Syllable Words

You can reexamine vowel sounds in two-syllable words as a way to review those patterns and extend students' understanding of how those patterns work in polysyllabic words. For example, look at the familiar long-*a* patterns in the sort in Figure 7.7. Students in the syllables and affixes stage learn to listen for the accented syllable and see the familiar vowel patterns (*ai, ay,* and *a-e*) they learned in the within word pattern stage.

Students fully master a number of vowel patterns within single-syllable and polysyllabic words during the within word pattern stage. These are often called **ambiguous vowels** because they represent a range of sounds and spellings. For example, the vowel sound is the same in *cause, lawn,* and *false,* but is spelled three different ways (*au, aw, al*). The *ou* spelling pattern has four different sounds in *shout, touch, through,* and *thought.* These variations are often cited as examples of the irregularity of English spelling, but word sorting allows students to see that they form consistent categories just like other vowel patterns (Johnston, 2001).

By paying attention to the position of ambiguous vowels, students can often determine which spelling pattern occurs most often. For example, *aw* and *oy* usually occur at the ends of words or syllables (*straw, boycott*), whereas *au* and *oi* are found within syllables (*fault, voice*). If

FIGURE 7.7 Common Long-*a* Spellings in Two-Syllable Words

maintain	dismay	debate
raisin	crayon	bracelet
dainty	decay	parade
trainer	layer	mistake
sailor	toda	escape

these patterns persist as problems into the syllables and affixes stage, then it is appropriate to take a step back and spend a little more time with these vowels in one-syllable words. You can also examine them, with other vowel patterns, in two-syllable words like *mouthful*, *counter*, and *lousy* versus *coward*, *chowder*, and *brownie*.

Accent or Stress

In most words of two or more syllables, one syllable is emphasized—**stressed** or **accented**—more than the others. Why do we teach accent? First, it helps students learn how to pronounce new words when they check in the dictionary. Some dictionaries use apostrophes to show which syllables are accented, while others boldface the accented syllable; teach your students both systems. (Digital dictionaries help with pronunciation because students can click on the speaker icon to hear the correct pronunciation.) The second, more important, reason for teaching accent, or stress, is that it provides the language for us to talk about a number of spelling challenges. Different syllables or parts of words are more challenging to spell because they are either unaccented or receive less stress in a word. A final reason pertains to word meanings, as in the case of homographs or words that are spelled the same but are pronounced differently, according to which syllable is accented. We may sign a ***contract*** when we buy a house, but we might ***contract*** a ***contractor*** to build it.

Determining the accented syllable may be a challenge, but sorting students' names is a good way to introduce the concept. When we pronounce a familiar name, where do we put the most emphasis? Which syllable seems to "sound louder" than the others? We pronounce Molly's name "***moll** ee*," not "*mo **lee**.*" We say "***jen** ifer*," not "*je **ni** fer*" or "*jenni **fer**.*" One way to test for accent is to hold the back of your hand lightly under your chin as you say a two-syllable word such as *a-round*. Your jaw probably drops more for the accented syllable. Now try this with certain homographs, words that are spelled alike but whose meanings and parts of speech change with a shift in accent:

> Would you pre**sent** the **pres**ent to the guest of honor?
> It is a good idea to re**cord** your expenses so you have a **rec**ord of them.
> The landfill might re**fuse** the **ref**use.

When examining multisyllable words, knowing about accent helps students identify what they need to pay particular attention to. For example, when students pronounce the word *market*, they realize they know the spelling of the accented syllable (*mar*), yet may be uncertain about the vowel spelling in the final **unaccented syllable** (*ket* or *kit*?). When students grasp the concept of an accented syllable they also learn about the other side of this concept, the unaccented syllable. The unaccented syllable is the one in which the spelling of the vowel is not clearly long or short, so students need to pay close attention to it. The sound in this syllable is often represented by the **schwa** sound—the upside down *e* in a dictionary pronunciation key (ə). By the middle of the syllables and affixes stage, word study can focus on these unaccented final syllables.

> /ər/ as in *super*, *actor*, and *sugar*
> /əl/ as in *angle*, *angel*, *metal*, *civil*, and *fertile*
> /ən/ as in *sudden*, *human*, *basin*, *apron*, and *captain*
> /chər/, /yər/, and /zhər/ as in *lecture*, *figure*, and *treasure*
> /ĭj/ as in *village* and *damage*
> /ē/ as in mon**ey**, cook**ie**, and stor**y**

When sorting words with unaccented final syllables, you will find there is often no tidy generalization that governs the spelling and students may have to simply commit many of these words to memory. However, sometimes a part is related to the ending. For example, verbs and adjectives tend to end in *-en* (*waken*, *golden*), whereas nouns end in *-on* (*prison*, *dragon*). Comparative adjectives are always spelled with *-er*, as in *smarter*, *faster*, and *taller*. (Sorting words by parts of speech as well as by spelling patterns is an important extension when studying words like these.) What is most useful for students to discover is that some spellings are simply more common than others. For example, there are over 1,000 words that end in *-le* but only about 200 that end in *-el*. The ending *-er* is much more common than *-ar* or *-or*. An excellent follow-up to sorting these words is creating class lists that give students insight into the frequencies. Then they might use a "best guess" strategy when spelling an unfamiliar word.

Identifying the vowel in unaccented syllables is one of the biggest challenges we all face as spellers. As our colleague Tom Gill explains to students, "You can't trust sound when your voice goes down." However, as we have discussed briefly and shall see further in the next chapter, the spelling of the schwa in the unaccented syllable can sometimes be explained in terms of meaning or parts of speech. At this stage, introduce and begin discussing how the "spelling–meaning connection" may explain some of these spellings. The *-el* ending in *angel*, for example, also occurs in the related adjective *angelic*; the *-al* in *metal* occurs in the adjective *metallic*; and the *-an* in *human* occurs in the adjective *humane*. The accented syllables in these related words often provide a clue to the spellings of unaccented syllables, as well as expanding students' vocabularies.

Further Exploration of Consonants

Consonants continue to be revisited in more difficult words during this stage. Consider words like *circus* or *garbage*, in which *c* and *g* represent two different sounds. (They might be spelled phonetically as /sər-kəs/ and /gär-bĭj/.) Generalizations about the spelling of hard and soft *g* and *c* reveal an underlying logic. As in one-syllable words, the sounds of *g* and *c* depend on the vowel that follows (*a*, *o*, and *u* follow the hard sound, whereas *e*, *i*, and *y* follow the soft sound), which results in some interesting spellings. Why is there a silent *u* in *tongue*? Without it, the *g* would become soft (/tɔnj/). The sound of /k/ can be spelled with *ck* (*shamrock*), *c* (*magic*), *x* (*index*), and *qu* (*antique*), and many words contain silent consonants such as *t* (*moisten*), *h* (*honest*), *k* (*knuckle*), *gh* (*daughter*), and *h* again (*rhythm*). Studying silent consonants foreshadows the in-depth study of spelling–meaning connections explored in the next stage, derivational relations, in which silent letters like the *t* in *moisten* can be explained by its connection to *moist*.

Base Words and Simple Derivational Affixes

While students spend time examining and consolidating their word knowledge at the syllable level, they should also focus on base words and simple **derivational affixes** (both prefixes and suffixes). Inflectional suffixes such as *–s*, *-ed*, and *–ing* do not significantly affect the meaning or part of speech of the base word to which they are attached; *helps*, *helped*, and *helping* are still verbs. However, derivational affixes often do affect the meanings and grammatical functions of the bases to which they are attached. For example, adding derivational affixes such as *-ful*, *-ly*, or *-ness* to the base word *help* changes it from a verb to an adjective, adverb, or noun, as in *helpful*, *helpfully*, or *helpfulness*. Students benefit from learning about the meanings of derivational affixes as well as their role in changing the meaning and grammatical function of the base word.

The terms *base word* and *root word* are often used interchangeably. We prefer using *base word* when referring to words that stand on their own after all prefixes and suffixes have been removed (*govern* in *government*; *agree* in *disagreement*). Base words such as these are also known as **free morphemes**. We use the term *root* to refer to a word part that remains after all prefixes and suffixes have been removed but usually is *not* itself a word that can stand alone (*vis* in *visible* and *spec* in *spectator*). These roots, also known as **bound morphemes**, usually come from Greek or Latin.

Lay the groundwork for this study during the within word pattern stage when you talk about simple prefixes and suffixes in reading vocabulary. At the syllables and affixes stage, students explore in depth how prefixes and suffixes combine with base words and word roots to create new words, and how to spell many of those words. This helps students analyze unknown words they encounter in their reading, leading to expansive and elaborate vocabularies.

The sort in Figure 7.8 shows one way to introduce prefixes and base words in a systematic way. Unlike most sorts, we do not recommend talking about the meaning of words until *after* the sort. Instead, encourage students to

FIGURE 7.8 Simple Prefix Sort

unfair	retell	disagree
unable	replay	disorder
uncover	research	disobey
unplug	reuse	disarm
undress	retrain	disown
unkind	return	disappear

develop their own hypotheses about the prefix meanings as they consider the word list. Using the words in sentences, such as "I must *obey* my parents because if I *disobey* them I get in trouble," helps to focus on the shifts in meaning. Explore the **generative** aspect of combining prefixes and bases by constructing different words through combining and recombining prefix and base word cards or tiles in various ways: combine *dis-*, *re-*, *un-* with *able* and *order* to produce *disable*, *disorder*, *reorder*, and *unable*.

Introduce suffixes through sorts in which students discover how the derivational suffixes affect the meanings of known words as well as parts of speech. For example, add *-y* to the noun *guilt* to produce the adjective *guilty*; adding *-ly* produces the adverb *guiltily*. Some derivational suffixes to study in this stage for both vocabulary and spelling include:

> *-er* as in *farmer* and *-or* as in *professor* (both denote "agents or someone or something who does something"; words of Latin origin use the *-or* spelling)
>
> *-y*, *-ly*, *-ful*, *-less*, and *-ness* (these suffixes generally change the meaning and part of speech, creating adjectives, adverbs, and nouns)

Students should revisit the rules that govern e-drop and doubling as they add suffixes to base words. *Brave* becomes *bravely* with no change (the prefix *-ly* begins with a consonant), but when adding *-er* or *-est* (which begin with a vowel), the doubling rule applies, as in *flatter* and *flattest*. In addition, *y* must be changed to *i* before adding suffixes (*silly* to *sillier*, *silliest*, *silliness*).

Spelling Strategies

By the syllables and affixes stage, expectations for correct spelling include a large percentage of the words students use when writing. A good activity to do with students is to brainstorm a list of the many things they can do when they do not know how to spell a word they need for writing. A list can include the following: listen for the sounds and spell as best you can; ask a friend; ask the teacher; look around the room; try it and see if it looks right; think of a word that sounds like it (spell by analogy); and look it up in a dictionary. Help students to prioritize these options, and throughout this stage show them how to think of related words and see if there is a spelling–meaning connection they can make.

HELP CHILDREN DEVELOP A SPELLING CONSCIENCE. We want to create a desire in students to improve their spelling and have pride in what they can do correctly. There are several ways to do this, keeping in mind there needs to be a balance between expectations for correct spelling and encouraging students to spell as best they can in order to write with real purpose.

1. Talk with students about *why* good spelling matters (to be sure readers can understand what we write; to give a good impression) and *when* it matters. Brainstorm with them a list of the kinds of writing that need to be correctly spelled.
2. Meet with students during and after their independent writing time and talk about their spelling. Compliment them on the words they got right (or almost right) and ask them what they did. You may be surprised at the wide range of strategies they already use (Chandler, 1999). Talk about a few words that you think they might be able to add to their personal lists or dictionaries, or spell correctly with a bit more attention. For example, Ruth wrote, "The wind blue all through the night." The teacher began by saying, "You got that tough word *through*. How did you know that?" Ruth replied that when she spelled it as THRU that it did not look right so she found it in her spelling dictionary. Then the teacher pointed to the word *blue*. "That names the color but there is a homophone for the word you need. Let's check our homophone collection."
3. Expect students at this stage to edit their written work for spelling errors but only when you take the time to teach spelling and editing strategies. Simply saying, "Read your paper and find your spelling mistakes," is not particularly helpful. Modeling is important: when you write for students, think aloud about spelling, and model spelling strategies as

well as proofreading techniques such as rereading to check spelling. Occasionally, project a student's writing sample (with permission) and model with the class how you go about proofreading it using the tips in Figure 3.25, on page 83 in Chapter 3.

DOES IT LOOK RIGHT? Intermediate readers have seen many words and can use the strategy of writing a word and then considering whether it looks right. Introduce this using the "Have-a-Go" sheet (see Figure 6.10, on page 210 in Chapter 6), but as students progress, they can use the strategy less formally. They need only to write one or two attempts anywhere that is handy.

Look it up in the dictionary. Let's be honest: few of us turn to a thick heavy dictionary to look up the spelling of a word if other resources are more easily available, like spell check or asking the person beside you. Still, we want students to practice this skill so that it is available to them. Spelling dictionaries contain lists of commonly used words without definitions so they are much easier to use. (See page 210 in Chapter 6 for a list of spelling dictionaries). If you have students who are literate in a language other than English they may find a bilingual dictionary handy. They can look up a word they know in their own language to find the English spelling (2008).

for **English Learners**

Spell check using software. Some educators and parents worry that using spell check discourages students from learning to spell. There is no evidence that this is true and besides, if word study is an ongoing part of your curriculum, then your students are getting the spelling instruction they need. Once students reach the syllable and affixes stage, they should be spelling most words correctly. While they continue to invent spellings for words they don't know, the process is less valuable.

If students are using word processing software, teach them how to use spell check but also to be aware of its shortcomings. Point out that homophone errors are not likely to be caught (*hear/here*), similarly spelled words are often skipped (*fat/fate, cut/cute*) and that unusual proper names may be incorrectly identified as misspellings (Leesa, Garrie). (Rare technical terms might also be identified but this is probably not an issue for your students). For most competent spellers, errors are often due to poor typing skills, but it is also the case that students may not know how to spell a word. Spell check may help in both cases. Explain that students can correct underlined errors right away or ignore them until the editing stage.

Regardless of which digital devices your students use, you need to teach them how to use them. Introduce spell check using an interactive white board or LCD projector to walk through the steps. Provide students with a sample document that has multiple spelling errors and assign them the task of correcting the errors using spell check. Be explicit about the following:

- Encourage students to make an effort to spell a word using what they already know—something they should have been doing for a long time. Spell check will not work unless there is a good approximation of the word.
- Encourage students to carefully study the suggestion(s) to not only select the correct word but to note the mistake they made so that the next time they will be more likely to spell the word correctly. As handy as spell check may be, it is still much faster to spell words correctly the first time.
- Clarify the limitations of spell check.
- Remind students that spell check is a useful tool but it will not replace the careful rereading needed for a polished paper.

Word Study Instruction for the Syllables and Affixes Stage

Too often, spelling instruction at the intermediate level and above lacks systematic attention to generalizations. Without a good understanding of the features that require instruction at this level, teachers in the upper grades often give students lists of spelling words from content areas that are really vocabulary words (*amphibian, vertebrates, metamorphosis, carnivore*). While such words are important for understanding content and concepts, they lack any common spelling features and may not be appropriate for students who are in different spelling stages.

We hope you have come to understand from this chapter that systematic word study targeted to meet student needs can advance students' spelling knowledge, their vocabularies, and their strategies for figuring out unknown words in reading. At the intermediate and middle grades, the following principles should guide instruction:

- Actively involve students in the exploration of words. They are more likely to develop a positive attitude toward learning words, and a curiosity about words—what is known as *word consciousness*.
- Engage students' prior knowledge. This is especially important if they are learning specialized vocabulary in different disciplines or content areas.
- Ensure students have many exposures to words in meaningful contexts, both in and out of connected text.
- Provide students with systematic instruction of structural elements and how these elements combine; elements include syllables, affixes, and the effects of affixes on the base words to which they are attached.

Guidelines for Creating Sorts in the Syllables and Affixes Stage

PD **TOOLKIT**™

for Words Their Way®

Many sorts for this stage can be found to print or sort online.

Throughout this chapter, we discuss directions for word sorting, particularly in the *Routines and Management* section that follows. There are a few cautions for you to consider during this upper-level word study.

There is a visual simplicity to the sorts in this stage. The sorts are a starting point, with the ultimate goal of students understanding the meaning and function of spelling patterns, like the meaning of prefixes and suffixes. Some students think that once they sort and record words in their word study vocabulary notebooks, their work is done; in fact, the study has just begun. For example, think of how easy it is for students to sort words that begin with particular prefixes or suffixes, like *dis-*, *ex-* or *mis-*, and how much more goes into adding examples and making meaning connections for these prefixes. Many sorts during this stage hinge on making spelling–meaning connections. Once the spelling aspect becomes apparent, have students try to figure out the meaning connection to the spelling. For this reason, we discuss ways for you to increase students' exposure to words that share a specific spelling–meaning connection.

Consider the difficulty of the vocabulary in word sorts during this stage. It is likely that intermediate-grade students in the syllables and affixes stage can read many words whose meanings elude them so it is important to consider the semantic difficulty of the words as much as the spelling challenge when selecting words and features to study at this stage. For example, the old saying "*i* before *e* except after *c* or when sounded like *a* as in *neighbor* and *weigh*" may be worthwhile to teach, but many of the examples of words that follow the rule may not be in the speaking vocabulary of elementary students (*conceive, perceive, conceited, receipt*). It is fine to select a few words whose meanings students might not know, or words that they only know tenuously, but do not overburden sorts with these words.

Sequence and Pacing of Word Study in the Syllables and Affixes Stage

For students in the elementary grades who have reached the syllables and affixes stage, there is less urgency than in earlier stages because they have mastered much of what is typically considered "phonics" (consonants, blends, digraphs, and vowels) and they can spell most single-syllable and high-frequency words. However, students still have much to master in spelling, and knowing how to tackle unfamiliar multisyllabic words they encounter in reading.

TABLE 7.4   **Sequence of Word Study: Syllables and Affixes**

Patterns and Features	Examples
Early	
Plural endings -*s* and -*es*	*books/dishes*
Unusual plurals	*goose/geese, knife/knives, fish, sheep*
Inflectional endings:	
Sort by sound of -*ed* suffix	*walked /t/, wagged /d/, shouted /əd/*
Doubling	*stopping, stopped* (CVC)
e-Drop	*skating, skated* (CVCe)
No change	*walking, walked* (CVCC) and *nailing, nailed* (CVVC)
Change final *y* to *i* and add -*ed* or -*s*	*cried* (*y* after a consonant), *plays* (*y* after a vowel)
Compound words	*pancake, sidewalk*
Middle	
Open and closed syllables:	
VCCV doublet at juncture	*button, happy*
VCCV different consonants at juncture	*window, sister*
V/CV open with long vowel	*bacon, lazy*
VC/V closed with short vowel	*river, camel*
VCCCV blend or digraph at juncture	*pilgrim, tangle*
V/V	*giant, diet*
Vowel patterns in accented syllables:	
Common vowel patterns in accented syllable	*lonely, toaster, owner*
Less common and ambiguous vowels in accented syllables	*fountain, powder, laundry, awful, marble, prepare, repair, narrow*
Final unaccented syllables:	
/ər/	*beggar, barber, actor*
/ən/	*captain, human, frighten, basin, apron*
/əl/	*angel, able, central, civil, fertile*
/chər/ and /zhər/	*culture, measure, teacher*
Spelling /j/	*badger, major, village*
Two-syllable homophones	*pedal, petal, peddle*
Two-syllable homographs	*rebel, rebel*
Special consonants in two-syllable words	hard and soft *g* and *c*
	silent consonants (*written, knuckle, rhythm*)
	ph (*dolphin*), *gh* (*laughter, daughter*)
	qu (*question, antique*)
Late	
Simple prefixes and base words	*un-* (not–*unlock*), *re-* (again–*remake*), *dis-* (opposite–*dismiss*), *in-** (not–*indecent*), *non-* (not–*nonfiction*), *mis-* (wrong–*misfire*), *pre-* (before–*preview*), *ex-* (out–*exclude*), *uni-* (one–*unicycle*), *bi-* (two–*bicycle*), *tri-* (three–*tricycle*)
Suffixes	-*y* (*adjective*–like, tending, toward: *jumpy*), -*ly* (*adverb*–like: *gladly*), -*er*, -*est* (comparatives), -*ful* (full: *graceful*), -*less* (without: *penniless*), -*ness* (condition: *happiness*)
	-*ment* (action, process, or *result* of an action or process: *excitement*), -*ion* (action, process, or *result* of an action or process: *action*)

A word study sequence for this stage is presented in Table 7.4. The sequence touches on the important spelling patterns and features to consider, and is based on what students do developmentally. Normally, achieving students in the intermediate grades will take at least two years and more to progress through this stage. In addition, studying generative morphology using base words, roots, and affixes is explored through vocabulary study: the powerful role that knowledge of processes of word combination plays in vocabulary development as well as spelling.

The Elementary Spelling Inventory (ESI) described in Chapter 2 helps identify students in the syllables and affixes stage. Some teachers find that the Upper-Level Spelling Inventory (USI) provides better information about students in the later part of the stage. If students appear to be in the late syllables and affixes or derivational relations stage on the ESI, be sure to move on to the USI. Use the spell checks on the PDToolkit and in the *Words Their Way* supplements to more accurately identify what features students are ready to study. Use Table 7.1 (see page 249) to determine what features they are using but confusing to plan instruction. If in doubt about where to place students, remember it is best to take a step back and study earlier features that students may not fully understand even if they are spelling many words with those features correctly.

At advanced spelling stages (both syllable and affixes and derivational relations) you may find students "leveling out" on their spelling inventory results; that is, they are instructional on a range of spelling features at the same time and a few features are missing completely. This means that a strict sequence of instruction is not as important as in previous stages, and you can form larger groups for instructing certain features. For example, you can teach prefixes any time in the recommended sequence as well as to students in early derivational relations. However, do not rush students in the elementary grades through the syllables and affixes stage, into the derivational relations stage, because they may not be ready for the more advanced vocabulary used in the word sorts. At the same time, students in the middle grades who are still in the syllables and affixes stage should be moved along at a steady pace and might skip the late features, because they are covered again in early derivational relations. Students in the middle grades and high school who are in this stage may need the extra support suggested in *Words Their Way® with Struggling Readers: Word Study for Reading, Vocabulary and Spelling Instruction, Grades 4–12* (Flaniganet al., 2011).

EARLY, MIDDLE, OR LATE PLACEMENT. Identifying whether students are in the early, middle, or late part of the stage (see Table 7.4) will help you target where in the sequence of features to begin word study instruction.

Early. Students early in this stage know how to spell the vowel patterns in most single-syllable words but make errors when adding inflectional endings, as in SHOPING for *shopping* and CARRYES for *carries*. They are ready to explore the "double, drop, or nothing" principles that govern the place where base word and inflection meet.

Middle. Students in the middle of the stage usually add inflectional endings correctly but make mistakes with syllable junctures within words and with unaccented final syllables, as in RIPPIN for *ripen* and BOTEL for *bottle*. They are ready to extend their understanding of doubling to syllable junctures within words as they study open and closed syllables. Vowel patterns that students learned in the within word pattern stage are reviewed within the accented syllable. After studying accented syllables, students in the middle of the syllables and affixes stage look at the final unstressed syllable and two-syllable homophones and homographs. They also examine some unusual consonant sounds and spellings.

Late. Students who can spell most words correctly in the syllables and affixes categories on the inventory are at the end of the stage. In word study, the focus is on simple prefixes and derivational suffixes that affect the meanings of familiar base words in straightforward ways (*rebuild, dislike*) as an introduction to the spelling–meaning connection that is the focus in the derivational relations stage. For a faster pace, students in middle grades or

high school might skip this introduction and go to the sorts recommended for early derivational relations in which they review these affixes in more advanced words (*reconsider*, *discourage*).

Assess and Monitor Progress in the Syllables and Affixes Stage

Involve students in the upper elementary grades in their own progress monitoring, which, as they track their progress over time, can be very motivating.

Weekly Assessments and Spell Checks

Weekly spelling tests and unit assessments are described in Chapter 6 as a means by which you can monitor student progress. Call out 10 sorting words each week, but also include some words that assess transfer of a feature (e.g., more words to which students must add *-ing* or *-ed*) or words from a previous week's sort to send the message that students are not just responsible for the set of words they sorted that week. When students make errors on these assessments, you can ask them to go back to their word study notebooks to review the generalizations they explored and then to analyze their errors in an attempt to determine why they misspelled. Figure 7.9 shows two examples from a lesson on hard and soft *g*.

Monitoring Progress and Goal Setting

To assess retention over time, prepare an assessment that samples words from previous lessons, or use the unit spell checks on the website or in *Words Their Way®: Word Sorts for Syllables and Affixes Spellers*. Review and grade students' word study notebooks once a week. In addition, the student contract and grading form (see Figures 3.17 and 3.20 in Chapter 3) help to monitor progress. Use the assessments' results to determine whether students have met the goals in the goal-setting charts available on the website.

Figure 7.10 is an example of the goal-setting chart for early syllables and affixes. We recommend that you meet with students individually to go over the spelling inventory you used to assess them initially and to identify where to begin the study of features listed on the chart. When students score 90 to 100 percent on weekly tests and 80 to 100 percent on unit spell checks, that feature can be considered "mastered." If students do not meet these goals you should consider whether they were appropriately placed for instruction or whether they got adequate practice each week with the words. It may be necessary to reteach using different sets of words or increase the number of times students sort their words during the week.

MONITORING PROGRESS

PD TOOLKIT™

for Words Their Way®

Syllables and Affixes Stage Spell Check and **Syllables and Affixes Goal Setting Chart**
Progress monitoring assessments are available to download and print.

FIGURE 7.9 **Error Reflections**

Word	Error	What went wrong
guide	giude	I reversed the u and i. The u keeps the g from taking the soft j sound before an i.
iceberg	iceberge	Don't need an e on the end of this word because the sound is hard g, not the soft j sound.

FIGURE 7.10   Goal-Setting Chart

SYLLABLE AND AFFIXES MONITORING CHART

Name _____   Teacher _____   Date_____

Goals for Early Syllables and Affixes

18. Spell inflected endings   Double _____   *e*-drop _____   Nothing _____
     (*ed, ing, s*)   Change *y* to *i* _____   *es* _____

Criterion Met   Spell Check 18

19. Spell syllable juncture   VCV _____   VCCV_____   VCV _____   VCCCV _____   VV _____
     patterns

Criterion Met   Spell Check 19

Goals for Middle Syllables and Affixes

20. Spell long vowel   *a-e/ai/ay* _____   *e-e/ea/ee* _____   *i-e/igh* _____
     patterns in accented
     syllables   *o-e/oa/ow* _____   *oo/u-e/ew* _____

Criterion Met   Spell Check 20

Word Study with English Learners in the Syllables and Affixes Stage

for **English Learners**

English learners in the syllables and affixes stage have mastered many of the basic phonics and spelling generalizations of English and are ready to study the more advanced features of this stage. However, many of the words used in sorts at this stage may be new vocabulary. For this reason, it is especially important to make word study a language-learning event. Words that are featured due to spelling issues should be defined and used in conversational speech as a part of every lesson. The suggestions in Chapter 6 to support English learners apply to this stage as well. (See also Helman, Bear, Templeton, Invernizzi, & Johnston, 2012; Templeton & Gehsmann, 2014.)

Many features in the syllables and affixes stage may present some conceptual difficulty for English learners. Verb forms may be constructed differently in the native language, particularly inflected verbs. In Spanish, for example, the corresponding equivalent to the English *-ing* is often an infinitive used as an abstract noun (e.g., *To sleep is good for you*). As a result, English learners may have difficulty understanding English sentences that use the *-ing* form as the subject of the sentence (e.g., *Sleeping is good for you*) or perceiving the pronunciation of *-ing* or *-ed* at the ends of English words (Swan & Smith, 2001).

Plurals may also be formed differently in the native language. Perceiving and producing the pronunciations of *-s* or *-es* at the end of a word may require explicit attention. Learning the small subset of English nouns, verbs, and adjectives that involve unusual internal spelling–sound changes (*knife/knives, leave/left, child/children*) may not be as simple as it seems. Comparatives may also be constructed differently. Instead of being signaled by spelling changes or different words altogether, comparatives may be signaled by changes in accent.

In contrast to many other languages, English spellings are full of double letters that might puzzle English learners so studying doubling issues is important. In addition, the compounding and generative aspects of English may not occur in the native language. Compound words like *outsmart* or *windfall* may seem strange to English learners, especially when they are metaphoric (*headstrong*) rather than literal (*sundown*). Similarly, the common use of affixes and base words in English to generate new words may be rare in other languages. Studying these features in detail is important in helping English learners not only learn the spellings and meanings of words but also understand *why* words work the way they do in English.

WORD STUDY *Routines and Management*

Organizing differentiated instructional-level groups for word study is challenging but will best serve students' needs, especially those who are below grade level. The key to finding time for meeting with small groups is establishing routines. When students learn weekly word study routines, they become responsible for completing much of their work independently (both in class and at home) or with partners, leaving you free to work with other small groups. You can find more organization tips in Chapter 3.

The Word Study Lesson Plan in the Syllables and Affixes Stage

We recommend the basic word study lesson plans described in detail in Chapters 3 and 6 for this stage as well. Teacher-directed sorts are a good way to introduce new features but open sorts involve students in more active thinking. You may be skeptical about using word sorts with older students, but experience proves the value of sorts at this level. Even adults who are poor spellers enjoy and benefit from hands-on sorting activities (Massengill, 2006). Use the following basic routines for sorts:

1. Model a sort, or have students sort, and lead them in a discussion of the generalizations revealed by the sort as Ms. Radcliffe did at the beginning of this chapter. You should also discuss word meanings before or after (in the case of prefixes) sorting.
2. Have students sort their own set of words and check their sorts. Sorting the weekly words, not once but four or five times across the week, is a valuable routine for students and should be at the heart of systematic developmental word study.
3. Encourage students to clarify and summarize their understandings with oral and written reflections.
4. Use extension activities across the week to reinforce and broaden students' understandings. Activities include homework and working with partners in blind sorts, writing sorts, and timed sorts as described in Chapter 3. Games and other activities are another way to engage students in further exploration and review of the features they are learning in their sorts.

Word Study Notebooks in the Syllables and Affixes Stage

Using word study notebooks in this stage continues to be an easy way to help you and your students manage the routines and organization of word study (see Chapters 3 and 6). Word sorts should continue to be recorded in columns of contrasting categories; for example, words that drop the *e* before adding a suffix versus words that do not drop the *e*. Exemplars can be

added as they are found in word hunts and lists of base words and their derivations can also be formed—for example, *compete, competing, competed, competitor*.

In addition to basic word sorting routines, develop a list of additional word study notebook activities from which students select when they work independently or for homework. Some of these may be more appropriate at times than others, and some can be done to review previous lessons.

- Find words that have base words and underline the base word.
- Break words into syllables and underline the accented syllables.
- Make appropriate words on your lists plural or add *-ing* or *-ed*.
- Circle or underline any prefixes or suffixes you find in the words on your list.
- Add a prefix and/or suffix, when possible, to words on your list.
- Select five words and use them in sentences or illustrate them.
- Sort your words by parts of speech or subject areas and record your sort.
- Go for speed. Sort your words three times and record your times.
- Select five words to look up in the dictionary. Record the multiple meanings you find for each word.

With the increased emphasis on vocabulary learning, you may want to have your students divide their word study notebooks into two sections. In Tamara Barnen's class, the first section is titled "Word Study," and contains the assigned sorts. This section includes weekly records of sorts, word hunts, lists generated in small groups, written reflections of sorts, timed sorts, and writing sorts. The second section is called "Looking into Language" and contains lists of words related to themes and units, words categorized by parts of speech, graphic organizers, and semantic webs of content area studies. Students can create synonym and antonym wheels in their word study notebook, as shown in Figure 7.11. Some teachers include a third section, called a "Personal Dictionary," in which students record words they frequently need to use in writing. Because these notebooks will be used constantly, many teachers recommend stiff-backed, stitched composition books. Other teachers have students use loose leaf paper inserted into either a 1½-inch, three-ring binder or a less expensive cardboard folder with three pre-inserted brads. Notebook paper, handouts and worksheets can be added at any time and place, making a notebook a more flexible choice.

FIGURE 7.11	**Synonym and Antonym Wheels**

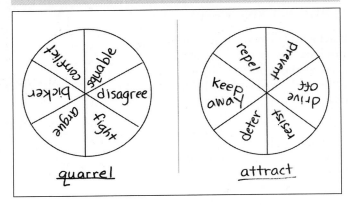

RESOURCES FOR IMPLEMENTING WORD STUDY *in Your Classroom*

You can find prepared sorts on the website and in Appendix D. These resources offer sample sorts, and lists of words for other sorts or to modify the suggested sorts.

Words Their Way®: Word Sorts for Syllables and Affixes Spellers (Johnston, Invernizzi, Bear, & Templeton, 2009) has

over 50 prepared sorts divided into eight study units with spell checks. Use the spell checks to better identify what students are ready to study and also for pre- and post-testing to monitor progress.

Appendix D has sample sorts and Appendix E has words listed by features that can be used in sorts.

ACTIVITIES for the Syllables and Affixes Stage

Several vocabulary activities are described first in this section followed by some dictionary activities. The remaining games and activities are designed to extend and reinforce spelling sorts. Common Core State Standards for Foundational Skills and Language are listed for grades 3, 4, and 5.

Vocabulary Activities

Refer back to vocabulary activities in Chapter 6 (Activities 6.1 to 6.5) that are also appropriate for this stage.

7.1 Semantic Maps

Semantic maps provide an excellent way to activate students' background knowledge on a topic by asking them to brainstorm words related to a topic, which gives you an idea of how much students already know. During or after the brainstorming session, organize the terms into categories using a graphic map such as the one in Figure 7.12. Keep the map posted and add new terms throughout the unit; "Animals" is the example used here. (CCSS Language (3rd–5th) 6)

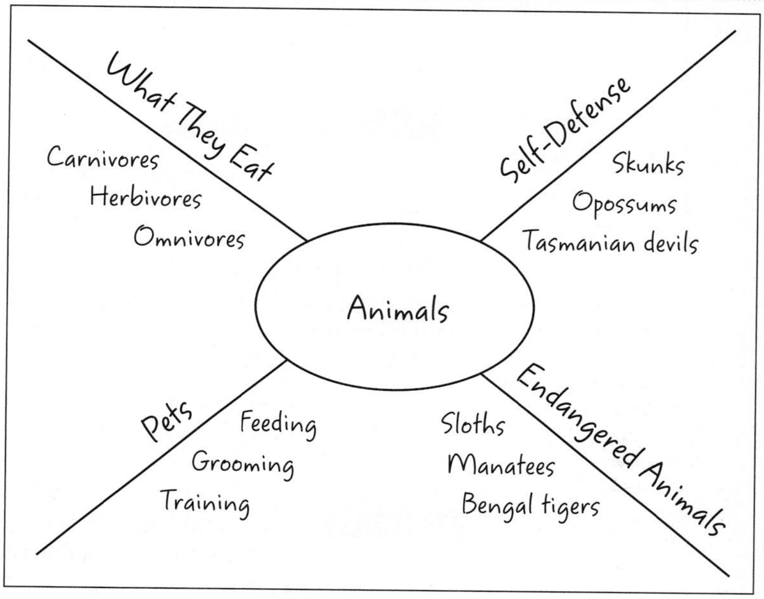

PROCEDURES

1. To kick off a unit on animals, write the word *animals* on the board and then asks students what words or ideas they associate with animals. Write the words on a chart; afterward, add a few more terms that were not mentioned but are important terms in the unit.

2. Next, talk with the students about different ways in which these words may be categorized and then arrange the words, with students' input, along the appropriate "leg" (category) of the map. This may lead students to think of more terms. As they talk and read further, they are growing their understanding of the new terms and their relationships to more familiar words and concepts. Have students make their own copy of the map as a follow-up activity and add to it over time.

3. Keep the maps posted throughout the unit, prominently displayed, and have students add terms as they move through the unit. Students may also decide that a particular term belongs to a different category, and if they can justify it, then they can move the term to the new category.

FIGURE 7.12   Semantic Map for Animals Unit

7.2 Concept Mapping

Concept or word maps focus on a specific term and visually represent its place in a conceptual hierarchy using guided questions. In Figure 7.13, the word *colony* is the focus. When you first present the map, the ovals are blank except for the headings: What is it? What is it like? What are some examples? What are some non-examples? As you discuss each question, fill the ovals with ideas offered by students. (CCSS Language (3rd–5th) 6)

FIGURE 7.13 **Concept or Word Map:** *Colony*

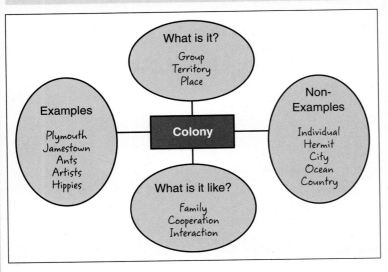

What is it?
Group
Territory
Place

Examples
Plymouth
Jamestown
Ants
Artists
Hippies

Colony

Non-Examples
Individual
Hermit
City
Ocean
Country

What is it like?
Family
Cooperation
Interaction

7.3 Vocabulary Jeopardy

Students enjoy playing the familiar Jeopardy game after brainstorming terms related to a study unit. (CCSS Language (3rd–5th) 6)

MATERIALS Create vocabulary cards for a study unit. Start with the vocabulary students generate on their own, followed by a scan through texts and materials. Determine four to five categories, such as "What Comes Out of a Volcano?" with terms such as *pumice, sulfur, ash, lava,* and *molten rock.* With these cards, students make a Jeopardy game. (Activity 6.18, in Chapter 6 contains a sample game board.) Students write items on cards that relate to facts and concepts they have studied and write correct responses on the backside. For example, *Material that comes out of a volcano* could take responses that include *What is ash?* or *What is molten rock?* Teams of students play the game as a whole-class vocabulary review of the unit.

7.4 Word Roots

Examining how Greek and Latin roots combine with affixes helps students build their generative morphological knowledge. This examination builds on the earlier investigation of how base words combine with affixes. This activity, adapted from Templeton & Gehsmann (2014), illustrates how the initial presentation and discussion of the Latin roots *vis/vid* and *dict* may be planned over the course of a week's instruction. See Table 7.5 for additional Greek and Latin roots to explore at this stage. (CCSS Foundational Skills (3rd) 3.b, (3rd–5th) 3.a, Language (4th–8th) 4.b)

TABLE 7.5 **Greek and Latin Roots: Generative Vocabulary Instruction at the Syllables and Affixes Stage**

Common Greek Roots	Common Latin Roots
tele (far, distant: *telegraph*)	*aud* (hear: *audible*)
therm (heat: *thermometer*)	*dict* (say: *predict*)
photo (light: *photograph*)	*spec* (look: *inspect*)
gram (thing that is written: *diagram*)	*vis/vid* (see: *vision, video*)
graph (writing: *digraph*)	*port* (carry: *portable*)
meter, metr (measure: *barometer, metric*)	*struct* (build: *structure*)
micro (small: *microscopic*)	*rupt* (break: *interrupt*)
scop (view, see: *telescopic*)	*fract* (break: *fracture*)
phon (sound: *homophone*)	*scrib/script* (write: *transcribe, transcription*)
bio (life: *biography*)	
auto (self: *autobiography*)	

PROCEDURES

Day 1.

1. Share with the students that they'll begin looking at roots that come from Latin, and present the word *predict*.

   Ask the students what it means if they *predict* something. Then, ask them if they see a prefix in *predict* (pre). What does it mean? (before) Cover *pre-*, and tell the students that they're left with *dict*, which is not a word that can stand by itself, but which is the *root* of *predict*. Explain that *dict* comes from a Latin word that means "to say or speak," and that when we "predict" something [display the whole word] we *say* [point to *dict*] that something will happen *before* [point to *pre*] it actually happens.

   If you feel your students don't need such an explicit walk-through, after you present the word *predict* ask them what they think the root means. Then, ask them that if they *predict* that something will happen, what they think that means.

2. Display the words *vision* and *revision*.

   Discuss the meaning of *vision*, emphasizing that it has to do with "seeing." Then, ask the students about *revision*, and what's involved during the *revision* step in writing. Ask them to turn to a partner and talk about what they think *revision* has to do with "seeing." You are guiding them to the realization that, when they *revise* their writing, they are "seeing" [point to *vis*] it "again" [point to *re-*].

Day 2.

1. Display the words from Day 1, and ask the students how they defined *dict* and *vis*. Then, display the following words:

visit	dictate
visor	dictionary
visibility	contradict
supervise	dictionary

2. Ask the students to talk with a partner about how the meaning of each root works in each of these words. For example, how does the meaning of "say" or "speak" work in the word *dictionary*? When someone *supervises* you, what does that have to do with the meaning of "see"? Circulate around the room as your students are talking, then bring the whole class back together to share their ideas.

Day 3. With *vis* or *dict* as a root, have students create a word using any of the prefixes and/or suffixes they have explored up to this point. In their word study notebook, have them write the word, a definition for it, and—if it can be illustrated—include an illustration. Be sure to follow up and have the students share their new words.

• •

Dictionary Skills for Syllable and Affixes Spellers

Because of their ease of use, online dictionaries and dictionary apps have the potential to bring students more easily and engagingly into the exploration of words. You should base instruction in the organization and use of the dictionary on a print version. See the list of resources for dictionaries and other books that will enhance word consciousness on page 268. Online versions of dictionaries include a "speaker"-type icon that, when clicked, provides an audio pronunciation of the word. For the upper elementary grades, some dictionaries include information about a word's origin in the entry. At the time of this writing, probably the best dictionary app for upper elementary students and beyond is the website "Vocabulary." It is part of a more expansive vocabulary instruction app—it provides accessible definitions, context sentences, and more importantly, morphologically-related word families for most entry words.

7.5 **Teaching the Dictionary**

Model how to use a dictionary regularly as part of word study lessons, read-alouds, subject area lessons, or any time a question might arise that can be answered in a dictionary. (CCSS Language (3rd) 2.g, 4.d, (4th–5th) 4.e)

PROCEDURES Walk through the dictionary features with your students, projecting pages on a white board or screen. Introduce the many different kinds of information that they can find:

- Introductory pages addressing how to use the dictionary, including important terminology (e.g., guide words, entry words)
- Introduction of special features throughout the dictionary; boxes that address synonyms, morphology, word histories
- Pronunciation guides are discussed in the introduction and also usually appear on every other page in the dictionary.
- Information presented in each word entry:

  - Parts of speech
  - Definitions with context sentences that help students make the important distinctions for multiple-meaning words
  - Syllable breaks
  - Accent or stress (sometimes with accent marks and sometimes with bolded letters)
  - Inflected forms (e.g., *editing*, *edited*)

Here are some resources you might use in your classroom. Often schools have a set of dictionaries on a rolling cart, but having a few in your classroom is important. Consider a variety of dictionaries instead of multiple copies because then students can compare entries and features.

Online:

Longman Dictionary of Contemporary English
Merriam-Webster Online Dictionary
The website Vocabulary

Print:

Longman dictionary of American English (5th ed.). Pearson.
The American Heritage children's dictionary. Boston: Houghton Mifflin Harcourt.
Ayto, J. (2009). *Oxford school dictionary of word origins: The curious twists & turns of the cool and weird words we use*. Oxford: Oxford University Press.
Fine, E. H. (2004). *Cryptomania! Teleporting into Greek and Latin with the Cryptokids*. Berkeley, CA: Tricycle. (Also see the Cryptokids website.)

7.6 **Weekly Word Study Notebook Dictionary Assignments**

Once students learn how to find things in a dictionary, be sure they get practice doing so by assigning activities such as these that require them to use the dictionary. (CCSS Language (3rd) 4.d, (4th & 5th) 4.c)

PROCEDURES Studying in weekly sorts suggests different assignments that students can complete in their word study notebooks, such as:

1. Write 10 of the week's words according to the syllable breaks in the dictionary (*tab-let*, *ta-ble*).
2. Write 10 words and indicate where the accent falls on the stressed syllable. Homographs like *pro'duce* and *produce'* are interesting to look up.
3. List more words that begin with a certain prefix. Caution students to be sure the words do indeed contain a prefix. (e.g., *reappear* has the *re-* prefix meaning "again", but *reason* does not).

4. Select five words to look up and record the definition(s). You might select these yourself or let students choose. Finding new definitions for words students already know sometimes makes this worthwhile. For example, students are likely to say they already know what *table* means (a piece of furniture) but of course it can mean other things, such as a chart or to put something aside.

7.7 Dictionary Bees

These drills are designed to help students develop skills in using the dictionary but keep them fast and fun. You can make these competitive or not. If one student is consistently the fastest make that student an announcer or referee so others can be first. (CCSS Language (3rd) 4.d, (4th–5th) 4.c)

MATERIALS Every student should have an elementary dictionary.

PROCEDURES Here are several different drills:

- How many turns? Announce a word for everyone to find using the fewest number of page turns. Remind students to first think about where the word is likely to come in the alphabetic sequence and then to use guidewords at the top. Tell them to keep track of how many tries it takes. Model this for the students first, and then do it yourself at the same time they do; after a while they might beat you at the game! Students can work in teams—one keeps score of the number of times the page is turned by the other student.
- Look up the spelling. Announce a word that students are not likely to know how to spell (e.g., *legitimate* or *foreign*) and challenge them to find the word in the dictionary. The first one to find the word, write it on a whiteboard or card, and hold up the written word is the winner. Even if students know how to spell the word they cannot write it until they find the word.
- Find information. Write an unfamiliar word on the board (perhaps one from an upcoming unit in science or social studies) and challenge them to find the definition, part of speech, pronunciation, or origin.

SPELLING ACTIVITIES These activities and games are designed to reinforce the word study introduced first in sorting activities. There are many games described in previous chapters that are adaptable for use with the features studied in this stage.

1. The Spelling Game (Activity 6.13, in Chapter 6) can be used with any feature, as it involves asking a player to spell a word before moving on the board. The word cards from any sort can be used as the playing cards for the game.
2. Go Fish (5.28, in Chapter 5), and The Racetrack Game (6.12), "I'm Out" (6.14), Jeopardy (6.18), Declare Your Category! (6.20), Word Study Uno (6.22), and Homophone Rummy (6.23) in Chapter 6 work well with the many features in this stage that have three or more categories: syllable patterns, vowel patterns in stressed syllables, unaccented final syllables, silent consonants, hard and soft *g* and *c*, prefixes, suffixes, and so on.

Adaptable
for Other Stages
● ● ● ● ●

7.8 Compound Word Activities

When examining compound words, consider the difficulty of the base words they use. *Cupcake* and *outfit* consist of two words that have common one-syllable patterns mastered in the within word pattern stage, but *cheeseburger* and *grandparent* include two-syllable words that students may find challenging to spell (*burger* and *parent*). Following are ways you can explore these words. (CCSS Foundational Skills (3rd) 3, 3.c, (4th–5th) 3, 3.a, Language (3rd) 2.e, (4th) 2.9, 4, (5th) 2.e)

- Share some common compound words with the students (e.g., *cookbook* and *bedroom*). Discuss their meanings, pointing out how each word in the compound contributes to the meaning of the whole word. You might ask students to draw pictures for illustration. For example, a student might draw a horse and a shoe, and then a horseshoe.

ACTIVITIES | SYLLABLES AND AFFIXES STAGE

- Using the compound word list in Appendix E, prepare word sorts that can be sorted in a variety of ways. The sort can focus on shared words (**head**light, **head**band, **head**ache, **head**phones versus **foot**ball, **foot**hill, **foot**print, **foot**step). You might also conduct concept sorts; for example, words that have to do with people (*anyone, someone, somebody, anybody*) or things we find outdoors (*sunlight, airplane, waterfall, airport*).
- Have students cut a set of compound words apart. Then challenge them to create as many new compound words as they can. Some words will be legitimate words (*mailbox*); others will be words that do not formally exist but could (*bookbox*). Have students share and discuss their words. Students might then write sentences using the pseudo-words and draw pictures that illustrate the meaning of each.
- Give students a word such as *fire, man, head, book,* or *rain* and challenge them to see how many related compound words they can brainstorm (*fireplace, firefighter, cookbook, bookmark, rainbow, raincoat*). Teams compete to see who can come up with the longest list in a variation of Scattergories (6.21). Let the team with the longest list read it aloud. Everyone crosses out any word that another team has also thought of. Only words that no other team thinks of earn points. Repeat until every team has had a chance to read the words remaining on their list. Remember that each part of the word must stand alone as a free morpheme.
- Challenge the more advanced students at this stage to sort compound words according to their underlying structure (Bravo, Hiebert, & Pearson, 2005). For example, noun + noun (*headlight, wasteland*); noun + verb (*windswept, handshake*); adjective + noun (*anyplace, hardwood*).
- Create a year-long class collection of compound words on a chart or in word study notebooks. This collection can include hyphenated words (*good-bye, show-off, push-up,* etc.).

7.9 Double Scoop

This board game helps students review and master consonant doubling and *e*-drop when adding inflectional endings. It is appropriate for small groups of two to four students. (CCSS FS: (3rd) 3.a, L: (3rd) 1.e, (4th) L: 2, 2.d)

MATERIALS Prepare a game board as shown in Figure 7.14 and write sentences, such as the examples below, on small cards to go into a deck. You will also need playing pieces, a

PD TOOLKIT™
for Words Their Way®

Double Scoop
This and other word study games are ready to print; blank templates are also available.

FIGURE 7.14   Double Scoop Game Board

spinner or die, and a small whiteboard or paper on a clipboard for writing answers under the categories of *e-Drop*, *Double*, and *No Change*.

The bunny was <u>hopping</u> down the road.
The cat is <u>sunning</u> herself on the chair.
Brittany <u>shopped</u> at her favorite store.

I was <u>hoping</u> to get new shoes.
He is <u>diving</u> into the pool.
She <u>glided</u> across the ice.

PROCEDURES

1. Players put their pieces on the sun to start. Player 2 (the reader) reads a sentence card and repeats the underlined word.
2. Player 1 (the writer) spells the underlined word under the correct heading on the whiteboard or paper.
3. Player 2 checks the answer by comparing it with the sentence card. If it is correct, player 1 spins and moves that number of spaces on the playing board.
4. Play then moves to the next student, who must spell and sort the underlined word given by the next player. If there are only two players, they simply switch roles.
5. The first player to reach the double scoop of ice cream wins.

7.10 Freddy, the Hopping, Diving, Jumping Frog

In this board game for two to four players, students review generalizations for adding *-ing*. (CCSS Foundational Skills (3rd) 3.a, Language (3rd) 1.e, (4th) 2, 2.d)

MATERIALS Create a game board using one or more of the follow-the-path templates in Appendix F, or by arranging green circles in a path to represent lily pads much like the game board for the Hopping Frog game in Activity 5.29 in Chapter 5. On each space, write either *Double*, *e-Drop*, or *Nothing*. Prepare playing cards by writing a variety of words with *-ing* added until there is an equal number for each rule (e.g., *hopping*, *diving*, *jumping*). Use words that students have been sorting and add more words from the syllables and affixes word lists in Appendix D. You can also add penalty or bonus cards such as the following:

You have the strongest legs. Jump ahead to the next lily pad.
You are the fastest swimmer. Skip 2 spaces.
Your croaking made me lose sleep. Move back 2 spaces.
You ate too many flies. Move back 2 spaces.

PROCEDURES

1. Place playing cards face-down and put playing pieces on the starting space.
2. Each player draws a card, reads the card aloud, and moves to the closest space that matches. For example, if the card says *hopping*, the player moves to the nearest space marked *Double*.
3. A player who draws a penalty or bonus card must follow the directions on the card.
4. The winner is the first to reach the home lily pad.

VARIATIONS Players can draw for each other, read the word aloud, and the player whose turn it is must spell the word correctly before moving to the appropriate space. You can write uninflected forms on cards (*hop*, *jump*, *dive*), and have players write how the word should be spelled before moving to the appropriate place. Include an answer sheet with words in alphabetical order to check if there is disagreement.

7.11 Slap Jack

This card game for two people may be used to contrast open- and closed-syllable words as represented by any of the syllable spelling patterns (V/CV vs. VCCV; V/CV vs. VC/V). The object of the game is for one player to win all 52 cards. (CCSS Foundational Skills (3rd–5th) 3, 3.a, Language (3rd) 2.f, (4th) 2, 2.d)

MATERIALS On 52 small cards, write the words that you want to be contrasted. For example, 26 words that follow the open-syllable VCV pattern (*pilot*, *human*) and 26 that follow the closed-syllable VCCV pattern (*funny*, *basket*); see word lists in Appendix E. Write the words on both ends of the cards so that neither player has to read the words upside down.

PROCEDURES

1. Deal the cards one at a time until the deck is gone. Players keep their cards face-down in a pile in front of them.
2. Each player turns a card face-up in a common pile at the same time. When two words with either open syllables or closed syllables are turned up together, the first player to slap the pile takes all the cards in the common pile and adds them at the bottom of his or her pile. Turning cards and slapping must be done with the same hand.
3. A player who slaps the common pile when there are not two open- or closed-syllable words must give both cards to the other player.
4. Play continues until one player has all the cards. If time runs out, the winner is the player with the most cards.

VARIATIONS Additional syllable juncture patterns may be added to the deck—for example, closed-syllable VCV (*cabin*, *water*) and VV (*riot*, *diet*). Word cards could be prepared for any feature that has two or three categories, such as inflected forms with -*ed* that players would slap when both words represent *e*-drop, double, or no change.

7.12 Double Crazy Eights

This activity for two to three players is based on the traditional card game Crazy Eights and works well to review vowel patterns, syllable juncture, and accented syllables. The object of the game is to get rid of all the cards in your hand. (CCSS Foundational Skills (3rd–5th) 3, 3.a, Language (3rd) 2.f, (4th) 2, 2.d)

MATERIALS Prepare 40 or more word cards comprising four suits and four Crazy Eight cards designated by the numeral 8. In this example, words with long-*a* are used: *rainbow, painter, raisin, complain, remain, explain, trainer, daisy, exclaim, regain, refrain, waiter, crayon, mayor, maybe, decay, today, payment, player, prayer, delay, hooray, dismay, replay, grateful, bracelet, mistake, parade, amaze, basement, escape, vibrate, baseball, insane, replace, neighbor, weightless, freighter, eighteen, eighty.*

PROCEDURES

1. The dealer gives each player eight cards. The remaining cards become the draw pile. The dealer turns the top card of the draw pile over and places it beside the deck. This card becomes the starter card and is the first card in the discard pile.
2. The player to the left of the dealer begins by placing a card that matches the starter card onto the discard pile. Matches may be made in three ways:
   - By pattern: **cray**on/hoo**ray** or **wait**er/com**plain**
   - By accent: first syllable **train**er/**pray**er or second syllable de**cay**/com**plain**
   - By unaccented syllable: **dai**sy/**eigh**ty or pay**ment**/base**ment**
3. With a Crazy Eight card, the player can change the suit to anything he or she chooses.
4. If the player does not have a match, he or she must draw from the draw pile until one is found.
5. If all the cards in the draw pile are used up, reserve the top card from the discard pile, shuffle the rest of the cards, and place them face-down on the table as the new draw pile.
6. Play continues until one player has discarded all of his or her cards.

VARIATIONS This game can be adapted simply by making up a new deck using words that focus on another spelling feature. Remember that the deck must have four suits and allow for matching by at least two different elements.

7.13 Pair Them Up

In this version of Memory or Concentration, students match up unusual plurals. (CCSS Language (3rd) 1.b)

Adaptable
for Other Stages
● ● ● ● ○

MATERIALS Create 11 sets of cards using word pairs such as the following: *wife/wives, leaf/leaves, life/lives, wolf/wolves, knife/knives, man/men, woman/women, mouse/mice, goose/geese, tooth/teeth, child/children*. Make one card each of *fish, sheep,* and *deer*.

PROCEDURES
1. Shuffle the cards and lay them all out face-down in a 5 × 5 array.
2. Each player turns over two cards at a time. If the cards make a match, the player keeps them and turns over two more.
3. If *fish, sheep,* or *deer* are turned over, there is no match and the player automatically gets to keep the card and go again.

VARIATIONS Create a similar game for two-syllable homophones (*berry, bury*) or for irregular past-tense pairs: *sleep/slept, slide/slid, shine/shone, freeze/froze, say/said, think/thought,* and so on.

7.14 The Apple and the Bushel

The purpose of this board game is to give students added practice in differentiating between *-le* and *-el* endings. (CCSS Language (3rd) 2.e, (4th) 2.d, (5th) 2.e)

MATERIALS Prepare the Apple and Bushel game board (see Figure 7.15) and word cards with words that end in *-el* and *-le* (*bushel, angel, apple, angle*).

PROCEDURES
1. Players draw for each other and read the word aloud.
2. Players must spell the word orally or in writing correctly and then move the marker to the nearest *-le* or *-el* ending that spells the word.
3. The game continues until one player reaches the bushel. (*Note*: To get in the bushel, an *-el* word must be drawn. A player who draws an *-le* word must move backward and continue playing from that space.)

VARIATION Add words that end with *-il* (*pencil*) and *-al* (*pedal*).

FIGURE 7.15   Apple and Bushel Game Board

7.15 Prefix Spin

This game for two to four players reinforces the idea that prefixes and base words can be combined in different ways. Let students play this after they have sorted words with the featured prefixes. (CCSS Foundational Skills (3rd–5th) 3.a)

MATERIALS Make a spinner using the directions in Appendix F. Divide the spinner into six sections and write each of these prefixes in a section: *mis-, pre-, un-, dis-,* and *re-* (use *re-* twice because it can be used in twice as many words as the others; see Figure 7.16). Prepare a deck of 24 cards with the following base words written on them: *judge, match, take, wrap, set, test, view, charge, pay, able, like, form, count, place, use, order, cover,* and *pack* (you can duplicate the last six to enlarge

FIGURE 7.16 **Prefix Spin**

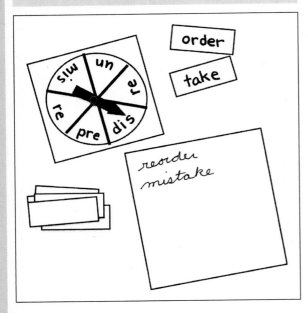

the deck; each can combine with three of the prefixes—for example, *misplace*, *replace*, and *displace*). Include paper and pencil for each player to record their matches. You may also want to include a list of allowable words to solve disputes. Matches include the following:

> miscount, misjudge, mismatch, misplace, mistake, misuse, prejudge, preset, pretest, preview, preform, preorder, prepay, recount, rematch, replace, retake, reuse, reset, retest, review, recharge, reform, reorder, repay, recover, repack, rewrap, unable, uncover, unlike, unpack, unwrap, discount, displace, discharge, disorder, disable, discover, dislike, disuse

PROCEDURES

1. Turn the base word cards face-down in a deck in the center of the playing area. Turn up one card at a time.
2. The first player spins for a prefix (such as *un-*). If the prefix can be added to the base word to form a real word (such as *unwrap*), the player takes the card and records the whole word on paper.
3. If the first player spins a prefix that cannot be added (such as *mis-*), the next player spins and hopes to land on a prefix that will work with the base word. This continues until someone can form a word.
4. A new base word is turned up for the next player and the game continues.
5. The winner is the player who has the most base word cards at the end of the game.

VARIATIONS

1. Use two spinners with suffixes written on the second one, such as *-s*, *-ed*, *-ing*, and *-able*. Award a bonus point when a player can use both the prefix and suffix with a base word, as in *replaceable* or *discovering*.
2. Make two sets of cards with the base words and pass out four words to each player that are laid out face-up. Each player spins and tries to match the prefix with one of the words he or she has. A word that is successfully matched can be turned over in a point pile and another card drawn so the player always has four cards for possible matches. This works well with prefixes that might not be as common as the original five.

7.16 Homophone Solitaire

Building on the traditional game of Solitaire, this simple card game requires flexible thinking and versatile attention to words. Word cards are matched by homophone, syllable pattern, or whether the homophonic spelling change is in the stressed or unstressed syllable. The object of the game is to end up with all the words in one pile. (CCSS Foundational Skills (3rd–5th) 3, Language (3rd–5th) 4)

MATERIALS You will need 52 word cards using two-syllable homophones. The cards are composed of two suits: (a) homophones in the accented syllable, and (b) homophones in the unaccented syllable. There are 13 pairs of matching homophones from each suit. (See the homophone list in Appendix E.)

PROCEDURES

1. Shuffle the deck, then turn one card over at a time. Say the word, observe the pattern, and place the card down, face-up.

2. Turn over the next card. Place it on top of the previous card if it matches by any of the following three features:

- Exact homophone (e.g., *alter/altar*).
- Syllable pattern: VCCV doublet (e.g., *mussel* could be placed on *lesson*); VCCV different (e.g., *canvas* could be placed on *incite*); open V/CV (e.g., *miner* could be placed on *rumor*); closed VC/V (e.g., *baron* could be placed on *profit*).
- Spelling change in the accented or unaccented syllable. For example, suppose *sender* was the last card played; the homophone for *sender* is *cinder*—the spelling change in the *sender/cinder* homophone pair occurs in the accented syllable. If a student is holding the card *morning*, she could place it on *sender* because the homophone for *morning* is *mourning*, which also has the spelling change in the accented syllable. Alternately, if the student is holding the card *presents*, he could play it on *miner* because the homophone for *presents* is *presence* and the homophone for *miner* is *minor*—the spelling change occurs in the *un*stressed syllables.

3. If there is no match, place the card to the right of the last card played.

4. Continue play in this way, placing cards with no matches to the right of the last card played. Stacks may be picked up and consolidated at any time. The top card played on a stack determines the movement.

5. Players may move back no more than four stacks for play.

6. Play continues until the entire deck is played. Then shuffle and play again!

Word Study for Advanced Readers and Writers

THE DERIVATIONAL RELATIONS STAGE

Derivational relations describes the type of word knowledge that more advanced readers and writers develop in the final stage. The term emphasizes how spelling and vocabulary knowledge at this stage grow primarily through processes of *derivation*—from a single base word or word root, we derive related words by adding prefixes and suffixes. Though students start exploring these processes in the within word pattern and syllables and affixes stages, their understanding expands and becomes much more elaborate at the derivational relations stage. Exploring words at the derivational relations stage draws on extensive experiences in reading and writing (e.g., Berninger, Abbott, Nagy, & Carlisle, 2009; Cunningham & Stanovich, 2003; Mahony, Singson, & Mann, 2000; Smith, 1998). The word sorts that students do at this level, together with their exploration of words, generally have more to do with *vocabulary* development than simply spelling development.

We will visit the sixth- and seventh-grade classrooms of Jorge Ramirez and Kelly Rubero several times in this chapter. Here, Mr. Ramirez illustrates how a teacher can guide students to understand how thinking about the base word and its meaning can be a clue to spelling a word.

Writing the misspelled word COMPISITION on the board, Mr. Ramirez begins: "I'd like to point something out to you: Words that are related in meaning are often related in spelling as well. For example [pointing to COMPISITION], everything is correct in this word except for the letter *i* in the second syllable. However, there's a related word in meaning and spelling that actually provides a clue to the correct spelling. Any ideas what this word might be?"

No one responds. Mr. Ramirez continues. "Well, let's look at this word [writes *compose* directly above COMPISITION]. Are *compose* and *composition* related in meaning? Yes, they are! Can you hear the long *o* sound in *compose*? You know how to spell this sound, and because *compose* and *composition* are related in meaning, the *o* in *compose* is the clue to the spelling of what we call the schwa sound in *composition*.

"Keeping this fact in mind can help you spell a word you may not be sure of, like *composition*. Why? Because schwas don't give you any clue to the spelling—they can be spelled with any of the vowel letters. You've got a powerful strategy you can use, though: thinking of a related word, like *compose*, gives you a clue.

"Let's try another one. Here's a misspelling I've seen a lot." He writes OPPISITION on the board. "Is there a word that is related in meaning and spelling that can give you a clue about how to spell the schwa sound?" He points to the *i* in the second syllable of OPPISITION.

There are a few seconds of silence before Darci tentatively responds, "*Oppose*?"

"Could be! Let's check it out." He writes *oppose* directly above OPPISITION. "We can clearly hear the sound that *o* in the second syllable of *oppose* stands for, and sure enough, *opposition* comes from *oppose*—they're similar in meaning—so Darci is right! *Oppose* gives us the clue for remembering the spelling of *opposition*. This week we will be looking at more words that are related in meaning and spelling as well. By looking at words that are related to ones you're trying to spell, you will discover a helpful clue to the spelling." ●

Development of Students in the Derivational Relations Stage

We find students in the derivational relations stage in upper elementary, middle school, high school, and into adulthood. Students at this level are fairly competent spellers, so the errors they make are "high level," requiring a more advanced foundation of spelling and vocabulary. However, misspellings such as INDITEMENT, ALLEDGED, IRELEVANT, and ACCOMODATE occur even among highly skilled and accomplished readers and writers. (Indeed, the persistence of such misspellings leads many adults to lament that, though they are good readers, they are "terrible" spellers!) Exploring the logic underlying correct spellings of these words not only helps us learn and remember the correct spelling but, more importantly, leads to a deeper understanding and appreciation of how words work. This understanding and appreciation leads in turn to the growth and differentiation of concepts—to vocabulary development.

Reading in the Derivational Relations Stage

The type of word knowledge that underlies advanced reading and writing includes an ever-expanding conceptual foundation and the addition of words that represent these concepts. Advanced readers can explore the Greek and Latin word elements that are the important morphemes out of which thousands of words are constructed. This is a **generative** process (Templeton, 2011/2012; Templeton et al., 2015), and linguists estimate that 60 to 80 percent of English vocabulary is generated by combining roots, prefixes, and suffixes (Nagy & Anderson, 1984). Over 90 percent of science and technology vocabulary is generated through this process (Green, 2008). Students who understand this generative process are in a position to analyze and understand the unfamiliar domain-specific academic vocabulary they will encounter in the reading materials of middle school and high school. Reading is the primary means by which students gain access to these words; the words simply do not occur as often in oral language. The explicit, generative, and deep study of written vocabulary adds to students' reading experience and conceptual development.

Readers at the derivational stage develop their understanding of the "meaning" layer of orthography quite extensively. This understanding, based primarily on morphological knowledge, supports their perception and identification of polysyllabic words. During the reading process at this stage, in addition to the syllabic chunks that intermediate readers and students in the syllables and affixes stage find in longer words, the advanced reader picks up **morphemic** or meaning chunks as well (Taft, 2003; Templeton, 1992). For example, an intermediate reader attempting to read the word *morphology* analyzes it syllable by syllable, picking up the letter sequences *mor-pho-lo-gy*. The advanced reader likely uses **morphemic analysis**, picking up on the meaning chunks in *morph-ology*, which cross syllable boundaries and offer insights into the meaning of the word (*morph* = structure, *ology* = study of).

Writing in the Derivational Relations Stage

Proficient writers have the potential to use the forms and functions—structures and purposes—of different genres. Together with their expanding vocabularies, this knowledge of form and function helps to inform their voice, or stance, which in turn guides their word choice when they write and revise. This understanding and sensitivity is often evident in their informal writing as well, such as in journals. Figure 8.1 presents an excerpt from a sixth-grader's response journal; her literature response group has been reading Scott O'Dell's *Island of the Blue Dolphins*. Her writing shows literary insights ("Every once in a while, the book gives you hints about things that will happen . . .") and a humorous stance ("Sometimes this book is Eerrie with a capital E").

FIGURE 8.1   Sixth-Grader's Response Journal—*Island of the Blue Dolphins*

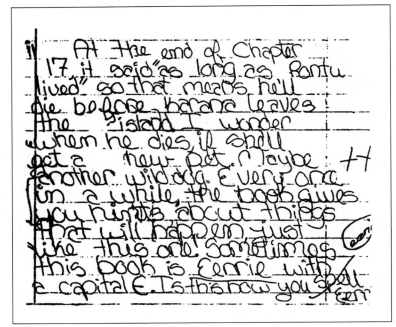

Source: From S. Templeton. *Children's Literacy Text*, 1st ed. Copyright © 1995 Wadsworth, a part of Cengage Learning, Inc. Reproduced by permission. www.cengage.com/permissions

Vocabulary Learning in the Derivational Relations Stage

Through wide reading and study in specific content domains, students' growth in general academic, as well as domain-specific, vocabulary accelerates dramatically during the derivational relations stage. It is important to note the distinction between *word-specific* and *generative* vocabulary instruction at this stage. There are effective activities for teaching a deep understanding of the concepts that specific words represent, which has been the traditional objective of vocabulary instruction (Beck, McKeown, & Kucan, 2013). It is equally important, however, to teach *about* words—the generative morphological processes by which meaningful word parts combine (Bowers & Kirby, 2010; Nagy, 2007; Templeton, 2011/2012; Templeton et al., 2015). Although students are introduced to the base word/word root distinction during the syllables and affixes stage, their understanding of the generative features of Greek and Latin affixes and roots really takes off during the derivational relations stage.

Flanigan et al. (2011) note that developing students' generative understanding is like the old saying, "Give someone a fish, they can eat for a day. Teach them to fish, they can eat for a lifetime." Word-specific instruction gives students the fish; generative instruction teaches them *how* to fish. For this reason, most of this chapter emphasizes generative instruction—giving students the keys to fully unlock the meaning code in the structure of English words.

Word sorts continue to be an effective context in which meaning and structure are explored. We will examine the relationships between spelling and meaning in some depth, because these relationships are generative and apply to most words in the English language. Word sorts also help students remember the spellings and meanings of specific words.

CONCEPT SORTS. An excellent framework for developing word-specific knowledge as well as relationships among the concepts that the words represent, concept sorts help activate background knowledge and generate interest in and questions about the topic. Based on the students' level of background knowledge, concept sorts may be closed or open, depending on whether categories are defined. Usually, the words to be sorted are the key vocabulary and important related words for a topic of study.

For example, the following vocabulary terms are for a science unit focusing on "Heavenly Bodies:"

> planet star sun moon asteroid comet meteorite meteoroid nebula white dwarf supernova black hole neutron star galaxy

The teacher has selected words the students know (*planet*, *star*, *moon*, *sun*), as well as some of the new words for the unit (*asteroid*, *neutron star*, *white dwarf*). Because the students have some background knowledge about space and astronomy, the teacher asks them to work with a partner to see how many different ways they can think of to sort the words or concepts, producing the following possibilities:

- In or out of our solar system
- Single bodies or members of a group
- Generating light or reflecting light

The following is one possible Single Body/Member of a group concept sort.

Single Body	Member of a Group	Not Sure
sun	planet	meteoroid
star	moon	nebula
asteroid	meteorite	white dwarf
comet		
supernova		
black hole		
galaxy		
neutron star		

As students discuss the sort, they can move the words and concepts in one category to any of the other two categories. In the process, more background information is engaged and uncertainties clarified.

DICTIONARIES. Because students use dictionaries frequently in the derivational relations stage, ensure that they understand the features — pronunciation guides, multiple definitions, sample sentences, parts of speech, and so on (see Chapter 7). Have at least one dictionary in the classroom that has information about word origins. This information is usually in brackets at the end of a main entry. Online dictionaries, such as OneLook and YourDictionary, are also useful. The following materials should always be readily available to students:

- Intermediate and collegiate dictionaries; enough copies for six to eight students to work in a small group
- Thesaurus collection: enough for six to eight students in small-group and whole class study
- Several word origin (etymological) dictionaries and root books (see next section)

Older students are often interested in the history of dictionaries. An excellent book that is accessible to many middle-grade advanced readers and writers is Joshua Kendall's *The Forgotten Founding Father: Noah Webster's Obsession and the Creation of an American Culture* (2010). Books that provide fascinating insights to share with students as they explore dictionaries more extensively are Simon Winchester's *The Professor and the Madman: A Tale of Murder, Insanity, and the Making of the Oxford English Dictionary* (1998) and *The Meaning of Everything: The Story of the Oxford English Dictionary* (2003).

Continue to model your own use and curiosity about dictionaries, including the serendipitous discoveries you can make—this helps develop your students' word consciousness. When looking up *graph*, for example, a note about *grafitti* caught seventh-grade teacher Kelly Rubero's eye and she was delighted to learn (and share with her students) that *graffiti* is an Italian plural form of *graffito* and both, like *graph*, are related to Greek *graphein* (to write). While electronic dictionaries have their place, one advantage of books is that students end up browsing the page and coming across other interesting facts about words.

Keep dictionaries handy when introducing word sorts so that students can check the accuracy of their morphological analyses. For example, after sorting words by the root *spec* and hypothesizing that it means "to look," students were unsure about how *speculate* fit that meaning. After looking at definitions and illustrative uses of *speculate* in several dictionaries they decided that one would be likely to look closely at something in the process of thinking about it or before taking a chance on buying it (Flanigan, Templeton, & Hayes, 2012).

PD TOOLKIT™
for Words Their Way®

Vocabulary With Root Tree
Observe how Ms. Robero explores word origins with a Root Tree.

WORD ORIGINS. Exploring dictionaries and the information they provide leads into the more sustained study of word origins. Exploring word origins and the processes of creating words provides a powerful knowledge base for learning vocabulary and spelling, as well as for facilitating more effective reading and writing. **Etymology**, the study of word origins (from the Greek *etymon*, meaning "true sense of a word"), may develop into a lifelong fascination for many students. As you engage students in examining word roots and affixes, the groundwork for more focused exploration of etymology and a lifelong love of word histories and vocabulary.

Students develop a real sense of how words work at this level as well as a general sense of how words can move through history. Ms. Rubero often reminds her students of the depth of their insights as they engage in this type of exploration during word study. Using resources like those presented here, and particularly in Shipley's *Origins of English Words* (2001), students can explore the derivations of words. These explorations invariably bring a wealth of additional words and relationships to students' attention. In Shipley, for example, the entry for *peter*, the original Indo-European root for "father," explains how the Romans created the name of the god *Jupiter* from the Greeks' *Zeus* + *peter*. Although all students benefit from these types of investigations, more verbally advanced students in the intermediate grades often become true "word nerds" once they are initiated. Studying word roots extends into the even more ancient Indo-European root forms (Templeton et al., 2015), a topic touched on briefly in the very last activity in this chapter.

Resources for Word Study—Greek and Latin Elements, and Word Origins

Greek and Latin Elements

Ayers, D. M. (1986). *English words from Latin and Greek elements* (2nd ed., revised by Thomas Worthen). Tucson: The University of Arizona Press.

Bear, D. R., Flanigan, K., Hayes, L. , Helman, L., Invernizzi, M., Johnston, F. J., & Templeton, S. (2014). *Vocabulary Their Way*: *Words and Strategies for Academic Success*. Glenview, IL: Pearson.

Crutchfield, R. (1997). *English vocabulary quick reference*: *A comprehensive dictionary arranged by word roots*. Leesburg, VA: LexaDyne.

Danner, H., & Noel, R. (2004). *Discover it*! *A better vocabulary the better way* (2nd ed.). Occoquan, VA: Imprimis Books.

Fine, E. H. (2004). Illustrated by K. Donner. *Cryptomania*: *Teleporting into Greek and Latin with the Cryptokids*. Berkeley, CA: Tricycle Press.

Fry, E. (2004). *The vocabulary teacher's book of lists*. San Francisco: Jossey Bass.

Kennedy, J. (1996). *Word stems*: *A dictionary*. New York: Soho Press.

Moore, B., & Moore, M. (1997). *NTC's dictionary of Latin and Greek origins*: *A comprehensive guide to the classical origins of English words*. Chicago: NTC Publishing Group.

Rasinski, T., Padak, N., Newton, R., & Newton, E. (2008). *Greek and Latin roots*: *Keys to building vocabulary*. Huntington Beach, CA: Shell Education.

Templeton, S., Bear, D. R., Invernizzi, M., Johnson, F., Flanigan, K., Townsend, D. R., Helman, L., & Hayes, L. (2015). *Vocabulary their way*: *Word study with middle and secondary students* (2nd ed.). Boston: Pearson.

Word Origins

Asimov, I. (1961). *Words from the myths*. Boston: Houghton Mifflin. (The most readable and interesting resource of this kind, available on any website that sells out-of-print books; such as Daedalusbooks and Alibris.)

Ayto, J. (1993). *Dictionary of word origins*. New York: Arcade. (Accessible for some students in the intermediate grades and most in the middle and secondary grades.)

Ayto, J. (2009). *Oxford school dictionary of word origins: The curious twists & turns of the cool and weird words we use*. Oxford: Oxford University Press. (Excellent for elementary and middle grades.)

Cousineau, P. (2012) *The painted word*: *A treasure chest of remarkable words and their origins*; and (2010) *Word catcher*: *An odyssey into the world of weird and wonderful words*. Berkeley, CA: Viva Editions.

D'Aulaire, I., & D'Aulaire, E. (1980). *D'Aulaires' book of Greek myths*. New York: Doubleday. (Of interest to third-graders and up; upper-intermediate reading level.)

Fisher, L. (1984). *The Olympians*: *Great gods and goddesses of ancient Greece*. New York: Holiday House. (Of interest to third-graders and up; third-grade reading level.)

Green, T. M. (2008). *The Greek and Latin roots of English* (4th ed.). Lanham, MD: Rowman & Littlefield Publishers, Inc.

Jones, C. F. (1999). Illustrated by J. O'Brian. *Eat your words*: *A fascinating look at the language of food*. New York: Delacorte Press.

Merriam-Webster new book of word histories. (1995). Springfield, MA: Merriam-Webster. (Of interest to most middle grade and secondary students.)

(continued)

(continued)

Robinson, S. (1989). *Origins* (Volume 1: *Bringing words to life*; Volume 2: *The word families*). New York: Teachers and Writers Collaborative. (Fascinating explorations for elementary students of selected Indo-European roots.)

Shipley, J. (2001). *The origins of English words*. Baltimore: Johns Hopkins University Press. (For teachers who are truly dedicated wordsmiths, Shipley's book is the ultimate source. A delightful read!)

Tompkins, G., & Yaden, D. (1986). *Answering students' questions about words*. Urbana, IL: National Council of Teachers of English.

Watkins, C. (2011). *The American Heritage dictionary of Indo-European roots* (3rd ed.). Boston: Houghton Mifflin Harcourt.

PD TOOLKIT™

for Words Their Way®

Greek Mythology: A Very Brief Primer
Students will enjoy reading this summary of Greek mythology.

Although the spelling of a word may appear odd, understanding its origin provides the most powerful key to remembering the spelling. Knowing that so many words have come from mythology, literature, and historical events and famous figures provides important background knowledge for students' reading in the various subject matter domains. The books and websites listed in Resource Connections: Resources for Word Study—Greek and Latin Elements, and Word Origins (this and previous page) also help. To stimulate students' curiosity about word origins, read aloud excerpts from such books when you have a few extra minutes.

Another way to add interest to studying word origins is to talk about words we imported from other countries. A significant number of words have recently come into American English from other contemporary languages, primarily Spanish (*quesadilla, chili con carne*) but some from French (*bistro, à la carte*) and Italian (*al fresco, cappuccino*) as well. As you may have guessed, such words initially turn up on our menus (Venezky, 1999). Given enough time, such "borrowed" words or "loanwords" become so familiar they don't strike us as foreign: *algebra* and *algorithm* from Arabic, *adventure* and *marine* from French, *husband* and *window* from Scandinavian, *canyon* and *ranch* from Spanish, *tomato* and *chocolate* from Native American languages. A popular classroom activity is to post a large world map on the wall and display words according to their country of origin. For example, where would you post the word *segue*?

ONLINE RESOURCES. The number of vocabulary- and word-themed websites seems to be increasing exponentially. Some of our favorites are listed in Resource Connections: Web Resources about Words (page 283). One in particular, *Visual Thesaurus*, offers significant potential for students' explorations. Users type in a word, and the word is then presented in a "Thinkmap" web that displays the meaning relationships shared by the target word or concept and other terms. Clicking on any word in these web-based resources reveals definitions and examples in context, as well as a new web of relationships. Figure 8.2 shows the thinkmap for the word *tranquil*. Clicking on the node above *tranquil* reveals the definition as it applies to individuals; clicking on the lower node describes *tranquil* in relation to a body of water. Figure 8.3 displays the thinkmap for *lithosphere*, an important term in a science unit on the four earth systems. Exploring the different nodes and the word or conceptual relationships they reveal provides students with a framework for exploring in breadth and depth an understanding of the lithosphere and its relationship to the other three earth systems, as well as their characteristics and functions. Another very helpful resource in the website is the "Vocabgrabber," an excellent tool for helping analyze the type, frequency, and relevance of the vocabulary in any text you use.

We must offer a cautionary note about any website that we recommend: although they are powerful tools, they do not know your students. *How* you use them and the information they provide ultimately rests on your judgment. For example, though "Vocabgrabber" will generate lists of important vocabulary words, *which* words you include is based on your judgment and knowledge of your students.

You can find additional ideas about word-specific activities for derivational relations students in Resource Connections: Teacher Resources for Word-Specific Vocabulary Activities.

Web Resources about Words

Do an Internet search for the following resources:

- American Corpus: The Corpus of American English (Davies, 2008) is an invaluable online resource for locating related words in English. It may be used to search for the occurrence of words in different types of texts.

- Etymology Online: Useful for exploring word histories, this site includes accessible etymological information. The site's author, Douglas Harper, updates it on a regular basis.

- OneLook: A comprehensive dictionary website on which most of the major dictionaries are available. This site also has excellent search capabilities for locating words that contain specific roots and affixes, as well as words that relate to a particular concept.

- Real Spellers: The educator who developed this website, Peter Bowers, shares lesson plans, lesson videos, and information about all aspects of English orthography; particularly strong are the morphological/etymological components.

- Verbivore: An excellent site for wordplay, containing many links to informative and engaging language and word sites.

- Visual Thesaurus: One of the most comprehensive interactive sites available. There is an annual subscription fee, but the benefits are more than worth the modest price.

- Visuwords: Similar in format to Visual Thesaurus, this site offers a more abbreviated web display. One significant feature is that, at the time of this writing, the site is free.

- Wordsmith: Subscribe for free and receive a new word in your inbox every day. Each week, words follow a particular theme. The categories of words discussed in this chapter—for example, eponyms and mythology—are represented.

FIGURE 8.2 Thinkmap for *tranquil*

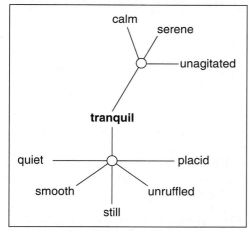

Source: Image from the Visual Thesaurus, http://www.visualthesaurus.com. Copyright © 2011 Thinkmap, Inc. All rights reserved.

FIGURE 8.3 Thinkmap for *lithosphere*

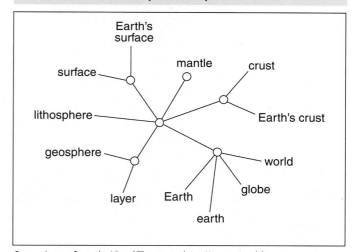

Source: Image from the Visual Thesaurus, http://www.visualthesaurus.com. Copyright © 2011 Thinkmap, Inc. All rights reserved.

Teacher Resources for Word-Specific Vocabulary Activities

Beck, I., McKeown, M., & Kucan, L. (2008). *Creating robust vocabulary: Frequently asked questions.* New York: Guilford.

Beck, I. L., McKeown, M. G., & Kucan, L. (2013). *Bringing words to life: Robust vocabulary instruction* (2nd ed.). New York: Guilford.

Blachowicz, C., & Fisher, P. (2009). *Teaching vocabulary in all classrooms* (4th ed.). Boston: Allyn & Bacon.

Blachowicz, C., Fisher, P., Ogle, D., & Watts-Taffe, S. (2013). *Teaching academic vocabulary, K–8: Effective practices across the curriculum.* New York: Guilford.

Diamond, L., & Gutlohn, L. (2007). *Vocabulary handbook.* Baltimore: Paul Brookes.

Flanigan, K., Hayes, L., Templeton, S., Bear, D. R., Invernizzi, M., & Johnston, F. (2011). *Words their way with struggling readers: Word study for reading, vocabulary, and spelling instruction, grades 4–12.* Boston: Pearson/Allyn & Bacon.

Nilsen, A. J., & Nilsen, D. L. F. (2004). *Vocabulary plus high school and up: A source-based approach.* Boston: Allyn & Bacon.

Stahl, S., & Nagy, W. (2006). *Teaching word meanings.* Mahwah, NJ: Erlbaum.

Templeton, S., Bear, D. R., Invernizzi, M., Johnson, F., Flanigan, K., Townsend, D. R., Helman, L., & Hayes, L. (2015). *Vocabulary their way: Word study with middle and secondary students* (2nd ed.). Boston: Pearson.

Templeton, S., & Flanigan, K. (2014). *Exploring words with advanced and verbally gifted students. Vocabulary Their Way: Words and Strategies for Academic Success* (Teacher Edition) (pp. T47–T51). Glenview, IL: Pearson .

Templeton, S., & Gehsmann, K. (2014). *Teaching reading and writing: The developmental approach (preK–8).* Boston: Pearson.

Orthographic Development in the Derivational Relations Stage

Table 8.1 summarizes some of the characteristics of spellers in this stage. At first glance, misspellings at the derivational relations stage appear similar to those at the syllables and affixes stage. Errors occur at the **syllable juncture** and with the vowel in unaccented or unstressed syllables. In contrast to the two-syllable words in which these errors occur at the syllables and affixes stage, derivational relations errors occur primarily in words of three or more syllables.

The Upper-Level Spelling Inventory (USI) is useful for collecting spelling errors for analysis and better identifying the spelling-meaning "landscape" that students are exploring. Specific spelling errors characteristic of this stage fall into three main categories:

1. Polysyllabic words often have **unaccented** syllables in which the vowel is **reduced** to the *schwa* sound, as in the second syllable of *opposition*. Remembering the root from which this word is derived (*oppose*) often helps students choose the correct vowel.
2. Several suffixes have different spellings despite similar pronunciations. For example, *-tion* in *opposition* is easily confused with *-ian* (*clinician*) and *-sion* (*tension*), which sound the same.
3. Other errors occur in the feature known as an **absorbed** or **assimilated prefix**. The prefix in *opposition* originally comes from *ob*, but because the word root starts with the letter

TABLE 8.1 Characteristics of Derivational Relations Spelling

	What Students Do Correctly	What Students Use but Confuse	What Is Absent
Early Derivational Relations *trapped, humor, sailor* CONFUDENSE for *confidence* OPISISION for *opposition*	Spell most words correctly Vowel patterns in accented syllables Doubling and *e*-drop at syllable juncture	Unaccented vowels in derivationally related pairs—CONFUDENT Some suffixes and prefixes— MONARCHIE/*monarchy* Other spelling–meaning connections—CRITISIZE/*critic*	*Note:* No features are completely absent
Middle Derivational Relations CLOROFIL for *chlorophyll*	All of the above plus: Common Latin suffixes and prefixes Spelling constancy of most bases and word roots	Some Greek letter–sound relationships— EM<u>F</u>ASIZE/*emp<u>h</u>asize* Greek and Latin elements—CIRCUM<u>F</u>RENCE/ *circum<u>fe</u>rence*	
Late Derivational Relations COMOTION for *commotion* DOMINENCE for *dominance*	All of the above	Absorbed prefixes— ILITERATE/*illiterate* ACCOMODATE/ *accommodate* SUPRESSION/*suppression*	

p (*pos*), the spelling has changed to reflect an easier pronunciation. (Try pronouncing *ob-position*—it's awkward to move rapidly from a /b/ to a /p/ sound.)

The Spelling–Meaning Connection

The spelling–meaning connection is another way of referring to the generative understanding of words—the significant role that morphology plays in the spelling system and in learning vocabulary. As we begin to explore spelling–meaning relationships, we help students become aware of this principle as it applies in English. Words that are related in *meaning* are often related in *spelling* as well, despite changes in sound (Chomsky, 1970; Templeton, 1983, 1992, 2012). As Mr. Ramirez pointed out to his students, this supports a powerful spelling strategy. If you do not know how to spell a word, try to think of a word that is similar in meaning and structure that you *do* know how to spell. Conversely, if you are unsure of the meaning of a word, or if you want to expand your vocabulary, think of words that are spelled alike and look for a meaning that is common across them. This consistency presents an excellent opportunity to integrate spelling and vocabulary instruction.

Being aware of logical spelling–meaning connections that apply to most words in the English language results in far more productive and reassuring word learning than the traditional one-word-at-a-time approach—demonstrating the "teach someone *how* to fish" aphorism here as well. For example, a general academic vocabulary word like *paradigmatic* is better learned, understood, and retained when related to *paradigm*, as well as providing a helpful clue to remembering the silent *g* in *paradigm*; in the same way, *mnemonic* can be related to *amnesia* and *amnesty*, all of which have to do with memory.

AFFIXES. Students first explore the spelling–meaning connection when studying affixes in the syllables and affixes stage, and review it in derivational relations with more advanced vocabulary and additional affixes. Table 8.2 presents the most frequently occurring prefixes and suffixes.

PD TOOLKIT™

for Words Their Way®

Assessment of Students in the Derivational Relations Stage

Ms Robero discusses her assessment results and the range of development in her class.

TABLE 8.2   **Sequence of Word Study**

AFFIXES: Prefix and Suffix Study

Review and explore affixes introduced during the syllables and affixes stage (*in-*, *un-*, *dis-*, *mis-*, *re-*, *ex-*, *pre-* ,*-er*, *-est*, *-ful*, *-ness*,*–less*, *-ly*) in more advanced vocabulary.

Additional Suffixes and Prefixes

-er/-or/-ian/-ist	people who do or believe			defender, creator, guardian, specialist		
-ary/-ory/-ery	having to do with (whatever it is affixed to)			stationary, victory, machinery		
-ity	quality, condition			mora*lity* matu*rity*		
-al/-ic	relating to, characterized by			fiction*al*, magnet*ic*		
inter-	between	*counter-*	opposing	*fore-*	before	*sub-* under
intra-	within	*anti-*	against	*post-*	after	*quadr-* four
super-	over, greater	*ex-*	out, former	*pro-*	in front of, forward	*pent-* five

Consonant and Vowel Alternations/Vowels in Unaccented Syllables

A number of suffixes affect the pronunciations of bases to which they are attached. These are examined in the context of consonant and vowel alternations.

Consonant Alternations		**Vowel Alternations/Unaccented Syllables**	
silent/sounded	*sign/signal, condemn /condemnation, soften/soft*	Long to short	*crime/criminal, **ignite/ignition**, humane/humanity*
/t/ to /sh/	*connect/connection, select/selection*	Long to schwa	*compete/competition, define/definition gene/genetic*
/k/ to /sh/	*music/musician, magic/magician*		
/k/ to /s/	*critic/criticize, political/politicize*	Schwa to short	*local/locality, legal/legality, metal/metallic*
/s/ to /sh/	*prejudice/prejudicial, office/official*		

Predictable Spelling Changes in Consonants and Vowels

/t/ to /sh/	*permit/permission, transmit/transmission*	/sh/ to /s/	*ferocious/ferocity, precocious/precocity*
/t/ to /s/	*silent/silence, absent/absence*	Long to short	*vain/vanity, receive/reception, retain/retention*
/d/ to /zh/	*explode/explosion, decide/decision*	Long to schwa	*explain/explanation, exclaim/exclamation*

Greek and Latin Word Elements

Review and explore Greek and Latin roots introduced during the syllables and affixes stage (see Table 7.5). Move to frequent Latin roots with the aim of gaining a working understanding of a few frequently occurring roots with relatively concrete and constant meanings: *tract* (draw, pull), *ject* (throw), *bene* (good, well), *gress* (move), *duc/duct* (lead), *vers/vert* (turn), *fac/fec/fic/fy* (make), *ven/vent* (come). (See lists in Appendix E for examples and additional roots.)

Greek Suffixes

Suffix	Meaning
-crat/-cracy	rule: *democracy*—rule by the *demos*, people
-ism/-ist	belief in; one who believes: *communism/communist, capitalism/capitalist*
-logy/-logist	science of; scientist: *geology*—science of the earth, studying the earth; *geologist*—one who studies the earth
-pathy/-path	feeling emotion, suffer/disease; *sympathy*—feeling with; *apathetic*—no feeling; *sociopath*—someone with a personality disorder
-phobia	abnormal fear: *claustrophobia*—fear of being closed in or shut in (*claus*)

(continued)

| **TABLE 8.2** | **Sequence of Word Study** *(Continued)* |

Advanced Suffix Study

1. *-able/-ible*   *respectable, favorable* versus *visible, audible*
2. *-ant/-ance*   *fragrant/fragrance, dominant/dominance*
   -ent/-ence   *dependent/dependence, florescent/florescence*
3. Consonant   *occurred, permitted* versus *traveled, benefited*
   doubling
   and accent

Absorbed Prefixes

1. Prefix + base   *in + mobile = immobile; ad + count = account*
   word
2. Prefix +   *ad + cept = accept, in + mune = immune*
   word root

ADDING *-ION* TO WORDS. The suffix pronounced "shun" can be spelled several ways, as in *protection, invasion, admission,* and *musician.* Hundreds of words in English end with this suffix, which means "act, process, or the result of an act or process." Usually a verb is changed to a noun by adding *-ion,* as in *elect* to *election* or *create* to *creation.* In the case of *-ian* it means "person" (*clinician, dietician*). This suffix affects sounds in interesting ways—it sometimes causes a final consonant sound to alternate (as in *detect/detection,* in which the /t/ becomes /sh/) or a vowel to alternate (as in *decide/decision*).

The generalizations governing changes in spelling when this suffix is added are complex, but you can address them early in the derivational relations stage because there are so many familiar words to examine. In order to spell the /shən/ suffix (the symbol ə stands for the "schwa" sound, which is the least-accented vowel sound in a word), consider the ending of the base word. The following list summarizes the generalizations about this suffix and the order in which they can be introduced and explored.

1. Base words that end in *-ct* or *-ss,* just add *-ion* (*traction, expression*)
2. Base words that end in *-ic,* add *-ian* (*magic/magician*)
3. Base words that end in *-te,* drop the *e* and add *-ion* (*translate/translation*)
4. Base words that end in *-ce,* drop the *e* and add *-tion* (*reduce/reduction*)
5. Base words that end in *-de* and *-it,* drop those letters and add *-sion* or *-ssion* (*decide/decision, admit/admission*)
6. Sometimes *-ation* is added to the base word, which causes little trouble for spellers because it can be heard (*transport/transportation*)

In Figure 8.4, students first pair the base word (the verb) with its derivative (the noun) and then group the pairs by the spelling patterns to determine the generalization (e.g., words ending in *de,* drop the *de* and add *sion*). Students should also look for the type of vowel or consonant alternations that have occurred.

FIGURE 8.4   Word Sort to Explore *-ion* Ending

divide	division	produce	production
delude	delusion	reduce	reduction
deride	derision	introduce	introduction
allude	allusion	reproduce	reproduction

Sound Alternations

An excellent way to explore the spelling–meaning connection is to examine more directly how the sound of vowels and consonants change or alternate in related words. Despite these changes in sounds, the spelling often remains the same to preserve the meaning connection.

CONSONANT ALTERNATION. Consonants that are silent in one word are sometimes "sounded" in a related word, as in the words *sign, signal,* and *signature.* Other times, as we've just seen, the pronunciation of consonants changes when a suffix is added to words. Listen how the sound of the *t* in *prevent* changes in *prevention.* The *t* now has the /sh/ sound. Other examples include /s/ to /sh/ in *compress* to *compression,* and /k/ to /sh/ in *magic* to *magician.* This phenomenon is known as **consonant alternation.**

Begin examining consonant alternation with silent/sounded pairs such as *bomb/bombard, crumb/crumble, muscle/muscular, hasten/haste, soften/soft.* As students move through the grades, they will encounter more words that follow this pattern, thereby expanding their vocabularies (*column/columnist, solemn/solemnity, assign/assignation*). Rather than trying to remember the spelling of one silent consonant in one word, students learn the strategy: try to think of a word related in spelling and meaning; you may get a clue from the consonant that is sounded.

VOWEL ALTERNATION AND REDUCTION. In the pair *revise/revision,* the long-*i* in the base word (*revise*) changes to a short-*i* in the derived word (*revision*). **Vowel alternation** occurs in related words in which the spelling of the vowels remains the same despite an alternation or change in the sound represented by the spelling. These alternations occur as suffixes are added and the accented syllables change (e.g., *im POSE / IM po SI tion*). Students benefit most from the study of vowel alternation patterns when these patterns are presented in a logical sequence. Begin by studying related words containing simple vowel alternations that change from long to short vowel sounds as suffixes are added, as in *nature* to *natural, sane* to *sanity,* and *divine* to *divinity.*

Next, have students explore in depth the spelling of the schwa, or least accented vowel sound, known as **reduced vowels.** As affixes are added to words, the accented syllables change—*con FIDE* to *CON fi dent*—and the reduction in accent influences the sound of the vowel. The long-*i* is reduced to schwa in *reside* to *resident, oppose* to *opposition,* and *invite* to *invitation.* In many words, the vowel is reduced from the short sound to the schwa: *allege* to *allegation, excel* to *excellent, habitual* to *habit.*

Help students notice that often *multiple* alternations occur in a group of related words. This insight might lead to an investigation of how many vowel and consonant alternations they can find within a group of words, such as the following:

ferocious	ferocity
diplomatic	diplomacy
specific	specificity

In *ferocious* and *ferocity,* for example, there is a long-to-short-*o* vowel alternation and a /sh/-/s/ consonant alternation.

The spelling–meaning connection explored through consonant and vowel alternations plays an important role in fine-tuning spelling knowledge and expanding students' vocabularies. Once students understand how the principle operates in known words, show them how it applies in unknown words. For example, let's say a student understands but misspells the word *solemn* as SOLEM in his writing. Show him the related word *solemnity.* In so doing, you can address two important objectives. First, the reason for the so-called silent-*n* in *solemn* becomes clear—the word is related to *solemnity,* in which the *n* is pronounced. Second, because he already knows the meaning of *solemn,* he can understand the meaning of the new but related word *solemnity.* You have just used the spelling system to expand this student's vocabulary.

Greek and Latin Elements

For purposes of vocabulary development, as we saw in Chapter 7, we begin to explore Greek and Latin elements at the syllables and affixes stage. In the derivational relations stage, the advanced study of Greek and Latin word roots, along with spelling challenges, offers an incredibly rich terrain to explore, extending through middle school, high school, and beyond. Importantly, most significant vocabulary terms within specific academic domains comprise these Greek and Latin elements. If you are studying forms of government, words like *democracy, monarchy,* and *plutocracy* suggest examining the common roots.

It is important to note that, over the years, educators and linguists have used different terms to refer to these elements and to make distinctions between roots of Greek or Latin origin (Dale, O'Rourke, & Bamman, 1971; Henry, 2003; Moats, 2000; Templeton & Gehsmann, 2014). For example, roots of Greek origin are often labeled "combining forms," and those of Latin origin are simply "roots." This is to distinguish the flexibility of Greek elements from Latin elements. Greek roots such as *photo* and *graph* may combine in different places in words—at the beginning, middle, or end (*telephoto*, **graph**ic, **photo**graph). Latin roots, on the other hand, tend to stay in one place, with prefixes and suffixes attached (**cred**ible, **cred**ence, in**cred**ible). After students understand these word parts and how they work, it may be helpful—as well as interesting—to point out this distinction between Greek and Latin roots. You may also encounter the term **stem**, which usually refers to a base or word root together with any derivational affixes that have been added, and to which inflectional endings may be added. (Yes, that's a mouthful, and that's why we usually avoid the term in our instruction!) Here are some examples: *function* is a stem to which *-s*, *-ed*, or *-ing* may be added; *dysfunction* is also a stem to which these same inflectional endings may be added. As with so much of word study, we need to know the various terms and usages but must use them judiciously and consistently with our students so as not to overwhelm them with labels when they are first learning a concept.

In the following lesson, Mr. Ramirez shows his students how Latin word roots function within words. He begins by passing out a sheet of words and asks students for ideas about how to sort them. The students quickly discover that the words contain similar word parts—*struct* and *fract*. Mr. Ramirez writes the key words *fracture* and *construct* and then writes the rest into categories as students call them out.

Mr. Ramirez points out *fracture* and *fraction* on the board. "We know what these two words are and what they mean. What happens when you *fracture* your arm?"

Students respond, "You break it."

"What do you do when you divide something into *fractions*?" Mr. Ramirez elicits from the students that you break whole numbers down into fractions.

"Good! Now, both words *fracture* and *fraction* have *fract* in them. Is *fract* a word?"

Students respond, "No."

"It's a very important part of the words *fracture* and *fraction*, however. We call *fract* a *word root*. *Fract* comes from a word in Latin that means 'to break.' Remember our discussion about the history of English and how so many words and word parts in English come from the Greek and Latin languages? *Fract* lives on in the words *fracture* and *fraction*. Word roots are everywhere! Let's look at these words."

Mr. Ramirez points to the words under *construct: construction, structure.* "What's the same in these three words?"

Students point out *struct.*

"Good! You've found the word root! Now, let's think about what this word root might mean. Think about what happens when construction workers construct a building or structure." Students engage in a brief discussion in which the meaning "to build" emerges. "Right! *Construct* means 'to build something,' and *structure* is another term we often use to refer to a building or something that has been built."

Next, Mr. Ramirez points to the word *instruct* and asks the students how the meaning of "build" might apply to the word. Through discussion, students come to the realization that *instruct* refers to how learning or knowledge is "built."

Mr. Ramirez assigns his students the task of finding more words with the *fract* and *struct* roots over the next few days. Students brainstorm, use the class dictionary, and consult an online dictionary to develop a long list of words including **fract**ious, **fract**als, in**fract**ion, re**fract**ion, super**struct**ure, recon**struct**ion, un**struct**ured, de**struct**ion, inde**struct**ible, ob**struct**ion, and in**struct**ional. Students record the words they find in the word study section of their vocabulary notebooks and come together to compare their findings. ●

for Words Their Way®

Sample Generative Lessons
These lessons introduce
and develop middle and
high school students'
understanding of the
generative power of Greek
and Latin roots.

Word roots nestle within longer words and are the meaningful anchor to which prefixes and suffixes may attach. Roots also follow the basic spelling–meaning premise that words with similar meanings are usually spelled similarly. It is important to point out to students that spelling *visually* represents the meanings of these elements and preserves the meaning relationships among words that at first may appear quite different. The consistent spelling of word roots is students' best clue to identifying them and examining how they function within words (*inspect*, *spectator*, *predict*, *indict*). Occasionally, the spelling of the roots may vary—both *vid* (in *video* and *evident*) and *vis* (in *visible* and *television*) come from the Latin word *videre*, meaning "to see." Students may already have noted some of these variations. For example, ask them to think about how *receive* and *reception* are related in meaning. Students can now examine these words while attending to the meaning of the root within the related words (*ceiv* and *cep* both mean "take"). It also helps that these changes are usually predictable (see the next section).

At the derivational relations stage, exploring Greek and Latin elements begins with those that occur with greatest frequency in the language and are most transparent in the words in which they occur. They should be sequenced according to the abstractness of their meanings, from concrete to abstract (Templeton, 2004, 2012). For example, the Greek roots *therm* (heat) and *photo* (light) and the Latin roots *spect* (to look), *rupt* (to break, burst), and *dict* (to speak, say) are introduced and explored early in the sequence because their meaning is transparent or straightforward. The way in which other roots function within words is often not as transparent, so those roots are explored later—for example, the Latin roots *fer* (to carry) in *defer* and *spir* (to breathe) in *inspiration* are somewhat abstract or metaphorical. Table 8.2 lists appropriate Greek and Latin roots; more Greek and Latin roots are in Appendix E.

Predictable Spelling Changes in Vowels and Consonants

After students have systematically explored some word roots and their derivational relatives that share the same spelling, they can begin examining related words in which both the sound *and* spelling change. This change is predictable or occurs regularly in families. For example, the spelling change of the long-*a* in *explain* from *ai* to a reduced-*a* in the derived word *explanation* is not the only word pair in which this type of change occurs; it also occurs in *exclaim/exclamation* and *proclaim/proclamation*; a similar change from long to short-*e* occurs in *receive/reception* and *deceive/deception*. Students learn that, if the base word has the *ai* or *ei* spelling, the derived word's spelling is simply *a* or *e*. Students can examine these words after they understand the spelling–meaning patterns presented earlier. As noted in the previous section, they also are learning that these spelling changes occur within word roots.

Students first conduct a word sort in which each base word is paired with its derivative, and then sort the word pairs according to the specific spelling change that occurs. The following sort illustrates this feature:

receive/reception	exclaim/exclamation	detain/detention
conceive/conception	proclaim/proclamation	retain/retention
deceive/deception	reclaim/reclamation	
perceive/perception	acclaim/acclamation	

Advanced Suffix Study

A handful of suffixes present occasional challenges even for advanced readers and writers. The adjective-forming suffix *-able/-ible* seems to be a classic for misspelling. However, there is a generalization that usually helps determine whether this suffix is spelled *-able* or *-ible*. Consider the sort below and look for the root or base word from which each word is derived.

dependable	credible
profitable	audible
agreeable	edible
predictable	visible

If the suffix is attached to a base word or **free morpheme** (*depend*), it is usually spelled *-able*; if it is attached to a word root or **bound morpheme** (*cred*), it is usually spelled *-ible*. Base words that end in *e* usually drop the *e* and add *-able* (*desire/desirable*); however, soft *c* or *g* endings may be followed by *-ible*, as in *reducible*, and sometimes a final *e* is retained to keep the soft sound, as in *noticeable* and *manageable*. These investigations generate discussions of how taking words apart or morphological analysis leads to roots and the words they generate. For example, the root *ten* in *pretend*, *contend*, *tennis*, *tense*, *tent*, and *tendon*; the Latin root *facere* (for *do* or *make*) in words with the root forms *fac-*, *-fic-*, *fact*, and *-fect,-* as seen in words like *artifact*, *defect*, *factory*, and *manufacture*.

Students can understand the connection between the suffixes *-ant/-ance* and *-ent/-ence* when pairs are examined: *brilliant/brilliance*, *confident/confidence*. Sound is no clue, but if you know the spelling of a word that ends in one of these suffixes, that word is a clue to the spelling of the suffix in the related word (Templeton, 1980). At this level, most students know how to spell one of the words in such pairs correctly; making this spelling–meaning relationship explicit is extremely helpful.

Whether consonants are doubled when inflectional endings are added, in words like *committed* and *benefited*, is revisited in the derivational relations stage with words of more than one syllable. Mr. Ramirez provides a collection of words that double and words that do not, and challenges his students to figure out why. See Table 7.2 for a summary of the rules.

"Okay, we've got a few words here to sort. What do you notice about these words? That's right, they all end in *-ed*. What do you notice about the base words?" He and his students discuss the fact that in some cases the final consonant has been doubled before adding *-ed*, and in others it has stayed the same. He has them sort the words into two columns by those features:

excelled	edited
occurred	limited
submitted	orbited
referred	conquered

Mr. Ramirez asks the students to work in pairs to talk about what they see and hear when they contrast the words in both columns. He encourages them to read the base words in each column several times. If no one brings up "accent" as a possible explanation, he asks them to listen as he reads the base words in each column, emphasizing the accented syllable: *excel*, *occur*, *submit*, *refer*. Then he reads *edit*, *limit*, *orbit*, *conquer*.

"I get it, I get it!" yells Silvio. "The accent is on a different syllable! When it is on the last syllable you have to double!"

Silvio has uncovered the generalization that Mr. Ramirez is working toward: if the last syllable of the base word is accented, double the final consonant before adding *-ed* (and *-ing* as well). If the last syllable is not accented, then do not double the final consonant.

Mr. Ramirez follows up the sort with a bit of history:

"Remember when Elsa brought in the British copy of *Harry Potter and the Goblet of Fire* that her grandma bought for her in England and we noticed how the spelling of some of the words was different than in American English? For example, there were a lot of doubled consonants that we don't have—*benefited* had two *ts*. Actually, in just about every situation where we in the United States do not double the final consonant, people in other English-speaking countries do. Do you know who we can blame for making it so that Americans have to think about whether or not to double? Would you believe it was Noah Webster? Yes! The man who brought us our first dictionary!

"Actually, what Webster wanted to do was make English spoken and written in the United States different from English spoken and written in Britain. When he did this, our country wasn't getting along too well with Britain—after all, we had fought a war to become independent not long before! So in his dictionary of American English—the first of its kind—Webster decided to change many spellings. One of the most obvious ways was to take out the *u* in words such as *honour* and *behaviour*." Mr. Ramirez writes these words on the board. "He also switched the *re* in words such as *theatre* and *centre*." He writes these on the board. ●

When students notice exceptions to this principle—when they see the spelling *travelled* or *benefitted*, for example—ask them to check the dictionary. Though they will see the correct spelling they will also see the alternative spelling, perhaps with the label *Brit* because final consonants like *l* are more likely to be doubled in British English whether they are accented or not. (By the way, Mr. Ramirez was able to work the information about Noah Webster into his lesson because he had recently read Kendall's *The Forgotten Founding Father*, to which we referred earlier.)

Assimilated Prefixes

Students study prefixes first in the within word pattern stage, and explore them more systematically at the syllables and affixes stage. Some prefixes are obvious visual and meaning units that are easy to see and understand, as in *unlikely* or *inactive*. Students at the derivational relations stage examine a group of prefixes that is somewhat disguised, as in the word *illegal*. The only clue to the prefix is the doubled letters. Known as **assimilated** or **absorbed** prefixes, their spellings may pose a significant challenge for students because they depend on considerable prior knowledge about other basic spelling–meaning patterns, processes of adding prefixes to base words, and simple Greek and Latin roots. Most adults are unaware of how assimilated prefixes work, but such knowledge can resolve many spelling dilemmas—such as how to spell *accommodate*, one of the most frequently misspelled words in the English language.

The following sort explores the idea of absorbed prefixes. Present the words in a random list and ask students to discuss their meanings. Students are likely to conclude that they all seem to mean "not" or "the opposite of." When asked how they might sort the words, the following categories emerge:

ineffective	illiterate	immature	irregular	impossible
inorganic	illegal	immobile	irrational	impatient
inactive	illogical	immortal	irrelevant	improper
infinite	illegible	immodest		

Ask students what they notice about the base words in each column. You might suggest they try saying "inmobile" or "inrelevant." Though it's possible to pronounce them, it's definitely awkward—moving from the *n* to *m* in *inmobile* and the *n* to *r* in *inrelevant* is cumbersome. At this point, some students will realize that the particular spelling of the prefix *in-* often depends on the first letter of the base word, taking on the same spelling (i.e., being "absorbed"). In fact, if they go to the dictionary to look up the prefixes or the words, they will be referred back to the original prefix *in-*.

Mr. Ramirez describes the process for his students, beginning by posing the question, "If all these prefixes mean the same thing, why do we spell them in different ways?" The students notice that the spelling seems to be related to the base word; *il-* is used before words starting with *l* and *ir-* before words starting with *r*. "Good observations," he responds. "Let's take the word *immobile*. A long time ago, the prefix *in-* was combined with the word *mobile* to create a new word that meant 'not mobile.' Now, try pronouncing the word like it was pronounced when it first came into existence: *inmobile*. Does that feel kind of weird? Does your tongue kind of get stuck on the beginning of *mobile*? Mine sure does! Over time it became easier for people to leave out the /n/ sound when pronouncing the word. The sound of the *n* became 'absorbed' into the /m/ sound at the beginning of the base word *mobile*. Before long, the spelling of the *n* changed to indicate this change in pronunciation—but it's important to remember

PD TOOLKIT™

for Words Their Way®

Prefix Assimilation
In these two videos over two days, Ms Robero guides a small group discussion.

that this letter didn't disappear. They knew it was necessary to keep the two letters in the prefix to indicate that it was still a prefix. If the last letter of the prefix had been dropped, then the meaning of the prefix might have been lost."

Primarily Latin in origin, assimilated or absorbed prefixes are widespread in English; an extensive list of assimilated prefixes is in Appendix E. By the way, *accommodate* has two assimilated prefixes: the *d* in the prefix *ad-* is absorbed into the first letter sound of the second prefix *con-*, and the *n* in *con-* is absorbed into the first letter sound of the word root *-mod-* (literally, "to fit with").

Spelling Strategies

Students in the derivational relations stage can use a range of strategies to spell unfamiliar words. The sixth-grader whose writing appears in Figure 8.1 is certainly thinking about spelling in the final sentence—evidence of a spelling conscience. The proofreading tips described in Chapter 3 and strategies described in Chapter 7, such as using spell check, apply in this stage as well.

Word Study Instruction for the Derivational Relations Stage

The principles for instructing intermediate readers and writers also guide our instruction at the advanced level. As at the intermediate level, word study for advanced readers emphasizes actively exploring words and applying word knowledge to spelling, vocabulary development, and analyzing unknown words encountered in reading. We can initiate word study for advanced readers by observing, "You know, when you first learned to read you had to learn how spelling stands for sounds. Now you're going to learn how spelling stands for meaning."

Sequence and Pacing

Table 8.2 presents a general sequence for word study in the derivational relations stage. Just as at the syllables and affixes stage, deciding what features to teach is often restricted by the difficulty of the word meanings rather than any problems with reading or spelling the words. For example, assimilated prefixes are examined later because many of the words that contain them will not occur with much frequency in the reading materials or be in the speaking vocabularies of most upper elementary students (e.g., *immunity* or *innumerable*). Although you can include some new vocabulary words in every sort at this level, there should still be a good number of familiar words from which students can begin to make generalizations, moving from the known to the unknown.

An important caution: You may wish to confirm that students who seem to be at the derivational stage based on the Elementary Spelling Inventory (ESI) are indeed at that level. Administering the Upper-Level Spelling Inventory (USI) more accurately identifies what features students need to study in the late syllables and affixes and early derivational relations stages. While we suggest a sequence of study, you will probably find that most students can be instructed on a number of features at the same time, which allows some flexibility in terms of grouping and selecting topics of study.

EARLY/MIDDLE. Students in the early stage of derivational relations have mastered most syllable juncture conventions, including spellings of most prefixes and suffixes and what happens when they are affixed to bases; they are working through the juncture conventions that govern the spelling of the frequent suffix *-ion* (*-tion*, *-sion*, *-ssion*). Occasionally, a common prefix may be misspelled, such as *permission* spelled PURMISSION by analogy with words such as *purchase*, or *destroy* spelled DISTROY because of the pronunciation of the first syllable and the frequency of the prefix *dis-*. Students in the early phase are also still learning how meaning is a clue to spelling unstressed vowels, such as not realizing that IMPASITION (*imposition*) is explained by the related word *impose*. By the middle phase, the spellings of prefixes and most suffixes are fairly locked in, as are the spellings of most bases and roots across morphologically related words (*compete*/*competitive*/*competition*).

LATE. A few students in the upper elementary grades may be in the late derivational relations stage, but most will not reach this stage until at least middle school and high school. Students at this phase can spell most new academic vocabulary words correctly when first encountering them. They use but confuse assimilated prefixes, however, as well as the suffixes *-able*/*-ible*, *-ant*/*-ent*, and *-ance*/*-ence*. As we have noted, this phase is not an "end" to development but rather part of a never-ending, fascinating journey.

Assess and Monitor Progress in the Derivational Relations Stage

MONITORING PROGRESS

Students in the derivational relations stage generally are good spellers because they have already acquired a great deal of word knowledge. As we emphasize in this chapter, word study for these students focuses primarily on the generative aspects of morphology and how the structure of words is usually the key to their meanings. You should address more than spelling in assessments. When you do assess with a focus on spelling, you needn't call out all the words in a sort, but rather only 10 or 15. Every few weeks, administer a cumulative review consisting of selected words representing different elements and patterns. There are several ways to assess.

- Ask students to spell the words studied that week. This works well for endings such as *-ion*, *-ible*/*-able*, and *-ence*/*-ance*, in which sound is not a clue.
- Ask students to both spell and define words; definitions should be in their own words.
- Give students a base word and ask them to add suffixes, such as adding *-ion* to words like *separate* (*separation*), *invade* (*invasion*), and *commit* (*commission*). Use words that they have not sorted to test for understanding of generalizations.
- Ask students to generate words given a prefix, suffix, or root. For example, the root *tract* should yield words like *attract*, *traction*, and perhaps *tractor*.
- Ask students to generate a related word in which a consonant or vowel sound is heard. For example, "There is a silent letter in *moisten*. Write a related word in which you can hear the sound of the letter." (*moist*)
- Ask students to match elements to meaning, such as matching *hyper-* and *hypo-* to the meanings "over" and "under."
- Ask students to spell a word and then underline a prefix, suffix, or root and also define the element, such as *fracture* means "*break*."
- Provide a sentence and ask students to supply or select the target word, as in the following: He loved to learn *magic* tricks and wanted to become a _____.

As in the syllables and affixes stage, students at this stage can monitor their own progress. However, there is less urgency in this stage because word study for derivational relations is typically spread out over the middle school and high school years and beyond—literally for the rest of their lives. Think about the word sorts you do with students at this level as supporting their vocabulary knowledge, both word-specific and generative. Unlike earlier developmental stages, sorts at this level need not be one-week affairs. Rather, they often stretch across two and sometimes three weeks.

As at all stages, review and grade student vocabulary notebooks. Focus on the range of words collected during word hunts for particular patterns, the types of open sorts that are recorded, and how well new words have been collected and described. (See Templeton et al.,

PD **TOOLKIT**™

for Words Their Way®

Early Derivational Relations Spell Checks and **Early Derivational Relations Monitoring Chart**
These assessments for monitoring progress are available to print.

2015, for additional assessment ideas, including how to involve older students in effective self-assessments.)

Word Study with English Learners in the Derivational Relations Stage

English learners have the potential to be *more* sensitive to words than monolingual speakers simply because they must be more analytical—of their home language as well as English— in order to negotiate the nature of spelling–sound–meaning relationships (Templeton, 2010). The study of **cognates** is fruitful at the derivational relations stage and can also benefit native English speakers who might be learning Spanish, French, or German as a foreign language. Cognates are words in different languages that share similar structures and similar meanings because they share similar origins.

We know that a large number of words in English are derived from Latin; this is true for many other languages as well. You can see the spelling–meaning connection in *mater* (Latin), *madre* (Spanish), *mere* (French), *mutter* (German), and *mother* (English). Paying attention to cognates helps both English learners and native speakers of English see morphological similarities between their native language and their to-be-learned language. Just as with our word sorts in English, sorting English and Spanish cognates offers opportunities for examining spelling–meaning relationships and grammatical features. For example, students may notice the common suffixes and their spellings that key different parts of speech (Nash, 1997):

	Nouns	Adjectives	Verbs	Adverbs
English	alphabet	alphabetic	alphabetize	alphabetically
Spanish	alfabeto	alfabético	alfabetizar	alfabéticamente
English	favor	favorable	favor	favorably
Spanish	favor	favorable	favorecer	favorablemente

Opportunities for finding cognates abound in specific academic domains such as science (Bravo, Hiebert, & Pearson, 2005), math, and social studies (Templeton, 2010; Templeton et al., 2015). In science or math, for example, students may match and discuss what they notice about the following cognates:

English	polygon	quadrilateral	hexagon	pentagon	triangle
Spanish	polígono	cuadrilatero	hexágono	pentágono	triángulo

Word roots also offer a rich terrain for exploring cognates in other languages. Make it a point to look for cognates as you study the different Latin roots—*port* shows up in Spanish *importar* and *exportar* and means the same thing ("carry") as in *export* and *import*. Create a chart of cognates in your classroom that students can add to as they discover more words. While most cognates across languages have the same or similar meanings, it is also important to be aware of potential "false friends." For example, the Spanish word *suburbio* looks a lot like the English word *suburbia*, or *suburbs*, but the Spanish word *suburbio* refers to the slums (Swan & Smith, 2001). Likewise, the Spanish word *éxito* doesn't correlate with *exit* at all, but means "success." The following resource supports exploring words and patterns at the derivational relations level in Spanish, and supports extensive cognate study with English:

Helman, L., Bear, D. R., Invernizzi, M., Templeton, S., & Johnston, F. (2013). *Palabras a su paso—Derivaciones*. Glenview, IL: Pearson.

WORD STUDY *Routines and Management*

Keep three basic points in mind regarding students' word study at this level (Templeton, 1989, 1992, 2012):

1. Words and word elements selected for study should be *generative*, which means that, when possible, teach about words in "meaning families." This highlights the awareness that particular patterns of relationships can be extended or generalized to other words. For example, being aware of the long-to-short vowel alternation pattern in words such as *compete* and *competition* can generalize to words such as *reduce/reduction*.

2. The words that we initially select for students to explore should be based on how obvious the relationship is. For example, teach clearly related words, such as *represent/misrepresent*, before teaching words that are less clearly related, such as *expose/exposition*.

3. There should be a balance of teacher-directed instruction with students' exploration and discussion. See ideas about how to foster thoughtful active discussions in Chapter 3.

Teacher-Directed Word Study Instruction

Word study should take place all day long and in all content areas as you pause to examine words, talk about unusual spellings (e.g., *pneumonia*), search for clues to meaning in the word and in context, and look up and discuss words in the dictionary. But, as in other stages, students in the derivational relations stage still need in-depth systematic attention to features at their developmental level. We emphasize the importance of word study at this developmental level for middle and secondary students, especially if these students have not experienced this type of systematic word study in school prior to this time.

PD TOOLKIT™

for Words Their Way®

Weekly Schedules and Classroom Activities With Students in the Derivational Relations Stage and **Classroom Organization With Students in the Derivational Relations Stage** In these two videos, Ms. Rubero describes how she organizes word study and structures her weekly routines.

Routines

Consider the routines and word study notebook activities appropriate for earlier stages. Categorizing words through sorting is still a powerful learning activity; however, some teachers rely more on writing words into categories than on cutting out words and sorting them physically. Blind sorts still work well when spelling is an issue (as in *-able* and *-ible* sorts or when working with the /shən/ ending), but do not pose much of a challenge when the sort features prefixes and roots.

Word hunts should extend over longer periods of time. In addition to words and features pulled from literary and informational texts, brainstorming additional words (word hunts in the head) sometimes works well and dictionaries can become a place for word hunts. Students can be taught to search online dictionaries by using an asterisk before and/or after the word part to get a list of words (e.g., **cian* will give you words that end with *-cian*; **hydr** will yield the hundreds of words that contain this root).

Ongoing classroom displays of words provide continual review as words turn up in reading and in class discussions; these can be added to categories started weeks before. As students explore word histories, show them how to reference and read the entries in unabridged dictionaries and in the resources available for such exploration (see Resource Connections: Teacher Resources for Word-Specific Vocabulary Activities, page 284).

FIGURE 8.5   Illustrating Word Relationships

Routines that focus on the meanings of words are very important. For example, have students use the dictionary to look up and record definitions and word origins of selected words (but not 20 at a time!). Have students use words in sentences to demonstrate their understanding of meaning, but invite them also to try illustrations or cartoons. These visual representations can be powerful mnemonics, as shown in Figure 8.5. Having students work cooperatively and letting them share their sentences or drawings is engaging.

Games are a valuable way to review words not only for a test, but also over time. At this level students can create many games themselves based on popular games like Concentration, Rummy, War, Slap Jack, Uno, Trivial Pursuit, and Jeopardy. Give them blank game board templates from Appendix F or card stock for playing cards and they can do the rest. While creating games, they will remember the words and come to understand the feature better.

At this stage, exploring a particular group of words and the spelling–meaning patterns they represent offers a number of paths to explore. For this reason, some teachers adopt a two-week schedule that includes a word study contract such as the one in Chapter 3. Give students 20 to 40 words, and have them complete a selection of routines independently in school or for homework. Test students every two weeks and include an assessment of mastery of meaning as well as of spelling. Ask students to explain the meaning of a prefix, root, or particular words.

Word Study Notebooks

Word study notebooks are an integral part of students' word learning at this stage (Gill & Bear, 1989; Templeton et al., 2015). In this last stage of development, the word study notebooks may be called Vocabulary Notebooks. Students use the notebooks to record word sorts and add words to the sorts after going on word hunts. To begin, divide the notebooks into three sections:

1. *Word Study.* A weekly record of sorts, reflections, and homework, this is also the section to record words that consistently present spelling challenges. Thinking of related words is one way to help clarify spellings.
2. *Looking into Language.* Includes records of whole-group word study of related words, concept sorts, interesting word collections, investigations, and theme study words.
3. *New and Interesting Words.* Words that students encounter in their reading that really grab them (much as "golden lines" do in their reading) are *golden words* (Templeton et al., 2015). These are often new and perhaps difficult words. Teach the following steps to help older students collect golden words:

   - *Collect the word.* While reading, mark words that really grab you or that you find difficult. When you are through reading or studying, go back to these words. Read around each word, and think about its possible meaning.
   - *Record the word and sentence.* Write the word, followed by the sentence in which it was used, the page number, and an abbreviation for the title of the book. (At times the sentence will be too long; write enough of it to give a clue to meaning.) Think about the word's meaning.
   - *Look at word parts and think about their meanings.* Look at the different parts of the word—prefixes, suffixes, and base word or root word. Think about the meanings of the affixes and the base or root.
   - *Record related words.* Think of other words that are like this word, and write them underneath the part of the word that is similar.
   - *Use the dictionary.* Look the word up in the dictionary, read the various definitions, and record the one that applies to the word in the book you are reading. Look for similar words (both in form and meaning) above and below the target word and list them as well. Look at the origin of the word, and add it to your entry if it is interesting.
   - *Review the words.*

A realistic goal is to collect five to ten words a week. Students can share the word in class, as in the following example:

- Collect the word: *orthography*.
- Record the word and sentence: "English *orthography* is not crazy, and it carries the history of the word with it." p. 22, *Sounds of Language*.
- Look at word parts and think about their meanings: *ortho/graph* (may have something to do with writing).
- Record possible related words: *orthodontist, orthodox, graphics, orthographer*.
- Study the word in the dictionary, and record interesting information: "A method of representing the sounds of a language by letters; spelling." Origin: *ortho*—"correct;" *graph*—"something written."

When looking for meaning connections, related words include *orthodontist*, *orthopedist*, *orthodox*; *graph*, *graphics*. When you work with students to make the meaning connection for *ortho-*, say, "What does an orthodontist do? An orthodontist makes your teeth straight. And an orthopedist? An orthopedist makes your bones straight. And if you are orthodox, you live a 'straight' or correct life. And indeed when we look in the dictionary, *ortho-* means straight or correct."

Vocabulary Their Way® (2nd edition) by Templeton, Bear, Invernizzi, Johnston, Flanigan, Townsend, Helman, and Hayes (2015) provides background and a wealth of instructional support for students at this level, including engaging ways of developing and fully using word study/vocabulary notebooks. You should find this resource especially helpful for derivational level students at the intermediate grades, extending the types of activities and instruction presented in this chapter. In addition, you may find that it extends your own knowledge base as well and provides you with the confidence to explore words more deeply with your students.

Preparing Sorts in the Derivational Relations Stage

PD ToolKit™
for Words Their Way®

Print ready-made sorts, have students sort online or make sorts with the *Create Your Own* application.

There are a number of word sorts in Appendix D and on the PD Toolkit that are appropriate for more advanced derivational relations students. Additional words are in the lists in appendixes D and E, which suggest other sorts as well. These resources present avenues of word study that are engaging and rewarding for students who are verbally advanced. Students should already be able to spell and define at least half of the words. With more advanced students, a larger proportion of the words included in sorts may be unfamiliar, but the students usually are able to infer the meanings because these words share similar meaning elements with the known words.

When you consistently model this type of exploration and curiosity about words—*word consciousness*—it becomes part of students' learning repertories. Indeed, it is more a mindset than a strategy per se. Students who develop word consciousness become lifelong wordsmiths and almost automatically wonder about the relationships among words in general, and about a particular word specifically; for example, does the similarity in spelling between *applaud/plaudit* and *mordant/morsel* capture underlying meaning relationships? (Yes!) When you share this type of awareness and curiosity, you nourish the continual growth of vocabulary and conceptual networks.

RESOURCES FOR IMPLEMENTING WORD STUDY *in Your Classroom*

A sample of prepared sorts are on the website and in Appendix D. These resources offer sample sorts and lists of words for other sorts or to modify the sorts that are suggested.

Words Their Way®: *Word Sorts for Derivational Relations Spellers* (Templeton, Johnston, Bear, & Invernizzi, 2009) has prepared sorts divided into nine units of study with assessments. Although these assessments mainly tap spelling knowledge, they often bring out morphological or vocabulary knowledge as well (e.g., matching prefixes with their meanings).

Vocabulary Their Way® (Templeton, Bear, Invernizzi, Johnston, Flanigan, Townsend, Helman, & Hayes, 2015) offers guided walk-throughs in the appendixes that address the concrete-to-abstract spelling–meaning

continuum and Greek/Latin roots. These are particularly useful for working with middle-grade and secondary students.

Palabras a su paso—Derivaciones (Helman, Bear, Invernizzi, Templeton, & Johnston, 2013) supports exploring words and patterns at the derivational relations level in Spanish, and supports extensive cognate study with English.

Vocabulary Their Way™: *Words and Strategies for Academic Success* (Bear, Flanigan, Hayes, Helman, Invernizzi, Johnston, & Templeton, 2014). This resource addresses general academic and domain-specific vocabulary for the middle grades, as well as generative strategies that emphasize morphological analysis and etymology.

ACTIVITIES for the Derivational Relations Stage

Vocabulary activities presented in Chapter 7 work equally well at the derivational relations stage—for example, concept maps and concept sorts. Such activities are excellent for developing students' understanding of specific words. The activities we present here not only support word-specific learning, but further students' understanding of the generative characteristics of morphology. This understanding drives vocabulary development and more advanced features of English spelling. For each activity, applicable Common Core State Standards for Language (L) are listed for grades 6, 7, and 8.

8.1 You Teach the Word

The vocabulary demands of content domains are significant. One way to handle these is to assign one word to each student, who then becomes responsible for teaching that word to the rest of the class. Ask each student to create a small poster to add to a class word wall, such as the one in Figure 8.6, that includes a definition, a synonym and/or antonym, an etymology, a sentence, or an illustration. Students can share their posters, but also encourage them to think of creative ways to help each other learn the word, such as by acting it out. For more advanced students, see the "Word Museum" project in Templeton et al. (2015). (CCSS Language (5th–8th) 4.b, 4.c, 4.d)

FIGURE 8.6   Poster for Laissez Faire

laissez faire
/lay-zay fair/
definition: noninterference, lack of government intervention
origin: French laisser - to let + faire - to do
example: The teacher had a laissez faire attitude about chewing gum in school.

8.2 Break it Down

Conduct this as a group activity or as a game (Flanigan et al., 2011). Beginning with words the students have already studied, provide sentences containing each word. Using the questions provided in the template in Figure 8.7, each group analyzes—breaks down—a word and then justifies how their derived meaning fits in the context of the sentence. Later, after students have applied these questions with known words, extend to unfamiliar words. This way of thinking about words deepens the strategy for analyzing unfamiliar words they encounter when they are reading independently (Chapter 7). (CCSS [5th-8th] L: 4.b 4.c 4.d)

8.3 Words That Grow from Base Words and Word Roots

In this whole-class or small-group activity, students see directly how words "grow." It builds on and extends the understanding, begun during the syllables and affixes stage, of how word elements combine. (CCSS Language (6th–8th) 4.b)

MATERIALS You will need a drawing of a tree (see Figure 8.8).

PROCEDURES
1. Decide on a base word or a word root to highlight. Begin with more frequently occurring words; over time, move to less frequently occurring roots.
2. Write the base word or word root at the bottom of the tree, and think of as many forms as possible.
3. Write the different forms on individual branches.
4. Display the word tree in the classroom for several days and encourage students to think of, find, and record more derived words. At the end of the week wipe them off and begin again by introducing a new base or word root.

FIGURE 8.7 "Break It Down" Template

Breakdown Word: _____

How many meaning parts did you find in the word?
(write the word and circle roots, underline affixes)

How many prefixes, what were they, and what do they mean?

How many suffixes, what were they, and what do they mean?

How many roots/base words, what were they, and what do they mean?

Definition: Therefore, (explain what you think the words means and how the meaning elements combine to help you construct your predicted definition)

This fits the sentence because (explain how your predicted definition fits the sentence)

Source: Flanigan, K., Hayes, L., Templeton, S., Bear, D., Invernizzi, M., & Johnston, F. (2011). *Words Their Way with Struggling Readers*. Boston, MA: Allyn & Bacon.

VARIATIONS After making the words, students may use them individually in sentences and/or discuss their meanings. Confirm with the dictionary.

8.4 Latin Jeopardy

At least three students are needed for this game (a host and scorekeeper, as well as two players), but lots more can play as well; you can divide the whole class into two teams. (CCSS Language (6th–8th) 4.b)

MATERIALS Create a grid with five columns and six rows. Insert headers to indicate the categories. Make a clue card by writing the points on one side and the answer on the other. During the game, turn over the square that is requested so the answer can be read. An alternative for a large group is to use an interactive whiteboard version of the Latin Root Jeopardy and Double Latin Root Jeopardy boards shown in Figures 8.9 and 8.10.

PROCEDURES The game consists of two rounds: Jeopardy and Double Jeopardy.

1. The game is modeled after the *Jeopardy* television game. The clue is in the form of an answer and players must phrase their response in the form of a question: Answer clue: Coming from the Latin root *tract*, it means "a machine for pulling heavy loads." Question response: What is *tractor*?
2. Determine who goes first. The player selects a category and point value. The host uncovers the clue and reads it aloud.
3. The first player responding correctly adds the point amount of the question to his or her total or gets to keep the card that was turned over. He or she then chooses another category and point amount. An incorrect answer means that the points are subtracted.
4. The winner is the one with the most points.

VARIATIONS

1. Add rounds of Double Jeopardy and Final Jeopardy. When it is time for the Final Jeopardy question, players see the category, but not the answer. They then decide how many of their points they will risk. When they see the answer, they have 30 seconds to write the question. If they are correct, they add the number of points they risked to their total; if incorrect, that number of points is subtracted from their total.
2. Alternate from one player to the next, or from one team to the next, rather than who shouts out the response first. If one player misses, the other team gets a chance to respond. If they are correct, they also get another turn.
3. Include Daily Doubles. (The number of points for an answer is doubled and, if correct, added to the player's score; if incorrect, the doubled number of points is subtracted from the player's score.)
4. Develop a Vocabulary Jeopardy to accompany a study unit. Generate vocabulary cards from the unit that fit into four or five categories (e.g., "Food Groups" or "Habitats"). Write questions that relate to facts and concepts studied on cards. Teams of students play the game as a whole-class vocabulary review of the unit.

FIGURE 8.8 **Word Tree: Words That Grow from Base Words and Roots**

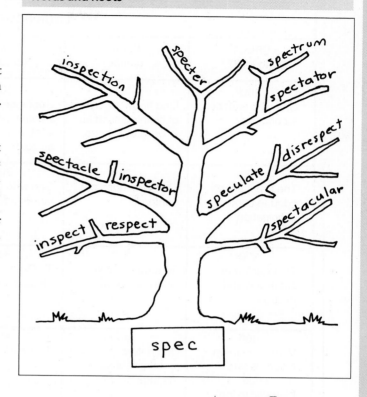

PD **pd** TOOLKIT™

for Words Their Way®

Greek and Latin Jeopardy
A ready to print version of this game is available

ACTIVITIES | DERIVATIONAL RELATIONS STAGE

FIGURE 8.9   **Latin Root Jeopardy Board**

LATIN ROOT JEOPARDY

SPECT (to look)	FORM (shape)	PORT (to carry)	TRACT (draw or pull)	DICT (to say, speak)
100 One who watches; an onlooker	100 One "form" or style of clothing such as is worn by nurses	100 Goods brought into a country from another country to be sold	100 Adjective: having power to attract; alluring; inviting	100 A book containing the words of a language explained
200 The prospect of good to come; anticipation	200 One who does not conform	200 One who carries burdens for hire	200 A powerful motor vehicle for pulling farm machinery, heavy loads	200 A speaking against, a denial
300 To regard with suspicion and mistrust	300 To form or make anew; to reclaim	300 To remove from one place to another	300 The power to grip or hold to a surface while moving, without slipping	300 A blessing often at the end of a worship service
400 Verb: to esteem Noun: regard, deference Literally: to look again	400 To change into another substance, change of form	400 To give an account of	400 An agreement: literally, to draw together	400 An order proclaimed by an authority
500 Looking around, watchful, prudent	500 Disfigurement, spoiling the shape	500 A case for carrying loose papers	500 To take apart from the rest, to deduct	500 To charge with a crime

8.5   Word Part Shuffle

Word Part Shuffle is a noncompetitive word-building activity (Moloney, 2008). A group of students receives a stack of cards consisting of most of the most generative prefixes, suffixes, and bases/word roots (see Figure 8.11). The group first creates words that may be found in a standard dictionary. Then the group coins a new word, using as many of the cards as they can. They create a definition for the new word and then share with other groups. Kara Moloney created a deck of these cards with color-coded margins indicating prefix, suffix, or base/root, which is available at on the verbum-struct-ion website. (CCSS Language (6th–8th) 4.b)

8.6   Quartet

Many games can be played with a deck of word cards made into suits of four. This game is much like "Go Fish," except the object is to collect and lay down a suit of four cards (or a quartet).

MATERIALS   Create 10 to 12 suits of four cards, composed of words that share a common root; for example, *biology, biography, biome, antibiotic.* Write the words at the top left so students can read the words when holding cards in their hands. (CCSS Language (6th–8th) 4.b)

FIGURE 8.10   Latin Root Double Jeopardy Board

LATIN ROOT DOUBLE JEOPARDY				
CRED (to believe)	DUCT (to lead)	FER (to bear, carry)	PRESS (to press)	SPIR (to breathe)
200 A system of doing business by trusting that a person will pay at a later date for goods or services	200 A person who directs the performance of a choir or an orchestra	200 (Plants) able to bear fruit; (Animals) able or likely to conceive young	200 A printing machine	200 An immaterial intelligent being
400 A set of beliefs or principles	400 To train the mind and abilities of	400 To carry again; to submit to another for opinion	400 Verb: to utter; Noun: any fast conveyance	400 To breathe out: to die
600 Unbelievable	600 To enroll as a member of a military service	600 To convey to another place, passed from one place to another	600 To press against, to burden, to overpower	600 To breathe through; to emit through the pores of the skin
800 Verb, prefix meaning "not"; word means to damage the good reputation of	800 The formal presentation of one person to another	800 Endurance of pain; distress	800 State of being "pressed down" or saddened	800 To breathe into; to instruct by divine influence
1000 An adjective, prefix *ac,* word means officially recognized	1000 An artificial channel carrying water across country	1000 Cone bearing, as the fir tree	1000 To put down, to prevent circulation	1000 To plot; to band together for an evil purpose

PROCEDURES

1. Each player is dealt seven cards; the rest are put in a deck. Each player looks through his or her cards for words in the same suit.
2. The first player turns to the next and asks for a particular root: "Give me any cards with the *bio* root." If the second player has any cards with the requested root, the player must give them up and the first player gets to go again. If the second player does not have any matches, he or she responds, "Draw one" and the first player draws from the deck.
3. Play proceeds in a clockwise fashion. When a player has a complete suit of four cards, he or she may lay them down. The player who has the most suits at the end—when someone runs out of cards—is the winner.

FIGURE 8.11   Word Shuffle Cards

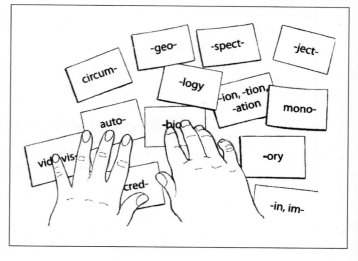

8.7 It's All Greek to Us

In this card game, the deck is composed of words derived from Greek roots. Three to five players may participate, one of whom will serve as game master, and hold and read definition cards. (CCSS Language (6th–8th) 4.b)

MATERIALS Using the list of Greek roots and derived words in Appendix E, prepare ten definition cards that consist of a root and definition, such as *derm* ("skin"). For each root, create four or more word cards (*epidermis, dermatology, taxidermist, hypodermic, pachyderm*). Write these words at the top so they can be seen when held in the hand.

PROCEDURES
1. The game master shuffles the word cards, deals ten cards per player, and places the remaining word cards face-down.
2. The game master reads a definition card and lays it down face-up. All players who are holding a card that matches the definition read it and place it below the corresponding Greek root. If no player can respond to the definition, the game master places the definition card on the bottom of his or her cards for rereading later in the game.
3. To begin the next round, a new definition card is laid down.
4. The player who discards all ten word cards first is the winner and becomes the next game master.

8.8 Brainburst

In this game, players compete to brainstorm as many words as they can that are derived from the same root. Only unique words earn points. (CCSS Language (6th–8th) 4.b, 4.c)

MATERIALS Write different roots on cards—such as *graph, phon, scope, aud, dict, port, tract, struct, spect*—roots that have a wide variety of possible derivations. Each team or player needs a pencil and sheet of paper. You will need a timer and a standard dictionary (condensed dictionaries may not have enough words).

PROCEDURES
1. Select one card and announce the root. Set the timer for two to three minutes. Each player or team tries to think of as many words as possible derived from that root.
2. When the timer goes off, players draw a line under their last words and count the number they have.
3. The player with the longest list reads the list aloud. If another player has the same word, it is crossed off of everyone's list. Any words that are not on another list (unique words) are checked.
4. Each player in turn reads aloud any words that no one else has called to determine if he or she has a unique word. Disputes should be settled with the help of a dictionary.
5. The player or team with the most unique words is the winner of the round.

VARIATIONS This game can also be played with prefixes (*ex-, sub-, pre-, post-*, etc.) and suffixes (*-ible, -able, -ant, -ent*, etc.).

8.9 Joined at the Roots

This concept sort is an effective extension of students' exploration of Latin and Greek word roots. It is appropriate for individuals, partners, or small groups. (CCSS Language (6th–8th) 4.b)

MATERIALS You will need a word sort board, word cards, and vocabulary notebook.

PROCEDURES
1. Model how to place words with appropriate roots under a particular category; for example, "Speaking and Writing," "Building/Construction," "Thinking and Feeling," and "Movement." Then involve students in the categorization.

2. Once students grasp how this categorization scheme works, they can work in small groups or in pairs. Each group or pair takes a different category and sorts words whose roots justify their membership in that category.

3. Have students write lists in vocabulary notebooks, and bring them to the larger group to share and discuss. (*Note*: Several of the words to be sorted may be placed under different categories.) Following are some examples of categories and a few illustrative words:

Speaking and Writing	Building/ Construction	Thinking and Feeling	Government	Movement	Travel
autobiography	technology	philanthropy	economy	synchrony	astronaut
photograph	construct	philosophy	demagogue	fracture	exodus
catalogue	tractor	attraction	politics		
emphasis					

8.10 Root Webs

Root webs like the one in Figure 8.12 are a graphic way to represent the links among words derived from a common root. (CCSS Language (6th–8th) 4.b)

PROCEDURES

1. Choose a set of common roots, such as *photo-*, *geo-*, *aqua-*, and *astro-*.
2. Model a web for students, as they complete their own webs in their vocabulary notebooks. Once students understand how to create the root webs, they can do them independently or in small groups.
3. Brainstorm related words. Students should use dictionaries to locate roots, verify their meanings, find their origins, and search for related words.
4. Honor all suggestions. Eliminate words that do not fit the meaning of a root. Lead students to examine parts and meaning.

VARIATION A progressive root web provides the context for a more systematic walk-through of how words are generated from a common word root. Figure 8.13 is an example of a completed progressive web for the root *ject*, meaning "throw." Walk through each addition of an affix on one strand of the web, writing the derived word and discussing its meaning with students. Invite students to complete the other strands, discussing the meaning of each derived word with the class. This model can then be used with other roots by students who work in pairs or small groups.

FIGURE 8.12 **"Root Web" in Student's Vocabulary Notebook**

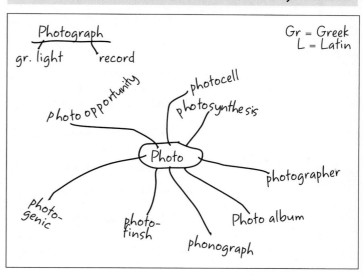

8.11 Identifying the Meanings of Word Roots

Given a series of words that share the same root, students analyze the words to determine the meaning of the root. Each group of three words can be finished with one of the words provided. For example, in item 1 of the first grouping, students look for which of the three words—*introspection*, *interrupt*, or *distract*—contains the same root as *spectator*, *inspect*, and *prospector* (*introspection*). In the next sentence, they write what they believe the root *spect* means. In the third sentence, they decide which of the remaining words—*interrupt* or *distract*—contains the same root as *corrupt*, *disrupt*, and *eruption*, and so on. This is an excellent activity for students to work on in pairs. (CCSS Language (6th–8th) 4.b)

FIGURE 8.13   Progressive Root Web

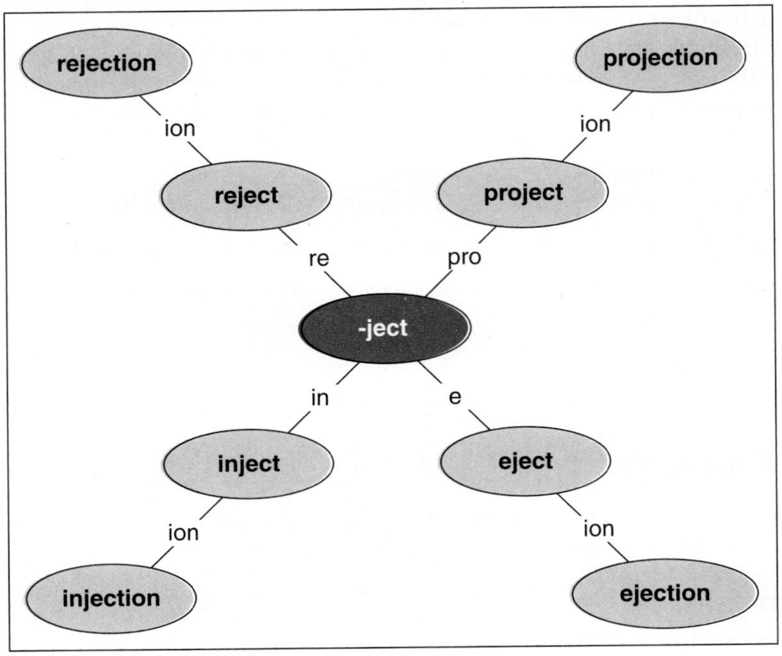

introspection   interrupt   distract

1. spectator, inspect, prospector, _____

The root *spect* means _____. (look, count, divide)

2. corrupt, disrupt, eruption, _____

The root *rupt* means _____. (speak, break, fall)

3. tractor, attract, extract, _____

The root *tract* means _____. (place, look, pull)

audience   refract   contradict

1. audible, auditory, audio, _____

The root *aud* means _____. (throw, hear, touch)

2. fraction, fracture, infraction, _____

The root *fract* means _____. (stretch, eat, break)

3. dictate, diction, predict, _____

The root *dict* means _____. (say, touch, fight)

dermatologist   nominative   invaluable

1. nominate, nominal, nominee, _____

The root *nom* means _____. (write, figure, name)

2. value, valor, devalue, _____

The root *val* means _____. (money, to be strong/to be worth, truth)

3. hypodermic, epidermis, dermatology, _____

The root *derm* means _____. (skin, medicine, platform)

VARIATIONS Following this format, groups of students can construct their own exercises and then swap with other groups. Appendix E has additional roots.

8.12 Combining Roots and Affixes

In a matrix such as the one in Figure 8.14, students indicate with an X words that can be made by combining the prefix and the root. Then they write the words below. A variation is to indicate with a "?" words that do not exist in English, but could. Students may write these words in a special section of their vocabulary notebooks, creating a definition and using each in a sentence. When students are uncertain about whether a word is an actual word in English, they may check it in the dictionary. (CCSS Language (6th–8th) 4.b, 4.c)

FIGURE 8.14 Matrix of Roots and Prefixes

	duce/duc/duct	port	spect	dict	tract
in/im		x			
trans					
ex					
pre					
		import			

8.13 From Spanish to English—A Dictionary Word Hunt

The purpose of this activity is to expand students' vocabularies through discovering relations among *cognates*. (CCSS Language (6th–8th) 4.b)

PROCEDURES

1. Look through a Spanish–English dictionary to find words in Spanish that remind you of words in English. Briefly note the definition or synonym (see Nash, 1997).
2. With an English dictionary, find words that share the same root or affix. Write these related words in your vocabulary notebook.
3. Record findings in the vocabulary notebook and create a class chart.

Following are sample entries on a class chart of cognates that one group of students collected in this activity.

for **English Learners**

Spanish (Translation)	English Relations	Spanish Relations
presumir (boast)	presume, presumption, presumptuous	presunción, presumido
extenso (extensive)	extend, extension	extensivo, extender
nocturno (nightly)	nocturnal, nocturne	noche, noctámbulo
polvo (powder)	pulverize (from Latin *pulvis*, meaning "dust")	polvillo, polvorear

8.14 The Synonym/Antonym Continuum

This activity encourages students to think about the subtle differences between word meanings as they work with antonyms and synonyms. (CCSS [6th-8th] L: 4.a, 4.b, 4.c, 4.d)

ACTIVITIES | DERIVATIONAL RELATIONS STAGE

MATERIALS Think of opposites like *hot/cold*, *brave/frightened*, *old/young*, *lazy/energetic*, and so on. Use a thesaurus to find synonyms for each word in the pair and write them on cards or in a list.

PROCEDURES Have students arrange the words along a continuum. At the ends of the continuum are the antonyms (words that are most opposite in meaning). Next to each of these words, students decide where to place synonyms (words that are closest to the meaning of the opposite words) and so on until all words are used.

For example, the words *balmy*, *frigid*, *chilly*, *boiling*, *frozen*, *tepid*, *hot*, *cool*, and *warm* can be arranged this way:

frigid frozen chilly cool tepid balmy warm hot

Students can first work individually and then compare their continua with one another. They should discuss differences and provide rationales for why they arranged particular words the way they did. The dictionary is the final judge of any disagreements. Encourage students to add other words, like *sweltering*, *steamy*, *balmy*, and so on, by brainstorming or using a thesaurus or dictionary. Give students a word pair of opposites and send them to a thesaurus to create a list of words. They can then order them as above or present them to another team to order.

8.15 Semantic Feature Analysis

This analysis (Anders & Bos, 1986) engages students in examining words and definitions in relation to each other. (CCSS Language (6th–8th) 4.b, 4.c, 4.d)

PROCEDURES
1. Write the words to be examined down the left margin of a matrix. (In this example, the words are *prefix*, *base word*, *affix*, *suffix*, and *word root*.) Then write the features of these words across the top. When you introduce this activity to students, list these features yourself. Later, after students understand how the analysis works, they have them suggest the features that will be listed.
2. Discuss the matrix with the whole class or with small groups. Students mark each cell with one of the following symbols: a plus sign (+) indicates a definite relationship between the word and a feature; a minus sign (−) shows the word does not have that feature; and a question mark (?) says that students feel they need more information before responding.
3. After students complete the matrix, point out (1) they now *really* know how much they know about each word, and (2) they also know what they still need to find out (Templeton, 1997). Figure 8.15 illustrates a semantic feature analysis completed by a group of sixth-grade students under a teacher's guidance to clarify the meanings of word study terms.

8.16 Which Suffix?

This activity is an excellent follow-up to previous work with base words, word roots, and suffixes. It is appropriate for individuals, buddies, or small groups. The suffixes included are *-tion/-sion*, *-ible/-able*, *-ence/-ance*, and *-ary/-ery*. (CCSS Language (6th–8th) 4.b, 4.c, 4.d)

FIGURE 8.15 Semantic Feature Analysis

	Cannot Stand Alone	Comes Before a Base Word or Root Word	Usually Comes from Greek or Latin	Can Stand Alone	Comes After Base Word or Word Root
Prefix	+	+	+	−	−
Base word	−	−	?	+	−
Affix	+	?	+	−	?
Suffix	+	−	+	−	+
Word root	+	−	+	−	−

MATERIALS You will need a word sort board, word cards, and a vocabulary notebook.

PROCEDURES

1. Decide how many suffix pairs to place at the top of the word sort board. (Note that several of the words to be sorted may be placed under different suffixes; for example, *permit*: *permissible*, *permission*.) Each card has the base word written on one side and the same word with allowable suffixes on the other side.
2. Mix up the word cards and place the deck with base words face-up. The students in turn choose the top card and decide in which suffix category it belongs.
3. After all the cards are placed, have students record in their vocabulary notebooks what they think is the correct spelling of the word.
4. After recording all the words, students turn over the cards to self-check the correct spelling.

VARIATIONS Students can work as buddies to explore a particular suffix "team" (e.g., *-tion* and *-sion*) to see what generalization(s) may underlie the use of a suffix.

8.17 Defiance or Patience?

The game Defiance (if using the *ant/ance/ancy* family), or Patience (if using the *ent/ence/ency* family), is for three to five players. The object of the game is to make as many groups of two, three, or four cards of the same derivation as possible and to run out of cards first. (CCSS Language (6th–8th) 2.b)

MATERIALS Using words from the lists in Appendix E, create a deck of 52 cards with suits of two, three, or four words (e.g., *attend*, *attendance*, and *attendant* is a set of three, and *radiate*, *radiant*, *radiance*, and *radiancy* for a set of four). Write each word across the top of a card, and your deck is prepared.

PROCEDURES

1. Each player is dealt five cards from the deck. The player to the left of the dealer begins the game. The player may first lay down any existing groups of two, three, or four held in his or her hand. This player then may ask any other player for a card of a certain derivation in his or her own hand: "Matthew, give me all of your *resistance*." (This could result in gaining *resistance*, *resistant*, *resistancy*, or *resist*.)
2. If a player does not have cards with the requested feature, he or she responds, "Be Defiant" (or "Be Patient," depending on which game is being played).
3. At this point, the requesting player must draw another card from the deck. If the card is of the same family being he or she is looking for, the player lays down the match and continues asking other players for cards. If the card is not a match, play passes to the person on the left and continues around the circle in the same manner. If the drawn card makes a match in the asking player's hand but was not in the group requested, he or she must hold the pair in hand until his or her turn comes up again. Of course, this means there is a risk of another player taking the pair before the next turn.
4. Play ends when one of the students runs out of cards. The player with the most points wins.
5. Players may play on other people's card groups, laying related cards down in front of themselves, not in front of the player who made the original match.
6. Scoring is as follows.

Singles played on other people's matches	1 point
Pairs	2 points
Triples	6 points
Groups of four	10 points
First player to run out of cards	10 points

VARIATIONS

1. Play a version called "Defy My Patience" that mixes sets of words from both lists to create an *ent*/*ant* deck.
2. "Challenge My Patience or Defy My Challenge." In this version, during scoring, before everyone throws down his or her hand, students should secretly write additional words that have not been played for groups they have laid down. Before hands are revealed, students share these lists and an additional point is added to the player's score for each related word he or she wrote. Any player who doubts the authenticity of a word claimed by an opponent may challenge the word. The challenger loses a point if the word is valid or gains a point if it is not. The player, likewise, counts the word if it is valid or loses a point if the challenger proves him or her wrong.
3. Encourage students to develop their own derivational families to add to this game, or another feature to substitute for the *ant*/*ent* contrast.

for Words Their Way®

Assimile
Download a ready-to-use version of this game.

FIGURE 8.16 **Assimile Game Board**

8.18 Assimile

This game can be played by two to six players. (CCSS Language (6th–8th) 2.b, 4.b, 4.c, 4.d)

MATERIALS The game board is modeled after a Monopoly board (see Figure 8.16). You will also need dice, game playing pieces, a deck of prefixes that can be assimilated (*ad-*, *sub-*, *in-*, *ex-*, *com-*, *ob-*), a deck of base words that can take assimilated prefixes (e.g., base words such as *company* [*accompany*] or *mortal* [*immortal*]), and a set of chance cards. The chance cards are similar to the base word cards but should be written on cards of a different color. Players will need a sheet of paper and pencil or pen to use in spelling words.

PROCEDURES This game is modeled after Monopoly.
1. Place base words face-down around the board, one in each space. One prefix is chosen as the focus and placed face-up in the center of the board. Chance cards are also placed in the middle.
2. Players roll the dice to see who goes first. The player with the highest number rolls again and moves that number of spaces on the board.
3. After landing on a particular space, the player turns up a word card and must determine whether this word can be assimilated to the prefix in the center of the board. If the card can be made into a word, the player attempts to both say the word and correctly spell it. A player who is able to correctly spell the word gets to keep the card. If the word cannot be assimilated, it is kept on the board face-up (this word will not be played again). However, if the word can be assimilated but the player misspells the word, the card is turned face-down to be played later in the game.
4. A player who is unable to come up with a word (for whatever reason) forfeits a turn, and play moves to the next player.
5. When a player passes "Go" or lands on a card that is face-up, he or she can draw from the chance pile. Chance cards provide players a chance to think of their own assimilated prefix word using the base word on the card and any assimilated prefix.
6. The game is over when all cards that can be played are played. The winner is the player with the most correctly spelled words.

VARIATIONS A separate set of Community Chest cards using all of the original assimilated prefixes can be placed in the middle of the board, from which players can draw after each round of turns. This ensures that all prefixes are studied. (Community Chest cards will have the prefixes *ad-*, *in-*, *com-*, *ob-*, *sub-*, *ex-*, *per-*, and *dis-*.) With this method, the word cards that cannot be played with one particular prefix are turned face-down until they can be played.

8.19 Rolling Prefixes

Players must be familiar with all types of assimilated prefixes to play this card game. (CCSS Language (6th–8th) 2.b, 4.b, 4.c, 4.d)

MATERIALS Create a deck of 32 word cards of assimilated prefixes (eight sets of four). Each group of four should consist of a mixed sort from each of the seven sets of assimilated prefixes: *ad-*, *in-*, *com-*, *ob-*, *sub-*, *ex-*, and *dis-*. One set must be a "wild set" (words with the aforementioned prefixes).

PROCEDURES

1. Each player is dealt eight cards—three cards to each player on the first round, two cards to each player on the second round, and three cards to each player on the third round.
2. The player on the dealer's left starts the game by putting a card face-up in the center of the table. It does not matter what the card is; the player must read the word and state the prefix.
3. The next player to the left and the others that follow attempt to play a card of the same suit (having the same prefix) as the first one put on the table. Players must read their word and state the prefix.
4. If everybody follows suit, the cards in the center of the table are picked up after all the players have added their cards, and put to the side. No one scores.
5. The game continues in the same fashion until someone is unable to follow suit. When this occurs, the player can look through his or her hand for a "wild card" and play it, changing the suit for the following players.
6. A player may change suit in this manner at any point in the game if he or she so chooses. For example, a player may play the word *collide* (prefix *com-*), and the next player may either play a *com-* prefix word (such as *concoct*) or a word with *com* elsewhere in the word, such as *accommodate*. If the player chooses *accommodate*, the prefix the following player must concentrate on is *ad-* or a form of *ad-*.
7. A player who is unable to follow suit must pick up the center deck of cards. The player who picks up the cards begins the next round. The game continues this way until someone runs out of cards.

VARIATIONS

- At first, players may not wish to state the original prefix of the words.
- Make multiple decks of assimilated prefixes, allowing for variation.
- Instead of ending the game after one person runs out of cards, the game can continue by the winner of the first round receiving one point for each card that the other players hold in their hands at the end of the round.

8.20 Eponyms: Places, Things, Actions

Eponyms are words that refer to places, things, and actions that are named after an individual (from Greek *epi-* for "after" + *noma* for "name"). Students' interest in word origins is often sparked by finding out where such words originate. As these words are discovered, they can be recorded in the "Looking into Language" section of the vocabulary notebook and/or displayed on a bulletin board. (CCSS Language (6th–8th) 4.c, 4.d)

Following is a sampler of common eponyms.

Bloomers	Amelia Bloomer, an American feminist in the late nineteenth century
Boycott	Charles Boycott, whose servants and staff refused to work for him because he would not lower their rents
Diesel	Rudolph Diesel, a German engineer who invented an alternative engine to the slow-moving steam engine
Ferris wheel	G. W. C. Ferris, designer of this exciting new ride for the 1893 World's Fair in Chicago
Guillotine	Joseph Guillotin, a French physician and the inventor of the device
Leotard	Jules Leotard, a French circus performer who designed his own trapeze costume
Magnolia	Pierre Magnol, French botanist
Pasteurize	Louis Pasteur, who developed the process whereby bacteria are killed in food and drink
Sandwich	John Montagu, the Earl of Sandwich, who requested a new type of meal
Sax	Antoine Joseph Sax, Belgian instrument maker, designer and builder of the first saxophone

The following resources include lists and information about eponyms:

Freeman, M. S. (1997). *A new dictionary of eponyms*. New York: Oxford University Press.

Marciano, J. (2009). *Anonyponymous: The forgotten people behind everyday words*. New York: Bloomsbury.

Terban, M. (1988.) *Guppies in tuxedos: Funny eponyms*. New York: Clarion.

8.21 Words That Grow from Indo-European Roots

The Indo-European Language
This resource can strengthen students' knowledge of roots and derivations.

The Indo-European (IE) language, spoken almost 8,000 years ago, is the "mother" language to over half of the world's languages (Watkins, 2011). This is one reason why the etymological information included for many entries in the *American Heritage Dictionary* (2012) includes not only the Latin or Greek roots from which they came but also their **Indo-European root**. Exploring these roots provides fascinating insights for students at the derivational level. You may wish to begin this exploration with the more concrete roots and activities provided in the "Origins" two-volume series by Sandra Robinson and her colleagues (1989). Using an Indo-European root such as *dhreu*, which meant "to fall," students come to appreciate how some of our English words with that root developed—*drop, droop, drip, drizzle*—as well as the more figurative meanings of *drowsy* and *dreary*.

Once students understand how the meanings of more common English words evolved from their Indo-European roots, you can extend their exploration to roots that have generated both transparent and more opaque meanings, words that occur most often in general academic and domain-specific vocabulary (Templeton, in press).

MATERIALS Have Watkins' *American Heritage Dictionary of Indo-European Roots* (2011) and Shipley's *Origins of English Words* (2001) on hand. Different groups of students may be assigned different Indo-European roots to examine.

PROCEDURE Each group selects English words derived from the root that they believe are good examples of how the "core" meaning of the Indo-European root functions in those words in present-day English. Then they construct a word tree like they did with Latin and Greek roots (see Figure 8.8). Figure 8.17 shows a word tree growing from the Indo-European root *-genə-*, which means "to give birth, beget; with derivatives referring to aspects and results of procreation and to familial and tribal groups" (Watkins, 2011, p. 27). Much of the activity's value lies in the conversation that surrounds the students' investigation. For example, first students wonder how *gentle* came from a root having to do with giving birth or beginning something. Then, when they check the etymological information in the *American Heritage* dictionary, they find that *gentle* comes from a Middle English word *gentil*, which in turn came from French. It meant "courteous," coming in turn from Latin *gentilis*, meaning "of the same clan." The students now understand the part of the Indo-European meaning of -*genə*- having to do with "familial and tribal groups." They discuss how you would be courteous to others who were in the same clan—the group you *began* your life with. Generative forms add up quickly, including *gentle, genteel, gently, gentleman, genealogy, gentry, generic, -genus, dehydrogenases,* and *hydrogen* to name a few. Students should be able to see into words with *gen* and begin to think of meaning connections. Students can dig as deeply as they wish, and 10 to 15 minutes at a time is usually enough time for a whole class or small group examination.

Students at this level are aware of how the spelling in related words sometimes changes (having examined, for example, pairs such as ex<u>claim</u>/ex<u>clam</u>ation, pro<u>claim</u>/pro<u>clam</u>ation). When they see the many different words that have evolved from a single Indo-European root they will notice how the spelling of the root has often changed. For example, the *e* in *cognate* has fallen away, but *gn* still functions as a meaningful root. Students may realize that so many cognates in different languages were, in a sense, "born together" (*co* + *gen*) because they came from the same Indo-European root!

FIGURE 8.17   Word Tree: Words That Grow from Indo-European Roots

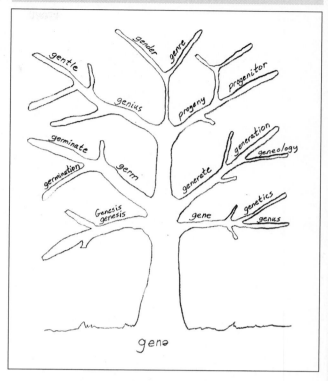

Appendices

This section of the text contains seven segments, or appendices. Appendix A provides the materials you will need for assessments. (Printable versions of these materials are also available on the website along with other assessments described in Chapter 2). Other Appendixes contain pictures, sample sorts, word lists, and templates that you can use to create your own word study activities.

Qualitative Spelling Checklist

Student _____   Observer _____

Use this checklist to analyze students' uncorrected writing and to locate their appropriate stages of spelling development. There are three gradations within each stage—early, middle, and late. Words in parentheses are examples.

The spaces for dates at the top of the checklist are used to follow students' progress. Check when certain features are observed in students' spelling. When a feature is always present check "Yes." The last place where you check "Often" corresponds to the student's stage of spelling development.

Dates: _____   _____   _____

Emergent Stage			
Early			
• Does the child scribble on the page?	Yes ____	Often ____	No ____
• Are letter-like forms arranged linearly?	Yes ____	Often ____	No ____
Middle			
• Are there random letters and numbers used in pretend writing? (4BT for *ship*)	Yes ____	Often ____	No ____
Late			
• Are key sounds used in syllabic writing? (/s/ or /p/ for *ship*)	Yes ____	Often ____	No ____
Letter Name–Alphabetic			
Early			
• Are salient sounds represented? (BD for *bed*)	Yes ____	Often ____	No ____
• Are blends and digraphs represented partially? (SP for *ship*)	Yes ____	Often ____	No ____
Middle			
• Are there logical vowel substitutions with a letter name strategy? (FLOT for *float*, BAD for *bed*)	Yes ____	Often ____	No ____
Late			
• Are some consonant digraphs and blends spelled correctly? (**ship**, **wh**en, **fl**oat)	Yes ____	Often ____	No ____
• Are short vowels spelled correctly? (b**e**d, sh**i**p, wh**e**n, l**u**mp)	Yes ____	Often ____	No ____
• Is the *m* or *n* included in front of other consonants? (l**u**mp, sta**n**d)	Yes ____	Often ____	No ____
Within Word Pattern			
Early			
• Are long vowels in single-syllable words used but confused? (FLOTE for *float*, TRANE for *train*)	Yes ____	Often ____	No ____
• Are the most common consonant digraphs and blends spelled correctly? (**sl**ed, **dr**eam, **fr**igh**t**)	Yes ____	Often ____	No ____
Middle			
• Are common vowel words spelled correctly, but some long vowel spelling and other vowel patterns used but confused? (SPOYL for spoil)	Yes ____	Often ____	No ____
Late			
• Are complex consonants spelled correctly? (spe**ck**, swi**tch**, smu**dge**)	Yes ____	Often ____	No ____
• Are most other vowel patterns spelled correctly? (sp**oi**l, ch**ew**ed, s**er**ving)	Yes ____	Often ____	No ____
Syllables & Affixes			
Early			
• Are inflectional endings added correctly to CVVC and CVCC words? (rain**ing**, walk**ed**)	Yes ____	Often ____	No ____
Middle			
• Are inflectional endings added correctly to base words? (chew**ed**, march**ed**, show**er**)	Yes ____	Often ____	No ____
• Are junctures between syllables spelled correctly? (ca**tt**le, ce**ll**ar, ca**rr**ies, bo**tt**le)	Yes ____	Often ____	No ____
Late			
• Are unaccented final syllables spelled correctly? (bott**le**, fortun**ate**, civi**lize**)	Yes ____	Often ____	No ____
• Are prefixes and suffixes spelled correctly? (fav**or**, rip**en**, cell**ar**, color**ful**)	Yes ____	Often ____	No ____
Derivational Relations			
Early			
• Are most polysyllabic words spelled correctly? (*fortunate, confident*)	Yes ____	Often ____	No ____
Middle			
• Are unaccented vowels in derived words spelled correctly? (conf**i**dent, civ**i**lize, cat**e**gory)	Yes ____	Often ____	No ____
Late			
• Are assimilated prefixes spelled correctly? (*illiterate, correspond, succeed*)	Yes ____	Often ____	No ____

General Directions for Administering the *Words Their Way* Inventories

Students should not study the words before a test. Assure students that they will not be graded on this activity, and that they will be helping you plan for their needs. Introduce the assessment to students; for example:

> *I am going to ask you to spell some words. Spell them the best you can. Some of the words may be easy to spell; some may be difficult. When you do not know how to spell a word, spell it the best you can.*

Ask students to number their paper (or prepare a numbered paper for kindergarten or early first grade). Call each word aloud and repeat it. Say each word naturally, without emphasizing phonemes or syllables. Use it in a sentence, if necessary, to be sure students know the exact word. Sample sentences are provided along with the words. After administering the inventory, use a Feature Guide, Class Composite Form, and, if desired, a Spelling-by-Stage Classroom Organization Chart to complete your assessment. Error Guide forms for the Primary and Elementary Inventories are available at PDToolkit for *Words Their Way*. The online assessment application helps complete the feature guide and create a class composite automatically.

Scoring the Inventory Using the Feature Guides

1. To score by hand, make a copy of the appropriate Feature Guide (PSI p. 320, ESI p. 324, USI p. 327) for each student. Draw a line under the last word used if you called fewer than the total number and adjust the possible total points at the bottom of each feature column.
2. Score the words by checking off the features spelled correctly that are listed in the cells to the right of each word. For example, if a student spells *bed* as BAD, he gets a check in the initial *b* cell and the final *d* cell, but not for the short vowel. Write in the vowel used (*a*, in this case), but do not give any points for it. If a student spells *train* as TRANE, she gets a check in the initial *tr* cell and the final *n* cell, but not for the long vowel pattern. Write in the vowel pattern used (*a–e* in this case), but do not give any points for it. Put a check in the "Correct" column if the word is spelled correctly. Do not count reversed letters as errors but note them in the cells. If unnecessary letters are added, give the speller credit for what is correct (e.g., if *bed* is spelled BEDE, the student still gets credit for representing the consonants and short vowel), but do not check "Correct" spelling.
3. Add the number of checks under each feature and across each word, double-checking the total score recorded in the last cell. Modify the ratios in the last row depending on the number of words called aloud.

Interpreting the Results of the Spelling Inventory

1. Look down each feature column to determine instructional needs. Students who miss only one (or two, if the features sample 8 to 10 words) can go on to other features. Students who miss two or three need some review work; students who miss more than three need careful instruction on this feature. If a student did not get any points for a feature, earlier features need to be studied first.
2. Determine a development stage by noting where students first make two or more errors under the stages listed in the shaded box at the top of the Feature Guide and circle the stage.
3. Use power scores or total number correct as a guide to calling the stage. Refer to the Power Scores and Estimated Stages table in Chapter 2.

Using the Classroom Composite and Spelling-by-Stage Classroom Organization Chart

1. Staple each Feature Guide to the student's spelling paper and arrange the papers in rank order from highest to lowest total points or use raw scores.
2. List students' names in this rank order in the left column of the appropriate Classroom Composite (PSI p. 320, ESI p. 324, USI p. 327) and transfer each student's total feature scores from the Feature Guide to the Classroom Composite. If you did not call out the total word list, adjust the numbers on the Possible Points row of the Classroom Composite.
3. Highlight cells where students make two or more errors on a particular feature to get a sense of your students' needs and to form groups for instruction.
4. You may find it easier to form groups using the Spelling-by-Stage Classroom Organization Chart (p. 322). List each student under the appropriate spelling stage (the stage circled on the Feature Guide) and determine instructional groups.

The online assessment tool on the website can automate many of these steps for you.

Note: See Chapter 2 for more detailed directions on choosing, administering, scoring, and interpreting the inventories, as well as using them to form instructional groups.

Primary Spelling Inventory (PSI)

The Primary Spelling Inventory (PSI) is used in kindergarten through third grade. The 26 words are ordered by difficulty to sample features of the letter name–alphabetic to within word pattern stages. Call out enough words so that you have at least five or six misspelled words to analyze. For kindergarten students or other emergent readers, you may only need to call out the first five words. In late kindergarten and early first-grade classrooms, call out at least 15 words so that you sample digraphs and blends; use the entire list for late first, second, and third grades. If any students spell more than 22 words correctly, you may want to use the Elementary Spelling Inventory.

Using the following list, call out the spelling word, then the sample sentence, then repeat the spelling word.

1. fan   A fan will keep you cool on a hot day. *fan*
2. pet   I have a pet cat who likes to play. *pet*
3. dig   Let's dig a hole in the sand. *dig*
4. rob   A raccoon will rob a bird's nest for eggs. *rob*
5. hope   I hope you will do well on this test. *hope*
6. wait   You need to wait for the letter. *wait*
7. gum   I stepped on some bubble gum. *gum*
8. sled   The dog sled was pulled by huskies. *sled*
9. stick   I used a stick to poke in the hole. *stick*
10. shine   He rubbed the coin to make it shine. *shine*
11. dream   I had a funny dream last night. *dream*
12. blade   The blade of the knife was very sharp. *blade*
13. coach   The coach called the team off the field. *coach*
14. fright   She was a fright in her Halloween costume. *fright*
15. chewed   The dog chewed on the bone until it was gone. *chewed*
16. crawl   You will get dirty if you crawl under the picnic table. *crawl*
17. wishes   In fairy tales, wishes often come true. *wishes*
18. thorn   The thorn from the rosebush stuck me. *thorn*
19. shouted   They shouted at the barking dog. *shouted*
20. spoil   The food will spoil if it sits out too long. *spoil*
21. growl   The dog will growl if you bother him. *growl*
22. third   I was the third person in line. *third*
23. camped   We camped down by the river last weekend. *camped*
24. tries   He tries hard every day to finish his work. *tries*
25. clapping   The audience was clapping after the program. *clapping*
26. riding   They are riding their bikes to the park today. *riding*

Words Their Way Primary Spelling Inventory Feature Guide

Student's Name _____ Teacher _____ Grade _____ Date _____

Words Spelled Correctly: _____ / 26   Feature Points: _____ / 56   Total: _____ / 82   Spelling Stage: _____

SPELLING STAGES →	EMERGENT LATE		LETTER NAME–ALPHABETIC			WITHIN WORD PATTERN			SYLLABLES AND AFFIXES	
	Consonants		EARLY	MIDDLE	LATE	EARLY	MIDDLE	LATE	EARLY	
Features →	Initial	Final	Short Vowels	Digraphs	Blends	Common Long Vowels	Other Vowels	Inflected Endings	Feature Points	Words Spelled Correctly
1. fan	f	n	A							
2. pet	p	t	E							
3. dig	d	g	I							
4. rob	r	b	O							
5. hope	h	p				o-e				
6. wait	w	t				ai				
7. gum	g	m	U							
8. sled			E		sl					
9. stick			I		st					
10. shine				sh		i-e				
11. dream					dr	ea				
12. blade					bl	a-e				
13. coach				ch		oa				
14. fright					fr	igh				
15. chewed				ch			ew	-ed		
16. crawl					cr		aw			
17. wishes				sh				-es		
18. thorn				th			or			
19. shouted				sh			ou	-ed		
20. spoil							oi			
21. growl							ow			
22. third				th			ir			
23. camped								-ed		
24. tries					tr			-ies		
25. clapping								-pping		
26. riding								-ding		
Totals	/7	/7	/7	/7	/7	/7	/7	/7	/56	/26

Words Their Way Primary Spelling Inventory Classroom Composite

Teacher _____ School _____ Grade _____ Date _____

SPELLING STAGES →	EMERGENT LATE	LETTER NAME–ALPHABETIC				WITHIN WORD PATTERN			SYLLABLES AND AFFIXES		
	Consonants		EARLY	MIDDLE	LATE	EARLY	MIDDLE	LATE	EARLY		
Students' ↓ Names	Initial	Final	Short Vowels	Digraphs	Blends	Common Long Vowels	Other Vowels	Inflected Endings	Correct Spelling	Total Rank Order
Possible Points	7	7	7	7	7	7	7	7	26	82
1.										
2.										
3.										
4.										
5.										
6.										
7.										
8.										
9.										
10.										
11.										
12.										
13.										
14.										
15.										
16.										
17.										
18.										
19.										
20.										
21.										
22.										
23.										
24.										
25.										
26.										
Highlight for instruction*										

*Highlight students who miss more than 1 on a particular feature; they will benefit from more instruction in that area.

Spelling-by-Stage Classroom Organization Chart

SPELLING STAGES →	EMERGENT			LETTER NAME–ALPHABETIC			WITHIN WORD PATTERN			SYLLABLES AND AFFIXES			DERIVATIONAL RELATIONS		
	EARLY	MIDDLE	LATE	EARLY	MIDDLE	LATE	EARLY	MIDDLE	LATE	EARLY	MIDDLE	LATE	EARLY	MIDDLE	LATE

CHAPTERS IN *WORDS THEIR WAY*	CHAPTER 4	CHAPTER 5	CHAPTER 6	CHAPTER 7	CHAPTER 8

Elementary Spelling Inventory (ESI)

The Elementary Spelling Inventory (ESI) covers more stages than the PSI. You can use it as early as first grade, particularly if a school system wants to use the same inventory across the elementary grades. The 25 words are ordered by difficulty to sample features of the letter name–alphabetic to derivational relations stages. Call out enough words so that you have at least five or six misspelled words to analyze. If any students spell more than 20 words correctly, use the Upper-Level Spelling Inventory to get a more accurate estimate of a student's ability; at the upper level, the ESI can overestimate the stage.

1. bed — I hopped out of bed this morning. *bed*
2. ship — The ship sailed around the island. *ship*
3. when — When will you come back? *when*
4. lump — He had a lump on his head after he fell. *lump*
5. float — I can float on the water with my new raft. *float*
6. train — I rode the train to the next town. *train*
7. place — I found a new place to put my books. *place*
8. drive — I learned to drive a car. *drive*
9. bright — The light is very bright. *bright*
10. shopping — She went shopping for new shoes. *shopping*
11. spoil — The food will spoil if it is not kept cool. *spoil*
12. serving — The restaurant is serving dinner tonight. *serving*
13. chewed — The dog chewed up my favorite sweater yesterday. *chewed*
14. carries — She carries apples in her basket. *carries*
15. marched — We marched in the parade. *marched*
16. shower — The shower in the bathroom was very hot. *shower*
17. bottle — The glass bottle broke into pieces on the tile floor. *bottle*
18. favor — He did his brother a favor by taking out the trash. *favor*
19. ripen — The fruit will ripen over the next few days. *ripen*
20. cellar — I went down to the cellar for the can of paint. *cellar*
21. pleasure — It was a pleasure to listen to the choir sing. *pleasure*
22. fortunate — It was fortunate that the driver had snow tires. *fortunate*
23. confident — I am confident that we can win the game. *confident*
24. civilize — They wanted to civilize the forest people. *civilize*
25. opposition — The coach said the opposition would be tough. *opposition*

Words Their Way Elementary Spelling Inventory Feature Guide

Student's Name _____   Grade _____   Date _____

Words Spelled Correctly: _____ /25   Teacher _____   Feature Points: _____ /62   Total: _____ /87   Spelling Stage: _____

SPELLING STAGES →	EMERGENT LATE		LETTER NAME–ALPHABETIC			WITHIN WORD PATTERN			SYLLABLES AND AFFIXES			DERIVATIONAL RELATIONS		
	Consonants		EARLY/MIDDLE	MIDDLE	LATE	EARLY	MIDDLE	LATE	EARLY	MIDDLE	LATE	EARLY/MIDDLE		
Features →	Initial	Final	Short Vowels	Digraphs	Blends	Common Long Vowels	Other Vowels	Inflected Endings	Syllable Junctures	Unaccented Final Syllables	Advanced Affixes	Bases or Roots	Feature Points	Words Spelled Correctly
1. bed	b	d	e											
2. ship		p	i	sh										
3. when			e	wh										
4. lump	l		u		mp									
5. float		t			fl	oa								
6. train		n			tr	ai								
7. place					pl	a-e								
8. drive		v			dr	i-e								
9. bright					br	igh								
10. shopping			o	sh				pping						
11. spoil					sp		oi							
12. serving							er	ving						
13. chewed				ch			ew	ed						
14. carries							ar	ies	rr					
15. marched				ch			ar	ed						
16. shower				sh			ow			er				
17. bottle									tt	le				
18. favor							or		v	or				
19. ripen									p	en				
20. cellar									ll	ar				
21. pleasure											ure	pleas		
22. fortunate											ate	fortun		
23. confident											ent	confid		
24. civilize											ize	civil		
25. opposition											tion	pos		
Totals	/7		/5	/6	/7	/5	/7	/5	/5	/5	/5	/5	/62	/25

Teacher _____ School _____ Grade _____ Date _____

Words Their Way Elementary Spelling Inventory Classroom Composite

SPELLING STAGES →	EMERGENT	LETTER NAME–ALPHABETIC			WITHIN WORD PATTERN			SYLLABLES AND AFFIXES			DERIVATIONAL RELATIONS			
	LATE	EARLY MIDDLE	LATE	EARLY	MIDDLE	LATE	EARLY	MIDDLE	LATE	EARLY	MIDDLE		
Students' Names ↓	Consonants	Short Vowels	Digraphs	Blends	Common Long Vowels	Other Vowels	Inflected Endings	Syllable Junctures	Unaccented Final Syllables	Advanced Suffixes	Bases or Roots	Correct Spelling	Total Rank Order
Possible Points	**7**	**5**	**6**	**7**	**5**	**7**	**5**	**5**	**5**	**5**	**5**	**25**	**87**
1.													
2.													
3.													
4.													
5.													
6.													
7.													
8.													
9.													
10.													
11.													
12.													
13.													
14.													
15.													
16.													
17.													
18.													
19.													
20.													
21.													
22.													
23.													
24.													
25.													
26.													
Highlight for instruction*													

*Highlight students who miss more than 1 on a particular feature; they will benefit from more instruction in that area.

Upper-Level Spelling Inventory (USI)

You can use the Upper-Level Spelling Inventory (USI) in upper elementary, middle school, high school, and postsecondary classrooms. The 31 words are ordered by difficulty to sample features of the within word pattern to derivational relations spelling stages. With normally achieving students, you can administer the entire list, but you may want to stop when students misspell more than eight words and are experiencing noticeable frustration. If any students misspell five of the first eight words, use the ESI to more accurately identify within word pattern features that need instruction.

1. switch	We can switch television channels with a remote control.	*switch*
2. smudge	There was a smudge on the mirror from her fingertips.	*smudge*
3. trapped	He was trapped in the elevator when the electricity went off.	*trapped*
4. scrape	The fall caused her to scrape her knee.	*scrape*
5. knotted	The knotted rope would not come undone.	*knotted*
6. shaving	He gave up shaving to grow a beard.	*shaving*
7. squirt	Don't let the ketchup squirt out of the bottle too fast.	*squirt*
8. pounce	My cat likes to pounce on her toy mouse.	*pounce*
9. scratches	We had to paint over the scratches on the car.	*scratches*
10. crater	The volcano crater was filled with bubbling lava.	*crater*
11. sailor	When he was young, he wanted to go to sea as a sailor.	*sailor*
12. village	My Granddad lived in a small seaside village.	*village*
13. disloyal	Traitors are disloyal to their country.	*disloyal*
14. tunnel	The rockslide closed the tunnel through the mountain.	*tunnel*
15. humor	You need a sense of humor to understand his jokes.	*humor*
16. confidence	With each winning game, the team's confidence grew.	*confidence*
17. fortunate	The driver was fortunate to have snow tires on that winter day. *fortunate*	
18. visible	The singer on the stage was visible to everyone.	*visible*
19. circumference	The length of the equator is equal to the earth's circumference. *circumference*	
20. civilization	We studied the ancient Mayan civilization last year.	*civilization*
21. monarchy	A monarchy is headed by a king or a queen.	*monarchy*
22. dominance	The dominance of the Yankees baseball team lasted for several years. *dominance*	
23. correspond	Many students correspond through e-mail.	*correspond*
24. illiterate	It is hard to get a job if you are illiterate.	*illiterate*
25. emphasize	I want to emphasize the importance of trying your best.	*emphasize*
26. opposition	The coach said the opposition would give us a tough game.	*opposition*
27. chlorine	My eyes were burning from the chlorine in the swimming pool. *chlorine*	
28. commotion	The audience heard the commotion backstage.	*commotion*
29. medicinal	Take cough drops for medicinal purposes only.	*medicinal*
30. irresponsible	It is irresponsible not to wear a seat belt.	*irresponsible*
31. succession	The firecrackers went off in rapid succession.	*succession*

Words Their Way Upper-Level Spelling Inventory Feature Guide

Student's Name _____

Words Spelled Correctly: _____ / 31   Teacher _____   Feature Points: _____ / 68   Total: _____ / 99   Grade _____   Date _____

Spelling Stage: _____

| SPELLING STAGES → | WITHIN WORD PATTERN | | | SYLLABLES AND AFFIXES | | | DERIVATIONAL RELATIONS | | | | |
| | EARLY | MIDDLE | LATE | EARLY | MIDDLE | LATE | EARLY | MIDDLE | LATE | | |
Features →	Blends and Digraphs	Vowels	Complex Consonants	Inflected Endings and Syllable Juncture	Unaccented Final Syllables	Affixes	Reduced Vowels in Unaccented Syllables	Greek and Latin Elements	Assimilated Prefixes	Feature Points	Words Spelled Correctly
1. switch	sw		tch								
2. smudge	sm	u	dge								
3. trapped	tr			pped							
4. scrape		a-e	scr								
5. knotted		o	kn	tted							
6. shaving	sh			ving							
7. squirt		ir	squ								
8. pounce		ou	ce								
9. scratches		a	tch	es							
10. crater	cr			t	er						
11. sailor		ai			or						
12. village				ll	age						
13. disloyal		oy			al	dis					
14. tunnel				nn	el						
15. humor				m	or						
16. confidence						con	fid				
17. fortunate					ate			fortun			
18. visible						ible		vis			
19. circumference						ence		circum			
20. civilization							liz	civil			
Subtotals	/ 5	/ 9	/ 7	/ 8	/ 7	/ 4	/ 2	/ 4	/ 0	/ 46	/ 20

(continued)

Words Their Way Upper-Level Spelling Inventory Feature Guide (Continued)

Student's Name _____

Words Spelled Correctly: _____ / 31

Teacher _____ Feature Points: _____ / 68

Grade _____ Total: _____ / 99

Date _____ Spelling Stage: _____

SPELLING STAGES →	WITHIN WORD PATTERN		SYLLABLES AND AFFIXES				DERIVATIONAL RELATIONS				
	EARLY	MIDDLE / LATE	EARLY	MIDDLE	LATE		EARLY	MIDDLE	LATE		
Features →	Blends and Digraphs	Vowels	Complex Consonants	Inflected Endings and Syllable Juncture	Unaccented Final Syllables	Affixes	Reduced Vowels in Unaccented Syllables	Greek and Latin Elements	Assimilated Prefixes	Feature Points	Words Spelled Correctly
21. monarchy								arch			
22. dominance						ance	min				
23. correspond							res		rr		
24. illiterate					ate				ll		
25. emphasize						size	pha				
26. opposition							pos		pp		
27. chlorine						ine		chlor			
28. commotion						tion			mm		
29. medicinal					al			medic			
30. irresponsible						ible	res		rr		
31. succession						sion			cc		
Subtotals	/ 0	/ 0	/ 0	/ 0	/ 2	/ 6	/ 6	/ 5	/ 3	/ 22	/ 11
Totals	/ 5	/ 9	/ 7	/ 8	/ 9	/ 10	/ 7	/ 7	/ 7	/ 68	/ 31

Teacher _____ School _____ Grade _____ Date _____

Words Their Way Upper-Level Spelling Inventory Classroom Composite

SPELLING STAGES →		WITHIN WORD PATTERN			SYLLABLES AND AFFIXES			DERIVATIONAL RELATIONS					
		EARLY / MIDDLE	LATE	EARLY	MIDDLE		LATE	EARLY	MIDDLE	LATE			
Students' Names ↓		Blends and Digraphs	Vowels	Complex Consonants	Inflected Endings and Syllable Juncture	Unaccented Final Syllables	Affixes	Reduced Vowels in Unaccented Syllables	Greek and Latin Elements	Assimilated Prefixes	Correct Spelling	Total Rank Order
Possible Points		**5**	**9**	**7**	**8**	**9**	**10**	**7**	**7**	**6**	**31**	**99**
1.												
2.												
3.												
4.												
5.												
6.												
7.												
8.												
9.												
10.												
11.												
12.												
13.												
14.												
15.												
16.												
17.												
18.												
19.												
20.												
21.												
22.												
23.												
24.												
25.												
26.												
27.												
Highlight for instruction*												

*Highlight students who miss more than 1 on a particular feature if the total is between 5 and 8. Highlight those who miss more than 2 if the total is between 9 and 10.

Sound Board for Beginning Consonants and Digraphs

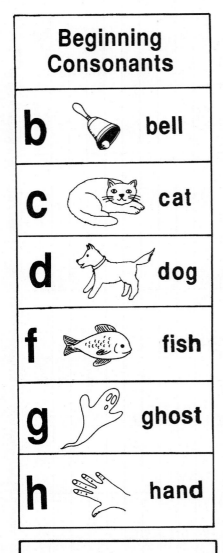

Beginning Consonants

b — bell

c — cat

d — dog

f — fish

g — ghost

h — hand

j — jug

k — key

l — lamp

m — mouse

n — net

p — pig

r — ring

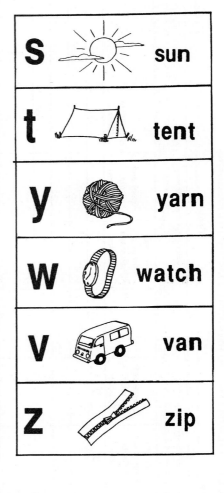

s — sun

t — tent

y — yarn

w — watch

v — van

z — zip

Beginning Digraphs

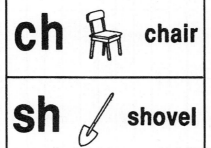

ch — chair

sh — shovel

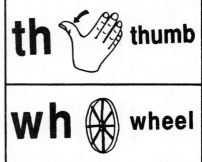

th — thumb

wh — wheel

Sound Board for Beginning Blends

Beginning Blends	**br** broom	**sc** scooter
bl block	**cr** crab	**sk** skate
cl cloud	**dr** drum	**sm** smile
fl flag	**fr** frog	**sn** snail
gl glasses	**gr** grapes	**sp** spider
sl slide	**pr** present	**st** star
pl 2+1=3 plus	**tr** tree	**sw** swing
tw twins	**qu** queen	

Sound Board for Long and Short Vowels

Short Vowels		Long Vowels			
a	cat	**a**	cake	**a**	tray
				a	rain
e	bed	**e**	feet	**e**	leaf
i	pig	**i**	kite	**i**	light
o	sock	**o**	bone	**o**	soap
u	cup	**u**	tube		

You can use the pictures that follow in a number of ways. For example, you can use them like clip art to create picture sorts. Refer to Chapters 4 and 5 for suggested contrasts for picture sorts , or create your own. Simply make copies of the pictures you need (combining two, three, or four sounds) and glue them randomly onto a template, such as the one in Appendix F on page 400. You will probably want to enlarge the pictures about 50 percent, and insert labels from the sound board boxes as headers. You may also want to make a complete set of pictures for modeling, small-group work, or centers. Glue or copy pictures to card stock, and perhaps color them, and laminate the card stock for durability. Use the pictures for games and other activities as well.

Pictures are grouped by beginning consonants, digraphs, blends, short vowels, and long vowels. The following list will help you find pictures for rhyme sorts, word families, additional short vowels, and long vowels. The picture names in bold type are in either the short or long vowel picture section, while the others can be found by their beginning sounds.

Long Vowel Picture Rhymes

tape	**game**	**soap**	**beach**	deer	**slide**	fire	
cape	**frame**	**rope**	**peach**	spear	**bride**	tire	
vine	**bone**	**toad**	pear	**moon**	**seal**	**cube**	**bead**
nine	**cone**	**road**	chair	spoon	**heel**	**tube**	**read**
suit	gate	**snake**	**glue**	jeep	school	**peas**	king
fruit	plate	**cake**	**shoe**	sheep	stool	**cheese**	ring
flute	skate	**rake**	zoo	sleep	spool	**keys**	sting
		lake	two	sweep			
hive	**rose**	**coat**	**three**	**hay**	**cane**	**pie**	**whale**
five	**nose**	**boat**	**bee**	**pay**	**rain**	**tie**	**tail**
dive	**toes**	**goat**	**knee**	pray	**chain**	**fly**	**mail**
drive	hose	**float**	tree	tray	plane	**cry**	snail
		note	key	play	train	fry	sail
							pail
							nail
							scale

Note: More long vowel pictures can be found among initial sounds: paint, vase, shave, blade, flame, grapes, braid, leaf, leash, steam, seal, key, wheel, sleeve, teeth, queen, dream, bike, dice, dime, kite, smile, prize, climb, price, globe, snow, comb, ghost, smoke, toast, flute.

Short Vowel Picture Rhymes

glass	lamp	four	bus	trunk	duck	switch	mitten
grass	stamp	door	plus	skunk	truck	witch	kitten
vest	**wig**	car	**leg**	**cut**	**sun**		
chest	**pig**	jar	egg	**hut**	**bun**		
nest	**dig**	star	peg	**nut**	**run**		
wall	**box**	hook	**pup**	jump			
saw	**fox**	book	**cup**	stump			
claw	socks						
hen	**bed**	kick	**gum**	dog	**pot**	**fin**	**net**
men	**sled**	stick	drum	log	**dot**	**pin**	**jet**
ten	shed	chick	plum	jog	**hot**	chin	**pet**
pen	bread	brick	thumb	frog	**cot**	twin	vet
bag	**can**	**cat**	king	**sock**	**shell**		
rag	**man**	**bat**	ring	**rock**	**bell**		
wag	**fan**	**hat**	wing	**lock**	**well**		
flag	pan	mat	sting	**clock**	smell		
tag	van	bat	swing	block			
cap	**mop**	**zip**	**jack**	**mug**	**pill**		
map	**hop**	**lip**	**sack**	**bug**	**hill**		
nap	**top**	**rip**	**pack**	**jug**	**mill**		
trap	**pop**	ship	shack	**tug**	spill		
clap	chop	whip	quack	**rug**	drill		
snap	shop	skip	track	plug	grill		
	stop	clip	crack				
		drip					
		flip					

Note: Bolded words may be found in vowel pictures. More short vowel pictures can be found among initial sounds: gas, ham, mask, match, glass, crab, sad, trash, desk, check, belt, web, dress, fish, six, bridge, swim, crib, flip, kiss, kit, twin, cup, gum, tub, brush.

Initial Consonants

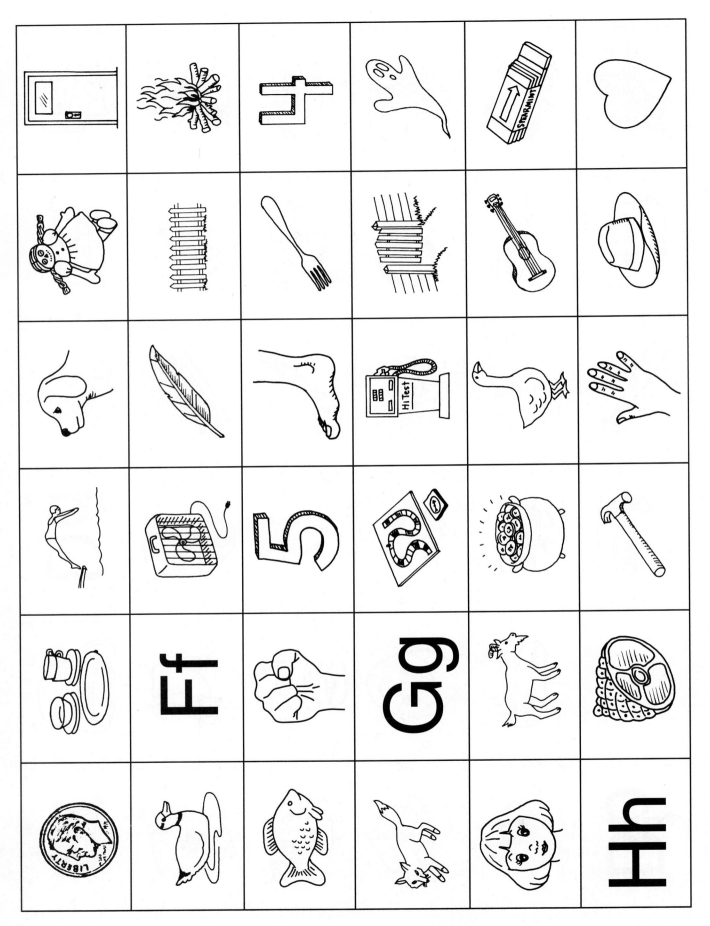

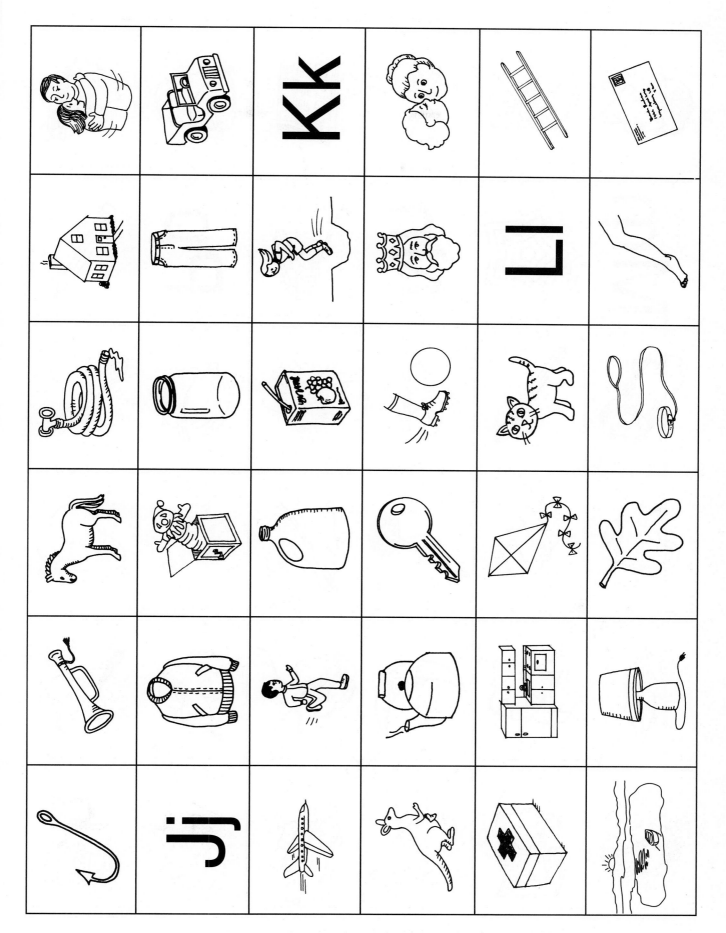

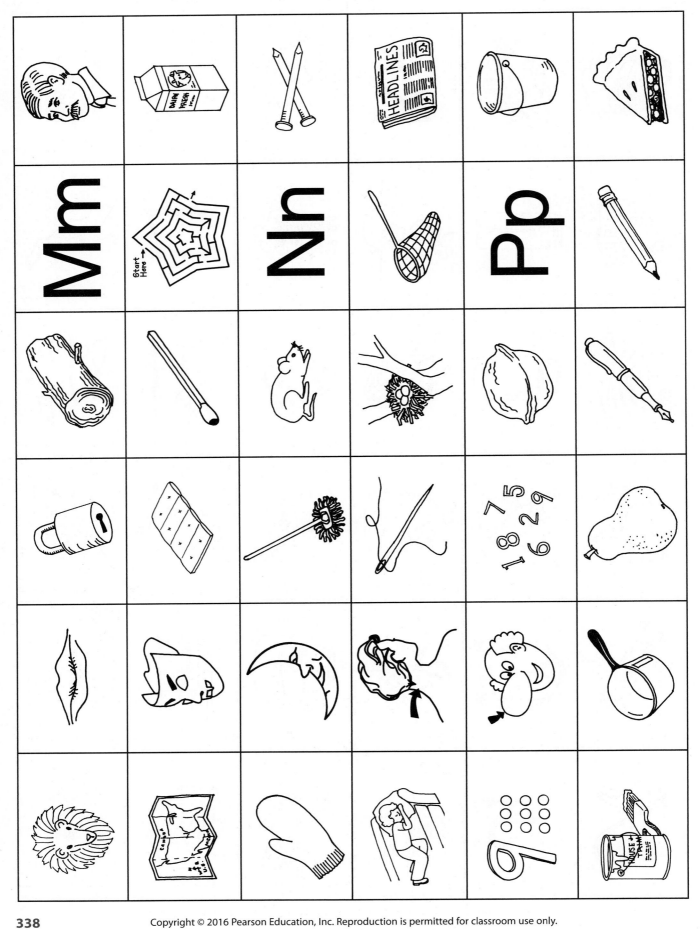

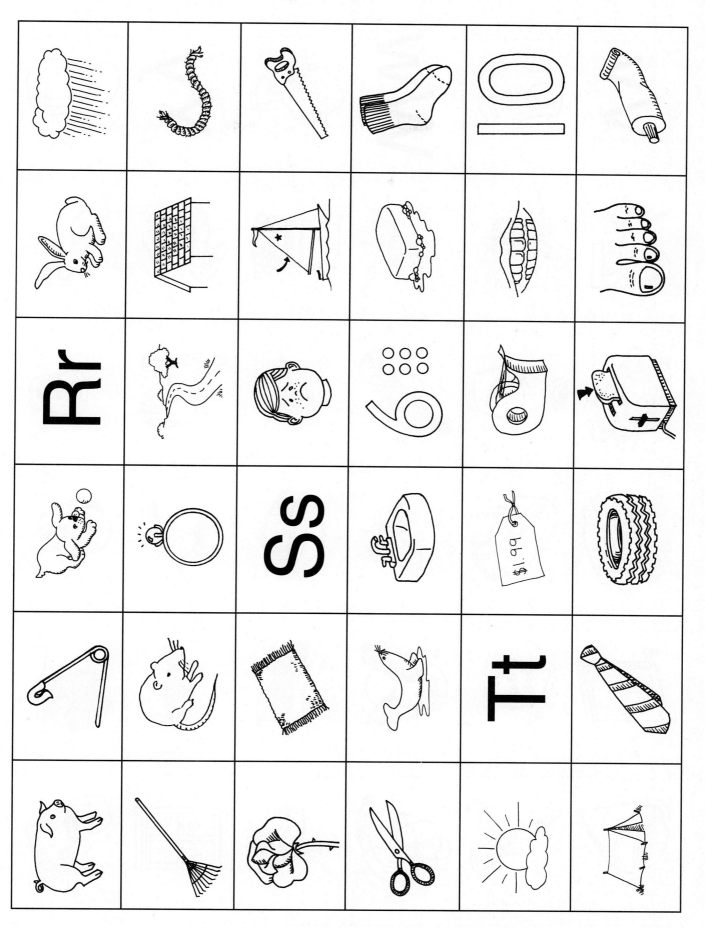

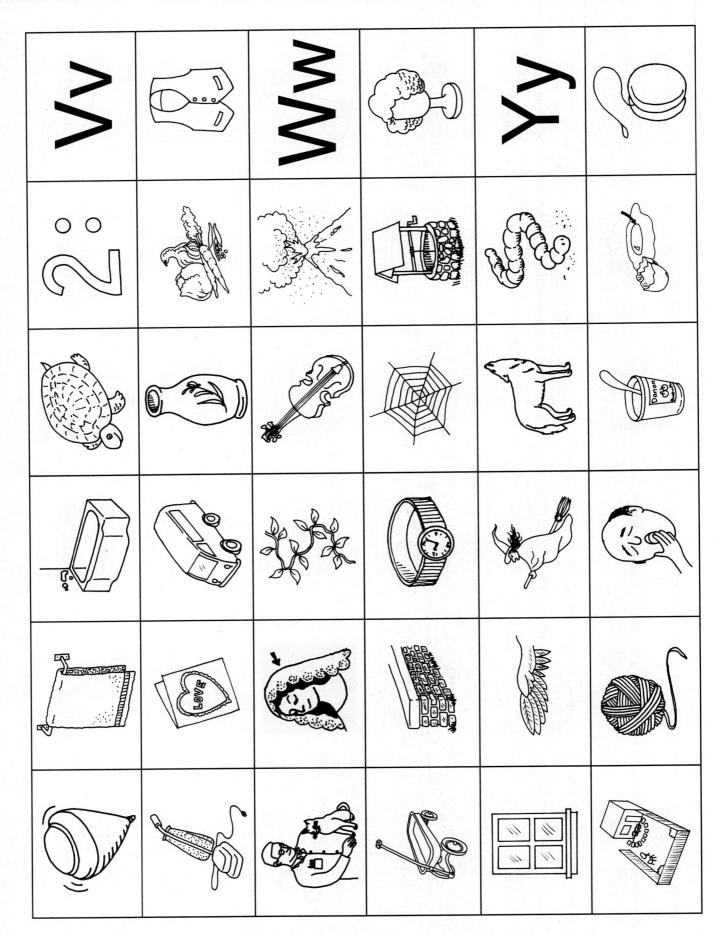

Zz					

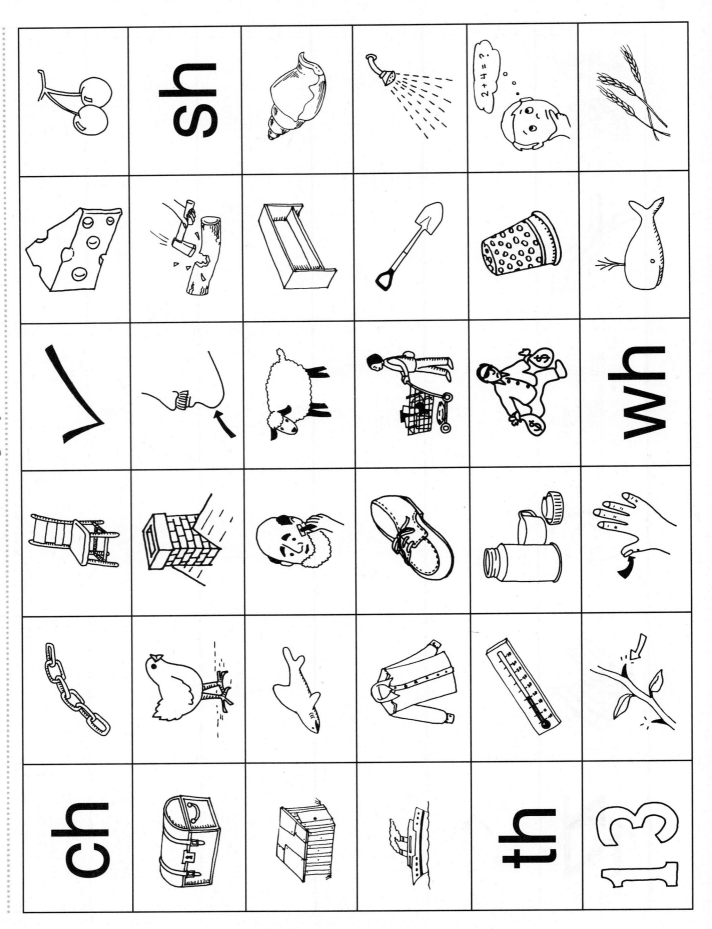

Initial Digraphs

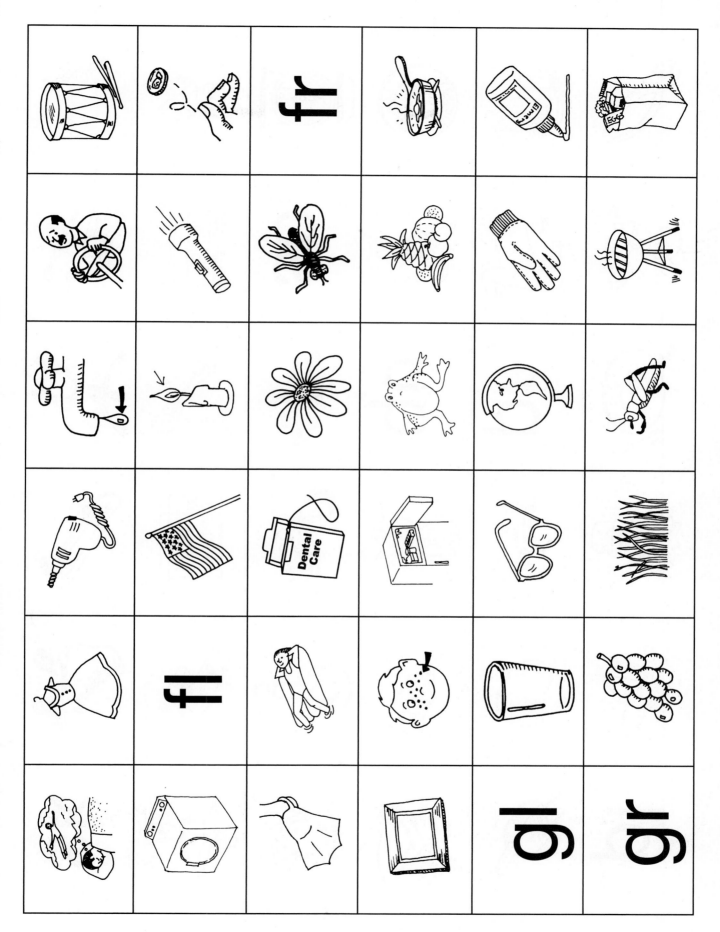

345

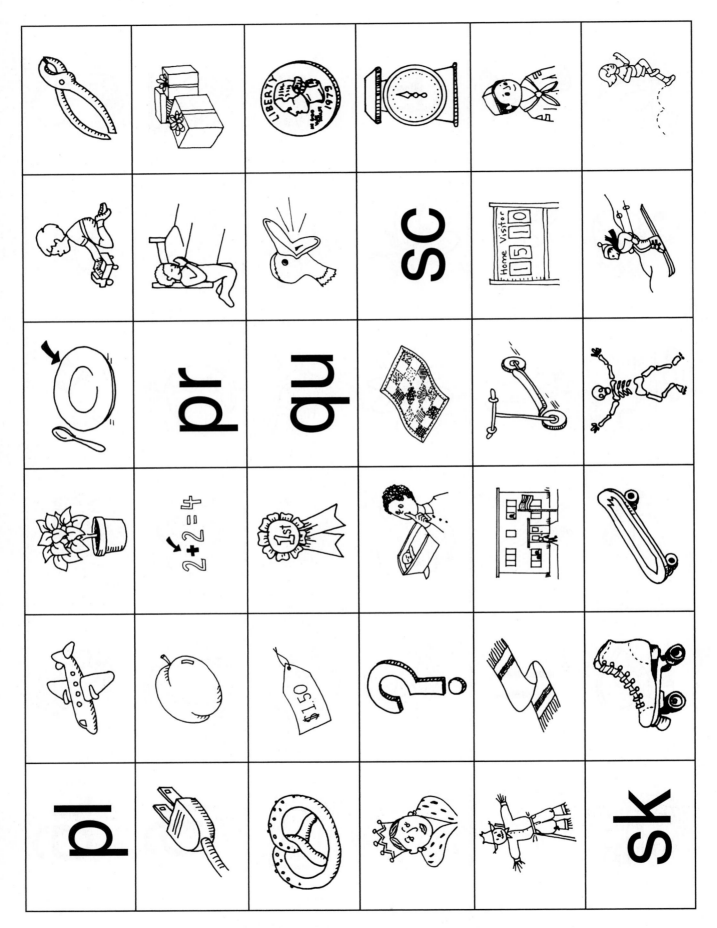

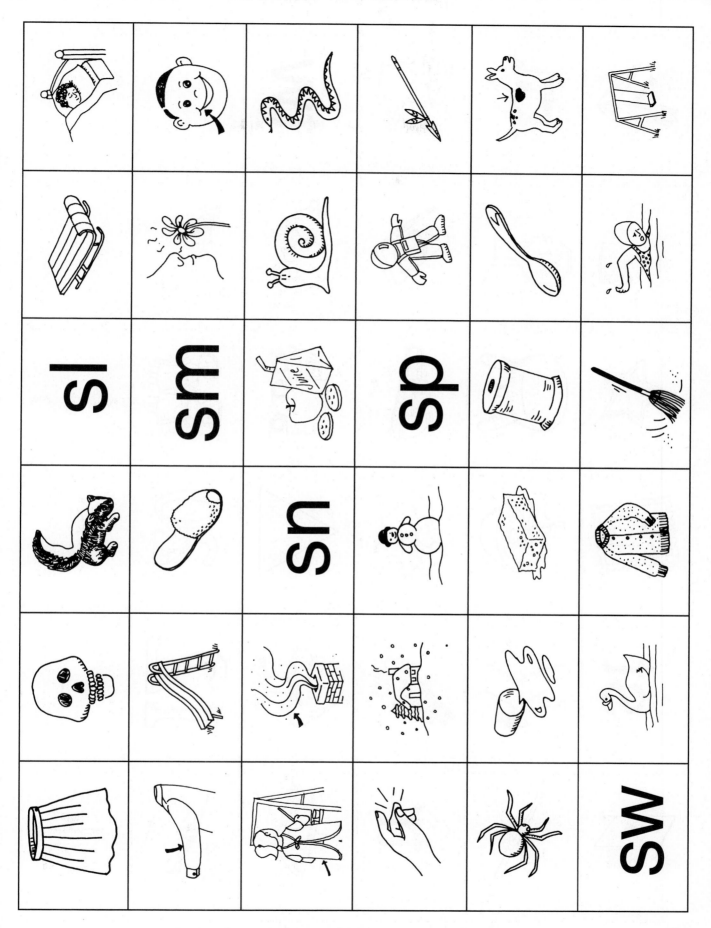

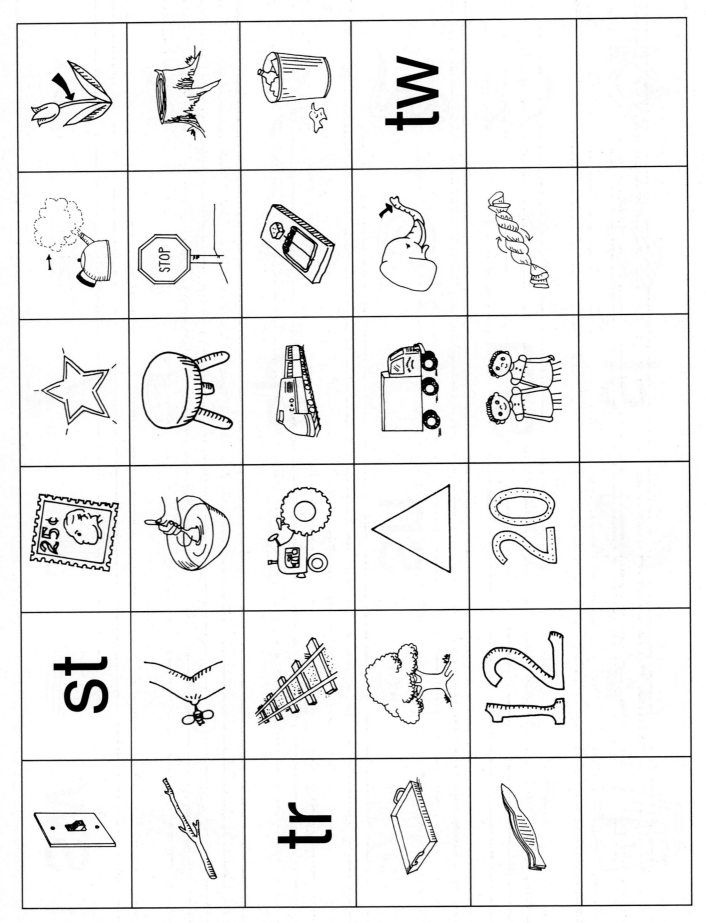

Medial Vowels

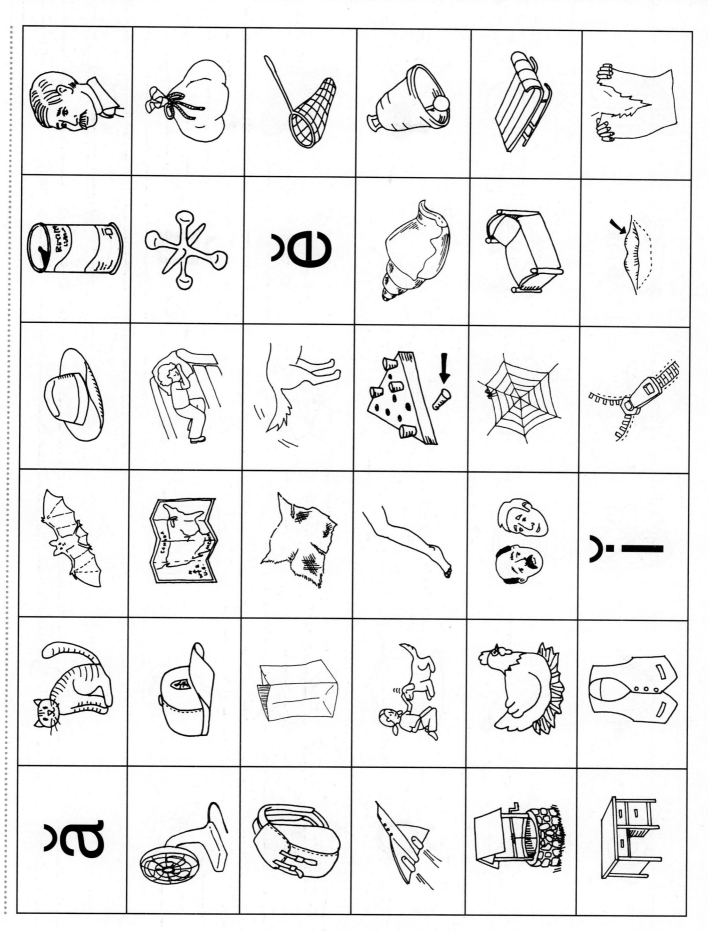

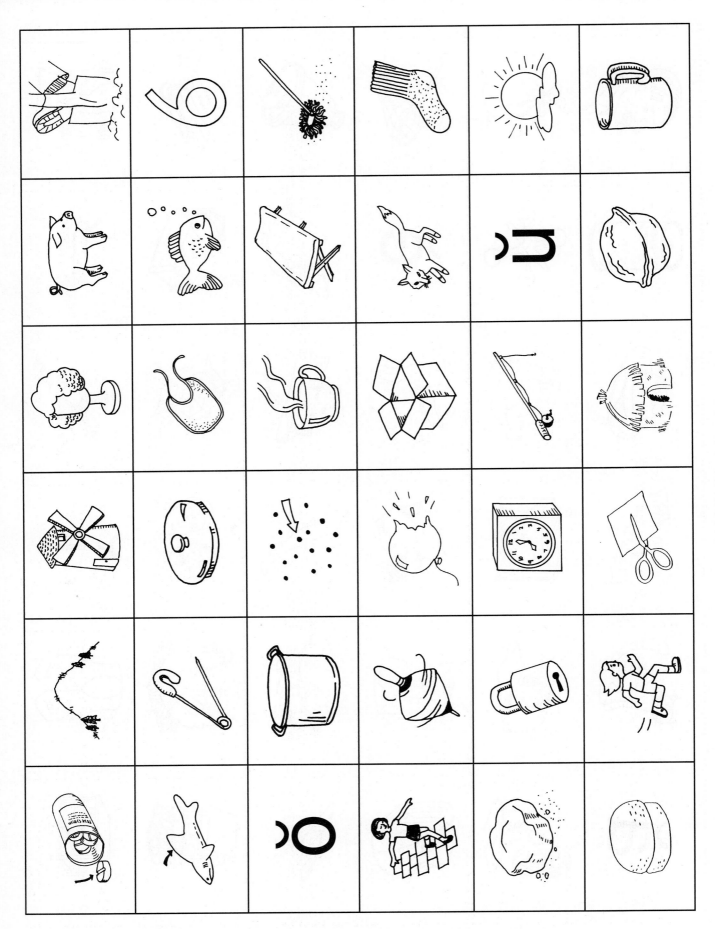

Copyright © 2016 Pearson Education, Inc. Reproduction is permitted for classroom use only.

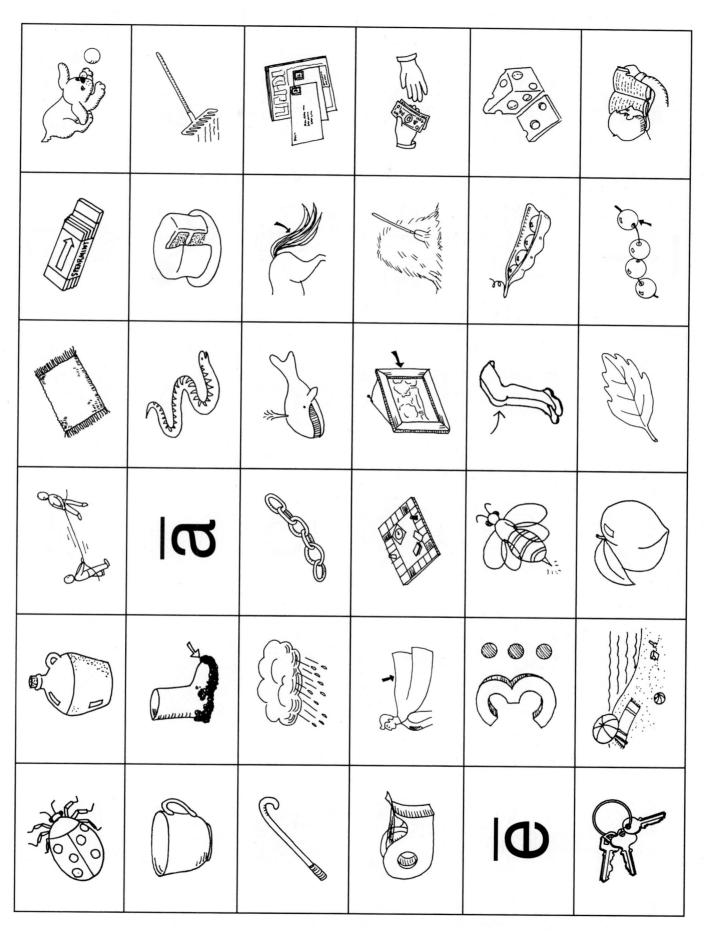

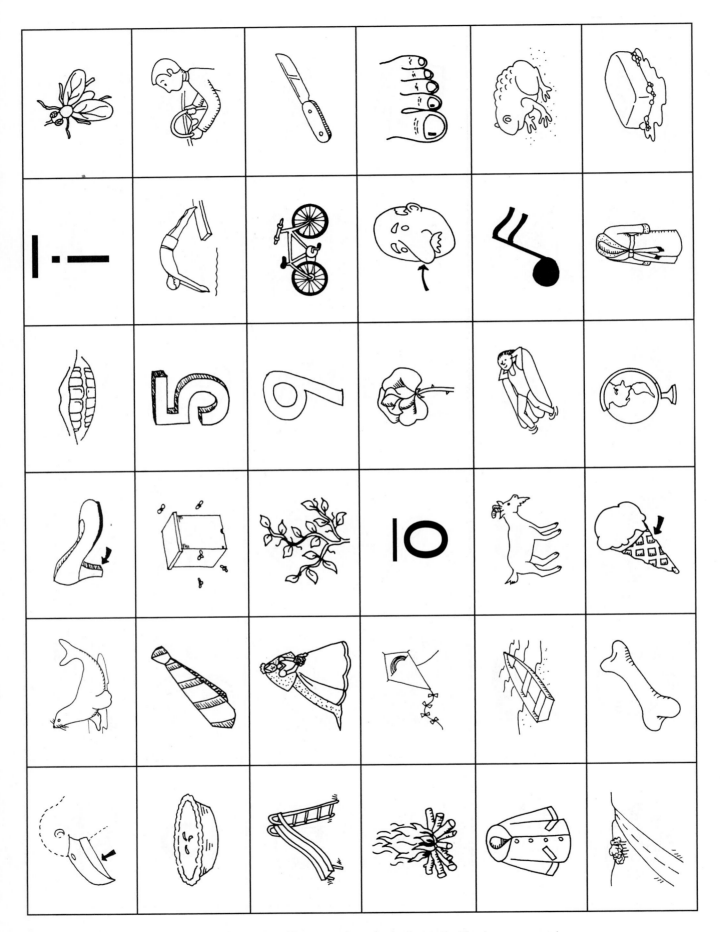

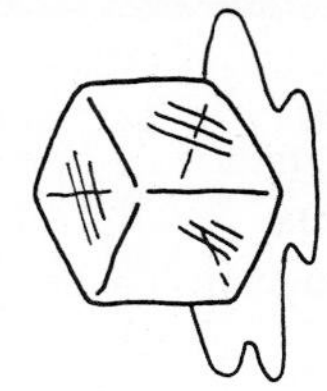	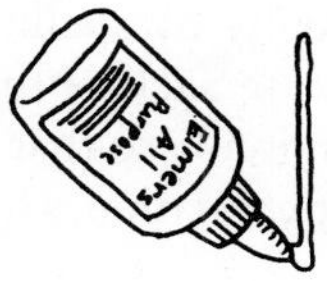				
ū	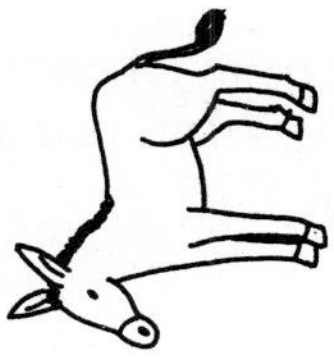				
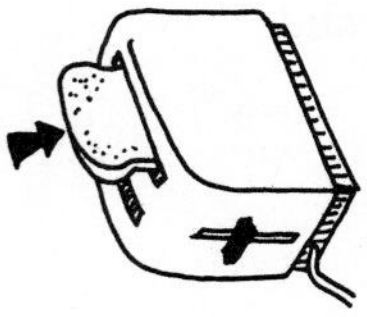	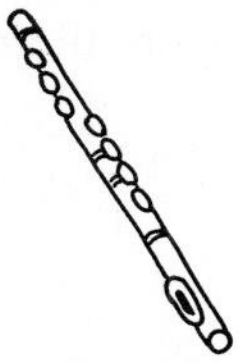				
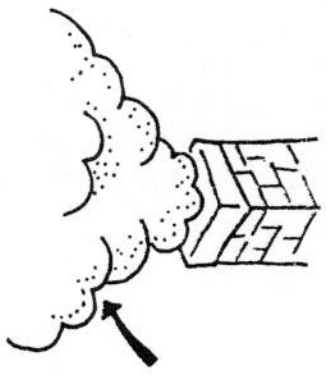	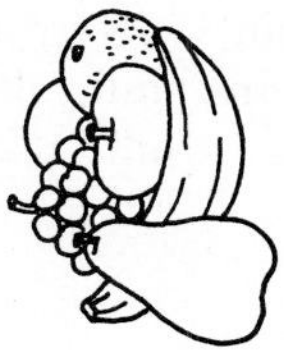				
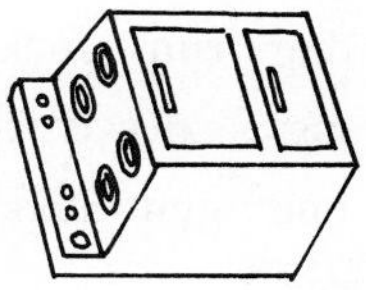	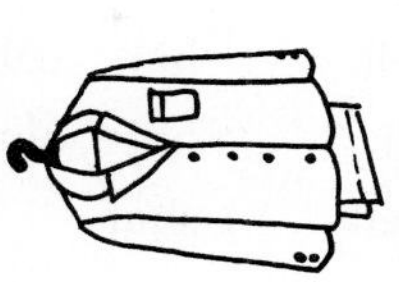	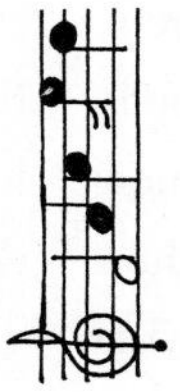			
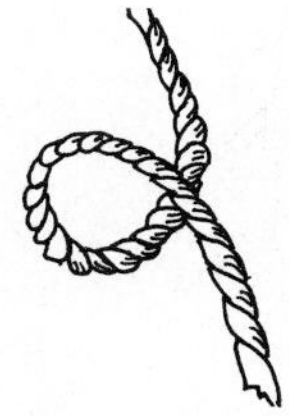	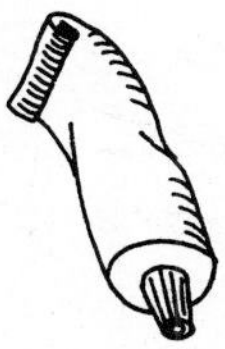	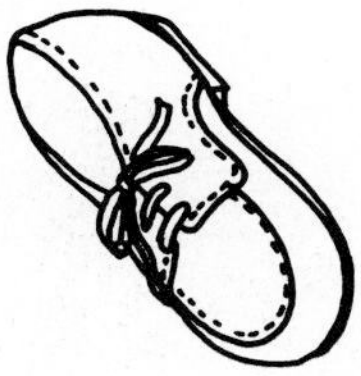			

The sample word sorts on the following pages are arranged sequentially by spelling stage. Prepare word sorts for your students by writing the words on a template such as the one in Appendix F on page 401. Be sure to write the words on the template randomly so that students can make their own discoveries as they sort. Consider the following information when using these sorts.

- These sorts are not intended to be a sequence for all students. Chapter 2 will help you match your students to the spelling stages. Each instruction chapter contains additional suggestions about the pacing and sequencing of word study for each stage. Choose appropriate sorts from among those presented here.
- This is not an exhaustive list of sorts, but it does give you a starting point for creating your own. You can adapt these sorts by adding, deleting, or substituting words that are more appropriate for your students. Word lists are provided in Appendix E.

Letter Name–Alphabetic Sorts

Letter name–alphabetic spellers will also need to study initial consonants, digraphs, blends, and short vowels with picture sorts. Use the pictures in Appendix C to create these sorts and refer to Chapter 5, Table 5.5, for a scope and sequence.

Same Short Vowel Word Families

1. Short *a*		2. More Short *a*'s			3. Short *i*		4. More Short *i*'s			
cat	man	sad	cap	bag	sit	big	pin	pill	rip	sick
bat	can	mad	tap	rag	bit	wig	win	will	lip	pick
sat	pan	dad	map	wag	hit	pig	fin	fill	hip	lick
fat	ran	had	nap	tag	fit	dig	thin	hill	zip	kick
mat	fan	pad	lap	flag	kit	fig	chin	mill	dip	tick
rat	van		rap		quit			bill		chick
hat	tan							kill		

5. Short *o*		6. More Short *o*'s			7. Short *e*				8. Short *u*				
not	hop	job	lock	dog	pet	ten	bed	bell	cut	tub	bug	fun	duck
got	pop	rob	rock	log	net	hen	red	tell	nut	rub	rug	bun	luck
hot	mop	cob	sock	frog	met	pen	fed	well	hut	cub	dug	run	suck
lot	cop	mob	dock	fog	set	men	led	fell	but	club	jug	sun	truck
pot	stop	blob	clock	jog	jet	then	sled	shell	shut		hug	gun	tuck
dot	shop	sob	block		bet	when					tug		
shot					get								

Mixed Short Vowel Word Families

9. Short *a, i, u*

man	pin	fun
can	win	run
fan	fin	sun
ran	thin	bun
than	grin	gun
plan	chin	
van	skin	

10. Short *a, i, o, u*

cat	sit	not	cut
mat	fit	hot	mutt
hat	hit	got	nut
sat	kit	pot	but
rat	bit	rot	hut
that	pit	cot	shut
	quit	dot	

11. Short *a, i, e*

bag	big	pill	bell
rag	wig	will	sell
wag	pig	hill	tell
flag	jig	fill	well
tag	dig	bill	fell
snag	fig	spill	shell
		drill	smell

12. Families with *ck*

back	sick	lock	duck	neck
sack	lick	rock	suck	peck
tack	pick	sock	tuck	deck
jack	tick	dock	truck	speck
pack	kick	clock		
black	chick	block		

13. Preconsonantal Nasals

camp	jump	band	sink
lamp	dump	hand	pink
ramp	hump	sand	think
stamp	stump	land	wink
damp	lump	stand	drink

14. Families Ending in *sh*

mash	fish	mush
cash	dish	hush
trash	wish	rush
rash	swish	gush
dash		brush
crash		
flash		

Short Vowels in CVC Words

15. Short *a, o*

		*
cat	not	
bag	job	was
mad	top	for
pan	fox	
pat	got	
cab	top	
jam	not	

16. Short *e, u*

		*
pet	but	
bell	sun	put
red	cup	push
yes	mud	
let	cut	
ten	hug	
beg	duck	
	gum	

17. Short *a, i, o*

hat	big	pop
fan	six	rock
cab	lip	box
tax	did	mom
bat	dig	stop
back	zip	lock
	will	hop
	win	hot

18. All Short Vowels

can	let	hit	sock	hug
that	fed	fish	mop	luck
lap	met	fill	dot	run
last	web	six	box	bus
sack	fell	this	rob	pup
	wet	sick		bun
		wig		rug

19. Short Vowels with Digraphs

that	ship	when
chat	chill	check
than	whip	shed
shall	this	shell
shack	whiz	then
chap	chip	them
wham	thin	
	thick	

20. Two-Step Sort with Blends and Short Vowels

a. Initial consonant and blends

rack	tack	dug	trick	drum
rag	tag	dip	track	drill
rash	tap	duck	trash	drag
rug	tick		trap	drug
rip			trip	drip
			truck	

b. Short vowels

tack	tick	truck
tap	trip	drum
trash	drill	dug
drag	dip	rug
rack	rip	duck
rag	trick	drug
rash	drip	
trap		

21. Two-Step Sort with Blends and Short Vowels

a. Blends

cram	slip	spill
crab	slid	spin
crash	slap	spot
crib	clock	snap
brag	blob	
brat	flag	
grip	flop	
	flock	

b. Vowels

crab	clip	trot
cram	slid	drop
brag	spill	spot
brat	grip	flop
slap	slip	clock
crash	spin	blob
flag	crib	flock
snap	twig	

22. Two-Step Sort with Presconsonantal Nasals

a. Preconsonantal Nasals

sang	camp	pant	pink	sand
king	lamp	plant	think	land
sing	stamp	print	junk	
swing	limp	hunt	trunk	
sting	jump	want		
sung	bump			

b. Short Vowels

			*
sang	king	jump	
camp	limp	sung	want
sand	print	bump	
lamp	pink	junk	
pant	sing	hunt	
land	think	trunk	
plant	swing	skunk	
stamp	sting		

Note: Oddballs are in columns marked with asterisks.

Within Word Pattern Sorts

23. Short/Long *a*

hat	name	*
jack	date	have
ask	race	what
slap	plane	
fast	cape	
lamp	page	
flag	same	
pass	safe	
path	gave	
glad	gate	

24. Short/Long *a*

cap	lake	rain
last	wave	wait
plan	late	nail
sat	tape	gain
flat	bake	fail
tax	base	pail
	shade	plain
	made	sail
	maze	
	sale	

25. Long-*a* Patterns

same	mail	day	*
whale	pain	say	said
flake	train	play	have
grape	paid	may	
stage	brain	pay	
grade	snail	stay	
chase	chain	clay	
shave	tail		
tale	waist		
waste			

26. Short/Long *e*

well	week	she
step	peel	he
west	weed	we
men	peek	me
bed	speed	
help	keep	
belt	pee	

27. Short/Long *e*

best	green	mean	*
left	wheel	team	been
neck	sheet	deal	head
bell	need	reach	
bled	bleed	beach	
yet	teeth	steam	
	creep	clean	
	speed	bean	

28. Short/Long *e*

mess	head	neat
rest	dead	meal
bell	deaf	speak
kept	breath	meat
nest	death	treat
shell	dread	sneak
vest	bread	heat

29. Short/Long *i*

dish	hike	*
chip	ride	give
kick	ripe	live
whip	nice	
twin	white	
miss	dime	
pick	fine	
rich	life	

30. Short/Long *i*

clip	mine	try	*
win	price	fly	eye
trick	spine	shy	buy
gift	lime	why	bye
list	wife	sky	
mitt	vine	dry	
thick	five		
swim			

31. Short/Long *o*

lock	home	*
odd	slope	move
crop	note	gone
shot	hose	some
clock	vote	
shock	joke	
knob	smoke	
slot	hope	
	choke	

32. Long-*o* Patterns

rope	road	blow	*
woke	boat	grow	now
close	soap	know	cow
stone	soak	slow	
bone	moan	throw	
phone	loaf	snow	
broke	coach	low	
hole	load	bow	
vote	toast	flow	

33. Short/Long *u*

bun	June	blue	*
fuss	cute	glue	truth
luck	rule	clue	
lump	tube	due	
trust	tune	true	
plum	huge		
crust	cube		

34. Long-*u* Patterns

rude	fruit	new	*
crude	suit	chew	fuel
flute	juice	drew	build
mule	bruise	knew	
fume	cruise	stew	
chute		few	
dune		dew	
use		brew	

35. Less Common Long *a*

hay	prey	eight	break
tray	they	weigh	great
stray	obey	vein	steak
pray	hey	veil	
sway		freight	
play		sleigh	
		neigh	

36. *r*-Influenced *a*

car	care	chair	*
star	share	pair	bear
bark	bare	hair	
card	mare	air	
far	rare		
dark	scare		
arm	hare		
start			

37. Less Common Long *e*

greed	chief	these	*
speech	field	scene	vein
greet	brief	theme	friend
creek	grief	eve	seize
fleet	shriek		
geese	piece		
cheese	thief		
	niece		

38. *r*-Influenced *e*

her	near	cheer	bear	*
fern	clear	deer	pear	heart
germ	dear	sneer	wear	
jerk	year	queer	swear	
herb	spear	peer		
herd	beard			
perch				

39. Long-*i* Patterns

kite	might	mind
bride	night	wild
write	right	kind
spice	bright	blind
hide	light	find
wipe	tight	child
mice	sight	mild
		grind

40. *r*-Blends/ *r*-Influenced *i*

grin	third	hire
bring	shirt	tire
drip	dirt	fire
grill	bird	wire
trick	skirt	tired
drink	girl	
brick		
crib		

41. Ambiguous/Long *o*

soft	roll	ghost	*
moth	cold	most	son
cost	stroll	host	from
cross	mold	post	
cloth	scold		
lost	fold		
toss	told		
frost	folk		
long			

42. *r*-Influenced *o*

for	more	door	*
born	store	poor	your
short	chore	floor	
porch	tore		
storm	shore		
north	score		
fort	wore		
torch	swore		

Note: Oddballs are marked with asterisks.

43. Other Long _u_

gloom	new	who
bloom	grew	to
roost	crew	too
smooth	flew	two
scoop	blew	
school	stew	
mood	dew	
pool	knew	

44. _r_-Influenced _u_

hurt	cure	heard
turn	pure	learn
church	sure	earn
burst	lure	pearl
curl		yearn
purr		earth
purse		search

45. _r_-Blends/Vowels

grill	girl
trap	tarp
crush	curl
fry	first
price	purse
track	dark
brag	bark
drip	dirt
frog	fort

46. _r_-Influenced Vowels

car	her	for
shark	first	short
farm	bird	corn
hard	burn	horn
card	word	scorn
yard	worm	torn
scar	world	
march	dirt	
	jerk	

47. _ck, k, ke_

lick	leak	like
lack	seek	lake
tack	soak	take
snack	sleek	snake
stuck	weak	stake
stick	week	strike
whack	croak	wake

48. CVCe Sorts across Vowels

cave	drive	drove	huge
crane	while	those	fume
taste	smile	throne	prune
stage	twice	phone	chute
trade	crime	wrote	flute
waste	guide	quote	mule

49. CVVC across Vowels

road	team	rain	*
boast	stream	strain	board
coach	sweet	claim	great
groan	queen	waist	
throat	peach	faith	
toast	thief	praise	
roast	peace	strain	
		trail	

Ambiguous Vowels and Complex Consonants

50. Diphthongs

toy	coin	town	sound
boy	foil	clown	mouth
joy	boil	brown	scout
	spoil	gown	round
	noise	frown	couch
	point	howl	loud

51. More Diphthongs

row	owl	out
snow	growl	found
blown	drown	shout
flown	crown	cloud
grown	plow	south
thrown	fowl	foul
	prowl	doubt

52. Ambiguous Vowels

salt	hawk	fault	*
bald	draw	caught	fought
chalk	lawn	cause	ought
stall	raw	taught	
false	crawl	sauce	
small	claw	haul	
walk	paw	pause	

53. Words Spelled with _w_

watch	war	wrap
swamp	warn	wreck
swan	warm	write
wand	dwarf	wrist
swat	swarm	wren
wash	wart	wrong

54. Complex Consonants

scram	straight	shrank	square
scrape	strange	shrink	squawk
scratch	stretch	shred	squint
screech	strict	shrunk	squash
screw	string	shriek	squeeze
screen	strong	shrimp	squirt
scrap			

55. _tch_ and _ch_

catch	reach	*
witch	coach	rich
patch	peach	such
fetch	roach	
hutch	screech	
itch	beach	
switch	pouch	
ditch		
latch		

56. _dge_ and _ge_

badge	page
ridge	stage
edge	huge
fudge	rage
bridge	cage
judge	
hedge	
lodge	

57. Hard and Soft _c_ and _g_ across Vowels

cave	coat	cute	cent	cyst
camp	coast	cup	cell	gym
cast	cost	cue	cease	
gave	gold	gum	gem	
gain	golf	gush	germ	
gasp	goof			

58. _ce, ge, ve, se_

dance	charge	glove	cheese
chance	large	give	please
prince	wedge	curve	tease
fence	dodge	shove	loose
since	ridge	live	choose
voice	edge	above	
juice	change	have	

Concept Sorts

59. What Lives in Water?

Yes	No
frog	toad
fish	lizard
whale	zebra
sea turtle	tortoise
clam	elephant
crab	horse

60. Edible Plants

Grain	Fruit	Vegetable
wheat	apples	carrots
oats	peaches	beans
rice	berries	lettuce
rye	pears	cucumber
barley	bananas	cabbage
	oranges	beets

61. Animal Attributes

Fish	Bird	Mammal
scale	feather	hair
eggs	eggs	born alive
gills	lungs	lungs
heart	heart	heart
no legs	two legs	legs
fins	wings	

62. States

East	West	North	South
Virginia	California	Maine	Florida
North	Nevada	Vermont	Mississippi
Carolina	Utah	New York	Texas
Maryland	Arizona		Alabama
Delaware			

63. Geometry Terms

Shapes	Lines	Measurements
triangle	ray	perimeter
rhombus	angle	degrees
square	line	diameter
rectangle	right angle	circumference
parallelogram	obtuse angle	area
isosceles triangle		radius

Syllables and Affixes Sorts

Inflected Endings (*ed* and *ing*), Consonant Doubling, and Plurals

64. Sort for Sound of *ed*

trapped	waited	played
mixed	dotted	mailed
stopped	patted	boiled
chased	treated	raised
cracked	traded	tried
walked	ended	filled
asked	handed	seemed
jumped	needed	yelled

65. Plural Words (*s* and *es*)

cows	boxes	buses	dishes
chicks	mixes	glasses	benches
farms	axes	dresses	watches
fences	foxes	passes	lashes
gates		gases	churches
horses		guesses	ashes
			brushes

66. Plurals with *y*

babies	plays
carries	monkeys
ponies	boys
bodies	trays
pennies	donkeys
worries	enjoys
daddies	turkeys
berries	valleys
parties	

67. Base Words + *ed* and *ing*

jump	jumped	jumping
hike	hiked	hiking
dress	dressed	dressing
wait	waited	waiting
stop	stopped	stopping
pass	passed	passing
live	lived	living
wag	wagged	wagging

68. Adding *ing* (double and *e*-drop)

batting	baking
shopping	skating
bragging	biting
hopping	hoping
humming	sliding
begging	waving
skipping	moving
swimming	caring

69. Adding *ed* (double, nothing)

slipped	picked	traded
grabbed	called	baked
stopped	tracked	wasted
wagged	peeled	liked
tripped	watched	stared
knotted	cheered	waved
rubbed	talked	skated
whizzed	dreamed	tasted

70. Adding *ing* (double, *e*-drop, nothing)

				*
trimming	diving	pushing	floating	
running	riding	jumping	raining	mixing
popping	sliding	finding	sleeping	taxing
dragging	driving	kicking	boating	
wagging	wasting	wanting	waiting	
quitting	whining	munching	cheering	

71. Past Tense Verbs

kneel	knelt	chase	chased
teach	taught	mix	mixed
bring	brought	walk	walked
deal	dealt	bake	baked
sweep	swept	shop	shopped
send	sent		
think	thought		
lend	lent		
drink	drank		

Note: Oddballs are in columns marked with asterisks.

Syllable Junction Sorts, Open and Closed Syllables (VCCV, VCV)

72. Compound Words

landfill	downtown	backyard	homework
homeland	downstairs	backbone	homemade
wasteland	lowdown	backpack	hometown
landlord	downcast	backward	homeroom
landslide	downfall	bareback	homesick
landscape	downpour	flashback	
landmark	breakdown	piggyback	
mainland	countdown	paperback	

73. VCCV at Junction (same/different)

button	market
sunny	garden
yellow	signal
happy	member
happen	basket
sitting	center
fellow	plastic
matter	tablet

74. Syllable Juncture (VCCV, open VCV)

tablet	baby
napkin	human
happen	music
winter	fever
foggy	silent
tennis	duty
sudden	writer
fossil	rival

75. VCV Open and Closed

meter	petal	*
human	rapid	water
secret	punish	busy
paper	magic	
lazy	shiver	
even	comet	
major	river	
climate	clever	
crater	proper	
clover	liquid	
bacon		

76. Closed VCCV/Open VCV

funny	picture	pilot
summer	expert	navy
pretty	until	nature
dollar	forget	music
butter	napkin	spoken
gossip	canyon	frozen
letter	sister	spider
pattern	army	student
	number	

77. Closed/Open with Endings

sadden	dusting	sliding
chipped	rented	shining
matted	helping	named
scarred	sifted	scaring
winner	faster	rider
biggest	longest	tamest
running	walker	moping

78. VCC/CV, VC/CCV, and V/V

athlete	pilgrim	create	*
pumpkin	control	poet	cruel
English	complete	riot	
kingdom	children	trial	
mushroom	monster	lion	
halfway	kitchen	diet	
	hundred		

Unaccented Syllable Sorts

79. *le* and *el*

fable	camel	*
angle	angel	pencil
little	model	journal
rattle	gravel	
settle	motel	
cattle	bushel	
nibble	level	
turtle	pretzel	
table	travel	
middle		

80. *er, ar, or*

bigger	burglar	doctor
freezer	grammar	favor
dreamer	collar	author
faster	dollar	editor
blister	lunar	tractor
jogger	solar	motor
speaker		mayor
skater		
smaller		

81. *er, ar, or*

Comparatives	Agents	Things
sweeter	worker	cellar
thinner	teacher	meter
smarter	waiter	river
slower	voter	pillar
younger	actor	anchor
gentler	beggar	vapor
steeper	barber	trailer
cheaper	skater	flower

82. Final *en/on/in/ain*

broken	dragon	cousin	mountain
hidden	weapon	cabin	captain
heaven	apron	napkin	fountain
chosen	ribbon	pumpkin	curtain
children	gallon		certain
eleven	cotton		

83. Unaccented First Syllables

again	decide	beyond
away	design	begin
another	defend	between
aloud	debate	behave
agree	depend	before
afraid		beside
awoke		

84. /j/ Sound

carriage	budget	magic
voyage	agent	engine
message	angel	region
postage	gorgeous	fragile
village	danger	margin
storage	legend	logic
sausage	pigeon	
savage	dungeon	
courage	gadget	

85. Changing *y* to *i*

cry	cries	cried
hurry	hurries	hurried
party	parties	partied
empty	empties	emptied
baby	babies	babied
reply	replies	replied
supply	supplies	supplied
carry	carries	carried
fry	fries	fried

86. *y* Words by Part of Speech

Long *i*	Long *e*		
Verb	Noun	Adjective	Adverb
try	celery	happy	happily
certify	candy	pretty	correctly
apply	gypsy	guilty	clearly
occupy	quarry	angry	safely
rely	country	silly	horribly
	cemetery		hourly
	category		certainly
	copy		sensibly

Sorts to Explore Accent/Stress

87. Stress in Homographs

re'cord n.	re cord' v.
protest n.	protest v.
conduct n.	conduct v.
subject n.	subject v.
extract n.	extract v.
permit n.	permit v.
insert n.	insert v.
desert n.	desert v.
rebel n.	rebel v.
combat n.	combat v.
conflict n.	conflict v.

88. Long *u* in Stressed Syllable

bu' gle	a muse'
future	compute
ruby	confuse
rumor	reduce
tulip	perfume
tuna	pollute
tutor	salute
super	excuse
pupil	abuse
ruler	include

Revisiting Vowel Patterns in Longer Words

89. Patterns for Long *a*

debate	explain	layer
mistake	dainty	dismay
amaze	trainer	payment
parade	complain	crayons
engage	acquaint	hooray
bracelet	raisin	decay
estate	refrain	betray
escape	painter	

90. Patterns for Long *u* and *o*

rooster	useful	toaster	suppose
cartoon	refuse	oatmeal	decode
scooter	amuse	approach	remote
balloon	reduce	loafer	erode
noodle	conclude	rowboat	tadpole
	pollute	goalie	lonesome
	perfume		explode

91. Patterns for Long *e* and *i*

needle	reason	polite	highway	*
succeed	eager	decide	lightning	sweater
fifteen	increase	advice	delight	believe
thirteen	defeat	invite	tonight	
canteen	season	surprise	resign	
steeple	conceal	survive		

92. Diphthongs in Multisyllable Words

moisture	joyful
appoint	boycott
poison	royal
turquoise	soybean
moisten	oyster
pointless	voyage
broiler	annoy
embroider	enjoy
rejoice	destroy
noisy	employ
avoid	
pointed	

93. More Diphthongs

county	flower	*
council	allow	double
lousy	brownie	
fountain	vowel	
mountain	shower	
scoundrel	towel	
counter	tower	
around	chowder	
bounty	coward	
mouthful	drowsy	
	powder	
	power	

Note: Oddballs are in columns marked with asterisks.

94. Spelling the *er* Sound in Accented and Unaccented Syllables

cer'tain	re verse'	sur prise'	lan'tern
person	observe	perhaps	concert
thirsty	alert	survive	modern
service	prefer	surround	western
hurry	emerge		govern
turkey			

95. Words with *ure* and *er*
(*ture, sure, cher*)

capture	measure	archer	*
creature	treasure	butcher	injure
fracture	pleasure	preacher	failure
mixture	closure	stretcher	
pasture	leisure	teacher	
texture		rancher	
future			
nature			

Affixes

96. Prefixes

unfair	retell	disagree
unable	replay	disappear
uncover	retrain	disgrace
unkind	return	disarm
undress	reuse	disorder
unplug	research	disobey
unequal	regain	disable
uneven	reword	displaced
unpack	rebuild	disloyal
unusual	remodel	dishonest

97. More Prefixes

preschool	explode	misspell
preview	exceed	mistreat
prevent	expose	misplace
preheat	explore	misuse
prefix	exile	misbehave
prepare	expand	mistake
predict	exclaim	

98. Number Prefixes

unicycle	bicycle	tricycle
unison	biweekly	trilogy
unicorn	bisect	triangle
unique	bilingual	tripod
uniform	biplane	triple
universe	bifocals	trio
		triplets

99. Suffixes

sunny	slowly	happily
rainy	quickly	angrily
foggy	sadly	nosily
guilty	calmly	busily
bossy	bravely	drily
dirty	hardly	daintily
messy	strangely	gaily
wordy	weakly	greedily

100. More Suffixes

darkness	harmless	colorful
kindness	fearless	faithful
illness	homeless	dreadful
weakness	restless	thankful
freshness	ageless	thoughtful
hardness	mindless	painful
blindness	helpless	

Derivational Relations Sorts

Adding Suffixes

101. Adding *-ion*

ct + -ion		ss + -ion	
act	action	express	expression
distinct	distinction	impress	impression
select	selection	process	procession
extinct	extinction	depress	depression
predict	prediction	success	succession
subtract	subtraction	profess	profession
contract	contraction	discuss	discussion
affect	affection		

102. *e*-Drop + *-ion*

te + -ion		ce + -ion		se + -ion	
educate	education	induce	induction	expulse	expulsion
congratulate	congratulation	introduce	introduction	convulse	convulsion
create	creation	produce	production	repulse	repulsion
decorate	decoration	deduce	deduction		
generate	generation	reproduce	reproduction		
imitate	imitation	reduce	reduction		
fascinate	fascination				
complicate	complication				
separate	separation				

103. -sion and Spelling Changes

t to s + -sion		de-drop, + -sion	
commit	commission	explode	explosion
transmit	transmission	collide	collision
permit	permission	conclude	conclusion
emit	emission	persuade	persuasion
omit	omission	erode	erosion
regret	regression	delude	delusion
remit	remission	include	inclusion
		divide	division
		intrude	intrusion

104. e-Drop + -ation or -ition

e-drop + -ation		e-drop + ition	
admire	admiration	compose	composition
determine	determination	define	definition
explore	exploration	dispose	disposition
combine	combination	oppose	opposition
declare	declaration	expose	exposition
inspire	inspiration	decompose	decomposition
organize	organization		
examine	examination		
perspire	perspiration		

105. -ible and -able

base + -able	root + -ible
dependable	audible
expendable	edible
breakable	visible
agreeable	feasible
predictable	terrible
remarkable	possible
readable	legible
profitable	plausible
perishable	horrible
punishable	tangible
laughable	credible

106. -able after e

e-drop	soft ce/ge	hard c/g
presumable	changeable	navigable
desirable	manageable	amicable
usable	peaceable	despicable
lovable	serviceable	impeccable
deplorable	noticeable	applicable
comparable		
excusable		

107. Assimilated Prefix Sort

com-	ad-	in-
compound	adverse	inactive
conform	affair	irresponsible
colleague	affront	immature
compact	assemble	irrational
context	affirm	immortal
correlate	arrange	illogical
constrain	acclaim	innumerable
	admit	illegal

Vowel Alternations and Reduced Vowels in Unaccented Syllables

108. Vowel Alternations in Related Pairs

Long a to Short a	Long a to Schwa
cave/cavity	major/majority
humane/humanity	narrate/narrative
nation/national	relate/relative
volcano/volcanic	famous/infamous
grave/gravity	able/ability
nature/natural	native/nativity
insane/insanity	educate/educable
flame/flammable	proclaim/proclamation
profane/profanity	stable/stability

109. Vowel Alternations in Related Pairs

Long e to Short e	Long e to Schwa
serene/serenity	compete/competition
brief/brevity	repeat/repetition
proceed/procession	remedial/remedy
recede/recession	
succeed/succession	
conceive/conception	
receive/reception	

110. Vowel Alternations in Related Pairs

Long i to Short i	Long i to Schwa
resign/resignation	invite/invitation
sign/signal	define/definition
divine/divinity	reside/resident
divide/division	recite/recitation
revise/revision	deprive/deprivation
deride/derision	admire/admiration
criticize/criticism	inspire/inspiration
arise/arisen	preside/president

111. Vowel Alternations in Related Pairs

Long to Short	Long to Schwa	Schwa to Short
induce/induction	compose/composition	metal/metallic
seduce/seduction	propose/proposition	brutal/brutality
reduce/reduction	impose/imposition	local/locality
produce/production	expose/exposition	spiritual/spirituality
telescope/telescopic	harmonious/harmony	vital/vitality
microscope/microscopic	compete/competition	fatal/fatality
prescribe/prescription	serene/serenity	total/totality
		final/finality
		original/originality

Sorting by Roots

112. Greek and Latin Science Vocabulary Sort

astro	astronomer, astronaut, astrology, astrolabe
bio	biology, biome, biosphere, biotic
chlor	chlorophyll, chloroplast, chlorine, chlorella
eco	ecology, economy, ecosystem, ecotype
hydro	hydrophobia, hydrology, hydrogen
hypo	hypodermis, hypodermic, hypothermia, hypotension
photo/phos	phosphorescent, photography, telephoto
vor	voracious, omnivore, carnivore

113. Greek Roots

autograph	telegram
automatic	telepathy
autobiography	telegraph
autonomy	televise
automobile	telephone
autonomous	teleconference

114. Latin Roots (contrast 3 or 4 at a time)

judge	traction	suspect	visual	formulate	credit	portable	dictate
adjudicate	contract	spectator	visionary	uniform	incredible	porter	contradict
judgment	attract	inspect	vision	reform	discredit	reporter	prediction
judicial	intractable	respect	vista	transform	creed	portfolio	verdict
prejudice	subtraction	spectacular	visible	deformed	credulous	export	dictionary
judicious	tractor	inspector	revise	nonconformist	accredit	import	dictator
prejudicial	contraction	spectacles	television				diction
judiciary	protractor	disrespect	supervise				
	distraction	expectation					
		circumspect					

conduct	fertile	pressure	respiration
induct	refer	express	spirit
educate	transfer	depression	expire
introduction	suffer	suppress	perspire
produce	conifer	impression	inspiration
reduce	conference	oppressive	conspire
induction			

Creating Your Own Word Sort Sheets

The following lists of words are organized by features students need to study in the letter name–alphabetic through derivational relations stages. Under each feature the words are generally grouped by frequency and complexity. For example, under short-*a*, the early part of the list offers words most likely encountered by first graders (*am, ran, that*). The latter part of the list contains words that may be obscure in meaning and spelled with blends or digraphs (*yam, brass, tramp*). Fry's 300 instant words listed on page 366 are the most frequent words and should be included in beginner sorts.

The lists include possible exceptions or oddballs that can be added to sorts. Sometimes the oddballs you include will be true exceptions (such as *said* in a sort with long-*a* patterns), but other times oddballs may represent a less common spelling pattern, such as *ey* representing long-*a* in *prey* and *grey*.

Prepare word sorts to use with students by writing the selected words on a template such as the one on page 401 in Appendix F. We recommend that you enlarge the template about 5 to 8 percent before writing in the words neatly. Be sure to insert the words randomly so students can make their own discoveries as they sort. Many people find it easy to create computer-generated word sort sheets using the "table" function in a word processing program. First, set the margins all around at 0.5 inches, and then insert a table that is three columns by six to eight rows. Save the blank template to use again. Type in words in each cell, leaving a blank line before and after each word. After typing in all words, "select" the entire table and click on the "center" button. Choose a simple font (Ariel and Geneva work well) and a large font size (26 works well). After creating the sort, save it using a name that defines the features such as "Short Vowels: a, o, e." You can contrast sounds, spelling patterns, word endings, prefixes, root words, and so on. Here are some reminders and tips about creating your own word sorts.

1. Create sorts that will help students form their own generalizations about how words work. Use a collection of 15 to 25 words so that there are plenty of examples to consider.
2. Contrast at least two, and up to four, features in a sort. There are many sample sorts in Appendix D to give you ideas.

   Examples of sound sorts:
   Contrast short-*o* and long-*o*.
   Contrast the sound of *ear* in *learn* and in *hear*.
   Contrast the sound of *g* in *guest* and *gym*.

   Examples of pattern sorts:
   Contrast long-*o* spelled with *oa, o-e,* and *ow*.
   Contrast words that end with *or, er,* and *ar*.
   Contrast words that double a consonant before *-ing* with those that do not.

   Examples of meaning sorts:
   Contrast words derived from *spect* and *port*.
   Contrast words with prefixes *sub, un,* and *trans*.

   The best sorts are those that combine a sound sort with a pattern sort. For example, a long-*o* and short-*o* sort can begin with a sound sort and then proceed to sort the long vowels by patterns—CVVC and CVCe.
3. Consider whether you want to underline key words or create headers for the sort. Your decision will depend on the level of support you feel your students need, as described in Chapter 3.
4. In most sorts, include up to three oddballs when possible—words that have the same sound or pattern but are not consistent with the generalization that governs the other words. For example, in a long-*o* sort, with words sorted by the *oa, o-e,* and *ow* patterns, the exceptions might include the words *now* and *love* since they look like they would have the long-*o* sound but do not. The best oddballs are high-frequency words students already know from reading. These are listed under *Oddballs* in the word lists in this appendix.

5. Words in a sort can be made easier or harder in a number of ways:

- Common words like *hat* or *store* are easier than uncommon words like *vat* or *boar*. It is important to use words students know from their own reading in the letter name–alphabetic and within word pattern stages to make sorts easier. This is less important when you get to syllables and affixes and derivational relations stages in which words sorts can help to extend a student's vocabulary.
- Add words with blends, digraphs, and complex consonant units (e.g., *ce*, *dge*, or *tch*) to make words harder. *Bat* and *blast* are both CVC words, but *blast* is harder to read and spell.
- Adding more oddballs to a sort makes the sort harder. But don't use oddballs students are not likely to know (like *plaid* in a long-*a* sort for students early in the within word pattern stage).

300 Instant High-Frequency Words

First Hundred

a	can	her	many	see	us
about	come	here	me	she	very
after	day	him	much	so	was
again	did	his	my	some	we
all	do	how	new	take	were
an	down	I	no	that	what
and	eat	if	not	the	when
any	for	in	of	their	which
are	from	is	old	them	who
as	get	it	on	then	will
at	give	just	one	there	with
be	go	know	or	they	work
been	good	like	other	this	would
before	had	little	our	three	you
boy	has	long	out	to	your
but	have	make	put	two	
by	he	man	said	up	

Second Hundred

also	color	home	must	red	think
am	could	house	name	right	too
another	dear	into	near	run	tree
away	each	kind	never	saw	under
back	ear	last	next	say	until
ball	end	leave	night	school	upon
because	far	left	only	seem	use
best	find	let	open	shall	want
better	first	live	over	should	way
big	five	look	own	soon	where
black	found	made	people	stand	while
book	four	may	play	such	white
both	friend	men	please	sure	wish
box	girl	more	present	tell	why
bring	got	morning	pretty	than	year
call	hand	most	ran	these	
came	high	mother	read	thing	

Third Hundred

along	didn't	food	keep	sat	though
always	does	full	letter	second	today
anything	dog	funny	longer	set	took
around	don't	gave	love	seven	town
ask	door	goes	might	show	try
ate	dress	green	money	sing	turn
bed	early	grow	myself	sister	walk
brown	eight	hat	now	sit	warm
buy	every	happy	o'clock	six	wash
car	eyes	hard	off	sleep	water
carry	face	head	once	small	woman
clean	fall	hear	order	start	write
close	fast	help	pair	stop	yellow
clothes	fat	hold	part	ten	yes
coat	fine	hope	ride	thank	yesterday
cold	fire	hot	round	third	
cut	fly	jump	same	those	

Copyright © 2000 Edward B. Fry. Used with permission.

Word Lists

a Families

at	ad	ag	an	ap	ab	am	all	ar	art
at*	had*	bag	man*	cap	cab	am**	all*	bar	cart
cat	bad	rag	than**	lap	dab	dam	ball**	car	dart
bat	dad	sag	ran**	gap	jab	ham	call**	far**	mart
fat	mad	wag	can*	map	nab	ram	tall	jar	part
hat	pad	nag	fan	nap	lab	jam	fall	par	tart
mat	sad	flag	pan	rap	tab	clam	hall	star	start
pat	rad	brag	tan	yap	blab	slam	mall		chart
rat	glad	drag	van	tap	crab	cram	wall		smart
sat	lad	shag	plan	zap	scab	wham	small		
that*		snag	clan	clap	stab	swam	stall		
flat		lag	scan	flap	grab	yam			
brat		tag		slap	slab	gram			
chat				trap					
gnat				chap					
				snap					
				wrap					
				strap					

and	ang	ash	ack	ank	amp	ast	ant	atch	ass
hand**	bang	bash	back**	bank	camp	fast	ant	batch	mass
band	fang	cash	pack	sank	damp	cast	pant	catch	pass
land	hang	dash	jack	tank	lamp	past	chant	hatch	class
sand	sang	gash	rack	yank	ramp	last**	slant	latch	grass
brand	rang	hash	lack	blank	champ	mast	grant	match	brass
grand	clang	mash	sack	plank	clamp	vast	plant	patch	glass
stand**		rash	tack	crank	cramp			snatch	bass
strand		sash	black**	drank	stamp			scratch	
		lash	quack	prank	tramp				
		trash	crack	spank	scamp				
		crash	track	thank					
		smash	shack						
		slash	snack						
		clash	stack						
		flash							

More Short-*a* Words

as*	wax	bath	fact	draft	ranch	*Oddballs*		
has*	ask	path	mask	shaft	grasp	want**		saw**
gal	yak	task	bask	craft	plant	what*		laugh
pal	tax	calf	raft	staff	shall**	was*		
gas	math	half	lamb	graph	branch			

*Occurs in first 100 instant words.

**Occurs in second 100 instant words.

e Families

et	en	ed	ell	eg	ess	eck	est	end	ent
get*	men**	red**	tell**	beg	less	deck	best**	end**	bent
let**	den	bed	bell	peg	mess	neck	nest	bend	dent
bet	hen	fed	cell	leg	guess	peck	pest	lend	cent
met	ten	led	fell	keg	bless	wreck	rest	mend	lent
net	pen	wed	jell		dress	speck	test	send	rent
pet	then*	bled	sell		press	check	vest	tend	sent
set	when*	fled	well		stress	fleck	west	blend	tent
wet	wren	sled	shell				chest	spend	vent
vet	Ben	shed	smell				jest	trend	went
fret	Ken	shred	spell				crest		scent
jet			swell				guest		spent
yet			dwell						

More Short-e Words

									Spelled ea	
yes	gem	pep	left**	melt	self	etch	clench	read**	death
web	them*	step	kept	pelt	shelf	fetch	drench	head	breath
egg	hem	held	slept	knelt	fresh	sketch	tempt	bread	dread
elm	stem	help	wept		flesh	wretch	tenth	dead	deaf
next**		desk	swept			stretch	debt	lead	wealth
								tread	health
								spread	

Short-i Families

it	id	ig	in	ill	im	ip	ick	ink	int	itch	ing
it*	did*	big**	in*	will*	dim	dip	lick	link	mint	itch	king
bit	hid	dig	fin	dill	him*	hip	kick	mink	lint	pitch	ping
fit	lid	fig	pin	fill	Jim	lip	pick	pink	hint	ditch	sing
hit	kid	jig	tin	hill	Kim	nip	sick	sink	print	hitch	ring
lit	bid	pig	din	kill	rim	rip	tick	rink	glint	witch	wing
pit	rid	rig	win	gill	Tim	sip	slick	wink	flint	switch	thing**
sit	slid	wig	bin	mill	trim	tip	quick	think**			bring**
kit	skid	zig	thin	pill	brim	zip	trick	blink			sling
wit		twig	twin	till	swim	whip	chick	drink			sting
skit			chin	bill	slim	clip	flick	stink			swing
spit			shin	drill	whim	flip	brick	clink			spring
slit			spin	grill	grim	slip	stick	shrink			string
quit			grin	chill	skim	skip	thick				cling
				skill		drip	click				fling
				spill		trip	prick				wring
				still		chip					
				thrill		ship					
				quill		snip					
						strip					

More Short-i Words

												Oddballs
if*	his*	mix	mitt	crib	cliff	rich	film	risk	swift	disc	child
is*	this*	six	hiss	fish	stiff	wind	tilt	brisk	inch	sixth	mind
with*	which*	fix	kiss	dish	lift	fist	limp	sift	pinch	fifth	find**
wish**	live**	whiz	milk	swish	gift	inn	limb	shift			climb

Short-*o* Families

ot		ob	og†	op	ock	ong	oss
not*	blot	bob	dog	cop	cock	long*	boss
got**	slot	cob	bog	hop	dock	bong	toss
hot	plot	job	fog	pop	lock	gong	moss
jot	shot	rob	hog	mop	mock	song	loss
lot	spot	gob	jog	top	rock	strong	gloss
pot	knot	mob	log	slop	sock	throng	cross
cot	trot	sob	clog	flop	tock		
dot		snob	frog	drop	block		
		blob		shop	clock		
		glob		stop	flock		
		knob		crop	smock		
		throb		plop	shock		
				prop	stock		

More Short-*o* Words

					Ambiguous Sounds of *o*†			Oddballs	
box**	rod	prod	fond	notch	on*	lost	moth	of*	for*
ox	sod	odd	bond	romp	off	cost	cloth	won	from*
fox	god	mom	blond	stomp	loft	frost	broth	son	cold
pox	plod	con	gosh	prompt	soft	doll	golf	front	post

u Families

ut	ub	ug	um	un	ud	uck	ump	ung
but*	cub	bug	bum	run**	bud	buck	bump	sung
cut	hub	dug	gum	fun	mud	duck	jump	rung
gut	rub	hug	hum	gun	stud	luck	dump	hung
hut	tub	jug	sum	bun	thud	suck	hump	lung
nut	club	mug	plum	sun		tuck	lump	swung
rut	grub	rug	slum	spun		yuck	pump	clung
jut	snub	tug	scum	stun		pluck	rump	strung
shut	stub	slug	chum			cluck	plump	slung
strut	scrub	plug	drum			truck	stump	sprung
	shrub	drug	strum			stuck	thump	wrung
		snug					clump	flung
							slump	stung
							grump	

uff	unk	ush	ust	unch	umb
buff	bunk	gush	must**	bunch	dumb
cuff	hunk	hush	just*	hunch	numb
huff	junk	mush	gust	lunch	crumb
muff	sunk	rush	dust	munch	thumb
ruff	chunk	blush	bust	punch	plumb
puff	drunk	brush	rust	crunch	
fluff	flunk	crush	crust	brunch	
stuff	skunk	flush	trust		
snuff	shrunk	slush			
scuff	stunk				
gruff	slunk				
bluff	trunk				

†These words do not have a short *o* in some dialects, but instead are pronounced as "aw."

More Short-u Words

					ul‡	ou = u	o = u	o-e =u	Oddballs
up*	much*	buzz	gull	hunt	gulp	tough	of*	come*	put*
us*	such**	fuzz	dull	grunt	bulge	rough	does	some*	push
pup	plus	tusk	mutt	stunt	bulk	touch	son	none	bush
cup	thus	dusk	butt	shucks	gulf	young	ton	done	truth
bus	fuss	husk	tuft		sulk		won	love	
					pulse		from*	dove	
							front	glove	

Long a Words

CVCe						CVVC			CVV-Open	CVVC
a-e						ai			ay	ei
made**	ate	wake	tame	ape	pane	rain	wait	snail	day	eight
name**	gate	fake	fame	gape	vane	pain	bait	frail	jay	neigh
same	hate	shake	flame	grape	mane	tail	gain	praise	may**	rein
came**	late	brake	blame	drape	slate	nail	vain	trail	play**	weigh
make*	date	flake	lame	trace	scale	mail	main	strait	say**	weight
take*	sale	base	lane	grace	stale	sail	plain	saint	stay	eighth
bake	male	vase	plane	space	gaze	pail	chain	quaint	way**	freight
cake	tale	chase	cane	waste	daze	rail	stain	strain	clay	reign
lake	whale	race	crane	paste	blaze	fail	drain	faith	gray	veil
age	pale	lace	rate	taste	graze	jail	grain	straight	pray	sleigh
cage	fade	place	fate	haste	haze	gain	brain		tray	beige
page	wade	pace	crate	sake	range	main	aim	Oddballs	slay	heir
face	shade	state	grate	quake	change	train	claim	said*		vein
gave	grade	plate	bathe	drake	strange	aid	ail	again*	Oddballs	
save	trade	skate	cave	phase		paid	aide	their*	they*	Oddballs
wave	shape	rage	grave	jade	Oddballs	maid	raid		prey	break
tape	cape	stage		blade	have*	laid	paint		grey	great
safe	mate				dance	braid	waist		hey	steak
					chance					

Long e Words

CVCe	CVVC											CVV-open
e-e	ea				ee						ie	
eve	read**	beak	east	leave**	seem**	deep	kneel	sheep	spree		thief	see*
scene	sea	leak	feast	weave	feed	beep	steel	sleep	geese		chief	bee
scheme	eat*	weak	least	flea	seep	seep	wheel	creep	cheese		grief	wee
theme	beat	peak	clean	peace	feel	jeep	speed	steep	sneeze		brief	free
these**	seat	lean	steal	please**	feet	keep	bleed	sweep	breeze		yield	tree**
	meat	heal	knead	cease	beet	seek	greed	creek	freeze		field	flee
Open	mean	real	sneak	crease	meet	week	breed	cheek	sleeve		shield	glee
me*	bean	deal	creak	grease	seen	beef	keen	sleek	screen		niece	knee
he*	seal	meal	steam	squeal	week	reef	green	speech	preen		piece	three*
we*	tea	heap	dream	league	peek	eel	queen	teeth			shriek	
be*	pea	leap	cream	breathe	seed	heel		sleet	Oddballs		priest	
the*	bead	seam	scream	squeak	need	reel		greet	been*		grieve	
she*	neat	each**	stream		peep	peel		sheet	seize		fierce	
	team	teach	plead	Oddballs		deed		sweet	weird		fiend	
	beam	beach	knead	head		weed		fleet	vein		siege	
	lead	reach	beast	dead				street	suite		pier	
	ear**	peach	treat	steak								
				great							Oddballs	
				break							friend**	

‡These words have a slightly different u sound before the l.

Long-*i* Words

CVCe

i-e

like*	five**	while**	wide	white**	tribe
bike	mine	ice	slide	quite	scribe
dime	fine	mice	pride	write	stride
time	nine	nice	tide	spite	stripe
hide	vine	rice	glide	site	strike
ride	shine	mile	wipe	lice	spine
side	drive	file	pipe	spice	whine
line	dive	pile	swipe	slice	prime
live	hive	smile	spike	twice	chime
kite	life	wise	lime	price	fife
size	ripe	rise	crime	guide	knife
bite	hike	wife	pine	prize	thrive

CVV-open

ie

lie
pie
tie
die

Oddballs

buy
guy
live**
give*
eye

CV-open

y/ye

my*
by*
why**
fly
cry
sky
try
dry
shy
sly
spry
dye
lye
rye

VCC

igh

high**	find**
night**	kind**
right**	mind
light	climb
might	child
bright	wild
fight	mild
sigh	blind
tight	grind
flight	hind
fright	sign
sight	bind
slight	wind
thigh	rind

Long-*o* Words

CVCe

o-e

home**	wove	rove	slope
nose	drove	cove	lope
hole	dome	stove	lone
rope	globe	whole	stroke
robe	cone	sole	throne
note	zone	wrote	quote
hose	role	choke	clothe
hope	stole	broke	
vote	doze	poke	
code	froze	smoke	
mole	pose	yoke	
pole	chose	spoke	
joke	those	tone	
stone	close	shone	
		phone	

C V VC

oa

boat	foam	float
coat	roam	coach
goat	goal	roach
road	coal	throat
toad	loaf	toast
load	coax	coast
soap	whoa	boast
oat	loan	roast
oak	moan	cloak
soak	groan	croak
whoa	moat	loaves

Oddballs

one*	love	some*
done	dove	come*
none	glove	move
gone	prove	lose
once	shove	whose
tomb		

CV-Open

o

go*
no*
so*
ho
yo-yo

oe

toe
woe
doe
hoe
foe

Oddballs

to*
do*
who*
two*
shoe
broad
sew

C V V

ow

bow
know*
show
slow
snow
crow
blow
glow
grow
sow
low
tow
flow
own**
flown
throw
thrown
blown
grown
bowl

VCC

oCC

old*	both**
gold	most**
hold	folk
cold	roll
told	poll
fold	stroll
mold	scroll
sold	post
bold	ghost
scold	host
bolt	comb
colt	
jolt	
volt	

Long-u Words

CVCe		CVVC	CVV	CVVC			CVV		Oddballs
u-e		*ui*	*ue*	*oo – /u_/*			*ew*		*Oddballs*
use**	nude	fruit	blue	too**	goof	whoop	new*	brew	do*
cute	crude	suit	due	zoo	soon**	scoop	dew	stew	you*
rude	dune	bruise	clue	moo	noon	school**	chew	crew	to*
rule	flute	cruise	glue	boot	moon	spoon	drew	whew	two*
mule	fume	juice	true	root	zoom	tooth	few	screw	build
tune	chute		flue	food	boom	shoot	flew	threw	built
June	mute		hue	mood	loom	smooth	knew	shrewd	guide
tube	plume		cue	tool	bloom	roost	grew	strewn	truth
cube	prune		sue	cool	gloom	proof			through
duke	muse		fuel	fool	loop	stool			guilt
huge	spruce		cruel	pool	troop	spook			suite
dude				roof		brood			

Ambiguous Vowels: ô sound

al	au	aw		o		ough	w + a
tall	caught	saw**	gnaw	on*	loss	cough	was*
wall	taught	paw	thaw	off	cross	ought	want**
mall	pause	law	caw	dog	gloss	fought	wash
talk	sauce	draw	bawl	frog	cloth	bought	wand
walk	fault	claw	awe	log	moth	thought	wasp
calm	haunt	dawn	drawn	fog	broth	brought	watt
palm	launch	lawn	crawl	bog	soft	trough	swap
bald	because**	yawn	shawl	hog	loft		swat
halt	fraud	fawn	sprawl	lost	golf		watch
salt	haul	hawk	squawk	cost	bong		
small	maul	raw	straw	frost	song		/w/ + a
stall	jaunt	gawk	scrawl	boss	long*		squash
stalk	gaunt			toss	strong		squat
chalk				moss	throng		squad
waltz	*Oddballs*						
false	aunt						
scald	laugh						

Ambiguous Vowels/Diphthongs (*ou/ow* and *oi/oy*)

ow		ou			oo‡		oi	oy
ow		*ou*			*oo‡*		*oi*	*oy*
how*	drown	out*	house**	*Oddballs*	book**	*Oddballs*	coin	boy*
now	frown	our*	about*	could**	look**	blood	join	toy
cow	crown	loud	mouse	would*	good*	flood	oil	joy
down*	crowd	ouch	foul	should**	cook		foil	enjoy
bow	fowl	cloud	mouth	touch	took		soil	soy
wow	scowl	proud	shout	young	foot		boil	ploy
town	prowl	count	pout	cough	wood		coil	
gown	growl	round	scout	tough	hook		point	
brown	vow	sound	snout	through	shook		joint	
clown		found**	stout	rough	stood		hoist	
owl		pound	sprout		wool		moist	
howl		mound	pouch		crook		toil	
sow		bound	couch		hood		broil	
plow		hound	crouch		hoof		voice	
		wound	drought		soot		noise	
		ground	doubt		brook		choice	
					nook			

‡Compare to *oo* words under long-u

r-Influenced Vowels

ar		ar + e	are	air	ear /ee/	eer	er	ear /@/	Oddballs
far**	dart	carve	care	fair	ear**	deer	her*	heard	very*
car	start	large	bare	hair	near**	cheer	fern	earth	their*
jar	bark	starve	dare	pair	hear	steer	herd	learn	there*
star	shark	barge	share	stair	dear**	queer	jerk	earn	were*
card	lark	charge	stare	flair	year**	jeer	term	search	here*
hard	scar		mare	chair	fear	sneer	germ	pearl	where**
yard	mar	Oddballs	flare	lair	tear	peer	stern	yearn	heart
art	barb	are*	glare		clear		herb		bear
part	harp	war	rare		beard		per		wear
cart	sharp	warm	scare		gear		perk		swear
bar	snarl		hare		spear		perch		pear
arm	scarf		snare		shear		clerk		hearth
harm	charm		blare		smear		nerve		
dark	arch		fare				serve		
park	march		square				verse		
spark	smart						swerve		
yarn	chart								

ur	ure	ir	ire	or	ore	our	oar	w + ar	w + or
burn	sure**	girl**	fire	or*	more**	your*	roar	warm	work*
hurt	cure	first**	tire	for*	store	four**	soar	war	word
turn	pure	bird	wire	born	shore	pour	boar	ward	world
curl	lure	dirt	hire	corn	bore	mourn	coarse	wharf	worm
curb		stir	sire	horn	chore	court	hoarse	quart	worth
burst	ur-e	sir		worn	score	fourth	board	swarm	worse
church	curve	shirt	ier	cord	sore	gourd		warp	
churn	nurse	skirt	drier	cork	before*	source	oor	wart	
surf	curse	third	pliers	pork	wore	course	door	warn	
purr	urge	birth	flier	fort	tore		poor		
burr		firm	crier	short	swore	Oddballs	floor		
blur		swirl		nor		our*			
lurch		twirl	iar	ford		flour			
lurk		chirp	liar	lord		hour			
spur		squirt	briar	storm		scour			
hurl		thirst	friar	porch		sour			
blurt		squirm		torch					
				force					
				north					
				horse					
				forth					
				scorn					
				chord					
				forge					
				gorge					

Complex Consonants

ch	tch	Cch		Hard g		Soft g	dge	Cge
teach	catch	ranch	arch	frog	guide	huge	edge	range
reach	patch	branch	march	drug	guard	cage	ledge	change
beach	hatch	lunch	starch	twig	guilt	age	hedge	barge
peach	latch	bunch	search	flag	guess	page	wedge	charge
coach	match	munch	perch	shrug	guest	stage	pledge	large
speech	watch	punch	lurch	gave	ghost	rage	badge	forge
couch	ditch	bench	church	game		orange	ridge	gorge
crouch	pitch	clench	birch	gain	*Oddballs*	gem	bridge	surge
pouch	witch	trench	torch	gauge	get*	germ	lodge	bulge
screech	switch	wrench	porch	gone	girl**	gene	dodge	strange
pooch	fetch	drench	scorch	goat	gift	gym	judge	sponge
	sketch	pinch		gold	gear	gyp	budge	plunge
Oddballs	clutch	finch		goose	geese	giant	fudge	hinge
rich	scratch	hunch		goof		gist	smudge	merge
such	stretch	mulch		golf			trudge	lounge
much*	stitch	gulch		gulp			grudge	
which*	twitch	launch		gull				
	blotch			gust				
				gulf				

Hard c	Soft c	ce	se /z/	se /s/	-ze	-z	-ve	Voiceless th	Voiced th
card	cell	rice	wise	cease	size	buzz	love	bath	bathe
cave	cent	face	chose	dense	haze	fizz	dove	cloth	clothe
cast	cease	place	close	false	doze	jazz	shove	booth	soothe
cause	cinch	brace	phase	geese	prize	frizz	glove	loath	loathe
caught	cyst	slice	muse	goose	froze	quiz	have*	teeth	teethe
couch	cite	price	those	loose	graze	quartz	give*	breath	breathe
core		truce	these**	moose	blaze	waltz	move		seethe
coin		trace	prose	mouse	gauze		weave	*Silent w*	
coast		since	cause	nurse	seize		leave	write	*Silent k*
cost		fence	noise	purse	freeze		curve	wrist	know*
coach		peace	pause	sense	sneeze		nerve	wrap	knew
cough		juice	raise	tense	snooze		serve	wrong	knee
curb		niece	tease	rinse	breeze		twelve	wreck	knit
curl		voice	cheese	verse	maize		solve	wring	knock
curve		sauce	please	chase	bronze		prove	who*	knife
cult		once	poise	close	wheeze		sleeve		knight
cuff		hence	browse	blouse	squeeze			*Silent g*	knob
		force	choose	house**				gnaw	knot
		ounce	bruise	pulse				gnome	
		dance	cruise	lapse				gnat	*Silent b*
		chance		worse				gnash	crumb
		prince		hoarse				gnu	comb
		fleece		glimpse					limb
		piece						*Silent h*	thumb
		bounce						ghost	climb
		source						herb	lamb
		choice						honest	doubt
		fierce						rhino	tomb
								rhyme	numb
								hour	

Homophones

be/bee	hey/hay	serial/cereal	Mary/marry/merry	browse/brows
blue/blew	made/maid	cheap/cheep	great/grate	bred/bread
I/eye/aye	male/mail	days/daze	seem/seam	guessed/guest
no/know	nay/neigh	dew/do/due	knew/new	rest/wrest
here/hear	oh/owe	doe/dough	stair/stare	beech/beach
to/too/two	pail/pale	heel/heal	hour/our	real/reel
hi/high	pair/pear/pare	horse/hoarse	rough/ruff	peel/peal
new/knew/gnu	peek/peak/pique	ho/hoe	poor/pour	team/teem
see/sea	reed/read/Reid	in/inn	haul/hall	leak/leek
there/they're/their	so/sew/sow	need/knead	piece/peace	sees/seas
bear/bare	root/route	lone/loan	ant/aunt	sheer/shear
by/buy/bye	shone/shown	we/wee	flair/flare	feet/feat
deer/dear	aid/aide	ring/wring	mist/missed	hymn/him
ate/eight	add/ad	peddle/petal/pedal	mane/main	whit/wit
for/four/fore	break/brake	straight/strait	wail/whale/wale	scents/cents/sense
our/hour	cent/sent/scent	pole/poll	died/dyed	tents/tense
red/read	flee/flea	earn/urn	manor/manner	gilt/guilt
lead/led	creak/creek	past/passed	pier/peer	knit/nit
meat/meet	die/dye	sweet/suite	Ann/an	tic/tick
plane/plain	fair/fare	ore/or	tacks/tax	sight/site/cite
rode/road/rowed	hair/hare	rain/reign/rein	cash/cache	rye/wry
sail/sale	heard/herd	role/roll	rap/wrap	style/stile
stare/stair	night/knight	sole/soul	maze/maize	might/mite
we'd/weed	steel/steal	seller/cellar	air/heir	climb/clime
we'll/wheel	tail/tale	shoo/shoe	bail/bale	fined/find
hole/whole	thrown/throne	soar/sore	ail/ale	side/sighed
wear/ware/where	fir/fur	steak/stake	prays/praise	tide/tied
one/won	waist/waste	some/sum	base/bass	vice/vise
flower/flour	week/weak	tow/toe	faint/feint	awl/all
right/write	we've/weave	vein/vane/vain	wade/weighed	paws/pause
your/you're	way/weigh	medal/metal/meddle	wave/waive	born/borne
lye/lie	wait/weight	wrote/rote	knave/nave	chord/cord
its/it's	threw/through	forth/fourth	whet/wet	foul/fowl
not/knot	vail/veil/vale	tea/tee	sell/cell	mall/maul
gate/gait	aisle/I'll/isle	been/bin	bell/belle	mourn/morn
jeans/genes	ball/bawl	board/bored	bowled/bold	rot/wrought
time/thyme	beat/beet	course/coarse	bough/bow	bald/balled
son/sun	bolder/boulder	boy/buoy		

Compound Words by Common Base Words

We have limited the list here to words that have base words across a number of compound words.

aircraft	checkbook	foothold	homesick	snowman	raincoat
airline	cookbook	footlights	homespun	fireman	raindrop
airmail	scrapbook	footnote	homestead	gentleman	rainfall
airplane	textbook	footprint	homework	handyman	rainstorm
airport	buttercup	footstep	horseback	policeman	roadblock
airtight	butterfly	footstool	horsefly	salesman	roadway
anybody	buttermilk	barefoot	horseman	nightfall	roadwork
anymore	butterscotch	tenderfoot	horseplay	nightgown	railroad
anyone	doorbell	grandchildren	horsepower	nightmare	sandbag
anyplace	doorknob	granddaughter	horseshoe	nighttime	sandbar
anything	doorman	grandfather	racehorse	overnight	sandbox
anywhere	doormat	grandmother	sawhorse	outbreak	sandpaper
backboard	doorstep	grandparent	houseboat	outcast	sandpiper
backbone	doorway	grandson	housefly	outcome	sandstone
backfire	backdoor	haircut	housewife	outcry	seacoast
background	outdoor	hairdo	housework	outdated	seafood
backpack	downcast	hairdresser	housetop	outdo	seagull
backward	downhill	hairpin	birdhouse	outdoors	seaman
backyard	download	hairstyle	clubhouse	outfield	seaport
bareback	downpour	handbag	doghouse	outfit	seasick
feedback	downright	handball	greenhouse	outgrow	seashore
flashback	downsize	handbook	townhouse	outlaw	seaside
hatchback	downstairs	handcuffs	landfill	outline	seaweed
paperback	downstream	handmade	landlady	outlook	snowball
piggyback	downtown	handout	landlord	outnumber	snowflake
bathrobe	breakdown	handshake	landmark	outpost	snowman
bathroom	countdown	handspring	landscape	outrage	snowplow
bathtub	sundown	handstand	landslide	outright	snowshoe
birdbath	touchdown	handwriting	dreamland	outside	snowstorm
bedrock	eyeball	backhand	farmland	outsmart	somebody
bedroom	eyebrow	firsthand	homeland	outwit	someone
bedside	eyeglasses	secondhand	highland	blowout	someday
bedspread	eyelash	underhand	wasteland	carryout	somehow
bedtime	eyelid	headache	wonderland	cookout	somewhere
flatbed	eyesight	headband	lifeboat	handout	something
hotbed	eyewitness	headdress	lifeguard	hideout	sometime
sickbed	shuteye	headfirst	lifejacket	workout	underline
waterbed	firearm	headlight	lifelike	lookout	undergo
birthday	firecracker	headline	lifelong	overall	underground
birthmark	firefighter	headlong	lifestyle	overboard	undermine
birthplace	firefly	headmaster	lifetime	overcast	underwater
birthstone	firehouse	headphones	nightlife	overcome	watercolor
childbirth	fireman	headquarters	wildlife	overflow	waterfall
blackberry	fireplace	headstart	lighthouse	overhead	watermelon
blackbird	fireproof	headstrong	lightweight	overlook	waterproof
blackboard	fireside	headway	daylight	overview	saltwater
blackmail	firewood	airhead	flashlight	playground	windfall
blacksmith	fireworks	blockhead	headlight	playhouse	windmill
blacktop	backfire	figurehead	moonlight	playmate	windpipe
bookcase	bonfire	homeland	spotlight	playpen	windshield
bookkeeper	campfire	homemade	sunlight	playroom	windswept
bookmark	football	homemaker	mailman	playwright	downwind
bookworm	foothill	homeroom	doorman	rainbow	headwind

Plurals

ch + es	sh + es	ss + es	x + es	y + s	Change y to i + es				f to ves
arches	bushes	bosses	foxes	plays	flies	babies	daisies	stories	wives
watches	dishes	classes	boxes	stays	fries	berries	guppies	buddies	knives
coaches	flashes	glasses	taxes	trays	cries	bodies	ladies	sixties	leaves
couches	brushes	crosses	axes	donkeys	tries	bunnies	parties		loaves
inches	ashes	guesses	mixes	monkeys	skies	cities	pennies	*Oddballs*	lives
peaches	wishes	kisses		jockeys	spies	copies	ponies	goalies	wolves
notches	crashes	passes		turkeys	dries	counties	supplies	taxies	calves
lunches	leashes	dresses		volleys		fairies	puppies	movies	elves
switches	lashes		**s + es**	valleys		duties	bullies	cookies	scarves
churches			gases	enjoys		armies	hobbies		selves
branches			buses	obeys		fairies	spies		shelves
benches				decays			skies		

Verbs for Inflected Ending Sorts

VCC		**C V V C**	***e*-Drop**		**C V C Words That Double**			**Don't Double**	**Irregular Verbs**
help	act	need	live**	dance	stop	drip	grab	level	see/saw
jump	add	wait	time	glance	pat	fan	hug	edit	fall/fell
want**	crash	boat	name	hike	sun	flop	jam	enter	feel/felt
ask	crack	shout	bake	hire	top	grin	kid	exit	tell/told
back**	block	cook	care	serve	hop	grip	log	limit	grow/grew
talk	bowl	head	close	score	plan	mop	map	suffer	know/knew
call**	count	meet	love	solve	pot	plod	nap	appear	draw/drew
thank	brush	peek	move	sneeze	shop	rob	nod	complain	blow/blew
laugh	bump	bloom	smile	trace	trip	shrug	pin	explain	throw/threw
trick	burn	cool	use**	trade	bet	sip	dip	repeat	find/found
park	climb	cheer	hate	vote	cap	skin	dim	attend	drink/drank
pick	camp	clear	hope	drape	clap	skip	rub	collect	sink/sank
plant	curl	dream	ice	fade	slip	slam	beg		hear/heard
rock	dash	float	joke	graze	snap	slap	blur	**Double**	break/broke
start	dust	flood	paste	praise	spot	snip	bud	admit	hold/held
bark	farm	fool	phone	scrape	tag	sob	chip	begin	stand/stood
work**	fold	join	prove	shave	thin	strip	chop	commit	build/built
walk	growl	lean	race	shove	trap	wrap	crop	control	ring/rang
yell	hunt	mail	scare	snare	trot	zip	strum	excel	sing/sang
wish**	kick	nail	share	cause	tug	brag	swap	forbid	sweep/swept
guess	land	moan	skate	cease	wag	chug	swat	forget	sleep/slept
turn	learn	scream	stare	pose	drop	hem		omit	keep/kept
smell	nest	pour	taste	quote	drum	jog	*Oddballs*	permit	drive/drove
track	lick	sail	wave	rove	whiz	mob	box**	rebel	shine/shone
push	lock	trail	carve	blame	flap	plot	fix	refer	feed/fed
miss	melt	zoom			flip	prop	wax		bleed/bled
paint	point				scar	blot	row	***e*-Drop**	lay/laid
wash	print				skim	chat	chew	arrive	pay/paid
wink	quack				slug	scan	sew	escape	say/said
rest	reach				stab	slop	show	excuse	speak/spoke
					throb		snow	nibble	send/sent
								rattle	buy/bought
								refuse	bring/brought
								amuse	tear/tore
								ignore	wear/wore
								retire	

Pairs to Contrast

hoping	hopping
taping	tapping
pining	pinning
griping	gripping
striping	stripping
moping	mopping
waging	wagging

Syllable Juncture

VCCV Doublet	VCCV		VCV Open	V VCV Open	VCV Closed	V V	V C C C V
pretty**	after*	campus	over**	season	never**	create	constant
better**	under**	frantic	open**	reason	present**	riot	dolphin
blizzard	number	magnet	baby	peanut	cabin	liar	laughter
blossom	chapter	mascot	writer	leader	planet	fuel	pilgrim
button	pencil	sandal	basic	sneaker	finish	poem	instant
cabbage	picnic	pretzel	even		robin	diary	complain
copper	basket	splendid	bacon	easy	magic	cruel	hundred
cottage	cactus	kidnap	chosen	floated	limit	trial	monster
dipper	canyon	wisdom	moment	waiter	manage	diet	orchard
fellow	capture	goblet	human	needed	prison	neon	orphan
foggy	center	goblin	pilot	reading	habit	lion	purchase
follow	window	tonsil	silent		punish	poet	complete
common	compass	finger	vacant	*Oddballs*	cover	giant	athlete
funny	contest	signal	navy	cousin	promise	chaos	kitchen
happen	costume	sister	music	water	closet	idea	children
mammal	doctor	subject	female	busy	camel	video	inspect
message	picture	Sunday	robot		cavern	meteor	pumpkin
office	plastic	temper	crater		comet	violin	English
pattern	public	thunder	climate		dozen	annual	kingdom
sudden	problem	trumpet	duty		finish	casual	bottle
tennis	reptile	twenty	famous		habit	radio	mumble
traffic	rescue	umpire	fever		honest	alien	sandwich
tunnel	sentence	walnut	final		level	piano	actress
valley	seldom	welcome	flavor		lever	area	enchant
village	fabric	whimper	humid		lizard	mosaic	congress
hollow	helmet	winter	labor		modern		ostrich
dessert	husband	wonder	legal		oven		subtract
butter	lumber	index	local		palace		pitcher
hammer	master	insect	pirate		timid		stretcher
attic	napkin	injure	private		panic		control
gallon	dentist	elbow	program		rapid		mushroom
rabbit	blanket	enter	recent		visit		thimble
gallop	tablet	velvet	rumor		solid		
lesson	bandit	chimney	siren		wagon		
banner			solar		vanish		
kitten			spiral		topic		
ribbon			crazy		travel		
mitten			bonus		study		
bonnet			lazy		seven		
bottom			paper		rigid		
cotton			secret		polish		
fossil			hero		legend		
gossip			zero		banish		
muffin			spider		gravel		
puppet			tiger		tragic		
yellow			rodent				
			super				
			bonus				
			tulip				
			sequel				

a Patterns in Accented Syllables

Long-*a* VCV open Accent in 1st	Long-*a* Accent in 1st	Long-*a* Accent in 2nd	Short-*a* in VCCV Accent in 1st	Short-*a* in VCW Accent in 1st	*ar* Accent in 1st	*air* Accent in 1st	*arr/are* Accent in 1st
baby	rainbow	complain	attic	wagon	artist	stairway	marry
nation	painter	contain	hammer	cabin	marble	fairway	parrot
vapor	raisin	explain	batter	planet	garden	airport	narrow
skater	railroad	remain	happen	magic	party	dairy	carrot
lazy	daisy	terrain	mammal	habit	carpet	haircut	sparrow
bacon	dainty	exclaim	valley	camel	pardon	fairy	narrate
wafer	sailor	refrain	cabbage	habit	market	airplane	barrel
raven	straighten	campaign	traffic	rapid	tardy	chairman	carry
famous	failure	regain	pattern	panic	harvest	prairie	parent
fatal	tailor	obtain	scatter	panel	parka		careful
navy	waiter	maintain	ballot	palace	charter	**Accent in 2nd**	barely
basic	traitor	decay	daddy	cavern	larva	repair	barefoot
flavor	mailbox	dismay	gallop	manage	garland	despair	
data	maybe	delay	massive	vanish	parcel	unfair	**Accent in 2nd**
crater	player	portray	napkin	travel	barber	impair	prepare
savor	crayon	mistake	basket	satin	starchy	affair	compare
raking	mayor	parade	fabric	tragic	charter		beware
labor	payment	amaze	plastic	falcon	garlic		aware
vacant	prayer	replace	master	shadow	margin		declare
radar	layer	dictate	cactus	chapel	hardly		
hazel	crayfish	crusade	chapter	facet	partner		
	bracelet	debate	canyon	radish	bargain		
Oddballs	pavement	behave	capture	tavern	carbon		
any*	basement	cascade	tadpole	statue	farther		
many*	baseball	escape	ambush		jargon		
water	grateful	disgrace	lantern	**Broad-*a* VCV**	scarlet		
	graceful	erase	scamper	bravo	parlor		
	safety	essay	canvas	father	sharpen		
	statement	foray	package	drama	sparkle		
	wakeful	invade	tablet	water	target		
	mayhem	insane	lather	plaza	tarnish		
	painless	sustain		llama	harbor		
	ailment	betray		squalid	partial		
		evade			marshal		
	Oddballs	disdain		**Broad-*a* in VCCV**	martyr		
	again*			swallow	carton		
	captain	*Oddballs*		wallet	darling		
	bargain	obey		wallow	varnish		
	postage	survey					
					Oddballs		
					toward		
					lizard		

e Patterns in Accented Syllables

Long-e VCV open Accent in 1st	Long-e Accent in 1st	Long-e Accent in 2nd	Long-ie Accent in 1st	Short-e in VCCV Accent in 1st	Short-e in VCV Accent in 1st	er = ur Accent in 1st	eer/ear/ere Accent in 1st
even	needle	succeed	briefly	better	medal	person	eerie
female	freedom	indeed	diesel	letter	metal	perfect	deerskin
fever	freezer	fifteen		fellow	level	nervous	cheerful
zebra	breezy	thirteen	**Accent in 2nd**	tennis	lever	sermon	earache
legal	cheetah	canteen	believe	message	never	serpent	fearful
meter	steeple	agree	achieve	penny	debit	hermit	earmuff
recent	tweezers	degree	retrieve	beggar	denim	thermos	spearmint
depot	beetle	between	relief	pencil	lemon	kernel	yearbook
cedar	feeble	proceed	besiege	dentist	melon	perky	dreary
detour	greedy	asleep	apiece	center	memo	permit	bleary
veto	sweeten	delete	relieve	helmet	pedal	sherbet	clearly
prefix	beaver	supreme	belief	reptile	petal	gerbil	nearby
tepee	eager	trapeze		rescue	seven	mermaid	hearsay
decent	easy	compete	**Long-ei Accent in 1st**	seldom	clever	certain	teardrop
preview	easel	extreme	either	sentence	credit	merchant	weary
prefix	season	stampede	ceiling	temper	senate	version	merely
evil	reason	deplete	leisure	twenty	tenor	servant	nearly
zenith	reader	recede	seizure	welcome	epic	verbal	clearing
	feature	convene	neither	velvet	relic	mercy	dearest
VV	creature	mislead		pesky		verdict	spearmint
neon	meaning	disease	**Accent in 2nd**		**Short ea**		
create	eastern	increase	receive		feather	**ear = ur**	**Accent in 2nd**
area	bleachers	defeat	perceive		heavy	early	career
idea	cleaner	repeat	receipt		steady	earnings	appear
video	eager	conceal	deceive		ready	earthworm	overhear
	treaty	ideal	conceive		leather	pearly	endear
	neatly	reveal	caffeine		weather	earnest	adhere
	peanut	ordeal			pleasant	yearning	austere
	weasel	appeal			sweater	rehearse	revere
	greasy	mislead			healthy	research	severe
	beacon	obese			weapon	earthquake	sincere
	beagle	esteem			sweaty	learner	interfere
	eagle	redeem			heaven		
	measles	retreat			heather		
		ordeal			meadow		
		decree			measure		
		complete			treasure		
					breakfast		

Oddballs
people
hearty
pretty
cherry
leopard
heifer
neighbor
reindeer

i Patterns in Accented Syllables

Long-*i* VCV open Accent in 1st	Long-*i* Accent in 1st	Long-*i* Accent in 2nd	Short-*i* in VCCV Accent in 1st	Short-*i* in VCV Accent in 1st	*ir* Accent in 1st	*ire* Accent in 1st	*y* = /ī/ Accent in 1st
pilot	ninety	polite	into**	finish	thirty	tiresome	typist
silent	driveway	surprise	kitten	limit	firmly	firefly	dryer
diner	sidewalk	decide	dipper	river	dirty	direful	flyer
writer	iceberg	advice	slipper	lizard	birthday		tyrant
tiger	lively	survive	mitten	timid	thirsty	**Accent in 2nd**	hydrant
siren	mighty	combine	dinner	visit	birdbath	require	bypass
pirate	slightly	arrive	silly	given	circle	rehire	nylon
private	frighten	invite	skinny	city	circus	attire	stylish
spiral	lightning	describe	ribbon	sliver	stirring	inquire	rhyming
biker	highway	divide	pillow	civil	firmly	expire	python
spider	brightly	excite	dizzy	digit	virtue	desire	cycle
visor	higher	provide	chilly	prison	stirrup	perspire	tryout
minus	nightmare	confide	bitter	wizard	twirler	admire	cyclone
rival	tighten	recline	minnow	quiver	skirmish	inspire	hybrid
bison	fighter	ignite	blizzard	figure	circuit	entire	hyphen
item	highlight	despite	tissue		irksome	acquire	stylish
Friday	sightsee	oblige	mixture		whirlpool	retire	skyline
sinus	blindfold	divine	fifty		chirping		hygiene
slimy	kindness	tonight	picnic		flirting		tycoon
icy	climber	resign	picture		squirrel		
climax	wildcat	design	chimney				**Accent in 2nd**
idol	wildlife	delight	frisky				defy
		guitar	windy				July
V V		rewind	signal				apply
lion		unkind	sister				rely
dial		behind	whimper				imply
diet		beside	finger				supply
riot		inside	winter				reply
pliers		recite	kidnap				deny
diary		collide	jigsaw				
vial		advise	window				**y = /i/ Accent in 1st**
triumph		confine	blister				crystal
friar			fiction				hymnal
liar			listen				pygmy
trial			scissors				rhythm
violin							symbol
client							system
science							sylvan
violet							cynic
							physics
Oddballs							cymbal
machine							
liter							
mirror							
pizza							
spirit							
busy							
women							

o Patterns in Accented Syllables

Long-*o* VCV open Accent in 1st	Long-*o* Accent in 1st	Long-*o* Accent in 2nd	Short-*o* in VCCV Accent in 1st	Short-*o* in VCV Accent in 1st	*or* Accent in 1st	*wor* Accent in 1st	*ore/oar/our* Accent in 1st
robot	lonely	alone	foggy	robin	morning**	worker	boredom
pony	lonesome	explode	follow	closet	forty	worry	shoreline
chosen	hopeful	erode	copper	comet	stormy	worthy	scoreless
donate	homework	awoke	blossom	promise	story	worship	hoarsely
motor	closely	decode	cottage	honest	corner		coarsely
soda	goalie	enclose	common	modern	border	**war/quar**	hoarding
notice	loafer	dispose	office	solid	torment	warning	sources
sofa	coaster	suppose	hollow	topic	forest	warden	fourteen
frozen	toaster	compose	nozzle	volume	fortress	warrior	pouring
local	coastal	remote	bottle	body	shortage	wardrobe	mournful
moment	soapy	unload	comma	novel	torrent	quarrel	foursome
rodent	roadway	approach	cotton	profit	tortoise	quarter	courtroom
grocer	owner	afloat	hobby	promise	portrait	reward	
potion	bowling	below	yonder	comic	forfeit		**Accent in 2nd**
ocean	rowboat	bestow	popcorn	logic	shorter		before*
rotate	snowfall	aglow	contest	proper	order		ignore
hoping	lower	disown	costume	novice	normal		restore
stolen	mower	enroll	doctor		northern		explore
solar	slowly	behold	bonfire	**Short-*o* /u/**	forward		galore
poem	towboat	revolt	bother	oven	corncob		aboard
	soldier	almost	cobweb	onion	chorus		ashore
	poster	expose	conquer	shovel	florist		adore
	hostess	oppose	problem	monkey	boring		
	postage	console	posture	mother	sporty		
	smolder		monster	nothing	hornet		
	molten	**Long-*o* V V**	congress	smother	organ		
	molding	poet	collar	wander	morsel		
	folder	poem	volley	dozen	mortal		
	oatmeal	boa	goblin	stomach	orbit		
		oasis			orchard		
	Long-*o* Unaccented	coerce	*Oddballs*				
	yellow		dolphin		**Accent in 2nd**		
	pillow	*Oddballs*	stomach		report		
	shadow	hotel	Europe		record		
	mellow	only**	sorry		perform		
	willow				inform		
	hollow				afford		
	fellow				reform		
	sparrow				absorb		
	follow				abhor		
	window				adorn		
					distort		
					endorse		

u Patterns in Accented Syllables

Long-u VCV open Accent in 1st	Long-u Accent in 1st	Long-u Accent in 2nd	Short-u in VCCV Accent in 1st	Short-u in VCV Accent in 1st	ur Accent in 1st	ure Accent in 2nd	V V
super	useful	amuse	supper	punish	sturdy	secure	fuel
music	Tuesday	misuse	button	suburb	purpose	assure	cruel
ruby	juicy	confuse	funny	pumice	further	endure	annual
tuna	chewy	reduce	sudden	study	hurry	impure	casual
truly	dewdrop	conclude	tunnel		purple	mature	usual
pupil	jewel	dilute	puppet	*Oddballs*	turtle	unsure	dual
rumor	pewter	exclude	buddy	cougar	furnish	obscure	duel
human	skewer	include	butter	beauty	Thursday	manure	fluent
humid	sewage	pollute	fuzzy	cousin	blurry	brochure	duet
future	poodle	excuse	guppy		turkey	unsure	
tutor	rooster	resume	ugly		current	disturb	
tumor	moody	compute	husband		purchase		
futile	doodle	abuse	lumber		burger		
student	noodle	perfume	number		furry		
tuba	scooter	protrude	public		murky		
tulip	toothache	salute	Sunday		mural		
unit	neutral	dispute	thunder		surfer		
ruler	sewer	askew	trumpet		burden		
	feudal	assume	umpire		bureau		
		immune	under**		burrow		
		consume	hundred		curfew		
		accuse	mumble		hurdle		
		intrude	lucky		jury		
		pollute	hungry		murmur		
		review	bucket		turnip		
		cartoon	bundle		burner		
		raccoon	public		gurgle		
		lagoon	custom		burglar		
		shampoo	juggle		curtain		
		balloon	luster		during		
		baboon	publish		further		
		cocoon	suffer		murder		
		maroon	yummy		surplus		
		tattoo					

Ambiguous Vowels in Accented Syllables

Accent in 1st

oy/oi	oo	ow	ou	ou = short u	au	aw	al
voyage	poodle	powder	county	trouble	saucer	awful	also**
loyal	foolish	power	counter	double	author	awkward	always
joyful	rooster	flower	thousand	southern	August	lawyer	almost
boycott	scooter	prowler	fountain	couple	autumn	awesome	halter
royal		coward	mountain	cousin	laundry	awfully	salty
soybean	**Accent in 2nd**	tower	council	touched	caution	gnawing	balky
oyster	balloon	drowsy	lousy	younger	faucet	gawking	balmy
moisture	cartoon	brownie	scoundrel	youngster	sausage	flawless	calmly
poison	shampoo	rowdy	bounty	moustache	auction	drawing	falter
noisy	baboon	chowder	boundary	nervous	haunted	jawbone	halting
pointed	caboose	vowel	founder	famous	cauldron	lawless	hallway
toilet	cocoon	dowdy	doubtful	country	gaudy	tawny	waltzing
ointment	harpoon	towel	southeast		daughter	yawning	alter
	igloo	shower	voucher	ou = long u	jaunty	clawed	asphalt
Accent in 2nd	platoon	cowboy	cloudy	coupon	naughty	brawny	walnut
annoy	raccoon	powwow	flounder	toucan	slaughter	bawdy	walrus
enjoy	typhoon	drowning	trousers	youthful	trauma	gnawed	
employ	papoose	trowel		cougar	pauper		
destroy	maroon		**Accent in 2nd**	crouton	nausea	*Oddball*	*Oddballs*
ahoy	tattoo	**Accent in 2nd**	about*	souvenir	laundry	drawer	laughed
appoint	lagoon	allow	without				all right
avoid			around	**Accent in 2nd**	**Accent in 2nd**		balloon
exploit			announce	routine	because**		gallon
rejoice			profound	acoustics	exhaust		
			surround	bouquet	assault		
					applause		

Final Unsaccented Syllables

al	il/ile	el	le		et	it
normal	stencil	model	fiddle	scribble	target	profit
central	April	angel	little*	people**	basket	audit
crystal	civil	barrel	able	hurdle	blanket	bandit
cymbal	council	bagel	ample	hustle	bucket	credit
dental	evil	bushel	angle	juggle	budget	digit
fatal	fossil	camel	ankle	jungle	carpet	edit
feudal	gerbil	cancel	apple	kettle	closet	exit
final	lentil	channel	battle	knuckle	comet	habit
focal	nostril	chapel	beagle	maple	cricket	hermit
formal	pencil	diesel	beetle	middle	faucet	limit
global	peril	flannel	bottle	needle	fidget	merit
journal	pupil	funnel	bramble	noodle	gadget	orbit
legal	tonsil	gravel	bridle	noble	hatchet	rabbit
mammal	docile	hazel	bubble	paddle	helmet	spirit
medal	facile	jewel	buckle	pebble	hornet	summit
mental	fertile	kennel	bundle	pickle	jacket	unit
metal	fragile	kernel	bugle	purple	locket	visit
nasal	futile	label	candle	puzzle	magnet	
naval	hostile	level	castle	riddle	vomit	
neutral	missile	morsel	cattle	saddle	planet	*-ate*
oval	mobile	nickel	cable	sample	poet	climate
pedal	sterile	novel	chuckle	settle	puppet	private
petal		panel	circle	single	racket	senate
plural		parcel	cradle	steeple	scarlet	pirate
rascal		quarrel	cripple	struggle	secret	chocolate
rival		ravel	cuddle	stumble	skillet	
royal		satchel	cycle	tackle	sonnet	*Oddball*
rural		sequel	dimple	tickle	tablet	biscuit
sandal		shovel	doodle	title	thicket	
scandal		shrivel	double	triple	toilet	
signal		squirrel	eagle	trouble	trumpet	
spiral		swivel	fable	twinkle	velvet	
tidal		tinsel	freckle	turtle	wallet	
total		towel	fumble	waffle	diet	
vandal		travel	gamble	whistle	market	
vital		tunnel	gargle	wrinkle	pocket	
vocal		vessel	gentle	muscle	quiet	
local		vowel	grumble	simple	rocket	
coastal			handle	temple	violet	
		Oddballs	idle	wrestle		
		motel	rattle	ripple		
		hotel	rifle	huddle		
			sprinkle	dribble		
			brittle	straddle		
			crinkle	stubble		
			gurgle			
			humble			
			pimple			
			puddle			
			sparkle			

er

er			er Agents	er Comparatives	ar	or	
other*	poster	bother	butcher	bigger	beggar	color**	rumor
under**	printer	center	robber	cheaper	burglar	actor	mirror
better**	shower	copper	swimmer	cleaner	scholar	author	horror
never**	timber	finger	runner	farther	cellar	doctor	humor
over**	toaster	power	drummer	quicker	cedar	editor	meteor
mother**	trouser	powder	jogger	slower	cheddar	mayor	motor
another**	ladder	proper	dreamer	younger	collar	neighbor	razor
banner	counter	quiver	dancer	older	cougar	sailor	scissors
blister	crater	roller	speaker	flatter	dollar	tailor	splendor
border	cancer	rubber	teacher	plainer	grammar	traitor	sponsor
clover	cider	sander	skater	lighter	hangar	tutor	terror
cluster	scorcher	saucer	marcher	darker	lunar	visitor	tractor
fiber	ledger	scooter	shopper	weaker	solar	donor	tremor
freezer	stretcher	shaver	racer	stronger	molar	armor	vapor
liter	pitcher	weather	grocer	wilder	polar	error	cursor
litter	answer	silver	barber	sweeter	sugar	favor	honor
lumber	blender		peddler	cooler	nectar	anchor	tumor
manner	flower		plumber	braver	pillar		harbor
spider			ranger		liar		
sister			usher				
brother			voter				
father			catcher				
lather			baker				

/chər/			/shər/	/yər/	/zhər/	/jər/	
culture	nurture	mixture	pressure	failure	leisure	conjure	
capture	rapture	moisture	fissure	manicure	measure	injure	
creature	sculpture	picture	reassure	figure	closure	procedure	
denture	stature	pasture			pleasure		
feature	stricture	posture			treasure		
fixture	texture	puncture			enclosure		
fracture	tincture	nature			exposure		
future	torture	furniture			composure		
gesture	venture	miniature			disclosure		
juncture	adventure	premature					
lecture	departure	signature			Oddballs		
injure					senior		
					danger		

ain	an	en Verb	en Noun	en Adjective	in	on	
captain	human	frighten	chicken	golden	basin	apron	bacon
certain	organ	sharpen	children	open**	cabin	button	carton
curtain	orphan	shorten	garden	rotten	cousin	cannon	cotton
fountain	slogan	sweeten	kitten	spoken	margin	common	gallon
mountain	urban	thicken	mitten	sunken	pumpkin	dragon	lemon
villain	woman	widen	women	swollen	raisin	wagon	lesson
bargain		deafen	heaven	wooden	robin	pardon	prison
chieftain		flatten	oxygen	broken	dolphin	person	poison
		lengthen	siren	hidden	muffin	reason	ribbon
		open**	linen	chosen	penguin	season	weapon
			eleven	stolen	satin	salmon	
					napkin		

/ij/		/is/		/ē/ = ey	/ē/ = ie	/ē/ = y	
voyage	sausage	justice	furnace	chimney	cookie	very*	berry
bandage	cabbage	practice	surface	donkey	movie	pretty**	body
village	rummage	service	palace	turkey	brownie	early	beauty
message	savage	office	necklace	jockey	genie	crazy	drowsy
cottage	passage	crevice	menace	valley	goalie	candy	empty
wreckage	image	notice	grimace	volley	sweetie	daisy	guilty
courage	marriage	novice	terrace	journey	zombie	forty	tidy
storage	manage	bodice		honey	birdie	envy	treaty
luggage	sewage	crisis		money	eerie	worry	carry
damage	language	tennis	*Oddballs*	jersey	bootie	gravy	bossy
postage	package	axis	lettuce	pulley	rookie	sorry	trophy
garbage		basis	porpoise	hockey	pinkie	dizzy	stingy
hostage	*Oddballs*	iris	tortoise	galley	prairie	cherry	bury
storage	knowledge			monkey		funny	easy
shortage	cartridge			alley		happy	story
						hurry	icy

Prefixes and Suffixes

mis-	*pre-*	*re-*	*un-*	*dis-*	*in* ("not")	*non-*
misbehave	precook	rebound	unable	disable	incomplete	nonsense
misconduct	predate	recall	unafraid	disagreeable	incorrect	nonstop
miscount	prefix	recapture	unarmed	disappear	indecent	nonfiction
misdeed	pregame	recharge	unbeaten	disarm	indirect	nonfat
misfit	preheat	reclaim	unbroken	discharge	inexpensive	nonprofit
misgivings	prejudge	recopy	uncertain	disclose	inflexible	nondairy
misguide	premature	recount	unclean	discolor	informal	nonstick
misjudge	prepay	recycle	unclear	discomfort	inhuman	nonviolent
mislay	preschool	reelect	uncommon	discontent	injustice	nonskid
mislead	preset	refill	uncover	discover	insane	nonstandard
mismatch	preteen	refinish	undone	dishonest	invalid	
misplace	pretest	reform	unequal	disinfect	invisible	*de-*
misprint	preview	refresh	unfair	dislike	inept	deflate
misspell	prewash	relearn	unkind	disloyal		defrost
mistake	predict	remind	unlike	disobey	*in* ("in" or "into")	deprive
mistreat	precede	remodel	unlock	disorder	income	decrease
mistrust	prehistoric	renew	unpack	displace	indent	delete
misuse	prepare	reorder	unreal	disregard	indoor	deport
mischief	prevent	repay	unripe	disrespect	inset	detract
	precaution	reprint	unselfish	distaste	insight	deficient
	preschool	research	unstable	distrust	inside	degrading
	prenatal	restore	unsteady	disgrace	inlaid	denounce
	prescribe	retrace	untangle		inmate	depleted
		return	untie		ingrown	deprived
		review	unwrap		inboard	detached
		rewrite	unbutton		inland	deviate
		rebuild	uneven		infield	deodorant
		report	unhappy		inflate	decongestant
		recall	unopened		inhale	dehydrated
		refuel	unheated		insert	desegregated
		reject	unattached		inspect	decaffeinated
		reassure	unplanned		inspire	demerits
		reconsider	unplug		intake	

uni-	*bi-*	*tri-*	*fore-*	*sub-*	*ex-*	*en-*
unicorn	biceps	triangle	forearm	subset	expel	enable
unicycle	bicycle	triple	forecast	subtract	express	endanger
uniform	bifocals	triceps	foretell	subdivide	explore	enact
unify	bilingual	triceratops	foresee	subgroup	exceed	enclose
union	binoculars	tricycle	foresight	submerge	excerpt	encourage
unique	bisect	trilogy	forehand	submarine	exclaim	enforce
unison	biweekly	trio	forehead	submerse	exclude	enjoy
universal	biannual	triceratops	foreman	submit	excrete	enslave
universe		triplets	forethought	subway	exhale	enlarge
		tripod	foreshadow	subtotal	exile	enlist
		triad	forepaw	subtitle	expand	enrage
		trinity	foremost	sublet	explode	enrich
		trident	forefathers	subsoil	exit	enroll
		triathlon		subject	extend	entrust
		trillion			exempt	
					exhaust	

-ly		*-y*		*-er/-est*	*-less*	*-ful*	*-ness*
badly		breezy	rainy	blacker/blackest	ageless	careful	awareness
barely	nightly	bumpy	sandy	bigger/biggest	breathless	cheerful	closeness
bravely	safely	chilly	soapy	bolder/boldest	careless	colorful	coolness
closely	friendly	choppy	snowy	braver/bravest	ceaseless	fearful	darkness
costly	gladly	cloudy	stormy	calmer/calmest	endless	graceful	firmness
cruelly	lonely	dirty	sweaty	closer/closest	helpless	harmful	goodness
deadly	nearly	dusty	thirsty	cheaper/cheapest	homeless	hopeful	openness
loudly	quickly	easy	windy	cleaner/cleanest	lawless	lawful	ripeness
proudly	quietly	floppy	dressy	cooler/coolest	painless	peaceful	sickness
smoothly	slowly	frosty	skinny	colder/coldest	powerless	playful	sharpness
kindly	surely	gloomy	speedy	smaller/smallest	priceless	powerful	stiffness
nicely	lively	greasy	floppy	thinner/thinnest	reckless	tasteful	stillness
		grouchy	lucky	fewer/fewest	spotless	thoughtful	thinness
		gritty	grubby	finer/finest	tasteless	truthful	weakness
Change *y* to *i*		noisy		hotter/hottest	useless	useful	moistness
noisily				harder/hardest	fearless	wasteful	vastness
lazily				sadder/saddest	lifeless	wonderful	dullness
angrily				newer/newest	speechless	youthful	kindness
busily				quicker/quickest	thankless	beautiful	dampness
easily				lighter/lightest	cloudless	armful	blindness
happily				louder/loudest	fruitless	dreadful	tenderness
luckily				larger/largest	jobless	respectful	eagerness
daily				meaner/meanest	scoreless	faithful	
gaily					sleeveless	grateful	
bodily				Change *y* to *i*	pointless	hateful	Change *y* to *i*
readily				funnier/funniest	restless	helpful	dizziness
steadily				noisier/noisiest	worthless	joyful	emptiness
				prettier/prettiest		painful	laziness
				dirtier/dirtiest		skillful	readiness
				easier/easiest	Change *y* to *i*	thankful	fussiness
				juicier/juiciest	penniless	wishful	happiness
				lazier/laziest	pitiless	fretful	ugliness
				luckier/luckiest	merciless		clumsiness
				busier/busiest			liveliness
				crazier/craziest			
				heavier/heaviest			
				clumsier/clumsiest			

Special Consonants

Hard g	Soft g	Hard c	Soft c	Final c	que	k / ke	ph	Silent Letters
gadget	genie	cabin	city	attic	antique	namesake	trophy	wrinkle
gallon	genius	cafe	cider	music	unique	cupcake	dolphin	wreckage
gallop	genre	cactus	civil	topic	clique	earthquake	orphan	wriggle
gamble	general	campus	cinder	zodiac	opaque	forsake	phonics	wryly
garage	gentle	candle	circle	clinic	critique	keepsake	gopher	wrestle
gully	gerbil	canyon	circus	comic	physique	mistake	nephew	answer
golden	gesture	cavern	citric	cynic	mystique	pancake	phantom	
gossip	giant	carpet	cedar	toxic	brusque	provoke	pheasant	knuckle
guilty	ginger	cable	celery	panic	conquer	slowpoke	phony	knowledge
gorilla	giraffe	comma	cement	picnic	boutique	turnpike	physics	
gopher	gypsy	copy	census	classic		evoke	triumph	gnaw
gather	gyrate	cozy	center	critic	*x*	homework	photo	gnarl
gutter	gently	cocoa	cereal	elastic	relax	embark	telephone	gnome
guitar	gender	comet	ceiling	exotic	complex	landmark	alphabet	gnostic
gobble		coffee	certain	frantic	index	network		gnu
goggles		corner	cycle	graphic	perplex	berserk		
gaily		county	cynic	hectic	reflex			ghetto
gallery		cubic	cymbal	garlic	vortex			ghastly
		cuddle	cyclist	fabric	vertex			ghoul
Oddballs		culprit	cyclone	frolic	prefix			
giggle		curtain	cylinder	logic	phoenix			honest
geyser		custom	cellar	drastic	annex			honor
gecko		concern		scenic				rhombus
		concert		basic	*ck*			rhyme
		cancel		plastic	attack			rhythm
		cancer		public	gimmick			shepherd
				traffic	hammock			
				arctic	ransack			solemn
				mystic	padlock			column
				skeptic	potluck			autumn
				metric	hemlock			condemn
				mimic	carsick			
					haddock			castle
								thistle
								whistle
								fasten
								listen
								often*
								soften
								moisten
								daughter
								naughty
								height
								weight
								freight
								assign
								design
								resign

Alternations and Reduced Vowels in Unaccented Syllables

Silent to Sounded Consonant	Long to Short	Long to Schwa	Short to Schwa
bomb/bombard	cave/cavity	able/ability	metallic/metal
column/columnist	flame/flammable	famous/infamous	academy/academic
soften/soft	grave/gravity	major/majority	malice/malicious
crumb/crumble	nature/natural	native/nativity	periodic/period
debt/debit	athlete/athletic	prepare/preparation	emphatic/emphasis
damn/damnation	please/pleasant	relate/relative	celebrate/celebrity
design/designate	crime/criminal	stable/stability	democratic/democracy
decide/decision	decide/decision	compete/competition	excel/excellent
fasten/fast	revise/revision	combine/combination	perfection/perfect
hasten/haste	wise/wisdom	define/definition	critic/criticize
hymn/hymnal	know/knowledge	invite/invitation	habit/habitat
malign/malignant	episode/episodic	recite/recitation	mobility/mobile
moisten/moist	assume/assumption	reside/resident	prohibit/prohibition
muscle/muscular	produce/production	compose/composition	geometry/geometric
resign/resignation	convene/convention	expose/exposition	
sign/signal	volcano/volcanic	custodian/custody	
condemn/condemnation	serene/serenity	pose/position	
	ignite/ignition	social/society	
	humane/humanity		
	divide/division		

Adding /shun/ to base words

ct + ion	ss + ion	t + ion	d, de to sion	e-drop + ion	it to ission
action	expression	assertion	explosion	creation	admission
subtraction	oppression	digestion	decision	decoration	omission
distinction	possession	invention	division	generation	permission
election	profession	suggestion	invasion	imitation	submission
prediction	confession	adoption	conclusion	illustration	transmission
extinction	compression	insertion	intrusion	indication	
detection	obsession	congestion	protrusion	translation	e-drop + tion
selection	digression	prevention	allusion	congratulation	production
rejection	impression	distortion	collision	frustration	introduction
reaction	discussion	exhaustion	evasion	operation	reduction
connection	aggression	eruption	erosion	location	reproduction
distraction	depression	exception	seclusion	vibration	deduction
objection	procession	desertion	persuasion	circulation	seduction
infection	recession		expansion	pollution	
instruction		t + ation	ascension	dictation	be to p + tion
protection	c + ian	adaptation	suspension	hesitation	description
conviction	magician	temptation	exportation	donation	prescription
correction	musician	presentation	consultation	devotion	inscription
detection	optician	indentation		graduation	subscription
abstraction	logician	plantation		migration	transcription
inspection	clinician	infestation		navigation	
injection	diagnostician	lamentation		isolation	
reflection	electrician	confrontation			
	politician	expectation			
	technician				

Vowel Alternations with Change in Accent When Adding Suffixes

Schwa to Short with ity	Long to Short with cation	Long to Schwa with ation
mental/mentality	apply/application	declare/declaration
general/generality	certify/certification	degrade/degradation
moral/morality	clarify/clarification	prepare/preparation
brutal/brutality	classify/classification	admire/admiration
central/centrality	gratify/gratification	combine/combination
eventual/eventuality	imply/implication	define/definition
personal/personality	notify/notification	deprive/deprivation
neutral/neutrality	purify/purification	derive/derivation
original/originality	modify/modification	incline/inclination
normal/normality	unify/unification	invite/invitation
mental/mentality	simplify/simplification	recite/recitation
formal/formality	multiply/multiplication	compile/compilation
equal/equality	magnify/magnification	perspire/perspiration
vital/vitality	specify/specification	explore/exploration
legal/legality	verify/verification	
local/locality	qualify/qualification	
hospital/hospitality	identify/identification	
personal/personality	justify/justification	
	beautify/beautification	

Adding the Suffix able/ible

Root Word + ible	Base Word + able	e-drop + able	y to i + able
audible	affordable	achievable	variable
credible	agreeable	admirable	reliable
edible	allowable	adorable	pliable
eligible	avoidable	advisable	pitiable
feasible	breakable	believable	justifiable
gullible	comfortable	comparable	identifiable
horrible	dependable	conceivable	deniable
invincible	expandable	consumable	enviable
legible	favorable	debatable	remediable
plausible	laughable	deplorable	
possible	payable	desirable	Drop *ate* in Base
terrible	preferable	disposable	tolerable
visible	predictable	excitable	vegetable
indelible	profitable	lovable	operable
intangible	punishable	notable	navigable
compatible	reasonable	pleasurable	abominable
combustible	refillable	recyclable	negotiable
responsible	remarkable	valuable	educable
defensible	respectable		estimable
divisible	transferable	*ce/ge* + able	irritable
plausible		manageable	appreciable
tangible		enforceable	
accessible		noticeable	
		changeable	

Adding *ant/ance/ancy* and *ent/ence/ency*

hesitant/hesitance/hesitancy
abundant/abundance/abundancy
relevant/relevance/relevancy
extravagant/extravagance/extravagancy
malignant/malignance/malignancy
petulant/petulance/petulancy
radiant/radiance/radiancy
brilliant/brilliance/brilliancy
defiant/defiance
reluctant/reluctance
exuberant/exuberance
fragrant/fragrance
instant/instance
elegant/elegance
vigilant/vigilance
resistant/resistance
significant/significance
tolerant/tolerance
observant/observance
resistant/resistance

competent/competence/competency
dependent/dependence/dependency
emergent/emergence/emergency
equivalent/equivalence/equivalency
excellent/excellence/excellency
expedient/expedience/expediency
lenient/lenience/leniency
resident/residence/residency
resilient/resilience/resiliency
convenient/convenience
different/difference
diligent/diligence
evident/evidence
impatient/impatience
independent/independence
patient/patience
innocent/innocence
intelligent/intelligence
obedient/obedience
indulgent/indulgence
violent/violence

Using *ary*, *ery*, and *ory*

ary	ery	ary with Schwa	ery with Schwa	ory	ory with Schwa
customary	very	anniversary	artery	allegory	compulsory
fragmentary	cemetery	boundary	bribery	auditory	cursory
extraordinary	stationery	documentary	celery	category	directory
hereditary	confectionery	elementary	discovery	dormitory	memory
imaginary		glossary	gallery	explanatory	satisfactory
legendary		salary	grocery	inventory	theory
literary		summary	machinery	observatory	victory
military		burglary	mystery	territory	history
missionary		diary	nursery	circulatory	memory
necessary		infirmary	scenery	derogatory	accessory
ordinary		auxiliary	surgery	laboratory	compulsory
revolutionary		documentary	drapery	mandatory	victory
secretary		rudimentary	forgery	respiratory	
solitary			misery		
stationary					
temporary					
vocabulary					
primary					
dictionary					

Accent in Polysyllabic Words

First Syllable			Second Syllable			Third Syllable
anything	cantaloupe	aptitude	December	asparagus	whoever	constitution
somebody	comedy	architect	November	attorney	accountant	population
beautiful	customer	artery	October	computer	agility	planetarium
families	engineer	avalanche	September	election	amphibian	Sacramento
grandfather	evidence	calculator	uncommon	endurance	apprentice	Tallahassee
January	forestry	camera	unusual	executive	deliver	understand
libraries	generator	carpenter	unwanted	erosion	remember	imitation
Wednesday	improvise	everything	protection	ignition	whenever	regulation
wonderful	iodine	colorful	reduction	judicial	tomorrow	California
populate	meteorite	gasoline	romantic	mechanic	abilities	definition
acrobat	navigator	everywhere	unable	banana	apartment	diagnosis
amateur	average	hamburger	providing	department	companion	hippopotamus
			vacation	important	condition	irrigation
						Mississippi
						declaration
						exclamation

Prefixes

anti ("against")	auto ("self")	circum ("around")	inter ("between")	intra ("within")	mal ("bad")
antifreeze	autograph	circumference	interact	intramural	malice
antidote	automation	circumvent	intercede	intravenous	malignant
antitoxin	autobiography	circumstance	interfere	intrastate	maltreated
antibiotic	automobile	circumspect	interloper		malpractice
anticlimactic	autocrat	circumscribe	interchange		maladjusted
antisocial	autonomy	circumlocution	interject		malnutrition
antigen	autopsy	circumnavigate	interrupt		malcontent
antipathy			intercede		malfunction
antiseptic			intercom		malady
			international		
			interlocking		
			intermission		
			international		
			intermural		

peri ("around")	post ("after")	pro ("before," "forward")		super ("higher")	trans ("across")
perimeter	posterior	proceed	profile	superpower	transfer
period	posterity	propel	promotion	supervision	transport
periphery	posthumous	produce	prohibit	supermarket	transmit
periscope	postpone	progress	procreate	supernatural	transplant
peripatetic	postscript	provide	propitious	superman	translate
periodontal	postmortem	program	pronounce	supersede	translucent
	postgraduate	projector	promulgate	supersonic	transparent
	postmeridian	protective	propensity	superstition	transform
	postseason	proclaim	proficient	superficial	transient
	postdated	profess	protracted	supercilious	transcend
					transact

Number-Related Prefixes (see also *uni*, *bi*, and *tri* under "Prefixes and Suffixes" on page 388)

mon, mono	*cent*	*mil*	*oct*	*poly*	*semi*	*multi*
monarchy	centigrade	million	octagon	polygon	semiannual	multitude
monastery	centimeter	millimeter	octopus	polygamy	semicolon	multiply
monogram	centipede	milligram	October	polychrome	semicircle	multicolored
monologue	centennial	millennium	octave	polyhedron	semisolid	multipurpose
monorail	century	millionaire	octahedron	polyglot	semiconscious	multicultural
monotone	percent		octogenarian	polyester	semifinal	multimedia
monotonous	bicentennial	*deca/deci*	octane	polygraph	semiweekly	multiplex
monolith		decade		polymath	semiprecious	multifaceted
monopoly	*sex/hex*	December	*pent*	polymers		multivitamin
monochrome	sextant	decahedron	pentagon	polyp	*quad*	multifarious
monogamy	sextuplets	decagon	pentameter	polytechnic	quadrangle	multiplication
	hexagon	decimal	pentacle		quadrant	
		decathlon			quarter	

Assimilated or Absorbed Prefixes

in ("not")	*il*	*im*		*ir*
inaccurate	illogical	immature	impure	irrational
inefficient	illegal	immaterial	impaired	irreconcilable
inoperable	illiterate	immobile	impartial	irreparable
insecure	illegible	immodest	impossible	irregular
innumerable	illicit	immoderate	impediment	irrelevant
inactive	illustrious	immoral	imperfect	irreplaceable
inappropriate	illegitimate	immortal	impersonal	irresistible
incompetent	illuminate	immovable	improper	irresponsible
indecent		immigrant	impractical	irreversible
		immediate		irradiate
		immerse		irreligious

sub ("under" or "lower")		*suf*	*sup*	*sur*
subversion	subatomic	suffix	supplant	surreal
subterranean	subcommittee	suffuse	suppliant	surrender
suburban	subdivision	suffer	support	surrogate
substitute	submarine	suffice	supposition	surreptitious
substandard	subconscious	sufficient	suppress	
subsidize	subcontractor	suffocate	supplicant	*suc*
subclass	subjugate		supplement	succumb
sublease	subscribe			succeed
subscript	subscription			success
subtract	submarine			succinct
subdue	submit			successive

com ("with" or "together")
common
community
combination
committee
company
comply
compress
compound
companion
compact
complete
comrade
combine

col
collection
collide
collision
collage
collaborate
colleague
collapse
collusion
collate
collateral
colloquial
collect

con
conspire
concert
connect
congress
congestion
congregation
conclude
condense
construct
constellation
connote

cor
correlate
corroborate
correct
correspond
corrupted
corrugated

co
coagulate
coexist
coalition
coauthor
coeducational
cohabit
cohesion
cohort
coincide
cooperate
coordinate

ad ("to" or "toward")
adjacent
adjoining
addicted
adhesive
adjacent
adaptation
additional
adjective
adjust
admire
admission
advocate

at
attend
attune
attract
attach
attack
attain
attention
attempt
attitude
attribute
attrition

ac
accompany
acceptable
access
accident
accommodate
accomplish
accumulate
accelerate
acquisition
acquire
acquisitive

af
affinity
affable
affection
affluence
affiliate
affricative
affirmation

ag
aggregate
aggravate
aggression
aggrieved

al
alliance
alliteration
allowance
allusion
alleviate
allotment

an
annex
annihilate
announce
annul
annotate

ap
approach
approximate
appropriate
apprentice
apprehend
appreciate
application
applause
appetite
appendix
appear
appeal

as
assemble
associate
assimilate
assent
assault
assertion
assessment
assume
assiduous
assistance
assuage
assumption

ar
arrange
arrest
array
arrive
arrogant

dis ("not" or "opposite of" or "apart")
disadvantage
dissatisfied
disillusioned
disaster
disability
disagreeable
disseminate
disappoint
discern
disdain

disarray
disconcerted
discharged
disclaimer
disconsolate
discouraged
disregard
disenchanted
disoriented

dif
difficult
diffusion
different
diffidence

ex ("out or "from")
extract
excavate
exceed
exception
excerpt
excursion
exhale
exile
expansion
expenditure
exclaim

explode
excrete
exhume
extinct
expand
extend
exclude
exhaust
extension
explosion

ef
efface
effect
efferent
efficiency
effrontery
effusive
effort
effront
effluent
effervescent

ec
ecstasy
eccentric
ecclesiastical

ob ("to," "toward," or "against")
oblong
objection
obligation
obliterate
oblivious

obscure
observant
obstruction
obstreperous
obstinate

obscure
oblique
obstacle
obsolete
obnoxious

op
opponent
opposite
opportunity
opposition
oppress

of
offend
offensive
offering
offense
officious

oc
occurrence
occasion
occupation
occupy
occlude

Greek Roots

aer	"air" aerate, aerial, aerobics, aerodynamic, aeronautics, aerosol, aerospace
arch	"rule, chief" monarchy, anarchy, archangel, archbishop, archetype, architect, hierarchy, matriarch, patriarch
aster, astr	"star" aster, asterisk, asteroid, astrology, astronomy, astronaut, astronomical, astrophysics, disaster
bi, bio	"life" biology, biography, autobiography, biopsy, symbiotic, biodegradable, antibiotic, amphibious, biochemistry
centr	"center" center, central, egocentric, ethnocentric, centrifuge, concentric, concentrate, eccentric
chron	"time" chronic, chronicle, chronological, synchronize, anachronism
cosm	"world" cosmic, cosmology, cosmonaut, cosmopolitan, cosmos, microcosm
crat	"rule" democrat, plutocrat, bureaucrat, idiosyncratic, technocrat
crit	"judge" critic, criticize, critique, criterion, diacritical, hypocrite
cycl	"circle" cycle, bicycle, cyclone, tricycle, unicycle, recycle, motorcycle, cyclical, encyclopedia
dem	"people" demagogue, democracy, demographics, endemic, epidemic, epidemiology
derm	"skin" dermatologist, epidermis, hypodermic, pachyderm, taxidermist, dermatitis
geo	"earth" geology, geophysics, geography, geothermal, geocentric, geode
gram	"to write" diagram, program, telegram, anagram, cryptogram, epigram, grammar, monogram
graph	"to write" graph, paragraph, autograph, digraph, graphics, topography, biography, bibliography, calligraphy, choreographer, videographer, ethnography, phonograph, seismograph, lexicographer
homo	"same" homophone, homograph, homosexual, homogeneous
hydra	"water" hydra, hydrant, hydrate, hydrogen, hydraulic, hydroelectric, hydrology, hydroplane, hydroponics, anhydrous, hydrangea, hydrophobia
logo	"word, reason" logic, catalogue, dialogue, prologue, epilogue, monologue
logy	"study" biology, geology, ecology, mythology, pathology, psychology, sociology, theology, genealogy, etymology, technology, zoology
meter	"measure" centimeter, millimeter, diameter, speedometer, thermometer, tachometer, altimeter, barometer, kilometer
micro	"small" microscope, microphone, microwave, micrometer, microbiology, microcomputer, microcosm
ortho	"straight, correct" orthodox, orthodontics, orthography, orthodontists, orthopedic
pan	"all" pandemic, panorama, pandemonium, pantheon, Pan-American
path	"feeling, suffer" sympathy, antipathy, apathetic, empathize, pathogen, pathologist, pathetic, pathos, osteopath
ped	"child" (see Latin *ped* for "foot") pedagogy, pediatrician, pedophile, encyclopedia
phil	"loving" philosophy, philharmonic, bibliophile, Philadelphia, philanderer, philanthropy, philatetic, philter
phobia	"fear" phobia, acrophobia, claustrophobia, xenophobia, arachnophobia, agoraphobia
phon	"sound" phonics, phonograph, cacophony, earphone, euphony, homophone, microphone, telephone, xylophone, saxophone, phoneme, symphony
photo	"light" photograph, telephoto, photocopier, photographer, photosynthesis, photocell, photogenic, photon
phys	"nature" physics, physical, physician, physiology, physique, astrophysics, physiognomy, physiotherapy
pol	"city" politics, police, policy, metropolis, acropolis, cosmopolitan, megalopolis, Minneapolis
psych	"spirit, soul" psyche, psychology, psychoanalyst, psychiatry, psychedelic, psychosis, psychosomatic, psychic
scope	"see" microscope, periscope, scope, telescope, stethoscope, gyroscope, horoscope, kaleidoscope, stereoscope
sphere	"ball" sphere, atmosphere, biosphere, hemisphere, ionosphere, stratosphere, troposphere
tech	"build, art, skill" technical, technician, technology, polytechnic
tele	"far" telecast, telegraph, telegram, telescope, television, telethon, teleconference, telepathy
therm	"heat" thermal, geothermal, thermometer, thermonuclear, thermos, thermostat, thermodynamic, exothermic
typ	"to beat, to strike" typewriter, typist, typographical, archetype, daguerreotype, prototype, stereotype, typecast
zo	"animal" zoo, zoology, protozoan, zodiac, zoologist

Latin Roots

aud	"hear" audio, auditorium, audience, audible, audition, inaudible, audiovisual
bene	"well" benefactor, benevolent, beneficial, benefit, benign, benefactress, benediction
cand, chand	"shine" candle, chandelier, incandescent, candelabra, candid, candidate
cap	"head" captain, capital, capitol, capitalize, capitulate, decapitate, per capita, captivity
cide	"cut, kill" incise, incision, concise, circumcise, excise, fungicide, herbicide, pesticide, insecticide, suicide, homicide, genocide
clud, clos, clus	"shut" close, closet, disclose, enclose, foreclose, conclude, exclude, exclusive, preclude, occlude, seclude, seclusion, recluse
cogn	"know" recognize, incognito, cognizant, cognition, recognizance
corp	"body" corpse, corporal, corporation, corpus, corpulent, incorporate, corpuscle
cred	"trust, believe" credit, credible, credentials, incredible, accredited, credulous
dent, dont	"tooth" dentist, dentures, orthodontist, indent
dic, dict	"speak" dictate, diction, dictionary, predict, verdict, benediction, contradict, dedicate, edict, indict, jurisdiction, valedictorian, dictation
doc	"teach" documentary, indoctrinate, doctorate, doctor, docent, docile, doctrine
duc, duct	"lead" abduct, conductor, deduct, aqueduct, duct, educate, educe, induct, introduction, reduce, reproduce, viaduct

equa, equi	"equal" equal, equality, equation, equator, equity, equivalent, equilibrium, equivocate, equidistant, equinox
fac, fec	"do" factory, manufacture, faculty, artifact, benefactor, confection, defect, effect, facile, facilitate, facsimile, affect, affection
fer	"carry" ferry, transfer, prefer, reference, suffer, vociferous, inference, fertile, differ, conifer, conference, circumference
fid	"trust" fidelity, confidant, confidence, diffident, infidelity, perfidy, affidavit, bona fide, confidential
fin	"end" final, finale, finish, infinite, definitive
flex, flect	"bend, curve" flex, flexible, inflexible, deflect, reflection, inflection, circumflex, genuflect
flu	"flow" fluid, fluent, influx, superfluous, affluence, confluence, fluctuate, influence
form	"shape" conform, deform, formal, formality, format, formation, formula, informal, information, malformed, platform, reform, transform, uniform
grac, grat	"thankful" grace, gratuity, gracious, ingrate, congratulate, grateful, gratitude, ingratiate, persona non grata, gratify
grad, gress	"go, step" graduate, gradual, gradient, grade, retrograde, centigrade, degraded, downgrade, digress, aggressive, congress, egress, ingress, progress, regress, transgression
ject	"throw" eject, injection, interject, object, objection, conjecture, abject, dejected, projection, projectile, projector, reject, subjective, trajectory
jud	"judge" judge, judgment, prejudice, judiciary, judicial, adjudge, adjudicate, injudicious
junct	"join" junction, juncture, injunction, conjunction, adjunct, disjunction
langu, lingu	"tongue" language, bilingual, linguistics, linguist, linguine, lingo
lit	"letter" literature, illiterate, literal, literacy, obliterate, alliteration, literary
loc, loq	"speak" elocution, eloquent, loquacious, obloquy, soliloquy, ventriloquist, colloquial, interlocutor
mal	"bad" malady, malignant, maladroit, malaria, malcontent, malicious, malign, maladjusted, malevolent, malfunction, malnourished, malpractice
man	"hand" manual, manufacture, manicure, manuscript, emancipate, manacle, mandate, manipulate, manage, maneuver
mem	"memory, mindful" remember, memory, memorize, memorial, memorandum, memento, memorabilia, commemorate
min	"small" diminish, mince, minimize, minute, minuscule, minus, minor, minnow, minimum
miss, mit	"send" transmission, remission, submission, admit, transmit, remit, submit, omit, mission, missile, demise, emission, admission, commission, emissary, intermission, intermittent, missionary, permission, promise
mob, mot	"move" mobile, motion, motor, remote, automobile, promote, motivate, motel, locomotion, immobile, emotion, demote, commotion
pat	"father" paternal, patrimony, expatriate, patron, patronize
ped	"foot" pedal, pedestal, pedicure, pedigree, biped, centipede, millipede, moped, impede, expedite, orthopedic, pedestrian, quadruped
pens, pend	"hang" appendage, appendix, pending, pendulum, pension, suspended, suspense, compensate, depend, dispense, expend, expensive, pensive, stipend, impending, pendant
port	"carry" porter, portfolio, portage, portable, export, import, rapport, report, support, transport, comportment, deport, important, portmanteau
pos, pon	"put, place" pose, position, positive, apropos, compose, composite, compost, composure, disposable, expose, impose, imposter, opposite, postpone, preposition, proponent, proposition, superimpose, suppose
prim, princ	"first" prime, primate, primer, primeval, primitive, prima donna, primal, primary, primogeniture, primordial, primrose, prince, principal, principality, principle
quir, ques	"ask" inquire, require, acquire, conquer, inquisition, quest, question, questionnaire, request, requisite, requisition
rupt	"break" rupture, abrupt, bankrupt, corrupt, erupt, disrupt, interrupt
sal	"salt" salt, saline, salary, salami, salsa, salad, desalinate
sci	"know" science, conscience, conscious, omniscience, subconscious, conscientious
scrib, script	"write" scribble, script, scripture, subscribe, transcription, ascribe, describe, inscribe, proscribe, postscript, prescription, circumscribe, nondescript, conscription
sect, seg	"cut" bisect, dissect, insect, intersect, section, sector, segment
sent, sens	"feel" sense, sensitive, sensory, sensuous, sentiment, sentimental, assent, consent, consensus, dissent, resent, sensation
sequ, sec	"follow" sequel, sequential, consequence, consecutive, non sequitur, persecute, second, sect, subsequent
son	"sound" sonic, sonnet, sonorous, unison, ultrasonic, assonance, consonant, dissonant, resonate, sonate
spec, spic	"see" spectacle, spectacles, spectacular, specimen, prospect, respect, retrospective, speculate, suspect, suspicion, aspect, auspicious, circumspect, inspector, introspection
spir	"breathe" spirit, respiration, perspire, transpire, inspire, conspire, aspirate, dispirited, antiperspirant
sta, stis	"stand" stable, state, station, stationary, statistic, statue, stature, status, subsist, assist, consistent, desist, insistent, persistent, resist
stru	"build" construct, instruct, destruction, reconstruction, obstruct
tain, ten	"hold" detain, obtain, pertain, retain, sustain, abstain, appertain, contain, entertain, maintain
tang, tact	"touch" tangible, intangible, tangent, contact, tactile
tend, tens	"stretch" distend, tendon, tendril, extend, intend, intensify, attend, contend, portend, superintendent
term	"end" term, terminal, terminate, determine, exterminate, predetermine
terra	"earth" terrain, terrarium, terrace, subterranean, terrestrial, extraterrestrial, Mediterranean, terra cotta, terra firma
tort, torq	"twist" contort, distort, extort, torture, tortuous, torque
tract	"pull" tractor, traction, contract, distract, subtract, retract, attract, protracted, intractable, abstract, detract

vac	"empty" vacant, vacuum, evacuate, vacation, vacuous, vacate
val	"strong, worth" valid, valiant, validate, evaluate, devalue, convalescent, valedictorian, invalid
ven, vent	"come" vent, venture, venue, adventure, avenue, circumvent, convention, event, intervene, invent, prevent, revenue, souvenir, convenient
vers, vert	"turn" revert, vertex, vertigo, convert, divert, vertical, adverse, advertise, anniversary, avert, controversy, conversation, extrovert, introvert, inverse, inverted, perverted, reverse, subvert, traverse, transverse, universe, versatile, versus, vertebra
vid, vis	"see" video, vista, visage, visit, visual, visa, advise, audiovisual, envision, invisible, television, supervise, provision, revision, improvise
voc	"call" vocal, vociferous, evoke, invoke, advocate, avocation, convocation, equivocal, invocation, provoke, revoke, vocabulary, vocation
vol, volv	"roll" revolve, evolve, involve, volume, convoluted, devolve

Game Boards

This appendix contains templates for picture and word sorts as well as games. Figures F.1 through F.8 are templates that you can use to create some of the games described throughout the book. Note that there are two sides for each game board. When the two sides are placed together, they form a continuous track or path. These games can be adapted for different features and levels. Here are some general tips for creating the games.

1. Photocopy the game boards (enlarge slightly) and mount them on colored manila file folders, making them easy to create and store. Place game materials, such as spinners, word cards, or game markers, in plastic bags or envelopes labeled with the name of the game and stored in the folder. You might mark the flip side of word cards in some way so that lost cards can be returned to the correct game. Rubber stamp figures work well.

2. When mounting a game board in a folder, be sure to leave a slight gap (about an eighth of an inch) between the two sides so that the folder will still fold. If you do not leave this gap, the paper will buckle. Trim the sheets of paper so the two new sides line up neatly, or cut around the path shape and line up the two pieces of the pathway.

3. Various objects (buttons, plastic discs, coins, and bottle caps) can be used for game markers or pawns that the students will move around the board. Flat objects store best in the folders, or you may want to put a collection of game markers, dice, and spinners in a box. Store the box near the games, and students can take what they need.

4. Add pizazz to games with pictures cut from magazines or old workbooks, stickers, comic characters, clip art, and so on. Rubber stamps, your drawings, or students' drawings can be used to add interest and color. Create catchy themes such as Rabbit Race, Lost in Space, Through the Woods, Mouse Maze, Rainforest Adventure, and so forth.

5. Include directions and correct answers (when appropriate) with the game, stored inside along with playing pieces or glued to the outside of the folder.

6. Label the spaces around the path or track according to the feature you want to reinforce, and laminate the board for durability. If you want to create open-ended games that can be adapted to a variety of features, laminate the path before you label the spaces. Then you can write in letters or words with a washable overheard pen and change them as needed. Permanent marker can also be used and removed with hairspray or fingernail polish remover.

7. Add interest to the game by labeling some spaces with special directions (if you are using a numbered die or spinner) or add cards with special directions to the deck of words. Special directions can offer the students a bonus in the form of an extra turn or a penalty such as losing a turn. These bonus or penalty directions can tie in with your themes. For example, in the Rainforest Adventure the player might forget a lunch and be asked to go back to the starting space. Keep the reading ability of your students in mind as you create these special directions.

Spinners

Many of the word study games described in this book use a game spinner. Figure F.8 provides simple directions for making a spinner.

Templates for Sorts

TEMPLATE FOR PICTURE SORTS

TEMPLATE FOR WORD SORTS

FIGURE F.1 Racetrack and Game Board (left and right)

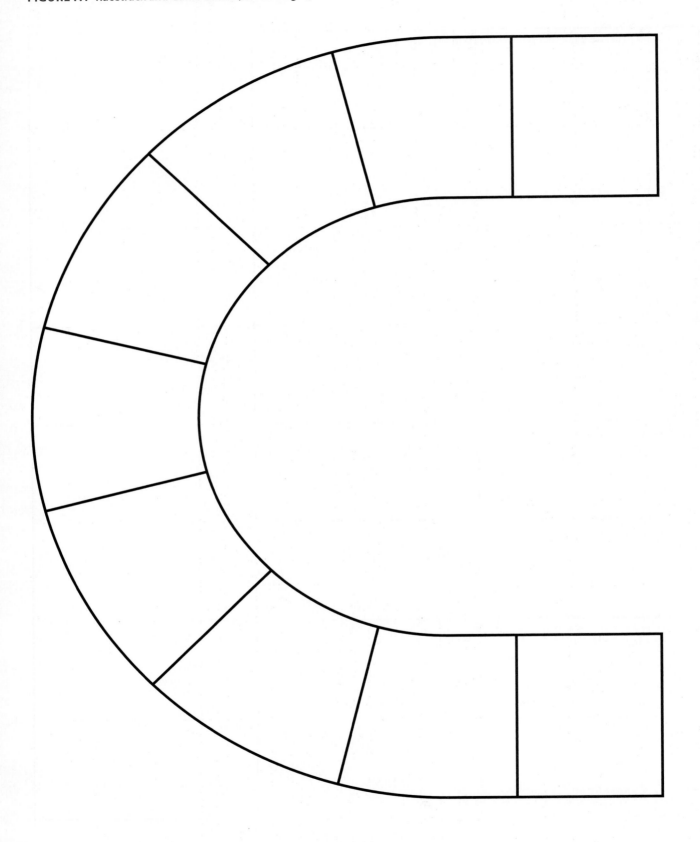

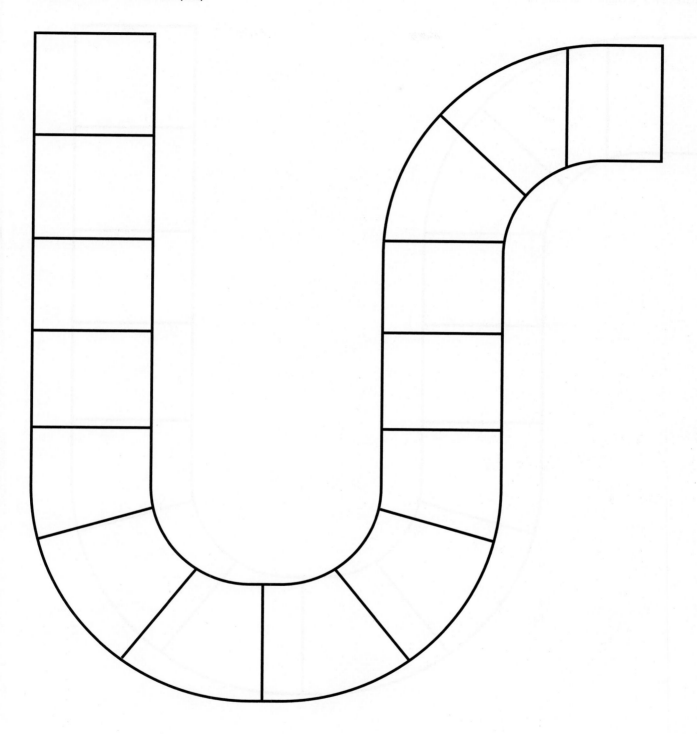

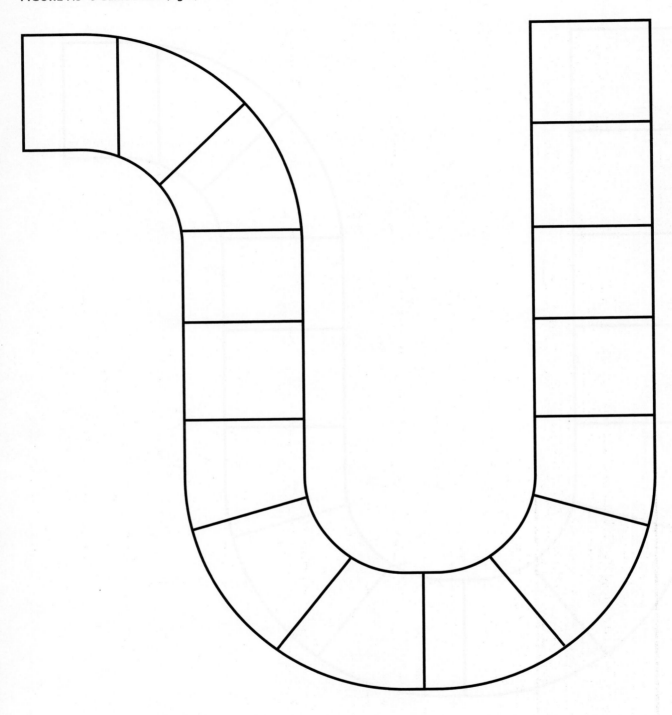

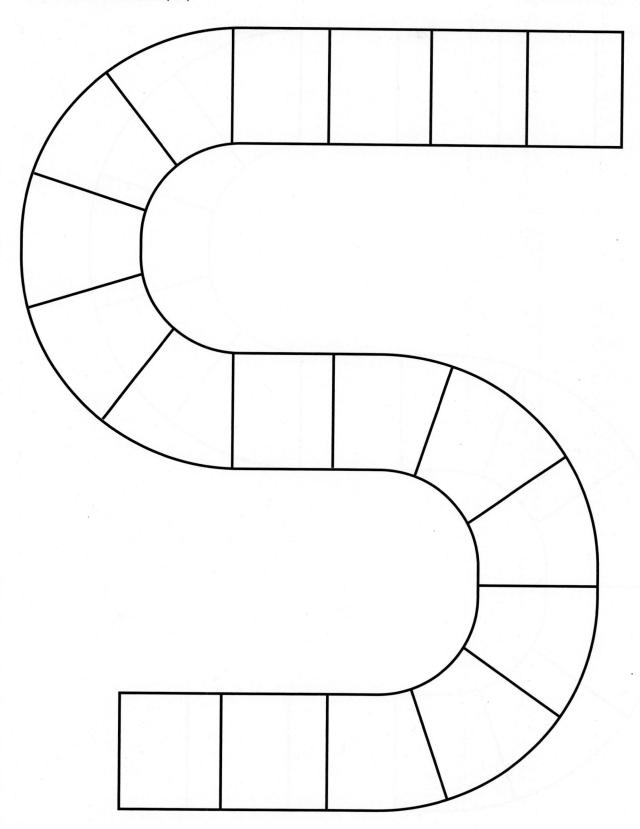

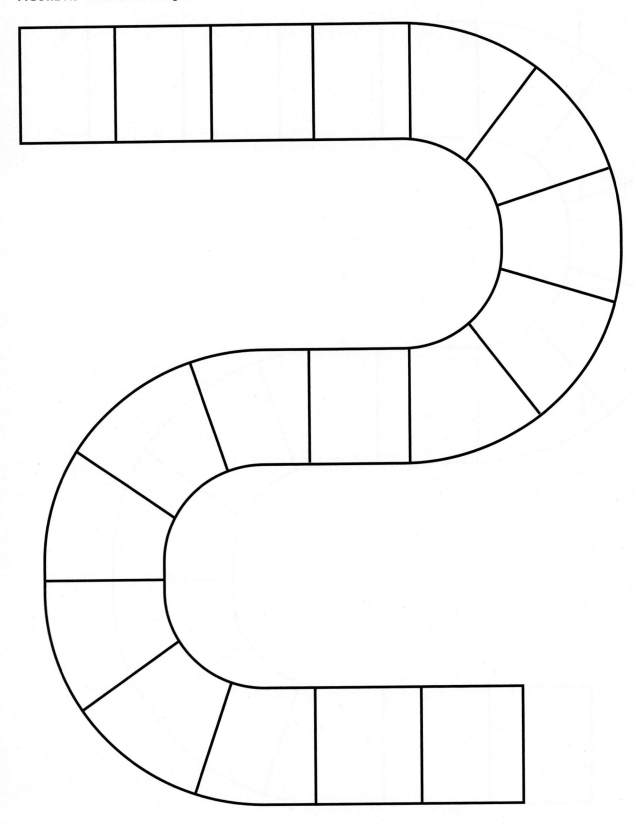

FIGURE F.6 Rectangle Game Board (left)

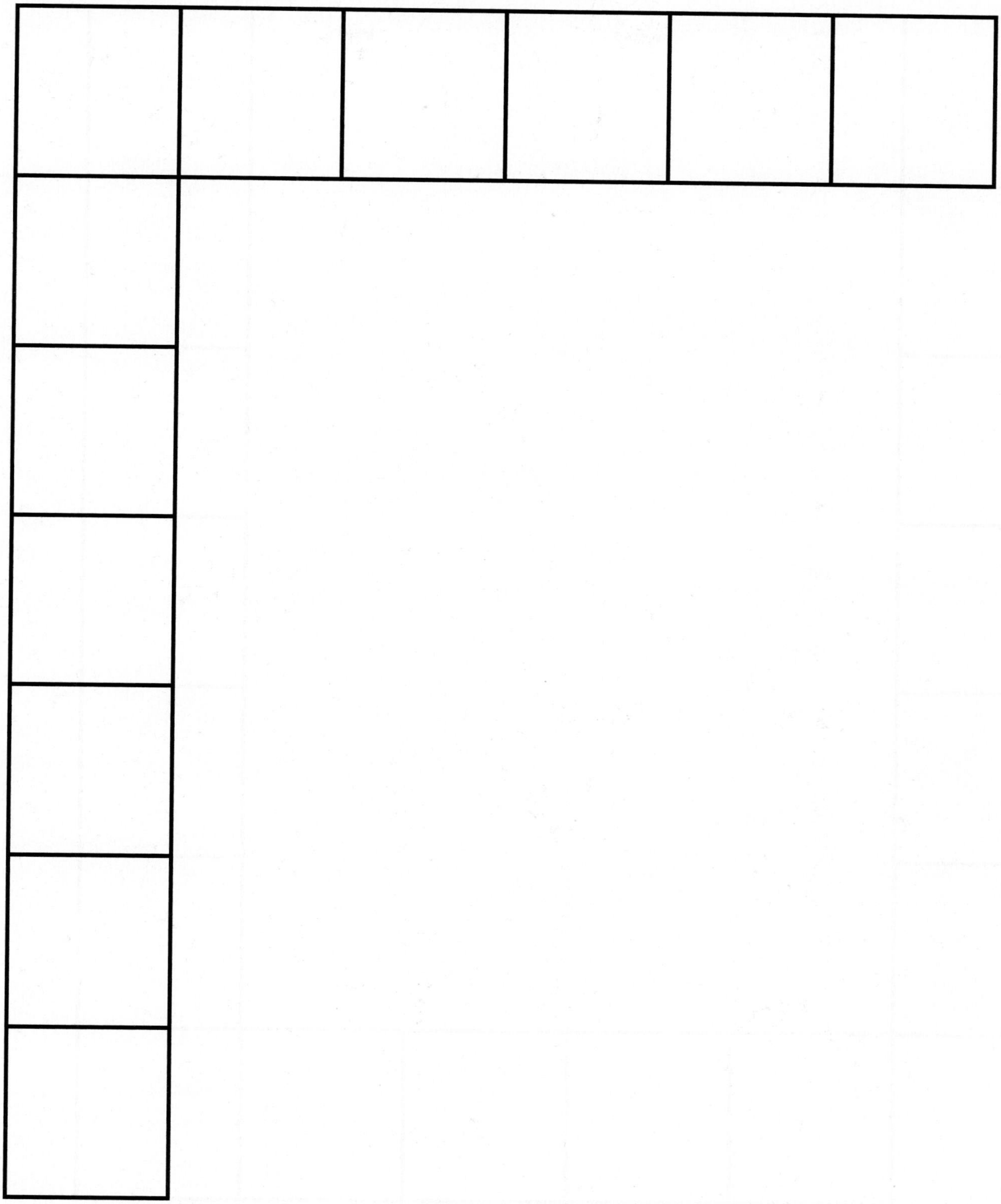

FIGURE F.7 Rectangle Board (right)

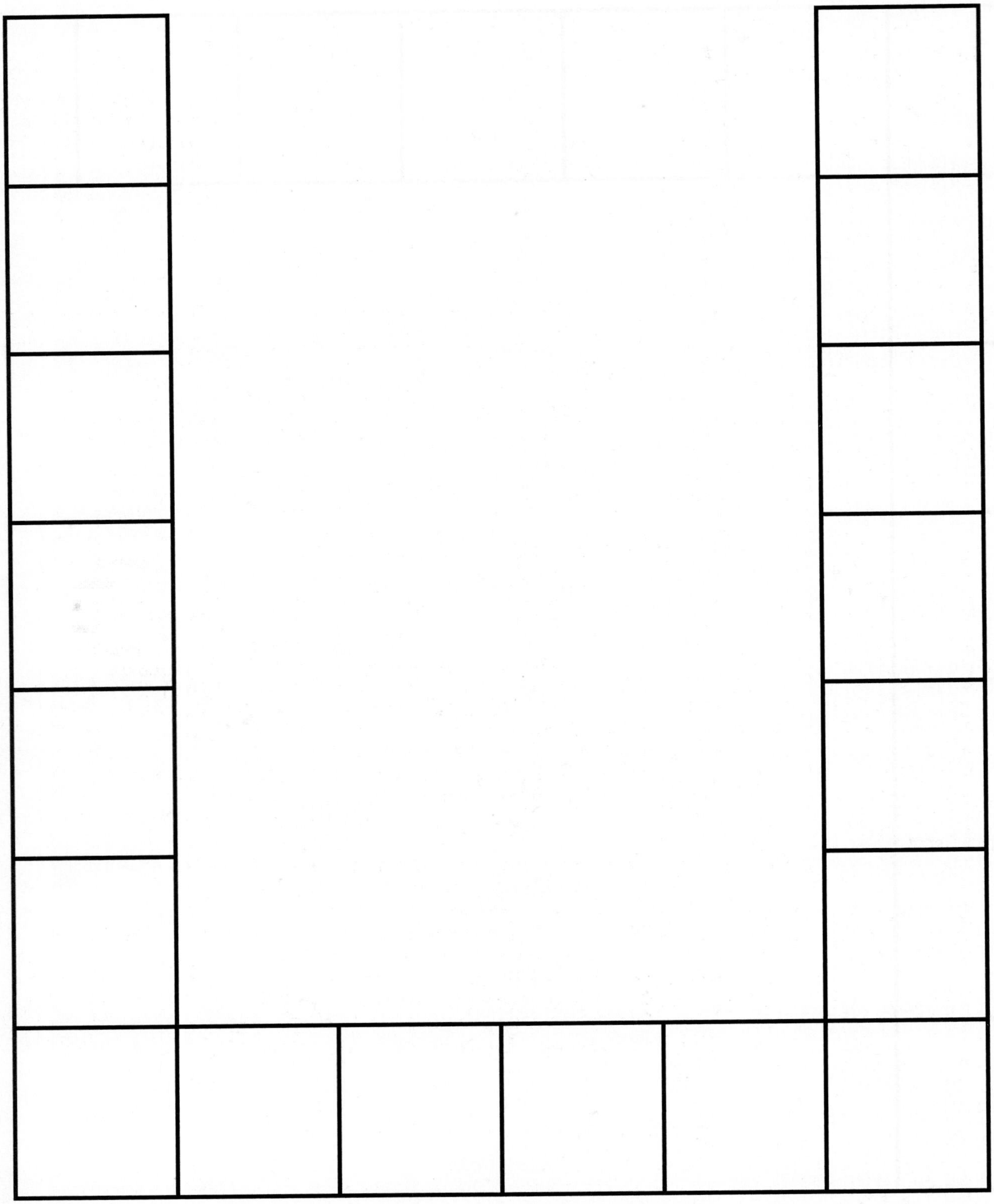

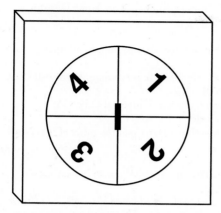

1. Glue a circle 3" to 4" in diameter onto a square of heavy cardboard or foamcore that is about 5" square. Square spinner bases are easier to hold than round ones.

2. Cut a narrow slot in the center of the circle with the point of a sharp pair of scissors or a razor blade.

pointer
pattern

3. Cut the pointer from soft plastic (such as a milk jug) and make a clean round hole with a hole punch.

4. A washer, either a metal one from the hardware store or one cut from the same plastic as the spinner, helps the pointer move freely.

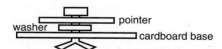

washer · pointer · cardboard base

5. Push a paper fastener through the round hole of the pointer, the washer, and the slot in the spinner base. Flatten the legs, leaving space for the pointer to spin easily. Put a piece of tape over the flattened legs of the paper fastener.

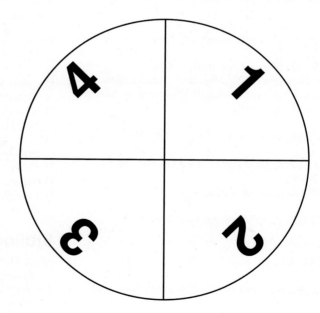

Children's Literature

Azarian, M. (1981). *A farmer's alphabet*. Boston: David Godine.

Base, G. (1986). *Animalia*. New York: Harry Abrams.

Blume, J. (1971). *Freckle juice*. New York: Yearling.

Blume, J. (2003). *Superfudge*. New York: Penguin.

Brett, J. (2003). *Town mouse, country mouse*. New York: Putnam.

Bruna, D. (1978). *B is for bear*. New York: Price Stern Sloan.

Cameron, P. (1961). *I can't, said the ant*. New York: Putnam Publishing.

Carle, E. (1974). *My very first book of shapes*. New York: HarperCollins.

Carle, E. (1987). *Have you seen my cat?* Picture Books.

Christelow, E. (1989). *Five little monkeys jumping on the bed*. Boston: Clarion Books.

Cleary, B. (1968). *Ramona the pest*. New York: HarperCollins.

Clements, A. (1996). *Frindle*. New York: Atheneum.

Crews, D. (1995). *Ten black dots*. New York: Harper Trophy.

Dahl, R. (1988). *Fantastic Mr. Fox*. New York: Puffin Books.

Fleming, D. (1993). *In the small small pond*. New York: Henry Holt and Company.

Florian, D. (1987). *A winter day*. New York: Scholastic.

Florian, D. (1990). *A beach day*. New York: Greenwillow.

Frasier, D. (2007). *Miss Alaineus: A vocabulary disaster*. Sandpiper.

Freeman, D. (1968). *Corduroy*. New York: Viking Juvenile Books.

Galdone, P. (1973). *The three billy goats gruff*. New York: Clarion Books.

Galdone, P. (2006). *The little red hen*. Boston: Clarion.

Garten, J. (1994). *The alphabet tale*. New York: Greenwillow.

Guarina, D. (1989). *Is your mama a llama?* Illustrated by Steven Kellogg. New York: Scholastic.

Heller, R. (1993). *Chickens aren't the only ones*. New York: Putnam.

Hoban, T. (1978). *Is it red? Is it yellow? Is it blue?* New York: Greenwillow Books.

Hutchins, P. (2005). *Rosie's walk*. Fullerton, CA: Aladdin.

Juster, N. (1961/2005). *The phantom tollbooth*. New York: Yearling.

Langstaff, J. (1974). *Oh, a hunting we will go*. New York: Atheneum.

Lionni, L. (1969). *Alexander and the wind-up mouse*. New York: Pantheon.

Martin, B., & Archambault, J. (1989). *Chicka chicka boom boom*. New York: Simon & Schuster.

Marshall, E., & Marshall, J. (1994). *Fox and his friends*. New York: Puffin Books.

McCloskey, R. (1948). *Blueberries for Sal*. New York: Puffin Books.

McGovern, A. (1996). *Stone soup*. New York: Scholastic.

McMillan, B (1990). *One sun: A book of terse verse*. New York: Holiday House.

Milne, A. A. (2009). *Winnie the Pooh*. New York: Dutton Juvenile.

O'Dell, S. (2010). *Island of the blue dolphins*. Sandpiper.

Raffi. (1976). *Singable songs for the very young*. Universal City, CA: Troubadour Records.

Raffi. (1985). *One light, one sun*. Universal City, CA: Troubadour Records.

Rowling, J. K. (2000). *Harry Potter and the goblet of fire*. New York: Scholastic.

Schotter, R. (2006). *The boy who loved words*. New York: Schwartz & Wade.

Scieszka, J. (1992). *The good, the bad, and the goofy*. New York: Viking Press.

Seuss, Dr. (1963). *Dr. Seuss's ABC*. New York: Random House.

Seuss, Dr. (1974). *There's a wocket in my pocket*. New York: Random House.

Sharmat, M. (1980). *Gregory the terrible eater*. New York: Four Winds Press.

Shaw, N. (1986). *Sheep in a jeep*. Boston: Houghton Mifflin.

Slepian, J., & Seidler, A. (1967). *The hungry thing*. New York: Follet.

Slepian, J., & Seidler, A. (1990). *The hungry thing returns*. New York: Scholastic.

Slobodkina, E. (1947). *Caps for sale*. New York: Harper Trophy.

Steig, W. (1978). *Amos and Boris*. New York: Farrar, Straus and Giroux.

The tree (A First Discovery Book). (1992). New York: Cartwheel Books.

Wagener, G. (1991). *Leo the lion*. New York: New York: HarperCollins.

Wallner, J. (1987a). *City mouse–country mouse*. New York: Scholastic.

Wallner, J. (1987b). *The country mouse and the city mouse and two more mouse tales from Aesop*. New York: Scholastic.

Wells, N. (1980). *Noisy Nora*. New York: Dial Press.

White, E. B. (1945). *Stuart Little*. New York: Harper Row.

Wildsmith, B. (1982). *The cat on the mat*. New York: Oxford Press.

Bibliography of Word Study Books

Allen, M. S., & Cunnigham, M. (1999). *Webster's new world rhyming dictionary*. New York: Simon & Schuster.

The American heritage book of English usage: A practical and authoritative guide to contemporary English. (1996). Boston: Houghton Mifflin.

Asimov, I. (1959). *Words of science, and the history behind them*. Boston: Houghton Mifflin.

Asimov, I. (1962). *Words on the map*. Boston: Houghton Mifflin.

Balmuth, M. (1992). *The roots of phonics: An historical introduction*. Austin, TX: Pro-Ed.

Black, D. C. (1988). *Spoonerisms, sycophants and sops; A celebration of fascinating facts about words.* New York: Harper & Row.

Byson, B. (1990). *The mother tongue: English and how it got that way.* New York: Morrow.

Byson, B. (1994). *Made in America: An informal history of the English language in the United States.* New York: Morrow.

Ciardi, J. (1980). *A browser's dictionary: A compendium of curious expressions and intriguing facts.* New York: Harper & Row.

Collis, H. (1981). *Colloquial English.* New York: Regents Pub.

Collis, H. (1986). *101 American English idioms.* New York: McGraw Hill.

Crystal, D. (1987). *The Cambridge encyclopedia of language.* New York: Cambridge University Press.

Cummings, D. W. (1988). *American English spelling.* Baltimore: Johns Hopkins University Press.

Editors of the American Heritage Dictionaries. (2008). *Curious George's dictionary.* Boston: Houghton Mifflin Harcourt.

Editors of the American Heritage Dictionaries. (2009). *The American Heritage first dictionary.* Boston: Houghton Mifflin Harcourt.

Folsom, M. (1985). *Easy as pie: A guessing game of sayings.* New York: Clarion.

Franlyn, J. (1987). *Which is witch?* New York: Dorset Press.

Fry, E. B., & Kress, J. E. (2006). *The reading teacher's book of lists* (5th ed.). San Francisco: Jossey-Bass.

Funk, C. E. (1948). *A hog on ice and other curious expressions.* New York: Harper & Row.

Funk, C. E. (1955). *Heavens to Betsy and other curious sayings.* New York: Harper & Row.

Funk, W. (1954). *Word origins and their romantic stories.* New York: Grosset & Dunlap.

Gwynne, F. (1970). *The king who rained.* New York: Simon & Schuster.

Gwynne, F. (1976). *A chocolate moose for dinner.* New York: Simon & Schuster.

Gwynne, F. (1980). *A sixteen hand horse.* New York: Simon & Schuster.

Gwynne, F. (1988). *A little pigeon toad.* New York: Simon & Schuster.

Harrison, J. S. (1987). *Confusion reigns.* New York: St. Martin's Press.

Heacock, P. (1989). *Which word when?* New York: Dell Pub.

Heller, R. (1987). *A cache of jewels and other collective nouns.* New York: Grosset & Dunlap.

Heller, R. (1988). *Kites sail high.* New York: Grosset & Dunlap.

Heller, R. (1989). *Many luscious lollipops: A book about adjectives.* New York: Grosset & Dunlap.

Heller, R. (1990). *Merry-go-round: A book about nouns.* New York: Grosset & Dunlap.

Heller, R. (1991). *Up, up and away: A book about adverbs.* New York: Grosset & Dunlap.

Heller, R. (1995). *Behind the mask: A book about prepositions.* New York: Grosset & Dunlap.

Hoad, T. F. (1986). *The concise Oxford dictionary of English etymology.* New York: Oxford University Press.

Kinsley, C. (1980). *The heroes.* New York: Mayflower.

Kress, J. E. (2002). *The ESL teacher's book of lists.* San Francisco, CA: John Wiley & Sons.

Lewis, N. (1983). *Dictionary of correct spelling.* New York: Harper & Row.

Maestro, G. (1983). *Riddle romp.* New York: Clarion.

Maestro, G. (1984). *What's a frank frank? Easy homograph riddles.* New York: Clarion.

Maestro, G. (1985): *Razzle-dazzle riddles.* New York: Clarion.

Maestro, G. (1986). *What's mite might? Homophone riddles to boost your word power.* New York: Clarion.

Maestro, G. (1989). *Riddle roundup: A wild bunch to beef up your word power.* New York: Clarion.

Merriam-Webster children's dictionary. (2008). New York: DK Publishing.

Nash, R. (1991). *NTC's dictionary of Spanish cognates thematically organized.* Chicago: NTC Publishing Group.

The Oxford English Dictionary on CD-ROM. (1994). Oxford: Oxford University Press.

Partridge, E. (1984). *Origins: A short etymological dictionary of modern English.* New York: Greenwich House.

Pei, M. (1965). *The story of language.* Philadelphia: Lippincott.

Presson, L. (1996). *What in the world is a homophone?* Hauppauge, NY: Barron's.

Presson, L. (1997). *A dictionary of homophones.* New York: Barron's.

Randall, B. (1992). *When is a pig a hog? A guide to confoundingly related English words.* New York: Prentice Hall.

Robinson, S. R. (1989). *Origins, Volume 1: Bringing words to life.* New York: Teachers & Writers Collaborative.

Robinson, S. R., with Lindsay McAuliffe (1989). *Origins, Volume 2: The word families.* New York: Teachers & Writers Collaborative.

Room, A. (1992). *NTC's dictionary of word origins.* Lincolnwood, IL: National Textbook.

Safire, W. (1984). *I stand corrected: More on language.* New York: Avon.

Sarnoff, J., & Ruffins, R. (1981). *Words: A book about word origins of everyday words and phrases.* New York: Charles Scribner's Sons.

Schleifer, R. (1995). *Grow your own vocabulary: By learning the roots of English words.* New York: Random House.

The Scholastic dictionary of synonyms, antonyms, homonyms. (1965). New York: Scholastic.

Scragg, D. G. (1974). *A history of English spelling.* Manchester, England: Manchester University Press.

Shipley, J. T. (1967). *Dictionary of word origins.* Lanham, MD: Rowman & Littlefield.

Shipley, J. (2001). *The origins of English words.* Baltimore: Johns Hopkins University Press.

Terban, M. (1982). *Eight ate: A feast of homonym riddles.* New York: Clarion.

Terban, M. (1983). *In a pickle and other funny idioms.* New York: Clarion.

Terban, M. (1984). *I think I thought and other tricky verbs.* New York: Clarion.

Terban, M. (1986). *Your foot's on my feet! And other tricky nouns.* New York: Clarion.

Terban, M. (1987). *Mad as a wet hen! And other funny idioms.* New York: Clarion.

Terban, M. (1988a). *The dove dove: Funny homograph riddles.* New York: Clarion.

Terban, M. (1988b). *Too hot to hoot: Funny palindrome riddles.* New York: Clarion.

Terban, M. (1991). *Hey, hay! A wagonful of funny homonym riddles.* New York: Clarion.

Terban, M. (1992). *Funny you should ask: How to make up jokes and riddles with wordplay.* New York: Clarion.

Venesky, R. (1970). *The structure of English orthography.* The Hague: Mouton.

Venezky, R. L. (1999). *The American way of spelling: The structure and origins of American English orthography.* New York: Guilford Press.

Watkins, C. (2011). *The American Heritage Dictionary of Indo-European Roots, Third Edition.* Boston: Houghton Mifflin Harcourt.

Webster's dictionary of word origins. (1992). New York: Smithmark.

Weiner, S. (1981). *Handy book of commonly used American idioms.* New York: Regents Pub.

Winchester, S. (1998). *The professor and the madman: A tale of murder, insanity, and the making of the Oxford English dictionary.* New York: HarperCollins.

Winchester, S. (2003). *The meaning of everything: The story of the Oxford English Dictionary.* New York: Oxford University Press.

Yopp, H. K., & Yopp, R. E. (2000). *Oo-pples and boo-noo-noos.* Portsmouth, NH: Heineman.

Young, S. (1994). *Scholastic rhyming dictionary.* New York: Scholastic

Glossary

absorbed (assimilated) prefixes Prefixes in which the spelling and sound of the consonant has been absorbed into the spelling and sound at the beginning of the base or root to which the prefix is affixed (e.g., *ad* + *tract* = *attract*).

academic vocabulary Academic vocabulary includes domain-specific vocabulary found in content area, specialized, disciplinary texts (e.g., *dendrite* in biology, *coordinates* and *equilateral* in geometry, *electoral college* in government), as well as general academic vocabulary used across content areas and disciplines (e.g., *analyze, define, factors, method, principle*).

accented/stressed syllable The syllable in a word that receives more emphasis when spoken and usually has a clearly pronounced vowel sound. Compare to *unaccented syllable*.

affix Most commonly a suffix or prefix attached to a base word, stem, or root.

affixation The process of attaching a word part, such as a prefix or suffix, to a base word, stem, or root.

affricate A speech sound produced when the breath stream is stopped and released at the point of articulation, usually where the tip of the tongue rubs against the roof of the mouth just behind the teeth, such as when pronouncing the final sound in the word *such* or the beginning sound in the word *trip*. Includes the sounds for /ch/, /sh/, /j/, and /tr/.

alliteration The occurrence in a phrase or line of speech of two or more words having the same beginning sound (e.g., Big burly bears bashed berry baskets.).

alphabetic A writing system containing characters or symbols representing individual speech sounds.

alphabetic layer The first layer of word study instruction, focusing on letter–sound correspondences. Old English was phonetically regular to a great extent.

alphabetic principle The concept that letters and letter combinations are used to represent phonemes in orthography. See also *orthography; phoneme*.

ambiguous vowels A vowel sound represented by a variety of different spelling patterns, or vowel patterns that represent a wide range of sounds (e.g., the *ou* in *cough, through,* and *could*).

analytic phonics Word study that divides words into their elemental parts through phonemic, orthographic, and morphological analysis.

articulated/articulation Sounds are physically shaped in the mouth during speech using the tongue, teeth, lips, and the roof of the mouth. Some confusions are made in spelling based on similarities in articulation (e.g., *tr* for *dr*).

assimilated prefixes See *absorbed (assimilated) prefixes*.

automaticity Refers to the speed and accuracy of word recognition and spelling. Automaticity is the goal of word study instruction and frees cognitive resources for comprehension.

base word A word to which prefixes and/or suffixes are added. For example, the base word of *unwholesome* is *whole*. See *free morphemes*.

blends A phonics term for an orthographic unit of two or three letters at the beginning or end of words that are blended together. There are *l*-blends such as *bl, cl* and *fl*; *r*-blends such as *gr, tr,* and *pr*; *s*-blends such as *pc, scr,* and *squ*; and final blends such as *ft, rd,* and *st*. Every sound represented in a blend is pronounced, if only briefly.

blind sort A word sort done with a partner in which students who are responsible for sorting cannot see the word. They must instead attend to the sounds and sometimes visualize the spelling pattern to determine the category.

blind writing sort A variant of a blind sort in which one student (or teacher) names a word without showing it to another student, who must write it in the correct category under a key word.

bound morphemes Meaning units of language (morphemes) that cannot stand alone as a word. *Respected* has three bound morphemes: *re+spect+ed*. Compare to *free morphemes*.

center time Work completed independently in prepared areas within a classroom.

choral reading Oral reading done in unison with another person or persons.

circle time Group work conducted under the teacher's direction.

classroom composite A classroom profile that organizes students into instructional groups by features to be taught within each stage.

closed sorts Word or picture sorts based on predetermined categories. Compare to *open sorts*.

closed syllable A syllable that ends with or is "closed" by a consonant sound. In polysyllabic words, a closed syllable contains a short-vowel sound that is closed by two consonants (e.g., *rabbit, racket*). Compare to *open syllable*.

cognates Words in different languages derived from the same root.

complex consonant patterns Consonant units occurring at the end of words determined by the preceding vowel sound. For example, a final *tch* follows the short-vowel sound in *fetch* and *scotch*, while a final *ch* follows the long-vowel sound in *peach* and *coach*. Other complex consonant patterns include final *ck* (*pack* vs. *peak*) and final *dge* (*badge* vs. *cage*).

compound words Words made up of two smaller words. A compound word may or may not be hyphenated, depending on its part of speech.

concept of word in text (COW-T) The ability to match spoken words to printed words, as demonstrated by the ability to point to, or track, the words of a memorized text while reading.

concepts about print (CAP) Understandings about how books are organized (front-to-back page turning, titles, illustrations), how print is oriented on the page (top to bottom, left to right), and features of print such as punctuation and capitalization.

concept sorts A categorization task in which pictures, objects, or words are grouped by shared attributes or meanings to develop concepts and vocabulary.

consolidated alphabetic phase Ehri's fourth phase of word recognition, in which readers use patterns, chunks, and other word parts to figure out unfamiliar words.

consonant alternation The process in which the pronunciation of consonants changes in the base or root of derivationally related words while the spelling does not change (e.g., the silent-to-sounded *g* in the words *sign* and *signal*; the /k/ to /sh/ pattern in the words *music* and *musician*).

consonant blend See *blends*.

consonant digraph See *digraph*.

consonants Letters that are not vowels (*a, e, i, o,* and *u*). Whereas vowel sounds are thought of as musical, consonant sounds are known for their noise and the way in which air is constricted as it is stopped and released or forced through the vocal tract, mouth, teeth, and lips.

continuant sound A consonant sound, such as /ssssss/ that can be prolonged as long as the breath lasts without distorting the sound quality. Includes the consonant sounds for /f/, /l/, /m/, /n/, /r/, /s/, /v/, /w/, and /th/. See *stop consonants*.

cut and paste activities A variation of picture sorting in which students cut out pictures from magazines or catalogs and paste them into categories.

derivational affixes Affixes added to base words that affect the meaning (*sign*, **resign**; *break*, *break**able***) and/or part of speech (*beauty*, *beaut**iful***). Compare to *inflected/inflectional endings*.

derivational relations The last stage of spelling development, in which spellers learn about derivational relationships preserved in the spelling of words. *Derivational* refers to the process by which new words are created from existing words, chiefly through affixation, and the development of a word from its historical origin. *Derivational constancy* refers to spelling patterns that remain the same despite changes in pronunciation across derived forms. For example, *bomb* retains the *b* from *bombard* because of its historical evolution.

developmental level An individual's stage of spelling development: emergent, letter name–alphabetic, within word pattern, syllables and affixes, or derivational relations.

developmental spelling Spelling that reflects the current word knowledge of students who spell "as best they can." Also called *invented spelling*.

dialogic reading An approach to reading aloud that is designed to stimulate oral language and dialogue while enhancing students' ability to retell stories.

digraph Two letters that represent one sound. There are consonant digraphs and vowel digraphs, though the term most commonly refers to consonant digraphs. Common consonant digraphs include *sh, ch, th,* and *wh*. Consonant digraphs at the beginning of words are *onsets*.

diphthong A complex speech sound beginning with one vowel sound and moving to another within the same syllable. The *oy* in *boy* is a diphthong, as is the *ou* in *cloud*.

directionality The left-to-right direction used for reading and writing English.

domain-specific academic vocabulary See *academic vocabulary*.

draw and label activities An extension activity for a picture sort in which students draw pictures of things that begin with the sounds under study. The pictures are drawn in the appropriate categories and labeled with the letter(s) corresponding to that sound.

echo reading Oral reading in which the student echoes or imitates the reading of the teacher or partner to offer support for beginning readers and to model fluency.

emergent A period of literacy development ranging from birth to beginning reading. This period precedes the letter name–alphabetic stage of spelling development.

eponyms Places, things, and actions that are named after an individual.

etymology The study of the origin and historical development of words.

feature analysis More than scoring words right and wrong, feature analyses provide a way of interpreting students' spelling errors by taking into account their knowledge of specific orthographic features such as consonant blends or short vowels. Feature analyses inform teachers what spelling features to teach.

feature guide A tool used to classify students' errors within a hierarchy of orthographic features. Used to score spelling inventories to assess students' knowledge of specific spelling features at their particular stage of spelling development, and to plan word study instruction to meet individual needs.

free morphemes Meaning units of language (morphemes) that stand alone as words. (*Workshop* has two free morphemes: *work* and *shop*.) Compare to *bound morphemes*.

frustration level A dysfunctional level of instruction where there is a mismatch between instruction and what an individual is able to grasp. This mismatch precludes learning and often results in frustration.

full alphabetic readers/phase Ehri's third phase of word recognition, in which readers are able to sound out words using letter–sound correspondences or phonics they know.

general academic vocabulary See *academic vocabulary*.

generative The approach to word study that emphasizes orthographic principles that apply to *many* words, as opposed to an approach that focuses on individual words. Generative instruction addresses the combination of base words, Greek and Latin word roots, and affixes in order to *generate* students' understanding of how most words in the English language work.

headers Words, pictures, or other labels used to designate categories for sorting.

high-frequency words Words that make up roughly 50 percent of any text—those that occur most often (e.g., *the, was, were, is*).

homographs Words that are spelled alike but have different pronunciations and different meanings (e.g., "*tear* a piece of paper" and "to shed a *tear*"; "*lead* someone along" and "the element *lead*").

homonyms Words that share the same spelling but have different meanings (tell a *yarn*, knit with *yarn*). See *homographs*; *homophones*; *polysemous*.

homophones Words that sound alike, are spelled differently, and have different meanings (e.g., *bear* and *bare*, *pane* and *pain*, and *forth* and *fourth*).

independent level That level of academic engagement in which an individual works independently, without need of instructional support. Independent-level behaviors demonstrate a high degree of accuracy, speed, ease, and fluency.

Indo-European (IE) root Indo-European is the "mother" language to over half of the world's languages.

inflected/inflectional endings Suffixes that change the verb tense (*walks*, *walked*, *walking*) or number (*dogs*, *boxes*) of a word.

instructional level A level of academic engagement in which instruction is comfortably matched to what an individual is able to grasp. See also *zone of proximal development (ZPD)*.

interactive read-alouds A reading format to support emergent reading where the teacher reads aloud to the students and invites discussion and other participation.

interactive writing A cooperative instructional strategy whereby a text is composed with student input and the writing is done largely by the students under supervision to create an accurately spelled final version. It can be used to model writing strategies and concepts about print.

invented spelling Also known as spelling "as best you can"; allows students to write even before they can read during the emergent stage.

key pictures Pictures placed at the top of each category in a picture sort. Key pictures act as headers for each column and can be used for analogy.

key words Words placed at the top of each category in a word sort. Key words act as headers for each column and can be used for analogy.

kinetic reversal An error of letter order (PTE for *pet*).

language experience approach An approach to teaching reading, in which students dictate to a teacher, who records their language. Dictated accounts can then be used as familiar reading materials.

lax Lax vowels are commonly known as the short-vowel sound.

letter name–alphabetic spelling stage The second stage of spelling development, in which students represent beginning, middle, and ending sounds of words with phonetically accurate letter choices, often based on the sound of the letter name itself, rather than learned letter–sound associations. The letter name *h* (aitch), for example, produces the /ch/ sound, and is often selected to represent that sound (HEP for *chip*).

liquids The consonant sounds for /r/ and /l/, which, unlike other consonant sounds, do not obstruct air in the mouth. The sounds for /r/ and /l/ are more vowel-like in that they do not involve direct contact between the lips, tongue, and the roof of the mouth as other consonants do. Instead, they "roll around" in the mouth, as if liquid.

long vowels Every vowel (*a*, *e*, *i*, *o*, and *u*) has two sounds, commonly referred to as "long" and "short." The long-vowel sound "says its letter name" and frequently are paired with other vowels as in *bake* and *beak*. See *tense*.

meaning layer The third layer of English orthography, including meaning units such as prefixes, suffixes, and word roots. These word elements were acquired primarily during the Renaissance, when English was overlaid with many words of Greek and Latin derivation.

meaning sorts A type of word sort in which the categories are determined by semantic categories or by spelling–meaning connections.

memory reading An accurate recitation of text accompanied by fingerpoint reading.

mock linear A kind of pretend writing where children beginning to write approximate the broader contours of the writing system, starting with the linear arrangement of print.

morphemes (or morphemic) Meaning units in the spelling of words, such as the suffix *-ed*, which signals past tense, or the root *graph* in the words *autograph* or *graphite*. See also *bound morphemes*; *free morphemes*.

morphemic analysis The process of analyzing or breaking down a word in terms of its meaning units or morphemes (e.g., *in-struct-or*).

morphology The study of word parts related to syntax and meaning.

nasals A sound, such as /m/, /n/, or /ng/, produced when the air is blocked in the oral cavity but escapes through the nose. The first consonants in the words *mom* and *no* represent nasal sounds.

oddballs Words that do not fit the targeted feature in a sort.

onset The initial consonant(s) sound of a single syllable or word. The onset of the word *sun* is /s/. The onset of the word *slide* is /sl/. See *rimes*.

open sorts A type of picture or word sort in which the categories for sorting are left open. Students sort pictures or words into groups according to the students' own judgment. See *closed sorts*.

open syllable Syllables that end with a long-vowel sound (e.g., *la-bor*, *sea-son*). Compare to *closed syllable*.

orthography The writing system of a language—specifically, the correct sequence of letters, characters, or symbols.

other vowels Vowels that are neither long nor short and include *r*-influenced vowels and diphthongs, such as *oy* or *ou*.

partial alphabetic readers/phase Ehri's second phase of word recognition, in which students use partial clues, primarily initial consonants, to identify words. Also known as selective cue stage.

pattern A letter sequence that functions as a unit to represent a sound (such as *ai* in *rain*, *pain*, and *train*) or a sequence of vowels and consonants, such as the consonant-vowel-consonant (CVC) pattern in a word such as *rag* or at a syllable juncture such as the VCCV pattern in *button*.

pattern layer The second layer or tier of English orthography, in which patterns of letter sequences, rather than individual letters themselves, represent vowel sounds. This layer of information was acquired during the period of English history following the Norman invasion. Many of the vowel patterns of English are of French derivation.

pattern sort   A word sort in which students categorize words according to similar spelling patterns.

personal readers   Individual books of reading materials for beginning readers. Group experience charts, dictations, rhymes, and short excerpts from books comprise the majority of the reading material.

phoneme   The smallest unit of speech that distinguishes one word from another. For example, the *t* of *tug* and the *r* of *rug* are two phonemes.

phoneme segmentation   The process of dividing a spoken word into the smallest units of sound within that word. The word *bat* can be divided or segmented into three phonemes: /b/, /ă/, /t/.

phonemic awareness   The ability to consciously manipulate individual phonemes in a spoken language. Phonemic awareness is often assessed by the ability to tap, count, or push a penny forward for every sound heard in a word like *cat*: /c/, /ă/, /t/.

phonetic   Representing the sounds of speech with a set of distinct symbols (letters), each denoting a single sound. See also *alphabetic principle*.

phonics   The systematic relationship between letters and sounds.

phonics readers   Beginning reading books written with controlled vocabulary that contain recurring phonics elements.

phonograms   Often called *word families*, phonograms end in high-frequency rimes that vary only in the beginning consonant sound to make a word. For example, *back*, *sack*, *black*, and *track* are phonograms with the rime *-ack*.

phonological awareness   An awareness of various speech sounds such as syllables, rhyme, and individual phonemes.

picture sort   A categorization task in which pictures are sorted into categories by sound or by meaning. Pictures cannot be sorted by pattern.

polysemous (or polysemy)   The characteristic of words to have multiple meanings; derived from *poly-* ("many") + *sem-* the Latin root referring to "meaning").

prealphabetic readers phase   Ehri's first phase of word recognition, in which students use nonalphabetic clues, like word length or distinctive print, to identify words. Also known as logographic.

preconsonantal nasals   Nasals that occur before consonants, as in the words *bump* or *sink*. The vowel is nasalized as part of the air escapes through the nose during pronunciation. See also *nasals*.

predictable   Text for beginning readers with repetitive language patterns, rhythm and rhyme, and illustrations that make it easy to read and remember.

prefix   An affix attached at the beginning of a base word or word root that changes the meaning of the word.

prephonetic   Writing that bears no correspondence to speech sounds; literally, "before sound." Prephonetic writing occurs during the emergent stage and typically consists of random scribbles, mock linear writing, or hieroglyphic-looking symbols.

pretend reading   A paraphrase or spontaneous retelling told by students as they turn the pages of a familiar story book.

print referencing   The practice of referring to features of print such as punctuation, capital letters, directionality, and so forth as a way to teach students concepts about print. See also *concepts about print* (*CAP*).

prosodic/prosody   The musical qualities of language, including intonation, expression, stress, and rhythm, that contribute to fluency.

reduced vowel   A vowel occurring in an unstressed syllable. See also *schwa*.

rimes   A unit composed of the vowel and any following consonants within a syllable. For example, the rime unit in the word *tag* is *ag*. See also *onset*.

r-influenced (r-controlled) vowels   In English, *r* colors the way the preceding vowel is pronounced. For example, compare the pronunciation of the vowels in *bar* and *bad*. The vowel in *bar* is influenced by the *r*.

root word/roots   Words or word parts, often of Latin or Greek origin, that are often combined with other roots to form words such as *telephone* (*tele* and *phone*). See also *stem*.

salient sound   A prominent sound in a word or syllable that stands out because of the way it is made or felt in the mouth.

schwa   A vowel sound in English that often occurs in an unstressed syllable, such as the /uh/ sound in the first syllable of the word *above*.

seatwork   School work that is completed at the student's own desk. Seatwork is usually on a student's independent level and is usually assigned for practice. See also *independent level*.

semiphonetic   Writing that demonstrates *some* awareness that letters represent speech sounds (literally, "part sound"). Beginning and/or ending consonant sounds of syllables or words may be represented, but medial vowels are usually omitted (e.g., ICDD for *I see Daddy*). Semiphonetic writing occurs at the end of the emergent stage or the very outset of the early letter name–alphabetic stage.

shared reading   An activity in which the teacher prereads a text and then invites students join in on subsequent readings.

short vowels   Every vowel (*a, e, i, o,* and *u*) has two sounds, commonly referred to as "long" and "short." The vocal cords are more relaxed when producing the short-vowel sound than the long-vowel sound. Because of this, short-vowel sounds are often referred to as *lax*. The five short vowels can be heard at the beginning of these words: *apple, Ed, igloo, octopus,* and *umbrella*. Compare to *long vowels*.

sight words/sight vocabulary   Printed words stored in memory by the reader that can be read immediately, "at first sight," without having to use decoding strategies.

sound board   Charts used by letter name–alphabetic spellers that contain pictures and letters for the basic sound–symbol correspondences (e.g., the letter *b*, a picture of a bell, and the word *bell*).

sound sort   Sorts that ask students to categorize pictures or words by sound as opposed to visual patterns.

speed sorts   Pictures or words that are sorted under a timed condition. Students try to beat their own time.

spelling-by-stage classroom organization chart   A classroom composite sheet used to place students in a developmental spelling stage and form groups.

spelling inventories   Assessments that ask students to spell a series of increasingly difficult words used to determine what features students know or use but confuse, as well as a specific developmental stage of spelling.

spelling–meaning connections Words that are related in meaning often share the same spelling despite changes in pronunciation from one form of the word to the next. For example, the word *sign* retains the *g* from *signal* even though it is not pronounced, thus "signaling" the meaning connection through the spelling.

static reversal A handwriting error that is the mirror image of the intended letter (*b* for *d*, or *p* for *d*).

stem This usually refers to a base or word root together with any derivational affixes that have been added, and to which inflectional endings may be added.

stop consonants A consonant sound such as /t/ that is formed by briefly obstructing air in the vocal track followed by a puff of air; stop consonant sounds (/b/, /d/, /g/, /k/, /p/, and /t/) cannot be prolonged without distorting the sound. Also known as plosives.

stressed/accented syllable The syllable in a word that is given an added emphasis when spoken and marked with bold letters or accent marks in the dictionary (e.g., ap' ple or **ap** ple).

structural analysis The process of determining the pronunciation and/or meaning of a word by analyzing word parts including syllables, base words, and affixes.

suffix An affix attached at the end of a base word or word root.

syllable juncture The transition from one syllable to the next. Sometimes this transition involves a spelling change such as consonant doubling or dropping the final -*e* before adding -*ing*.

syllable juncture patterns The alternating patterns of consonants (C) and vowels (V) at the point where syllables meet. For example, the word *rabbit* follows a VCCV syllable pattern at the point where the syllables meet.

syllables Units of spoken language that consist of a vowel that may be preceded and/or followed by several consonants. Syllables are units of sound and can often be detected by paying attention to movements of the mouth. Syllabic divisions indicated in the dictionary are not always correct because the dictionary will always separate meaning units regardless of how the word is pronounced. For example, the proper syllable division for the word *naming* is *na-ming*; however, the dictionary divides this word as *nam-ing* to preserve the *ing*.

syllables and affixes stage The fourth stage of spelling development, which coincides with intermediate reading. Syllables and affixes spellers learn about the spelling changes that often take place at the point of transition from one syllable to the next. Frequently this transition involves consonant doubling or dropping the final -*e* before adding a suffix.

synchrony Occurring at the same time. In this book, stages of spelling development are described in the context of reading and writing behaviors occurring at the same time.

synthetic phonics Phonics instruction that begins with individual sounds and the blending of sounds to form words.

teacher-directed sorts An explicit word study lesson in which the teacher models and leads students through the sorting process, offers explanations, and facilitates a discussion about the features and the meaning of words.

tense A vowel sound that is commonly known as the long-vowel sound. Long-vowel sounds are produced by tensing the vocal cords.

tracking The ability to fingerpoint read a text, demonstrating concept of word in text. See *concept of word in text (COW-T)*.

unaccented/unstressed syllable The syllable in a word that gets little emphasis and may have an indistinct vowel sound, such as the first syllable in *about*, the second syllable in *definition*, or the final syllables in *doctor* or *table*. See also *schwa*.

unvoiced (or voiceless) A sound that, when produced, does not cause the vocal cords to vibrate. For example, the *t* in *at* is unvoiced. Voiced/voiceless consonant contrasts include these pairs: [/p/ /b/], [/t/ /d/], [/k/ /g/], [/ch/ /g/], [/f/ /v/], [/s/ /z/]. In most languages, vowels are voiced.

voice pointing A strategy used by emergent readers to identify a word in a memorized rhyme or familiar text. They go back to the beginning of the text and start reciting it in their heads (or out loud) while mentally pointing to each word as it is recited until they arrive at the word in question.

voiced A sound that, when produced, vibrates the vocal cords. The letter sound of *d* in *add*, for example, vibrates the vocal cords. Compare to *unvoiced*.

vowel A speech sound produced by the easy passage of air through a relatively open vocal tract. Vowels form the most central sound of a syllable. In English, vowel sounds are represented by the following letters: *a*, *e*, *i*, *o*, *u*, and sometimes *y*. Compare to *consonants*.

vowel alternation The process in which the pronunciation of vowels changes in the base or root of derivationally related words, while the spelling does not change (e.g., the long-to-short vowel change in the related words *crime* and *criminal*; the long-to-schwa vowel change in the related words *impose* and *imposition*).

vowel digraphs A phonics term for pairs of vowels that represent a single vowel sound (such as *ai* in *rain*, *oa* in *boat*, *ue* in *blue*). Compare to *digraph*.

vowel marker A silent letter used to indicate the sound of the vowel. In English, silent letters are used to form patterns associated with specific vowel sounds. Vowel markers are usually vowels, as the *i* in *drain* or the *a* in *treat*, but they can also be consonants, as the *l* in *told*.

whole-to-part model A technique for fostering early literacy development using the shared reading of a whole texts followed activities involving the parts (sentences, words, letters, and sounds).

within word pattern spelling stage The third stage of spelling development, which coincides with the transitional period of literacy development. Within word pattern spellers have mastered the basic letter–sound correspondences of written English and they grapple with letter sequences that function as a unit, especially long-vowel patterns that include silent letters.

word A unit of meaning. A word may be a single syllable or a combination of syllables. A word may contain smaller units of meaning within it. In print, a word is separated by white space. In speech, several words may be strung together in a breath group. For this reason, it takes a while for young students to develop a clear concept of word. See also *concept of word*.

word bank   A collection of known words harvested from frequently read beginning reading materials. Word bank words are written on small cards and stored for review and use in word study games and word sorts.

word cards   Words written on 2-by-1-inch pieces of cardstock or paper.

word consciousness   An attitude of curiosity and attention to words critical for vocabulary development.

word families   Phonograms or words that share the same rime. (For example, *fast*, *past*, *last*, and *blast* all share the *ast* rime.) In the derivational relations stage, *word families* refers to words that share the same root or origin, as in *spectator*, *spectacle*, *inspect*, and *inspector*. See *phonograms*; *rimes*.

word hunts   A word study activity in which students go back to texts they have previously read to hunt for other words that follow the same spelling features examined during the word or picture sort.

word root   See *root word/roots*.

word sort   A basic word study routine in which students group words into categories. Word sorting involves comparing and contrasting within and across categories. Word sorts are often cued by key words placed at the top of each category.

word study   A learner-centered, conceptual approach to instruction in phonics, spelling, word recognition, and vocabulary, based on a developmental model.

word study notebooks   Notebooks in which students write their word sorts into columns and add other words that follow similar spelling patterns throughout the week. Word study notebooks may also contain lists of words generated over time, such as new vocabulary, homophones, cognates, and so on.

writing sorts   An extension activity in which students write the words they have sorted into categories.

zone of proximal development (ZPD)   A term coined by the Russian psychologist Vygotsky, referring to the ripe conditions for learning something new. A person's ZPD is that zone which is neither too hard nor too easy. The term is similar to the concept of *instructional level*.

References

Adams, M. J. (1990). *Beginning to read: Thinking and learning about print*. Cambridge, MA: MIT Press.

Allen, R. V. (1976). *Language experiences in communication*. Boston: Houghton Mifflin.

Allington, R. L., & Cunningham, P. M. (2006). *Schools that work: Where all children read and write*. (3rd ed.). Boston: Allyn & Bacon.

Anders, P., & Bos, C. (1986). Semantic feature analysis: An interactive strategy for vocabulary development and text comprehension. *Journal of Reading, 29*, 610–616.

Aram, D., & Biron, S. (2004). Intervention programs among low SES Israeli preschoolers. The benefits of joint storybook reading and joint writing to early literacy. *Early Childhood Research Quarterly, 19*, 588–610.

Armbruster, B. B., Lehr, F., & Osborn, J. (2001). *Put reading first: The research building blocks for teaching children to read*. Washington, DC: The Partnership for Reading.

Bahr, R. H., Silliman, E. R., & Berninger, V. (2009). What spelling errors have to tell about vocabulary learning. In C. Wood & V. Connelly (Eds.), *Contemporary perspectives on reading and spelling* (pp. 177–210). London: Routledge.

Ball, E. W., & Blachman, B. A. (1988). Phoneme segmentation training: Effect on reading readiness. *Annals of Dyslexia, 38*, 208–225.

Balmuth, M. (1992). *The roots of phonics: A historical introduction*. Austin, TX: Pro-Ed.

Barrentine, S. J. (1996). Engaging with reading through interactive read-alouds. *The Reading Teacher, 50*, 36–42.

Baumann, J. F., Edwards, E. C., Font, G., Tereshinski, C. A., Kame'enui, E. J., & Olejnik, S. (2003). Teaching morphemic and contextual analysis to fifth-grade students. *Reading Research Quarterly, 37*(2), 150–176.

Bear, D. (1982). *Patterns of oral reading across stages of word knowledge*. Unpublished manuscript, University of Virginia, Charlottesville.

Bear, D. (1989). Why beginning reading must be word-by-word. *Visible Language, 23*(4), 353–367.

Bear, D. (1991a). Copying fluency and orthographic development. *Visible Language, 25*(1), 40–53.

Bear, D. (1991b). "Learning to fasten the seat of my union suit without looking around": The synchrony of literacy development. *Theory into Practice, 30*(3), 149–157.

Bear, D. (1992). The prosody of oral reading and stage of word knowledge. In S. Templeton & D. Bear (Eds.), *Development of orthographic knowledge and the foundations of literacy: A memorial Festschrift for Edmund H. Henderson* (pp. 137–186). Hillsdale, NJ: Lawrence Erlbaum.

Bear, D. R., Caserta-Henry, C., & Venner, D. (2004). *Personal readers and literacy instruction with emergent and beginning readers*. Berkeley, CA: Teaching Resource Center.

Bear, D., & Cathey, S. (1989, November). *Reading fluency in beginning readers and expression in practiced oral reading: Links with word knowledge*. Paper presented at National Reading Conference, Austin, TX.

Bear, D. R., Flanigan, K., Hayes, L., Helman, L., Invernizzi, L., Johnston, F., & Templeton, S. (2014). *Vocabulary their way: Words and strategies for academic success*. Boston: Pearson. Middle School Vocabulary Program for Classroom Use Includes Teacher Editions, Teacher Resource DVD-ROM, Student Games DVD-ROM, and Routine Cards [Grades 6–8].

Bear, D. R., & Helman, L. (2004). Word study for vocabulary development: An ecological perspective on instruction during the early stages of literacy learning. In J. F. Baumann & E. J. Kame'enui (Eds.), *Vocabulary instruction: Research to practice* (pp. 139–158). New York: Guilford Press.

Bear, D. R., Helman, L., & Woessner, L. (2009). Word study assessment and instruction with English learners in a second grade classroom: Bending with students' growth. In J. Coppola & E. V. Primas (Eds.), *One classroom, many learners: Best literacy practices for today's multilingual classrooms* (pp. 11–40). Newark, DE: International Reading Association.

Bear, D. R., Invernizzi, M., Johnston, F., & Templeton, S. (2010). *Words their way: Letter and picture sorts for emergent spellers* (2nd ed.). Boston: Allyn & Bacon.

Bear, D., Invernizzi, M., Johnston, F., & Templeton, S. (2012). *Words Their Way: The Developmental Approach*. Glenview, IL: Pearson Education.

Bear, D. R., Negrete, S., Cathey, S. (2012). Developmental literacy instruction with struggling readers across three stages. *New England Journal of Reading, 48*(1), 1–9.

Bear, D., & Templeton, S. (1998). Explorations in developmental spelling: Foundations for learning and teaching phonics, spelling and vocabulary. *The Reading Teacher, 52*, 222–242.

Bear, D., & Templeton, S. (2000). Matching development and instruction. In N. Padak & T. Rasinski (Eds.), *Distinguished Educators on Reading: Contributions that have shaped effective literacy instruction* (pp. 363–376). Newark, DE: International Reading Association.

Bear, D., Templeton, S., Helman, L., & Baren, T. (2003). Orthographic development and learning to read in different languages. In G. Garcia (Ed.), *English learners: Reaching the highest level of English literacy* (pp. 71–95). Newark, DE: International Reading Association.

Bear, D., Truex, P., & Barone, D. (1989). In search of meaningful diagnoses: Spelling-by-stage assessment of literacy proficiency. *Adult Literacy and Basic Education, 13*(3), 165–185.

Beaver, J., & Carter, M. (2003). *Developmental reading assessment*. Parsippany, NJ: Celebration Press, Pearson Learning Group.

Beck, I., McKeown, M., & Kucan, L. (2008). *Creating robust vocabulary: Frequently asked questions*. New York: Guilford.

Beck, I. L., McKeown, M. G., & Kucan, L. (2013). *Bringing words to life: Robust vocabulary instruction* (2nd ed.). New York: Guilford Press.

Beers, J. W., & Henderson, E. H. (1977). A study of developing orthographic concepts among first grade children. *Research in the Teaching of English, 11*, 133–148.

Berninger, V. W., Abbott, R. D., Nagy, W., & Carlisle, J. (2009). Growth in phonological, orthographic, and morphological awareness in grades 1 to 6. *Journal of Psycholinguistic Research*, *39*(2), 141–163.

Biemiller, A. (1970). The development of the use of graphic and contextual information as children learn to read. *Reading Research Quarterly*, 6, 1, 75–96.

Biemiller, A. (2001). Teaching vocabulary: Early, direct, sequential. *American Educator*, *25*(1), 24–28.

Biemiller, A. (2004). Teaching vocabulary in the primary grades: Vocabulary instruction ,needed. In J. F. Baumann & E. J. Kame'enui (Eds.), *Vocabulary instruction: Research to practice* (pp. 28–40). New York: Guilford Press.

Biemiller, A. (2005). Size and sequence in vocabulary development: Implications for choosing words for primary grade vocabulary instruction. In E. H. Hiebert & M. L. Kamil (Eds.), *Teaching and learning vocabulary: Bringing research to practice* (pp. 223–242). Mahwah, NJ: Lawrence Erlbaum.

Biemiller, A., & Slonim, N. (2001). Estimating root word vocabulary growth in normative and advantaged populations: Evidence for a common sequence of vocabulary acquisition. *Journal of Educational Psychology*, *93*, 498–520.

Bissex, G. L. (1980). *Gnys at wrk: A child learns to read and write*. Cambridge, MA: Harvard University Press.

Blachman, B. A. (1994). What we have learned from longitudinal studies of phonological processing and reading, and some unanswered questions: A response to Torgeson, Wagner, and Rashotte. *Journal of Learning Disabilities*, *27*, 287–291.

Blachman, B. A. (2000). Phonological awareness. In M. L. Kamil, P. B. Mosenthal, D. P. Pearson, & R. Barr (Eds), *Handbook of reading research*, *Volume III*/pp. 483–502. Mahwah, NJ: Lawrence Erlbaum.

Blachowicz, C., & Fisher, P. J. (2009). *Teaching vocabulary in all classrooms* (4th ed.). Boston: Allyn & Bacon.

Blackwell-Bullock, R., Invernizzi, M., Drake, A. E., & Howell, J. L. (2009). A concept of word in text: An integral literacy skill. *Reading in Virginia*, *31*, 30–35.

Bowers, P. N., & Kirby, J. R. (2010). Effects of morphological instruction on vocabulary acquisition. *Reading and Writing: An Interdisciplinary Journal*, *23*(5), 515–537.

Bravo, M. A., Hiebert, E. H., & Pearson, P. D. (2005). Tapping the linguistic resources of Spanish/English bilinguals: The role of cognates in science. In R. K. Wagner, A. E. Muse, & K. R. Tannenbaum (Eds.), *Vocabulary acquisition: Implications for reading comprehension* (pp. 140–156). New York: Guilford Press.

Bryant, P., Nunes, T., & Bindman, M. (1997). Backward readers' awareness of language: Strengths and weaknesses. *European Journal of Psychology of Education*, *12*(4), 357–372.

Button, K., Johnson, M. J., & Furgerson, P. (1996). Interactive writing in a primary classroom. *The Reading Teacher*, *49*, 446–454.

Cabell, S. Q., Tortorelli, L. S., & Gerde, H. K. (2013). How do I write . . . ? Scaffolding preschoolers' early writing skills. *The Reading Teacher*, *66*(8), 650–659.

Cantrell, R. J. (2001). Exploring the relationship between dialect and spelling for specific vocalic features in Appalachian first-grade children. *Linguistics and Education*, *12*(1), 1–23.

Carlisle, J. F. (2010). Effects of instruction in morphological awareness on literacy achievement: An integrative review. *Reading Research Quarterly*, *45*(4), 464–487.

Carlisle, J. F., Kelcey, B., & Berebitsky, D. (2013). Teachers' support of students' vocabulary learning during literacy instruction in high poverty elementary schools. *American Educational Research Journal*, *50*(6), 1360–1391.

Carnine, D., Silbert, J., Kame'enui, E. J., & Tarver, S. G. (2009). *Direct instruction reading* (5th ed.). Upper Saddle River, NJ: Prentice Hall.

Carpenter, K. (2010). *The relationships among concept sorts, storybook reading, language-based print awareness, and language proficiency in the vocabulary learning of kindergarten children*. Unpublished doctoral dissertation, University of Nevada, Reno.

Cartwright, K. B. (2006). Fostering flexibility and comprehension in elementary students. *The Reading Teacher*, *59*: 628–634. doi: 10.1598/RT.59.7.2

Cartwright, K. B. (Ed.). (2008). *Literacy processes: Cognitive flexibility in learning and teaching*. New York: Guilford Press.

Cartwright, K. B. (2010). *Word Callers: Small-group and one-to-one interventions for children who read but don't comprehend*. Portsmouth, NH: Heinemann.

Cathey, S. S. (1991). *Emerging concept of word: Exploring young children's abilities to read rhythmic text*. Doctoral dissertation, University of Nevada, Reno, NV, UMI #9220355.

Chall, J. S. (1983). *Stages of reading development*. New York: McGraw-Hill.

Chandler, K. (1999) *Spelling inquiry: How one elementary school caught the mnemonic plague*. Portland, ME: Stenhouse.

Chomsky, C. (1970). Reading, writing, and phonology. *Harvard Educational Review*, *40*(2), 287–309.

Chomsky, C. (1971). Write first read later. *Childhood Education*, *47*, 296–299.

Clarke, L. K. (1988). Invented versus traditional spelling in first graders' writing: Effects on learning to spell and read. *Research in the Teaching of English*, *22*, 281–309.

Clay, M. (1975). *What did I write?* Exeter, NH: Heinemann.

Clay, M. M. (1979a). *Stones: The concepts about print test*. Portsmouth, NH: Heinemann.

Clay, M. M. (1979b). *The early detection of reading difficulties: A diagnostic survey and reading recovery procedures*. Aukland, New Zealand: Heinemann Publishers.

Clay, M. (2009). *An observation survey of early literacy achievement* (2nd ed). Portsmouth, NH: Heinemann.

Clay, M. M. (1991). Introducing a new storybook to young readers. *The Reading Teacher*, *45*, 264–273.

Common Core State Standards for English Language Arts & Literacy in History/Social Studies, Science, and Technical Subjects. (2010, March 10). Retrieved January 25, 2011, from www.corestandards.org/assets/CCSSI_ELA%20Standards.pdf

Conrad, N. J. (2008). From reading to spelling and spelling to reading: Transfer goes both ways. *Journal of Educational Psychology*, *100*(4), 869–878.

Coxhead, A. (2000). A new academic word list. *TESOL Quarterly*, *34*, 213–238.

Cunningham, A. E., & Stanovich, K. E. (2003). Reading matters: How reading engagement influences cognition. In J. Flood, D. Lapp, J. Squire, & J. Jensen (Eds.), *Handbook of research on teaching in the English language arts* (vol. 2, pp. 857–867). Mahwah, NJ: Lawrence Erlbaum.

Cunningham, P. M. (2012). *What really matters in spelling: Research-based strategies and activities*. Boston, MA: Pearson.

Cunningham, P. (2013). *Phonics they use: Words for reading and writing* (6th ed.) Boston, MA: Pearson.

Dale, E., O'Rourke, J., & Bamman, H. (1971). *Techniques of teaching vocabulary*. Palo Alto, CA: Field Educational Publications.

Daniels, H. (2002). *Literature circles: Voice and choice in book clubs and reading groups*. Portland ME: Stenhouse Publishers.

Delpit, L. D. (1988). The silenced dialogue: Power and pedagogy in educating other people's children. *Harvard Educational Review, 58,* 280–298.

Diamond, L., & Gutlohn, L. (2006). *Vocabulary handbook*. Berkeley, CA: Consortium on Reading Excellence.

Dixon, L.Q., Zhao, J., & Joshi, R. M. (2012). One dress, two dress: Dialectical influence on spelling of English words among kindergarten children in Singapore. *System, 40,* 214 – 225.

Dolch, E. W. (1942). *Better spelling*. Champaign, IL: The Garrard Press.

Dorr, R. E. (2006). Something old is new again: Revisiting language experience. *The Reading Teacher, 60*(2), 138–146.

Doyle, G. B., & Bramwell, W. (2006). Promoting emergent literacy and social–emotional learning through dialogic reading. *The Reading Teacher, 59*(6), 554–564.

Duffy, G. G. (2009). *Explaining reading: A resource for teaching concepts, skills and strategies* (2nd ed.). New York: Guilford Press.

Ehri, L. (1992). Review and commentary: Stages of spelling development. In S. Templeton & D. Bear (Eds.), *Development of orthographic knowledge and the foundations of literacy: A memorial Festschrift for Edmund H. Henderson* (pp. 307–332). Hillsdale, NJ: Lawrence Erlbaum.

Ehri, L. C. (1997). Learning to read and learning to spell are one and the same, almost. In C. A. Perfetti, L. Rieben, & M. Fayol (Eds.), *Learning to spell: Research, theory, and practice across languages* (pp. 237–269). Mahwah, NJ: Lawrence Erlbaum.

Ehri, L. (2000). Phases of acquisition in learning to read words and implications for teaching. *British Journal of Educational Psychology: Monograph Series, 1,* 7–28.

Ehri, L. C. (2005). Learning to read words: Theory, findings, and issues. *Scientific Studies of Reading, 9*(2), 167–188.

Ehri, L. C. (2006). Alphabetics instruction helps children learn to read. In R. M. Joshi & P. G. Aaron (Eds.), *Handbook of orthography and literacy* (pp. 649–678). Mahwah, NJ: Lawrence Erlbaum.

Ehri, L. C. (2014). Orthographic mapping in the acquisition of sight word reading, spelling memory, and vocabulary learning. *Scientific Studies of Reading, 18*(1), 5–21.

Ehri, L. C., & Roberts, T. (2006). The roots of learning to read and write: Acquisition of letters and phonemic awareness. In D. K. Dickinson & S. B. Neuman (Eds.), *Handbook of early literacy research* (vol. 2, pp. 113–131). New York: Guilford Press.

Ehri, L. C., & Wilce, L. S. (1980). Do beginning readers learn to read function words better in sentences or lists? *Reading Research Quarterly, 15,* 675–685.

Elkonin, D. B. (1973). U.S.S.R. In J. Downing (Ed.), *Comparative reading*. New York: Macmillan.

Farstrup, A. E., & Samuels, S. J. (Eds.). (2008). *What research has to say about vocabulary instruction*. Newark, DE: International Reading Association.

Fashola, O., Drum, P. A., Mayer, R. E., & Kang, S. J. (1996). A cognitive theory of orthographic transitioning: Predictable errors in how Spanish-speaking children spell English words. *American Educational Research Journal, 33,* 825–843.

Ferreiro, E., & Teberosky, A. (1982). *Literacy before schooling*. Portsmouth, NH: Heinemann.

Fisher, D., & Frey, N. (2008). *Better learning through structured teaching: A framework for gradual release of responsibility*. Alexandria, VA: Association for Supervision and Curriculum Development.

Flanigan, K. (2006). "Daddy, where did the words go?": How teachers can help emergent readers develop a concept of word in text. *Reading Improvement, 43*(1), 37–49.

Flanigan, K. (2007). A concept of word in text: A pivotal event in early reading acquisition. *Journal of Literacy Research, 39*(1), 37–70.

Flanigan, K., Hayes, L., Templeton, S., Bear, D. R., Invernizzi, M., & Johnston, F. (2011). *Words their way with struggling readers: Word study for reading, vocabulary, and spelling instruction, grades 4–12*. Boston: Allyn & Bacon.

Flanigan, K., Templeton, S., & Hayes, L. (2012). What's in a word? Using content vocabulary to generate growth in general academic vocabulary knowledge. *Journal of Adolescent and Adult Literacy, 56*(2), 132–140. doi: 10.1002/JAAL.00114

Foorman, B. R., & Petscher, Y. (2010). Development of spelling and differential relations to text reading in grades 3–12. *Assessment for Effective Intervention, 36*(1), 7–20. doi: 10.1177/1534508410379844

Ford, K., & Invernizzi, M. (2009). *Phonological Awareness Literacy Screening for Kindergarteners in Spanish* (PALS español-K). Charlottesville, VA: University of Virginia.

Fountas, I., & Pinnell, G. (2001). *Guiding readers and writers (grades 3–6): Teaching, comprehension, genre, and content literacy*. Portsmouth, NH: Heinemann.

Fresch, M. J., & Wheaton, A. F. (2004). *The spelling list and word study resource book*. New York: Scholastic.

Fry, E. (1980). The new instant word list. *The Reading Teacher, 34,* 284–289.

Fry, E. B., & Kress, J. E. (2006). *The reading teacher's book of lists: K–12* (5th ed.). San Francisco: Jossey-Bass.

Fuchs, L. S., Fuchs, D., & Maxwell, L. (1988). The validity of informal reading comprehension measures. *Remedial & Special Education, 9*(2), 20–28.

Ganske, K. (1999). The developmental spelling analysis: A measure of orthographic knowledge. *Educational Assessment, 6,* 41–70.

Ganske, K., & Jocius, R. (2013) Small-group word study: Instructional conversations or mini-interrogations? *Language Arts, 19,* 23–39.

Gee, J. P. (2005). *An introduction to discourse analysis: Theory and method*. New York: Routledge.

Gehsmann, K. M., Millwood, K., & Bear, D. R. (2012, December). *Validating a classroom observation tool for studying developmental word study instruction*. Presentation at the 62nd annual conference of the Literacy Research Association, San Diego, CA.

Gehsmann, K., & Templeton, S. (2011/2012). Of stages and standards in literacy: Teaching developmentally in the age of accountability. *Journal of Education, 192*(1), 5–16.

Gehsmann, K., & Templeton, S. (2013). Foundational skills. In L. M. Morrow, T. Shanahan, & K. K. Wixson (Eds.), *Teaching with the Common Core Standards for English Language Arts: PreK-2* (pp. 67–84). New York: Guilford Press.

Gibson, J. J., & Yonas, P. M. (1968). A new theory of scribbling and drawing in children. In *The analysis of reading skill: A program of basic and applied research* (Final Report, Project No. 5-1213, Cornell University and the U.S. Office of Education, pp. 335–370). Ithaca, NY: Cornell University.

Gill, C. (1980). *An analysis of spelling errors in French*. Unpublished doctoral dissertation. University of Virginia.

Gill, C. H., & Scharer, P. L. (1996). Why do they get it on Friday and misspell it on Monday: Teachers inquiring about their students as spellers. *Language Arts, 73*, 89–96.

Gill, J. T. (1992). Focus on research: Development of word knowledge as it relates to reading, spelling, and instruction. *Language Arts, 69*(6), 444–453.

Gill, J. T., & Bear, D. (1988). No book, whole book, and chapter DR-TAs: Three study techniques. *Journal of Reading, 31*(5), 444–449.

Gillet, J. W., & Kita, M. J. (1979). Words, kids, and categories. *The Reading Teacher, 32*, 538–542.

Goswami, U. (2008). Reading, complexity, and the brain. *Literacy, 42*(2), 67–74.

Graham, S., Harris, K. R., & Fink, B. (2000). Is handwriting causally related to learning to write? Treatment of handwriting problems in beginning writers. *Journal of Educational Psychology, 92*(4), 620–633.

Graham, S., Morphy, P., Harris, K. R., Fink-Chorzempa, B., Saddler, B., Moran, S., & Mason, L. (2008). Teaching spelling in the primary grades: A national survey of instructional practices and adaptations. *American Education Research Journal, 45*(3), 796–825.

Graves, M. F. (1986). Vocabulary learning and instruction. In *Review of Research in Education, 13* (pp. 49–89). Washington, DC: American Educational Research Association.

Green, T. M. (2008). *The Greek and Latin roots of English* (4th ed). Lanham, MD: Rowman & Littlefield Publishers.

Hall, M. (1980). *Teaching reading as a language experience*. Columbus, OH: Merrill.

Halladay, J. L. (2012). Revisiting key assumptions of the reading level framework. *The Reading Teacher, 66*(1), 53–62.

Hanna, P. R., Hanna, J. S., Hodges, R. E., & Rudorf, H. (1966). *Phoneme-grapheme correspondences as cues to spelling improvement*. Washington, DC: United States Office of Education Cooperative Research.

Harré, R., & Moghaddam, F. (Eds.). (2003). *The self and others: Positioning individuals and groups in personal, political, and cultural contexts*. Westport, CT: Praeger.

Harris, M. L., Schumaker, J. B., & Deshler, D. D. (2011). The effects of strategic morphological analysis instruction on the vocabulary performance of secondary students with and without disabilities. *Learning Disability Quarterly, 34*(1), 17–33.

Harste, J. C., Woodward, V. A., & Burke, C. L. (1984). *Language stories and literacy lessons*. Portsmouth, NH: Heinemann.

Hart, B., & Risley, T. R. (1995). *Meaningful differences in the everyday experience of American children*. Baltimore: Paul C. Brookes.

Hasbrouck, J., & Tindal, G. A. (2006). Oral reading fluency norms: A valuable assessment tool for reading teachers. *The Reading Teacher, 59*(7), 636–644.

He, T-h., & Wang, W-l. (2009). Invented spelling of EFL young beginning writers and its relation with phonological awareness and grapheme-phoneme principles. *Journal of Second Language Writing, 18*(1), 44–56.

Helman, L. (2004). Building on the sound system of Spanish. *The Reading Teacher, 57*, 452–460.

Helman, L. A. (Ed.). (2009). *Literacy development with English learners: Research-based instruction in grades K–6*. New York: Guilford Press.

Helman, L. A., & Bear, D. R. (2007). Does an established model of orthographic development hold true for English learners? In D. W. Rowe, R. Jimenez, D. L. Compton, D. K. Dickinson, Y. Kim, K. M. Leander, & V. J. Risko (Eds.), *56th Yearbook of the National Reading Conference* (pp. 266–280).

Helman, L., Bear, D. R., Invernizzi, M., Templeton, S., & Johnston, F. (2009a). *Words their way: Emergent sorts for Spanish-speaking English learners*. Boston: Allyn & Bacon.

Helman, L., Bear, D. R., Invernizzi, M., Templeton, S., & Johnston, F. (2009b). *Words their way: Letter name-alphabetic sorts for Spanish-speaking English learners*. Boston: Allyn & Bacon.

Helman, L., Bear, D. R., Invernizzi, M., Templeton, S., & Johnston, F. (2011). *Words their way: Emergent sorts for Spanish-speaking English learners*. Boston: Allyn & Bacon.

Helman, L. A., Bear, D. R., Templeton, S., Invernizzi, M., & Johnston, F. (2012). *Words their way with English learners* (2nd ed.). Boston: Pearson/Allyn & Bacon.

Helman, L., Bear, D. R., Invernizzi, M., Templeton, S., & Johnston, F. (2013). *Palabras a su paso: El estudio de palabras en acción-Etapa alfabética*. Glenview, IL: Pearson.

Henderson, E. H. (1981). *Learning to read and spell: The child's knowledge of words*. DeKalb: Northern Illinois Press.

Henderson, E. H. (1990). *Teaching spelling* (2nd ed.). Boston: Houghton Mifflin.

Henderson, E. H., & Beers, J. (Eds.). (1980). *Developmental and cognitive aspects of learning to spell*. Newark, DE: International Reading Association.

Henderson, E. H., Estes, T., & Stonecash, S. (1972). An exploratory study of word acquisition among first graders at midyear in a language experience approach. *Journal of Reading Behavior, 4*, 21–30.

Henderson, E. H., & Templeton, S. (1986). The development of spelling ability through alphabet, pattern, and meaning. *Elementary School Journal, 86*, 305–316.

Henry, M. (1988). Beyond phonics: Integrated decoding and spelling instruction based on word origin and structures. *Annals of Dyslexia, 38*, 258–275.

Henry, M. (2003). *Unlocking literacy: Effective decoding and spelling instruction*. Baltimore: Paul H. Brookes.

Hiebert, E. H. (2005). In pursuit of an effective, efficient vocabulary curriculum for elementary students. In E. H. Hiebert & M. L. Kamil (Eds.), *Teaching and learning vocabulary: Bringing research to practice* (pp. 243–263). Mahwah, NJ: Lawrence Erlbaum.

Holmes, V. M., & Davis, C. W. (2002). Orthographic representation and spelling knowledge. *Language and Cognitive Processes, 17*, 345–370.

Honig, A. S., & Shin, M. (2001). Reading aloud with infants and toddlers in child care settings: An observational study. *Early Childhood Education Journal, 28*(3), 193–197.

Horn, E. (1954). *Teaching spelling*. Washington, DC: National Education Association.

Huang, F. L., Tortorelli, L. S. & Invernizzi, M. (2014). An investigation of factors associated with letter-sound knowledge at kindergarten entry. *Early Childhood Research Quarterly, 29*(2), 182–192.

Invernizzi, M. (1992). The vowel and what follows: A phonological frame of orthographic analysis. In S. Templeton & D. Bear (Eds.), *Development of orthographic knowledge and the foundations of literacy: A memorial Festschrift for Edmund H. Henderson* (pp. 106–136). Hillsdale, NJ: Lawrence Erlbaum.

Invernizzi, M. (2002). Concepts, sounds, and the ABCs: A diet for a very young reader. In D. M. Barone & L. M. Morrow (Eds.), *Literacy and young children* (pp. 140–157). New York: Guilford Press.

Invernizzi, M. (2009). Virginia's Early Intervention Reading Initiative (EIRI) and Response to Intervention (RtI). *Reading in Virginia, 36–39.*

Invernizzi, M., Abouzeid, M., & Gill, T. (1994). Using students' invented spellings as a guide for spelling instruction that emphasizes word study. *Elementary School Journal, 95*(2), 155–167.

Invernizzi, M., & Hayes, L. (2004). Developmental-spelling research: A systematic imperative. *Reading Research Quarterly, 39*, 2–15.

Invernizzi, M., & Hayes, L. (2010). Word recognition. In D. Allington & A. McGill-Franzen (Eds.), *Handbook of reading disabilities.* Newark, DE: International Reading Association.

Invernizzi, M., Juel, C., Swank, L., & Meier, J. (2006). *Phonological Awareness Literacy Screening for Kindergartners* (PALS-K). Charlottesville, VA: University Printing Services.

Invernizzi, M., Juel, C., Swank, L., & Meier, J. (2008). *Phonological Awareness Literacy Screening–Kindergarten (PALS-K): Technical Reference.* Charlottesville, VA: University of Virginia.

Invernizzi, M., Justice, L., Landrum, T., & Booker, K. (Winter, 2005). Early literacy screening in kindergarten: Widespread implementation in Virginia. *Journal of Literacy Research, 36*, 479–500.

Invernizzi, M., Meier, J., & Juel, C. (2003). *PALS 1–3 Phonological Awareness Literacy Screening* (4th ed.). Charlottesville, VA: University Printing Services.

Invernizzi, M. A. & Tortorelli, L.S. (2013). Phonological awareness and alphabet knowledge: The foundations of early reading. In M. Mallette & D. Barone (Eds.), *Best Practices in Early Literacy Instructions.* New York, NY: Guilford.

Invernizzi, M., & Worthy, J. W. (1989). An orthographic-specific comparison of the spelling errors of LD and normal children across four levels of spelling achievement. *Reading Psychology, 10*, 173–188.

James, W. (1958). *Talks to teachers on psychology and to students on some of life's ideals.* New York: Norton. (Original work published 1899.)

Johnston, F. R. (1998). The reader, the text, and the task: Learning words in first grade. *The Reading Teacher, 51*, 666–675.

Johnston, F. R. (2000). Word learning in predictable text. *Journal of Educational Psychology, 92*, 248–255.

Johnston, F. R. (2001). The utility of phonic generalizations: Let's take another look at Clymer's conclusions. *The Reading Teacher, 55*, 132–143.

Johnston, F. R. (2003, December). *The Primary Spelling Inventory: Exploring its validity and relationship to reading levels.* Paper presented at the National Reading Conference, Scottsdale, AZ.

Johnston, F., Invernizzi, M., Bear, D. R., & Templeton, S. (2009). *Words their way: Word sorts for syllables and affixes spellers.* Boston: Pearson/Allyn & Bacon.

Johnston, F., Invernizzi, M., Helman, L., Bear, D. R., & Templeton, S. (2015). *Words Their Way for PreK and Kindergarten.* Boston: Pearson.

Johnston, F., Invernizzi, M., Juel, C., & Lewis-Wagner, D. (2009). *Book buddies: A tutoring framework for struggling readers.* New York: Guilford Press.

Johnston, P. H. (2004) *Choice words: How our language affects children's learning.* Portland, ME.: Stenhouse.

Johnston, P. H. (2012). *Opening minds: Using language to change lives.* Portland, ME: Stenhouse.

Jones, C. D., Clark, S. K., & Reutzel, D. R. (2013). Enhancing alphabet knowledge instruction: Research implications and practical strategies for early childhood educators. *Early Childhood Education Journal, 41*(2), 81-89.

Joseph, L. M. (2002). Facilitating word recognition and spelling using word boxes and word sort phonic procedures. *School Psychology Review, 3*, 122–129.

Juel, C., Biancarosa, G., Coker, D., & Deffes, R. (2003). Walking with Rosie: A cautionary tale of literacy instruction. *Educational Leadership, 60*(7), 12–18.

Juel, C., & Minden-Cupp, C. (2000). Learning to read words: Linguistic units and instructional strategies. *Reading Research Quarterly, 35*, 458–492.

Justice, L. M. (2006). *Communication sciences and disorders: An introduction.* Upper Saddle River, NJ: Pearson/Merrill/Prentice Hall.

Justice, L. M., & Ezell, H. K. (2004). Print referencing: An emergent literacy enhancement technique and its clinical applications. *Language, Speech, and Hearing Services in Schools, 35*, 185–193.

Justice, L. M., Kaderavek, J. N., Fan, X., Sofka, A., & Hunt, A. (2009). Accelerating preschoolers' early literacy development through classroom-based teacher child story book reading and explicit print referencing. *Language, Speech, & Hearing Services in Schools, 40*, 67–85.

Justice, L. M., & Pullen, P. (2003). Promising interventions for promoting emergent literacy skills: Three evidence-based approaches. *Topics in Early Childhood Special Education, 23*, 99–113.

Justice, L. M., & Sofka, A. E. (2010). *Engaging children with print: Building early literacy skills through quality read alouds.* New York: Guilford Press.

Kim, Y., Petscher, Y., Foorman, B., & Zhou, C. (2010). The contributions of phonological awareness and letter name knowledge to letter-sound acquisition—a cross-classified multilevel model approach. *Journal of Educational Psychology, 102*, 313–326.

Kirk, C., & Gillon, G. T. (2009). Integrated morphological awareness intervention as a tool for improving literacy. *Language, Speech, and Hearing Services in Schools, 40*(2), 341–351.

Labbo, L. D. (2004). Author's computer chair [Technology in Literacy Department]. *The Reading Teacher, 57*(7), 688–691.

Labbo, L. D., Eakle, A. J., & Montero, M. K. (2002, May). Digital Language Experience Approach: Using digital photographs and software as a Language Experience Approach innovation. *Reading Online, 5*(8). http://www.readingonline.org/electronic/elec_index.asp?HREF=labbo2/index.html

Lane, H. B., & Allen, S. A. (2010). The vocabulary-rich classroom: Modeling sophisticated word use to promote word consciousness and vocabulary growth. *The Reading Teacher, 63*(5), 362–370.

Larkin, R. F., & Snowling, M. J. (2008). Morphological spelling development. *Reading & Writing Quarterly, 24,* 363–376.

Lerer, S. (2007). *Inventing English: A portable history of the language.* New York: Columbia University Press.

Liberman, I., & Shankweiler, D. (1991). Phonology and beginning reading: A tutorial. In L. Rieben & C. Perfetti (Eds.), *Learning to read: Basic research and its implication.* Hillsdale, NJ: Lawrence Erlbaum.

Liberman, I. Y., Shankweiler, D., & Liberman, A. M. (1989). "The alphabetic principle and learning to read." *Meeting of the International Academy for Research on Learning Disabilities, Oct, 1986, Northwestern U, Evanston, IL, US.* The University of Michigan Press.

Lobo, Y. B., & Winsler, A. (2006). The effects of a creative dance and movement program on the social competence of Head Start preschoolers. *Social Development, 15*(3), 501–519.

Lubliner, S., & Scott, J. (2008). *Nourishing vocabulary: Balancing words and learning.* Thousand Oaks, CA: Corwin Press.

Lundberg, I., Frost, J., & Peterson, O. (1988). Effects of an extensive program for stimulating phonological awareness in preschool children. *Reading Research Quarterly, 23,* 267–284.

Mages, W. K. (2008). Does creative drama promote language development in early childhood? A review of the methods and measures employed in the empirical literature. *Review of Educational Research, 78*(1), 124–152.

Mahony, D., Singson, M., & Mann, V. (2000). Reading ability and sensitivity to morphological relations. *Reading and Writing: An Interdisciplinary Journal, 12,* 191–218.

Marzano, R. J. (1992). *A different kind of classroom: Teaching with dimensions of learning.* Alexandria, VA: ASCD.

Massengill, D. (2006). Mission accomplished . . . It's learnable now: Voices of mature challenged spellers using a Word Study approach. *Journal of Adolescent and Adult Literacy, 49*(5), 420–431.

Mathews, M. (1967). *Teaching to read: Historically considered.* Chicago: University of Chicago Press.

McCabe, A. (1996). *Chameleon readers: All kinds of good stories.* New York: Webster/McGraw-Hill.

McCracken, M. J., & McCracken, R. A. (1995). *Reading, writing, and language* (2nd ed.). Winnipeg, Canada: Peguis.

McGee, L. M., & Richgels, D. J. (2011). *Literacy's beginnings: Supporting young readers and writers* (6th ed.). Boston, MA: Pearson.

Mesmer, H. A., Cunningham, J. W., & Heibert, E. H. (2012). Toward a theoretical model of text complexity for the early grades: Learning from the past, anticipating the future. *Reading Research Quarterly, 47*(3), 235–258.

Moats, L. (2000). *Speech to print: Language essentials for teachers.* Baltimore: Paul H. Brookes.

Moloney, K. (2008). *"I'm not a big word fan": An exploratory study of ninth-graders' language use in the context of word consciousness-oriented vocabulary instruction.* Unpublished doctoral dissertation, University of Nevada, Reno.

Morais, J., Cary, L., Alegria, J., & Bertelson, P. (1979). Does awareness of speech as a sequence of phonemes arise spontaneously? *Cognition, 7,* 323–331.

Morgan, R. K., & Meier, C. R. (2008). Dialogic reading's potential to improve children's emergent literacy skills and behavior. *Preventing School Failure, 52,* 11–16.

Morris, D. (1980). Beginning readers' concept of word. In E. Henderson & J. Beers (Eds.), *Developmental and cognitive aspects of learning to spell* (pp. 97–111). Newark, DE: International Reading Association.

Morris, D. (1981). Concept of word: A developmental phenomenon in the beginning reading and writing process. *Language Arts, 58*(6), 659–668.

Morris, D. (1992). Concept of word: A pivotal understanding in the learning-to-read process. In S. Templeton, & D. R. Bear (Eds.), *Development of orthographic knowledge and the foundations of literacy: A memorial Festschrift for Edmund H. Henderson* (pp. 53–77). Hillsdale, NJ: Lawrence Erlbaum Associates.

Morris, D. (1993). The relationship between children's concept of word in text and phoneme awareness in learning to read: A longitudinal study. *Research in the Teaching of English, 27*(2), 133–154.

Morris, D. (1999). *The Howard Street tutoring manual* (2nd ed.). New York: Guilford Press.

Morris, D. (2013). *Diagnosis and correction of reading problems* (2nd ed.). New York: Guilford Press.

Morris, D., Blanton, L., Blanton, W., & Perney, J. (1995). Spelling instruction and achievement in six elementary classrooms. *The Elementary School Journal, 96,* 145–162.

Morris, D., Bloodgood, J. W., Lomax, R. G., & Perney, J. (2003). Developmental steps in learning to read: A longitudinal study in kindergarten and first grade. *Reading Research Quarterly, 38,* 302–328.

Morris, D., Nelson, L., & Perney, J. (1986). Exploring the concept of "spelling instructional level" through the analysis of error-types. *Elementary School Journal, 87,* 181–200.

Morris, D., Trathen, W., Frye, E. M., Kucan, L., Ward, D., Schlagal, R., & Hendrix, M. (2013). The role of reading rate in the informal assessment of reading ability. *Literacy Research and Instruction, 52*(1), 52–64.

Nagy, W. (2007). Metalinguistic awareness and the vocabulary-comprehension connection. In R. K. Wagner, A. E. Muse, & K. R. Tannenbaum (Eds.), *Vocabulary acquisition: Implications for reading comprehension* (pp. 52–78). New York: Guilford Press.

Nagy, W., & Anderson, R. C. (1984). How many words are there in printed school English? *Reading Research Quarterly, 19,* 304–330.

Nagy, W., Berninger, V. W., & Abbott, R. D. (2006). Contributions of morphology beyond phonology to literacy outcomes of upper elementary and middle-school students. *Journal of Educational Psychology, 98,* 134–147.

Nagy, W., Berninger, V., Abbott, R., Vaughan, K., & Vermeulen, K. (2003). Relationship of morphology and other language skills to literacy skills in at-risk second-grade readers and at-risk fourth-grade writers. *Journal of Educational Psychology, 95*(4), 730–742.

Nagy, W., & Townsend, D. (2012). Words as tools: Learning academic vocabulary as language acquisition. *Reading Research Quarterly, 47*(1), 91–108.

Nash, R. (1997). *NTC's dictionary of Spanish cognates thematically organized.* Chicago: NTC Publishing Group.

Nathenson-Mejia, S. (1989). Writing in a second language: Negotiating meaning through invented spelling. *Language Arts, 66,* 515–526.

National Early Literacy Panel. (2008). *Report on a synthesis of early predictors of reading.* Louisville, KY: National Institute of Family Literacy.

National Reading Panel (NRP). (2000). *Teaching children to read: An evidence-based assessment of the scientific research literature on reading and its implications for reading instruction.* Washington, DC: National Institute of Child Health and Human Development.

Nessel, D., & Jones, M. (1981). *The language-experience approach to reading.* New York: Teachers College Press.

Neuman, S. B., & Roskos, K. (2012). More than teachable moments: Enhancing oral vocabulary instruction in your classroom. *The Reading Teacher, 66*(1), 63–67.

Nunes, T., & Bryant, P. (2006). *Improving literacy by teaching morphemes.* London: Routledge.

Nunes, T., & Bryant, P. (2009). *Children's reading and spelling: Beyond the first steps.* London: Wiley-Blackwell.

O'Connor, R. (2007). *Teaching word recognition: Effective strategies for students with learning difficulties.* New York: Guilford Press.

Ouellette, G. P., & Sénéchal, M. (2008). A window into early literacy: Exploring the cognitive and linguistic underpinnings of invented spelling. *Scientific Studies of Reading, 12*(2), 195–219.

Palmer, J., & Invernizzi, M. (2014). *No more phonics and spelling worksheets.* Portsmouth, NH: Heinemann.

Papandropoulou, I., & Sinclair, H. (1974). What is a word? *Human Development, 17*(4), 241–258.

Parry, J., & Hornsby, D. (1988). *Write on: A conference approach to writing.* Portsmouth, NH: Heinemann.

Pearson, P. D., & Gallagher, M. (1983). The instruction of reading comprehension. *Contemporary Educational Psychology, 8,* 317–344.

Pearson, P. D., Hiebert, E. H., & Kamil, M. (2007). Vocabulary assessment: What we know and what we need to learn. *Reading Research Quarterly, 42*(2), 282–296.

Pense, K. L., & Justice, L. M. (2008). *Language development from theory to practice.* Upper Saddle River, NJ: Pearson/Merrill/Prentice Hall.

Perfetti, C., Beck, I., Bell, L., & Hughes, C. (1987). Phonemic knowledge and learning to read are reciprocal. *Merrill-Palmer Quarterly, 33,* 283–319.

Piasta, S. B., & Wagner, R. K. (2010). Developing early literacy skills: A meta-analysis of alphabet learning and instruction. *Reading Research Quarterly, 45*(1), 8–38.

Phenix, J. (1996). *The spelling teacher's book of lists.* Ontario: Pembroke.

Pressley, M. (2006). *Reading instruction that works: The case for balanced teaching* (3rd ed.). New York: Guilford Press.

Pufpaff, L. (2009). A developmental continuum of phonological sensitivity skills. *Psychology in the Schools, 46*(7), 679–691.

Pullen, P. C., & Justice, L. M. (2003). Enhancing phonological awareness, print awareness, & oral language skills in preschool children. *Intervention in School & Clinic, 39*(2), 87–98.

Puranik, C. S., Lonigan, C. J., & Kim, Y. S. (2011). Contributions of emergent literacy skills to name writing, letter writing, and spelling in preschool children. *Early Childhood Research Quarterly, 26*(4), 465–474.

Raphael, T. E., Pardo, L. S., Highfield, K., & McMahon. (2013). *Book club: A literature-based curriculum* (2nd ed.). Lawrence, MA: Small Planet Communications, Inc.

Rasinski, T. (2010). *The fluent reader: Oral and silent reading strategies for building word recognition, fluency, and comprehension* (2nd ed.). New York: Scholastic.

Rayner, K., Foorman, B. R., Perfetti, C. A., Pesetsky, D., & Seidenburg, M. S. (2001). How psychological science informs the teaching of reading. *Psychological Science in the Public Interest, 2,* 31–74.

Read, C. (1971). Pre-school children's knowledge of English phonology. *Harvard Educational Review, 41*(1), 1–34.

Read, C. (1975). *Children's categorization of speech sounds in English.* Urbana, IL: NCTE Research Report No. 17.

Richgels, D. J. (1995). Invented spelling ability and printed word learning in kindergarten. *Reading Research Quarterly, 30,* 96–109.

Richgels, D. J. (2001). Invented spelling, phonemic awareness, and reading and writing instruction. In S. B. Neuman & D. K. Dickenson (Eds.), *Handbook of early literacy research* (pp. 142–155). New York: Guilford Press.

Robb, L. (1999). *Easy mini-lessons for building vocabulary.* New York: Scholastic.

Roberts, B. S. (1992). The evolution of the young child's concept of word as a unit of spoken and written language. *Reading Research Quarterly, 27*(2), 125–138.

Robinson, S. R. (1989). *Origins, Volume 1: Bringing words to life.* New York: Teachers & Writers Collaborative.

Rosenthal, J., & Ehri, L. (2008). The mnemonic value of orthography for vocabulary learning. *Journal of Educational Psychology, 100*(1), 175–191. Retrieved from Education Abstracts (H. W. Wilson) database.

Samuels, S. (1979). The method of repeated readings. *The Reading Teacher, 32,* 403–408.

Sawyer, D. J., Lipa-Wade, S., Kim, J., Ritenour, D., & Knight, D. F. (1997). *Spelling errors as a window on dyslexia.* Paper presented at the 1997 annual convention of the American Educational Research Association, Chicago.

Sawyer, D. J., Wade, S., & Kim, J. K. (1999). Spelling errors as a window on variations in phonological deficits among students with dyslexia. *Annals of Dyslexia, 49,* 137–159.

Schlagal, R. (1992). Patterns of orthographic development into the intermediate grades. In S. Templeton & D. Bear (Eds.), *Development of orthographic knowledge and the foundations of literacy: A memorial Festschrift for Edmund H. Henderson* (pp. 31–52). Hillsdale, NJ: Lawrence Erlbaum.

Schlagal, R. (2013). Best practices in spelling and handwriting. In S. Graham, C. A. MacArthur, & J. Fitzgerald (Eds.), *Best practices in writing instruction* (2nd ed., pp. 257–283). New York: Guilford Press.

Scott, J. A., Skobel, B. J., & Wells, J. (2008). *The word-conscious classroom: Building the vocabulary readers and writers need.* New York: Scholastic.

Sharp, A. C., Sinatra, G. M., & Reynolds, R. E. (2008). The development of children's orthographic knowledge: A microgenetic perspective. *Reading Research Quarterly, 43*(3), 206–226.

Shen, H., & Bear, D. R. (2000). The development of orthographic skills in Chinese children. *Reading and Writing: An Interdisciplinary Journal, 13,* 197–236.

Shipley, J. T. (2001). *The origins of English words.* Baltimore, MD: The Johns Hopkins University Press.

Smith, M. L. (1998). Sense and sensitivity: An investigation into fifth-grade children's knowledge of English derivational morphology and its relationship to vocabulary and reading ability. University Microfilms No. AAM9830072. *Dissertation Abstracts International, 59*(4-A), 1111.

Smith, N. B. (2002). *American reading instruction* (special edition). Newark, DE: International Reading Association.

Smith, S. B., Simmons, D. C., & Kame'enui, E. J. (1995). *Synthesis of research on phonological awareness: Principles and implications for reading acquisition* (Tech. Rep. No. 21). Eugene, OR: University of Oregon, National Center to Improve the Tools of Educators.

Snow, C. E., Burns, M. S., & Griffin, P. (Eds.). (1998). *Preventing reading difficulties in young children.* Washington, DC: National Academy Press.

Spear-Swerling, L., & Sternberg, R. J. (Contributor) (1997). *Off track: When poor readers become "learning disabled."* Boulder, CO: Westview Press.

Stahl, S. A., & Nagy, W. E. (2006). *Teaching word meanings.* Mahwah, NJ: Lawrence Erlbaum.

Stauffer, R. (1980). *The language-experience approach to the teaching of reading* (2nd ed.). New York: Harper & Row.

Steffler, D. J. (2001). Implicit cognition and spelling development. *Developmental Review, 21,* 168–204.

Stever, E. (1976). Dialectic and socioeconomic factors affecting the spelling strategies of second-grade students. *Dissertation Abstracts International, 37*(07A), 4120. (University Microfilms No. AAG7700149.)

Sterbinsky, A. (2007). *Words their way spelling inventories: Reliability and validity analyses.* Memphis, TN: University of Memphis Center for Research in Educational Policy. http://assets.pearsonschool.com/asset_mgr/current/201034/Reliability_and_Validation_Study_Report.pdf

Strickland, D., & Morrow, L. (1989). Environments rich in print promote literacy behavior during play. *Reading Teacher, 43,* 178–179.

Sulzby, E. (1986). Writing and reading organization. In W. H. Teale & E. Sulzby (Eds.), *Emergent literacy: Writing and reading* (pp. 50–89). Norwood, NJ: Abex.

Swan, M., & Smith, B. (2001). *Learner English: A teacher's guide to interference and other problems* (2nd ed.). New York: Cambridge University Press.

Taft, M. (1991). *Reading and the mental lexicon.* London: Lawrence Erlbaum.

Taft, M. (2003). Morphological representation as a correlation between form and meaning. In E. G. H. Assink & D. Sandra (Eds.), *Reading complex words: Cross language studies* (pp. 113–137). New York: Kluwer Academic.

Temple, C. S. (1978). *An analysis of spelling errors in Spanish.* Unpublished doctoral dissertation, University of Virginia.

Templeton, S. (1979). Spelling first, sound later: The relationship between orthography and higher order phonological knowledge in older students. *Research in the Teaching of English, 13,* 255–264.

Templeton, S. (1980). Logic and mnemonics for demons and curiosities: Spelling awareness for middle- and secondary-level students. *Reading World, 20,* 123–130.

Templeton, S. (1983). Using the spelling/meaning connection to develop word knowledge in older students. *Journal of Reading, 27*(1), 8–14.

Templeton, S. (1989). Tacit and explicit knowledge of derivational morphology: Foundations for a unified approach to spelling and vocabulary development in the intermediate grades and beyond. *Reading Psychology, 10,* 233–253.

Templeton, S. (1992). Theory, nature, and pedagogy of higher-order orthographic development in older children. In S. Templeton & D. Bear (Eds.), *Development of orthographic knowledge and the foundations of literacy: A memorial Festschrift for Edmund H. Henderson* (pp. 253–278), Hillsdale, NJ: Lawrence Erlbaum.

Templeton, S. (1997). *Teaching the integrated language arts* (2nd ed.). Boston: Houghton Mifflin.

Templeton, S. (2002). Effective spelling instruction in the middle grades: It's a lot more than memorization. *Voices from the Middle, 9*(3), 8–14.

Templeton, S. (2003). Spelling. In J. Flood, D. Lapp, J. R. Squire, & J. M. Jensen (Eds.), *Handbook of research on teaching the English language arts* (2nd ed., pp. 738–751). Mahwah, NJ: Lawrence Erlbaum.

Templeton, S. (2004). The vocabulary-spelling connection: Orthographic development and morphological knowledge at the intermediate grades and beyond. In J. F. Baumann & E. J. Kame'enui (Eds.), *Vocabulary instruction: Research to practice* (pp. 118–138). New York: Guilford Press.

Templeton, S. (2008). Foreword. *Curious George's Dictionary.* Boston, MA: Houghton Mifflin Harcourt.

Templeton, S. (2010). Spelling–meaning relationships among languages: Exploring cognates and their possibilities. In L. Helman (Ed.), *Literacy development with English learners: Research-based instruction in grades K–6* (pp. 196–212). New York: Guilford Press.

Templeton, S. (2011/2012). Teaching and learning morphology: A reflection on generative vocabulary instruction. *Journal of Education, 192*(2/3), 101–107.

Templeton, S. (2012). The vocabulary-spelling connection and generative instruction: Orthographic development and morphological knowledge at the intermediate grades and beyond. In J. F. Baumann & E. J. Kame'enui (Eds.), *Vocabulary instruction: Research to Practice* (2nd ed., pp.116–138). New York: Guilford Press.

Templeton, S. (2013). *Learning and reading words closely and deeply, The archaeology of thought.* In Sisk, D. A. (Ed.), *Accelerating and extending literacy for diverse learners: Using culturally responsive teaching.* Lanham, MD: Rowman & Littlefield.

Templeton, S., & Bear, D. (Eds.). (1992). *Development of orthographic knowledge and the foundations of literacy: A memorial Festschrift for Edmund H. Henderson.* Hillsdale, NJ: Lawrence Erlbaum.

Templeton, S., & Bear, D. R. (2006). *Spelling and vocabulary.* Boston: Houghton Mifflin.

Templeton, S., & Bear, D. R. (2011). Phonemic awareness, word recognition, and spelling. In T. Rasinski (Ed.), *Developing reading instruction that works* (pp. 153–178). Bloomington, IN: Solution Tree Press.

Templeton, S., Bear, D. R., Invernizzi, M., Johnson, F., Flanigan, K., Townsend, D. R., Helman, L., & Hayes, L. (2015). *Vocabulary their way: Word study with middle and secondary students* (2nd ed.). Boston: Pearson.

Templeton, S., Bear, D. R., Johnston, F., & Invernizzi, M. (2010). *Vocabulary their way: Word study for middle and secondary students.* Boston: Pearson/Allyn & Bacon.

Templeton, S., & Gehsmann, K. (2014). *Teaching reading and writing: The developmental approach (preK-8).* Boston: Pearson.

Templeton, S., & Ives, R. T. (2007). The nature and development of spelling. In B. Guzetti (Ed.), *The encyclopedia of early childhood literacy education* (pp. 111–122). Westport, CT: Praeger.

Templeton, S., & Morris, D. (2000). Spelling. In M. Kamil, P. Mosenthal, P. D. Pearson, & R. Barr (Eds.), *Handbook of reading research* (vol. 3, pp. 525–543). Mahwah, NJ: Lawrence Erlbaum.

Templeton, S., Smith, D., Moloney, K., Van Pelt, J., & Ives, B. (2009). *Generative vocabulary knowledge: Learning and teaching higher-order morphological aspects of word structure in grades 4, 5, and 6.* Symposium presented at the 59th annual meeting of the National Reading Conference, Albuquerque, December.

Templeton, S., & Spivey, E. M. (1980). The concept of "word" in young children as a function of level of cognitive development. *Research in the Teaching of English, 14*(3), 265–278.

Townsend, D., Bear, D. R., Smith, D., Morency, A., Sweeney, M., Crawford-Ferre, H., Wulfing, K, Burton, A. (2013). *Morphological awareness and academic language in the content areas.* American Educational Research Association.

Townsend, D., Filippini, A., Collins, P., & Biancarosa, G. (2012). Evidence for the importance of academic word knowledge for the academic achievement of diverse middle school students. *Elementary School Journal, 112*(3), 497–518.

Treiman, R. (1985). Onsets and rimes as units of spoken syllables: Evidence from children. *Journal of Educational Psychology, 77*(4), 417–427.

Treiman, R. (1993). *Beginning to spell.* New York: Oxford University Press.

Treiman, R., Goswami, U., Tincoff, R., & Leevers, H. (1997). Effects of dialect on American and British children's spelling. *Child Development, 68,* 229–245. doi:10.2307/1131847.

Treiman, R. Stothard, S. E., & Snowling, M. J. (2013). Instruction matters: Spelling of vowels by children in England and the US. *Reading and Writing: An Interdisciplinary Journal, 26,* 473–487.

Tunmer, W. E. (1991). Phonological awareness and literacy acquisition. In L. Rieben & C. A. Perfetti (Eds.), *Learning to read: Basic research and its implications* (pp. 105–120). Hillsdale, NJ: Lawrence Erlbaum.

Turbil, J. (2000) Developing a spelling conscience. *Language Arts, 77,* 209–216.

Uhry, J. K. (1999). Invented spelling in kindergarten: The relationship with finger-point reading. *Reading and Writing: An Interdisciplinary Journal, 11*(5–6), 441–464.

Uhry, J. K. (2002). Finger-point reading in kindergarten: The role of phonemic awareness, one-to-one correspondence, and rapid serial naming. *Scientific Studies of Reading, 6*(4), 319–342.

Uhry, J. K., & Shepherd, M. J. (1993). Segmentation/spelling instruction as part of a first-grade reading program: Effects on several measures of reading. *Reading Research Quarterly,* 219–233.

Venezky, R. L. (1970). *The structure of English orthography.* The Hague: Mouton.

Venezky, R. L. (1999). *The American way of spelling: The structure and origins of American English orthography.* New York: Guilford Press.

Viise, N. (1994). *Feature word spelling lists: A diagnosis of progressing word knowledge through an assessment of spelling errors.* Unpublished doctoral dissertation, University of Virginia.

Viise, N. (1996). A study of the spelling development of adult literacy learners compared with that of classroom children. *Journal of Literacy Research, 28*(4), 561–587.

Vygotsky, L. S. (1962). *Thought and language.* Cambridge, MA: MIT Press.

Ward, A. (2009). *A formative study investigating interactive reading activities to develop kindergartners' science vocabulary.* Unpublished dissertation, University of Virginia.

Wasik, B. A., Bond, M. A., & Hindman, A. (2006). The effects of a language and literacy intervention on Head Start children and teachers. *Journal of Educational Psychology, 98*(1), 63–74.

Watkins, C. (2011). *The American heritage dictionary of Indo-European roots* (3rd ed.) Boston: Houghton Mifflin Harcourt.

Welsch, J., Sullivan, A., & Justice, L. (2003). That's my letter: What preschoolers' name writing representation can tell us about emergent literacy knowledge. *Journal of Literacy Research, 35*(2), 757–776.

White, T. G. (2005). Effects of systematic and strategic analogy-based phonics on grade 2 students' word reading and reading comprehension. *Reading Research Quarterly, 40*(2), 234–255.

White, T. G., Sowell, J., & Yanagihara, A. (1989). Teaching elementary students to use word-part clues. *The Reading Teacher, 42,* 302–308.

Whitehurst, G. J. (1979). Meaning and semantics. In G. J. Whitehurst & B. J. Zimmerman (Eds.), *The functions of language and cognition* (pp. 115–139). New York: Academic Press.

Whitehurst, G. J., Arnold, D. S., Epstein, J. N., Angell, A. L., Smith, M., & Fiscehl, J. E. (1994). A picture book reading intervention in day care and home for children from low-income families. *Developmental Psychology, 30,* 679–689.

Worthy, M. J., & Invernizzi, M. (1989). Spelling errors of normal and disabled students on achievement levels one through four: Instructional implications. *Bulletin of the Orton Society, 40,* 138–149.

Worthy, M., & Viise, N. M. (1996). Morphological, phonological and orthographic differences between the spelling of normally achieving children and basic literacy adults. *Reading and Writing: An Interdisciplinary Journal, 8,* 138–159.

Wylie, R. E., & Durrell, D. D. (1970). Teaching vowels through phonograms. *Elementary English, 47,* 787–791.

Yang, M. (2005). Development of orthographic knowledge among Korean children in grades 1 to 6. (Doctoral dissertation, University of Virginia). *Dissertation Abstracts International, 66/05,* 1697.

Young, K. (2007). Developmental stage theory of spelling: Analysis of consistency across four spelling-related activities. *Australian Journal of Language and Literacy, 30*(3), 203–220.

Zeno, S. M., Ivens, S. H., Millard, R. T., & Duvvuri, R. (1996). *The educator's word frequency guide.* New York: Touchstone Applied Science Associates.

Ziegler, J. C., & Goswami, U. (2005). Reading acquisition, developmental dyslexia, and skilled reading across languages: A psycholinguistic grain size theory. *Psychological Bulletin, 13*(1), 3–29.

Zucker, T.A., & Invernizzi, M. (2008). eSorts and digital extensions of word study. *The Reading Teacher, 61*(8), 654–658. doi:10.1598/RT.61.8.7

Zutell, J. (1996). The directed spelling thinking activity (DSTA): Providing an effective balance in word study instruction. *The Reading Teacher, 50,* 98–107.

Zutell, J., & Allan, V. (1988). The English spelling strategies of Spanish-speaking bilingual children. *TESOL Quarterly, 22,* 333–340.

Zwiers, J. (2008). *Building academic language: Essential practices for content classrooms.* San Francisco: Jossey-Bass.